Jews and Christians – Parting Ways in the First Two Centuries CE?

Beihefte zur Zeitschrift
für die neutestamentliche
Wissenschaft

Edited by

Matthias Konradt, Judith Lieu, Laura Nasrallah,
Jens Schröter, and Gregory E. Sterling

Volume 253

Jews and Christians – Parting Ways in the First Two Centuries CE?

Reflections on the Gains and Losses of a Model

Edited by
Jens Schröter, Benjamin A. Edsall, and Joseph Verheyden

DE GRUYTER

ISBN 978-3-11-127462-1
e-ISBN (PDF) 978-3-11-074221-3
e-ISBN (EPUB) 978-3-11-074224-4
ISSN 0171-6441

Library of Congress Control Number: 2021932862

Bibliographic Information published by the Deutsche Nationalbibliothek
The Deutsche Nationalbibliothek lists this publication in the Deutsche Nationalbibliografie;
Detailed bibliographic data are available in the Internet at http://dnb.dnb.de.

© 2023 Walter de Gruyter GmbH, Berlin/Boston
This volume is text- and page-identical with the hardback published in 2021.
Printing and binding: CPI books GmbH, Leck

www.degruyter.com

Table of Contents

Jens Schröter, Benjamin A. Edsall, and Joseph Verheyden
Introduction —— 1

Christoph Markschies
From "Wide and Narrow Way" to "The Ways that Never Parted"? Road Metaphors in Models of Jewish-Christian Relations in Antiquity —— 11

Anders Runesson
What Never Belonged Together Cannot Part: Rethinking the So-Called Parting of the Ways between Judaism and Christianity —— 33

Jan N. Bremmer
***Ioudaismos, Christianismos* and the Parting of the Ways —— 57**

Jens Schröter
Was Paul a Jew Within Judaism? The Apostle to the Gentiles and His Communities in Their Historical Context —— 89

Matthias Konradt
Matthew within or outside of Judaism? From the 'Parting of the Ways' Model to a Multifaceted Approach —— 121

Kylie Crabbe
Character and Conflict: Who Parts Company in Acts? —— 151

Jörg Frey
"John within Judaism?" Textual, Historical, and Hermeneutical Considerations —— 185

James Carleton Paget
The Epistle of Barnabas, Jews and Christians —— 217

Benjamin A. Edsall
Justin Martyr without the "Parting" or the "Ways" —— 249

Paul R. Trebilco
Beyond "The Parting of the Ways" between Jews and Christians in Asia Minor to a Model of Variegated Interaction —— 273

Joseph Verheyden
Living Apart Together: Jews and Christians in Second-Century Rome – Re-visiting Some of the Actors Involved —— 307

Tobias Nicklas
Jews and Christians? Sketches from Second Century Alexandria —— 347

List of Contributors —— 381

Index of Ancient Sources —— 383

Index of Modern Authors —— 399

Index of Subjects —— 407

Jens Schröter, Benjamin A. Edsall, and Joseph Verheyden

Introduction

The contributions in this volume go back to a conference held in December 2019 at the Faculty of Theology of Humboldt University Berlin. The conference was the initiation of a larger project on "Jews and Christians in the First Three Centuries CE," jointly organized by Australian Catholic University, which graciously sponsored the meeting, Catholic University Leuven and Humboldt University Berlin.

We want to thank Konrad Schwarz (Berlin) and Charlotte von Schelling (Regensburg) for their cooperation in preparing the manuscript, including many helpful suggestions which have contributed substantially to the publication of the present volume. Alexandra Priesterath and Janina Skóra did an excellent job in preparing and hosting the Berlin meeting, for which we are very grateful. Last, but not least, we would like to thank the publishing house Walter de Gruyter, especially Alice Meroz and Sabina Dabrowski, for friendly and reliable collaboration during the publication process.

The idea of the Berlin conference was neither to defend nor to refute the model of the "parting(s) of the ways." Instead, the well-known metaphor which is still used today, served as a starting point to reflect on the relationship of Jews and Christians in the first three centuries.

1 Challenging the Idea of "Parting Ways"

The relationship between "Jews" and "Christians" in the first three centuries CE belongs to the most burning issues in current scholarship. Already the terminology for an adequate historical description is disputed. It may be questioned whether it is appropriate to use terms such as "Christians" and "Christianity" for the earliest years of the Jesus movement and the Christ groups of the Mediterranean world, as there was a great variety of such groups in the early period.[1] Likewise, "Judaism" was a multifaceted phenomenon with diverse strands and

---

[1] The diversity of early Christianity has often been pointed out in recent research by referring to the manifold views represented by the writings inside and outside of the New Testament. This includes the so-called "Apostolic Fathers," the apocryphal writings and other early Christian texts which reveal a great variety of early perceptions of the confession to Jesus Christ. See e.g. D. Brakke, *The Gnostics. Myth, Ritual, and Diversity in Early Christianity* (Cambridge, MA, and London: Harvard University Press, 2010).

perspectives on the law, messianic expectations, and attitudes towards gentiles.[2] Against this background, the relationships between the Christ groups (or "Christianities"[3]) and Synagogue communities (or "Judaisms"[4]) was complex and varying. An undifferentiated use of the designations "Christians" and "Jews" is therefore in danger of projecting back a historically later situation when such a juxtaposition was a political and sociological reality into a time without clear-cut social and religious boundaries between Jews who venerated Jesus as Messiah and Son of God, other Jews who refused to do so, and gentiles who joined the Christ groups. Moreover, opposing terms such as "particularism and universalism," "synagogue vis à vis church," and "law versus gospel" (let alone terms with negative connotations such as "Spätjudentum") introduce judgements which are likely to obscure the historical reality.[5] In other words: to speak of a separation of "Jews" and "Christians" in the first centuries CE is an abstraction that is likely to simplify the complex relationships of Synagogue communities and Christ groups in the Roman empire.[6]

---

[2] The meaning of "Jew" and "Judaism" in antiquity is discussed in S.J.D. Cohen, *The Beginnings of Jewishness: Boundaries, Varieties, Uncertainties* (Berkeley: University of California Press, 1999); S. Freyne, "Behind the Names: Samaritans, Ioudaioi, Galileans," in *Text and Artefact in the Religions of Mediterranean Antiquity. Essays in Honour of Peter Richardson*, ed. S.G. Wilson and M. Desjardins (Waterloo, ON: Wilfried Laurier University Press, 2000), 389–401. See also S. Mason, "Jews, Judeans, Judaizing, Judaism: Problems of Categorization in Ancient History," *JSJ* 38 (2007): 457–512. Mason argues that in antiquity "Ioudaioi" denoted a people (*ethnos*), its land and its culture, not a system of religious convictions which could be abstracted from this ethnic group. Whether this hypothesis holds, can be left open here.
[3] The plural "Christianities" is used by B.D. Ehrman, *Lost Christianities. The Battles for Scripture and the Faiths We Never Knew* (Oxford: Oxford University Press, 2003).
[4] See J. Neusner et al., eds., *Judaisms and Their Messiahs at the Turn of the Christian Era* (Cambridge: Cambridge University Press, 1987); A.F. Segal, *The Other Judaisms of Late Antiquity* (Atlanta: Scholars Press, 1987).
[5] On the problem of terminology see A. Runesson, "The Question of Terminology: The Architecture of Contemporary Discussions on Paul," in *Paul Within Judaism: Restoring the First-Century Context to the Apostle*, ed. M. Nanos and M. Zetterholm (Minneapolis: Fortress, 2015), 53–77; idem, "Particularistic Judaism and Universalistic Christianity? Some Critical Remarks on Terminology and Theology," *StTh* 54 (2000): 55–75; P. Fredriksen, "Mandatory Retirement: Ideas in the Study of Christian Origins whose Time has Come to Go," *Studies in Religion* 35 (2006): 231–246.
[6] See P. Fredriksen, "What 'Parting of the Ways'? Jews, Gentiles, and the Ancient Mediterranean City," in *The Ways that Never Parted. Jews and Christians in Late Antiquity and the Early Middle Ages*, ed. A.H. Becker and A.Y. Reed, TSAJ 95 (Tübingen: Mohr Siebeck, 2003), 35–64; A. Runesson, "Inventing Christian Identity: Paul, Ignatius, and Theodosius I," in *Exploring Early Christian Identity*, ed. B. Holmberg, WUNT 226 (Tübingen: Mohr Siebeck, 2008), 59–92.

These observations have called into question the model of a "parting of the ways," used some thirty years ago by the late James Dunn, to describe the relationship between Christianity and Judaism in the earliest period. With this metaphor Dunn wanted to describe the historical processes that can be traced back to the Hellenists and Paul and came in its decisive stage in the period between 70 and 135.[7] To be sure, Dunn consciously did not speak of "*a* parting," but of several "partings," to emphasize that the separation of Christians and Jews was a cumulation of several historical processes in which "Christianity" and "Judaism" became distinct and clearly demarcated.[8] In a later publication Dunn even emphasized that "the imagery of 'the parting of the ways' is more misleading than helpful" and that "no single imagery can adequately describe such a complex historical process or development."[9] However, the terminology of a "parting" or several "partings" (in German: "Trennungen" or "Trennungsprozesse") remains attractive for scholars up to more recent publications.[10]

In recent years, scholarship has gravitated toward replacing the idea of a "parting" or several "partings" with other models.[11] As already indicated, it is commonly objected that in the period of emerging Christianity there were no fixed entities called "Judaism" and "Christianity" or clear-cut social groups of "Jews" and "Christians,"[12] but complex and often overlapping social phenomena which recommend the use of more flexible metaphors, as e.g. "a criss-crossing

---

[7] See J.D.G. Dunn, *The Partings of the Ways between Christianity and Judaism and their Significance for the Character of Christianity*, 2nd ed. (London: SCM Press, 2006).
[8] Dunn, *Partings* (see n. 7), 301–318. Dunn emphasizes that also after the period of several "partings" Christianity remained "Jewish Christianity", as is proven by shared basic convictions such as the confession to the one God of Israel and the meaning of Scripture; the preservation and adaptation of Jewish writings such as Fourth Ezra, Second Baruch, the Psalms of Solomon and many others; and by the continuing contact between Christians and Jews the (307–11).
[9] See J.D.G. Dunn, *Neither Jew nor Greek. A Contested Identity*, vol. 3 of *Christianity in the Making* (Grand Rapids and Cambridge, U.K.: Eerdmans, 2015), 598–602.
[10] U. Schnelle, *Die getrennten Wege von Römern, Juden und Christen* (Tübingen: Mohr Siebeck, 2019). He describes five models which have been developed in scholarship for the "parting" of Jews and Christians (3–6) and concentrates on Roman religious politics as the decisive factor for the relationship of Judaism and Christianity in the first and second centuries. See also B. Wander, *Trennungsprozesse zwischen Frühem Christentum und Judentum*, 2nd ed., TANZ 16 (Tübingen: Francke, 1997).
[11] See the schematic diagrams by M. Goodman, "Modeling the 'Parting of the Ways'," in *The Ways that Never Parted* (see n. 6), 119–29.
[12] As is well known, the opposition was first used by Ignatius in Magn. 8:1; 10:1.3; Phld. 6:1. See K.-W. Niebuhr, "'Judentum' und 'Christentum' bei Paulus und Ignatius von Antiochien," *ZNW* 85 (1994): 218–233.

of muddy tracks,"[13] "a multi-lane highway,"[14] or a dance.[15] There is evidence that a number of Jewish followers of Jesus did not abandon their affiliation to the Synagogue after joining the Jesus movement. Among the members of early Christ groups there were almost certainly not a few who did not give up their Jewish way of life, including Sabbath observance, food laws and circumcising their male offspring. There is evidence for such strands in early Christianity, e.g. in the Gospel of Matthew,[16] the Didache,[17] the so-called Jewish-Christian Gospels,[18] or even the Pauline communities.[19] Thus, in the first centuries CE we are facing not two religious movements, but diverse groups of Jesus followers with different social and religious crossovers and interactions.

The questioning of the model of a "parting (or several partings) of the ways" has even led to the counter-formulation that the ways of Judaism and Christianity "never parted."[20] The intention behind this approach is to highlight the fact that

---

[13] J.M. Lieu, "The Parting of the Ways: Theological Construct or Historical Reality?," in eadem, *Neither Jew nor Greek. Constructing Early Christianity*, 2nd ed. (London et al.: T&T Clark, 2016), 31–49.
[14] A. Reinhartz, "A Fork in the Road or a Multi-Lane Highway? New Perspectives on the 'Parting of the Ways' Between Judaism and Christianity," in *The Changing Faces of Judaism, Christianity, and other Greco-Roman Religions in Antiquity*, ed. I.H. Henderson and G.S. Oegema, JSHRZ Studien 2 (Gütersloh: Gütersloher Verlagshaus, 2006), 280–295.
[15] See T. Nicklas, "Parting of the Ways? Probleme eines Konzepts," in *Juden – Heiden – Christen? Religiöse Inklusion und Exklusion in Kleinasien bis Decius*, ed. S. Alkier and H. Leppin, WUNT 400 (Tübingen: Mohr Siebeck, 2018), 21–41: 37–38.
[16] See A.J. Saldarini, *Matthew's Christian-Jewish Community*, CSHJ (Chicago: University of Chicago Press, 1994); A. Runesson, "Re-Thinking Early Jewish–Christian Relations: Matthean Community History as Pharisaic Intragroup Conflict," *JBL* 127:1 (2008): 95–113.
[17] See B. ter Haar Romeny, "Hypotheses on the Development of Judaism and Christianity in Syria in the Period after 70 C.E.," in *Matthew and the Didache. Two Documents from the Same Jewish-Christian Milieu?*, ed. H. van de Sandt (Assen: Royal Van Gorcum and Minneapolis: Fortress Press, 2005), 13–33; J. Verheyden, "Jewish Christianity, A State of Affairs: Affinities and Differences with Respect to Matthew, James, and the Didache," in *Matthew, James, and the Didache. Three Related Documents in Their Jewish and Christian Setting*, ed. H. van de Sandt and J.K. Zangenberg (Atlanta: Scholars Press, 2008), 123–135.
[18] See J. Frey, "Fragmente judenchristlicher Evangelien," in *Antike Christliche Apokryphen in deutscher Übersetzung I: Evangelien und Verwandtes*, ed. C. Markschies and J. Schröter (Tübingen: Mohr Siebeck, 2012), 560–660; idem, "Gospels of the Nazarenes," in *From Thomas to Tertullian*, ed. J. Schröter and C. Jacobi, vol. 2 of *The Reception of Jesus in the First Three Centuries*, ed. C. Keith et al. (London: T&T Clark, 2020), 163–172; idem, "Gospel of the Ebionites," ibid., 173–182; idem, "Gospel of the Hebrews," ibid., 183–192.
[19] See K.-W. Niebuhr, "Offene Fragen zur Gesetzespraxis bei Paulus und seinen Gemeinden (Sabbat, Speisegebote, Beschneidung)," *BThZ* 25 (2008): 16–51.
[20] See the provocative title of the volume edited by Becker and Reed, *The Ways that Never Parted* (see n. 6).

Christianity is deeply embedded in Jewish traditions and "impregnated" by its Jewish legacy. At the same time, there can be no doubt that the Jesus followers engaged the Scriptures and Jewish traditions in their own way, which eventually led to the formation of groups with a distinct social profile. While the metaphor of "parting ways" can be questioned, then, it is also seen to be useful in helping to describe the historical processes of the formation of Rabbinic Judaism and Christianity.[21] Nevertheless, it is important to be aware of the terminological pitfalls which attend descriptions of the complex reality of Christ groups and Synagogue communities in the Roman Empire of the first three centuries CE. Terms or metaphors can emphasize commonalities or differences between Jews and Christians; they can simplify complex historical realities; they evoke the idea of a targeted process that inevitably resulted in a bifurcation of Judaism and Christianity as separated religious and social entities; or they can highlight that Jews and Christians did not simply "part" from each other, but formed groups with various perspectives on the authoritative Scriptures of Israel, the meaning of the Torah and the salvation of humankind, the relationship of this world to the otherworld, etc.

2 Summary of the Individual Chapters

Given the broad, complex, and shifting nature of social and theological identities among early Jews and Christians, the contributions in this volume, far from claiming to present a complete survey, offer soundings in the ocean of early Christian and Jewish interactions. In the course of the book, the chapters progress from a focus on broader conceptual and terminological matters to discussions of particular writers, to close with a series of investigations oriented geographically around Asia Minor, Rome and Alexandria.

Christoph Markschies opens the collection fittingly with an extended reflection on the usefulness of "road metaphors" in modeling early Jewish-Christian relations. In tracing the history of their use, he notes that the simplicity of the metaphor is usually not matched by simplicity in the available material. He shows that, even by the time of John Chrysostom at the end of the 4th century, the rhetoric of separation itself provides evidence for ongoing interaction and shared religious observance between Jews and Christians. Identities are complex, at both institutional and individual levels, and this complexity is also seen in most of the contributions to the book.

---

21 See L. Baron, et al., eds., *The Ways that Often Parted: Essays in Honor of Joel Marcus* (Atlanta: SBL Press, 2018).

Anders Runesson and Jan Bremmer seek to illuminate the complexity of the issues by looking at socio-institutional and terminological aspects of Jewish-Christian relations, respectively. Runesson argues, provocatively, that the entire debate about the "parting" (or "partings," or lack thereof) is based on a simplistic, monolithic understanding of the role of the synagogue and a confusion between different groups of Christ associations: non-Jewish Christ associations never shared an institutional context with rabbinic Judaism. For his part, Bremmer traces the development in the use of the terms *Ioudaismos* and *Christianismos* from 2 Maccabees (for the former) through the early 3rd century. It emerges that these terms signify a way of life in that period and that, at least in Christian sources, they are developed in tandem, with their use signifying distance between Jewish and Christian communities to different degrees in different places.

After these conceptual and terminological discussions, the following six chapters turn to texts or figures who have in the past been identified as clear witnesses to the "parting," ranging from Paul to Justin Martyr. Jens Schröter's investigation of Paul approaches the question in two principal ways, first by inquiring into Paul's own self-presentation and his articulation of the relation between Christ-believers and non-believing Jews and, second, by addressing practical considerations related to Torah observance and the life of these Christian communities. Similarly, Matthias Konradt organizes his chapter on the Gospel of Matthew – within or outside of Judaism? – around the twin poles of evidence for its strong and ongoing connections with contemporary Judaism and its interest in the inclusion of gentiles *qua* gentiles. In the case of Acts, Kylie Crabbe emphasizes the consistently hybrid identity of the various literary characters – Timothy, Apollos, Paul et al. When one takes the complex of overlapping identities together with the literary aspect of the work, where characters fulfill particular plot functions without unambiguous external, historical referents, it becomes increasingly clear that the possibility of holding together multiple identities is what enables the inclusion of Jewish and Gentile believers within the same community. For all three authors, the question of "inside or outside" operates on too binary a logic to adequately address the historical situations.

Turning to the Gospel of John, Jörg Frey takes up an even more contested document in the history of discussions of Jewish-Christian relations, not only one in which an exit from Judaism is often considered done and dusted, but one that is at times considered *anti*-Jewish. Frey surveys manifold issues: from the vexed question of the ἀποσυνάγωγος (John 9:22; 12:42; 16:2) to the theological parallels with Qumran materials, to the evidence for ongoing Jewish practices in John and the Johannine letters. He admits, of course, that John does engage in powerfully negative rhetoric against "the Jews," though even here matters are not without complicating positive examples.

James Carleton Paget and Benjamin Edsall offer two investigations of the "parting" beyond the confines of the New Testament, in the *Epistle of Barnabas* and the works of Justin Martyr. In both instances, the history of scholarship has been dominated by the view that these works represent a final rupture with Judaism, even if not one already long accomplished. While taking readers through a kaleidoscope of interpretations – from those that see Barnabas as demonstrating a "parting" to those that deny this – Carleton Paget importantly notes that if many scholars increasingly agree that Barnabas does not reflect an accomplished separation between Jews and Christians, there is yet little agreement on what the alternative interpretation should be. The historical and historiographical complexities remain unsolved. In the case of Justin Martyr, Edsall distinguishes between Justin's theological arguments for Christian legitimacy – oriented around the claim to be "the true Israel" – and the evidence he provides of ongoing interaction and integration between Jewish and Christian communities.

The final essays, by Paul Trebilco, Joseph Verheyden and Tobias Nicklas, address the issue of Jewish-Christian relations in particular locales. Trebilco explores the epigraphic, liturgical and literary evidence in Asia Minor for continued interaction and communal overlap between Jews and Christians, arguing for a variegated model of interaction that includes other non-Jewish communities in place of the binary frame of the "parting." In relation to Rome, Verheyden acknowledges the sociological mixture of Jews and Christians there but emphasizes that the two groups were not solely or even primarily concerned with differentiating from one another. By the middle of the 2nd century, he argues, Jewish and Christian communities become more distinguishable and yet they remained somehow connected. Nicklas addresses the dearth of evidence about early 2nd century Jewish and Christian communities in Alexandria. While things are muddy, he argues it is likely that the destruction of the Alexandrian Jewish community in AD 117 led to a Gentile Christian community that was no longer in contest with the remaining Jewish population.

A number of common themes run through the essays. These include, for example, a critique of the "parting" model as overly binary, tending to impede sound historical analysis rather than enable it. Because the metaphor lacks nuance, it must always be tested and corrected against the historical material in question. Furthermore, the difficulties of demarcating the boundaries of Jewish and Christian identities – on the scale of the individual and of the community – should not be underestimated. Some communities were separate from others, in some places, and these separations do not fall neatly along clear borders of Christianity and Judaism. Indeed, as the essays on Asia Minor, Rome and Alexandria emphasize, if focusing on Jewish-Christian relations appears to be a pressing concern for contemporary scholars, it was not consistently so for the early Jewish and Christian communities. What finally emerges from these points, at least in the view of the editors, is that the answer to whether or not Christians and Jews had "parted" ways depends a great deal on the perspective one adopts in asking the question. If some find this a rather unsatisfying conclusion, it is nevertheless preferable to confess one's uncertainty than to claim having reached a final verdict in matters that – for lack of more complete evidence and context, among other things – continue to elude us.

Bibliography

Baron, L., et al., eds., *The Ways that Often Parted: Essays in Honor of Joel Marcus* (Atlanta: SBL Press, 2018).
Becker, A. H., and A. Y. Reed, eds., *The Ways that Never Parted. Jews and Christians in Late Antiquity and the Early Middle Ages*, TSAJ 95 (Tübingen: Mohr Siebeck, 2003).
Brakke, D., *The Gnostics. Myth, Ritual, and Diversity in Early Christianity* (Cambridge, MA, and London: Harvard University Press, 2010).
Cohen, S. J. D., *The Beginnings of Jewishness: Boundaries, Varieties, Uncertainties* (Berkeley: University of California Press, 1999).
Dunn, J. D. G., *The Partings of the Ways between Christianity and Judaism and their Significance for the Character of Christianity*, 2nd ed. (London: SCM Press, 2006).
Dunn, J. D. G., *Neither Jew nor Greek. A Contested Identity*, vol. 3 of *Christianity in the Making* (Grand Rapids and Cambridge, U.K.: Eerdmans, 2015).
Ehrman, B. D., *Lost Christianities. The Battles for Scripture and the Faiths We Never Knew* (Oxford: Oxford University Press, 2003).
Fredriksen, P., "What 'Parting of the Ways'? Jews, Gentiles, and the Ancient Mediterranean City," in *The Ways that Never Parted. Jews and Christians in Late Antiquity and the Early Middle Ages*, ed. A. H. Becker and A. Y. Reed, TSAJ 95 (Tübingen: Mohr Siebeck, 2003), 35–64.
Fredriksen, P., "Mandatory Retirement: Ideas in the Study of Christian Origins whose Time has Come to Go," *Studies in Religion* 35 (2006): 231–246.
Frey, J., "Fragmente judenchristlicher Evangelien," in *Antike Christliche Apokryphen in deutscher Übersetzung I: Evangelien und Verwandtes*, ed. C. Markschies and J. Schröter (Tübingen: Mohr Siebeck, 2012), 560–660.
Frey, J., "Gospels of the Nazarenes," in *From Thomas to Tertullian*, ed. J. Schröter and C. Jacobi, vol. 2 of *The Reception of Jesus in the First Three Centuries*, ed. C. Keith et al. (London: T&T Clark, 2020), 163–172.
Frey, J., "Gospel of the Ebionites," in *From Thomas to Tertullian*, ed. J. Schröter and C. Jacobi, vol. 2 of *The Reception of Jesus in the First Three Centuries*, ed. C. Keith et al. (London: T&T Clark, 2020), 173–182.

Frey, J., "Gospel of the Hebrews," in *From Thomas to Tertullian*, ed. J. Schröter and C. Jacobi, vol. 2 of *The Reception of Jesus in the First Three Centuries*, ed. C. Keith et al. (London: T&T Clark, 2020), 183–192.

Freyne, S., "Behind the Names: Samaritans, Ioudaioi, Galileans," in *Text and Artefact in the Religions of Mediterranean Antiquity. Essays in Honour of Peter Richardson*, ed. S. G. Wilson and M. Desjardins (Waterloo, ON: Wilfried Laurier University Press, 2000), 389–401.

Goodman, M., "Modeling the 'Parting of the Ways'", in *The Ways that Never Parted. Jews and Christians in Late Antiquity and the Early Middle Ages*, ed. A. H. Becker and A. Y. Reed, TSAJ 95 (Tübingen: Mohr Siebeck, 2003), 119–129.

Lieu, J. M., "The Parting of the Ways: Theological Construct or Historical Reality?," in eadem, *Neither Jew nor Greek. Constructing Early Christianity*, 2nd ed. (London et al.: T&T Clark, 2016), 31–49.

Mason, S., "Jews, Judeans, Judaizing, Judaism: Problems of Categorization in Ancient History," *JSJ* 38 (2007): 457–512.

Neusner, J., et al., eds., *Judaisms and Their Messiahs at the Turn of the Christian Era* (Cambridge: Cambridge University Press, 1987).

Nicklas, T., "Parting of the Ways? Probleme eines Konzepts," in *Juden – Heiden – Christen? Religiöse Inklusion und Exklusion in Kleinasien bis Decius*, ed. S. Alkier and H. Leppin, WUNT 400 (Tübingen: Mohr Siebeck, 2018), 21–41.

Niebuhr, K.-W., "'Judentum' und 'Christentum' bei Paulus und Ignatius von Antiochien," *ZNW* 85 (1994): 218–233.

Niebuhr, K.-W., "Offene Fragen zur Gesetzespraxis bei Paulus und seinen Gemeinden (Sabbat, Speisegebote, Beschneidung)," *BThZ* 25 (2008): 16–51.

Reinhartz, A., "A Fork in the Road or a Multi-Lane Highway? New Perspectives on the 'Parting of the Ways' Between Judaism and Christianity," in *The Changing Faces of Judaism, Christianity, and other Greco-Roman Religions in Antiquity*, ed. I. H. Henderson and G. S. Oegema. JSHRZ Studien 2 (Gütersloh: Gütersloher Verlagshaus, 2006), 280–295.

Romeny, B. ter Haar, "Hypotheses on the Development of Judaism and Christianity in Syria in the Period after 70 C.E.," in *Matthew and the Didache. Two Documents from the Same Jewish-Christian Milieu?*, ed. H. van de Sandt (Assen: Royal Van Gorcum and Minneapolis: Fortress Press, 2005), 13–33.

Runesson, A., "Particularistic Judaism and Universalistic Christianity? Some Critical Remarks on Terminology and Theology," *StTh* 54 (2000): 55–75.

Runesson, A., "Inventing Christian Identity: Paul, Ignatius, and Theodosius I," in *Exploring Early Christian Identity*, ed. B. Holmberg, WUNT 226 (Tübingen: Mohr Siebeck, 2008), 59–92.

Runesson, A., "Re-Thinking Early Jewish–Christian Relations: Matthean Community History as Pharisaic Intragroup Conflict," *JBL* 127:1 (2008): 95–113.

Runesson, A., "The Question of Terminology: The Architecture of Contemporary Discussions on Paul," in *Paul Within Judaism: Restoring the First-Century Context to the Apostle*, ed. M. Nanos and M. Zetterholm (Minneapolis: Fortress, 2015), 53–77.

Saldarini, A. J., *Matthew's Christian-Jewish Community*, CSHJ (Chicago: University of Chicago Press, 1994).

Schnelle, U., *Die getrennten Wege von Römern, Juden und Christen* (Tübingen: Mohr Siebeck, 2019).

Segal, A. F., *The Other Judaisms of Late Antiquity* (Atlanta: Scholars Press, 1987).
Verheyden, J., "Jewish Christianity, A State of Affairs: Affinities and Differences with Respect to Matthew, James, and the Didache," in *Matthew, James, and the Didache. Three Related Documents in Their Jewish and Christian Setting*, ed. H. van de Sandt and J. K. Zangenberg (Atlanta: Scholars Press, 2008), 123–135.
Wander, B., *Trennungsprozesse zwischen Frühem Christentum und Judentum*, 2nd ed., TANZ 16 (Tübingen: Francke, 1997).

Christoph Markschies
From "Wide and Narrow Way" to "The Ways that Never Parted"? Road Metaphors in Models of Jewish-Christian Relations in Antiquity

Abstract: Der Beitrag gliedert sich in zwei Teile: Im ersten Teil werden die Vorgeschichte der Metaphorik "Parting of the Ways" und die problematischen theoretischen Implikationen des Modells behandelt. Es wurde nach allem, was sich ermitteln lässt, erstmals in der ersten Hälfte des zwanzigsten Jahrhunderts in England gebraucht. Wie alle Modellbildungen vereinfacht es radikal die historischen Befunde. Um zu einer angemesseneren Sicht der historischen Verhältnisse – jenseits der Alternativen von getrennten und niemals getrennten Wegen – beizutragen, werden die Homilien gegen die Juden, die Johannes Chrysostomus Ende des vierten Jahrhunderts in Antiochia hielt, analysiert und insbesondere die Spannungen zwischen Rhetorik, Realitätskonstruktion und so thematisierten Realitäten in den Blick genommen.

Keywords: Jewish Christianity, Model, Metaphor, Road, Didache, John Chrysostom, Antijudaism

Behind the metaphoric duality of "The parting of the ways" and "The ways that never parted" are in reality, according to a system devised by Udo Schnelle in a more or less recently published book, *"five ideal type models"* for the parting of Judaism and Christianity.[1] We can for the time being set aside the obvious ques-

---

[1] U. Schnelle, *Die getrennten Wege von Römern, Juden und Christen: Religionspolitik im 1. Jahrhundert n. Chr.* (Tübingen: Mohr Siebeck, 2019), 3; cf. also T. Nicklas, *Jews and Christians? Second Century 'Christian' Perspectives on the 'Parting of the Ways,'* Annual Deichmann Lectures 2013 (Tübingen: Mohr Siebeck, 2014); idem, "Parting of the Ways? Probleme eines Konzepts," in *Juden – Heiden – Christen? Religiöse Inklusion und Exklusion in Kleinasien bis Decius*, ed. S. Alkier and H. Leppin, WUNT 400 (Tübingen: Mohr Siebeck, 2018), 21–41; and S.J.D. Cohen, "The Ways That Parted: Jews, Christians, and Jewish-Christians, ca. 100–150 CE," in *Jews and Christians in the First and Second Centuries: The Interbellum 70–132 CE*, ed. J. Schwartz and P.J. Tomson, CRINT 15 (Leiden and Boston: Brill, 2017), 307–339; cf. G.G. Stroumsa, "Als sich der Orient nach Osten bewegte: Judentum und Islam in der Wissenschaft des neunzehnten Jahrhunderts/When the Orient moved East: Judaism and Islam in Nineteenth-Century Scholarship," in *Eine dreifältige*

tion of whether Schnelle, with his five type models, really took seriously the provocation of Annette Yoshiko Reed and Adam H. Becker, who dispute – whether with an ironic undertone typical for French poststructuralism or deadly German seriousness – that the ways really ever parted. For nobody can dispute talk of a "way" that Judaism and Christianity have travelled along and subsequently that the metaphor of a fork in the road at which the different ways initially arose also constitutes a model that uses a metaphor. Only people can of course travel along roads or paths in the actual sense, groups travel along roads occasionally also in the real sense but here we are not thinking about a physical retreat by some apocalypticists or other into the desert, but about a development described using the metaphorical idea of a road.

To begin with, I would like to take a brief look at what dealing with a model – according to Schnelle – with an "ideal type model" even, actually means. Thereafter I would like to query the history of this model, i.e. of a model for the development of Judaism and Christianity using the metaphor of a road. And finally I would like to examine this very model with the aid of some historical observations as to whether it provides us with what it promises or, to put it better maybe, whether it is suitable for delivering what we expect from it. To do this, I have deliberately chosen a very late example, that is, certain homilies by the Antiochian preacher John Chrysostom from the late fourth century. A brief summarizing section concludes my explanations.

1 The parting of the ways – a model for the development of religion(s)

Models are essential in academic discourse while at the same time their effects are highly ambivalent. We use ideas of models in our attempt to illustrate reality. We deliberately reduce the complexity of reality in order to be able to look at something that is overly complex for our imagination and to be able to portray this to others. In this way, thinking can detach itself from a usually rather confusing variety of phenomena so that these can initially be classified by being reduced and subsequently understood, though at the price of our being bound to the power of the models, which is restricted due to this reduction.[2] Occasionally,

---

Schnur: Über Judentum, Christentum und Islam in Geschichte und Wissenschaft, ed. M. Tilly, Lucas-Preis 2018 (Tübingen: Mohr Siebeck, 2020), 126–209.
[2] I here paraphrased and slightly modified the first sentences of H. Bredekamp and K. Pinkau, "Einladung zum akademischen Gespräch – Rundbrief," in *Modelle des Denkens. Streitgespräch*

our being bound to the models – as described superbly by Gottfried Wilhelm Leibniz – even becomes a type of shackle where the model that reduces the reality pushes itself to the fore beyond this in fact irreducible variety of phenomena, obscuring that which inhibits reduction and simplification. As a result of this observation, it is clear that some models are not so good while others are better. When scholarship functions based on ideal types, the model will be selected that maps the variety of reality with the least possible loss of differentiation yet which incorporates the greatest possible reducibility – or even, as in the case of our model, reduces it to a single term or a single metaphor. Good models enable us to simplify complex structures and illustrate abstract or scattered structures efficiently, as Jürgen Mittelstraß once explained.[3] I would like here to add to this modelling typology familiar from scientific theory the observation that, in classical and ancient studies, modelling is occasionally used not to help structure a confusing variety of phenomena but to help deal with a lack of sources. For the first few centuries of our common era – compared to sources at our disposal for German foreign policy in the twentieth century for instance – the number of sources is often woefully low, which only allows us to reconstruct situations locally, for the most part only from a very specific, individual viewpoint, too. It is only in late antiquity that the situation improves somewhat. Rather than merely classifying it, models therefore replace a sizeable chunk of reality here.

One final comment on the theoretical implications of the modelling, which once again links to the last German article known to me on the topic. Allow me to introduce this comment using a question: Why does Schnelle, in his systematisation of five methods of access, additionally distinguish – assuming he does this deliberately – the subclass of ideal type models within the models? If Schnelle has used the term deliberately, he thereby follows, implicitly or explicitly, the categorical differentiation of *ideal typical* models of social phenomena and their *real typical* empirical description, which Max Weber introduced to scientific theory and which in turn (as so often) referenced the Neo-Kantian

---

in der Wissenschaftlichen Sitzung der Versammlung der Berlin-Brandenburgischen Akademie der Wissenschaften am 12. Dezember 2003, ed. Präsident der Berlin-Brandenburgischen Akademie der Wissenschaften, Debatte Heft 2 (Berlin: Berlin-Brandenburgische Akademie der Wissenschaften, 2005), 9–12, see 9. Cf. also S. Alkier and H. Leppin, "Einleitung – Juden, Christen, Heiden?," in *Juden – Heiden – Christen? Religiöse Inklusionen und Exklusionen im Römischen Kleinasien bis Decius*, ed. S. Alkier and H. Leppin, WUNT 400 (Tübingen: Mohr Siebeck, 2018); M. Vogel, "Ein Streit nicht nur um Worte: Begriffsgeschichtliche Beobachtungen zu frühchristlichen Strategien der Exklusion," ibid., 45–52.

3 J. Mittelstraß, "Anmerkungen zum Modellbegriff," in *Modelle des Denkens* (see n. 2), 65–67, see 65.

Heinrich Rickert. Ideal typical modelling is – to cite Weber – a "unilateral augmentation of one or several aspects," which takes place a priori, before all empirical events, by abstracting conceptually and objectively from features of social reality.[4] Typical examples of an ideal type of this kind are, according to Weber, "stock market crashes" or "bureaucracy." Regardless of what Udo Schnelle actually meant and what the implications of Max Weber's distinction are, a great deal speaks for the theory that modelling the emergence of a religion according to the comparatively straightforward model of a fork in the road is an ideal typical construction of a social development and not a real typical systematisation of phenomena based on empirical observations. An original unit is separated off, which always gives rise to a new element. The previous element that is now minus the new element did not, of course, really stay the same but also changed itself. One thus becomes two. And in this way an ideal typical innovation in religious history arises (but not just here – one might think for example of the division of the Roman Catholic Church in the Middle Ages during the Reformation, the splitting of the Social Democratic Party in Germany after 1918 and so forth), this is how a new religion arises. I would like to note very briefly here that, of course – if we already think in terms of such ideal types – new aspects can in reality not only arise due to the splitting off from an earlier, prior unit but, presumably also rather spontaneously, in a group that does not originate from a uniform framework at all. If this is so, however, the ideal type reconstruction of the history of the Jewish and Christian religions in imperial antiquity with its model of a fork in the road in particular is highly presumptuous because it assumes an original unit that somehow or other splits off – I deliberately use the term "somehow or other" here, for in reality, the metaphor is indeed fairly diffuse. A fork in the road might be what we call a bifurcation, the splitting off of one road into two equally justified continuations, but may also be a clear hierarchical divergence of a side road from a main road. With regard to an implied hierarchy of the two paths of "Judaism" and "Christianity" (initially in inverted commas), the metaphor of the fork in the road is certainly imprecise and indeed rather diffuse and, in this respect at least, in its literal German translation "die Trennung der Wege" (the parting of the ways) is highly problematic.

Following these general comments on model theory, we shall now come to the second section on the history of this model.

---

[4] M. Weber, "Die Objektivität sozialwissenschaftlicher und sozialpolitischer Erkenntnis," in idem, *Gesammelte Aufsätze zur Wissenschaftslehre*, 3rd ed. (Tübingen: Mohr Siebeck, 1968), 146–214, here 191.

2 The parting of the ways – a model with a history

To the best of my knowledge there is no history of the model of the parting of the ways. There are, of course, countless stories of the development of Christianity, what is known as Jewish Christianity, and, meanwhile, even stories about the development of Judaism from Christianity, though I by no means wish to conflate the respective ideas of Daniel Boyarin and Peter Schäfer[5] with this brief reference. But there is no proper history of the scholarship on the formulation and the concept itself of "the parting of the ways," and of course I will not be able to hastily construct one for the purposes of this conference.

Nevertheless, I would like to make a few remarks on the backstory of the metaphorical use of the image of the path and what is arguably the most famous use thereof in the past century. To this purpose, I will revisit some stations from the history of the scholarship working backwards. I do this because we cannot, of course, start our consideration of the formulation "the parting of the ways" in the year 1989. In September of that momentous year, it was principally exegetes from Tübingen and Durham who gathered for the second "Durham-Tübingen Research Symposium on Earliest Christianity and Judaism".[6] There was a remembrance marking the one-hundred-and-tenth anniversary of the death of Joseph Barber Lightfoot (1828–1889), who in 1879 had come to Durham as bishop from Cambridge, where he had first been the Hulsean Professor of Divinity and later, from 1875, the Lady Margaret Professor. Such international collaborations were by no means common at the time; the Tübingen-based New Testament scholar Martin Hengel (1926–2009) was well acquainted with the by then retired Charles Kingsley Barrett (1917–2011) and passionately enjoyed discussing the history of Christianity with intelligent and interested colleagues in England and France. If I recall it correctly from conversations during my days

---

[5] E.g. D. Boyarin, *Abgrenzungen. Die Aufspaltung des Judäo-Christentums*, trans. by G. Palmer, ANTZ 10 = ABU 1 (Berlin and Dortmund: Institut Kirche und Judentum/Lehrhaus e.V., 2009); P. Schäfer, *Die Geburt des Judentums aus dem Geist des Christentums. Fünf Vorlesungen zur Entstehung des rabbinischen Judentums*, Tria Corda 6 (Tübingen: Mohr Siebeck, 2010).
[6] J.D.G. Dunn, ed., *Jews and Christians. The parting of the ways A.D. 70 to 135. – The Second Durham-Tübingen Research Symposium on Earliest Christianity and Judaism, Durham, September, 1989*, WUNT 66 (Tübingen: Mohr Siebeck, 1992).

as a student and assistant, the idea for the symposium had been his.[7] William Horbury of Cambridge and Peter Stuhlmacher of Tübingen were also present. In the foreword, the man chiefly responsible for the symposium in Durham, James D. G. Dunn, described the relationship between the great Tübingen theologian Ferdinand Christian Baur (1792–1860) and Durham's Lightfoot. The salient thing for our context is that Dunn, beyond a concise summary of the main differences between the two scholars, asserted that *Jewish Christianity*, for both Baur and Lightfoot, was the truly interesting phenomenon between early Judaism and Christianity. It is noteworthy that the metaphor of the "parting of the ways" does not appear in this foreword by James D. G. Dunn, and it is only in the "concluding summary" that Dunn returns to it in the context of revisiting the presentations of the symposium. His concluding metaphors caution against an overly literal understanding of the metaphor in the sense of a sudden and comprehensive divergence of Judaism and Christianity. It would be interesting to find out whether the monograph *The Partings of the Ways Between Christianity and Judaism and their Significance for the Character of Christianity*, which was published three years later,[8] had been largely finished in its rough conception during the symposium or only took shape later, inspired as it were by the event. As it was in 1991 and 1992 that both monographs, the edited volume of the 1989 symposium and the cited work by Dunn, were published, the term "the parting(s) of the ways" and the corresponding model as interpreted by Dunn certainly travelled quickly. Remarkably, Dunn admitted in the foreword to the second edition of his monograph from the year 2006 that the criticism by his New Testament colleague Judith Lieu was justified and the model he had actually used in order to replace the idea of a fixed date for the break between Judaism and Christianity with the image of a pathway was too static. What is more, Dunn wrote, there are more than two rigid options for "Judaism" and "Christianity."[9]

But the history of the metaphor does not begin with Dunn. In their intelligent and witty polemic against the concept of the "parting of the ways," Annette Yoshiko Reed and Adam H. Becker point to an earlier usage by James Parkes

---

[7] J. Frey, "Friedrich Avemarie (1960–2012) und sein wissenschaftliches Vermächtnis," in F. Avemarie, *Neues Testament und frührabbinisches Judentum*, ed. J. Frey and A. Standhartinger, WUNT 316 (Tübingen: Mohr Siebeck, 2013), XI–XXXIII, here XIII.
[8] J.D.G. Dunn, *The Partings of the Ways between Christianity and Judaism and their Significance for the Character of Christianity* (London: SCM Press, 1991).
[9] J.M. Lieu, "'The Parting of the Ways': Theological Construct or Historical Reality?," in eadem, *Neither Jew nor Greek? Constructing Early Christianity* (London and New York: T&T Clark, 2002), 11–30.

(1896–1981), an English cleric, independent scholar and (church-)political activist, who in one of his publications on Jewish-Christian relations and the history of anti-Semitism had headed a chapter with the words "The Parting of the Ways." This was in the book *The Conflict of the Church and the Synagogue. A Study in the Origins of Antisemitism* from the year 1934, which traces the history into the early Middle Ages and examines the first two centuries following the death of Paul through the death of Origen in the middle of the third century. At the beginning of this period, according to Parkes, Christianity is still a Jewish sect;[10] for him, Jewish Christianity is an archaic phenomenon after the divergence of Judaism and Christianity, for which citations are taken from the Gospel of John and the apologist Justin. Oddly enough, the metaphor really only occurs in the chapter title and the headings printed on every second page. There is therefore reason to suspect that the phrase had not yet been assimilated into common use in the thirties, not least in view of the fact that books by Parkes are, and were at the time, certainly not mainstream literature.

Some time ago, Judith Lieu cited an even earlier, somewhat related instance of the metaphorical imagery of a divergence from the year 1912; in that year, Frederick John Foakes Jackson (1855–1941) and colleagues from the Jesus College Cambridge edited a volume of papers titled *The Parting of the Roads. Studies in the Development of Judaism and Early Christianity*, dedicated to the Master of the college, Henry Arthur Morgan.[11] Foakes Jackson, a student of Joseph Barber Lightfoot, is still best known for a work he began in 1920 with Kirsopp Lake (1872–1946), which went on to be reprinted multiple times, titled *The Beginnings of Christianity*, which was essentially a translated and commented edition of the Acts of the Apostles. He personally, however, contributes no more to the volume and thus the paradigm of "The Parting of the Roads" than his role as publisher. The second publisher is another story. If one reads the introductory essay to the volume, which was written by the second editor alongside Foakes Jackson – the little known, at least in this country, Dean of London's St. Paul's Cathedral, William R. Inge (1890–1954) – one is struck as a modern reader by the pronounced, and all-too-familiar, to German listeners, at least, from the bleakest periods of German New Testament scholarship, by the differentiation between Galilee and Judaea, which Inge goes so far as to specify in terms of blood: "In speaking of the Jewish element in Christianity, it must be remembered that the cradle of our faith was not Judaea but Galilee, and that the Galileans had probably hardly

---

10 J. Parkes, *The Conflict of the Church and the Synagogue. A Study in the Origins of Anti-Semitism* (London: Soncino Press, 1934), 77.
11 F.J. Foakes Jackson and W.R. Inge, eds., *The Parting of the Roads: Studies in the Development of Judaism and Early Christianity* (London: Edward Arnold, 1912).

a drop of Jewish blood in their veins."[12] I shall refrain from revisiting the, as we regard it today, anti-Jewish and indeed anti-Semitic portrayal of the Jewish religion as legalistic and nationalistic, which Inge uses, in spite of his recognition for the Biblical texts of the Psalms and the prophets, as a means of constructing a strict contrast between "Hebraic and Hellenic views of life."[13] Likewise, his prejudices concerning Hellenism are not worth expounding upon ("Christianity had to build its house out of the traditions of ruined and embittered Judaism and a degenerated and barbarized Hellenism"[14]); all that emerges clearly from this architecture is that in the end, Jesus of Nazareth provides the synthesis: "the divine founder of Christianity was above this antithesis."[15] If one may refer jointly to the works of Foakes Jackson and Inge, to use the metaphor of "The Parting of the Roads," then this rather gives rise to the idea that, in the one Christianity both paths of Judaism and Hellenism come together to make one, rather than one single Jewish path forking off onto two paths. It appears to me that, unlike Judith Lieu, Foakes Jackson and Inge don't really belong to the prehistory of the two volumes from the years 1991/1992 that were edited or even wholly written by Dunn. Nevertheless, the volume still retains its importance in the history of the research work on the separation between Judaism and Christianity, alone due to the fact that it contains another essay by the later (orthodox) Rabbi from London's New West End Synagogue, Ephraim Levine, titled "The Breach between Judaism and Christianity," in which one of the rare early Jewish views of the subject is presented.[16]

My thesis, however, is now that the applied model is clearly older and, in view of its age, it should come as no surprise when New Testament scholars apply it and speak of a "Parting of the Roads" or a "Parting of the Ways." What I mean is that practically every New Testament scholar who grew up in the English system (perhaps unlike an entire generation of German New Testament scholars) knows the concisely formulated terms of the original Jewish "two-paths teaching" from the Didache. I quote here the beginning of this very early church order, perhaps still from the late first century Anno Domini:

---

12 W.R. Inge, "Introductory," in *The Parting of the Roads: Studies in the Development of Judaism and Early Christianity,* ed. F.J. Foakes Jackson and W.R. Inge (London: Edward Arnold, 1912), 4.
13 Inge, "Introductory" (see n. 12), 8.
14 Inge, "Introductory" (see n. 12), 13.
15 Inge, "Introductory" (see n. 12), 11.
16 E. Levine, "The Breach between Judaism and Christianity," in *The Parting of the Roads: Studies in the Development of Judaism and Early Christianity,* ed. F.J. Foakes Jackson and W.R. Inge (London: Edward Arnold, 1912), 283–310; cf. E. Levine, *The History of the New West End Synagogue. 1879–1929* (Aldershot: Drew, 1929).

> There are two paths, one of life and one of death, and the difference is great between the two paths. 2. Now the path of life is this: ... But the path of death is this: ...[17]

There is little dispute that this notion of two paths, at the junction of which those being addressed in the text now stand, asked to make a clear decision for the right path (in the double meaning of the word), has been taken from the contemporary Jewish literature. In his commentary on the Didache, Kurt Niederwimmer speaks of a "two-path tractate" the traces of which, in his opinion, can also be found in the Epistle of Barnabas, which is a lecture subject at this congress and proof of which is provided in more or less independent adaptations in five other church orders and related texts from antique Christianity[18]. The discovery of the Qumran texts after the Second World War in particular confirmed the older hypothesis that it is a Jewish text or at least a Jewish idea. In the meantime, a dissertation has even been submitted about the connections – by Jonathan Draper in Cambridge in the year 1983, titled "A Commentary on the Didache in the Light of the Dead Sea Scrolls and Related Documents."[19] However, in addition to the Qumran texts and The Rule of the Congregation, one could also refer to passages from the Targum Neofiti I and The Sentences of Pseudo-Phocylides as evidence. The first English and German literature on the Didache appeared at the turn of the twentieth century and the 'two-paths teaching' nearly always enjoyed special attention.

With this, we can now move to our announced example and the third and last section of this contribution.

---

17 Did. 1:1–3: Ὁδοὶ δύο εἰσί, μία τῆς ζωῆς καὶ μία τοῦ θανάτου, διαφορὰ δὲ πολλὴ μεταξὺ τῶν δύο ὁδῶν. Ἡ μὲν οὖν τῆς ζωῆς ἐστιν αὕτη· πρῶτον ἀγαπήσεις τὸν θεὸν τὸν ποιήσαντά σε, δεύτερον τὸν πλησίον σου ὡς σεαυτόν· πάντα δὲ ὅσα ἐὰν θελήσῃς μὴ γίνεσθαί σοι, καὶ σὺ ἄλλῳ μὴ ποίει. 3. Τούτων δὲ τῶν λόγων ἡ διδαχή ἐστιν αὕτη· εὐλογεῖτε τοὺς καταρωμένους ὑμῖν καὶ προσεύχεσθε ὑπὲρ τῶν ἐχθρῶν ὑμῶν, νηστεύετε δὲ ὑπὲρ τῶν διωκόντων ὑμᾶς. Did. 5:1: Ἡ δὲ τοῦ θανάτου ὁδός ἐστιν αὕτη·.
18 K. Niederwimmer, *Die Didache, erklärt*, Kommentar zu den Apostolischen Vätern 1 (Göttingen: Vandenhoeck & Ruprecht, 1989), 83–157.
19 Cf. the Thesis of Jonathan Draper, *A Commentary on the Didache in the Light of the Dead Sea Scrolls and Related Documents*, https://www.academia.edu/11195007/A_Commentary_on_the_Didache_in_the_Light_of_the_Dead_Sea_Scrolls_and_Related_Documents_Part_I (accessed 31 July 2020).

3 The Parting of the ways – on the usefulness of the model

One will hopefully forgive a historian who studies the history of antique Christianity when, in his concluding third section, he tests the usefulness of the model that is linked to the metaphor of "The Parting of the Ways" based on a very late example, that is, the situation in the large antique city of Antioch, which we have been able to reconstruct from the sermons of John Chrysostom, more precisely his *Homilies against Jews*, a series of sermons that Chrysostom held in the year 386 A.D. in the cathedral of Antioch.

The words of this star preacher seem to fully confirm that a parting of the ways had already long since taken place – one can at least interpret the downright hostile and viciously spiteful attitude of the prominent Christian theologian and well-known preacher towards the Jewish people and the Jewish synagogue in this way, which is also how it is interpreted in most parts of secondary literature. Here are only a few examples: John did not shy away from describing Jewish citizens from his own city as "dogs." On the one hand, he accused them of being "stiff-necked" due to what he considered to be exaggerated observation of the law and yet maintained, on the other hand, that they regularly became ill due to overeating and excessive drinking, thus at the same time contradicting their observance of the law – and these comments came from the same sermon. At the end of the introductory passage, he literally says: "Although such beasts are unfit for work, they are fit for killing" (*Adversus Judaeos* 1.2–3).[20]

If one considers at this point that up to fifteen percent of the six-hundred thousand inhabitants of the city belonged to the Jewish community, certainly more than fifty thousand, and that the Jewish community owned several synagogues and places of prayer, among these the synagogue in which the highly distinguished graves of the seven Maccabean martyrs and their mother were displayed and worshipped by many pilgrims, then one must regard Chrysostom's

---

20 John Chrysostom, *Adv. Jud.* 1.2 (PG 48, 846): οὕτω καὶ ὁ τῶν Ἰουδαίων δῆμος, ὑπὸ τῆς μέθης καὶ πολυσαρκίας εἰς κακίαν ἐσχάτην κατενεχθέντες, ἐσκίρτησαν, καὶ οὐκ ἐδέξαντο τὸν ζυγὸν τοῦ Χριστοῦ, οὐδὲ τὸ ἄροτρον τῆς διδασκαλίας εἵλκυσαν. Ὅπερ οὖν καὶ ἄλλος προφήτης αἰνιττόμενος ἔλεγεν, Ὡς δάμαλις παροιστρῶσα παροίστρησεν Ἰσραήλ (Hos 4:16). Ἕτερος δὲ αὐτὸν μόσχον ἀδίδακτον ἐκάλει (Jer 31:18). Τὰ δὲ τοιαῦτα ἄλογα, πρὸς ἐργασίαν οὐκ ὄντα ἐπιτήδεια, πρὸς σφαγὴν ἐπιτήδεια γίνεται. Ὅπερ οὖν καὶ οὗτοι πεπόνθασι, καὶ πρὸς ἐργασίαν ἀχρήστους ἑαυτοὺς καταστήσαντες, πρὸς σφαγὴν ἐπιτήδειοι γεγόνασι. Διὰ τοῦτο καὶ ὁ Χριστὸς ἔλεγεν· Τοὺς ἐχθρούς μου, τοὺς μὴ θελήσαντάς με βασιλεῦσαι ἐπ' αὐτῶν, ἀγάγετε ὧδε, καὶ κατασφάξατε αὐτούς (Luke 19:27).

tirades as nothing less than a boycott of this group in the city, and his words can even be seen as an incitement to civil war. Here only a few examples: while Chrysostom says that Jewish physicians may be able to heal the body, he nevertheless adds that the Christian soul of their patients is doomed. And that is why Chrysostom likens them to kidnappers who entice children with sweets and whispers in order to then sell them as slaves (1.7).[21] And their successes, he maintains, come from magic and sorcery. It is therefore better for a Christian to die than to be healed in this way (8.5).[22] But physicians are not the only profession subject to scorn and derision by Chrysostom. All Jews are to his mind uncultivated, shameless, ungrateful, and recalcitrant. They are rebellious against the political authorities and at loggerheads with one another. They are braggarts and a disgrace to the city, poor devils, robbers, and cheats. And allegations of sexual deviance are of course not missing from this chamber of horrors full of hateful and polemic accusations: Jews dance on the marketplace with bare feet, keep company with "harlots" and "effeminates." They love going to the theatre (to watch cheaply erotic comedies),[23] they are lecherous, and no better than swine and rams, because they have intercourse like dogs and stallions.

I now depart from this extremely unpleasant compilation from the eight homilies from the series, which is only a small excerpt from the excellent compilation by Rudolf Brändle,[24] and add as a direct quotation the worst accusation

---

[21] John Chrysostom, *Adv. Jud.* 1.7 (PG 48, 855): Καὶ καθάπερ οἱ ἀνδραποδισταὶ τραγήματα καὶ πλακοῦντας καὶ ἀστραγάλους καὶ ἕτερά τινα τοιαῦτα πολλάκις τοῖς μικροῖς προτεινόμενοι παιδίοις καὶ δελεάζοντες, τῆς ἐλευθερίας αὐτὰ καὶ τῆς ζωῆς ἀποστεροῦσιν αὐτῆς· οὕτω δὴ καὶ οἱ δαίμονες, μέλους ὑπισχνούμενοι θεραπείαν, ὅλην τῆς ψυχῆς καταποντίζουσι τὴν σωτηρίαν.
[22] John Chrysostom, *Adv. Jud.* 8.5 (PG 48, 935): Ἐγὼ δὲ ὑπερβολὴν ποιοῦμαι πολλήν, καὶ ἐκεῖνο λέγω, ὅτι εἰ καὶ θεραπεύουσιν ἀληθῶς, βέλτιον ἀποθανεῖν, ἢ τοῖς ἐχθροῖς τοῦ Θεοῦ προσδραμεῖν, καὶ τοῦτον θεραπευθῆναι τὸν τρόπον. Τί γὰρ ὄφελος, σῶμα θεραπεύεσθαι τῆς ψυχῆς ἀπολλυμένης; τί δὲ κέρδος, ἐνταῦθά τινος τυγχάνειν παραμυθίας, μέλλοντας εἰς τὸ ἀθάνατον παραπέμπεσθαι πῦρ.
[23] Cf. S.-P. Bergjan, "'Das hier ist kein Theater, und ihr sitzt nicht da, um Schauspieler zu betrachten und zu klatschen' – Theaterpolemik und Theatermetaphern bei Johannes Chrysostomos," *ZAC* (2005): 567–592.
[24] Johannes Chrysostomus, *Acht Reden gegen Juden*, ed. and trans. R. Brändle and V. Jegher-Bucher, Bibliothek der Griechischen Literatur 41 (Stuttgart: Hiersemann, 1995), 72–73. Cf. also W. Kinzig, "'Non-separation': Closeness and Co-operation Between Jews and Christians in the Fourth Century," *VC* 45 (1991): 27–53; R. Brändle, "Christen und Juden in Antiochien in den Jahren 386/87. Ein Beitrag zur Geschichte altkirchlicher Judenfeindschaft," in idem, *Studien zur Alten Kirche*, ed. M. Heimgartner, T.K. Kuhn, and M. Sallmann (Stuttgart, Berlin, and Köln: Kohlhammer, 1999), 68–84; A.M. Ritter, "Erwägungen zum Antisemitismus in der Alten Kirche. Johannes Chrysostomos' 'Acht Reden wider die Juden'," in idem, *Studia Chrysostomica. Aufsätze zu Weg, Werk und Wirkung des Johannes Chrysostomus (ca. 349–407)*, STAC 71 (Tübingen:

of all, namely the charge that the Jews – thus maintained by the well-known Antiochian preacher – killed Christ and therefore God:

> If a man were to have slain your son, would you endure to look upon him, or accept his greeting? Would you not shun him as a wicked demon, as the devil himself? They slew the Son of your Lord; do you have the boldness to enter with them under the same roof? (1.7).[25]

One occasionally reads in the secondary academic literature that these terrible allegations were already to be found long before that in the Christian literature of the antique and that John Chrysostom was by no means particularly original with his vicious attacks. Similarly, one could also point out that it was certainly widespread in contemporary imperial rhetoric to use very direct and not particularly discerning language to describe an object of reprimand as absolutely shameful and horrible.[26] At that time, such rhetorical excesses in critiques and reprimands were the negative reverse side of the coin to equally exaggerated positive descriptions in public speeches of people or objects that were loved, which we nowadays would regard as over-the-top adulation.

This practice of the eulogy was exercised, for example, in the addresses on the occasion of the Emperor's birthday and at other speeches honouring rulers and great politicians.[27] We can find examples of such defamatory language in political speeches right up to the present day (in the past years increasingly

---

Mohr Siebeck, 2012), 16–33; idem, "John Chrysostom and the Jews," in idem, *Studia Chrysostomica*, 105–116; G. Bady, "Quelques éléments de réflexion sur les Sermons contre les juifs et les judaïsants de Jean Chrysostome," in *L'Antijudaïsme du Pères: Mythe et/ou réalité?*, ed. J.-M. Auwers, R. Burnet, and D. Luciani, Théologie Historique 125 (Paris: Beauchesne Editeur, 2017), 101–118.

25 John Chrysostom, *Adv. Jud.* 1.7 (PG 48, 854): Εἴ τις τὸν υἱὸν ἀνεῖλε τὸν σόν, εἰπέ μοι, ἆρα ἂν αὐτὸν ἰδεῖν ὑπέμεινας; ἆρα ἂν ἀκοῦσαι τῆς προσηγορίας; ἀλλ' οὐχ ὡς δαίμονα πονηρὸν, ἀλλ' οὐχ ὡς αὐτὸν τὸν διάβολον ἔφυγες ἄν; Τοῦ Δεσπότου σου τὸν Υἱὸν ἀνεῖλον, καὶ τολμᾷς αὐτοῖς εἰς ταυτὸν συνιέναι;

26 R.L. Wilken, *John Chrysostom and the Jews. Rhetoric and Reality in the Late 4th Century*, The Transformation of the Classical Heritage 4 (Berkeley: University of California Press, 1983), 73–122 and A. Finkelstein, "Taming the Jewish Genie. John Chrysostom and the Jews of Antioch in the Shadow of Emperor Julian," in *From Strength to Strength: Essays in Appreciation of Shaye J. D. Cohen*, ed. M.L. Satlow, Brown Judaic Studies 363 (Providence, RI: Brown University Press), 555–575. Cf. now: W. Mayer, "Preaching Hatred? John Chrysostom, Neuroscience, and the Jews," in *Revisioning John Chrysostom. New Approaches, New Perspectives*, ed. C. De Wet and W. Mayer, Critical Approaches to Early Christianity 1 (Leiden and Boston: Brill, 2019), 58–136.

27 Cf. e. g. D. Lassandro, "Bibliographia dei Panegyrici Latini," *Invigilata lucernis* 11 (1989): 219–259.

often, and not only in America, unfortunately), but it shocks us of course when we read them from an antique sermon in the Christian church. An explanation about the rhetorical or ecclesiastical conventions of the time does not excuse, from our point of view, such words by any means. What is more, one must be clear about the fact that the hateful tone used by John Chrysostom was not only a matter of rhetoric. In the antique, for example, anyone who accused a fellow citizen of magic and sorcery was charging him with a crime and thus reporting him to the city authorities. And certain forms of magic and sorcery were punishable by death. The same applied for what were considered to be deviant sexual practices, which was also punishable under certain circumstances. And accusing Jewish citizens of rebellion and insurrection was highly dangerous. This was something to what the authorities reacted very fast and brutally, mercilessly persecuting any insurgents with military violence. When John Chrysostom (an highly influential Christian intellectual in the city) delivered his sermons in the cathedral, the biggest and most prestigious church in the city, speaking out such serious (and completely unfounded) allegations, then he not only exposed innocent people to observation and persecution by the Roman authorities. He also incited his fellow Christians to spy on and denounce others and thus actively destroyed peace in the society of the metropolis. If I were a cynic, I would say it is a wonder that the eight homilies against the Jews by Chrysostom did not lead to a pogrom against the Jewish community. To put it in other words, and less cynically, what we have just seen is a highly skilled, experienced rhetorician apply stereotypes that had long been there in the Christian congregation in order to disturb the public peace and to eradicate the existence of the Jewish community within urban society. By doing so, he radicalized in a horrible manner certain already widespread, anti-Jewish stereotypes. Considering that, precisely in the month in which Chrysostom held his sermons against the Jews, the military entered the city in order to brutally suppress troublemakers who (presumably under the influence of alcohol) had destroyed public monuments, the Christian preacher's hateful polemics were even more treacherous.[28] Did he perhaps want to present new scapegoats to the military in that heated atmosphere? One can at least presume that that was indeed his intention.

However, can one now read the just cited or referred-to passages as something other than evidence of the "parting of the ways of Jews and Christians," to refer back to the title of the small book by Udo Schnelle (and Shaye J. D.

---

28 Johannes Chrysostomus, *Acht Reden gegen Juden* (see n. 24), 37–39. Cf. also G. Downey, *A History of Antioch in Syria from Seleucus to the Arab Conquest* (Princeton, NJ: Princeton University Press, 1961), 410–417.

Cohen)? I would like, perhaps somewhat surprisingly, to actually see these passages more as evidence of the point of view propagated by Annette Yoshiko Reed, Adam H. Becker, and others like Tobias Nicklas, and probably founded by Daniel Boyarin and Peter Schäfer, and speak of ways "that never parted."[29] Even if this talk of the parting of the ways in the second century already represented a revision of the clearly more difficult, older models formed using kinship analogies (whereby Christianity is understood as the daughter religion of the Jewish mother religion and therefore implicitly of course as more modern and contemporary than Judaism), it has become clear in more recent times how little the still existing closeness and the still existing related common dynamics in their development are evident when such metaphors about the parting of ways in the second century are assumed to be true. That is why, despite all the hateful polemics we find from the likes of Chrysostom, and despite the fact that at that time another well-known Christian preacher in the west, namely Bishop Ambrosius of Milan, even defended the burning down of a Jewish synagogue by radical Christians and wanted to protect the perpetrators from their deserved punishment, Judaism and Christianity nevertheless remained closely linked with one another and they had still not definitively parted ways – at least not nearly in all regions of the Empire and not in all social strata or in all church groups.[30]

What becomes evident more clearly when one applies this newer way of looking at things instead of the old perspective is easy to recognize when one takes another look at the eight homilies of Chrysostom, this time reading them 'against the grain,' so to speak, and not just describing how the Antiochian "star preacher" viewed the relationship between Christianity and Judaism. One might also ask the question about what actual circumstances in the city and in his Christian congregation he was reacting to – and these observations corroborate excellently the new, somewhat provocative notion of ways that never parted. The article, in which Paula Fredriksen introduces the aforementioned, now

---

29 Dunn, *The Partings of the Ways* (see n. 8); Lieu, "'*The Parting of* the Ways'" (see n. 9); and A.Y. Reed and A.H. Becker, "Introduction: Traditional Models and New Directions," in *The Ways that Never Parted: Jews and Christians in Late Antiquity and the Early Middle Ages*, ed. A.H. Becker and A.Y. Reed, TSAJ 95 (Tübingen: Mohr Siebeck 2003), 1–33.
30 Cf. e.g. N.B. McLynn, *Ambrose of Milan. Church and Court in a Christian Capital*, The Transformation of the Classical Heritage 22 (Berkeley, Los Angeles, and London: University of California Press, 1994), 298–307.

classic collected edition by Annette Yoshiko Reed and Adam H. Becker,[31] describes the interaction between Jewish, Christian, and pagan inhabitants of the city during the Roman Empire and their continuation into late antiquity. However, it is about far more than just everyday interaction: Antiochian Judaism was apparently highly attractive for the members of the Christian congregation (or to put it perhaps more tentatively: for individual members of the Christian congregation). In his first *Homily Against the Jews*, John Chrysostom admits this openly and honestly: "Many, I know, respect the Jews and think that their present way of life is a venerable one" (1.3).[32] Christian men and women went to Jewish physicians and by no means preferred practitioners of medicine from their own faith (8.5–6).[33] They also went, without seeing any problem with this, to the synagogues, celebrated Sabbat together with Jewish people and obviously very naturally took part in the series of large holy day festivities in late summer and early autumn, in Rosh Hashanah, the New Year's celebrations, in the ten days of penance and in Yom Kippur, the day of atonement, as well as in the Feast of Tabernacles, Sukkot, five days later. People used magic papyri with Hebrew texts and the names of angels from the Jewish tradition.[34] Some of these Christian men and women even considered circumcision. Chrysostom refers to such Christians using a Greek term that had long since been introduced in his time, namely ἰουδαΐζοντες, which in English means: 'Judaizing Christian,' that is, Christians who "want to fall back into Judaism" (or more neutral: Christians at least partially observe Jewish laws, involve themselves into certain rituals and liturgies, and share certain parts of Jewish all day life).[35]

Modern research also described them for a long time as ἰουδαΐζοντες, and then even pointed out that, according to the testimonies of Chrysostom, this group included a lot of slaves and women. But when we take a closer look, we notice that this circle did actually bring forth theological reasons explaining why they not only went to church on Sundays, but also to the Sabbat in the syn-

---

31 P. Fredriksen, "What 'Parting of the Ways'? Jews, Gentiles, and the Ancient Mediterranean City," in *The Ways that Never Parted. Jews and Christians in Late Antiquity and the Early Middle Ages*, ed. A.H. Becker and A.Y. Reed, TSAJ 95 (Tübingen: Mohr Siebeck, 2003), 35–64.
32 John Chrysostom, *Adv. Jud.* 1.3 (PG 48, 847): Οἶδα ὅτι πολλοὶ αἰδοῦνται Ἰουδαίους, καὶ σεμνὴν νομίζουσιν εἶναι τὴν ἐκείνων πολιτείαν νῦν· διὸ τὴν ὀλεθρίαν ὑπόληψιν πρόρριζον ἀνασπάσαι ἐπείγομαι.
33 John Chrysostom, *Adv. Jud.* 1.3 (PG 48, 934–935).
34 A. von Stockhausen, "Christian Perception of Jewish Preaching in Early Christianity?," in *Preaching in Judaism and Christianity. Encounters and Developments from Biblical Times to Modernity*, Studia Judaica 41 (Berlin and New York, De Gruyter, 2008), 49–70, here especially 67–70.
35 C. Markschies, "Der Heilige Chrysostomus und die 'Halbchristen'," *Revista Teologică* (Sibiu). Serie Nouă 17 (2007): 250–268.

agogue and celebrated the Jewish high holy days. John Chrysostom quoted their arguments in question form and I here cite him verbatim: "Is the gap between us and the Jews so negligible? Is our dispute over such a trivial thing that you think it's one and the same?" (5.9).³⁶ Those who criticized Chrysostom, therefore, accepted precisely the model of the paths that did not part. They were of the opinion that there was only a small difference between Judaism and Christianity, and that between the church and the synagogue people only argued about trivial matters and both were one and the same: "The ways that never have parted."

We are used to regarding people who went to both the synagogue and the church, whose festive calendar included both the Jewish and the Christian high holy days and who lived very naturally in both communities from Chrysostom's perspective: we refer to them as "Judaizers" and accuse them of having a lack of knowledge about their own religion and of the Jewish religion, too.³⁷ But perhaps our views are simply too strongly influenced by Chrysostom. And this Antiochian star preacher perhaps polemicized to such a terrible extent because an entire section of his cathedral congregation did not draw such a distinct line between Christianity and Judaism as he would have liked. It is possible that those members of the congregation who were familiar with and appreciated their Jewish brothers and sisters in faith were so shocked by these unbridled polemics, because they knew better. It must have been clear to them that their Jewish physicians were not charlatans or sorcerers, that those of the Jewish faith sitting next to them on the benches and those who were their hosts on holy days were not "amorous stallions," troublemakers and thieves. If this were not the case, then the star preacher would pretty much have been talking in vain in the cathedral of Antioch. And an entire section of the congregation would have gone home either confused or amused, at best entertained, to then go to the synagogue again on the next Sabbat and to the church again on Sunday. One can only refer to this group as "Judaizing" if one considers the separation processes that have no doubt existed since the second century to be irreversible

---

36 John Chrysostom, *Adv. Jud.* 5.9 (PG 48, 897: Ἆρα τί τούτου σαφέστερον γένοιτ' ἄν; Ὥρα δὴ λοιπὸν, εἰ μὴ δοκοῦμεν διενοχλεῖν, ἐπ' αὐτὸ τὸ ζητούμενον ἐλθεῖν, τὴν παροῦσαν αἰχμαλωσίαν, καὶ τὴν δουλείαν ταύτην δὲ τὴν σήμερον, δι' ἣν ἅπαντα ταῦτα ἐκινήσαμεν. Ἀλλὰ διανάστητέ μοι νῦν· οὐδὲ γὰρ ὑπὲρ τῶν τυχόντων ἡμῖν ὁ ἀγών.

37 But cf. S.J.D. Cohen, "Judaize/Judaizing," in *The Eerdmans Dictionary of Early Judaism*, ed. J.J. Collins and D.C. Harlow (Grand Rapids: Eerdmans, 2010), 847–848. Cohen has argued that Christians in Antioch, "were not betraying their Christianity, as Chrysostom and his modern followers would have it, so much as they, as Christians secure in their Christianity, were simply participating in the riches of their municipal culture" (https://www.berliner-antike-kolleg.org/fellows/shaye_cohen/index.html; accessed 31 July 2020).

and inscribed into the nature of Christianity. Otherwise, one must conversely say that the Christians attacked by Chrysostom in such a polemic manner positioned themselves on the side of their Jewish brothers and sisters who had likewise been so polemically attacked by him, simply refusing to allow the clergy to tear them apart. They would then – to express this in somewhat pointed terms – be true Christians in the succession of Jesus, closer to him than the preacher John Goldenmouth, and this would also make them the predecessors of all Christians interested in a dialogue with Judaism today.

Now, the new research paradigm of the ways that have never parted is not only based on the analysis of eight homilies by an Antiochian star preacher named John Goldenmouth. It is also not based only on the act of reading hateful polemics quasi 'against the grain' and asking what was really going on below the pulpit on which the theatrical thunder of sermons against the Jews were set forth. There are, of course, all kinds of further arguments in favour of the view of "the ways that never parted." The American scholar of Judaism, Daniel Boyarin, in particular has pointed out[38] that the classic strict distinctions between two entities "Judaism" and "Christianity," which have become separated by the model that talks of lineage or forks in the road, can hardly describe the many actually existing mixed phenomena and hybrid forms. What can we imagine an Antiochian synagogue congregation to be like? One that also welcomed members of the Christian cathedral community of Antioch, inviting them afterwards to the Sabbat meal? There were likely also synagogue congregations that saw things in a stricter light. Antioch's Judaism was diverse, colourful, one can indeed speak of 'Judaisms.' And the same applies for Christianity, for the 'Christianities.' And between the more open congregations and (if I may speak in such brief terms) the Rabbis and clergy who were liberal and more open to dialogue, there was an exchange and not only polemics in matters relating to biblical texts and liturgical practices, about the organization of people's lives and political strategies. If one (like Israel Yuval[39] or Clemens Leonhardt[40])

---

38 D. Boyarin, *Dying for God. Martyrdom and the Making of Christianity and Judaism* (Stanford: Stanford University Press, 1999), 1–21.
39 I.J. Yuval, "Passover in the Middle Ages," in *Passover and Easter. Origin and History to Modern Time*, ed. P. F. Bradshaw and L. A. Hoffman, Two Liturgical Traditions 5 (Notre Dame, IN: University of Notre Dame Press, 1999), 127–160; I.J. Yuval, "Christianity in Talmud and Midrash: Parallelomania or Parallelophobia?," in *Transforming Relations. Essays on Jews and Christians Throughout History in Honor of Michael A. Signer* (Notre Dame, IN: University of Notre Dame Press, 2010), 50–74.
40 C. Leonhard, *The Jewish Pesach and the Origins of the Christian Easter: Open Questions in Current Research*, Studia Judaica 35 (Berlin and New York: De Gruyter, 2006); cf. A. Gerhards and C.

compares the respective calendar of holy days and corresponding liturgical texts in antique Judaism and Christianity, then it becomes apparent how strongly the congregations remained interconnected with one another like a kind of network – congregations which many like to portray as dual entities. The Antiochian Christians who attended the series of Jewish holy day celebrations from Rosh Hashanah to Sukkot were only a small part of this great Jewish-Christian network in late antiquity, towards the end of the antique era.

In this third part of my contribution, my aim was to test the "parting of the ways" model as to its usefulness. In conclusion, one more thing is important to me – the fact that it is difficult anyway to capture the scattered observations on Jewish and Christian identity in one single model. And "identity" is also a difficult concept that is highly contentious in research.[41] Let us here understand it simply, without making too much of a fuss, as the entirety of specific characteristics that make up a person or a group of people. Looking at the example of the antique large city and imperial residence, it has become clear that there is no such thing as one single Christian identity; rather, the star preacher John Chrysostom was in dispute with individual members of the congregation about that identity and about the supposed necessity of establishing a boundary towards Judaism, and it was a pretty brutal dispute at that. One could also show the same thing for the Jewish identities, although the situation regarding sources is more difficult here. Also, here, there was not merely one identity but rather multiple identities. How important are shared characteristics between Jewish people and Christian people, and how important are different characteristics? Chrysostom attacks a Christian identity that holds the shared characteristics to be much more important than the differences. Am I mistaken or has this dispute in history never ceased since the end of antiquity? And has the question of whether one should speak of "parting of the ways" or of "the ways that never have parted" not remained a matter of dispute in the Christian churches and therefore also in Christian theology right up to the present day? If this, my concluding observation, should hold true, then one might regard the controversies surrounding this model a little more calmly – and not only because models are by nature never without problems. This may be a pretty sobering conclusion

---

Leonhard, ed., *Jewish and Christian Liturgy and Worship: New Insights into its History and Interaction*, Jewish and Christian Perspectives Series 15 (Leiden and Boston: Brill, 2007).

41 C. Markschies, *Christian Theology and its Institutions in the Early Roman Empire. Prolegomena to a History of Early Christian Theology* (Waco, TX: Baylor Press, 2015), 335–345 and W. Mayer, "Shaping the Sick Soul: Reshaping the Identity of John Chrysostom'," in *Christians Shaping Identity from the Roman Empire to Byzantium. Studies inspired by Pauline Allen*, ed. G.D. Dunn and W. Mayer, VCSup 132 (Leiden and Boston: Brill, 2015), 140–164.

at the beginning of a congress about such a model, but then, what speaks against taking a more sober view in an academic environment when the thing itself deserves plain and simple enthusiasm, while the model pertaining to the thing – being rather problematic – does not.

Bibliography

Alkier, S., and H. Leppin, "Einleitung – Juden, Christen, Heiden?," in *Juden – Heiden– Christen? Religiöse Inklusionen und Exklusionen im Römischen Kleinasien bis Decius*, ed. idem, WUNT 400 (Tübingen: Mohr Siebeck, 2018), 1–17.

Bady, G., "Quelques éléments de réflexion sur les Sermons contre les juifs et les judaïsants de Jean Chrysostome," in *L'Antijudaïsme du Pères: Mythe et/ou réalité?*, ed. J.-M. Auwers, R. Burnet, and D. Luciani, Théologie Historique 125 (Paris: Beauchesne Editeur, 2017), 101–118.

Bergjan, S.-P., "'Das hier ist kein Theater, und ihr sitzt nicht da, um Schauspieler zu betrachten und zu klatschen' – Theaterpolemik und Theatermetaphern bei Johannes Chrysostomos," *ZAC* (2005): 567–592.

Brändle, R., "Christen und Juden in Antiochien in den Jahren 386/87. Ein Beitrag zur Geschichte altkirchlicher Judenfeindschaft," in idem, *Studien zur Alten Kirche*, ed. M. Heimgartner, T. K. Kuhn, and M. Sallmann (Stuttgart, Berlin, and Köln: Kohlhammer, 1999), 68–84.

Brändle, R., and V. Jegher-Bucher, J., *Chrysostomus – Acht Reden gegen Juden*, Bibliothek der Griechischen Literatur 41 (Stuttgart: Hiersemann, 1995).

Bredekamp, H., and K. Pinkau, "Einladung zum akademischen Gespräch – Rundbrief," in *Modelle des Denkens. Streitgespräch in der Wissenschaftlichen Sitzung der Versammlung der Berlin-Brandenburgischen Akademie der Wissenschaften am 12. Dezember 2003*, ed. Präsident der Berlin-Brandenburgischen Akademie der Wissenschaften, Debatte Heft 2 (Berlin: Berlin-Brandenburgische Akademie der Wissenschaften, 2005), 9–12.

Boyarin, D., *Dying for God. Martyrdom and the Making of Christianity and Judaism* (Stanford: Stanford University Press, 1999).

Boyarin, D., *Abgrenzungen. Die Aufspaltung des Judäo-Christentums*, trans. by G. Palmer, ANTZ 10 = ABU 1 (Berlin and Dortmund: Institut Kirche und Judentum/Lehrhaus e.V., 2009).

Cohen, S. J. D., "Judaize/Judaizing," in *The Eerdmans Dictionary of Early Judaism*, ed. J. J. Collins and D. C. Harlow (Grand Rapids: Eerdmans, 2010), 847–848.

Cohen, S. J. D., "The Ways That Parted: Jews, Christians, and Jewish-Christians, ca. 100–150 CE," in *Jews and Christians in the First and Second Centuries: The Interbellum 70–132 CE*, ed. J. Schwartz and P. J. Tomson, CRINT 15 (Leiden and Boston: Brill, 2017), 307–339.

Downey, G., *A History of Antioch in Syria from Seleucus to the Arab Conquest* (Princeton, NJ: Princeton University Press, 1961), 410–417.

Draper, J., *A Commentary on the Didache in the Light of the Dead Sea Scrolls and Related Documents*, https://www.academia.edu/11195007/

A_Commentary_on_the_Didache_in_the_Light_of_the_Dead_Sea_Scrolls_and_Related_-Documents_Part_I (accessed 31 July 2020).
Dunn, J. D. G., *The Partings of the Ways between Christianity and Judaism and their Significance for the Character of Christianity* (London: SCM Press, 1991).
Dunn, J. D. G., ed., *Jews and Christians. The parting of the ways A.D. 70 to 135. – The Second Durham-Tübingen Research Symposium on Earliest Christianity and Judaism, Durham, September, 1989*, WUNT 66 (Tübingen: Mohr Siebeck, 1992).
Finkelstein, A., "Taming the Jewish Genie. John Chrysostom and the Jews of Antioch in the Shadow of Emperor Julian," in *From Strength to Strength: Essays in Appreciation of Shaye J. D. Cohen*, ed. M. L. Satlow, Brown Judaic Studies 363 (Providence, RI: Brown University Press), Pages 555–575.
Fredriksen, P., "What 'Parting of the Ways'? Jews, Gentiles, and the Ancient Mediterranean City," in *The Ways that Never Parted. Jews and Christians in Late Antiquity and the Early Middle Ages*, ed. A. H. Becker and A. Y. Reed (Tübingen: Mohr Siebeck, 2003), 35–64.
Frey, J., "Friedrich Avemarie (1960–2012) und sein wissenschaftliches Vermächtnis," in F. Avemarie, *Neues Testament und frührabbinisches Judentum*, ed. J. Frey and A. Standhartinger, WUNT 316 (Tübingen: Mohr Siebeck, 2013), XI–XXXIII.
Foakes Jackson, F. J., and W. R. Inge, eds., *The Parting of the Roads: Studies in the Development of Judaism and Early Christianity* (London: Edward Arnold, 1912).
Gerhards, A., and C. Leonhard, *Jewish and Christian Liturgy and Worship: New Insights into its History and Interaction*, Jewish and Christian Perspectives Series 15 (Leiden and Boston: Brill, 2007).
Inge, W. R., "Introductory," in *The Parting of the Roads: Studies in the Development of Judaism and Early Christianity*, ed. F. J. Foakes Jackson and W. R. Inge (London: Edward Arnold, 1912), 1–14.
Kinzig, W., "'Non-separation': Closeness and Co-operation Between Jews and Christians in the Fourth Century," *VC* 45 (1991): 27–53.
Lassandro, D., "Bibliographia dei Panegyrici Latini," *Invigilata lucernis* 11 (1989): 219–259.
Leonhard, C., *The Jewish Pesach and the Origins of the Christian Easter: Open Questions in Current Research*, Studia Judaica 35 (Berlin and New York: De Gruyter, 2006).
Levine, E., "The Breach between Judaism and Christianity," in *The Parting of the Roads: Studies in the Development of Judaism and Early Christianity*, ed. F. J. Foakes Jackson and W. R. Inge (London: Edward Arnold, 1912), 283–310.
Levine, E., *The History of the New West End Synagogue. 1879–1929* (Aldershot: Drew, 1929).
Lieu, J. M., "'The Parting of the Ways': Theological Construct or Historical Reality?," in eadem, *Neither Jew nor Greek? Constructing Early Christianity* (London and New York: T&T Clark, 2002), 11–30.
Markschies, C., "Der Heilige Chrysostomus und die 'Halbchristen'," *Revista Teologică* (Sibiu), Serie Nouă 17 (2007), 250–268.
Markschies, C., *Christian Theology and its Institutions in the Early Roman Empire. Prolegomena to a History of Early Christian Theology* (Waco, TX: Baylor Press, 2015), 335–345.
Mayer, W., "Shaping the Sick Soul: Reshaping the Identity of John Chrysostom'," in *Christians Shaping Identity from the Roman Empire to Byzantium. Studies inspired by Pauline Allen*, ed. G. D. Dunn and W. Mayer, VCSup 132 (Leiden and Boston: Brill, 2015), 140–164.

Mayer, W., "Preaching Hatred? John Chrysostom, Neuroscience, and the Jews," in *Revisioning John Chrysostom. New Approaches, New Perspectives*, ed. C. De Wet and W. Mayer, Critical Approaches to Early Christianity 1 (Leiden and Boston: Brill, 2019), 58–136.

McLynn, N. B., *Ambrose of Milan. Church and Court in a Christian Capital*, The Transformation of the Classical Heritage 22 (Berkeley, Los Angeles, and London: University of California Press, 1994), 298–307.

Mittelstraß, J., "Anmerkungen zum Modellbegriff," in *Modelle des Denkens. Streitgespräch in der Wissenschaftlichen Sitzung der Versammlung der Berlin-Brandenburgischen Akademie der Wissenschaften am 12. Dezember 2003,* ed. Präsident der Berlin-Brandenburgischen Akademie der Wissenschaften, Debatte Heft 2 (Berlin: Berlin-Brandenburgische Akademie der Wissenschaften, 2005), 65–67.

Nicklas, T., *Jews and Christians? Second Century 'Christian' Perspectives on the 'Parting of the Ways'*, Annual Deichmann Lectures 2013 (Tübingen: Mohr Siebeck, 2014).

Nicklas, T., "Parting of the Ways? Probleme eines Konzepts," in *Juden – Heiden – Christen? Religiöse Inklusion und Exklusion in Kleinasien bis Decius*, ed. S. Alkier and H. Leppin, WUNT 400 (Tübingen: Mohr Siebeck, 2018), 21–41.

Niederwimmer, K., *Die Didache, erklärt*, Kommentar zu den Apostolischen Vätern 1 (Göttingen: Vandenhoeck & Ruprecht, 1989), 83–157.

Parkes, J., *The Conflict of the Church and the Synagogue. A Study in the Origins of Anti-Semitism* (London: Soncino Press, 1934).

Reed, A. Y., and A. H. Becker, "Introduction: Traditional Models and New Directions," in *The Ways that Never Parted: Jews and Christians in Late Antiquity and the Early Middle Ages*, ed. idem, TSAJ 95 *(Tübingen*: Mohr Siebeck 2003), 1–33.

Ritter, A. M., "Erwägungen zum Antisemitismus in der Alten Kirche. Johannes Chrysostomos' 'Acht Reden wider die Juden'," in idem, *Studia Chrysostomica. Aufsätze zu Weg, Werk und Wirkung des Johannes Chrysostomus (ca. 349–407)*, STAC 71 (Tübingen: Mohr Siebeck, 2012), 16–33.

Ritter, A. M., "John Chrysostom and the Jews," in idem, *Studia Chrysostomica. Aufsätze zu Weg, Werk und Wirkung des Johannes Chrysostomus (ca. 349–407)*, STAC 71 (Tübingen: Mohr Siebeck, 2012), 105–116.

Schäfer, P., *Die Geburt des Judentums aus dem Geist des Christentums. Fünf Vorlesungen zur Entstehung des rabbinischen Judentums*, Tria Corda 6 (Tübingen: Mohr Siebeck, 2010).

Schnelle, U., *Die getrennten Wege von Römern, Juden und Christen: Religionspolitik im 1. Jahrhundert n. Chr.* (Tübingen: Mohr Siebeck, 2019).

Stockhausen, A. von, "Christian Perception of Jewish Preaching in Early Christianity?," in *Preaching in Judaism and Christianity. Encounters and Developments from Biblical Times to Modernity*, Studia Judaica 41 (Berlin and New York, De Gruyter, 2008), 49–70.

Stroumsa, G. G., "Als sich der Orient nach Osten bewegte: Judentum und Islam in der Wissenschaft des neunzehnten Jahrhunderts/When the Orient moved East: Judaism and Islam in Nineteenth-Century Scholarship," in *Eine dreifältige Schnur: Über Judentum, Christentum und Islam in Geschichte und Wissenschaft*, ed. M. Tilly, Lucas-Preis 2018 (Tübingen: Mohr Siebeck, 2020), 126–209.

Vogel, M., "Ein Streit nicht nur um Worte: Begriffsgeschichtliche Beobachtungen zu frühchristlichen Strategien der Exklusion," in *Juden – Heiden– Christen? Religiöse Inklusionen und Exklusionen im Römischen Kleinasien bis Decius*, ed. S. Alkier and H. Leppin, WUNT 400 (Tübingen: Mohr Siebeck, 2018), 43–69.

Weber, M., "Die Objektivität sozialwissenschaftlicher und sozialpolitischer Erkenntnis," in idem, *Gesammelte Aufsätze zur Wissenschaftslehre*, 3rd ed. (Tübingen: Mohr Siebeck, 1968), 146–214.

Wilken, R. L., *John Chrysostom and the Jews. Rhetoric and Reality in the Late 4th Century*, The Transformation of the Classical Heritage 4 (Berkeley: University of California Press, 1983), 73–122.

Yuval, I. J., "Passover in the Middle Ages," in *Passover and Easter. Origin and History to Modern Time*, ed. P. F. Bradshaw and L. A. Hoffman, Two Liturgical Traditions 5 (Notre Dame, IN: University of Notre Dame Press, 1999), 127–160.

Yuval, I. J., "Christianity in Talmud and Midrash: Parallelomania or Parallelophobia?," in *Transforming Relations. Essays on Jews and Christians Throughout History in Honor of Michael A. Signer* (Notre Dame, IN: University of Notre Dame Press, 2010), 50–74.

Anders Runesson

What Never Belonged Together Cannot Part: Rethinking the So-Called Parting of the Ways between Judaism and Christianity

Abstract: Sowohl in der Kirche als auch in der Forschung wurde lange Zeit die Ansicht vertreten, Judentum und Christentum hätten sich sehr früh voneinander getrennt, wobei zumeist das Wirken von Paulus oder sogar von Jesus als Ursprung dieser Spaltung vermutet wurden. In jüngerer Zeit hat sich diese Sicht jedoch bei der Mehrheit der Forschung deutlich verschoben. Viele Forscher*innen nehmen nun einen sehr späten Zeitpunkt für diesen Prozess an, der zudem als komplex und langwierig beschrieben wird. Einige Forscher*innen, die auf eine andauernde Interaktion zwischen Christen und Juden im Lauf der Jahrhunderte hinweisen, gehen sogar noch weiter und vertreten die Auffassung, dass sich die Wege von Judentum und Christentum überhaupt nicht getrennt haben. In diesem Aufsatz möchte ich die Diskussion dadurch voranbringen, dass ich meiner Analyse die Interaktionen in antiken jüdischen und griechisch-römischen Institutionen zugrunde lege. Dadurch möchte ich zeigen, dass die Metapher der ‚Trennung' im Kern irreführend ist und den historischen Befund von Anfang unzutreffend wiedergibt.

Keywords: Second temple Judaism, Rabbinic Judaism, Jesus movement, Non-Jewish Christianity, synagogues, associations, civic institutions, diversity, anachronism, history, theology, hermeneutics

1 Introduction: Theological Discourse and its Methodological Pitfalls

In the past, numerous – and still a few – scholars have claimed that Judaism and Christianity parted ways already as Jesus launched his program, breaking away, as it were, from 'Judaism' and the 'synagogue.' Or at least – and slightly more popular today – this departure is claimed to have happened once Paul, a couple of decades later, had declared 'Christianity' to be a religion of surpassing value, leaving Judaism behind together with all other things 'rubbish' (as Phil 3:9 has often been made to mean). More recently, however, the majority view has shifted significantly, and the parting is now considered late, or even later than late –

that is, as never really occurring at all, since continued interaction through the centuries has been suggested as a criterion on which to decide the issue.[1]

It is not difficult to see how some of these claims and conclusions, whether historically reliable or not, match rather well the general concerns of the various faith communities within which, and often to which, scholars have spoken and continue to speak. While theories of continued interaction and a lack of parting may align more or less closely with a larger modern context in which Christians and Jews seek common ground in dialogue, hypotheses considering Jesus or Paul or the New Testament to be departing from 'Judaism,' understood as a monolithic entity, serve well those (Jewish and Christian) communities today that seek to emphasise distinctive identities. But the problem of identity as related to the Jewish and Christian reality is multi-layered and complex, resisting simple models, regardless of whether they respond or not to modern anxieties related to contemporary (religious) identity politics.[2]

In this essay, I will argue that the events significant for the development of what is today Judaism and Christianity were *both* very late *and* very early. This type of conclusion in itself rests on, among other things, the claim that the whole idea of a 'parting' between what is today Judaism and Christianity, as if embedded in some historically verifiable event, is flawed, since it cannot be shown beyond reasonable doubt that these modern traditions ever belonged together in the first place. While the many aspects forming the foundation of the theory I shall suggest here cannot be discussed in detail due to space constraints, the conclusions that shall be drawn emerge as likely, in my view,

---

[1] Cf. A.Y. Reed and A.H. Becker, "Introduction: Traditional Models and New Directions," in *The Ways that Never Parted: Jews and Christians in Late Antiquity and the Early Middle Ages*, ed. A.H. Becker and A.Y. Reed, TSAJ 95 (Tübingen: Mohr Siebeck, 2003), 1–33.

[2] See, e.g., the contributions in Becker and Reed, *The Ways that Never Parted* (see n. 1), and, more recently, those in L. Baron, J. Hicks-Keeton, and M. Thiessen, eds., *The Ways that Often Parted: Essays in Honor of Joel Marcus* (Atlanta, GA: Society of Biblical Literature Press, 2018). Despite the seemingly contradictory book titles, the editors of the latter volume explicitly state that the findings presented in their book provide additional evidence for, and support the overall aim of, the former (L. Baron, J. Hicks-Keeton, and M. Thiessen, "Introduction," in *The Ways that Often Parted: Essays in Honor of Joel Marcus*, ed. eidem [Atlanta, GA: Society of Biblical Literature Press, 2018], 1–14, here 4). The history of scholarship on parting issues, from F.C. Baur onwards, is discussed by J.E. Burns in *The Christian Schism in Jewish History and Jewish Memory* (Cambridge: Cambridge University Press, 2016), 19–60. Of special interest to this issue is the modern construct of the category 'Jewish Christianity,' which rests, originally, on apologetic foundations, but which has made its way into critical scholarship, too, including especially studies concerned with the so-called parting of the ways. See the recent and important study by M. Jackson-McCabe, *Jewish Christianity: The Making of the Christianity-Judaism Divide* (New Haven, CT: Yale University Press, 2020).

once we: a) move beyond theology as an indicator of a supposed split, b) introduce instead socially measurable criteria responding to identifiable ways in which humans organise society, and, finally, c) consider seriously the fact that our question takes as a point of departure our own present reality, and that we do so *before* we start digging through layers of time to reach a conjectured stratum where it all would have begun. In the following, I shall summarise some of the key points of the approach, with the aim of setting the stage for the discussion to follow.

Our first 'checkpoint' as we approach these complex issues is related to the third problem just mentioned and concerns the question itself and its implications for the conclusions it will allow us to draw; that is, the question of *if* or *when* there was a "parting of the ways" between Judaism and Christianity. The point is this: The 'parting' metaphor assumes what remains to be proven, namely that *rabbinic Judaism*, the mother of all modern mainstream forms of Judaism – originating in the early 2nd century CE and becoming mainstream Judaism sometime around the 4th century or later[3] – once belonged in some sort of tangible way with *non-Jewish Christianity*, which emerged in the early 2nd century with some traces going back to the mid-1st century, and which is the mother of all modern forms of mainstream Christianity.[4] When we ask the question this way, it becomes clear that the modern context in which we ask the question of "parting" defines 'Judaism' and 'Christianity' in ways often dissimilar from the historical realities in the ancient period in which we seek our answers. The result is a methodological asymmetry caused by a lack of attention to the relationship between the present and the past inherent in the question itself.

To give an example of a difficulty that might occur as a result of such methodological asymmetry, we may refer to a common but, in my view, problematic interpretive trajectory, namely the idea advanced by J. Louis Martyn about the Johannine *aposynagōgos* passages as a key to our understanding of a parting process between Judaism and Christianity.[5] In brief,[6] for Martyn, taking his

---

[3] The late date for the rise to power and influence of the rabbis in Jewish society is today a consensus among scholars. See, e.g., L.I. Levine, *The Ancient Synagogue: The First Thousand Years*, 2nd ed. (New Haven, CT: Yale University Press, 2005), 466–498; G. Stemberger, *Jews and Christians in the Holy Land: Palestine in the Fourth Century* (Edinburgh: T&T Clark, 2000), 269–297. See also S. Schwartz, *Imperialism and Jewish Society, 200 B.C.E.–640 C.E.* (Princeton, NJ: Princeton University Press, 2001), 259.

[4] The earliest evidence we have access to which explicitly names and defines *Christianismos* as an entity outside of and incompatible with *Ioudaismos* – thus foreshadowing in some way the modern situation – is Ignatius of Antioch (Ign.*Magn*.10).

[5] John 9:22; 12:42; 16:2. J.L. Martyn, *History and Theology in the Fourth Gospel*, 3rd ed. (Louisville, KY: Westminster John Knox, 2003). For a comprehensive and critical discussion of Martyn's theo-

point of departure in John 9:22, these passages in John are to be seen in the context of the rabbinic prayer *birkat haminim*, in which (Jewish) Christians, after 70 CE, are cursed. The idea is that, if such cursing takes place in a synagogue setting, there is no room for Christians in the synagogue. Consequently, a parting of ways is forced by the Rabbis behind the prayer.

Disregarding for the moment the complex history of the *birkat haminim* and the dating of its different portions, which invalidates this part of Martyn's theory,[7] the fundamental problem here relates to a lack of definition of the institutional setting in which all of this would have taken place, as well as assumptions made about who would have been in charge in those institutions. More specifically, the hypothesis that the rabbis would have been in some sort of control of public synagogue settings in the late 1st century when the Gospel of John was produced, an idea foundational to Martyn's theory, has been shown by numerous synagogue scholars, perhaps most forcefully by Lee Levine, to be incorrect.[8]

---

ry, see J. Bernier, *Aposynagogos and the Historical Jesus in John: Rethinking the Historicity of the Johannine Expulsion Passages* (Leiden: Brill, 2013). See also most recently W.V. Cirafesi, *John within Judaism: Religion, Ethnicity, and the Shaping of Jesus-Oriented Jewishness in the Fourth Gospel*, AJEC (Leiden: Brill, forthcoming 2021). A critical discussion but from a different angle is given by A. Reinhartz, *Cast Out of the Covenant: Jews and Anti-Judaism in the Gospel of John* (Lanham, MD: Lexington Books/Fortress Academic, 2018). M.C. de Boer, "Expulsion from the Synagogue: J. L. Martyn's *History and Theology in the Fourth Gospel* Revisited," *NTS* 66.3 (2020): 367–391, has made an attempt at reviving Martyn's hypothesis regarding the issue of formal expulsion from synagogues, in which he leaves aside the problem of the *birkat haminim*. Unfortunately, de Boer does not interact with Bernier's critique of Martyn, which is based on recent synagogue studies, and this weakens his argument. See further below.

6 I will here disregard the many methodological problems that, in my view, weakens Martyn's argument as well as some of the later iterations of it, including the assumption that it would be possible, in detail, to 'excavate' different layers of the text, suggesting these layers would represent windows into specific historical contexts in the one Johannine community which supposedly would have produced the text for internal use.

7 For discussion, see R. Langer, *Cursing the Christians? A History of the Birkat Haminim* (New York, NY: Oxford University Press, 2012).

8 See Levine, *The Ancient Synagogue* (see n. 3), 40–41 (regarding the Pharisees and their lack of leading roles in public synagogues), and 466–498 (dealing with the rabbis). Undisputable rabbinic control of religious matters in synagogues came only under Muslim rule in the Middle Ages (498). De Boer, "Expulsion" (see n. 5), argues that local synagogue authorities are represented in John's narrative by Pharisees, which creates a historical conundrum with regard to the socio-religious location of the people behind the production of the Gospel. Indeed, it seems that de Boer's argument oscillates between understanding the Pharisees in John as a narrative construction, where they represent historical "local synagogue authorities" (e.g., 367, 384) on the one hand, and very real historical Pharisees who influence the local synagogue authorities, on the other hand (e.g., 378, 385). The problem is not solved by attempts at conflating Pharisees and

Thus, at the time when John's Gospel was authored, there was no rabbinic authority in public synagogue settings, which could have, officially and by decree, forced such expulsions. The problem is not solved, either, if we shift the focus from public synagogue institutions, where all Jews gathered (cf. John 18:20), to the separate rabbinic associations (the *batei midrash*), where the rabbis were indeed in control.[9] Such a shift in institutional setting, which would be necessary in order to account for a context in which the rabbis were in charge and could make decisions resulting in exclusions of individuals from their meetings, would produce a very unlikely historical scenario. For if we were to relate John's gospel to such rabbinic association-like institutions, we would have to assume that the people generating and/or reading John's Gospel would have been institutionally affiliated with rabbinic Jews, a minority group within Judaism at the time without much interest in influencing Jewish society.

To this should be added that the idea of a 'Christianity' is terminologically and conceptually absent from John, which makes terms like 'Jewish Christianity' inappropriate for historical analysis.[10] As with the rest of the New Testament,[11]

---

rabbis ("Pharisaic/rabbinic"; 386, 387), both because the rabbis, as stated, did not aim for influence in the public sphere in this early period, and because the evidence for rabbinic control in the Diaspora is slim, or non-existent, at this time (if indeed this 'layer' of John's Gospel is to be placed in the Diaspora).

9 It is a significant problem in de Boer's "Expulsion" (see n. 5) that he does not define what he understands the nature of the synagogue institutions, from which the Johannines were expelled, to be. He does refer to J.S. Kloppenborg's study of the *aposynagōgos* passages, which treats the institutions in question as (diaspora) associations (379), but he also seems to accept L.I. Levine's reconstruction of ancient synagogues, which understands them as public civic institutions (cf. 385, n. 93). The social effects of being expelled, or ostracised, from civic institutions (cf. the Greek phenomenon of ostracising by popular vote unpopular citizens) would be quite different from being expelled from an association, as discussed by Bernier, *Johannine Expulsion Passages* (see n. 5). See also the discussion by Cirafesi, *John within Judaism* (see n. 5), on the transition from Johannine presence in public assemblies to the formation of their association, an argument based also on an analysis of the letters of John. Of course, none of these socio-institutional processes undermines the Jewish ethno-religious identity of those who produced and/or identified with the Johannine literature.

10 See most recently the convincing argument against the use of this designation by Jackson-McCabe, *Jewish Christianity* (see n. 2).

11 *Christianoi*, however, as referring to believers in Jesus (perhaps best translated as 'messianics'), occurs in Acts 11:26 and 26:28 as well as in 1 Pet 4:16. Cf. Did. 12:4. Pliny the Younger also uses the Latin version of this word in his letter to Trajan (Pliny the Younger, *Ep.* 10.96–97). We should be careful, though, not to equate the earliest uses of this term with its later meaning. For a discussion, see A. Runesson, "The Question of Terminology: The Architecture of Contemporary Discussions on Paul," in *Paul Within Judaism: Restoring the First-Century Context to the Apostle*, ed. M.D. Nanos and M. Zetterholm (Minneapolis, MN: Fortress, 2015), 53–77.

the term is never used, which creates a conceptual and socio-institutional distance between modern historians and the earliest followers of Jesus. Of course, there are no rabbis either in John's Gospel. Arguably, instead of reading rabbis into the story, it would first of all be important to try to make sense of the text based on the groups that are actually named in the narrative, and then define their historical roles in late-first century Jewish institutions designated by synagogue terms.[12] The impulse more generally, however, to look at institutions rather than at assumed distinctive theological[13] and/or ritual patterns, is, I would argue, to be commended as a way forward; such an approach, however, clearly locates John within Judaism based on the interactions described in the text, which makes historical sense of the narrative. We shall return to this shortly.

This brief example of the difficulties involved has foregrounded John's Gospel, but similar things could be said, from different perspectives, about the problem of terminological, institutional, and other anachronisms in the study of Matthew, Mark, and Luke.[14] And, of course, Paul.[15] In other words, since a shared historical ('original') setting for what is today (rabbinic) Judaism and (non-Jewish) Christianity cannot be proven – the origins of these separate traditions seem indeed to be separate, and Christianity, in fact, to be the slightly older of the two

---

12 To solve this issue, de Boer, "Expulsion" (see n. 5), 385, n. 92 and 385–386, n. 95, argues for a close continuity between the Pharisees and the Rabbis, so that the former becomes the latter's "immediate predecessors" (n. 95). This, however, does not solve the problem regarding the rabbis's lack of interest in influencing public Jewish society in the early period, or how such an attitude could be reconciled with the argument that the Pharisees were very intent on doing just that. De Boer's argument that Pharisees would have aimed at influencing local synagogue authorities – assuming he intends these institutions to be the civic institutions of the land of Israel (?) – is worth pursing further, though, as it avoids placing the Pharisees as directly in charge of such institutions (see above, n. 8).

13 Such as, e.g., High Christology.

14 Matthew: See, e.g., M. Konradt, *Israel, Church, and the Gentiles in the Gospel of Matthew*, trans. by K. Ess, BMSEC 2 (Waco, TX: Baylor University Press, 2014); A. Runesson, *Divine Wrath and Salvation in Matthew: The Narrative World of the First Gospel* (Minneapolis, MN: Fortress, 2016); idem and D.M. Gurtner, eds., *Matthew Within Judaism. Israel and the Nations in the First Gospel*, ECL 27 (Atlanta, GA: Society of Biblical Literature Press, 2020). Mark: J. VanMaaren, *The Gospel of Mark Within Judaism: Reading the Second Gospel in its Ethnic Landscape* (PhD diss., McMaster University, 2019). Luke: I. Oliver, *Luke's Jewish Eschatology: The National Restoration of Israel in Luke-Acts* (Oxford: Oxford University Press, 2021). On John, see also the important discussion by Cirafesi, *John within Judaism* (see n. 5).

15 See, e.g., the contributions in Nanos and Zetterholm, *Paul Within Judaism* (see n. 11). Note also, importantly, M. Thiessen, *Paul and the Gentile Problem* (Oxford: Oxford University Press, 2016); P. Fredriksen, *Paul: The Pagans' Apostle* (New Haven, CT: Yale University Press, 2017); W.S. Campbell, *The Nations in the Divine Economy: Paul's Covenantal Hermeneutics and Participation in Christ* (Lanham, MD: Lexington Books/Fortress Academic, 2018).

– we need to approach the issue from a different angle. This brings me to my second point about the institutional matrices that formed the Jesus movement and other early Jewish groups, and shaped the interaction between them. To these institutions we now turn. As we shall see, taking seriously what is known about such ancient Jewish and Graeco-Roman institutions will allow us to reconstruct some basic social parameters, which moulded both Jewish and non-Jewish expressions of communal life and interactions. This in turn will shed light on the socio-religious options at disposal to the ancients at the time when the Jesus movement emerged and later.

2 Distinguishing Ancient Institutions from Modern

If theological and even ritual behaviour does not provide us with enough solid ground to move the question of the so-called parting of the ways forward, then, in order to explain how the modern situation came into being, it seems to me prudent to turn to investigating instead the socio-institutional frameworks within which the ancients produced and expressed their communal identities; these institutional frameworks are, indeed, tangible, and the limits they set for social interaction are, at least to a certain degree, measurable. After an initial brief sketch of the relevant institutions we will proceed with a discussion of the so-called partings issue.

People in Mediterranean societies were understood by the ancients themselves as operating within three basic spheres: the public/civic, the domestic/private, and the social space in-between these two, which was inhabited by what is today often referred to as associations, in lack of a better term.[16] These associations frequently mimicked the terminology used in the civic sphere, both in

---

[16] It should be noted that this is an etic term, not one that the ancients would have used, and that it refers to a variety of phenomena existing between the public and the private. Still, the category is, from an analytical point of view, useful to think with. As R. Ascough, "Methodological Reflections on Synagogues and Christ Groups as 'Associations': A Response to Erich Gruen," *JJMJS* 4 (2017): 118–126, here 126, has formulated it in relation to Pauline studies, "[t]he issue is not really whether synagogues or Pauline Christ groups were or were not associations. The real issue is whether we learn anything useful by comparing data from a variety of different ancient groups." See also J.S. Kloppenborg, *Christ's Associations: Connecting and Belonging in the Ancient City* (New Haven, CT: Yale University Press, 2019), 18–19; on the organisation of ancient life around the two poles of *polis* and family and the location of associations in-between, see p. 23.

terms of group names and elected officers.[17] In order to better understand these small face-to-face groups, or social units, all of which had their patron deities, recent scholarship has categorised them according to the networks from which they drew their membership. Based on the work of John Kloppenborg, Philip Harland has suggested five such types of networks, with some overlap: ethnic/ geographical/immigrant; cultic; occupational; neighbourhood; and household.[18] The size of such groups could vary, but a common number of members would be between 15 and 25.[19]

As Egyptian and other adjacent societies did, Jewish society also mirrored, in several ways, this basic social structure with its three operational spheres. Like Graeco-Roman associations, Jewish associations imitated the terminology used by Jewish (and Graeco-Roman) civic institutions.[20] In the past, however, and still in the work of some scholars, these aspects of Jewish society, and thus also the different social dynamics that come with them, have been obscured through a lack of attention to how Jewish society intersects with other Mediterranean ways of construing social, cultic, and political life.[21] This very likely has to do with more general and often anachronistic assumptions about the nature

---

[17] For sources, see J.S. Kloppenborg and R.S. Ascough, *Greco-Roman Associations: Texts, Translations, and Commentary. I: Attica, Central Greece, Macedonia, Thrace*, BZNW 181 (Berlin: de Gruyter, 2011); P.A. Harland, *Greco-Roman Associations: Texts, Translations, and Commentary. II: North Coast of Black Sea, Asia Minor*, BZNW 204 (Berlin: de Gruyter, 2014). See also the recent discussions of associations and how they operated in Graeco-Roman society by Kloppenborg, *Christ's Associations* (see n. 16), and R. Last and P.A. Harland, *Group Survival in the Ancient Mediterranean: Rethinking Material Conditions in the Landscape of Jews and Christians* (London: T&T Clark, 2020).

[18] P.A. Harland, *Associations, Synagogues and Congregations: Claiming a Place in Ancient Mediterranean Society* (Minneapolis, MN: Fortress, 2003), 28–53; cf. Last and Harland, *Group Survival* (see n. 17), 9–13; Kloppenborg, *Christ's Associations* (see n. 16), 25–40.

[19] Kloppenborg, *Christ's Associations* (see n. 16), 2, 106–130. Cf. R. Last, *The Pauline Church and the Corinthian* Ekklēsia: *Greco-Roman Associations in Comparative Context* (Cambridge: Cambridge University Press, 2016), 20, 71–80. Cultic groups tended to be the smallest, with a median of 24 and mode of 15. Occupational associations were often twice that size, and some associations could count their members in the hundreds, even if such large numbers were unusual.

[20] On the distinction between public/civic Jewish institutions and Jewish associations, see A. Runesson, *The Origins of the Synagogue: A Socio-Historical Study*, CBNT 37 (Stockholm: Almqvist & Wiksell, 2001); J.J. Ryan, *The Role of the Synagogue in the Aims of Jesus* (Minneapolis, MN: Fortress, 2017), 23–35.

[21] On the ancient city, see P. Fredriksen, *Augustine and the Jews: A Christian Defense of Jews and Judaism* (New Haven, CT: Yale University Press, 2010), 79–102. On the categorisation of Jewish institutions as associations, see the recent debate between E. Gruen, R.J. Korner, and R.S. Ascough in *JJMJS* (2016 and 2017) (http://www.jjmjs.org/issues.html, accessed 1 March 2021).

of ancient synagogues, since, contrary to Graeco-Roman associations and civic structures, synagogues still exist today as religious institutions; the modern is all the more easily read back into the ancient. Indeed, the word 'synagogue' is used by most scholars for both the modern and the ancient period, despite the fact that in antiquity Jews used a total of twenty-five terms, with some overlap, to designate both their civic institutions and their associations.[22] The most common of these, used for both types of institution, were *synagōgē*, *ekklēsia*, and *proseuchē*.[23]

The fact that our harmonising translation habits conceal the difference in nature between these two types of institution has obscured for us the distinct social dynamics nurtured by each, and thus also made almost impossible a historically sound reconstruction of the developments we seek to understand. As for Jewish civic assemblies, they were local political and administrative units, through which cities and towns were run. The archaeological remains of structures housing such institutions demonstrate that these were public buildings reminiscent of the *bouleuteria*. They had stepped benches lining three or four walls, constructing a space which had its focal point in the empty centre of the room, highlighting communication between those gathered as the purpose of the architectural shape. Further, these buildings show no signs of divisions between the sexes. This is important to note, as the literary texts that describe activities taking place in these civic institutions speak of both men and women as present. The New Testament gospels refer frequently to these institu-

---

[22] Seventeen of these are in Greek, five in Hebrew, and three in Latin. For sources, see A. Runesson, D.D. Binder, and B. Olsson, *The Ancient Synagogue From its Origins to 200 C.E.: A Source Book*, AJEC 72 (Leiden: Brill, 2008; hereafter abbreviated *ASSB*). Graeco-Roman associations also used a variety of terms to designate their institutions, including the Greek *synagōgē* (e.g., IPerinthos 49=GRA I.86, which also mentions an *archisynagōgos*, an office translated by Kloppenborg and Ascough as "chief-convener"). See also the discussion in R. Last, "The Other Synagogues," *JSJ* 47.3 (2016): 330–363.

[23] For example, Philo uses *synagōgē* for the association of the Essenes (*Prob.* 81=*ASSB* no. 40); Josephus uses *proseuchē* and *ekklēsia* for public assemblies (e.g., *Vita* 276–281=ASSB no. 43; *A.J.* 16.62; cf. Josephus's political use of *ekklēsia* for a non-Jewish assembly in *A.J.* 14.252); the Gospels use *synagōgē* for public assemblies (e.g., Matt 13:54; Mark 1:21; Luke 12:11; John 18:20), and Matthew's Gospel, alone among the four but together with Paul, uses *ekklēsia* for (Jewish) associations worshipping the God of Israel through a messianic lens (Matt 16:18; 18:17); papyri from Egypt (e.g., *CPJ* 1.134=*ASSB* no. 148) and inscriptions from the Black Sea (e.g., *IJO* 1=*ASSB* no. 124) use *proseuchē* for Jewish association buildings. On *ekklēsia* as a 'synagogue' term, see the comprehensive study by R.J. Korner, *The Origin and Meaning of Ekklēsia in the Early Jesus Movement*, AJEC 98 (Leiden: Brill, 2017). On Josephus's use of the same term for public Jewish assemblies, see especially A.R. Krause, *Synagogues in the Works of Flavius Josephus: Rhetoric, Spatiality, and First-Century Jewish Institutions*, AJEC 97 (Leiden: Brill, 2017).

tions as platforms for Jesus and his movement as they tried to convince other Jews to accept the idea that a new kingdom was on its way.²⁴ The very nature of the space in which this message of the kingdom was proclaimed would have stressed the political aspects of whatever was said or done.

The other type of institution designated by the same or similar terms as the civic, the associations whose patron deity was the God of Israel, were, just as their Graeco-Roman counterparts, first and foremost for members (and their guests). Like their Graeco-Roman counterparts, these small face-to-face groups would have drawn their membership from similar types of networks, such as, e.g., occupational, neighbourhood, or immigrant connections. This means that, in addition to giving up the idea of a monolithic Jewish institution called 'synagogue' – often patterned on modern assumptions about synagogues as religious institutions – in favour of understanding institutions designated by synagogue terms as being of two basic types, the civic and the association type, we also need to step away from a uniform understanding of Jewish associations. The social dynamics of an association whose main purpose was to cater to the needs of a network of professionals, and whose patron deity was the God of Israel, would thus have been quite different from an association whose network was formed more exclusively around the cult of this same deity.

Looking at specific examples in the ancient material, we hear of Jewish associations in Philo and Josephus, but also in the New Testament and in rabbinic literature. Acts 6:9 describes the *synagōgē* of the Freedmen in Jerusalem, and possibly, depending on how one interprets the Greek in that passage, either one or four more *synagōgai* in that city, drawing their membership from immigrant groups originating from Cyrenaica, Alexandria, Cilicia, and Asia.²⁵ The Tosefta also mentions a "synagogue of the Alexandrians" in Jerusalem (t. Meg. 2:17). In a similar way, Leviticus Rabbah (35:12) identifies a "synagogue of the weavers"²⁶ in Lydda (Lod), prompting the editors of the English translation of Midrash Rabbah to comment that "synagogues were often formed of members

---

24 See, e.g., Mark 1:39; Matt 4:23; 9:35; 10:17; John 18:20.
25 For discussion, see *ASSB*, no. 18 (see n. 22). For the passage as referring to five 'synagogues,' see Levine, *Ancient Synagogue* (see n. 8), 52–54. The term *proseuchē* is used in Acts 16:13 for a different kind of association.
26 כנישתא דטרסיא דלוד. Note, though, the ambivalence of the Hebrew here. While H. Freedman and M. Simon (see n. 27 below) translate "mine workers," *tarsia* could also refer to weavers or bronze-workers or, indeed, simply to people from Tarsus. M. Jastrow, *A Dictionary of the Targumim, the Talmud Babli and Yerushalmi, and the Midrashic Literature* (London: Luzac & Co., 1903), ad loc., lists weavers first, which seems reasonable if that trade in common parlance was connected with the city, which appears to have been the case.

engaged in a particular craft," i.e., what we would call occupational associations, or guilds.²⁷ Although debated, from Rome, as discussed by Peter Richardson, inscriptional evidence may suggest twelve or thirteen Jewish associations ('synagogues'), the names of which indicate the network from which they drew their membership, and/or what they wished to foreground as markers of their identity (beyond being Jewish, or perhaps better, beyond putting their trust in the God of Israel as their patron deity).²⁸

In terms of associations defining their membership based on occupational networks, we have an interesting passage in the Tosefta describing the "Great Synagogue" of Alexandria, a huge basilica-like structure, we are told, in which people are said to have gathered according to occupation, making it easier for newcomers to quickly find a suitable network that could assist them in finding a job.²⁹ While we must reckon with considerable diversity, thus, in terms of the membership of Jewish associations and what purposes they served,³⁰ what sets these institutions apart from other Graeco-Roman or Egyptian associations was that their patron deity was the God of Israel. Some of these Jewish associations paid homage to the same deity through a lens of transmitted teachings by Jesus, understood as the messiah. Such Christ-groups, as we may call them, consequently drew their membership from the same five types of networks that we have noted above.³¹ With or without a Christ-oriented lens through which worship and teaching would have been organised, however, Jewish associations

---

27 H. Freedman and M. Simon, eds., *The Midrash Rabbah: Translated into English with Notes, Glossary and Indices*, vol. 2: *Exodus & Leviticus* (London: Soncino, 1977), 453.
28 P. Richardson, *Building Jewish in the Roman East* (Waco, TX: Baylor University Press, 2004), 120–124. See also, idem, "Augustan Era Synagogues in Rome?," in *Judaism and Christianity in First-Century Rome*, ed. K.P. Donfried and P. Richardson (Grand Rapids, MI: Eerdmans, 1998), 17–29. Some of this evidence is uncertain and the dates of the inscriptions are debated. For the sources, see D. Noy, *Jewish Inscriptions of Western Europe*, vol. 2: *The City of Rome* (Cambridge: Cambridge University Press, 1995).
29 T. Sukkah 4:6. On the size of buildings used for gatherings, cf. Josephus, *Vita* 267–281; 294–295, on the *proseuchē* of Tiberias, also described as a very large edifice. (The Tiberias building was, however, as described by Josephus, a public institution used for civic assemblies.)
30 See also the recent study by M.E. Stone, *Secret Groups in Ancient Judaism* (Oxford: Oxford University Press, 2018). While Stone does not address the issue of associations more explicitly, his study, as well as the earlier study of Y.M. Gillihan (*Civic Ideology, Organization, and Law in the Rule Scrolls: A Comparative Study of the Covenanters' Sect and Contemporary Voluntary Associations in Political Context*, STDJ 97 [Leiden: Brill, 2012]), shows that these types of groups could vary considerably in terms of their nature and purpose. Stone does, however, relate and compare these Jewish groups with similar non-Jewish groups, as we have also done here under the modern umbrella term 'associations.'
31 Cf. discussion in Kloppenborg, *Christ's Associations* (see n. 16), ch. 2.

were rarely exclusively Jewish in terms of the ethnicity of their membership.[32] Just as non-Egyptians had found Isis a powerful deity and, accordingly, had begun to join her worship, non-Jews, in a similar process that removed ethnic requirements for participation, sought the benefits associated with what they believed to be a powerful deity, the God of Israel. This did not change when the Jesus movement entered the scene. As with other Graeco-Roman associations, then, we should envision associations honouring the God of Israel as their patron deity, with or without a Messiah, as mixed groups: Jews and non-Jews, slaves and free, men and women.[33]

In sum, and this is worth repeating: All this means that, in addition to giving up the idea of a monolithic Jewish religious institution called 'synagogue' in favour of understanding institutions designated by synagogue terms as being of two basic types, the civic and the association type, we must also step away from a uniform understanding of Jewish associations. *There was no such thing in antiquity as the synagogue.* It is within these diverse institutional matrices that we need to reconstruct the developments which eventually lead to the present-day situation. As we shall see, when read within this context, the evidence is, in my opinion, organised best in separate chronological trajectories, in which what is today Judaism is shaped alongside the formation of Christianity. The following reconstruction also problematises theories positing either early or late separations, as I will argue that the process was *both* quite early and rather late, and should, further, not be described as a parting. Indeed, the ancient interactions between these traditions have as little to do with mediaeval and modern dynamics between Judaism and Christianity as apples have with oranges.

---

32 On the term God-fearers, see the recent study by P. Fredriksen, "'If it Looks Like a Duck, and Quacks Like a Duck...': On Not Giving Up the Godfearers," in *A Most Reliable Witness: Essays* in *Honor of Ross Shepard Kraemer*, ed. H.S. Ashbrook et al. (Providence, NJ: Brown University Press, 2016), 25–33; cf. J.G. Gager, "Jews, Gentiles, and Synagogues in the Book of Acts," *HTR* 79.1–3 (1986): 91–99. In order to distinguish between such God-fearers and those aligning their cultic interests with the Jewish messianic option, I have suggested the term Christ-fearers for the latter; see A. Runesson, "Inventing Christian Identity: Paul, Ignatius, and Theodosius I," in *Exploring Early Christian Identity*, ed. B. Holmberg, WUNT 226 (Tübingen: Mohr Siebeck, 2008), 59–92, here 73.
33 This institutional reality seems to be echoed in Gal 3:28, which consequently is best understood as Paul theologising a widespread Graeco-Roman and Jewish institutional pattern. For discussion, see A. Runesson, "Placing Paul: Institutional Structures and Theological Strategy in the World of the Early Christ-believers," *SEÅ* 80 (2015): 43–67.

3 The Impact of Institutional Contexts on the Birth of (Modern) Christianity and Judaism

It is obviously impossible to summarise in a short essay the five centuries-worth of socio-institutional interaction that are relevant to the developments leading us from antiquity to today. In order to overcome some of the obstacles related to word-limits, I have, perhaps in a rather unorthodox manner,[34] produced a chart (fig. 1). The intention of this chart is not, of course, to present reality in any sort of absolute way, but rather to provide the reader with a suggested approximation of the broader outlines of history, which can be easily summarised on one page and which highlights the key stages that I discuss below.[35]

3.1 Land of Israel

We shall begin our discussion in the land of Israel (to the left in the chart), since that is where Jesus and his earliest followers operated. As the reader will immediately realise, the selection of institutions included in the chart is not comprehensive, but has been made based on their importance for our question and the developments in later centuries.

At the centre, we have the local civic assemblies which we have discussed above and in which we find, from the very beginning, Jesus and his movement encountering and interacting with other Jews. For our purposes, it is of importance to emphasise the obvious, namely that at this time, the rabbinic movement did not exist. The Jews with which Jesus and his earliest followers interacted were either not aligned with any other particular group or association (the majority; usually referred to in the gospels as *hoi ochloi*, 'crowds')[36] or were mem-

---

[34] But cf. M. Goodman, "Modeling the 'Parting of the Ways'," in *The Ways that Never Parted: Jews and Christians in Late Antiquity and the Early Middle Ages*, ed. A.H. Becker and A.Y. Reed, TSAJ 95 (Tübingen: Mohr Siebeck, 2003), 119–129.
[35] I am grateful to K. Hedner Zetterholm for the discussion of several details of this chart.
[36] Cf. E.P. Sanders's definition and discussion of "common Judaism" in *Judaism: Practice and Belief, 63 BCE–66 CE* (London: SCM, 1992), 47–314: "What the priests and the people agreed on" (47). After considerable debate about whether such a categorisation would contribute to concealing the significant diversity evident within Judaism in the 1st century, Sanders defended his reconstruction in "Common Judaism Explored," in *Common Judaism: Explorations in Second-Temple Judaism*, ed. W.O. McCready and A. Reinhartz (Minneapolis, MN: Fortress, 2008), 11–23. As he emphasises in this latter publication, talk about a 'common Judaism' does in no way assume either uniformity or normativity.

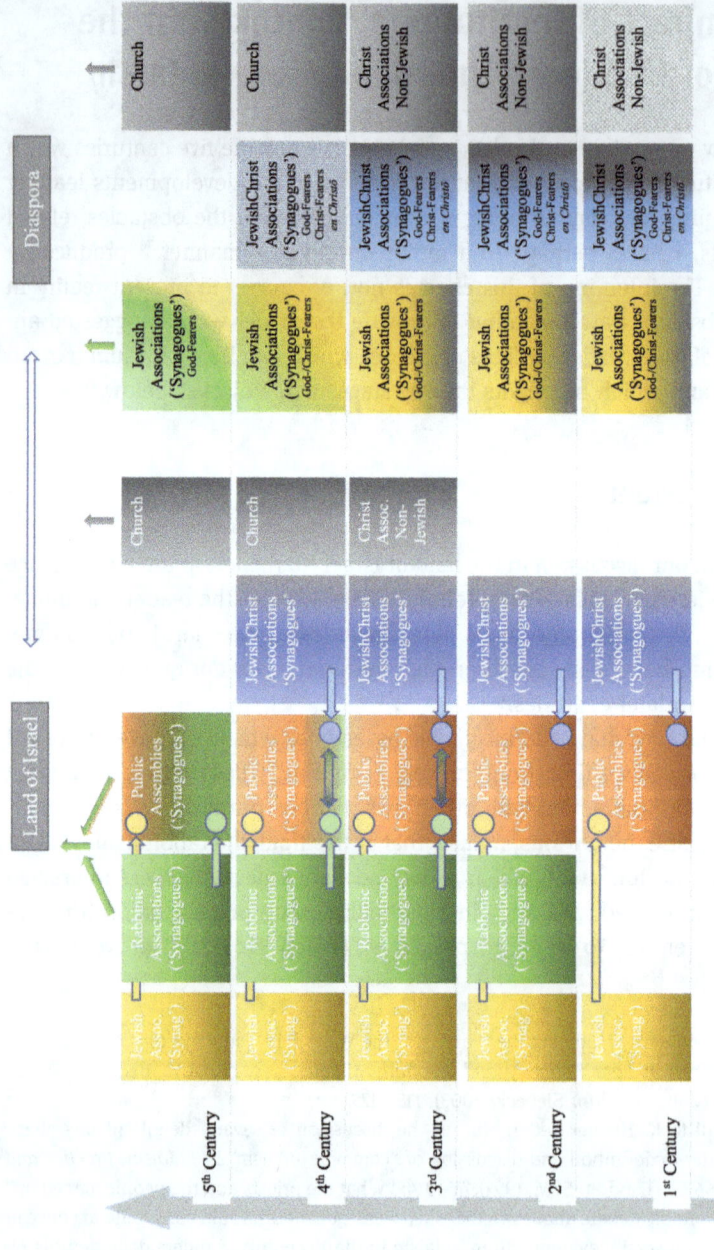

Figure 1: The early history of what became Judaism and Christianity as seen from the perspective of their institutional contexts. Since the purpose of the chart is to enable an overview of developments that led to the modern variants of Judaism and Christianity, it does not include, e.g., the Samaritans, who played an important role in antiquity, but were only minimally involved in the developments that produced the later relationship between Jews and Christians.

bers of such groups (e.g., the Pharisees; a minority, whose influence at the time is still debated[37]). Further, while Jesus never established what we would call an association (he aimed, it seems, at creating a religio-political mass movement, which may be assumed based on his choice of these civic institutions as a platform from which to make his proclamations), his followers did so after his death. We see traces of such developments in, e.g., Matthew's mentioning that Jesus's followers are to establish their own *ekklēsia*, in which they themselves decide halakhic matters and have their own penal code (Matt 16:18 and 18:18). This did not, however, lead to the absence of these followers of Jesus in the public assemblies, as we see, not least, in the several references in the gospels to corporal punishment executed in these civic institutions or 'synagogues.' Rather, this group just as other groups, such as the Pharisees, met both individually in their separate associations and encountered one another in the civic assemblies.[38]

An essential observation here, based on the institutional realities of ancient Jewish society, is thus that the origin of these Christ-associations was independent of any parting processes that would have generated what we would call a new religion, or even a departure from Jewish society and engagement in its civic institutions. The origin of an association does not necessarily require that its members had parted from other associations, even though this may also at times have occurred.[39] Most importantly, the processes that led to the emergence of these Christ-groups were independent of the later developments that led to the origins of the Rabbinic Judaism, whose beginnings were also unrelated to parting processes. On the contrary, it seems that the consolidation of rabbinic forms of Judaism were the result of a coalition, i.e., a movement in the opposite social direction; a coming together of various other groups, among which we find also some Pharisees.[40]

---

[37] See, e.g., the contributions in J. Neusner and B.D. Chilton, eds., *In Quest of the Historical Pharisees* (Waco, TX: Baylor University Press, 2007).

[38] It is instructive here to compare how different factions met and interacted with one another in the *proseuchē* of Tiberias, as recounted by Josephus in *Vita* 276–281; 294–295 (*ASSB* [see n. 22], no. 43).

[39] I have argued earlier that the Gospel of Matthew shows evidence of having been produced within an association whose members had previously belonged to the Pharisaic party; see A. Runesson, "Re-Thinking Early Jewish–Christian Relations: Matthean Community History as Pharisaic Intragroup Conflict," *JBL* 127.1 (2008): 95–132.

[40] See, e.g., the discussion in J. Neusner, "The Use of the Later Rabbinic Evidence for the Study of First-Century Pharisaism," in *Approaches to Ancient Judaism: Theory and Practice*, ed. W.S. Green (Missoula, MT: Scholars Press, 1978), 215–228. It is of some interest to note that the only Jewish group which is reported in the New Testament to have generated believers in Jesus is also the Pharisees (e.g., John 3:1–2; 9:16; 19:39; Acts 15:5; 23:6; Phil 3:5; cf. Luke

When the rabbis began to show interest in influencing Jewish society around the 3rd century and thus engaged competitively in interaction with others in public assemblies ('synagogues') – a competition the rabbis would eventually win – Jewish Christ-followers had already been labelled heretical and become marginalised by non-Jewish Christians, a topic to which we shall return shortly. Key to our quest, however, which is concerned with tracing developments that may form a bridge (or not) to the modern period where we find 'Judaism' and 'Christianity' as two distinct traditions, is that while there is a continuous trajectory from the rabbis through the mediaeval period and until today, their counterpart in the 3rd century, the groups against which they to various degrees defined themselves, and from which they distanced themselves,[41] disappeared from the historical scene. This, in and of itself, disqualifies any theory of partings between (rabbinic) Judaism and (non-Jewish) Christianity as asymmetric, since the latter is institutionally irrelevant to the former,[42] and the part of the Jesus movement that did in fact interact with the rabbis in shared institutional settings vanished.

3.2 Diaspora

Turning to the Diaspora (the columns to the right on the chart), the situation looks quite different, especially in the early period, and especially as in the Di-

---

13:31). It seems, thus, that the Pharisees split in at least two directions, at different points in time.

[41] See discussion by K. Hedner Zetterholm, "Alternate Visions of Judaism and Their Impact on the Formation of Rabbinic Judaism," *JJMJS* 1 (2014): 127–153.

[42] Cf. Burns, *Christian Schism* (see n. 2), 55, who argues that "[t]he only Christianity of which the rabbis knew was the type practiced by Jews." See, similarly, S.J.D. Cohen, "The Ways That Parted: Jews, Christians, and Jewish-Christians, ca. 100–150 CE," in *Jews and Christians in the First and Second Centuries: The Interbellum 70–132 CE*, ed. J. Schwartz and P. Tomson, CRINT 15 (Leiden: Brill, 2018), 307–339, here 333. This claim should perhaps be slightly rephrased to better match the evidence, though, as we have archaeological remains dating to the 3rd century of non-Jews practicing some form of Christ-cult in Kefar 'Othnay, Galilee (see the excavators's report, Y. Tepper and L. Di Segni, *A Christian Prayer Hall of the Third Century CE at Kefar 'Othnay [Legi]: Excavations at the Megiddo Prison* [Jerusalem: IAA, 2006]). It may be better to argue, thus, that the only 'Christianity' the rabbis made an effort to engage was the type practiced by Jews. Still, the terminology used by Burns is somewhat problematic, as he speaks of a 'Christianity' practiced by Jews. While the term 'Christianity' from the 2nd century onwards came into use, mostly by non-Jews, Jewish followers of Jesus and very likely also those Jews who disagreed with them would have understood Christ-centred Judaism precisely as a form of Judaism.

aspora there were no shared civic institutions controlled by Jews but only various forms of associations whose patron deity was the God of Israel.

It is likely that already in the 1st century we find non-Jewish followers of Jesus as members of Jewish associations otherwise not inclined towards things messianic.[43] There would also have been separate groups dedicated to the worship of the God of Israel exclusively through the lens provided by Jesus traditions. Indeed, if the dating of Ignatius's letters to the early 2nd century will withstand scrutiny, and if we take into account the letters of Pliny the Younger to Trajan, dated around the same time,[44] as well as consider the multifaceted nature of associations in the Mediterranean world, it is also likely that before the 1st century was over, perhaps even soon after Paul wrote in the 60s,[45] we find Christ-groups consisting exclusively of non-Jews, who would understand their cosmic allegiances to be quite different from – and even excluding – adherence to Jewish ancestral customs. It is the contention of this essay that these latter associations, and the processes that birthed them, provide us with our earliest connecting point between the present and the past of Christianity.

To be noted in this regard, though, is that the Jewish Christ-groups practising forms of Christ-centred Judaism, such as those related to Palestine, discussed above, slowly recede into the background and eventually disappear, leading to a historical and institutional break between the present and the past; one of many socio-religious dead-ends, as it were, in the history of religions.[46] Importantly, and in a similar manner, the less messianically inclined Jewish associations, within which and/or against which Christ-followers debated – interactions generating the hostile Christian rhetoric of the many texts that have survived to

---

[43] The Book of Acts includes several instances in its narrative, in which we find such scenarios described. For examples and discussion, see *ASSB*, e.g., nos. 72 (Acts 15:19–21), 91 (18:4–8), 107 (19:8–9), 173 (14:1–7), 174 (13:42–48), 184 (17:10–12), 186 (17:1–4).

[44] Pliny the Younger, *Ep. Tra.*, 10.96.9–10.

[45] I am thinking here of those non-Jewish Christ-followers whom Paul considers arrogant in Rom 11:17–24. To be sure, it seems clear from Paul's argument in Romans that the non-Jews he is addressing were closely related to Jewish Christ-followers. Paul's rhetoric seems also to imply that they had close interaction with other, non-Messianic Jews. It is not difficult to see, however, how the sentiments among the non-Jews that Paul is combating in Rome in the 60s could, and probably would, begin to spread and lead to the establishment of Christ-groups exclusively consisting of what Paul regarded as 'wild olive shoots,' who had forgotten, or refused to accept, that they received their nourishment from the root, and not the other way around (11:17–18). See further below.

[46] I am not concerned here with variants of Hebrew Christians through later centuries or with modern variants of messianic Judaism; these phenomena need to be studied in their own right and in their own historical and institutional contexts.

our own days – these Jewish (non-rabbinic) associations and their forms of embodying Jewish tradition disappeared from the scene of history too, as eventually the rabbis conquered also the diaspora.

Thus, again, we discover an asymmetrical situation that frustrates theories claiming common origins and a later split between what is today referred to as 'Judaism' and 'Christianity.' While there are significant trajectories of continuity between the emerging non-Jewish and even anti-Jewish cult of Christ in the 2nd century diaspora on the one hand, and the church that eventually triumphed in the Roman Empire and reached the modern Western world via Medieval Europe on the other hand, the Judaism against which they defined themselves vanished, giving way to the rabbis. In other words, if we are interested in understanding in which ways rabbinic Judaism, the mother of all modern mainstream forms of Judaism, was shaped by and interacted with followers of Jesus, we need to study the forms of Christ-centred Judaism that the Church Fathers decried as heretical. And, vice versa, understanding how (modern) Christianity was formed in polemic against Judaism, we must, especially for the early period, pay special attention to those forms of Judaism that the rabbis competed against and eventually defeated. This is why, in my view, the early history of modern Judaism and Christianity cannot be studied through the lens provided by the metaphor of a parting of the ways.

But what, then, of Paul, we might ask – is it not true that we find in his letters traces of some sort of parting? And do we not find similar traces also in Acts?[47] What has Paul (and Acts) to do with (modern) Christianity? Taking an institutional perspective and foregrounding key passages such as Romans 11 and 1 Cor 7:17–24, one would have to conclude: not much.[48] Contrary to what we see in Ignatius's letters, the tensions visible in these texts make most sense if understood as created from within Judaism, from a position where the definition of Judaism is what is at stake, not the creation of a new 'religious' entity.[49] Such struggles were by no means isolated to messianic groups defining themselves in

---

[47] See above, n. 45 and 43.

[48] Also from an institutional perspective, Paul was, as P. Eisenbaum would say, not a Christian (*Paul was not a Christian: The Original Message of a Misunderstood Apostle* [New York, NY: HarperOne, 2009]).

[49] On Paul, see the discussion in A. Runesson, "Paul and the Joining of the Ways: Ordering the Eschaton, Preparing for Judgment," in *Israel and the Nations: Paul's Gospel in the Context of Jewish Expectation*, ed. F. Abel (Lanham, MD: Lexington/Fortress Academic, 2021). On Luke-Acts, cf. Oliver, *Luke's Jewish Eschatology* (see n. 14). It is, in my view, within such institutional and discursive contexts that we see, too, the dynamics which come to the fore in the Johannine literature, as discussed in the introductory section above.

relation to other ways of being Jewish. Other movements, such as the covenanters in Qumran and, if Philo's account is to be believed, the Therapeutae in Egypt, embodied Judaism in their own specific ways for their own specific reasons, and they did so in relation to other forms of Judaism from which they distanced themselves. The same is true of the Pharisees. Such developments do not create new 'religions,' and the parting of the ways processes discernible take place within Judaism.

If, as we noted above, the non-Jewish Christ-groups in the 2nd century constitute the earliest connecting point with what later became 'Christianity,' a phenomenon socio-institutionally and rhetorically distinguishable from 'Judaism,' then the question would be: From where did such groups emerge? This is a complex issue to address, but it seems reasonable, given the diversity of the institutional networks available in antiquity, that they either parted not from Judaism generally, but from messianic-Jewish groups specifically,[50] or were simply never part of a messianic-Jewish group at all.

As we enter the mid-2nd century, we find in the writings of Justin Martyr evidence that would seem to reflect a similar situation.[51] Here, Justin declares himself to be of the opinion that Messianic Jews and non-Jews should be able to coexist, as long as the former do not missionize the latter with regard to the keeping of Mosaic law. His position thus rejects the necessity of a parting of ways between Christ-followers of different persuasions, and at the same time identifies what he believes to be the deal-breaker that would force such as parting. It is not about the keeping of the Mosaic law in and of itself (which to his mind does not carry any salvific significance, either for Jews or non-Jews), but the Mosaic law as applied to, and missionized to non-Jewish Christ-followers. As he makes his argument, Justin also identifies another position on this issue among his contemporaries, one which he opposes, namely that non-Jewish Christ-followers should have nothing to do with Messianic Jews. Needless to say, the latter position – a far cry from Paul's olive-tree metaphor in Rom 11, but aligning well with the trajectory within which we find Ignatius – eventually won the day.

In sum, we have been unable to locate an ancient institutional context, either in the land of Israel or in the Diaspora, shared between what is today Judaism and Christianity, resulting in the conclusion that we cannot frame the issue as a parting of ways between the two. The cause behind the antagonistic relation-

---

50 Cf. M. Zetterholm, *The Formation of Christianity in Antioch: A Social-Scientific Approach to the Separation Between Judaism and Christianity* (London: Routledge, 2003), 3, 231; Cohen, "The Ways that Parted" (see n. 42), 310.
51 Justin, *Dial.* 47.

ship between these two modern religions must therefore be sought elsewhere, beyond origin myths, as these developments seem to rather inhabit the discursive and political realm of appropriation and colonisation.

4 Conclusion: History and Hermeneutics

As the various writings of the New Testament indicate in no uncertain terms, the questions addressed in this paper, and which were dealt with more broadly in the conference from which the present volume originates, have been debated for some 2000 years. To me, this fact alone suggests that the only stable historical trajectory throughout the centuries, in Judaism and Christianity, and among "the dangerous ones in-between," as John Gager once called them, is the one which speaks of diverse voices struggling, but ever failing, to establish hegemony. Academia, for its part, has invented new game-rules, putatively beyond the normative, feeding them into these age-old endeavours to understand both the past and, by implication, the present.

I suspect that the intensity of the debates orbiting the so-called 'parting' issue has often been fuelled by the assumption that modern-day identities are somehow determined and controlled by origin myths. While I would certainly agree that the past is intertwined with the present in ways more numerous than the cells of our bodies, approaches essentialising historical developments are as deceptive as the etymological fallacy; indeed, potentially even more so, as they tend to condemn us to discursive servitude, opening up the interpretive abyss of divisive modern identity politics. I agree, thus, with Joshua Ezra Burns and many others that the type of questions we deal with here are entangled in all sorts of ways with concerns about the present and – for Burns and for most – the well-being of both Jews and Christians (and, by implication, society as such, with all its distinct religious communities).[52] I would, though, even more than Burns does, emphasise the importance of an acute hermeneutical awareness as the past is brought out from the shadows it inhabits, insisting on its de-essentialised and heuristic application in contemporary dialogues. One thing is for certain, however, and that is that "Christian triumphalist theology was not inevitable," as Baron, Hicks-Keeton, and Thiessen express it in the introduction to their volume *The Ways that Often Parted*.[53] Even a short meditation over this simple fact

---

52 Burns, *Christian Schism* (see n. 2), 15.
53 Baron/Hicks-Keeton/Thiessen, "Introduction" (see n. 2), 1.

may instil humility and inspire new ways of understanding the relationship between history and theology.

Antiquity is, indeed, ground best trodden carefully, but the present is a minefield, as current developments in Europe, North America, and the Middle East show with such dismal clarity. In such a landscape – which is our own – history can only be one voice among many as a theology of the other is formed. The question is, then, not only in which way that voice is re-created, but also *how* we bring it into the conversation.

Bibliography

Ascough, R. S., "Methodological Reflections on Synagogues and Christ Groups as 'Associations': A Response to Erich Gruen," *JJMJS* 4 (2017): 118–126.

Baron, L., J. Hicks-Keeton, and M. Thiessen, eds., *The Ways that Often Parted: Essays in Honor of Joel Marcus* (Atlanta, GA: Society of Biblical Literature Press, 2018).

Baron, L., "Introduction," in *The Ways that Often Parted: Essays in Honor of Joel Marcus*, ed. idem, J. Hicks-Keeton, and M. Thiessen (Atlanta, GA: Society of Biblical Literature Press, 2018), 1–14.

Bernier, J., *Aposynagogos and the Historical Jesus in John: Rethinking the Historicity of the Johannine Expulsion Passages* (Leiden: Brill, 2013).

Burns, J. E., *The Christian Schism in Jewish History and Jewish Memory* (Cambridge: Cambridge University Press, 2016).

Campbell, W. S., *The Nations in the Divine Economy: Paul's Covenantal Hermeneutics and Participation in Christ* (Lanham, MD: Lexington Books/Fortress Academic, 2018).

Cirafesi, W. V., *John within Judaism: Religion, Ethnicity, and the Shaping of Jesus-Oriented Jewishness in the Fourth Gospel*, AJEC (Leiden: Brill, forthcoming 2021).

Cohen, S. J. D., "The Ways That Parted: Jews, Christians, and Jewish-Christians, ca. 100–150 CE," in *Jews and Christians in the First and Second Centuries: The Interbellum 70–132 CE*, ed. J. Schwartz and P. J. Tomson, CRINT 15 (Leiden: Brill, 2018), 307–339.

de Boer, M. C., "Expulsion from the Synagogue: J. L. Martyn's *History and Theology in the Fourth Gospel* Revisited," *NTS* 66.3 (2020): 367–391.

Eisenbaum, P., *Paul Was Not a Christian: The Original Message of a Misunderstood Apostle* (New York, NY: HarperOne, 2009).

Fredriksen, P., *Augustine and the Jews: A Christian Defense of Jews and Judaism* (New Haven, CT: Yale University Press, 2010).

Fredriksen, P., "'If it Looks Like a Duck, and Quacks Like a Duck…': On Not Giving Up the Godfearers," in *A Most Reliable Witness: Essays* in *Honor of Ross Shepard Kraemer*, ed. H. S. Ashbrook et al. (Providence, NJ: Brown University Press, 2016), 25–33.

Fredriksen, P., *Paul: The Pagans' Apostle* (New Haven, CT: Yale University Press, 2017).

Freedman, H., and M. Simon, eds., *The Midrash Rabbah: Translated into English with Notes, Glossary and Indices,* vol. 2: *Exodus & Leviticus* (London: Soncino, 1977).

Gager, J. G., "Jews, Gentiles, and Synagogues in the Book of Acts," *HTR* 79.1–3 (1986): 91–99.

Gillihan, Y. M., *Civic Ideology, Organization, and Law in the Rule Scrolls: A Comparative Study of the Covenanters' Sect and Contemporary Voluntary Associations in Political Context*, STDJ 97 (Leiden: Brill, 2012).

Goodman, M., "Modeling the 'Parting of the Ways'," in *The Ways that Never Parted: Jews and Christians in Late Antiquity and the Early Middle Ages*, ed. A. H. Becker and A. Y. Reed, TSAJ 95 (Tübingen: Mohr Siebeck, 2003), 119–129.

Harland, P. A., *Associations, Synagogues and Congregations: Claiming a Place in Ancient Mediterranean Society* (Minneapolis, MN: Fortress, 2003).

Harland, P. A., *Greco-Roman Associations: Texts, Translations, and Commentary. II: North Coast of Black Sea, Asia Minor*, BZNW 204 (Berlin: de Gruyter, 2014).

Hedner Zetterholm, K., "Alternate Visions of Judaism and Their Impact on the Formation of Rabbinic Judaism," *JJMJS* 1 (2014): 127–153.

Jackson-McCabe, M., *Jewish Christianity: The Making of the Christianity-Judaism Divide* (New Haven, CT: Yale University Press, 2020).

Jastrow, M., *A Dictionary of the Targumim, the Talmud Babli and Yerushalmi, and the Midrashic Literature* (London: Luzac & Co., 1903).

Kloppenborg, J. S., *Christ's Associations: Connecting and Belonging in the Ancient City* (New Haven, CT: Yale University Press, 2019).

Kloppenborg, J. S., and R. S. Ascough, *Greco-Roman Associations: Texts, Translations, and Commentary. I: Attica, Central Greece, Macedonia, Thrace*, BZNW 181 (Berlin: de Gruyter, 2011).

Konradt, M., *Israel, Church, and the Gentiles in the Gospel of Matthew*, trans. by K. Ess, BMSEC 2 (Waco, TX: Baylor University Press, 2014).

Korner, R. J., *The Origin and Meaning of Ekklēsia in the Early Jesus Movement*, AJEC 98 (Leiden: Brill, 2017).

Krause, A. R., *Synagogues in the Works of Flavius Josephus: Rhetoric, Spatiality, and First-Century Jewish Institutions*, AJEC 97 (Leiden: Brill, 2017).

Langer, R., *Cursing the Christians? A History of the Birkat Haminim* (New York, NY: Oxford University Press, 2012).

Last, R., "The Other Synagogues," *JSJ* 47.3 (2016): 330–363.

Last, R., *The Pauline Church and the Corinthian* Ekklēsia: *Greco-Roman Associations in Comparative Context* (Cambridge: Cambridge University Press, 2016).

Last, R., and P. A. Harland, *Group Survival in the Ancient Mediterranean: Rethinking Material Conditions in the Landscape of Jews and Christians* (London: T&T Clark, 2020).

Levine, L. I., *The Ancient Synagogue: The First Thousand Years*, 2nd ed. (New Haven, CT: Yale University Press, 2005).

Martyn, J. L., *History and Theology in the Fourth Gospel*, 3rd ed. (Louisville, KY: Westminster John Knox, 2003).

Neusner, J., "The Use of the Later Rabbinic Evidence for the Study of First-Century Pharisaism," in *Approaches to Ancient Judaism: Theory and Practice*, ed. W. S. Green (Missoula, MT: Scholars Press, 1978), 215–228.

Neusner, J., and B. D. Chilton, eds., *In Quest of the Historical Pharisees* (Waco, TX: Baylor University Press, 2007).

Noy, D., *Jewish Inscriptions of Western Europe*, vol. 2: *The City of Rome* (Cambridge: Cambridge University Press, 1995).

Oliver, I., *Luke's Jewish Eschatology: The National Restoration of Israel in Luke-Acts* (Oxford: Oxford University Press, 2021).
Reed, A. Y., and A. H. Becker, "Introduction: Traditional Models and New Directions," in *The Ways that Never Parted: Jews and Christians in Late Antiquity and the early Middle Ages*, ed. A. H. Becker and A. Y. Reed, TSAJ 95 (Tübingen: Mohr Siebeck, 2003), 1–33.
Reinhartz, A., *Cast Out of the Covenant: Jews and Anti-Judaism in the Gospel of John* (Lanham, MD: Lexington Books/Fortress Academic, 2018).
Richardson, P., "Augustan Era Synagogues in Rome?," in *Judaism and Christianity in First-Century Rome*, ed. K. P. Donfried and P. Richardson (Grand Rapids, MI: Eerdmans, 1998), 17–29.
Richardson, P., *Building Jewish in the Roman East* (Waco, TX: Baylor University Press, 2004).
Runesson, A., *The Origins of the Synagogue: A Socio-Historical Study*, CBNT 37 (Stockholm: Almqvist & Wiksell, 2001).
Runesson, A., "Inventing Christian Identity: Paul, Ignatius, and Theodosius I," in *Exploring Early Christian Identity*, ed. B. Holmberg, WUNT 226 (Tübingen: Mohr Siebeck, 2008), 59–92.
Runesson, A., "Re-Thinking Early Jewish–Christian Relations: Matthean Community History as Pharisaic Intragroup Conflict," *JBL* 127.1 (2008): 95–132.
Runesson, A., "Placing Paul: Institutional Structures and Theological Strategy in the World of the Early Christ-believers," *SEÅ* 80 (2015): 43–67.
Runesson, A., "The Question of Terminology: The Architecture of Contemporary Discussions on Paul," in *Paul Within Judaism: Restoring the First-Century Context to the Apostle*, ed. M. D. Nanos and M. Zetterholm, (Minneapolis, MN: Fortress, 2015), 53–77.
Runesson, A., *Divine Wrath and Salvation in Matthew: The Narrative World of the First Gospel* (Minneapolis, MN: Fortress, 2016).
Runesson, A., "Paul and the Joining of the Ways: Ordering the Eschaton, Preparing for Judgment," in *Israel and the Nations: Paul's Gospel in the Context of Jewish Expectation*, ed. F. Abel (Lanham, MD: Lexington/Fortress Academic, 2021).
Runesson, A., and D. M. Gurtner, eds., *Matthew Within Judaism. Israel and the Nations in the First Gospel*, ECL 27 (Atlanta, GA: Society of Biblical Literature Press, 2020).
Runesson, A., D. D. Binder, and B. Olsson, *The Ancient Synagogue From its Origins to 200 C.E.: A Source Book*, AJEC 72 (Leiden: Brill, 2008).
Ryan, J. J., *The Role of the Synagogue in the Aims of Jesus* (Minneapolis, MN: Fortress, 2017).
Sanders, E. P., *Judaism: Practice and Belief, 63 BCE–66 CE* (London: SCM, 1992).
Sanders, E. P., "Common Judaism Explored," in *Common Judaism: Explorations in Second-Temple Judaism*, ed. W. O. McCready and A. Reinhartz (Minneapolis, MN: Fortress, 2008), 11–23.
Schwartz, S., *Imperialism and Jewish Society, 200 B.C.E.–640 C.E.* (Princeton, NJ: Princeton University Press, 2001).
Stemberger, G., *Jews and Christians in the Holy Land: Palestine in the Fourth Century* (Edinburgh: T&T Clark, 2000).
Stone, M. E., *Secret Groups in Ancient Judaism* (Oxford: Oxford University Press, 2018).
Tepper, Y., and L. Di Segni, *A Christian Prayer Hall of the Third Century CE at Kefar 'Othnay [Legi]: Excavations at the Megiddo Prison* (Jerusalem: IAA, 2006).
Thiessen, M., *Paul and the Gentile Problem* (Oxford: Oxford University Press, 2016).

VanMaaren, J., *The Gospel of Mark Within Judaism: Reading the Second Gospel in its Ethnic Landscape* (PhD diss., McMaster University, 2019).
Zetterholm, M., *The Formation of Christianity in Antioch: A Social-Scientific Approach to the Separation Between Judaism and Christianity* (London: Routledge, 2003).

Jan N. Bremmer
Ioudaismos, Christianismos and the Parting of the Ways

Abstract: In den Diskussionen über das Modell des "Parting of the Ways" wurde den Begriffen *Ioudaismos* und *Christianismos* in der Regel wenig Aufmerksamkeit gewidmet. *Ioudaismos* ist dabei der ältere Begriff, der sich allmählich von der Charakterisierung einer bestimmten Form judäischer Lebensweise zu einer statischeren Bedeutung entwickelte, die dem modernen Begriff "Judentum" näherkommt. Allerdings wurde der Begriff in jüdischen und christlichen Kreisen unterschiedlich aufgefasst. *Christianismos* wurde, wahrscheinlich von Marcion, als Gegensatz zu *Ioudaismos* geprägt, allerdings auf der Grundlage des Begriffs *Christianos/us*, der seinen Ursprung wahrscheinlich in Rom hat. Im Osten wird *Christianismos* bis heute verwendet, im Westen wurde der Begriff jedoch bald durch *Christianitas* ersetzt. Diese Bedeutungsverschiebungen lassen sich nicht vom Prozess des "Parting of the Ways" trennen, aber sie wurden auch von den politischen Entwicklungen im Römischen Reich beeinflusst.

Keywords: Ioudaismos; Christianismos; Chrestiani; Christianoi; Christiani; Christianitas; Maccabees; Parting of the Ways.

1 Introduction

What can we say about the Parting of the Ways that is actually new? Hasn't really everything been said? Looking at the bibliography, one can only be sceptical about any claims of originality. Yet, that is not everybody's reaction. In 2019, Udo Schnelle, the meritorious New Testament chair of Halle-Wittenberg, published a concise analysis of the Parting, which he called *The Separated Ways of Romans, Jews and Christians*.[1] In this book, he concentrates on the 1st century, which is not surprising for the author of a popular study on the first hundred years of Christianity.[2] Yet, it is good to realise that one can also look at the be-

---

[1] U. Schnelle, *Die getrennten Wege von Römern, Juden und Christen* (Tübingen: Mohr Siebeck, 2019), to be read with the comments by T. Nicklas, "Diversität, Dynamik und Differenzierung: Eine Diskussion mit Udo Schnelles Modell der 'getrennten Wege von Römern, Juden und Christen'," *EvTh* 80 (2020), 444–454.
[2] U. Schnelle, *Die ersten 100 Jahre des Christentums 30–130 n.Chr.: Die Entstehungsgeschichte einer Weltreligion*, 3rd ed. (Göttingen: Vandenhoeck & Ruprecht, 2019).

ginning of the Jesus movement from a different perspective. For example, in his attractive study of the beginning of Christianity until Constantine, Hartmut Leppin hardly discusses the 1st century at all and consciously refrains from doing so because, as he argues, Jesus was not yet a Christian.[3]

More recent discussions have focused on all kinds of aspects, but they have not concentrated in detail on some important terms of the debate. It is obvious that the terms 'Romans' and 'Christians' do not necessarily have to be exclusive of one another in this debate, as some early Jesus followers, such as possibly the apostle Paul,[4] may well have been Roman citizens, too. This simple example has made me ask in this contribution what the terms usually employed in the discussions, such as Judaism and Christianity, Jews and Christians, actually can say for the theme of the present book. We cannot, though, leave it with the Jews and Christians only, as Schnelle concludes his just mentioned study by stating regarding the Romans that their "christentumfeindliche Haltung forderte geradezu die Distanzierung des Judentums vom entstehenden Christentum. Deshalb konnte es auch keine 'Trennung der Wege' geben, denn alle drei sind nie gemeinsame, sondern von Anfang an getrennte Wege gegangen."[5]

Schnelle rightly points to the Romans as important, but whether they actually performed the role he attributes to them remains to be seen. Even the impact of the tax levied for the *fiscus Iudaicus* has been downplayed recently. Following Martin Goodman, who already had argued its impact on the Parting of the Ways, the tax has been ascribed an important role in a well-known study by Marius Heemstra,[6] who has been followed by Jörg Frey.[7] The tax had certainly been increased by Vespasian. Whereas the Jewish temple tribute used to be imposed on

---

[3] H. Leppin, *Die frühen Christen: Von den Anfängen bis Konstantin*, 2nd ed. (München: Beck, 2019), to be read with my review in *ARYS* 17 (2019): 402–416.
[4] P. van Minnen, "Paul the Roman Citizen," *JSNT* 56 (1994): 43–52; E.A. Judge, *Paul and the Conflict of Cultures: The Legacy of His Thought Today*, ed. J.R. Harrison (Eugene, OR: Cascade, 2019), 68–69.
[5] Schnelle, *Die getrennten Wege* (see n. 1), 190.
[6] M. Goodman, "Nerva, the *Fiscus Judaicus* and Jewish Identity," *JRS* 79 (1989): 40–44 and "The Meaning of '*Fisci Iudaici Calumnia Sublata*' on the Coinage of Nerva," in *Studies in Josephus and the Varieties of Ancient Judaism*, ed. S.J.D. Cohen and J. Schwartz, AGJU 67 (Leiden: Brill, 2007), 81–89; M. Heemstra, *The Fiscus Judaicus and the Parting of the Ways*, WUNT II/277 (Tübingen: Mohr Siebeck, 2010) and "The Interpretation and Wider Context of Nerva's Fiscus Judaicus Sestertius," in *Judaea and Rome in Coins, 65 BCE–135 CE*, ed. D.M. Jacobsen and N. Kokkinos (Oxford: Oxbow, 2012), 187–201.
[7] See J. Frey, "Die Juden im Johannesevangelium und die Frage nach der Trennung der Wege zwischen der johanneischen Gemeinde und der Synagoge," in idem, *Die Herrlichkeit des Gekreuzigten. Studien zu den Johanneischen Schriften I*, ed. J. Schlegel (Tübingen: Mohr Siebeck, 2013), 339–377, esp. 367–370.

male Jews between 20 and 50 years of age, it now also included women, children, and even slaves. Yet, the fact remains that in Rome and Italy the tax must have been levied mainly on the upper classes, as the very few texts and few excavated coins suggest.[8] A role in the Parting of the Ways is hard to see when one does not share Heemstra's precise dating of some New Testament writings, such as of the Apocalypse and Hebrews, and the postulation of a persecution by Domitian.[9] In any case, it is clear that the Romans played a role and that their literature is an important source for our knowledge of early Christianity (§ 1 and 4).

What is lacking in Schnelle is a more incisive analysis of the terms 'Judaism' and 'Christianity' and their ancient equivalents. Modern anthropological and historical research has stressed that the meaning of terms can differ between insiders and outsiders or, in modern jargon, between emic and etic perspectives.[10] One only needs to think of the developments of terms for Americans of African descent and the danger in using a term no longer considered to be acceptable in order to realise that designations of people need not be harmless. There is another term as well, which needs to be taken into consideration here, and that is 'religion.' As several recent studies have stressed, antiquity did not know the term 'religion' in the modern sense of the world.[11] As far as I can see, the term has hardly played any role in recent discussions, but it will be hard to avoid using it, and we have to see to what extent it is useful and/or enlightening to use this modern term. I will start with a fresh look at the term Ἰουδαισμός/*Judaismus*

---

8 Texts: S. Günther, "Ein politischer Skandal als mediales Ereignis. Der fiscus Iudaicus zwischen Domitian und Nerva," *Numismatisches Nachrichtenblatt* 63 (2014): 10–13 and "The Fiscus Iudaicus: A Hypothetical Scholarly Construct," in *Religio licita? Rom und die Juden*, ed. G. Hasselhoff and M. Strothmann (Berlin and Boston, MA: de Gruyter, 2017), 175–189. Coins: N.T. Elkins, "Roman Emperor Nerva's Reform of the Jewish Taks" = https://www.biblicalarchaeology.org/daily/ancient-cultures/daily-life-and-practice/roman-emperor-nervas-reform-of-the-jewish-tax/, accessed 3 December 2019.
9 See the critical review of Heemstra by W. Ameling, *ZKG* 122 (2011): 336–337; R. Couzin, "A Modern Look at the Roman Imperial 'Jewish Tax'," *Canadian Tax Journal / Revue fiscale canadienne* 65 (2017): 333–352.
10 Cf. C. Ginzburg, "Our Words, and Theirs: A Reflection on the Historian's Craft, Today," in *Historical Knowledge. In Quest of Theory, Method and Evidence*, ed. S. Fellman and M. Rahikainen (Cambridge: Cambridge University Press, 2012), 97–119; M. Sahlins, "In Anthropology, It's Emic all the Way Down," *Hau: Journal of Ethnographic Theory* 7 (2017): 157–163.
11 B. Nongbri, *Beyond Belief* (New Haven, CT, and London: Yale University Press, 2012); C. Barton and D. Boyarin, *Imagine no Religion* (New York, NY: Fordham University Press, 2016), to be read with the review by A.K. Petersen, *BMCR* 2017.06.14; T. Whitmarsh, "The Invention of Atheism and the Invention of Religion in Classical Athens," in *Sceptic and Believer in Ancient Mediterranean Religions*, ed. B. Edelmann-Singer et al., WUNT 443 (Tübingen: Mohr Siebeck, 2020), 37–51.

(§ 1), continue with the term Χριστιανοί/*Christiani* as we have had several recent studies of the term, which have paid more attention to the onomastic and palaeographical aspects of the early occurrences of the name than previous analyses (§ 2),[12] go on with Χριστιανισμός/*Christianismus* (§ 3), and end with some concluding observations (§ 4).

2 Ἰουδαισμός/Judaismus

For an outsider, one of the most interesting developments in the field of Second Temple Judaism is undoubtedly the polemics concerning the terms 'Jew' and 'Judaean,' as initiated by Steve Mason.[13] His path-breaking article has focused attention on a previously fairly unreflected usage of the terms.[14] Although Mason's argument has been fiercely contested,[15] a considerable number of scholars nowadays has accepted his point of view and prefers 'Judaean' over 'Jew' for the period of the centuries around the beginning of the Christian era. However, as far

---

12 See, most recently, B. van der Lans and J.N. Bremmer, "Tacitus and the Persecution of the Christians: An Invention of Tradition?," *Eirene* 53 (2017): 299–331, esp. 317–322; J.N. Bremmer, *Maidens, Magic and Martyrs in Early Christianity* (Tübingen: Mohr Siebeck, 2017), 7–12; J.G. Cook, "Chrestiani, Christiani, Χριστιανοί: A Second Century Anachronism?," *VigChris* 74 (2020): 237–264; still useful, R.A. Lipsius, *Über den Ursprung und den ältesten Gebrauch des Christennamens* (Jena: Neuenhahn, 1873).
13 For the epigraphical evidence, see R.S. Kraemer, "On the Meaning of the Term 'Jew' in Greco-Roman Inscriptions," *HThR* 81 (1989): 35–53; M.H. Williams, *Jews in a Graeco-Roman Environment*, WUNT 312 (Tübingen: Mohr Siebeck, 2013), 267–286.
14 S. Mason, "Jews, Judaeans, Judaizing, Judaism: Problems of Categorization in Ancient History," *JSJ* 38 (2007): 457–512 and, in response to criticisms of his thesis, "Ancient Jews or Judeans? Different Questions, Different Answers," *Marginalia* 26–8–2014 = https://marginalia.lareviewofbooks.org/ancient-jews-judeans-different-questions-different-answers-steve-mason/, accessed 22 November 2019.
15 See, for example, C. Baker, "A 'Jew' by Any Other Name?," *JAJ* 2 (2011): 153–180; S. Schwartz, "How Many Judaisms Were There? A Critique of Neusner and Smith on Definition and Mason and Boyarin on Categorization," ibid., 208–238; M. Satlow, "Jew or Judaean?," in *'The One Who Sows Bountifully': Essays in Honor of Stanley K. Stowers*, ed. C.J. Hodge et al. (Providence, RI: Society of Biblical Literature, 2013), 165–175; T.M. Law and C. Halton, eds., *Jew and Judean: A Forum on Politics and Historiography in the Translation of Ancient Texts* (Los Angeles, CA, 2014) = https://dl.orangedox.com/yTWsrMwDFZF3fqx2kt/Jew%20and%20Judean.pdf, accessed 29 November 2019; more nuanced, M. Öhler, "Judäer oder Juden? Die Debatte 'Ethnos vs. Religion' im Blick auf das 2. Makkabäerbuch," in *Die Makkabäer*, ed. F. Avemarie et al., WUNT 382 (Tübingen: Mohr Siebeck, 2017), 157–185. For the most recent survey of the debate, see P.J. Tomson, *Studies on Jews and Christians in the First and Second Centuries*, WUNT 418 (Tübingen: Mohr Siebeck, 2019), 187–220.

as I can see, virtually no supporters or opponents of Mason have looked for the meaning of *Ioudaios* and *Ioudaismos* in early Christian texts in the immediate centuries after Paul.[16] Yet, for a better understanding of the Parting of the Ways we should also consider texts later than those in the books of the later New Testament. We are assisted in our analysis by Mason himself as he has recently returned to the problem of using the term 'Judaism.'[17] I will gratefully, albeit not slavishly, make use of his analysis, but the focus of my discussion will be rather the combination *Ioudaismos/Iudaismus* with *Christianismos/us*.

According to Mason, "though the apostle Paul and Ignatius initiated Christian usage in narrowly restricted contexts, Christian writers from 200 to 500 C.E. did employ these terms liberally."[18] Given the recent discussions, though, regarding Ignatius's date and the books by Marcion (below), there is reason to take a fresh look and somewhat reconsider Mason's position concerning the 2nd century.

One of the striking insights of Mason's seminal article is "that ethnic -ίζω/-ισμός normally occur in explicit or implicit contrast with some other potential affiliation, movement, or inclination."[19] In itself, this is perhaps not that strange, as we usually define ourselves in comparison to others. Yet, as a principle it remains an important guideline. And indeed, Seth Schwartz has observed that Mason's

> argument that in some passages *Ioudaismos* has not the static sense of Judaism – a body of religious lore, belief and practice – but the dynamic sense of Judaizing – adopting or intensifying one's engagement with such lore, belief and practice, is proven true, and brilliantly so.[20]

Indeed, as Steve Mason clearly shows, *Ioudaismos* originally meant "not a general term for 'Judaism' but rather a certain kind of activity over against a pull in

---

[16] But see the discussion by M. Lowe, "Who were the ΙΟΥΔΑΙΟΙ?," *NovT* 18 (1976): 101–131, nuanced by T. Nicklas, "The 'Jews' in the Gospel of John. Past and Future Lines of Scholarship," in *Perceiving the Other in Ancient Judaism and Early Christianity*, ed. M. Bar-Asher Siegal et al., WUNT 394 (Tübingen: Mohr Siebeck, 2017), 49–66, here 54–55.
[17] S. Mason, "Paul Without Judaism: Historical Method over Perspective," in *Paul among Jews and Gentiles: essays in honour of Terence L. Donaldson*, ed. R. Charles (London: T&T Clark, 2021), 9–39, = https://www.academia.edu/40939312/Paul_Without_Judaism_Historical_Method_over_Perspective, accessed 11 June 2020.
[18] Mason, "Jews, Judaeans" (see n. 14), 461.
[19] Mason, "Jews, Judaeans" (see n. 14), 463.
[20] Schwartz, "How Many Judaisms were There?" (see n. 15), 225.

another, foreign direction." In other words, *Ioudaismos* originally had a dynamic meaning: Judaizing rather than Judaism.[21]

It seems important to me to modify Mason's argument in one detail. It is not the case that the dynamic sense of *Ioudaismos* occurs in all instances since and including the Maccabean revolt, but it certainly does occur in the older instances until Paul. As is well known, the term occurs first in 2 Maccabees. Mason states that the cognate verb ἰουδαΐζω is older than the noun.[22] This seems reasonable, but LXX Esther 8:17, where we first find the verb, is actually later than 2 Maccabees;[23] similarly, χριστιανίζω is attested first in Origen (*Cels.* 3.75, 80 etc.), that is, long after the coinage of Χριστιανισμός by Marcion and its usage by Polycarp and Ignatius (§ 3). It may thus well be that the noun was sometimes coined before the corresponding verb, presumably in analogy to other comparable terms, even though this does not affect Mason's argument that the verb denotes an activity and not a static position.

Given the absence of *Ioudaismos* in Philo and Josephus, it is rather surprising to see the term appear in Paul's Letter to the Galatians, although perhaps less surprising when we look at its content. The well-known passage, Gal 1:13–14, is as follows:

> [13] You have heard, no doubt, of my earlier life in *Ioudaismos*. I was violently persecuting the church of God and was trying to destroy it. [14] I advanced in *Ioudaismos* beyond many among my peers, being exceedingly zealous for the traditions of my ancestors.[24]

Evidently, for Paul, the content of *Ioudaismos* was related to a certain idea of his ancestral traditions and their importance. In that respect, he may well have thought to stand in the line of the Maccabees, as Mason plausibly suggests.[25] In the most detailed recent discussion of the passage, Matthew Novenson calls

---

21 Mason, "Jews, Judaeans" (see n. 14), 465–468.
22 Mason, "Jews, Judaeans" (see n. 14), 464.
23 M. Harl et al., *La Bible grecque des Septante*, 2nd ed. (Paris: Cerf, 1994), 111.
24 Gal 1:13–14: Ἠκούσατε γὰρ τὴν ἐμὴν ἀναστροφήν ποτε ἐν τῷ Ἰουδαϊσμῷ, ὅτι καθ' ὑπερβολὴν ἐδίωκον τὴν ἐκκλησίαν τοῦ θεοῦ καὶ ἐπόρθουν αὐτήν, καὶ προέκοπτον ἐν τῷ Ἰουδαϊσμῷ ὑπὲρ πολλοὺς συνηλικιώτας ἐν τῷ γένει μου, περισσοτέρως ζηλωτὴς ὑπάρχων τῶν πατρικῶν μου παραδόσεων; see also G.S. Oegema, "1 and 2 Maccabees in Paul's Letter to the Galatians," in *Die Makkabäer*, ed. F. Avemarie et al., WUNT 382 (Tübingen: Mohr Siebeck, 2017), 345–360, here 346–348; more detailed, but not always persuasive, D. Sänger, "Ἰουδαϊσμός – ἰουδαΐζειν – ἰουδαϊκῶς. Sprachliche und semantische Überlegungen im Blick auf Gal 1,13 f. und 2,14," *ZNW* 108 (2017): 150–185.
25 Mason, "Jews, Judaeans" (see n. 14), 468.

it a "sectarian political program."²⁶ However, that qualification seems too modern. There is no doubt that the programme of the Maccabees was also religious in our terms, and the close entanglement of religion and politics in the Maccabean movement should not be reduced to just politics. In fact, Paul's own confession that he used to persecute the church of God militates against this interpretation. However, in this case, the term *Ioudaismos* still presupposes a kind of activism, a propagation, if need be by violent means, of a certain way of life. Yet, this way of life also has clearly to be situated within the Judaean world, not in a gentile environment.

The next occurrence of *Ioudaismos* is in 4 Maccabees, which should be dated to around 100 AD at the earliest, given its medical vocabulary.²⁷ It is noted that King Antiochus IV, when his abolition of ancestral law met only active defiance, through torture tried to compel every member of the *ethnos* to eat polluted food and to swear off Ἰουδαϊσμός (4:26). Here, the author seems to use the term in a more static meaning, even if taken from 2 Maccabees, as he ascribes the *Ioudaismos* to 'every member' of the Judaeans. Such a development from a dynamic to a more static usage need not be surprising, as we can see the same development in the meaning of ἑλληνισμός, which developed from an initially active meaning 'imitating Greek'/'starting to speak Greek' to a more static meaning 'properly speaking Greek' in the 1ˢᵗ centuries of the Christian era.²⁸ And indeed, as the original Maccabean revolt gradually became an event of the past, there was room for a shift in meaning of the term, even within the Greek linguistic system.

There are no indications that 4 Maccabees influenced Marcion,²⁹ the next author to use the term *Ioudaismos*. Recently, about the same time but independently from one another, both Judith Lieu and Markus Vinzent have paid attention to

---

[26] M.V. Novenson, "Paul's Former Occupation in *Ioudaismos*," in *Galatians and Christian Theology: Justification, the Gospel, and Ethics in Paul's Letter*, ed. M.W. Elliott et al. (Grand Rapids, MI: Eerdmans, 2014), 24–39, here 39.

[27] I analyse this vocabulary in J.N. Bremmer, "The Date and Location of Ignatius: An Onomastic Approach," in *Das Baujahr hinter der Fassade. Probleme bei der Datierung neutestamentlicher Pseudepigraphen und neuere Lösungsansätze*, ed. W. Grünstäudl and M. Schmidt, WUNT (Tübingen: Mohr Siebeck, forthcoming 2021); it has not been taken into account by A.M. Schwemer, "Zu Entstehungszeit und -ort des 4. Makkabäerbuchs," in *Die Makkabäer*, ed. F. Avemarie et al., WUNT 382 (Tübingen: Mohr Siebeck, 2017), 245–327.

[28] M. Casevitz, "Hellenismos: formation et fonction des verbes en -IZΩ et de leur dérivés" and C. Daumier, "Sextus Empiricus contre les grammariens: ce que parler grec veut dire," in *Hellenismos. Quelques jalons pour une histoire de l'identité grecque*, ed. S. Said (Leiden: Brill, 1991), 9–16, 17–32, respectively.

[29] Marcion is not mentioned in A.Y. Reed, *Jewish-Christianity and the History of Judaism*, TSAJ 171 (Tübingen: Mohr Siebeck, 2018).

Tertullian's usage of the term in connection with Marcion. As Judith Lieu observed, nearly twenty-five years ago: "neither *Judaism* nor *Christianism* are found in Irenaeus or in Justin, two of Tertullian's principal sources and they appear together only in Books IV and V of the *Adv. Marc.*, which were written at the final stage of the work when Tertullian first had access to Marcion's *Antitheses*."[30] This analysis seems to me more precise than the argument in her *opus magnum* on Marcion:

> Although repeated elsewhere in the *Against Marcion*, this pair (*Christianismus* and *Iudaismus*) is not found outside it, and neither of the individual terms is common in Tertullian's work. This, together with the Greek origin of the terms, makes it likely that its association with Marcion was not entirely Tertullian's invention, although Irenaeus' apparent ignorance of the polarity indicates that it did not function as a significant 'head-line' for the former.[31]

Now Tertullian tells us that the antithesis in Marcion between Judaism and Christianity was supported by a statement in his *Gospel* (par. Luke 16:16–17; Matt 11:13):

> John [the Baptist] has been set as a form of boundary between old things and new, a line at which Judaism should cease and Christianity should begin, without, though, there having been, by an alien power, a cessation of the Law and the prophets, and the establishing of the Gospel in which is the reign of God, Christ himself.[32]

Lieu is somewhat hesitant as to Tertullian quoting Marcion's *ipsissima verba*,[33] and certainty at this point, as on many other ones of Marcion's texts, is unobtainable, but the repetition of the opposition makes it plausible that his text of the *Antitheses* contained the opposition of *Christianismos* and *Ioudaismos* (§ 3).[34] In

---

[30] J.M. Lieu, *Image and Reality: The Jews in the World of the Christians in the Second Century* (London and New York, NY: T&T Clark, 1996), 266 (some words in italics originally in bold); approvingly quoted by M. Vinzent, *Tertullian's Preface to Marcion's Gospel* (Leuven: Peeters, 2016), 345.

[31] J.M. Lieu, *Marcion and the Making of a Heretic* (Cambridge: Cambridge University Press, 2015), 408.

[32] Tertullian, *Marc.* IV.33.8: *Iohannem constitutum inter vetera et nova, ad quem desineret Iudaismus et a quo inciperet Christianismus, non tamen ut ab alia virtute facta sit sedatio legis et prophetarum, et initiatio evangelii in quo est dei regnum, Christus ipse*, cf. Vinzent, *Tertullian's Preface to Marcion's Gospel* (see n. 30), 342–347.

[33] Lieu, *Marcion* (see n. 31), 74–75, 231, 405–406, 409.

[34] *Christianismus/Iudaismus*: Tertullian, *Marc.* IV.6.3; IV.33.8; V.3.8; Vinzent, *Tertullian's Preface to Marcion's Gospel* (see n. 30), 344–345.

any case, as she notes, "Marcion most likely used the term 'Judaism' under the influence of Paul's reference to his 'past life in Judaism' (Gal 1:13–14), and his voice may be heard behind Tertullian's affirmation, 'we also claim Galatians as a primary letter against Judaism' (*AM* V.2.1)."[35]

It is much more difficult to see what *Ioudaismos* exactly meant in Marcion's work. When Tertullian argues that "Marcion in his *Antitheses* accuses of having been interpolated by the defenders of Judaism for the incorporation of the Law and the prophets that they might construct also Christ from this,"[36] the term still seems to contain a certain 'activist' significance, even though its pairing with *Christianismos* suggests a shading into a more static meaning. At the same time, though, as is perceptively noted by Lieu, *Ioudaismos* did not mean 'Judaism' for Marcion or refer to actual Jews in Rome, but clearly alludes to a group of Christians within the larger Church of Rome, who, apparently, wanted to stick to the Torah and other aspects of the Judaean tradition.[37]

It is not different for Ignatius, our next author to use the term *Ioudaismos*.[38] I know of course that the place and date of Ignatius is debated, but the dependence on 4 Maccabees, Hermas, and the Gnostics Ptolemaeus and Noetus points to a time between the 140s and about 180, the time of Lucian and Irenaeus, who both seem to know the Letters. Moreover, the onomastics of Ignatius's Letters suggests an origin in the corridor Smyrna–Ephesus, exactly the same region as proposed by Reinhard Hübner along a completely different route.[39] Evidently, Ignatius knew not only Paul's Letters but also 4 Maccabees.[40] In his writings, the active meaning still seems present in the Letter to the Magnesians, where Ignatius exhorts the faithful: "as we are his (Christ's) disciples, let us learn to live ac-

---

35 Lieu, *Marcion* (see n. 31), 408–409.
36 Tertullian, *Marc.* IV.4.4: *quod Marcion per* Antitheses *suas arguit ut interpolatum a protectoribus Iudaismi ad concorporationem legis et prophetarum, qua etiam Christum inde confingerent* […].
37 Lieu, *Marcion* (see n. 31), 409: "('Judaism') would have been for him more a danger within the Church than embodied in some outside group, such as the Jews of his own time."
38 For a full discussion, see Lieu, *Image and Reality* (see n. 30), 23–56, although less helpful because of her sticking to the traditional dating and location of Ignatius; see also T. Nicklas, *Jews and Christians? Second-Century 'Christian' Perspectives on the "Parting of the Ways,"* Annual Deichmann Lectures 2013 (Tübingen: Mohr Siebeck, 2014), 5–10.
39 R. Hübner, *Der paradox Eine. Antignostischer Monarchianismus im zweiten Jahrhundert*, VCSup 50 (Leiden: Brill, 1999), and idem, "Thesen zur Echtheit und Datierung der sieben Briefe des *Ignatius* von Antiochien," *ZAC* 1 (1997): 42–70, repr. in idem, Addenda et Corrigenda in *Kirche und Dogma im Werden* (Tübingen: Mohr Siebeck, 2018), 63–92; Bremmer, "The Date and Location of Ignatius" (see n. 27).
40 Cf. the classic study by O. Perler, "Das vierte Makkabäerbuch, Ignatius von Antiochien und die ältesten Märtyrerberichte," *RivAC* 25 (1949): 47–72.

cording to *Christianismos*," and the opposite of this way of life is *ioudaizein*, presumably propagating a kind of Jewish Christianity.[41] The static meaning is clearer in the Letter to the Philadelphians, where Ignatius says:

> But if anyone expounds *Ioudaismos* to you, do not listen to him; for it is better to hear *Christianismos* from a man who is circumcised than *Ioudaismos* from a man uncircumcised; both of them, if they do not speak of Jesus Christ, are to me tombstones and graves of the dead on which nothing but the names of men is written.[42]

Perhaps surprisingly, Ignatius mentions actual Judaeans only once (Ign.*Smyrn.* 1:2) and not in a derogatory manner, but apparently, like Marcion, he uses the term *Ioudaismos* for those Christ followers who still live by and stick to traditional Judaean ways and manners.[43] Consequently, it seems that in Ignatius's case *Ioudaismos* refers to a more theological position, even though that does not exclude a way of life, as exemplified by keeping the Sunday instead of the Sabbath (Ign.*Magn.* 9:1). It is also clear that it does not yet mean a whole belief system and lifestyle of the Judaeans, as the Ignatian 'Judaizers' also believe in Christ. However, the next century would see a thorough change.

Within Jewish circles, the more static meaning of *Ioudaismos*, which we saw in 4 Maccabees, remained current in some circles. This is shown by two inscriptions, of which the well-known donor inscription from Macedonian Stobi (second half of the 2nd century or first half of the 3rd century) mentions that Polycharmus, the father of the synagogue, had lived his whole life "according to the (prescriptions of) Judaism (κατὰ τὸν Ἰουδαϊσμόν)."[44] A slightly later inscription from Rome mentions a certain Kattia Ammia "who had lived a fine life in Judaism

---

[41] Ign.*Magn.* 10:1: μαθηταὶ αὐτοῦ γενόμενοι, μάθωμεν κατὰ Χριστιανισμὸν ζῆν; 10:3: Ἄτοπόν ἐστιν, Ἰησοῦν Χριστὸν λαλεῖν καὶ ἰουδαΐζειν.

[42] Ign.*Phld.* 6:1: Ἐὰν δέ τις Ἰουδαϊσμὸν ἑρμηνεύῃ ὑμῖν, μὴ ἀκούετε αὐτοῦ. Ἄμεινον γάρ ἐστιν παρὰ ἀνδρὸς περιτομὴν ἔχοντος Χριστιανισμὸν ἀκούειν, ἢ παρὰ ἀκροβύστου Ἰουδαϊσμόν. Ἐὰν δὲ ἀμφότεροι περὶ Ἰησοῦ Χριστοῦ μὴ λαλῶσιν, οὗτοι ἐμοὶ στῆλαί εἰσιν καὶ τάφοι νεκρῶν, ἐφ' οἷς γέγραπται μόνον ὀνόματα ἀνθρώπων.

[43] Cf. C.K. Barrett, "Jews and Judaizers in the Epistles of Ignatius," in *Jews, Greeks and Christians. Religious Cultures in Late Antiquity*, ed. R. Hamerton-Kelly and R. Scroggs (Leiden: Brill, 1976), 220–244; S.J.D. Cohen, "Judaism without Circumcision and 'Judaism' without Circumcision in Ignatius," *HThR* 95 (2002): 395–415; Nicklas, "The 'Jews' in the Gospel of John" (see n. 16), 63; D. Boyarin, "Why Ignatius Invented Judaism," in *The Ways That Often Parted: Essays in Honor of Joel Marcus*, ed. L. Baron et al. (Atlanta, GA: Society for Biblical Literature, 2018), 309–324.

[44] D. Noy et al., eds., *Inscriptiones Judaicae Orientis. Volume I: Eastern Europe*, TSAJ 101 (Tübingen: Mohr Siebeck, 2004), 63 (= Mac1, tr. Noy).

(καλῶς βιώσασα ἐν τῷ Ἰουδαϊσμῷ)."⁴⁵ Whereas in these inscriptions the term *Ioudaismos* clearly still has a positive meaning, it would be different in Christian circles.

With Tertullian and Origen, the term *Iudaismus/Ioudaismos* becomes more popular, as Tertullian uses it 24 and Origen about 33 times. In both of them, however, the term no longer means those within the Jesus movement, albeit on the wrong side, but those who adhere to a system of beliefs and practices that is no longer sustainable, even has to be rejected, as Mason notes.⁴⁶ As such, it is not only opposed to *Christianismus/os*, but since Eusebius it also becomes combined with *Hellenismos* as the great opponents of *Christianismos*.⁴⁷ It is clear that *Ioudaismos* now has become, to quote Mason, "this faith-based identity over *ethnos*- and *polis*-affiliation."⁴⁸ With the 3rd century, though, we have long reached a factual parting of the ways, and I will stop here, the more so as Daniel Boyarin has recently published a book on the history of 'Judaism,' although it is not wholly satisfactory for the earliest stages of the term.⁴⁹ But even if I stop here, it remains to say that 'Judaism' would be highly successful as a term until the present day, unlike 'Christianism,' because the Latin *Iudaismus* of the Vulgate was translated in 1425 as *Judaisme* in English, even though the French already had the term *Judaisme* since about 1231.⁵⁰

---

45 G. Sacco, *Iscrizioni greche d'Italia, Porto* (Rome: Quasar, 1984), 101–102; D. Noy, *Jewish Inscriptions of Western Europe II* (Cambridge: Cambridge University Press, 1995), 464–465 (no. 584).
46 Mason, "Jews, Judaeans" (see n. 14), 472: "now it contrasts a living system with a defunct precursor" (Tertullian), 475 (Origen).
47 Eusebius, *Dem. ev.* 1.2.1; 1.2.9; *Praep. ev.* 1.5.12, etc.
48 Mason, "Paul without Judaism" (see n. 17), 26 (in the Academia version).
49 D. Boyarin, *Judaism: The Genealogy of a Modern Notion* (New Brunswick, NJ: Rutgers University Press, 2019), on which see A.Y. Reed and S. Magid, "Daniel Boyarin's Judaism: A Forum," *Marginalia* 5-7-2019 = https://marginalia.lareviewofbooks.org/introduction-marginalia-forum-daniel-boyarin-judaism/, accessed 11 June 2020.
50 M.J. Powell, *The Pauline Epistles Contained in Ms. Parker 32, Corpus Christi College, Cambridge* (London: Kegan Paul, 1916, repr. London: Forgotten Books, 1973) Gal. i. 13: For ȝee hafe herde my conuersacyoun sum tyme in Iudaisme [L. *in iudaismo*]; G. de Coinci, *Miracles de Nostre Dame*, ed. V.F. Koenig, Vol. 4 (Geneva: Droz, 1970), 63: "Pluseurs Juïs par la cité Leur Judaïsme déguerpirent, De cuer amerent et servirent La douce mère au roy de gloire."

3 Χριστιανοί/Christiani

Let us now turn to the 'Christian' terminology and ask: when, where, and why do we first start to hear about the name 'Christian'?[51] As is well known, the where is answered by the author of the Acts of the Apostles in a kind of explanatory gloss in a passage in which Antioch is central. Here the author tells us: "and it was in Antioch that the disciples were called Christians for the first time" (χρηματίσαι τε πρώτως ἐν Ἀντιοχείᾳ τοὺς μαθητὰς Χριστιανούς: 11:26).[52] Unfortunately, the date of Acts is disputed. It seems reasonable, though, to follow the *Mehrheitsmeinung* and think of about 90 to 120 as a probable date, even though slightly later dates are not impossible either. In any case, we are at the end of the 1st century at the earliest.

The author does not tell us who coined the name but, given that the ending of *-ianus* is typically Latin, the most reasonable explanation would be that it was given by Romans. Now, it is well known that we have a number of similar names, such as Caesariani ('Caesar's army'), Pompeiani ('Pompey's followers'), Pisoniani ('Piso's soldiers'), Ciceroniani ('friends/*clientes* of Cicero'), Herodiani ('followers of Herodes'), Augustiani ('Nero's claque'),[53] and Galbiani ('Galba's troops'). As Theodor Zahn acutely noted, the type of name is typically popular and was avoided by some Roman authors such as Varro.[54] Virtually all these names, and certainly the earlier ones, do refer to political or military followers; none, it should be stressed, suggests a name with a religious meaning. The name *Christianos/us* thus refers to a person called Christus, who was supposed to be the leader of some kind of political or military movement. It is possible, therefore, as has been suggested more often,[55] that the name arose from a Roman intervention in

---

51 For the earlier *Forschungsgeschichte*, see A. Gercke, "Der Christenname ein Scheltname," in *Festschrift zur Jahrhundertfeier der Universität zu Breslau*, ed. T. Siebs (Breslau: Trewendt & Granier, 1911), 360–373.
52 For χρηματίσαι, see van der Lans and Bremmer, "Tacitus" (see n. 12), 319–320; for πρώτως, see L. Robert, *Hellenica VII* (Paris: Librairie Adrien-Maisonneuve, 1949), 211: "πρώτως signifie 'pour la premiere fois', comme πρῶτον dont il est une forme hellénistique"; C. Spicq, *Théologie morale du Nouveau Testament I* (Paris: Gabalda et Cie, 1965), 407 n. 4 (papyrological evidence). Note that Codex D has: καὶ τότε πρῶτον ἐχρημάτισαν ἐν Ἀντιοχείᾳ οἱ μαθηταὶ Χρειστιανοί.
53 See now M. E. Muñoz-Santos, "Los Augustiani: El peculiar coro de Nerón," *Anuari. AntMed* 8 (2018): 653–662.
54 For full references, see T. Zahn, *Einleitung in das Neue Testament*, 2 vols. (Leipzig: Deichert, 1897–1899), 2:42; add Bremmer, *Maidens, Magic and Martyrs* (see n. 12), 8, which I use and supplement here.
55 Cf. J. Taylor, "Why Were the Disciples First Called 'Christians' at Antioch? (Acts 11.26)," *RB* 101 (1994): 75–94.

a quarrel between Jesus followers and their opponents in one of the Antiochene synagogues. Nevertheless, if we accept the not implausible supposition that Acts was actually written in Antioch, we may become much more sceptical and assume that it is "an attempt to champion the Christian community in that city."[56] And indeed, why would an occasional usage of the term in this Syrian city take off in the rest of the Empire? Isn't it much more likely that the term was invented in Rome, where we clearly find most of the earliest examples by far?

Unfortunately, the note in Acts does not inform us about the time when the Romans introduced the term 'Christian' for the Jesus followers. We can go back for the term at least to the early nineties. It is noteworthy that in the discussions of the name, there rarely is a reference to Flavius Josephus's mention of it. In his famous, if not notorious, *Testimonium Flavianum*, Josephus tells us:[57]

> At that time there arose Jesus, a wise man, if indeed one should call him a man. For he was a performer of marvellous works, a teacher of those who receive with pleasure the truth. And he won over many Jews and many of the Greeks. He was the Christ. When Pilate, upon hearing him accused by the foremost men among us, condemned him to the cross, those who first loved him did not cease. For he appeared to them on the third day alive again, the holy prophets having foretold these things and many other marvels about him. And even now the tribe of the Christians, so called after him, has not disappeared.

The passage has caused much ink to be spilled, with most scholars having been interested in the mention of Jesus as the Christ, but much less in the name of the Christians. As is well known, the debate about the *Testimonium Flavianum* received a new impetus through the publication of Arabic and Syriac versions of this text; from these, the version of Michael the Syrian also reproduces the mention of the Christians.[58] In recent times, with gradually more balanced discus-

---

56 See, most recently, J.R. Howell, *The Pharisees and Figured Speech in Luke-Acts*, WUNT II/456 (Tübingen: Mohr Siebeck, 2017), 67, with a persuasive argument for Antioch as the place of composition of Acts (pp. 65–71), at this point following older scholars such as Harnack, even if attaching too much weight to late sources like Jerome.
57 Josephus, *A.J.* 18.63–64: Γίνεται δὲ κατὰ τοῦτον τὸν χρόνον Ἰησοῦς σοφὸς ἀνήρ, εἴγε ἄνδρα αὐτὸν λέγειν χρή· ἦν γὰρ παραδόξων ἔργων ποιητής, διδάσκαλος ἀνθρώπων τῶν ἡδονῇ τἀληθῆ δεχομένων, καὶ πολλοὺς μὲν Ἰουδαίους, πολλοὺς δὲ καὶ τοῦ Ἑλληνικοῦ ἐπηγάγετο· ὁ Χριστὸς οὗτος ἦν. καὶ αὐτὸν ἐνδείξει τῶν πρώτων ἀνδρῶν παρ' ἡμῖν σταυρῷ ἐπιτετιμηκότος Πιλάτου οὐκ ἐπαύσαντο οἱ τὸ πρῶτον ἀγαπήσαντες· ἐφάνη γὰρ αὐτοῖς τρίτην ἔχων ἡμέραν πάλιν ζῶν τῶν θείων προφητῶν ταῦτά τε καὶ ἄλλα μυρία περὶ αὐτοῦ θαυμάσια εἰρηκότων. εἰς ἔτι τε νῦν τῶν Χριστιανῶν ἀπὸ τοῦδε ὠνομασμένον οὐκ ἐπέλιπε τὸ φῦλον, trans. A. Whealey.
58 For a useful juxtaposition in parallel columns of the various versions, see L.L. Grabbe, "'Jesus Who Is Called Christ': references to Jesus outside Christian sources," in *"Is This Not*

sions of the text, the authenticity of the passage, or at least an authentic core, seems to be increasingly accepted, except perhaps that many scholars will agree that Jerome (*Vir. ill.* 13) may well have been right by translating: *credebatur esse Christus*, instead of the Greek text's ὁ Χριστὸς οὗτος ἦν, 'he was the Christ,' his translation being supported by the Syriac version.[59] For us, it is important to stress that in AD 93–94 (*Ant.* 20.267) Josephus wrote his *Judaean Antiquities* in Rome for a local audience,[60] even though his readers were probably Greek speaking. It seems therefore not unreasonable to accept that he would refer to the followers of Jesus with a Roman term and not with one of the many other names the early Christians used as a self-designation.[61]

But from whom did Josephus get the name of the Christians? I do not see this question posed in recent literature. Yet, once we start having doubts about the Antiochene origin, the question becomes urgent. Now there are of course various possibilities. Josephus may have learned of the name via personal contacts, which seems not implausible given the number of Christians present in Rome. Differently, he may also have picked up this specific term from contemporary Roman literature. As a recent study of his Greek notes, it

> seems that Latin exercised a steady, and rather extensive influence on the Greek of Josephus, while Aramaic influence seems to have waned with time. While the Latinity of Jose-

---

the Carpenter?" The Question of the Historicity of the Figure of Jesus, ed. T.-L. Thompson and T.S. Verenna (Sheffield: Sheffield University Press, 2012), 57–69.

59 See, most recently, S. Bardet, "Le Testimonium Flavianum, intraduisible et illimité?," in *Pierre Geoltrain ou comment faire l'histoire des religions*, ed. S.C. Mimouni and I. Ullern-Weité (Turnhout: Brepols, 2006), 207–214; J. Carleton Paget, *Jews, Christians and Jewish Christians in Antiquity* (Tübingen: Mohr Siebeck, 2010), 199–265, although he (p. 223) mistakenly states that the phrase εἰς ἔτι τε νῦν nowhere occurs in Eusebius: see the latter's *Generalis elementaria introductio* (= *Eclogae propheticae*), p. 168,15 Gaisford: εἰς ἔτι τε νῦν παρ' ὅλῳ τῷ ἔθνει προφήτας γεγονέναι τοῦ Θεοῦ πιστεύεσθαι; A. Whealey, "The *Testimonium Flavianum*," in *A Companion to Josephus*, ed. H.H. Chapman and Z. Rodgers (Oxford: Oxford University Press, 2016), 345–355. For the *Forschungsgeschichte* of the passage, see S. Bardet, *Le testimonium Flavianum. Examen historique, considérations historiographiques* (Paris: Cerf, 2002); A. Whealey, *Josephus on Jesus: The Testimonium Flavianum Controversy from Late Antiquity to Modern Times* (New York, NY: Lang, 2003).

60 Cf. S. Mason, "The Importance of the Latter Half of Josephus's *Judaean Antiquities* for His Roman Audience," in *Pentateuchal Traditions in the Late Second Temple Period*, ed. A. Moriya and G. Hata, JSJSup 158 (Leiden: Brill, 2012), 129–153.

61 Cf. P.R. Trebilco, *Self-designations and Group Identity in the New Testament* (Cambridge: Cambridge University Press, 2011).

phus' Greek has long been overlooked and underappreciated, it is clear that this influence extended into every part of his Greek from his syntax to his vocabulary in all of his works.[62]

We simply cannot answer the question due to lack of further information, but we do want to stress that the passage shows knowledge of this particular name for the Jesus followers in Rome in the early 90s.

Can we go back further down in time? We find a likely early source in Tacitus's famous report of the fate of the Christians after the Great Fire in Rome in his *Annales*, which is usually dated sometime around 115–120:[63]

> *ergo abolendo rumori Nero subdidit reos et quaesitissimis poenis adfecit, quos per flagitia invisos vulgus Chrestianos appellabat. auctor nominis eius Christus Tiberio imperitante per procuratorem Pontium Pilatum supplicio adfectus erat* (15.44.2–3)

Therefore, to abolish the rumour, Nero fraudulently substituted culprits and afflicted with the most elaborate punishments those whom, hated for their shameful acts, the crowd called 'Chrestians'. The source of this name was Christus who during the reign of Tiberius was executed by the procurator Pontius Pilate.

I am not interested here in the reality of the persecution or the connection between the Great Fire, as I have participated in that debate elsewhere,[64] but for our purpose it is important to note the spelling of the name given here to the Jesus followers: *Chrestiani* instead of *Christiani*.[65] Although older editions often corrected *Chrestiani*, palaeographical research on the archetype of the *Annales* has shown that, originally, the scribe clearly wrote *Chrestiani*, but that the *e* was erased and replaced by an *i*.[66] Now it has been persuasively argued that Tac-

---

62 J.S. Ward, "Roman Greek: Latinisms in the Greek of Flavius Josephus," *CQ* 57 (2007): 632–649, here 647.
63 For the date of the *Annales*, see R. Syme, *Tacitus*, 2 vols. (Oxford: Oxford University Press, 1958), 2:465–480.
64 Van der Lans and Bremmer, "Tacitus" (see n. 12). For the origin of the debate and further reactions, see B.D. Shaw, "The Myth of the Neronian Persecution," *JRS* 105 (2015): 73–100; C.P. Jones, "The Historicity of the Neronian Persecution: A Response to Brent Shaw," *NTS* 63 (2017): 146–152; B.D. Shaw, "Response to Christopher Jones: The Historicity of the Neronian Persecution," *NTS* 64 (2018): 231–242 is not really persuasive, as is also noted by Cook, "*Chrestiani*, *Christiani*, Χριστιανοί" (see n. 12).
65 I elaborate, correct and update here van der Lans and Bremmer, "Tacitus"(see n. 12), 321–322.
66 See the ultraviolet photograph in E. Zara, "The Chrestianos Issue in Tacitus Reinvestigated," 2009 = http://www.textexcavation.com/documents/zaratacituschrestianos.pdf, accessed 21 November 2019; in more detail and also with photo, Cook, "*Chrestiani*, *Christiani*, Χριστιανοί" (see n. 12).

itus intends a pun here by juxtaposing *flagitia* and *Chrestiani*, which Hildebrand Hommel (1899–1996) attractively translated with *Biedermänner*,[67] as Tacitus certainly will have noted the connection between *Chrestiani* and Greek χρῆστος, 'decent, honest.' At the same time, though, it is striking that the spelling does not conform to that of contemporary authors, such as Pliny the Younger, Suetonius and 1 Peter, authors to whom I will return momentarily. That makes it likely that Tacitus took the spelling from his source(s), whom we cannot identify with any certainty, but who may well have been either Pliny the Elder, Cluvius Rufus or Fabius Rusticus, all of whom had written histories of Nero's reign and whose works Tacitus had used.[68] It seems therefore plausible that we come close to Nero's reign for the term *Chrestiani*.

The less usual spelling can of course more easily be associated with the notice in Suetonius (*Claud.* 25.4) that Claudius *Iudaeos impulsore Chresto assidue tumultuantis Roma expulit*. By all accounts, the most likely interpretation, which most historians accept, is that Chrestus here refers to Christus.[69] At the time, Christus as a name must have been unknown to the Romans, and even the name Chrestus must have sounded fairly uncommon to most of them. Greek literature, inscriptions and papyri give us only two examples of the name Χρῆστος from the last century BC, and even those are from the last decades before the turn of the era,[70] whereas also in Rome itself the name does not predate the 1st century BC.[71] The unusual name, then, may have helped to preserve it for later times, even though the name Chrestus already became popular in the course of the 1st century AD. We can see this also from the fact that Roman inscriptions present two early examples of the name Chrestianus, which in this context must mean 'slave of' or 'having been slave of' Chrestus. The first one mentions Faustus, a slave of Antonia Minor (d. 1 May 37), who bought the rights of funerary urns from a certain Iucundus Chrestianus, whereas the second mentions an Epaphroditus, a *magister* of the college of the *ministri* of

---

[67] I owe this translation to A.M. Ritter, *Alte Kirche*, KTGQ 1, 12th ed. (Göttingen: Vandenhoeck & Ruprecht, 2019), 9.
[68] Syme, *Tacitus* 1.278–83.
[69] Cf. H. Botermann, *Das Judenedikt des Kaisers Claudius, Römischer Staat und Christiani im 1. Jahrhundert* (Stuttgart: Steiner, 1996), 57–102; J.G. Cook, *Roman Attitudes Toward the Christians* (Tübingen: Mohr Siebeck, 2010), 15–22; see also H.C. Teitler, *VC* 51 (1997): 217 with a collection of the most important later evidence in his review of Botermann.
[70] *Agora* XXI F 243 (ca. 50 BC); *BGU* 16.2610 (9 BC). Cook, "Chrestiani, Christiani, Χριστιανοί" (see n. 12), 256 n. 94 states: "A usage, from I BCE, is in Appian, *Mithr.* 2.10.32 (Χρηστός)," but the name is the nickname, 'Honest', of the Bithynian Socrates.
[71] H. Solin, *Die griechischen Personennamen in Rom: Ein Namenbuch*, 3 vols., 2nd ed. (Berlin: de Gruyter, 2003), 3:1004–1006.

the *domus Augusta* in the late 30s AD, presumably formerly a slave of a man called Chrestus.[72]

These names show that the name *Chrestiani* must have sounded normal to the inhabitants of Rome, and, given the well-known frequent interchange of η and ι throughout the Roman and Byzantine periods,[73] it should not be surprising that Suetonius spelled *Chrestus*, but, interestingly, also *Christiani* (*Nero* 16.2), just like Tacitus (*Ann.* 15.44) wrote *Chrestiani* and *Christus*.[74] Apparently, either the Romans themselves had realised, or Jesus followers had pointed out to them, that the name should not be *Chrestiani* but *Christiani*, that is, if these spellings are not already later corrections. We do not know when the latter form prevailed, but probably in the late Flavian and earlier Antonine period, as Josephus (above), Pliny the Younger (*Ep.* 10.96.1),[75] Suetonius (above), Acts of the Apostles (26:28), and 1 Peter (4:16),[76] all have Χριστιανοί/*Christiani*.

4 Χριστιανισμός/Christianismus

Having seen that in all the earliest cases we find the name *Christiani/oi* only in Rome, except for Luke's Acts, we will now turn to a closer look at the term *Christianismos/us*. The Roman base, so to speak, of the name 'Christian' explains why

---

[72] *CIL* VI.24944 (Iucundus); *CIL* X.6638 B (Epaphroditus), cf. M. Bile and B. Gain, "Une nouvelle étymologie de ΧΡΙΣΤΙΑΝΟΣ," *REAug* 58 (2012): 141–153; J.B. Pischedda, *Strani chrestiani? La fantastica pseudostoria dei chrestiani prima dei cristiani* (Rome: ELL, 2012), with photos of the inscriptions.

[73] Most recently, E. Pachoumi, "An Invocation of Chrestos in Magic. The Question of the Orthographical Spelling of Chrestos and Interpretation Issues in PGM XIII.288–95," *Hermathena* 188 (2010): 29–54; W. Shandruk, "The Interchange of ι and η in Spelling χριστ- in Documentary Papyri," *BASP* 47 (2010): 205–219. The interchange is probably also responsible for Ign.*Magn.* 2:10: τῆς χρηστότητος αὐτοῦ (i.e., Christ's).

[74] This has been overlooked by R. Carrier, "Prospect of a Christian Interpolation in Tacitus, 'Annals' 15.44," *VigChris* 68 (2014): 264–283, whose arguments against the authenticity of Tacitus's text are not convincing either.

[75] For the epistolary exchange of Pliny and Trajan, see most recently J. Corke-Webster, "Trouble in Pontus: The Pliny–Trajan Correspondence on the Christians Reconsidered," *TAPA* 147 (2017): 371–411, whose section on the name (pp. 402–404) is too brief and hardly persuasive.

[76] For a date close to Pliny, see O. Zwierlein, *Petrus in Rom. Die literarischen Zeugnisse. Mit einer kritischen Edition der Martyrien des Petrus und Paulus auf neuer handschriftlicher Grundlage*, UALG 96, 2nd ed. (Berlin and Boston, MA: de Gruyter, 2010), 308–315, who overlooked D.G. Horrell, "The Label Χριστιανός: 1 Peter 4:16 and the Formation of Christian Identity," *JBL* 126 (2007): 361–381, reprinted in idem, *Becoming Christian. Essays on 1 Peter and the Making of Christian Identity* (London: Bloomsbury T&T Clark, 2013), 164–210.

we probably find the term *Christianismos* first in Marcion, plausibly in his *Antitheses*.[77] As is well known, we are in the mist about the precise dates of Marcion's stay in Rome, but we will not be far amiss when we assume the middle of the 2nd century. Unfortunately, this uncertainty also means that we cannot be sure about the publication dates of Marcion's writings, but it seems reasonable to assume, with Sebastian Moll,[78] that his *Antitheses* dates from about 145–150 and that it preceded the publication of Marcion's Gospel.[79] Although we cannot reconstruct Marcion's *Antitheses* in any detail, Tertullian charged Marcion with establishing a big and total divide between the Christ who came under Tiberius and the one yet to come, "as great as that between the just and the good, between Law and Gospel, between *Judaismus* and *Christianismus*."[80] Admittedly, Judith Lieu recently did get second thoughts about the origin of the term. She now argues that Ignatius is the only indication that Tertullian would be drawing on earlier debates. However, she not only sticks to the traditional early dating of the former, but she also does not take into account her earlier observation that the opposition only occurs in the last two books of Tertullian's treatise against Marcion, whereas the term *Iudaismus* occurs about 20 times in the whole of his œuvre.[81]

Now, *Ioudaismos* existed before *Christianismos* was coined, as we have seen (§ 1), but the latter could not have been invented without the occurrence of *Christianoi/i*. Yet, there is a big difference now. Previously, the name *Christianoi/i* was not a self-designation of the Jesus followers – Tacitus even explicitly says: *vulgus Chrestianos appellabat* – but Marcion turned this outsider, negative designation into an insider, positive one, even though we cannot say that much about the precise contents of the term for Marcion, except that it apparently was connected to the Gospel and clearly more positive than *Ioudaismos*.

We also find a positive meaning in the *Martyrdom of Polycarp*, where the author has the bishop say to the Roman proconsul: "I am a Christian, and if you want to learn the doctrine of *Christianismos*, set a day and listen."[82] Unfortunately, the date of the *Martyrdom* is disputed and cannot be established with any cer-

---

77 Note that Marcion is still missing in the discussion of *Christianismos* in J.M. Lieu, *Neither Jew nor Greek?*, 2nd ed., (London: Bloomsbury T&T Clark, 2005), 70–71 (first published in 1995).
78 S. Moll, *The Arch-Heretic Marcion*, WUNT 250 (Tübingen: Mohr Siebeck, 2010), 114.
79 For the *Antitheses* preceding Marcion's Gospel, see Tertullian, *Marc.* 1.19.4; R. Braun, *Tertullien: Contre Marcion IV* (Paris: Cerf, 2001), 89, n. 6; Lieu, *Marcion* (see n. 31), 283–285.
80 Tertullian, *Marc.* 4.6.3: *Inter hos magnam et omnem differentiam scindit, quantam inter iustum et bonum, quantam inter legem et evangelium, quantam inter Iudaismum et Christianismum.*
81 Lieu, *Marcion* (see n. 31), 409–410.
82 Mart.Pol. 10:1: Χριστιανός εἰμι. εἰ δὲ θέλεις τὸν τοῦ Χριστιανισμοῦ μαθεῖν λόγον, δὸς ἡμέραν καὶ ἄκουσον.

tainty. Yet most scholars will agree to a date somewhere in the 160s or 170s.[83] As is well known, Irenaeus describes an encounter of Polycarp and Marcion when the latter was in Rome,[84] and it is therefore hard to believe that Polycarp would not have known the latter's writings. However, Polycarp probably knew the Letters of Ignatius, and we simply cannot be certain from where he got the term. In any case, it is remarkable that he (or, perhaps, the author of the *Martyrdom*) presupposes a certain familiarity with the term, which is not explained to the proconsul and simply used as if it were a kind of philosophical system. Moreover, it is noteworthy that Polycarp uses the term without any reference to *Ioudaismos*, which is unique, as that is not the case with Marcion, Ignatius, Tertullian, and Origen. This seems to suggest that the term was perhaps more familiar at that time than we can see now.

In any case, our next source, which is probably more or less contemporary with the *Martyrdom*, is Ignatius. In Ignatius, *Christianismos* occurs 5 times and *Ioudaismos* 4 times, mostly in the same Letters.[85] Given that, as Judith Lieu has noted, Ignatius was probably acquainted with Marcion's writings, it seems a plausible supposition that he derived his opposition of 'Christianity' versus 'Judaism' from Marcion, as she previously suggested,[86] and was not the inventor of the term *Christianismos*, as she now argues in her book on Marcion.[87] In any case, it is clear that for Ignatius, too, *Christianismos* is a kind of doctrine: one has to "learn to live according to *Christianismos*" (Ign.*Magn.* 10:1), but also a message, a speaking about Christ (Ign.*Rom.* 6:1). At the same time, Ignatius makes it crystal clear that *Christianismos* is superior to *Ioudaismos*. One can pass from *Ioudaismos* to *Christianismos* but not the other way around (Ign.*Magn.* 2:10).

The close connection between the two terms is again found in Tertullian, who probably found them in Marcion, as four of his five usages of the term occur in his *Adversus Marcionem*, and all four in opposition to *Iudaismus*. Yet, even here *Christianismus* is still more a doctrine – the superiority of Christ's Gos-

---

83 See, most recently, H.R. Seeliger and W. Wischmeyer, *Märtyrerliteratur* (Berlin and Boston, MA: de Gruyter, 2015), 28–30; É. Rebillard, *Greek and Latin Narratives about the Ancient Martyrs* (Oxford: Oxford University Press, 2017), 86–87; C. Markschies, "Martyrium als Imitation des leidenden Christus – Beobachtungen zum Polykarp-Martyrium und seiner Vorgeschichte," in *For Example. Martyrdom and Imitation in Early Christian Texts and Art*, ed. A. Bettenworth et al. (München: Fink, 2020), 99–122.
84 Irenaeus, *Haer.* 3.3–4, cf. Lieu, *Marcion* (see n. 31), 294–295.
85 *Christianismos:* Ign.*Magn.* 10:1, 3 (2x), Ign.*Rom.* 3:3, Ign.*Phld.* 5:6. *Ioudaismos:* Ign.*Magn.* 10:2 (2x), Ign.*Rom.* 5:6 (2x).
86 Lieu, *Image and Reality* (see n. 30), 266; with further arguments, Vinzent, *Tertullian's Preface to Marcion's Gospel* (see n. 30), 345.
87 Lieu, *Marcion* (see n. 30), 409–410.

pel above Moses's Law – than that we should translate it as 'Christianity.' Tertullian's usage of the term was so influential that later Latin exegetes of Paul, such as Marius Victorinus, Ambrosiaster and Jerome, used the term virtually only in combination with and in opposition to *Iudaismus* or *lex/disciplina Iudaica*. However, the narrow meaning of the term, its origin as a Greek loan word, and, probably, Tertullian's dubious orthodox status made that in the earlier 4th century a new term was coined, *Christianitas*, which very soon overtook *Christianismus* and, already in the same century, was used to translate *Christianismos*. Eventually, it pushed the older term out of the Latin linguistic pool.[88]

It was different, though, in the East, where the term soon proved to be enormously successful. In Origen, we find 120 uses of Χριστιανισμός, of which only five are in pair with Ἰουδαϊσμός, three of which occur in the *Contra Celsum* (1.1.25; 3.13.9 and 14.18), in which Jews play an important role (§ 4). In Eusebius, the term occurs 22 times, of which two are paired with *Ioudaismos* and three with *Hellenismos* and *Ioudaismos*. After Eusebius, the opposition clearly loses its actuality, and even in Chrysostom's voluminous work the opposition Χριστιανισμός/Ἰουδαϊσμός occurs only four times. The term now encompasses both belief and practices, and thus comes close to our 'Christianity,' and it will remain the term for 'Christianity' in modern Greek.

5 Concluding considerations

What conclusions can we draw from our survey regarding the Parting of the Ways? I would like to make the following observations:
1. When we now look at the terms discussed, we note that their meanings evolved over the centuries, also depending on the historical situations. *Ioudaismos* is a term coined by a Greek-writing Jew who uses it to denote an activist propagation of traditional ancestral customs, at least as perceived by the Maccabees, in a Judaean society confronted with the challenges of a Greek culture that some found attractive. Subsequently, it is used by a Jesus follower for his formerly zealously sticking to traditional Judaean beliefs and practices, as perceived by him, in a Judaea ruled by the Romans. In both these cases, the term is clearly used for inner-Judaean polemics. It then moves to a designation for those Jesus followers who, surely in different ways, still stuck to Jewish traditions and practices, as is visible in Marcion

---

[88] T. Geelhaar, *Christianitas. Eine Wortgeschichte von der Spätantike bis zum Mittelalter* (Göttingen: Vandenhoeck & Ruprecht, 2015), 37–63.

and Ignatius. Yet in the 3rd century it ended up in Christian circles as 'Judaism,' a complex of beliefs and practices that were seen as being opposed to the following of Christ and the developing system of Christian beliefs, rituals and organisations. In the course of late antiquity, 'Judaism' thus comes closer to something like a modern religion for the outside observers, even though it certainly wasn't conceptualised like that by the contemporaries and still was not yet a separate sphere of society as religion has become more and more in the Western world.[89]

2. It is different with *Christianismos*, which is clearly the younger term. In the beginning, as in, plausibly, Marcion and Ignatius, it is still a polemical term, which lays claim to the right following of Christ. Most likely, the term will have had different contents in the cases of Marcion, Polycarp and Ignatius, and it has taken some time before the term became widely accepted. It is interesting to see that the Jew in Celsus, about whom Maren Niehoff has persuasively argued that he was a real person (or composed from real persons) and not a figment of Celsus's imagination,[90] does refer to the Jesus followers as *Christianoi* and, sometimes, as 'believers in Christ,' but never uses the term *Christianismos*.[91] The latter term was either not yet known in Alexandria in the middle of the 2nd century or, less likely, the Jew did not want to use the term for some reason. Neither do we see the term used by Justin Martyr in his *Apology* or *Dialogue with Trypho*.[92] However, in the 3rd century, as we have seen with Tertullian and Origen, the term becomes more and more

---

[89] For this development, see E. Feil, *Religio*, 4 vols. (Göttingen: Vandenhoeck & Ruprecht, 1986–2012).

[90] M.R. Niehoff, "A Jewish Critique of Christianity from the Second Century: Revisiting the Jew Mentioned in *Contra Celsum*," *JECS* 21 (2013): 151–175, followed, nuanced and elaborated by J. Carleton Paget, "The Jew of Celsus and *adversus Judaeos* Literature," *ZAC* 21 (2017): 201–242; J. Arnold, *Der Wahre Logos des Kelsos. Eine Strukturanalyse*, JbAC.E 39 (Münster: Aschendorff, 2016), 85–90, 215–220, 341–387, 454–457; J. Carleton Paget, "Celsus's Jew and Jewish Anti-Christian Counter-Narrative: Evidence of an Important Form of Polemic in Jewish-Christian Disputation," in *Intolerance, Polemics, and Debate in Antiquity*, ed. G.H. van Kooten and J. van Ruiten (Leiden: Brill, 2019), 387–423 (updated and refocused version of 2017).

[91] Origen, *Cels.* 1.1; 1.3; 1.9; 2.8 (believers), etc.

[92] For these writings, see, most recently, H. Leppin, "Christlicher Intellektualismus und religiöse Exklusion – Justin und der Dialog mit Tryphon," in *Juden – Heiden – Christen?*, ed. S. Alkier and H. Leppin, WUNT 400 (Tübingen: Mohr Siebeck, 2018), 368–389; B. van der Lans, "The Written Media of Imperial Government and a Martyr's Career: Justin Martyr's *1 Apology*," in *Marginality, Media, and Mutations of Religious Authority in the History of Christianity*, ed. L. Feldt and J.N. Bremmer, Studies in the History and Anthropology of Religion 6 (Leuven: Peeters, 2019), 117–135; M.R. Niehoff, "A Jew for Roman Tastes: The Parting of the Ways in Justin Martyr's *Dialogue with Trypho* from a Post-Colonial Perspective," *JECS* 27 (2019): 549–578.

used as denoting Christianity as a complex of beliefs and practices, even though it is still lacking in Irenaeus and is never used by a pagan author. Apparently, as the Church became more organised and internationally connected, the emergence of a single term became more and more acceptable and accepted.

3. To what extent do the terms shed light on the Parting of the Ways? In the middle of the 2nd century, the Parting of the Ways seems to have progressed considerably, both in Rome and in Alexandria. In the latter city, as Niehoff notes, the Jew of Celsus "was alarmed by the situation of the Jewish community following a significant spread of Christianity, which was accompanied by separatist theology."[93] In Rome, though, we do not hear of an engagement of the Jesus followers with the local Judaeans. Both Hermas and Marcion do not seem to consider them as being relevant, but their concern is with the varieties of the Christian community, not with the Parting of the Ways. It fits this observation that Roman sources of the early 2nd century never associated Judaeans with the Christians and never persecuted them together.[94] By all accounts, this suggests an early Parting of the Ways in Rome itself. The same lack of interest in Judaeans seems to be the case with Ignatius, who clearly had close contacts with Rome and a Roman community in Asia Minor.[95]

4. Finally, what about the Romans, whose influence is so much stressed by Schnelle? In a stimulating recent contribution, Benedikt Eckhardt has noted that in the century before and after the turn of the Christian era, the *Iudaei* were primarily seen by the Romans as a group that was geographically determined, thus 'Judaeans.' However, from Tacitus and Juvenal onwards, as Eckhardt notes, we can see a trend of people taking over Judaean beliefs and practices. In other words, as Eckhardt observes, from the 120s or so onwards, we start noticing a gradual shift from a geographical to a reli-

---

93 Niehoff, "A Jewish Critique" (see n. 90), 175.
94 J.M.G. Barclay, "'Jews' and 'Christians' in the Eyes of Roman Authors c. 100 CE" and A. Baumgarten, "The Rule of the Martian in the Ancient Diaspora," in *Jews and Christians in the First and Second Centuries: How to Write Their Histories*, ed. P.J. Tomson and J. Schwartz, CRINT 13 (Leiden: Brill, 2013), 313–326 and 398–430, respectively; S.J.D. Cohen, "The Ways That Parted: Jews, Christians, and Jewish-Christians, ca. 100–150 CE," in *Jews and Christians in the First and Second Centuries: The Interbellum 70–132 CE*, ed. J. Schwartz and P.J. Tomson, CRINT 15 (Leiden: Brill, 2018), 307–339.
95 See, most recently, W. Schmithals, "Zu Ignatius von Antiochien," *ZAC* 13 (2009): 181–203, here 195–201; F.R. Prostmeier, "Cui bono?," in *Die Briefe des Ignatios von Antiochia: Motive, Strategien, Kontexte*, ed. T.J. Bauer and P. von Möllendorff, Millennium Studies 72 (Berlin and Boston, MA: de Gruyter, 2018), 169–200; Bremmer, "Date and Location of Ignatius" (see n. 27).

gious meaning of *Iudaei/Ioudaioi*.⁹⁶ This trend accelerated in the course of the second half of the 2ⁿᵈ century, as he argues.⁹⁷

Eckhardt's findings are corroborated and supplemented by an investigation of René Bloch in the meaning of *Iudaeus/Iudaicus* in classical Latin literature. Although these words occur 88 times in classical Roman literature until the end of the 2ⁿᵈ century, to which can be added about 50 times for Iudaea, there are virtually no passages where these words should primarily be translated with 'Jew' rather than 'Judaean.'⁹⁸ Even the passages which Bloch interprets as referring to 'Jews' rather than 'Judaeans' hardly support a 'Jewish' interpretation. Thus when Ovid in his *Ars amatoria* (1.75–76), written at the turn of the era, alerts his reader to the possibility of beginning an amorous experience at, amongst other places, the synagogues, he writes: *Nec te praetereat Veneri ploratus Adonis / cultaque Iudaeo septima sacra Syro* ("Nor let Adonis bewailed of Venus escape you, nor the seventh day that the Syrian [collective here] from Judaea holds sacred"). Bloch interprets *Iudaeo* as the noun instead of the adjective ("the Syrian Jew"), but the closely similar expression somewhat later in the *Ars* (1.415–16), *quaque die redeunt rebus minus apta gerendis / culta palaestino septima festa Syro* ("or on that day, less fit for business, whereon returns the seventh-day feast that the Syrian of Palestine observes," trans. Mozley/Goold, Loeb), clearly shows that we should translate 'Syrian from Iudaea,' the latter being part of the province Syria at that time.⁹⁹ Similarly, in Suetonius's passage on the *fiscus Iudaicus*, where he distinguishes between two categories, *qui vel inprofessi Iudaicam vitam viverent vel dissimulata origine imposita genti tributa non pependissent* ("those were prosecuted who without publicly acknowledging it lived a Judaean life or those who, concealing their origin, did not pay the tribute levied upon their people"), we have closely together *vita*, *origo*, *gens* and, immediately following, an anecdote about the circumcision. By all accounts, the geographical origin is

---

96 I would add that this trend perhaps started already under Domitian, given the well-known condemnation of his younger cousin Clemens: Suetonius, *Dom.* 15.1; Cassius Dio 67.14.1–2.
97 B. Eckhardt, "Rom und die Juden – ein Kategorienfehler? Zur römischen Sicht auf die Iudaei in später Republik und frühem Prinzipat," in *Religio licita? Rom und die Juden*, ed. G. Hasselhoff and M. Strothmann (Berlin and Boston, MA: de Gruyter, 2017), 13–53.
98 R. Bloch, "Jew or Judean: The Latin Evidence," in *Torah, Temple, Land: Constructions of Judaism in Antiquity*, ed. M. Witte, J. Schröter, and V. Lepper, TSAJ (Tübingen: Mohr Siebeck, 2021), 231–242.
99 For the province at that time, see F. Millar, *The Roman Near East 31 BC – AD 337* (Cambridge, MA, and London: Harvard University Press, 1993), 31–38.

still clearly present, as it seems to be in all passages dating to Suetonius and earlier Latin literature.

It is therefore not surprising that until the time of Marcion the *Iudaei* were not yet conceptualised as a primarily religious group. However, as time went on and the geographical connections with the former homeland must have become less and less felt and visible, the religious practices that separated the *Iudaei/Ioudaioi* from the rest of the population will have become more characteristic for them than their geographical origin. The shift in meaning, then, of *Ioudaismos* in Christian literature from an inner-church group to a completely separate group, which was religiously recognisable as such, conforms to developments in the Roman Empire, where the *Ioudaioi/Iudaei* became increasingly seen as people with different religious beliefs and practices, but no longer as emigrants from Judaea. This trend must have been strengthened by various developments, such as the privileges given by the Romans to the Judaeans,[100] the Judaean opposition to the imperial cult,[101] and, perhaps, the tax imposed upon the Judaeans by Vespasian (above, Introduction), but certainly solidified by the *Constitutio Antoniniana* of AD 212, which gave full Roman citizenship to all free inhabitants of the Empire.[102]

The concepts 'Judaism' and 'Christianity' are so normal today that we usually do not think when using them. Still, I hope to have shown that the terms developed only gradually into their modern meanings. As such, their developments reflected a fatal separation whose consequences still impact our lives in the troubled times of today.[103]

---

100 Eckhardt, "Rom und die Juden " (see n. 97), 22–28.
101 K. Czajkowski, "Jewish Attitudes towards the Imperial Cult," *SCI* 34 (2015): 181–194.
102 The edict has been much discussed, see, most recently, C. Ando, ed., *Citizenship and Empire in Europe, 200–1900: The Antonine Constitution after 1800 Years* (Stuttgart: Steiner, 2016); A. Imrie, *The Antonine Constitution: An Edict for the Caracallan Empire*, Impact of Empire 29 (Leiden: Brill, 2018); interesting also for Jewish reactions, K. Berthelot and J. Price, eds., *In the Crucible of Empire: The Impact of Roman Citizenship upon Greeks, Jews and Christians* (Leuven: Peeters, 2019).
103 This contribution was started in the stimulating environment of the Centre for Advanced Studies "Beyond Canon" of the University of Regensburg and finished in Groningen in corona quarantine. I am most grateful to Raphael Brendel, Ruurd Nauta, Tobias Nicklas and Steve Mason for comments and corrections, and to Tom Blanton for his insightful correction of my English.

Bibliography

Ameling, W., review of *The Fiscus Judaicus and the Parting of the Ways* by M. Heemstra, *ZKG* 122 (2011): 336–337.
Ando, C., ed., *Citizenship and Empire in Europe, 200–1900: The Antonine Constitution after 1800 Years* (Stuttgart: Steiner, 2016).
Arnold, J., *Der* Wahre Logos *des Kelsos. Eine Strukturanalyse*, JbAC.E 39 (Münster: Aschendorff, 2016).
Baker, C., "A 'Jew' by Any Other Name?," *JAJ* 2 (2011): 153–180.
Barclay, J. M. G., "'Jews' and 'Christians' in the Eyes of Roman Authors c. 100 CE," in *Jews and Christians in the First and Second Centuries: How to Write Their Histories*, ed. P. J. Tomson and J. Schwartz, CRINT 13 (Leiden: Brill, 2013), 313–326.
Bardet, S., *Le testimonium Flavianum. Examen historique, considérations historiographiques* (Paris: Cerf, 2002).
Bardet, S., "Le Testimonium Flavianum, intraduisible et illimité?," in *Pierre Geoltrain ou comment faire l'histoire des religions*, ed. S. C. Mimouni and I. Ullern-Weité (Turnhout: Brepols, 2006), 207–214.
Barrett, C. K., "Jews and Judaizers in the Epistles of Ignatius," in *Jews, Greeks and Christians. Religious Cultures in Late Antiquity*, ed. R. Hamerton-Kelly and R. Scroggs (Leiden: Brill, 1976), 220–244.
Barton C., and D. Boyarin, *Imagine no Religion* (New York, NY: Fordham University Press, 2016).
Baumgarten, A., "The Rule of the Martian in the Ancient Diaspora," in *Jews and Christians in the First and Second Centuries: How to Write Their Histories*, ed. P. J. Tomson and J. Schwartz, CRINT 13 (Leiden: Brill, 2013), 398–430.
Berthelot, K., and J. Price, eds., *In the Crucible of Empire: The Impact of Roman Citizenship upon Greeks, Jews and Christians* (Leuven: Peeters, 2019).
Bile, M., and B. Gain, "Une nouvelle étymologie de ΧΡΙΣΤΙΑΝΟΣ," *REAug* 58 (2012): 141–153.
Bloch, R., "Jew or Judean: The Latin Evidence," in *Torah, Temple, Land: Constructions of Judaism in Antiquity*, ed. M. Witte, J. Schröter, and V. Lepper, TSAJ (Tübingen: Mohr Siebeck, 2021), 231–242.
Botermann, H., *Das Judenedikt des Kaisers Claudius, Römischer Staat und Christiani im 1. Jahrhundert* (Stuttgart: Steiner, 1996).
Boyarin, D., "Why Ignatius Invented Judaism," in *The Ways That Often Parted: Essays in Honor of Joel Marcus*, ed. L. Baron et al. (Atlanta, GA: Society for Biblical Literature, 2018), 309–324.
Boyarin, D., *Judaism: the Genealogy of a Modern Notion* (New Brunswick, NJ: Rutgers University Press, 2019).
Braun, R., *Tertullien: Contre Marcion* IV (Paris: Cerf, 2001).
Bremmer, J. N., *Maidens, Magic and Martyrs in early Christianity* (Tübingen: Mohr Siebeck, 2017).
Bremmer, J. N., Review of *Die frühen Christen: Von den Anfängen bis Konstantin* by H. Leppin, *ARYS* 17 (2019): 402–416.
Bremmer, J. N., "The Date and Location of Ignatius: An Onomastic Approach," in *Das Baujahr hinter der Fassade. Probleme bei der Datierung neutestamentlicher Pseudepigraphen*

und neuere Lösungsansätze, ed. W. Grünstäudl and M. Schmidt, WUNT (Tübingen: Mohr Siebeck, forthcoming 2021).

Carleton Paget, J., *Jews, Christians and Jewish Christians in Antiquity* (Tübingen: Mohr Siebeck, 2010).

Carleton Paget, J., "Celsus's Jew and Jewish Anti-Christian Counter-Narrative: Evidence of an Important Form of Polemic in Jewish-Christian Disputation," in *Intolerance, Polemics, and Debate in Antiquity*, ed. G. H. van Kooten and J. van Ruiten (Leiden: Brill, 2019), 387–423 (repr. 2017).

Carleton Paget, J., "The Jew of Celsus and *adversus Judaeos* Literature," *ZAC* 21 (2017): 201–242.

Carrier, R., "Prospect of a Christian Interpolation in Tacitus, 'Annals' 15.44," *VigChris* 68 (2014): 264–283.

Casevitz, M., "Hellenismos: formation et fonction des verbes en -ΙΖΩ et de leur dérivés" in *Hellenismos. Quelques jalons pour une histoire de l'identité grecque*, ed. S. Said (Leiden: Brill, 1991), 9–16.

Cohen, S. J. D., "Judaism without Circumcision and "Judaism" without Circumcision in Ignatius," *HThR* 95 (2002): 395–415.

Cohen, S. J. D., "The Ways That Parted: Jews, Christians, and Jewish-Christians, ca. 100–150 CE," in *Jews and Christians in the First and Second Centuries: The Interbellum 70–132 CE*, ed. J. Schwartz and P. J. Tomson, CRINT 15 (Leiden: Brill, 2018), 307–339.

Cook, J. G., *Roman Attitudes Toward the Christians* (Tübingen: Mohr Siebeck, 2010).

Cook, J. G., "Chrestiani, Christiani, Χριστιανοί: a second century anachronism?," *VigChris* 74 (2020): 237–264.

Corke-Webster, J., "Trouble in Pontus: The Pliny–Trajan Correspondence on the Christians Reconsidered," *TAPA* 147 (2017): 371–411.

Couzin, R., "A Modern Look at the Roman Imperial 'Jewish Tax'," *Canadian Tax Journal / Revue fiscale canadienne* 65 (2017): 333–352.

Czajkowski, K., "Jewish Attitudes towards the Imperial Cult," *SCI* 34 (2015): 181–194.

Daumier, C., "Sextus Empiricus contre les grammariens: ce que parler grec veut dire," in *Hellenismos. Quelques jalons pour une histoire de l'identité grecque*, ed. S. Said (Leiden: Brill, 1991), 17–32.

de Coinci, G., *Miracles de Nostre Dame*, ed. V. F. Koenig, Vol. 4 (Geneva: Droz, 1970).

Eckhardt, B., "Rom und die Juden – ein Kategorienfehler? Zur römischen Sicht auf die Iudaei in später Republik und frühem Prinzipat," in *Religio licita? Rom und die Juden*, ed. G. Hasselhoff and M. Strothmann (Berlin and Boston, MA: de Gruyter, 2017), 13–53.

Elkins, N. T., "Roman Emperor Nerva's Reform of the Jewish Taks" =https://www.biblicalarchaeology.org/daily/ancient-cultures/daily-life-and-practice/roman-emperor-nervas-reform-of-the-jewish-tax/, accessed 3 December 2019.

Feil, E., *Religio*, 4 vols. (Göttingen: Vandenhoeck & Ruprecht, 1986–2012).

Frey, J., "Die Juden im Johannesevangelium und die Frage nach der Trennung der Wege zwischen der johanneischen Gemeinde und der Synagoge," in idem, *Die Herrlichkeit des Gekreuzigten. Studien zu den Johanneischen Schriften I* (Tübingen: Mohr Siebeck, 2013), 339–377.

Geelhaar, T., *Christianitas. Eine Wortgeschichte von der Spätantike bis zum Mittelalter* (Göttingen: Vandenhoeck & Ruprecht, 2015).

Gercke, A., "Der Christenname ein Scheltname," in *Festschrift zur Jahrhundertfeier der Universität zu Breslau*, ed. T. Siebs (Breslau: Trewendt & Granier, 1911), 360–373.

Ginzburg, C., "Our Words, and Theirs: A Reflection on the Historian's Craft, Today," in *Historical Knowledge. In Quest of Theory, Method and Evidence*, ed. S. Fellman and M. Rahikainen (Cambridge: Cambridge University Press, 2012), 97–119.

Goodman, M., "Nerva, the *Fiscus Judaicus* and Jewish Identity," *JRS* 79 (1989): 40–44.

Goodman, M., "The Meaning of '*Fisci Iudaici Calumnia Sublata*' on the Coinage of Nerva," in *Studies in Josephus and the Varieties of Ancient Judaism*, ed. S. J. D. Cohen and J. Schwartz, AGJU 67 (Leiden: Brill, 2007), 81–89.

Grabbe, L. L., "'Jesus Who Is Called Christ': references to Jesus outside Christian sources," in *"Is This Not the Carpenter?" The Question of the Historicity of the Figure of Jesus*, ed. T.-L. Thompson and T. S. Verenna (Sheffield: Sheffield University Press, 2012), 57–69.

Günther, S., "Ein politischer Skandal als mediales Ereignis. Der fiscus Iudaicus zwischen Domitian und Nerva," *Numismatisches Nachrichtenblatt* 63 (2014): 10–13.

Günther, S., "The *Fiscus Iudaicus*: A Hypothetical Scholarly Construct," in *Religio licita? Rom und die Juden*, ed. G. Hasselhoff and M. Strothmann (Berlin and Boston, MA: de Gruyter, 2017), 175–189.

Harl, M., et al., *La Bible grecque des Septante*, 2nd ed. (Paris: Cerf, 1994).

Heemstra, M., *The Fiscus Judaicus and the Parting of the Ways*, WUNT II/277 (Tübingen: Mohr Siebeck, 2010).

Heemstra, M., "The Interpretation and Wider Context of Nerva's Fiscus Judaicus Sestertius," in *Judaea and Rome in Coins, 65 BCE–135 CE*, ed. D. M. Jacobsen and N. Kokkinos (Oxford: Oxbow, 2012), 187–201.

Horrell, D. G., "The Label Χριστιανός: 1 Peter 4:16 and the Formation of Christian Identity," *JBL* 126 (2007): 361–381 (repr. in idem, *Becoming Christian. Essays on 1 Peter and the Making of Christian Identity* [London: Bloomsbury T&T Clark, 2013], 164–210).

Howell, J. R., *The Pharisees and Figured Speech in Luke-Acts*, WUNT II/456 (Tübingen: Mohr Siebeck, 2017).

Hübner, R., "Thesen zur Echtheit und Datierung der sieben Briefe des *Ignatius* von Antiochien," *ZAC* 1 (1997): 42–70 (repr. in idem, Addenda et Corrigenda in *Kirche und Dogma im Werden* [Tübingen: Mohr Siebeck, 2018], 63–92).

Hübner, R., *Der paradox Eine. Antignostischer Monarchianismus im zweiten Jahrhundert* VCSup 50 (Leiden: Brill, 1999).

Imrie, A., *The Antonine Constitution: An Edict for the Caracallan Empire*, Impact of Empire 29 (Leiden: Brill, 2018).

Jones, C. P., "The Historicity of the Neronian Persecution: A Response to Brent Shaw," *NTS* 63 (2017): 146–152.

Judge, E. A., *Paul and the Conflict of Cultures: The Legacy of His Thought Today*, ed. J. R. Harrison (Eugene, OR: Cascade, 2019).

Kraemer, R. S., "On the Meaning of the Term 'Jew' in Greco-Roman Inscriptions," *HThR* 81 (1989): 35–53.

Law, T. M., and C. Halton, eds., *Jew and Judean: A Forum on Politics and Historiography in the Translation of Ancient Texts* (Los Angeles, CA, 2014) = https://dl.orangedox.com/yTWsrMwDFZF3fqx2kt/Jew%20and%20Judean.pdf, accessed 29 November 2019.

Leppin, H., "Christlicher Intellektualismus und religiöse Exklusion: Justin und der Dialog mit Tryphon," in *Juden – Heiden – Christen?*, ed. S. Alkier and H. Leppin, WUNT 400 (Tübingen: Mohr Siebeck, 2018), 368–389.

Leppin, H., *Die frühen Christen: Von den Anfängen bis Konstantin*, 2nd ed. (München: Beck, 2019).

Lieu, J. M., *Neither Jew nor Greek?* 2nd ed. (London: Bloomsbury T&T Clark, 2005).

Lieu, J. M., *Image and Reality: The Jews in the World of the Christians in the Second Century* (London and New York, NY: T&T Clark, 1996).

Lieu, J. M., *Marcion and the Making of a Heretic* (Cambridge: Cambridge University Press, 2015).

Lipsius, R. A., *Über den Ursprung und den ältesten Gebrauch des Christennamens* (Jena: Neuenhahn, 1873).

Lowe, M., "Who were the ΙΟΥΔΑΙΟΙ?," *NovT* 18 (1976): 101–131.

Markschies, C., "Martyrium als Imitation des leidenden Christus – Beobachtungen zum Polykarp-Martyrium und seiner Vorgeschichte," in *For Example. Martyrdom and Imitation in Early Christian Texts and Art*, ed. A. Bettenworth et al. (München: Fink, 2020), 99–122.

Mason, S., "Jews, Judaeans, Judaizing, Judaism: Problems of Categorization in Ancient History," *JSJ* 38 (2007): 457–512.

Mason, S., "The Importance of the Latter Half of Josephus's *Judaean Antiquities* for His Roman Audience," in *Pentateuchal Traditions in the Late Second Temple Period*, ed. A. Moriya and G. Hata, JSJSup 158 (Leiden: Brill, 2012), 129–153.

Mason, S., "Ancient Jews or Judeans? Different Questions, Different Answers," *Marginalia* 26–8–2014 = https://marginalia.lareviewofbooks.org/ancient-jews-judeans-different-questions-different-answers-steve-mason/, accessed 22 November 2019.

Mason, S., "Paul Without Judaism: Historical Method over Perspective," in *Paul among Jews and Gentiles: essays in honour of Terence L. Donaldson*, ed. R. Charles (London: T&T Clark, 2021), 9–39, = https://www.academia.edu/40939312/Paul_Without_Judaism_Historical_Method_over_Perspective, accessed 11 June 2020.

Millar, F., *The Roman Near East 31 BC–AD 337* (Cambridge, MA, and London: Harvard University Press, 1993).

Moll, S., *The Arch-Heretic Marcion*, WUNT 250 (Tübingen: Mohr Siebeck, 2010).

Muñoz-Santos, M. E., "Los Augustiani: El peculiar coro de Nerón," *Anuari. AntMed* 8 (2018): 653–662.

Nicklas, T., *Jews and Christians? Second-Century 'Christian' Perspectives on the "Parting of the Ways,"* Annual Deichmann Lectures 2013 (Tübingen: Mohr Siebeck, 2014).

Nicklas, T., "The 'Jews' in the Gospel of John. Past and Future Lines of Scholarship," in *Perceiving the Other in Ancient Judaism and Early Christianity*, ed. M. Bar-Asher Siegal et al., WUNT 394 (Tübingen: Mohr Siebeck, 2017), 49–66.

Nicklas, T., "Diversität, Dynamik und Differenzierung: Eine Diskussion mit Udo Schnelles Modell der 'getrennten Wege von Römern, Juden und Christen'," *EvTh* 80 (2020): 444–454.

Niehoff, M. R., "A Jewish Critique of Christianity from the Second Century: Revisiting the Jew Mentioned in *Contra Celsum*," *JECS* 21 (2013): 151–175.

Niehoff, M. R., "A Jew for Roman Tastes: The Parting of the Ways in Justin Martyr's *Dialogue with Trypho* from a Post-Colonial Perspective," *JECS* 27 (2019): 549–578.
Nongbri, B., *Beyond Belief* (New Haven, CT, and London: Yale University Press, 2012).
Novenson, M. V., "Paul's Former Occupation in *Ioudaismos*," in *Galatians and Christian Theology: Justification, the Gospel, and Ethics in Paul's Letter*, ed. M.W. Elliott et al. (Grand Rapids, MI: Eerdmans, 2014), 24–39.
Noy, D., *Jewish Inscriptions of Western Europe II* (Cambridge: Cambridge University Press, 1995).
Noy, D., et al., eds., *Inscriptiones Judaicae Orientis. Volume I: Eastern Europe*, TSAJ 101 (Tübingen: Mohr Siebeck, 2004).
Oegema, G. S., "1 and 2 Maccabees in Paul's Letter to the Galatians," in *Die Makkabäer*, ed. F. Avemarie et al., WUNT 382 (Tübingen: Mohr Siebeck, 2017), 345–360.
Öhler, M., "Judäer oder Juden? Die Debatte 'Ethnos vs. Religion' im Blick auf das 2. Makkabäerbuch," in *Die Makkabäer*, ed. F. Avemarie et al., WUNT 382 (Tübingen: Mohr Siebeck, 2017), 157–185.
Pachoumi, E., "An Invocation of Chrestos in Magic. The Question of the Orthographical Spelling of Chrestos and Interpretation Issues in PGM XIII.288–95," *Hermathena* 188 (2010): 29–54.
Perler, O., "Das vierte Makkabäerbuch, Ignatius von Antiochien und die ältesten Märtyrerberichte," *RivAC* 25 (1949): 47–72.
Petersen, A. K., Review of *Imagine no Religion* by C. Barton and D. Boyarin, *BMCR* 2017.06.14.
Pischedda, J. B., *Strani chrestiani? La fantastica pseudostoria dei chrestiani prima die cristiani* (Rome: ELL, 2012).
Powell, M. J., *The Pauline Epistles Contained in Ms. Parker 32, Corpus Christi College, Cambridge* (London: Kegan Paul, 1916, repr. London: Forgotten Books, 1973).
Prostmeier, F. R., "Cui bono?," in *Die Briefe des Ignatios von Antiochia: Motive, Strategien, Kontexte*, ed. T. J. Bauer and P. von Möllendorff, Millennium Studies 72 (Berlin and Boston, MA: de Gruyter, 2018), 169–200.
Rebillard, É., *Greek and Latin Narratives about the Ancient Martyrs* (Oxford: Oxford University Press, 2017).
Reed, A. Y., *Jewish-Christianity and the History of Judaism*, TSAJ 171 (Tübingen: Mohr Siebeck, 2018).
Reed, A. Y., and S. Magid, "Daniel Boyarin's Judaism: A Forum," Review of *Judaism: the genealogy of a modern notion* by D. Boyarin, *Marginalia* 5–7–2019 = https://marginalia.lareviewofbooks.org/introduction-marginalia-forum-daniel-boyarin-judaism/, accessed 11 June 2020.
Ritter, A. M., *Alte Kirche*, KTGQ 1, 12th ed. (Göttingen: Vandenhoeck & Ruprecht, 2019).
Robert, L., *Hellenica VII* (Paris: Librairie Adrien-Maisonneuve, 1949).
Sacco, G., *Iscrizioni greche d'Italia, Porto* (Rome: Quasar, 1984).
Sänger, D., "'Ἰουδαϊσμός – ἰουδαΐζειν – ἰουδαϊκῶς Sprachliche und semantische Überlegungen im Blick auf Gal 1,13 f. und 2,14," *ZNW* 108 (2017): 150–185.
Sahlins, M., "In Anthropology, It's Emic all the Way Down," *Hau: Journal of Ethnographic Theory* 7 (2017): 157–163.

Satlow, M., "Jew or Judaean?," in *'The One Who Sows Bountifully': Essays in Honor of Stanley K. Stowers*, ed. C. J. Hodge et al. (Providence, RI: Society of Biblical Literature, 2013), 165–175.

Schmithals, W., "Zu Ignatius von Antiochien," *ZAC* 13 (2009): 181–203.

Schnelle, U., *Die ersten 100 Jahre des Christentums 30–130 n. Chr.: Die Entstehungsgeschichte einer Weltreligion*, 3rd ed. (Göttingen: Vandenhoeck & Ruprecht, 2019).

Schnelle, U., *Die getrennten Wege von Römern, Juden und Christen* (Tübingen: Mohr Siebeck, 2019).

Schwartz, S., "How Many Judaisms Were There? A Critique of Neusner and Smith on Definition and Mason and Boyarin on Categorization," *JAJ* 2 (2011): 208–238.

Schwemer, A. M., "Zu Entstehungszeit und -ort des 4. Makkabäerbuchs," in *Die Makkabäer*, ed. F. Avemarie et al., WUNT 382 (Tübingen: Mohr Siebeck, 2017), 245–327.

Seeliger, H. R., and W. Wischmeyer, *Märtyrerliteratur* (Berlin and Boston, MA: de Gruyter, 2015).

Shandruk, W., "The Interchange of ι and η in Spelling χριστ- in Documentary Papyri," *BASP* 47 (2010): 205–219.

Shaw, B. D., "The Myth of the Neronian Persecution," *JRS* 105 (2015): 73–100.

Shaw, B. D., "Response to Christopher Jones: The Historicity of the Neronian Persecution," *NTS* 64 (2018): 231–242.

Solin, H., *Die griechischen Personennamen in Rom: Ein Namenbuch*, 3 vols., 2nd ed. (Berlin: de Gruyter, 2003).

Spicq, C., *Théologie morale du Nouveau Testament I* (Paris: Gabalda et Cie, 1965).

Syme, R., *Tacitus*, 2 vols. (Oxford: Oxford University Press, 1958).

Taylor, J., "Why Were the Disciples First Called 'Christians' at Antioch? (Acts 11.26)," *RB* 101 (1994): 75–94.

Teitler, H. C., Review of *Das Judenedikt des Kaisers Claudius, Römischer Staat und Christiani im 1. Jahrhundert* by H. Botermann, *VC* 51 (1997): 217.

Tomson, P. J., *Studies on Jews and Christians in the First and Second Centuries*, WUNT 418 (Tübingen: Mohr Siebeck, 2019).

Trebilco, P. R., *Self-designations and Group Identity in the New Testament* (Cambridge: Cambridge University Press, 2011).

van der Lans, B., "The Written Media of Imperial Government and a Martyr's Career: Justin Martyr's 1 Apology," in *Marginality, Media, and Mutations of Religious Authority in the History of Christianity*, ed. L. Feldt and J. N. Bremmer, Studies in the History and Anthropology of Religion 6 (Leuven: Peeters, 2019), 117–135.

van der Lans, B., and J. N. Bremmer, "Tacitus and the Persecution of the Christians: an invention of tradition?," *Eirene* 53 (2017): 299–331.

van Minnen, P., "Paul the Roman Citizen," *JSNT* 56 (1994): 43–52.

Vinzent, M., *Tertullian's Preface to Marcion's Gospel* (Leuven: Peeters, 2016).

Ward, J. S., "Roman Greek: Latinisms in the Greek of Flavius Josephus," *CQ* 57 (2007): 632–649.

Whealey, A., *Josephus on Jesus: The Testimonium Flavianum Controversy from Late Antiquity to Modern Times* (New York, NY: Lang, 2003).

Whealey, A., "The *Testimonium Flavianum*," in *A Companion to Josephus*, ed. H. H. Chapman and Z. Rodgers (Oxford: Oxford University Press, 2016), 345–355.

Whitmarsh, T., "The Invention of Atheism and the Invention of Religion in Classical Athens," in *Sceptic and Believer in Ancient Mediterranean Religions*, ed. B. Edelmann-Singer et al., WUNT 443 (Tübingen: Mohr Siebeck, 2020), 37–51.

Williams, M. H., *Jews in a Graeco-Roman Environment* (Tübingen: Mohr Siebeck, 2013).

Zahn, T., *Einleitung in das Neue Testament*, 2 vols. (Leipzig: Deichert, 1897–1899).

Zara, E., "The Chrestianos Issue in Tacitus Reinvestigated," 2009 = http://www.textexcavation.com/documents/zaratacituschrestianos.pdf, accessed 21 November 2019.

Zwierlein, O., *Petrus in Rom. Die literarischen Zeugnisse. Mit einer kritischen Edition der Martyrien des Petrus und Paulus auf neuer handschriftlicher Grundlage*, UALG 96, 2nd ed. (Berlin and Boston, MA: de Gruyter, 2010).

Jens Schröter
Was Paul a Jew Within Judaism?
The Apostle to the Gentiles and His
Communities in Their Historical Context

Abstract: Vor dem Hintergrund der in der neueren Paulusforschung entwickelten "Paul within Judaism"-Perspektive und in kritischer Betrachtung des "Parting(s) of the Ways"-Modells fragt der vorliegende Beitrag, wie der Platz des Paulus im Judentum seiner Zeit zu bestimmen ist. Es lässt sich erkennen, dass die von Paulus vorausgesetzte und von ihm selbst propagierte soziale Realität in den Gemeinschaften christusgläubiger Menschen deutlich komplexer war, als es ein Neben- oder gar Gegeneinander von 'Juden' und 'Christen,' deren "Wege sich getrennt" hätten, suggeriert. Paulus verlangt von Heiden, dass sie sich von Verhaltensweisen, die mit dem Glauben an den Gott Israels unvereinbar sind, fernhalten; Juden sollen dagegen ihre Bräuche den Heiden nicht aufzwingen. Gleichzeitig lässt sich erkennen, dass Paulus ein eigenes Selbstverständnis der an Jesus Christus Glaubenden gegenüber Juden und Heiden entwickelt (1 Kor 9,20–21). Der Platz des Paulus im Judentum ist deshalb je nach Perspektive unterschiedlich zu beschreiben.

Keywords: Paul within Judaism, Works of the Law, 4QMMT, Paul's self-presentation, table fellowship of Jews and non-Jews, Israel as God's chosen people

Today it is widely agreed that Paul's mission and theology have to be understood as working within 1st-century Judaism. It is less clear, however, whether Paul's activity should also be considered as the beginning of a development which eventually led to a separation of Christianity from Judaism. Whereas some scholars trace the separation of Jews and Gentiles back to Paul, others are convinced that such a view would misinterpret Paul's own view of the meaning of Jewish traditions for faith in Jesus Christ. It is even debated whether the categories 'Judaism' and 'Christianity' should be applied to the 1st century at all.

Against the background of this debate in what follows I will ask how Paul's attitude towards Jewish rules such as food laws, Sabbath observance and circumcision can be determined. It will be argued that the question in the title of this article cannot be answered by defining from the outset who was considered a 'Jew' in the 1st century. There was a broad range of Jewish self-perceptions and perceptions of Jews and Judaism from outside, including different ways to delineate the relationship between Jews and non-Jews. As will be shown below, Paul's own view should be interpreted within this framework. Whether Paul was "a Jew within Judaism" may therefore be answered differently depending on which perspective one adopts, as was probably the case already in Paul's own time.

I will begin with some general remarks about the metaphor of the "parting of the ways" which is still in the background of the current discussion about Paul's place within Judaism. However, it will be shown that this imagery is less helpful and should perhaps be abandoned. In a second step, I will look at Paul's self-presentation as an apostle. It will be shown that Paul depicts himself and the Christ believers in distinction from Jews and non-Jews. This does not, however, lead to a distancing from Jewish traditions but rather to a new understanding of them. Third, the consequences of Paul's approach for Christ-believing communities of Jews and Gentiles will be examined. As will be shown, Paul's ethics demands a radical new orientation of the Gentiles whereas Jews are urged not to impose their rules of life on non-Jewish members of the community of Christ believers. I will conclude that the answer to the question in the title of this article was (and still is) a matter of perspective.

1 "Parting Ways"? Reflections on a Metaphor

As is well known, the metaphor of a parting – or several partings – of the ways between 'Jews' and 'Christians'[1] was introduced almost thirty years ago by James Dunn's study "The Partings of the Ways," followed by a collection of essays with a similar title.[2] Since then the imagery of parting ways has become a much dis-

---

[1] I will use the terminology 'Jews' and 'Christians' in this article, although I am aware that it is highly problematic with regard to the 1st and 2nd centuries, especially if the terms are set in opposition to or in distinction from each other. In historical perspective, it would be more appropriate to use descriptions like 'Jewish and non-Jewish Christ believers' or even to avoid such descriptions entirely because they may evoke the false perception of uniform religious movements. The use of such terms in the present article is therefore only for the sake of convenience. It should be kept in mind that both terms are abstractions which do not describe the historical reality in an appropriate way.

[2] J.D.G. Dunn, *The Partings of the Ways between Christianity and Judaism and their Significance for the Character of Christianity*, 2nd ed. (London: SCM Press, 2006); idem, ed., *Jews and Christians: The Parting of the Ways AD 70 to 135*, WUNT 66 (Tübingen: Mohr Siebeck, 1992). See also idem, *Neither Jew nor Greek. A Contested Identity*, vol. 3 of *Christianity in the Making* (Grand Rapids, MI, and Cambridge, UK: Eerdmans, 2015), 598–672. In this latter publication Dunn himself uses the singular.

cussed and contested issue.³ The historical process of the separation between Judaism and Christianity was of course already discussed before, and the image of parting ways or roads had also been used already in the early 20th century.⁴ However, the complex relationships between Jews and Christians – including the search for driving forces for the formation of a distinctive Christian identity, the questions about the extent to which Jewish believers in Jesus Christ remained faithful to their Jewish legacy and continued to follow a Jewish way of life after joining Christian communities, and how the diversity of Jewish groups and Christian strands in the 1st and 2nd centuries can be grasped by the metaphor of parting ways – were only considered in recent decades. To be sure, there are scholars who remained less convinced by this imagery since in their view it simplifies or even obscures the historical circumstances and tends to neglect that 'Judaism' and 'Christianity' are constructs that can hardly be applied to the actual historical circumstances of the 1st and 2nd centuries.⁵ At the outset it is therefore necessary to specify the image of "parting(s) of the ways" and its applicability to ancient Judaism and ancient Christianity.

The purpose of introducing the image in the early 90s was to study the complex relationships between Judaism and Christianity in a historically appropriate way, taking seriously the multifaceted character of Second Temple Judaism, the Jewishness of Jesus and the historical observation that Jewish believers in Jesus Christ remained faithful to their Jewish traditions also after becoming members of Christian communities. The concept of "parting ways," however, appears as a modern abstraction which compares 'Judaism' and 'Christianity' as distinctive religious systems; this reflects the social reality of Second Temple Judaism and for-

---

3 The literature about the "parting of the ways" model is abundant. For overviews see B. Wander, *Trennungsprozesse zwischen Frühem Christentum und Judentum*, 2nd ed., TANZ 16 (Tübingen: Francke, 1997), 8–53; U. Schnelle, *Die getrennten Wege von Römern, Juden und Christen. Religionspolitik im 1. Jahrhundert n. Chr.* (Tübingen: Mohr Siebeck, 2019), 1–10; S.J.D. Cohen, "The Ways that Parted: Jews, Christians, and Jewish-Christians, ca 100–150 CE," in *Jews and Christians in the First and Second Centuries: The Interbellum 70–132 CE*, ed. J. Schwartz and P.J. Tomson, CRINT 15 (Leiden and Boston, MA: Brill, 2017), 307–339. See now also the thematic issue "Parting of the Ways. Die Trennung der Wege von Juden und Christen in der neueren Forschung," *EvTh* 80/6 (2020).
4 See F.J. Foakes Jackson, ed., *The Parting of the Roads. Studies in the Development of Judaism and Early Christianity* (London: Arnold, 1912). The articles in this volume deal with the Old Testament, Second Temple Judaism ("Judaism in the Days of the Christ"), New Testament writings (Synoptics, Paul's Theology, Johannine Theology), and finally "The Breach between Judaism and Christianity" from a today outdated perspective.
5 See the fundamental criticism by J.M. Lieu, "The Parting of the Ways: Theological Construct or Historical Reality?," in *Neither Jew nor Greek. Constructing Early Christianity*, ed. eadem, 2nd ed. (London et al.: T&T Clark, 2016), 31–49.

mative Christianity only to a small extent, if at all.⁶ Moreover, there are divergent views on whether and how the model of parting ways may be applied to the developments of the 1ˢᵗ and 2ⁿᵈ centuries. Some scholars would relate actual "partings" of Jews and Christians to the period between 70 and 135, with the two Jewish revolts, the *birkat ha-minim* and the *fiscus Iudaicus* as decisive events, resulting in the juxtaposition of two social and religious movements.⁷ The beginnings of these developments are, however, often related to an earlier period: to the Hellenists and their critique of the Temple or to the formation of the community in Antioch and the designation of the Jesus followers as χριστιανοί.⁸

In the search for driving theological and sociological forces behind such a divide, Paul's turn from a Pharisee to an apostle – often called a 'conversion' –, the transformation of major Jewish categories and institutions (such as temple, sacrifice, priesthood, purity and Jerusalem), as well as the foundation of Pauline communities are also sometimes regarded as crucial steps in the formation of Christianity as an independent movement apart from Judaism.⁹ According to this view, Paul's mission and theology seem to have paved the way for the later separation of Jews and Christians.¹⁰

---

6 In *Partings* (see n. 2), James Dunn emphasizes that "there was no single, uniform type of Judaism in the first century of the common era" (24). However, he continues by identifying "four pillars of Second Temple Judaism" (monotheism, election, covenant focused in Torah, and land focused in temple) which were allegedly questioned or at least altered by the early Christians. In his later study (*Neither Jew nor Greek* [see n. 2]) he reiterates that "we are not dealing with two already well defined religions relating to each other" (599). He even concedes "that the imagery of 'the parting of the ways' is more misleading than helpful" (ibid.) and should be replaced by other imageries (602).

7 See Dunn, *Partings* (see n. 2), 312–318; M. Heemstra, *The Fiscus Iudaicus and the Parting of the Ways*, WUNT II/277 (Tübingen: Mohr Siebeck, 2010). With regard to John and the "parting of the ways" see A. Reinhartz, "'Common Judaism,' 'The Parting of the Ways,' and 'The Johannine Community'," in *Orthodoxy, Liberalism, and Adaptation. Essays on Ways of Worldmaking. Times of Change from Biblical, Historical and Systematic Perspectives*, ed. B. Becking, STAR 5 (Leiden and Boston, MA: Brill, 2011), 69–88.

8 See Dunn, *Partings* (see n. 2), 76–99; U. Schnelle, *Paulus. Leben und Denken*, 2ⁿᵈ ed. (Berlin and Boston, MA: de Gruyter, 2014), 160–174; W. Kraus, *Zwischen Antiochia und Jerusalem. Die "Hellenisten", Paulus und die Aufnahme der Heiden ins Gottesvolk*, SBS 179 (Stuttgart: Katholisches Bibelwerk, 1999).

9 See U. Schnelle, *Die ersten 100 Jahre des Christentums 30–130 n.Chr. Die Entstehungsgeschichte einer Weltreligion*, 2ⁿᵈ ed. (Göttingen: UTB, 2016), 296–303. See also G. Theissen, "Judentum und Christentum bei Paulus," in *Paulus und das antike Judentum*, ed. M. Hengel and U. Heckel, WUNT 58 (Tübingen: Mohr Siebeck, 1991), 331–356.

10 Dunn, *Partings* (see n. 2), 100–115. See his summary, ibid., 114–115: "In sum, as far as Paul was concerned, *the whole conception of sacred space, cultic, sacrifice, priestly ministry and the question of who may enter and engage in their eschatological equivalents had been wholly trans-*

Pauline scholarship of the last few decades, however, has fundamentally challenged this approach. In several recent studies, Paul's self-understanding and theology, his relationship to Judaism – or, more appropriately: his place *within* Second Temple Judaism – have been substantially reconsidered. Although the paradigms developed in recent scholarship – "the new perspective on Paul" and "Paul within Judaism" – have to be distinguished from each other, they share the opinion that common assumptions about Paul's view of the relationship between faith in Jesus Christ and God's covenant with Israel, his attitude towards Torah observance, his depiction of the relationship between Jews and non-Jews in communities of Christ believers, and his view of Israel's role within God's plan of salvation all need to be reassessed. Another common assumption of these approaches is that perspectives on Paul which prevailed in Christian theology for a long time are rooted in or at least influenced by anti-Jewish stereotypes of Christian, especially Protestant, theology: the opposition between "faith in Jesus Christ" and "works of the law," together with the caricature of ancient Judaism as a "religion of the law" and the assertion that "justification by works of the law" would have been a common Jewish conviction (although the phrase δικαιοῦσθαι ἐξ ἔργων νόμου was probably coined by Paul himself as an opposition to δικαιοῦσθαι ἐκ πίστεως Ἰησοῦ Χριστοῦ; for the possible analogy in 4QMMT see below).[11]

The appropriateness of a view that detaches Paul from Judaism has been called into question in particular by studies which underline that Paul was a Jew who never left Judaism and whose activity and thinking should be interpreted entirely within the framework of ancient Judaism, not as the point of depar-

---

formed" (his emphasis). A similar view can already be found in Protestant interpretations of Paul from the early 20th century which regarded Paul's theology as the decisive step in the formation of Christianity as a movement that has departed from Judaism as his mother religion. See R. Bultmann, *Theology of the New Testament*, 2 vols. (London: SCM Press, 1952, 1955); and even earlier by W. Wrede, *Paul* (London: Green, 1907).

[11] For the discussion about the "new perspective" see J.D.G. Dunn, *The New Perspective on Paul. Collected Essays*, WUNT 185 (Tübingen: Mohr Siebeck, 2005); idem, "A New Perspective on the New Perspective on Paul," *EC* 4 (2013): 157–182; M. Bachmann, ed., *Lutherische und neue Paulusperspektive. Beiträge zu einem Schlüsselproblem der gegenwärtigen exegetischen Diskussion*, WUNT 182 (Tübingen: Mohr Siebeck, 2005); F. Watson, *Paul, Judaism and the Gentiles. Beyond the New Perspective* (Grand Rapids, MI, and Cambridge: Eerdmans, 2008); S.J. Gathercole, *Where is Boasting? Early Jewish Soteriology and Paul's Response in Romans 1–5* (Grand Rapids, MI, and Cambridge: Eerdmans, 2002); S. Westerholm, *Perspectives Old and New on Paul. The 'Lutheran' Paul and his critics* (Grand Rapids, MI and Cambridge: Eerdmans, 2004); J. Frey, "Das Judentum des Paulus," in *Paulus: Leben – Umwelt – Werk – Briefe*, ed. O. Wischmeyer, 2nd ed. (Tübingen and Basel: Francke, 2012), 25–65.

ture for a separation of Judaism and Christianity. According to this view, which is introduced in a recent volume with collected essays as "a new perspective in Pauline scholarship," namely as the "Paul within Judaism"-perspective,[12] Paul did not cease to be a Jew after he began to preach the gospel nor was he a critic of Judaism. Instead, he should be regarded as "a radical Jew,"[13] "an anomalous Jew,"[14] "a Pharisaic Jew who converted to a new apocalyptic, Jewish sect"[15] or as "a thoroughly Jewish Paul, functioning entirely within the context of Judaism."[16] This approach thus calls into question the appropriateness of the model of parting ways by claiming that early Christ followers – including those in the Pauline tradition – have to be regarded as groups that did not depart *from* Judaism but formed specific factions *within* Judaism.

The imagery of parting ways may therefore simplify the historical reality of communities consisting of Jewish and non-Jewish Christ believers and their relationships to communities with Jewish non-believers and Jewish believers in Christ. In other words: The social realities in the first two centuries and beyond were much more complex than a juxtaposition of 'Judaism' and 'Christianity' implies. Such a view runs the risk of neglecting that Jews who became believers in Christ did not immediately or necessarily abandon their Jewish way of life. It is, by contrast, more likely that Jewish customs like circumcision, Sabbath observance and food laws were still practiced by Jews who became Jesus followers. These Jewish Christ believers may have entered mixed communities of Jews and non-Jews or even stayed within their Jewish communities. It is therefore quite possible that communities of Christ believers who called themselves ἐκκλησία, μαθηταί, οἱ πιστεύοντες or οἱ ἐπικαλούμενοι τὸ ὄνομα τοῦ κυρίου consisted

---

[12] See M.D. Nanos, "Introduction," in *Paul within Judaism. Restoring the First-Century Context of the Apostle*, ed. M.D. Nanos and M. Zetterholm (Minneapolis, MN: Fortress, 2015), 1–29, here 1. See also M.D. Nanos, "Paul *and* Judaism: Why not *Paul's Judaism?*," in idem, *Reading Paul within Judaism. Collected Essays, Vol. 1* (Eugene, OR: Cascade Books, 2017), 3–59; G. Boccaccini, "Introduction: The Three Paths to Salvation of Paul the Jew (with responses by Albert I. Baumgarten and Daniel Boyarin)," in *Paul the Jew. Rereading the Apostle as a Figure of Second Temple Judaism*, ed. idem and C.A. Segovia (Minneapolis, MN: Fortress, 2016), 1–29.
[13] D. Boyarin, *A Radical Jew. Paul and the Politics of Identity* (Berkeley, CA: University of California Press, 1994).
[14] M.F. Bird, *An Anomalous Jew. Paul among Jews, Greeks, and Romans* (Grand Rapids, MI: Eerdmans, 2016).
[15] A.F. Segal, *Paul the Convert. The Apostolate and Apostasy of Saul the Pharisee* (New Haven, CT, and London: Yale University Press, 1990), 6.
[16] M.D. Nanos, *The Mystery of Romans. The Jewish Context of Paul's Letter* (Minneapolis, MN: Fortress, 1996), 9.

of members who followed Jewish practices of circumcising their children, celebrating the Sabbath and observing food laws.[17]

Paul's letters support such a view. Paul strongly opposes an attitude that imposes Torah observance on non-Jews,[18] but he never demands that Jews should cease observing the Torah.[19] Instead, he develops a model of communities of Christ believers in which different attitudes towards Jewish regulations should be respected.[20] Writings such as the Gospel of Matthew, the Didache or the so-called Jewish-Christian Gospels substantiate the view that Jews followed Jewish customs also after they became members of Christian communities.[21] Thus, they probably understood their faith in Jesus Christ not as an alternative to their Jewish identity but as a specific type of it. For an appropriate description of the identity of Jewish Christ believers and the relationship to their fellow Jews it is therefore necessary to use the terms 'Jews' and 'Judaism' as well as 'Christians' and 'Christianity' as descriptions of broad, flexible and often overlapping social realities, not of distinct, separated groups.

Because of the obvious weaknesses of the "parting of the ways" model, it has been argued that the metaphor should only be used if it is acknowledged that "the notion Judaism is not a stable category, but a term that [...] has undergone important changes" in the period after 70 compared to the time before the destruction of the temple and the formation of Rabbinic Judaism.[22] It therefore

---

17 Sometimes they are called "Jewish Christians," belonging to a strand of "Jewish Christianity." See J. Carleton Paget, "Jewish Christianity," in *The Cambridge History of Judaism, vol. 3: The Early Roman Period*, ed. W. Horbury, W.D. Davies, and J. Sturdy (Cambridge: Cambridge University Press, 1999), 731–775.
18 This is the main topic in Galatians, but see also Phil 3:2–11.
19 See K.-W. Niebuhr, "Offene Fragen zur Gesetzespraxis bei Paulus und seinen Gemeinden (Sabbat, Speisegebote, Beschneidung)," *BThZ* 25 (2008): 16–51.
20 See especially Rom 14:1–15:13. I will return to this aspect below.
21 See H. van de Sandt, ed., *Matthew and the Didache. Two Documents from the Same Jewish-Christian Milieu?* (Assen: Royal van Gorcum; Minneapolis, MN: Fortress, 2005); J.A. Overman, *Matthew's Gospel and Formative Judaism. The Social World of the Matthean Community* (Minneapolis, MN: Fortress, 1990); A. Runesson, "Rethinking Early Jewish–Christian Relations: Matthean Community History as Pharisaic Intragroup Conflict," *JBL* 127 (2008): 95–132. Some communities of Christ believers may have consisted mainly or even exclusively of Jewish members.
22 See A.K. Petersen, "At the End of the Road. Reflections on a Popular Scholarly Metaphor," in *The Formation of the Early Church*, ed. J. Ådna, WUNT 183 (Tübingen: Mohr Siebeck, 2005), 45–72, here 60; P. Schäfer, *Zwei Götter im Himmel. Gottesvorstellungen in der jüdischen Antike* (München: Beck, 2017): "Das frühe Christentum und das rabbinische Judentum sind nicht zwei von Anfang an fest etablierte 'Religionen', sondern kristallisieren sich in einem längeren Prozess und im Diskurs mit- und gegeneinander erst langsam heraus, mit beträchtlichen Unter-

seems possible in principle that from a certain time 'Judaism' and 'Christianity' indeed became distinct social and religious systems. This does, however, not imply that the separation of the two movements or the driving forces behind it should be applied already to the period before 70 or to the 1st and 2nd centuries altogether.[23] Moreover, it should be noted that the bifurcation cannot only be viewed from a Christian perspective. Whether or not 'Judaism' was something 'other' than 'Christianity' and vice versa depends not only on the perception from the Christian, but also from the Jewish side.[24] In other words, from a certain period of time, Jewish communities perceived of themselves to be different from Christ groups and did depart from them. It was not only the other way around.[25]

It has also been argued that the metaphor of parting ways would be misleading because the ways of Jews and Christians "never parted."[26] This approach emphasizes that Judaism and Christianity, despite their differences, share common convictions and traditions such as the belief in the one God, the authority of the Torah, the Prophets and other writings, eschatological or apocalyptic views of history and the belief in resurrection.[27] Moreover, it draws attention to the fact that the "parting" was not an inevitable result of developments which commenced in the 1st century and therefore the imagery should be more flexible

---

schieden zwischen diesem neuen rabbinischen Judentum und dem Judentum des Zweiten Tempels" (156).

23 See Petersen, "End of the Road" (see n. 22), 71: "Whereas the model [of parting ways, J.S.] is obviously meaningful from the perspective of the history of reception, it is highly problematic from the strictly historical point of view."

24 The distinction of Judaism and Christianity is thus also a process of "construction of otherness." See Petersen, "End of the Road" (see n. 22), 63–64. On "Otherness" with regard to Judaism from a more general viewpoint see E. Benbassa, "Otherness, Openness and Rejection in Jewish Context," *JISMOR* 5 (2010): 16–25; Y.M. Rabkin and H. Rabkin, "Perspectives on the Muslim Other in Jewish Tradition," *JISMOR* 5 (2010): 26–45.

25 See P. Schäfer, *Die Geburt des Judentums aus dem Geist des Christentums. Fünf Vorlesungen zur Entstehung des rabbinischen Judentums*, Tria Corda 6 (Tübingen: Mohr Siebeck, 2010); idem, *Anziehung und Abstoßung. Juden und Christen in den ersten Jahrhunderten ihrer Begegnung*, Lucasz-Preis 2014 (Tübingen: Mohr Siebeck, 2015); M. Bar-Asher Siegal, *Early Christian Monastic Literature and the Babylonian Talmud* (Cambridge: Cambridge University Press, 2013).

26 See P. Fredriksen, "What 'Parting of the Ways'? Jews, Gentiles, and the Ancient Mediterranean City," in *The Ways that Never Parted. Jews and Christians in Late Antiquity and the Early Middle Ages*, ed. A.H. Becker and A.Y. Reed, TSAJ 95 (Tübingen: Mohr Siebeck, 2003), 35–63; D. Boyarin, *Border Lines. The Partition of Judaeo-Christianity* (Philadelphia, PA: University of Pennsylvania, 2006); idem, "Als Christen noch Juden waren. Überlegungen zu den jüdisch-christlichen Ursprüngen," *KuI* 16 (2001): 112–129.

27 See A.Y. Reed and A.H. Becker, "Introduction: Traditional Models and New Directions," in *The Ways that Never Parted. Jews and Christians in Late Antiquity and the Early Middle Ages*, ed. idem, TSAJ 95 (Tübingen: Mohr Siebeck, 2003), 1–33.

than that of ways that parted from one another.²⁸ The model of parting ways therefore tends to ignore that the divide between both Jewish non-believers in Christ and Jewish and non-Jewish Christ believers, which led to the formation of Judaism and Christianity, was not the only possible outcome of processes in the 1ˢᵗ and 2ⁿᵈ centuries. The relationships between Jewish Christ-believers, Jews who refused the message of Jesus Christ, Gentile sympathizers of Judaism, and Gentile Christ-believers without a Jewish background may have differed from one region to another and were assessed differently in various writings. The metaphor of parting ways was therefore replaced by other images, such as that of competing siblings,²⁹ a multi-lane highway³⁰ or a dance.³¹ Even Paul's image of an olive tree with different branches may be more appropriate – even if it may be used in a different way than Paul who speaks of branches broken off from the tree and others which were grafted in.³² It has also been argued that, against the background of a great variety of Second Temple Judaism and early Christianity, early Christ groups could be regarded as a specific form of Judaism, called "apostolic Judaism," alongside other 'Judaisms' such as Pharisaic Judaism, Essene Judaism, and later Rabbinic Judaism.³³

As these observations indicate, the use of the designations 'Jews' and 'Christians' with regard to historical developments that eventually resulted in the juxtaposition of the Christian church and Jewish synagogue is in danger of obscuring that in the first two centuries there was no fixed entity 'Judaism' from which Christ believers could depart.³⁴ Behind these terms lurks therefore a terminolog-

---

28 See T. Nicklas, *Jews and Christians? Second Century 'Christian' Perspectives on the 'Parting of the Ways'*, Annual Deichmann Lectures 2013 (Tübingen: Mohr Siebeck, 2014); idem, "Parting of the Ways? Probleme eines Konzepts," in *Juden – Heiden – Christen? Religiöse Inklusion und Exklusion in Kleinasien bis Decius*, ed. S. Alkier and H. Leppin, WUNT 400 (Tübingen: Mohr Siebeck, 2018), 21–42.
29 A.F. Segal, *Rebecca's Children. Judaism and Christianity in the Roman World* (Cambridge, MA, and London: Harvard University Press, 1986), 173.
30 See A. Reinhartz, "A Fork in the Road or a Multi-Lane Highway? New Perspectives on the 'Parting of the Ways' Between Judaism and Christianity," in *The Changing Faces of Judaism, Christianity, and other Greco-Roman Religions in Antiquity*, ed. I.H. Henderson and G.S. Oegema, JSHRZ Studien 2 (Gütersloh: Gütersloher Verlagshaus, 2006), 280–295.
31 Nicklas, *Jews and Christians* (see n. 28), 222–223.
32 Rom 11:17–24. The image may also be used without the distinction of the branches to describe the relationships of Jews and Christians in historical perspective.
33 See A. Runesson, "The Question of Terminology: The Architecture of Contemporary Discussions on Paul," in *Paul within Judaism. Restoring the First-Century Context of the Apostle*, ed. M.D. Nanos and M. Zetterholm (Minneapolis, MN: Fortress, 2015), 53–77, here 67–68.
34 See D. Boyarin, "Semantic Differences; or: 'Judaism'/'Christianity'," in *The Ways that Never Parted. Jews and Christians in Late Antiquity and the Early Middle Ages*, ed. A.H. Becker and A.Y.

ical problem, which affects the interpretation of 1ˢᵗ and 2ⁿᵈ century texts. The term 'Judaism' in modern languages does not have an equivalent in ancient Jewish texts – the Greek term Ἰουδαϊσμός in Jewish texts does not refer to 'Judaism' as an ἔθνος or a religion, but to a specific way of defending Jewish faith in the one God, the temple, and the Torah against renegades.[35] A similar meaning of Ἰουδαϊσμός and the related terms ἰουδαΐζειν and Ἰουδαϊκῶς ζῆν should be presupposed for Paul's usage in Gal 1:14 and 2:14. Paul describes himself as ζηλωτὴς [...] τῶν πατρικῶν μου παραδόσεων who persecuted the community of God. In Gal 2:14 he accuses Peter for imposing a Jewish way of life upon Gentiles. Both passages therefore indicate that for Paul, as in 2 and 4 Maccabees, the terminology refers to forcing others to live according to the Jewish law.

The terms χριστιανός and χριστιανοί were coined in the 1ˢᵗ century, as is attested by their use in Acts 11:26; 26:28 and 1 Pet 4:16, and were translated into Latin as *Christianus* and *Christiani* as is attested early in the 2ⁿᵈ century by Tacitus, *Ann.* 15.44 and Pliny the Younger, *Ep.* 10.96. The opposition of Ἰουδαϊσμός versus Χριστιανισμός first appears in Ignatius in a polemical context. Ignatius criticizes members of the communities in Magnesia and Philadelphia who still follow a Jewish way of life. He urges his readers not to follow the way of Ἰουδαϊσμός because it has been replaced by the Χριστιανισμός. In this context, he coins the term Χριστιανισμός as an opposition to Ἰουδαϊσμός.[36] The terminology, therefore, points to different views on how faith in Jesus Christ should be practiced, not to separate groups of Jews and Christians. This terminology also does not help to grasp Paul's view of communities of Christ believers and their relationship to Jews who did not believe in Jesus Christ. The terms 'Jews' and 'Christians' or 'Judaism' and 'Christianity' are therefore in danger of simplifying com-

---

Reed, TSAJ 95 (Tübingen: Mohr Siebeck, 2003), 65–85; idem, "*Ioudaismos* within Paul. A modified Reading of Gal 1:13–14," in *The Message of Paul the Apostle within Second Temple Judaism*, ed. F. Abel (Lanham et al.: Lexington Books/Fortress Academic, 2019), 167–178.

35 The term occurs only rarely in Jewish sources. Its use is limited to 2 Macc 2:21; 8:1; 14:38 and 4 Macc 4:26 where it refers to the conflicts between the Maccabeans and their adherents with Antioch IV. The Synagogue inscriptions from Stobi and Porto (Latium) are from a later period. See K.-W. Niebuhr, *Heidenapostel aus Israel*, WUNT 62 (Tübingen: Mohr Siebeck, 1992), 21–24; idem, "'Judentum' und 'Christentum' bei Paulus und Ignatius von Antiochien," *ZNW* 85 (1994): 218–233. For the Stobi inscription see H. Lietzmann, "Notizen," *ZNW* 32 (1933): 93–95; M. Hengel, "Die Synagogeninschrift von Stobi (mit einem Anhang von Hanswulf Bloedhorn)," in idem, *Judaica et Hellenistica. Kleine Schriften I*, WUNT 90 (Tübingen: Mohr Siebeck, 1996), 91–130. In non-Jewish literature the term Ἰουδαϊσμός is only attested in Plutarch, *Cic.* 7.6, p. 864C.

36 Ign.*Magn.* 8:1; 10:1, 3; Ign.*Phld.* 6:1. See Niebuhr, "'Judentum' und 'Christentum'" (see n. 35), 224–233; Nicklas, *Jews and Christians?* (see n. 28), 1–10.

plex, multifaceted social and religious circumstances.[37] Moreover, they do not help us to interpret the texts from the 1st and 2nd centuries.

The terminological problem can be applied also to other terms[38] such as "church," "bishop" or "Christ" as translations of ἐκκλησία, ἐπίσκοπος and χριστός. Although it is true that the early Jesus followers used these and other terms in a distinct way, the meaning of these terms in a 1st century context differs from later use. This should be kept in mind if these terms are used as translations for New Testament texts. Paul's and Matthew's ἐκκλησία was an assembly of Jewish and non-Jewish followers of Jesus, but certainly not an institution with an organizational structure of later churches alongside the Jewish synagogue.[39] The terms ἐκκλησία and συναγωγή are nowhere used in the New Testament in direct opposition, and as is well known, ἐκκλησία could also be used for the public assembly of the citizens of Ephesus,[40] as συναγωγή was used for the Christian assembly, synonymous to ἐκκλησία.[41] The ἐπίσκοποι of Phil 1:1 are certainly not "bishops," but "overseers" or "treasurers" whose function in the community of Philippi remains unclear. Finally, although χριστός became a proper name for Jesus very early as is demonstrated e.g., by 1 Cor 15:3, the term can also mean "the anointed one," as in Rom 9:5: ἐξ ὧν ὁ Χριστὸς τὸ κατὰ σάρκα which may be translated as "from whom comes the anointed one according to earthly descendance."

Paul's terminology and thinking should thus not be regarded as being detached from Judaism. This has to be noted also with regard to the "new perspective on Paul." Whereas representatives of this approach rightly dismissed the caricature of ancient Judaism as a "religion of the law" which served as a negative foil for Paul's theology of justification by grace, they were still convinced that Paul considered Judaism in need of correction. Ed Parish Sanders in comparing Palestinian Judaism and Paul's theology as two distinct "patterns of religion," concluded in a well-known statement that "this is what Paul finds wrong with

---

37 See Nicklas, *Jews and Christians?* (see n. 28), 15: "there is no simple answer for [sic] the question when, where, why and how exactly the 'parting of the ways' between 'Jews' and 'Christians' took its decisive starting point and when, where, why and how it was fixed."
38 See Runesson, "The Question of Terminology" (see n. 33). The problem is also raised by P. Fredriksen, "Mandatory Retirement: Ideas in the study of Christian origins whose time has come to go," *SR* 35.2 (2006): 231–246. She reflects on conversion, nationalism, *religio licita* and monotheism as terms that have to be reconsidered.
39 For the term ἐκκλησία in Greek, Roman and Jewish sources, in pre-Pauline tradition and in Paul see R.J. Korner, *The Origin and Meaning of Ekklēsia in the Early Jesus Movement*, AJEC 98 (Leiden and Boston, MA: Brill, 2017).
40 Acts 19:32, 39, 40.
41 Jas 2:2 (συναγωγή); 5:14 (ἐκκλησία).

Judaism: it is not Christianity."⁴² James Dunn interpreted the phrase "works of the law" in Paul's writings as referring to certain rules such as circumcision, Sabbath observance and food laws rather than adhering to the Torah in general. According to Dunn, Paul criticized Jews for regarding these precepts as identity and boundary markers which served to separate themselves from the other nations.⁴³ Whether this is an appropriate interpretation of Paul's view of the Torah and the phrase "works of the law" may be questioned. Thus, although the "new perspective" aimed at adjusting a negative image of ancient Judaism as a religion in opposition to Christianity in Paul's letters, its representatives still regarded Paul as being detached from Judaism or at least on the way from Judaism to Christianity.

Against this background, in what follows I will first look at Paul's self-understanding and his view of the relationship between Christ believers and Jews, and second at his view of the law and the life in a community of believers in Jesus Christ. In my conclusion I will return to the question about whether Paul should be described as a Jew within Judaism.

2 Paul's self-presentation and his view of the relationship between Christ believers and non-believing Jews

For Paul's self-presentation as an apostle of Jesus Christ, the distinction between his former life ἐν τῷ Ἰουδαϊσμῷ and his new life as an apostle is of crucial importance.⁴⁴ In the autobiographical passages in Galatians, 1 and 2 Corinthians

---

42 E.P. Sanders, *Paul and Palestinian Judaism. A Comparison of Patterns of Religion* (London: SCM Press, 1977), 552.
43 Dunn has developed this view in many contributions which are collected in his *Paul and the New Perspective* (see n. 11). In the introductory article of this volume ("The New Perspective: whence, what and wither," 1–88) Dunn discusses objections and qualifications which were raised against his approach. He writes: "In short, I do not want to narrow 'the works of the law' to boundary issues" (25) and "All I want to do is to remind those interested that there is *also* a social and ethnic dimension to Paul's own understanding and expression of the gospel" (27). There is certainly no doubt about that!
44 See M. Hengel and A.M. Schwemer, *Paulus zwischen Damaskus und Antiochien. Die unbekannten Jahre des Apostels*, WUNT 108 (Tübingen: Mohr Siebeck, 1998); idem, *Die Urgemeinde und das Judenchristentum. Geschichte des frühen Christentums*, vol. 2 (Tübingen: Mohr Siebeck, 2019), 203–224; A. Lindemann, "Paulus – Pharisäer und Apostel," in idem, *Glauben, Handeln, Verstehen. Studien zur Auslegung des Neuen Testaments*, vol. 2, WUNT 282 (Tübingen: Mohr Siebeck, 2011), 33–72; J.D.G. Dunn, *Beginning from Jerusalem*, vol. 2 of *Christianity in the Making*

and Philippians, the two stages of his biography are set in sharp opposition to each other. Where his former life was characterized by his persecution of the ἐκκλησία τοῦ θεοῦ (Gal 1:13, 23; 1 Cor 15:9; Phil 3:6) and he was blameless according to the righteousness in the law (Phil 3:6), his new life is grounded in God who set him apart before he was born and revealed his son to him. Paul describes this as a visionary event (1 Cor 15:8: Christ appeared to him; Gal 1:15: God's son was revealed to him) which is even comparable to the creation of light (2 Cor 4:6: God who said, "Let light shine out of darkness," has shone in our hearts to give the light of the knowledge of the glory of God in the face of Jesus Christ). Therefore, Paul can describe those who are in Christ as a "new creation" (2 Cor 5:17; Gal 6:15). His former life, which he regarded once as "gains" (κέρδη) he now considers as "loss" (ζημία; Phil 3:7). Thus, from the perspective of his new insight Paul regards his former life as persecutor of the ἐκκλησία as a time that was ended by God's revelation. Connected to this event is a new view of Israel's scriptures, of the community of believers in Jesus Christ, and of the relationship of Israel and the Gentiles.

The Acts of the Apostles elaborate the Pauline self-descriptions with a terminology that is used in Jewish texts for the turning of Gentiles to the God of Israel.[45] The turning from darkness to light, the rescue from the power of Satan, and the contrast between blindness and opening of the eyes are used in Jewish texts as metaphors to describe the turning of non-Jews to the God of Israel.[46] Thus, neither Paul nor Luke use a language for the turn in Paul's biography that would interpret it as a turning from Judaism to faith in Jesus Christ. One should therefore be careful to use the term 'conversion' for the turn in Paul's biography. It was certainly not a conversion from Judaism to Christianity, but a vision of the risen Christ, a new insight into God's plan of salvation and God's instruction for Paul to proclaim the gospel of Jesus Christ to the Gentiles.

Even though his calling as an apostle was a fundamental turn in his life, Paul as a missionary of the gospel has by no means abandoned the scriptures of Israel or Jewish traditions.[47] This is clarified by his use of the authoritative

---

(Grand Rapids, MI, and Cambridge: Eerdmans, 2009), 322–377; R.N. Longenecker, ed., *The Road from Damascus* (Grand Rapids, MI, and Cambridge: Eerdmans, 1997).
45 See J. Schröter, "Paulus als Modell christlicher Zeugenschaft: Apg 9,15f. und 28,30f. als Rahmen der lukanischen Paulusdarstellung und Rezeption des 'historischen' Paulus," in *Reception of Paulinism in Acts – Réception du Paulinisme dans les Actes des Apôtres*, ed. D. Marguerat, BETL 229 (Leuven: Peeters, 2009), 53–80; Hengel and Schwemer, *Urgemeinde* (see n. 44), 224–234.
46 See Isa 42:7; Jos.Asen. 8:10; T.Levi 19:1.
47 See Frey, "Judentum" (see n. 11), 44–55; idem, "Paul's Jewish Identity," in *Jewish Identity in the Greco-Roman World*, ed. idem, D.R. Schwartz, and S. Gripentrog, AJEC 71 (Leiden and Boston,

Jewish writings in the letters to the Corinthians, Galatians and Romans⁴⁸ as well as by the treatment of Torah regulations, including circumcision and food laws, the ethics of the communities of believers in Christ (see below) and of God's election of Israel.⁴⁹ Paul does not give up the characteristics of a Jewish way of life, but makes them applicable to a community of Jews and Gentiles: circumcision is re-defined as a "circumcision of the heart" (Rom 2:29) and subordinated to faith (Rom 4); food laws are regarded as a matter of perception (Rom 14:2–23); Gentile attitudes towards sexuality and food offered in sacrifice are criticized from a Jewish perspective as fornication (πορνεία; 1 Cor 5:1; 6:13, 18; 7:2) and idolatry (εἰδωλολατρία; 1 Cor 10:14; Gal 5:20). Thus, it is obvious that for Paul faith in Jesus Christ is not only deeply rooted in faith in the God of Israel, but also in Jewish rituals and ethics summarized in the Torah. It is questionable, then, that Paul's theology should be described as a commencement of an independent religious movement or a new system that was no longer compatible with a restricted Jewish identity.⁵⁰ Such a view disregards the deep roots of Paul's thinking in Israel's scriptures and Jewish faith and forces the separation of 'Judaism' and 'Christianity' from a much later period to an entirely different historical situation. Moreover, such a view gives the impression that the parting of the ways between Jews and Gentiles was a logical and necessary consequence of Paul's mission and theology, despite the fact that historical developments are not inevitable and without alternatives.

How does Paul describe himself and those who believe in Jesus Christ in contrast to those who do not? As we already saw, Paul does not use the terms 'Jews' and 'Christians' for such a distinction. The believers in Christ are called "the believers" (οἱ πιστεύοντες; e.g., 1 Cor 1:21; 14:22; Gal 3:22; Rom 3:22, often

---

MA: Brill, 2007), 286–321; P.J. Tomson, *Paul and the Jewish Law. Halakha in the Letters of the Apostle to the Gentiles*, CRINT 3/1 (Assen: Van Gorcum; Minneapolis, MN: Fortress, 1990); idem, "Paul and his Place in Judaism," in idem, *Studies on Jews and Christians in the First and Second Centuries*, WUNT 418 (Tübingen: Mohr Siebeck, 2019), 317–497.

48 See M. Tilly, "Paulus und die antike jüdische Schriftauslegung," *KuD* 63 (2017): 157–181; F. Wilk, *Die Bedeutung des Jesajabuches für Paulus*, FRLANT 179 (Göttingen: Vandenhoeck & Ruprecht, 1998); D.-A. Koch, *Die Schrift als Zeuge des Evangeliums. Untersuchungen zur Verwendung und zum Verständnis der Schrift bei Paulus*, BHT 69 (Tübingen: Mohr Siebeck, 1986).

49 See the contributions in: F. Wilk and J.R. Wagner, eds., *Between Gospel and Election. Explorations in the Interpretation of Romans 9–11*, WUNT 257 (Tübingen: Mohr Siebeck, 2010).

50 Thus Schnelle, *Paulus* (see n. 7), 170: "Dieses universale theologische Grundkonzept ist *nicht kombinierbar* mit einer an Erwählung, Tora, Tempel und Land orientierten partikularen jüdischen Identität" (his emphasis).

also in singular: ὁ πιστεύων),⁵¹ "those who are in Christ" (οἱ ἐν Χριστῷ Ἰησοῦ: Rom 8:1), "those who call on the name of the Lord" (οἱ ἐπικαλούμενοι τὸ ὄνομα τοῦ κυρίου Ἰησοῦ Χριστοῦ, 1 Cor 1:2; see also Rom 10:12–13; 2 Tim 2:22) or "those who are called as saints" (κλητοὶ ἅγιοι; 1 Cor 1:2; Rom 1:7). They are distinguished from "Jews and Gentiles" or "Jews and Greeks" (1 Cor 1:22–24; Rom 1:16; 2:9–10). In his self-description as an apostle of Jesus Christ, Paul occasionally emphasizes his Jewish origin.⁵² In the controversies with his opponents in Philippi, he refers to his circumcision on the eighth day, to his descendance from the people of Israel, "from the tribe of Benjamin, a Hebrew born of Hebrews, as to the law a Pharisee."⁵³ Although in Philippians this biographical background is described as a period which he has left behind and that is no longer relevant, in 2 Cor 11:22–23 in a sharp rejoinder to his Corinthian opponents Paul points out that – as they are – he as well is a Hebrew, an Israelite and a seed of Abraham also in his new life as διάκονος Χριστοῦ.⁵⁴ In Rom 11:1 Paul emphasizes that he is an Israelite, a descendant of Abraham, from the tribe of Benjamin. The self-presentation in Romans is not developed in a polemical discourse with other Jewish apostles as in 2 Corinthians and Philippians. Instead, in Romans it is part of Paul's reflection about God's plan of salvation for Israel. Paul, as an Israelite who is also a believer in Jesus Christ, serves as a proof that God has not rejected his people, because there is a "remnant, chosen by grace" (λεῖμμα κατ' ἐκλογὴν χάριτος, 11:5), i.e., a part of Israel that assures the salvation of all of Israel.⁵⁵ In his self-descriptions Paul therefore underlines

---

51 See M. Wolter, "Die Wirklichkeit des Glaubens. Ein Versuch zur Bedeutung des Glaubens bei Paulus," in *Glaube. Das Verständnis des Glaubens im frühen Christentum und seiner jüdischen und hellenistisch-römischen Umwelt*, ed. J. Frey et al., WUNT 373 (Tübingen: Mohr Siebeck, 2017), 347–367. Πιστεύειν and πίστις in Paul's letters is always determined as faith in Jesus Christ. Abraham's faith according to Romans 4 too is meaningful as a faith without works and thus as prefiguration of the faith of those who believe in God "who raised Jesus our Lord from the dead" (4:24).
52 See Frey, "Paul's Jewish Identity" (see n. 47), 289–294.
53 Phil 3:5: περιτομῇ ὀκταήμερος, ἐκ γένους Ἰσραήλ, φυλῆς Βενιαμίν, Ἑβραῖος ἐξ Ἑβραίων, κατὰ νόμον Φαρισαῖος.
54 2 Cor 11:22–23: Ἑβραῖοί εἰσιν; κἀγώ. Ἰσραηλῖταί εἰσιν; κἀγώ. σπέρμα Ἀβραάμ εἰσιν; κἀγώ. 23 διάκονοι Χριστοῦ εἰσιν; παραφρονῶν λαλῶ, ὑπὲρ ἐγώ.
55 On the concept of "remnant" in Romans in the context of Jewish sources (Damascus Document, 4 Ezra) see S. Sheinfeld, "Who is the righteous Remnant in Romans 9–11? The Concept of Remnant in Early Jewish Literature and Paul's Letter to the Romans," in *Paul within Judaism. Restoring the First-Century Context of the Apostle*, ed. M.D. Nanos and M. Zetterholm (Minneapolis, MN: Fortress, 2015), 33–50.

that also as an apostle he is a seed of Abraham and belongs to Israel, even if that origin now gains a new meaning.

Remarkably, however, Paul nowhere uses the designation "Jew" (Ἰουδαῖος) for his life as an apostle. The only exception is Gal 2:15 which, however, does not contradict this finding, as we will see below. Instead, he repeatedly points out that the difference between Jews and Greeks (or Gentiles) is no longer valid in Christ. In Galatians 3:28 he probably quotes a conviction that was developed in the community of Antioch, namely that in Christ there is no longer Jew or Greek, slave or free, male and female. This belief is developed further in Romans. According to Rom 1:16 the gospel is "God's power for salvation to everyone who has faith, to the Jew first and also to the Greek." This general claim serves as the basis for Paul's argument in Rom 1–11. Paul repeatedly points out that there is no difference between Jews and Gentiles anymore. God is the God not of the Jews only, but also of the Gentiles (3:30). Therefore, both Jews and Gentiles are equal with regard to their situation before Christ. Not only Gentiles, but also Jews are sinners. All will be judged according to the same standard, which is God's law, and only those who do good will be saved (Rom 2:9–10). Paul explicitly states that all, Jews and Gentiles, are under sin.[56] The reason for this harsh verdict is that with Adam, the first human being, sin came into the world and therefore all have sinned and must die (Rom 5:12–21).

Paul thus makes a distinction between Israel as God's chosen people on the one hand and, on the other, "Jews" (Ἰουδαῖοι) as those who belong to Israel but can nevertheless be detached from God's salvation for a certain period because they do not accept the gospel. This view is developed in Romans 11 in the image of the olive tree as the distinction between Israel and the community of believers in Jesus Christ, consisting of Jews and Gentiles. With this metaphor Paul indicates that Israel was God's chosen people before Christ, whereas since the coming of Christ salvation is granted to the believers in Jesus Christ among both Jews and Gentiles. Jews who do not belong to the community of Christ believers are nevertheless part of Israel and will eventually be saved, because all of Israel is and remains God's people. In other words: the divide which splits Israel in two will be overcome by God himself.

The difference between Israel on the one hand and the division of mankind in Jews and Gentiles on the other is also supported by 1 Cor 1:22–24. Here Paul develops a distinction between Jews, Greeks and "us who are the called, both Jews and Greeks." Similarly, in 1 Cor 10:32 he prompts the Corinthian community, "Give no offense to Jews or to Greeks or to the assembly (ἐκκλησία) of God."

---

56 Rom 3:9 προῃτιασάμεθα γὰρ Ἰουδαίους τε καὶ Ἕλληνας πάντας ὑφ' ἁμαρτίαν εἶναι.

Thus, Paul makes a difference between Jews and Greeks on the one hand and the ἐκκλησία on the other. Finally, in the description of his work for the gospel in 1 Cor 9:20–21, Paul states:

ἐγενόμην τοῖς Ἰουδαίοις ὡς Ἰουδαῖος,
ἵνα Ἰουδαίους κερδήσω·
τοῖς ὑπὸ νόμον ὡς ὑπὸ νόμον, μὴ ὢν αὐτὸς ὑπὸ νόμον,
ἵνα τοὺς ὑπὸ νόμον κερδήσω·
τοῖς ἀνόμοις ὡς ἄνομος, μὴ ὢν ἄνομος θεοῦ ἀλλ' ἔννομος Χριστοῦ,
ἵνα κερδάνω τοὺς ἀνόμους.[57]

In this passage, too, Paul distinguishes between Jews and Gentiles on the one hand – those under the law and those without the law – and himself on the other. However, the passage remains ambiguous: Paul does not formulate a negative phrase in the first section, as he does in the second and the third one, but he relates himself to "the Jews as a Jew" in a similar way as in the following two sections. Another important observation is that Paul distinguishes the two groups[58] with regard to their relationship to the law. This allows him to describe his own attitude as "not under the law" and "not without God's law but in Christ's law." The passage therefore demonstrates that Paul reformulates his stance towards the law from the perspective of the gospel. The law is not abolished but has to be redefined on the basis of God's revelation in Jesus Christ.

The question "Was Paul a Jew within Judaism?" has therefore to be answered in a differentiated way. Although Paul nowhere claims that he has parted from Judaism and he does not understand the gospel as an alternative to God's covenant to his chosen people, he develops a distinction between Jews and Gentiles who became believers in Jesus Christ on the one hand and those who belong to Israel, but do not believe in the proclamation of the gospel on the other.[59] The Jewish distinction of humankind into Jews and Gentiles (or pagans or non-Jews) is thus modified in Paul's letters. Gentiles who become Christ believers

---

57 "To the Jews I became as a Jew, so that I might win Jews. To those under the law I became as one under the law – though I myself am not under the law – so that I might win those under the law. To those without the law I became as one without the law – though I am not without God's law but am in Christ's law – so that I might win those without the law."

58 Probably, Paul has two groups in mind, not three. The first group (the Jews) is described in the second phrase as "those under the law" and distinguished from the Gentiles as "those without the law."

59 See J.A. Staples, *The Idea of Israel in Second Temple Judaism: A New Theory of People, Exile, and Israelite Identity* (Cambridge University Press, forthcoming 2020). I want to thank Ben Edsall for making me aware of this publication.

must also believe in the God of Israel. Jews who do not believe in Jesus Christ are currently hardened and even called "enemies,"⁶⁰ but will be saved in the future (Rom 11:26). Paul does not describe himself as a Jew, but as a member of Israel, more precisely: of the remnant part of Israel that guarantees the salvation of all of Israel.⁶¹

3 Paul, the law and the life of the community of Jewish and non-Jewish Christ believers

For Paul's understanding of salvation it is of crucial importance that the gospel has to be preached to Jews and Gentiles alike. As the account of his own commission to the Gentiles in Gal 1:16 and his self-description as ἐθνῶν ἀπόστολος in Rom 11:13 demonstrate, Paul sees his own task in preaching the gospel to the Gentiles, but he regards faith in Jesus Christ as indispensable for the salvation of all human beings, Jews and Gentiles alike. Thus, he develops a view of the gospel as God's saving power for all who believe, for the Jews first and also for the Gentiles (Rom 1:16), as well as of the ethics of Jewish and non-Jewish Christ believers in the community of Jesus Christ.

With regard to the first aspect, the much-debated passage in Gal 2:11–16 is of fundamental importance. In his report about the Antioch incident⁶² in Gal 2:11–14 Paul criticizes that Peter and his fellow-Jews forced the Gentiles to live like Jews. Apparently, the problem for Paul was not that Peter and the other Jews themselves observed Jewish food laws, but that, after "certain people from James" came to Antioch, they did not treat non-Jewish Christ believers equally to Jewish believers but instead left the table fellowship with them.⁶³

In v. 15 Paul continues with a sharp distinction between "us Jews" and "sinners from the Gentiles." He continues that "we" – which means "we as Jews" – "know that a person is justified not by the works of the law but through faith in Jesus Christ." As the phrase at the end of v. 16 (ἐξ ἔργων νόμου οὐ δικαιωθήσεται πᾶσα σάρξ) shows, Paul takes this insight from the Jewish scriptures, in this case from Ps 142:2 in the Septuagint. He modifies the Septuagint text which reads οὐ

---

60 Rom 11:25, 28.
61 See esp. Rom 11:1–2, where Paul justifies the claim that God has not rejected his people by referring to himself as an Israelite and descendant of Abraham.
62 For the dating of the Antioch incident see M. Konradt, "Zur Datierung des sogenannten antiochenischen Zwischenfalls," *ZNW* 102 (2011): 19–39. Konradt assumes a longer period of time between the Apostolic council and the Antioch incident and dates the latter around 52.
63 See M. Zetterholm, "Purity and Anger: Gentiles and Idolatry in Antioch," *IJRR* 1 (2005): 1–24.

δικαιωθήσεται ἐνώπιόν σου πᾶς ζῶν to ἐξ ἔργων νόμου οὐ δικαιωθήσεται πᾶσα σάρξ by emphasizing the relationship between ἔργα νόμου and justification. The phrase "no human being is justified by works of the law" raises the dispute with Cephas about table fellowship with gentiles to a general level.

With the opposition of "works of the law" and "faith in Jesus Christ" Paul points to two opposing Jewish views of justification. He ascribes the insight that justification is not by works of the law to those Jews who have become believers in Jesus Christ, such as himself, Kephas, and Barnabas. This view contradicts another notion of the relationship of law and righteousness. To elaborate this distinction, Paul uses the phrase ἐξ ἔργων νόμου as a modifier of δικαιοῦσθαι. With this phrase he enters a discussion about Torah practice in relation to righteousness. This becomes evident by the much-discussed letter 4QMMT which provides a remarkable Hebrew parallel to Paul's Greek phrase and may illuminate the context of this debate.[64] The letter, apparently written by an influential, authoritative person who instructs the addresses about issues of the law,[65] gives an overview of certain Torah practices which have led to a segregation of the writer and his group from the multitude of the people.[66] At the end of the

---

64 See J. Frey, "Contextualizing Paul's 'Works of the Law': MMT in New Testament Scholarship," in *Qumran, Early Judaism, and New Testament Interpretation. Kleine Schriften III*, ed. J.N. Cerone, WUNT 424 (Tübingen: Mohr Siebeck, 2019), 743–762, here 746–761; L. Doering, "4QMMT and the Letters of Paul: Selected Aspects of Mutual Illumination," in *The Dead Sea Scrolls and Pauline Literature*, ed. J.-S. Rey, STDJ 102 (Leiden and Boston, MA: Brill, 2014), 69–87; M.G. Abegg, "Paul, 'Works of the Law' and MMT," *BAR* 20.6 (1994): 52–55, 82. Idem, "4QMMT C 27, 31 and 'Works Righteousness'," *DSD* 6 (1999): 139–147. A relationship between MMT and ἔργα νόμου in Paul was also considered by M. Bachmann, "Rechtfertigung und Gesetzeswerke bei Paulus," *ThZ* 49 (1993): 1–33; J.D.G. Dunn, "4QMMT and Galatians," *NTS* 43 (1997): 147–153; idem, "Noch einmal: 'Works of the Law': The Dialogue Continues," in *Fair Play: Diversity and Conflicts in Early Christianity. FS H. Räisänen*, ed. I. Dunderberg and C. Tuckett (Leiden: Brill, 2002), 273–290 (both articles are reprinted in his *The New Perspective on Paul. Collected Essays*, WUNT 185 [Tübingen: Mohr Siebeck, 2005], 333–339; 407–422).
65 For a reflection on the genre of 4QMMT see L. Doering, *Ancient Jewish Letters and the Beginnings of Christian Epistolography*, WUNT 298 (Tübingen: Mohr Siebeck, 2012), 194–214. Doering sees an analogy of MMT to the Pauline letters as a writing that "is not a private letter, but represents authoritative communication from an addressor to an addressee, who may be representative of a wider group of addressees" (214). See also idem, "4QMMT" (see n. 64), 86–87; A. Reinhartz, "We, You, They: Boundary Language in 4QMMT and the New Testament Epistles," in *Text, Thought, and Practice in Qumran and Early Christianity*, ed. R.A. Clements and D.R. Schwartz, STDJ 84 (Leiden: Brill, 2009), 89–105. T. Kato, "4QMMT Reconsidered: Is it really a Sectarian Text?," *JISMOR* 15 (2020): 21–33.
66 4QMMT C 7. The phrase פרשנו מרוב העם[...]ש[("we have segregated ourselves from the multitude of the people") introduces the third part of the letter in which the author continues the outline of Torah regulations of the previous section with admonitions of the addressees.

letter the author describes these regulations as מעשי התורה whose observation will lead to joy at the end of time and will be reckoned as righteousness.[67] If Paul knew a Hebrew equivalent to the Greek expression ἔργα νόμου, it was probably this phrase.[68]

The attitude of Peter and his fellow Jews, at least in Paul's view, to cease table fellowship with non-Jews because of purity concerns can therefore be compared to the position taken by the author of 4QMMT.[69] In both cases Jews separate themselves from others (Jews or Gentiles) to live in accordance with Torah regulations in order to achieve righteousness from God. Paul refers to this conflict with Peter in his letter to the Galatians because he identifies a similar attitude among his opponents in Galatia which would result in Gentiles being subjected to Jewish Torah practices as food laws and circumcision. The Galatian opponents may even have used the phrase ἔργα νόμου or מעשי התורה in their teaching in the Galatian communities.[70] Paul argues that such a view would violate the insight that justification cannot be achieved by "works of the law" that will be reckoned by God as righteousness because Scripture says that no human being will be justified by works of the law. He thus develops his view of righteousness by faith without works of the law in a debate with other Christ believing Jews about the relationship of Torah observance and faith in Jesus Christ. This position can be situated within the broad range of Jewish attitudes towards table fellowship with Gentiles in the diaspora.[71]

Paul's view of righteousness without works of the law is accompanied by an ethics for the communities of Jews and Gentiles in which the law gets a new meaning as the "law of Christ" (Gal 6:20). An important concern of Paul's ethical teaching is to admonish his non-Jewish addressees to abstain from their former practices as Gentiles and to follow a way of life according to their new status as

---

[67] 4QMMT C 27–32. Similarly, 1QS 5.21; 6.18: מעשי בתורה.
[68] See Abegg, "4QMMT" (see n. 64), 139; Dunn, "4QMMT" (see n. 64), 150 (336); Frey, "Contextualizing" (see n. 64), 756.
[69] The difference is that MMT reflects a Jewish controversy about works of the law in relation to righteousness whereas the bone of contention between Paul and Kephas (and other Christ believing Jews) is the enabling of table fellowship between Jews and Gentiles.
[70] This is supported by the observations that 4QMMT and Galatians refer to the blessings and curses from Deuteronomy 27–28 which is another important analogy (MMT C 20).
[71] See J.M.G. Barclay, *Jews in the Mediterranean Diaspora. From Alexander to Trajan (323 BCD – 117 C)* (Edinburgh: T&T Clark, 1996), 434–437. The relevant texts include Tob 1:10–11 (Tobit's fellow Jews eat from the food of the Gentiles, but Tobit himself refrains from doing so); Jdt 12:1–4, 15–19 (Judith eats her own food at the table of Holofernes); Jos.Asen. 7:1 (Joseph avoids sitting at the same table with the Egyptians); Jub. 22:19–23 (fellowship of Jews and Gentiles is strictly refused). Other texts deal with special food that Jews would accept (see below).

those who "were bought with a high price."⁷² Paul praises the Thessalonians for turning from idols to the living and true God (1Thess 1:9); the Galatians are reminded that formerly they did not know God and were enslaved to beings that by nature are not gods (Gal 4:8); he raises the issues of fornication (πορνεία) and idolatry (εἰδωλολατρία),⁷³ and he addresses some of his readers as former fornicators, idolaters, adulterers etc. (1 Cor 6:9). He demands that Gentiles respect basic rules for foreigners in a Jewish environment such as abstaining from fornication and worship of idols. The reason is that for Paul faith in Jesus Christ is indispensably linked to faith in the God of Israel.⁷⁴ Therefore, veneration of other gods or goddesses by partaking in cultic meals of pagan religious associations – Paul calls this "partaking of the table of demons" (1 Cor 10:21) – and fornication are incompatible with the faith in the one God and the one Lord.⁷⁵

As was already mentioned above, Paul, by contrast, nowhere demands that Jews should abandon their life according to the law. Instead, he insists that every believer should remain in the status in which he or she was called and live accordingly. This includes circumcision and uncircumcision, slaves and freemen as well as married and unmarried members of the community.⁷⁶ It is therefore conceivable that Jewish members of a Pauline ἐκκλησία observed the Sabbath, circumcised their male children and followed Jewish food laws at home. However, Paul, strongly opposes that such regulations are imposed on Gentile members of the ἐκκλησία. To enable table fellowship of Jews and non-Jews, Jewish Christ believers would thus have to refrain from declaring Jewish food laws as compulsory for community gatherings.⁷⁷ In principle, though, Paul shows a remarkable indif-

---

72 1 Cor 6:20; 7:23.
73 1 Thess 4:3; 1 Cor 5:1; 6:13–20; 7:2; Gal 5:19; 1 Cor 10:14–20; Gal 5:20.
74 This is also attested by the so-called Apostolic decree in Acts 15:20, 29; 21:25. See R. Deines, "Das Aposteldekret – Halacha für Heidenchristen oder christliche Rücksichtnahme auf jüdische Tabus?," in *Jewish Identity in the Greco-Roman World*, ed. J. Frey, D.R. Schwartz and S. Gripentrog, AJEC 71 (Leiden and Boston, MA: Brill, 2007), 323–395.
75 Πορνεία and εἰδωλολατρία or βρῶσις τῶν εἰδωλοθύτων are terms which describe (and condemn) sexual and religious behavior from a Jewish perspective. See Exod 34:15; Jub. 16:5, 8; 20:3–4; 22:16–17; 25:1, 7–8; 39:6; 1 En. 7:1; 8:1–3; 10:7–8; T.Reub 1:6; 3:3; 4:6–11; 5:1–7; 6:1–4; T.Sim. 5:3–4; T.Levi 9:9; T.Jud. 14:2–6; 15:1–2; 18:2; T.Dan. 5:5–6; T.Benj. 8:2; 9:1; 4 Macc 5:2; Ps.-Phoc. 31. Both attitudes or terms are connected in Exod 34:16; Lev 17:7; Num 25:1; Deut 31:16; Ezek 16:26, 28; Hos 1–3; Wis 14:12; Philo, *Decal.* 8.
76 See 1 Cor 7:17–24.
77 This would also be the logical conclusion from the Antioch incident, mentioned above. Paul does not criticize Kephas for observing food laws himself, but for imposing them on the Gentiles by making table fellowship dependent on the observation of Jewish purity rules.

ference with regard to food laws, allowing to eat whatever is offered on the meat market without raising questions (1 Cor 10:25). This shall be inspected closer by looking at two crucial passages, 1 Cor 8–10 and Rom 14.

In 1 Cor 8–10 Paul deals with the problem whether food offered to idols (εἰδωλόθυτα) may be consumed by members of the Corinthian ἐκκλησία.[78] Apparently, in the Corinthian community it was discussed whether such meat would violate the commitment to the God of Israel as the one and only God. Since the discourse (and the letter as a whole) seems to presuppose Gentile readers, it is more likely that the issue was raised by Gentile members of the Corinthian ἐκκλησία who became attracted to the God of Israel – perhaps so-called "Godfearers"[79] – and were irritated by other Gentile believers who continued eating meat sacrificed to pagan gods or goddesses and sold on the meat market. The irritation about such behavior can be explained against the background of some Jewish texts.[80] In a general statement, the letter of Aristeas mentions food regulations among those rules with which God has fenced the Jewish people in order to protect them against defilement by any abomination. In several Jewish texts, purity regulations are extended beyond the avoidance of pork meat. According to 2 Macc 5:27 Judas Maccabaeus and his companions survive

---

[78] The issue is discussed with regard to several situations: defiling the conscience of the weak (1 Cor 8:1–13); participation at sacrificial meals (10:14–22); eating meat sold on the meat market (10:25–26); invitation by an unbeliever and made aware that the meat has being offered in sacrifice (10:27–30).
[79] This is not the place for a detailed discussion of the so-called "God-fearers." It has to be noted, however, that the term, taken from the Acts of Apostles (as translation of φοβούμενοι/σεβόμενοι τὸν θεόν), is contested and the religious contours of people called "God-fearers" are blurred. I use the term in its conventional sense for non-Jews who observed Torah regulations such as Sabbath observance, abstaining from pork and other purity laws as it is attested by authors like Josephus, Epictetus, Seneca, and Juvenal (who use σεβόμενος/σεβόμενοι or θεοσεβής/θεοσεβεῖς and *metuens/metuentes*). The term θεοσεβεῖς is also attested by the well-known inscriptions from Miletus and Aphrodisias. For the discussion about the God-fearers see R.S. Kraemer, "Giving up the Godfearers," *JAJ* 5 (2014): 61–87 (who analyses the evidence for the "God-fearers" and concludes with a critical note about the use of the term); J.M. Lieu, "The Race of the God-fearers," *JTS* 46 (1995): 483–501 (who investigates in detail the terms θεοσεβής and θεοσέβεια in early Christian sources); P. Fredriksen, "Judaizing the Nations: The Ritual Demands of Paul's Gospel," *NTS* 56 (2010): 232–252; eadem, "The Question of Worship: Gods, Pagans, and the Redemption of Israel," in *Paul within Judaism. Restoring the First-Century Context of the Apostle*, ed. M.D. Nanos and M. Zetterholm (Minneapolis, MN: Fortress, 2015), 175–201.
[80] See H. Löhr, "Speisenfrage und Tora im Judentum des Zweiten Tempels und im entstehenden Christentum," *ZNW* 94 (2003): 17–37.

in the mountains eating only grass-like food to avoid defilement.[81] The book of Daniel describes how Daniel is careful not to be defiled by the food offered to him by the king.[82] Therefore, he and his fellow Jews only eat vegetables and drink water.[83] Similarly, the book of Judith mentions wine, oil, parched grain, fig cake and fine bread, as food of pious Jews, which Judith eats at the table of Holofernes whereas she refuses to eat of what is offered by Holofernes himself.[84] Philo in *Spec.* 2.20 outlines a modest way of life and mentions as simple food of poor people small cheap loaves, olives, cheese, and vegetables. This can be supplemented with some texts by Greek and Roman authors and also by Josephus who report that non-Jews were influenced by Jewish food regulations which separated them from the rest of the society.[85]

These food regulations were not derived directly from the Torah, but should prevent defilement through contact with unclean food or pagan cult.[86] This is corroborated by texts which describe the conflicts of Jews with pagan authorities about the observance of Jewish purity rules, as e. g., the resistance of pious Jews against Antiochus's IV. efforts to force Jews to violate their laws.[87] In a similar way, Philo describes how the Jewish legation in Rome is ridiculed for abstaining from pork meat.[88] As these and other texts indicate, the position of those who are described by Paul as weak or having a weak consciousness[89] in 1 Cor 8 and Rom 14 may represent groups within the community that adhere to food regulations common in the Jewish diaspora and regarded the observation of purity rules as indispensable for the distinction of Christ groups from their pagan environment.

Paul's own position in 1 Cor 8–10 and Rom 14 is characterized by a remarkable freedom towards Jewish purity concerns. In 1 Cor 8 he settles with those who have the knowledge (γνῶσις) that idols do not really exist and that there is only one God. From this insight he concludes that eating of food offered to

---

[81] Ιουδας δὲ ὁ καὶ Μακκαβαῖος δέκατός που γενηθεὶς καὶ ἀναχωρήσας εἰς τὴν ἔρημον θηρίων τρόπον ἐν τοῖς ὄρεσιν διέζη σὺν τοῖς μετ' αὐτοῦ, καὶ τὴν χορτώδη τροφὴν σιτούμενοι διετέλουν πρὸς τὸ μὴ μετασχεῖν τοῦ μολυσμοῦ.
[82] Dan 1:3–17.
[83] Dan 1:12^{LXX} Πείρασον δὴ τοὺς παῖδάς σου ἐφ' ἡμέρας δέκα, καὶ δοθήτω ἡμῖν ἀπὸ τῶν ὀσπρίων (Theod.: σπέρματα) τῆς γῆς, ὥστε κάπτειν καὶ ὑδροποτεῖν. Cf. v. 16; Esth 4:17 (C28)^{LXX}.
[84] Jdt 10:5; 12:1–4. See also Josephus, *Vita* 14: figs and nuts.
[85] J.M.G. Barclay, "'Do we undermine the Law?' A Study of Romans 14.1–15.6," in idem, *Pauline Churches and Diaspora Jews*, WUNT 275 (Tübingen: Mohr Siebeck, 2011), 37–59, here 44–46.
[86] Niebuhr, "Offene Fragen" (see n. 19), 34.
[87] 1 Macc 1:41–64; 2 Macc 6–7 and 4 Macc 4:15–6:35.
[88] Philo, *Leg.* 361–363. See Löhr, "Speisenfrage" (see n. 80), 19–21.
[89] 1 Cor 8:7–12; Rom 14:1–2.

idols should be avoided only with regard to those who do not have this knowledge. According to Rom 14 Paul presupposes a community of Christ believers consisting of members with Jewish and non-Jewish backgrounds, although these groups are not necessarily identical with the "strong" and the "weak." Rather, there may be "strong" and "weak" among Jewish and non-Jewish Christ believers. In any case, Paul's position is not aimed at abolishing Jewish food laws. Instead, he develops the view "that nothing is unclean in itself; but it is unclean for anyone who thinks it unclean" (Rom 14:14) – a perception that can be reconciled with Jewish attitudes towards purity.[90] The "strong" in Paul's view are those who do not regard clean and unclean as ontological categories, but as a matter of judgement. Similarly, in Romans 14, the weak are characterized as eating only vegetables, whereas the strong, to whom Paul counts himself, eat anything.

The issue at stake in 1 Cor 8 and Rom 14 is neither table fellowship nor the requirement of certain food regulations in the ἐκκλησία. Instead, Paul declares the observance of food laws as of only secondary importance with regard to the faith in the one God and Jesus Christ. This may be explained against a background in which table fellowship between Jews and Gentiles was not generally prohibited,[91] although Jews – particularly those in the diaspora and also Jewish members and God-fearing Gentiles in communities of Christ believers – have refrained from participating in such meals and from defiling themselves by eating unclean food. Paul's advice, furthermore, does not undermine the food regulations of the Torah. Instead he develops a view of the ἐκκλησία which consists of believers in God and Jesus Christ from different backgrounds and in which different attitudes to food regulations can exist side by side.

4 Concluding Remarks

In his letters Paul develops a distinct view of communities of believers in Jesus Christ. They are distinguished from Jews and Gentiles as "the elect" or "the saints" who are justified by their faith in Jesus Christ. This corresponds to Paul's view of the whole of humankind as being under the power of sin before

---

90 See D. Rudolph, "Paul and the Food Laws," in *Paul the Jew. Rereading the Apostle as a Figure of Second Temple Judaism*, ed. G. Boccaccini and C.A. Segovia (Minneapolis, MN: Fortress, 2016), 151–181; K. Hedner-Zetterholm, "The Question of Assumptions: Torah Observance in the First Century," in *Paul within Judaism. Restoring the First-Century Context of the Apostle*, ed. M.D. Nanos and M. Zetterholm (Minneapolis, MN: Fortress, 2015), 79–103.
91 Cf. Philo, *Leg.* 3.156; *Ios.* 201–202.

Christ and therefore in need of God's gift of justification. From this general theological and anthropological perspective, there is no difference between Jews and Gentiles, neither with regard to their past nor to their present. All have sinned and lack the glory of God (Rom 3:24), all are justified by faith in Jesus Christ.

This general perspective does, however, not lead to an equidistance of the Christ believers to Jews and Gentiles. By contrast, Paul points out that they are committed to the faith in the God of Israel that separates them from their pagan environment.

How can this result be applied to the question of whether Paul was a "Jew within Judaism"? Depending on the perspective from which the question is asked, different answers are possible. From the view of a Roman citizen or a civic authority Paul may have been regarded as a Jew who followed Jewish customs, caused trouble among his fellow Jews and even tried to convince Romans to take over Jewish customs. This perspective is described in Acts 16 to 19, even if Luke's depiction of Paul's relationship to Jews and Gentiles follows a specific agenda of portraying Paul as a faithful Jew who brought the message of Jesus to the non-Jewish world.[92] From the perspective of his Jewish contemporaries Paul may have been regarded as an apostate who not only dismissed Jewish purity rules but also endangered the integrity of Jewish communities with his message of the elimination of the differences between Jews and Gentiles. From the perspective of communities of Christ believers Paul may have been regarded as a Jew with a remarkable freedom towards the openness of God's people for Gentiles who do not even need to be circumcised or to observe the Sabbath. Paul may also have appeared to them as very restrictive and conservative with regard to regulations for sexual behavior and table fellowship with their Greek or Roman fellows. Paul himself may have answered the question, "Are you a Jew?" with: "I am an Israelite, a son of Abraham, who believes in the one and only God and in his son Jesus Christ."

Finally, how can Paul's theology and mission be related to the "parting of the ways"? The observations of this article suggest that this metaphor should be used with caution (if at all), because it imposes a later perspective on the historical situation of Paul and his communities. It was not Paul's aim to establish a new pattern of religion besides Judaism nor to criticize Judaism for separating itself from the Gentiles. Paul's activity and thinking were, in the first instance, aimed at convincing Gentiles to convert to the God of Israel and to faith in

---

[92] For the portrait of Paul in Acts see J. Schröter, "Die Paulusdarstellung der Apostelgeschichte," in *Paulus Handbuch*, ed. F.W. Horn (Tübingen: Mohr Siebeck, 2013), 542–551; D. Marguerat, *Paul in Acts and in His Letters*, WUNT 310 (Tübingen: Mohr Siebeck, 2013).

Jesus Christ and to live accordingly. Only in his letter to the Romans does he develop a more general perspective on the gospel for Jews and Gentiles. Here he argues that Israel will be saved in two steps: first, the community of believers in Jesus Christ from Jews and Gentiles and second, the rest of Israel by another saving activity of the "deliverer from Zion."[93]

For Paul it is a necessary consequence of the gospel for Jews and Gentiles that different attitudes towards Torah regulations and Jewish purity rules exist side by side in the ἐκκλησία and should not jeopardize the integrity of the community. He demands that Gentiles must abandon their former way of life and live according to the basic rules for believers in the God of Israel, and he expects Jews not to impose Torah regulations on their non-Jewish fellows in the community. The relationship between Jewish and non-Jewish believers in the community according to Paul is, therefore, more complex than the model of a "parting of the ways" implies. This model is in danger of projecting a teleological development from Paul to the later separation of Jews and Gentiles that is historically questionable. It may instead be more appropriate to place Paul's view of the gospel for Jews and Gentiles in the wider context of the social, religious and ethical world of his addressees. Such an approach leads to a more nuanced view of Paul's theology and the situation of his communities in their Jewish and Greco-Roman context.

Bibliography

Abegg, M. G., "Paul, 'Works of the Law' and MMT," *BAR* 20.6 (1994): 52–55.
Abegg, M. G., "4QMMT C 27, 31 and 'Works Righteousness'," *DSD* 6 (1999): 139–147.
Bachmann, M., "Rechtfertigung und Gesetzeswerke bei Paulus," *ThZ* 49 (1993): 1–33.
Bachmann, M., ed., *Lutherische und neue Paulusperspektive. Beiträge zu einem Schlüsselproblem der gegenwärtigen exegetischen Diskussion*, WUNT 182 (Tübingen: Mohr Siebeck, 2005).
Bar-Asher Siegal, M., *Early Christian Monastic Literature and the Babylonian Talmud* (Cambridge: Cambridge University Press, 2013).
Barclay, J. M. G., *Jews in the Mediterranean Diaspora. From Alexander to Trajan (323 BCD–117 C)* (Edinburgh: T&T Clark, 1996).
Barclay, J. M. G., "'Do we undermine the Law?' A Study of Romans 14.1–15.6," in *Pauline Churches and Diaspora Jews*, idem, WUNT 275 (Tübingen: Mohr Siebeck, 2011), 37–59.
Benbassa, E., "Otherness, Openness and Rejection in Jewish Context," *JISMOR* 5 (2010): 16–25.

---

[93] Rom 11:1–32.

Bird, M. F., *An Anomalous Jew. Paul among Jews, Greeks, and Romans* (Grand Rapids, MI: Eerdmans, 2016).

Boccaccini, G., "Introduction: The Three Paths to Salvation of Paul the Jew (with responses by Albert I. Baumgarten and Daniel Boyarin)," in *Paul the Jew. Rereading the Apostle as a Figure of Second Temple Judaism*, ed. idem and C. A. Segovia (Minneapolis, MN: Fortress, 2016), 1–29.

Boyarin, D., *A Radical Jew. Paul and the Politics of Identity* (Berkeley, CA: University of California Press, 1994).

Boyarin, D., "Als Christen noch Juden waren. Überlegungen zu den jüdisch-christlichen Ursprüngen," *Kul* 16 (2001): 112–129.

Boyarin, D., "Semantic Differences; or: 'Judaism'/'Christianity'," in *The Ways that Never Parted. Jews and Christians in Late Antiquity and the Early Middle Ages*, ed. A. H. Becker and A. Y. Reed, TSAJ 95 (Tübingen: Mohr Siebeck, 2003), 65–85.

Boyarin, D., *Border Lines. The Partition of Judaeo-Christianity* (Philadelphia, PA: University of Pennsylvania, 2006).

Boyarin, D., "*Ioudaismos* within Paul. A modified Reading of Gal 1:13–14," in *The Message of Paul the Apostle within Second Temple Judaism*, ed. F. Abel (Lanham et al.: Lexington Books/Fortress Academic, 2019), 167–178.

Bultmann, R., *Theology of the New Testament*, 2 vols. (London: SCM Press, 1952, 1955).

Carleton Paget, J., "Jewish Christianity," in *The Cambridge History of Judaism*, vol. 3: *The Early Roman Period*, ed. W. Horbury, W. D. Davies and J. Sturdy (Cambridge: Cambridge University Press, 1999), 731–775.

Cohen, S. J. D., "The Ways that Parted: Jews, Christians, and Jewish-Christians, ca 100–150 CE," in *Jews and Christians in the First and Second Centuries: The Interbellum 70–132 CE*, ed. J. Schwartz and P. J. Tomson, CRINT 15 (Leiden and Boston, MA: Brill, 2017), 307–339.

Deines, R., "Das Aposteldekret – Halacha für Heidenchristen oder christliche Rücksichtnahme auf jüdische Tabus?," in *Jewish Identity in the Greco-Roman World*, ed. J. Frey, D. R. Schwartz, and S. Gripentrog, AJEC 71 (Leiden and Boston, MA: Brill, 2007), 323–395.

Doering, L., *Ancient Jewish Letters and the Beginnings of Christian Epistolography*, WUNT 298 (Tübingen: Mohr Siebeck, 2012).

Doering, L., "4QMMT and the Letters of Paul: Selected Aspects of Mutual Illumination," in *The Dead Sea Scrolls and Pauline Literature*, ed. J.-S. Rey, STDJ 102 (Leiden and Boston, MA: Brill, 2014), 69–87.

Dunn, J. D. G., *The Partings of the Ways between Christianity and Judaism and their Significance for the Character of Christianity*, 2nd ed. (London: SCM Press, 2006)

Dunn, J. D. G., ed., *Jews and Christians: The Parting of the Ways AD 70 to 135*, WUNT 66 (Tübingen: Mohr Siebeck, 1992).

Dunn, J. D. G., "4QMMT and Galatians," *NTS* 43 (1997): 147–153. (repr. in idem, *The New Perspective on Paul. Collected Essays*, WUNT 185 [Tübingen: Mohr Siebeck, 2005], 333–339.)

Dunn, J. D. G., "Noch einmal: 'Works of the Law': The Dialogue Continues," in *Fair Play: Diversity and Conflicts in Early Christianity. FS H. Räisänen*, ed. I. Dunderberg and C. Tuckett (Leiden: Brill, 2002), 273–290. (repr. in idem, *The New Perspective on Paul. Collected Essays*, WUNT 185 [Tübingen: Mohr Siebeck, 2005], 407–422.)

Dunn, J. D. G., *The New Perspective on Paul. Collected Essays*, WUNT 185 (Tübingen: Mohr Siebeck, 2005).
Dunn, J. D. G., "The New Perspective: Whence, What and Wither," in idem, *The New Perspective on Paul. Collected Essays*, WUNT 185 (Tübingen: Mohr Siebeck, 2005), 1–88.
Dunn, J. D. G., *Beginning from Jerusalem*, vol. 2 of *Christianity in the Making* (Grand Rapids, MI, and Cambridge: Eerdmans, 2009).
Dunn, J. D. G., "A New Perspective on the New Perspective on Paul," *EC* 4 (2013): 157–182.
Dunn, J. D. G., *Neither Jew nor Greek. A Contested Identity*, vol. 3 of *Christianity in the Making* (Grand Rapids, MI, and Cambridge: Eerdmans, 2015).
Foakes Jackson, F. J., ed., *The Parting of the Roads. Studies in the Development of Judaism and Early Christianity* (London: Arnold, 1912).
Fredriksen, P., "What 'Parting of the Ways'? Jews, Gentiles, and the Ancient Mediterranean City," in *The Ways that Never Parted. Jews and Christians in Late Antiquity and the Early Middle Ages*, ed. A. H. Becker and A. Y. Reed, TSAJ 95 (Tübingen: Mohr Siebeck, 2003), 35–63.
Fredriksen, P., "Mandatory Retirement: Ideas in the study of Christian origins whose time has come to go," *SR* 35.2 (2006): 231–246.
Fredriksen, P., "Judaizing the Nations: The Ritual Demands of Paul's Gospel," *NTS* 56 (2010): 232–252.
Fredriksen, P., "The Question of Worship: Gods, Pagans, and the Redemption of Israel," in *Paul within Judaism. Restoring the First-Century Context of the Apostle*, ed. M. D. Nanos and M. Zetterholm (Minneapolis, MN: Fortress, 2015), 175–201.
Frey, J., "Paul's Jewish Identity," in *Jewish Identity in the Greco-Roman World*, ed. idem, D. R. Schwartz, and S. Gripentrog, AJEC 71 (Leiden and Boston, MA: Brill, 2007), 286–321.
Frey, J., "Das Judentum des Paulus," in *Paulus: Leben – Umwelt – Werk – Briefe*, ed. O. Wischmeyer, 2nd ed. (Tübingen and Basel: Francke, 2012), 25–65.
Frey, J., "Contextualizing Paul's 'Works of the Law': MMT in New Testament Scholarship," in *Qumran, Early Judaism, and New Testament Interpretation. Kleine Schriften III*, ed. J. N. Cerone, WUNT 424 (Tübingen: Mohr Siebeck, 2019), 743–762.
Gathercole, S. J., *Where is Boasting? Early Jewish Soteriology and Paul's Response in Romans 1–5* (Grand Rapids, MI, and Cambridge: Eerdmans, 2002).
Hedner-Zetterholm, K., "The Question of Assumptions: Torah Observance in the First Century," in *Paul within Judaism. Restoring the First-Century Context of the Apostle*, ed. M. D. Nanos and M. Zetterholm (Minneapolis, MN: Fortress, 2015), 79–103.
Heemstra, M., *The Fiscus Iudaicus and the Parting of the Ways*, WUNT II/277 (Tübingen: Mohr Siebeck, 2010).
Hengel, M., "Die Synagogeninschrift von Stobi (mit einem Anhang von Hanswulf Bloedhorn)," in idem, *Judaica et Hellenistica. Kleine Schriften I*, WUNT 90 (Tübingen: Mohr Siebeck, 1996), 91–130.
Hengel, M., *Die Urgemeinde und das Judenchristentum. Geschichte des frühen Christentums*, vol. 2 (Tübingen: Mohr Siebeck, 2019).
Hengel, M., and A. M. Schwemer, *Paulus zwischen Damaskus und Antiochien. Die unbekannten Jahre des Apostels*, WUNT 108 (Tübingen: Mohr Siebeck, 1998).
Kato, T., "4QMMT Reconsidered: Is it really a Sectarian Text?," *JISMOR* 15 (2020): 21–33.
Koch, D.-A., *Die Schrift als Zeuge des Evangeliums. Untersuchungen zur Verwendung und zum Verständnis der Schrift bei Paulus*, BHT 69 (Tübingen: Mohr Siebeck, 1986).

Konradt, M., "Zur Datierung des sogenannten antiochenischen Zwischenfalls," *ZNW* 102 (2011): 19–39.
Korner, R. J., *The Origin and Meaning of Ekklêsia in the Early Jesus Movement*, AJEC 98 (Leiden and Boston, MA: Brill, 2017).
Kraemer, R. S., "Giving up the Godfearers," *JAJ* 5 (2014): 61–87.
Kraus, W., *Zwischen Antiochia und Jerusalem. Die "Hellenisten", Paulus und die Aufnahme der Heiden ins Gottesvolk*, SBS 179 (Stuttgart: Katholisches Bibelwerk, 1999).
Lietzmann, H., "Notizen," *ZNW* 32 (1933): 93–95.
Lieu, J. M., "The Race of the God-fearers," *JTS* 46 (1995): 483–501.
Lieu, J. M., "The Parting of the Ways: Theological Construct or Historical Reality?," in *Neither Jew nor Greek. Constructing Early Christianity*, ed. eadem, 2nd ed. (London et al.: T&T Clark, 2016), 31–49.
Lindemann, A., "Paulus – Pharisäer und Apostel," in idem, *Glauben, Handeln, Verstehen. Studien zur Auslegung des Neuen Testaments,* vol. 2, WUNT 282 (Tübingen: Mohr Siebeck, 2011), 33–72.
Löhr, H., "Speisenfrage und Tora im Judentum des Zweiten Tempels und im entstehenden Christentum," *ZNW* 94 (2003): 17–37.
Longenecker, R. N., ed., *The Road from Damascus* (Grand Rapids, MI, and Cambridge: Eerdmans, 1997).
Marguerat, D., *Paul in Acts and in His Letters*, WUNT 310 (Tübingen: Mohr Siebeck, 2013).
Nanos, M. D., *The Mystery of Romans. The Jewish Context of Paul's Letter* (Minneapolis, MN: Fortress, 1996).
Nanos, M. D., "Introduction," in *Paul within Judaism. Restoring the First-Century Context of the Apostle*, ed. M. D. Nanos and M. Zetterholm (Minneapolis, MN: Fortress, 2015), 1–29.
Nanos, M. D., "Paul *and* Judaism: Why not *Paul's Judaism?*," in idem, *Reading Paul within Judaism. Collected Essays,* vol. 1 (Eugene, OR: Cascade Books, 2017), 3–59.
Nicklas, T., *Jews and Christians? Second Century 'Christian' Perspectives on the 'Parting of the Ways'*, Annual Deichmann Lectures 2013 (Tübingen: Mohr Siebeck, 2014).
Nicklas, T., "Parting of the Ways? Probleme eines Konzepts," in *Juden – Heiden – Christen? Religiöse Inklusion und Exklusion in Kleinasien bis Decius*, ed. S. Alkier and H. Leppin, WUNT 400 (Tübingen: Mohr Siebeck, 2018), 21–42.
Niebuhr, K.-W., *Heidenapostel aus Israel*, WUNT 62 (Tübingen: Mohr Siebeck, 1992).
Niebuhr, K.-W., "'Judentum' und 'Christentum' bei Paulus und Ignatius von Antiochien," *ZNW* 85 (1994): 218–233.
Niebuhr, K.-W., "Offene Fragen zur Gesetzespraxis bei Paulus und seinen Gemeinden (Sabbat, Speisegebote, Beschneidung)," *BThZ* 25 (2008): 16–51.
Overman, J. A., *Matthew's Gospel and Formative Judaism. The Social World of the Matthean Community* (Minneapolis, MN: Fortress, 1990).
Petersen, A. K., "At the End of the Road. Reflections on a Popular Scholarly Metaphor," in *The Formation of the Early Church*, ed. J. Ådna, WUNT 183 (Tübingen: Mohr Siebeck, 2005), 45–72.
Rabkin, Y. M., and H. Rabkin, "Perspectives on the Muslim Other in Jewish Tradition," *JISMOR* 5 (2010): 26–45.

Reed, A. Y., and A. H. Becker, "Introduction: Traditional Models and New Directions," in *The Ways that Never Parted. Jews and Christians in Late Antiquity and the Early Middle Ages*, ed. A. H. Becker and A. Y. Reed, TSAJ 95 (Tübingen: Mohr Siebeck, 2003), 1–33.

Reinhartz, A., "A Fork in the Road or a Multi-Lane Highway? New Perspectives on the 'Parting of the Ways' Between Judaism and Christianity," in *The Changing Faces of Judaism, Christianity, and other Greco-Roman Religions in Antiquity*, ed. I. H. Henderson and G. S. Oegema, JSHRZ Studien 2 (Gütersloh: Gütersloher Verlagshaus, 2006), 280–295.

Reinhartz, A., "We, You, They: Boundary Language in 4QMMT and the New Testament Epistles," in *Text, Thought, and Practice in Qumran and Early Christianity*, ed. R. A. Clements and D. R. Schwartz, STDJ 84 (Leiden: Brill, 2009), 89–105.

Reinhartz, A., "'Common Judaism,' 'The Parting of the Ways,' and 'The Johannine Community'," in *Orthodoxy, Liberalism, and Adaptation. Essays on Ways of Worldmaking. Times of Change from Biblical, Historical and Systematic Perspectives*, ed. B. Becking, STAR 5 (Leiden and Boston, MA: Brill, 2011), 69–88.

Rudolph, D., "Paul and the Food Laws," in *Paul the Jew. Rereading the Apostle as a Figure of Second Temple Judaism*, ed. G. Boccaccini and C. A. Segovia (Minneapolis, MN: Fortress, 2016), 151–181.

Runesson, A., "Rethinking Early Jewish–Christian Relations: Matthean Community History as Pharisaic Intragroup Conflict," *JBL* 127 (2008): 95–132.

Runesson, A., "The Question of Terminology: The Architecture of Contemporary Discussions on Paul," in *Paul within Judaism. Restoring the First-Century Context of the Apostle*, ed. M. D. Nanos and M. Zetterholm (Minneapolis, MN: Fortress, 2015), 53–77.

Sanders, E. P., *Paul and Palestinian Judaism. A Comparison of Patterns of Religion* (London: SCM Press, 1977).

Schäfer, P., *Die Geburt des Judentums aus dem Geist des Christentums. Fünf Vorlesungen zur Entstehung des rabbinischen Judentums*, Tria Corda 6 (Tübingen: Mohr Siebeck, 2010).

Schäfer, P., *Anziehung und Abstoßung. Juden und Christen in den ersten Jahrhunderten ihrer Begegnung*, Lucasz-Preis 2014 (Tübingen: Mohr Siebeck, 2015).

Schäfer, P., *Zwei Götter im Himmel. Gottesvorstellungen in der jüdischen Antike* (München: Beck, 2017).

Schnelle, U., *Paulus. Leben und Denken*, 2nd ed. (Berlin and Boston, MA: de Gruyter, 2014).

Schnelle, U., *Die ersten 100 Jahre des Christentums 30–130 n. Chr. Die Entstehungsgeschichte einer Weltreligion*, 2nd ed. (Göttingen: UTB, 2016).

Schnelle, U., *Die getrennten Wege von Römern, Juden und Christen. Religionspolitik im 1. Jahrhundert n. Chr.* (Tübingen: Mohr Siebeck, 2019).

Schröter, J., "Paulus als Modell christlicher Zeugenschaft: Apg 9,15f. und 28,30f. als Rahmen der lukanischen Paulusdarstellung und Rezeption des 'historischen' Paulus," in *Reception of Paulinism in Acts – Réception du Paulinisme dans les Actes des Apôtres*, ed. D. Marguerat, BETL 229 (Leuven: Peeters, 2009), 53–80.

Schröter, J., "Die Paulusdarstellung der Apostelgeschichte," in *Paulus Handbuch*, ed. F. W. Horn (Tübingen: Mohr Siebeck, 2013), 542–551.

Segal, A. F., *Rebecca's Children. Judaism and Christianity in the Roman World* (Cambridge, MA, and London: Harvard University Press, 1986).

Segal, A. F., *Paul the Convert. The Apostolate and Apostasy of Saul the Pharisee* (New Haven, CT, and London: Yale University Press, 1990).

Sheinfeld, S., "Who is the righteous Remnant in Romans 9–11? The Concept of Remnant in Early Jewish Literature and Paul's Letter to the Romans," in *Paul within Judaism. Restoring the First-Century Context of the Apostle*, ed. M. D. Nanos and M. Zetterholm (Minneapolis, MN: Fortress, 2015), 33–50.

Staples, J. A., *The Idea of Israel in Second Temple Judaism: A New Theory of People, Exile, and Israelite Identity* (Cambridge University Press, forthcoming 2020).

Theissen, G., "Judentum und Christentum bei Paulus," in *Paulus und das antike Judentum*, ed. M. Hengel and U. Heckel, WUNT 58 (Tübingen: Mohr Siebeck, 1991), 331–356.

Tilly, M., "Paulus und die antike jüdische Schriftauslegung," *KuD* 63 (2017): 157–181.

Tomson, P. J., *Paul and the Jewish Law. Halakha in the Letters of the Apostle to the Gentiles*, CRINT 3/1 (Assen: Van Gorcum; Minneapolis, MN: Fortress, 1990).

Tomson, P. J., "Paul and his Place in Judaism," in idem, *Studies on Jews and Christians in the First and Second Centuries*, WUNT 418 (Tübingen: Mohr Siebeck, 2019), 317–497.

van de Sandt, H., ed., *Matthew and the Didache. Two Documents from the Same Jewish-Christian Milieu?* (Assen: Royal van Gorcum; Minneapolis, MN: Fortress, 2005).

Wander, B., *Trennungsprozesse zwischen Frühem Christentum und Judentum*, 2nd ed., TANZ 16 (Tübingen: Francke, 1997).

Watson, F., *Paul, Judaism and the Gentiles. Beyond the New Perspective* (Grand Rapids, MI, and Cambridge: Eerdmans, 2008).

Westerholm, S., *Perspectives Old and New on Paul. The 'Lutheran' Paul and his critics* (Grand Rapids, MI, and Cambridge: Eerdmans, 2004).

Wilk, F., *Die Bedeutung des Jesajabuches für Paulus*, FRLANT 179 (Göttingen: Vandenhoeck & Ruprecht, 1998).

Wilk, F., and J. R. Wagner, eds., *Between Gospel and Election. Explorations in the Interpretation of Romans 9–11*, WUNT 257 (Tübingen: Mohr Siebeck, 2010).

Wolter, M., "Die Wirklichkeit des Glaubens. Ein Versuch zur Bedeutung des Glaubens bei Paulus," in *Glaube. Das Verständnis des Glaubens im frühen Christentum und seiner jüdischen und hellenistisch-römischen Umwelt*, ed. J. Frey et al., WUNT 373 (Tübingen: Mohr Siebeck, 2017), 347–367.

Wrede, W., *Paul* (London: Green, 1907).

Zetterholm, M., "Purity and Anger: Gentiles and Idolatry in Antioch," *IJRR* 1 (2005): 1–24.

Matthias Konradt
Matthew within or outside of Judaism? From the 'Parting of the Ways' Model to a Multifaceted Approach

Abstract: In der "neuen Matthäusperspektive" findet die vieldiskutierte Frage der Verortung der matthäischen Gemeinden innerhalb oder außerhalb des Judentums eine dezidierte Antwort zugunsten der ersten Alternative. Wird hier auf der einen Seite zu Recht das jüdische Kolorit des Matthäusevangeliums betont, so ist auf der anderen Seite eine empfindliche Vernachlässigung nicht nur der Bedeutung der Völkermission für das Verständnis der matthäischen Gruppen, sondern auch ihrer Vernetzung innerhalb der christusgläubigen Bewegung und schließlich ihrer Einbettung in umfassendere gesellschaftliche Kontexte zu verzeichnen. Nicht zuletzt ist die Alternative, die matthäischen Gruppen entweder innerhalb oder außerhalb des Judentums zu verorten, mit ihrer binären Logik, die ebenso das Modell des "Parting of the Ways" charakterisiert, kaum geeignet, die komplexe Koexistenz von Facetten einer tiefgehenden Integration in das Judentum mit Momenten organisatorischer und theologischer Eigenständigkeit in der nötigen Differenziertheit einzufangen und die Aspekte wechselseitiger Beeinflussungen und produktiver Konkurrenz innerhalb des umfassenderen Beziehungsnetzwerkes der matthäischen Gemeinden, die insbesondere die Verbindung zu anderen christusgläubigen Gruppen (an anderen Orten) einschließt, einzuordnen und zu gewichten.

Keywords: Matthew within Judaism, Parting of the Ways, Torah, Gentile Mission, circumcision

In the last three to four decades of Matthean research, a *new perspective* on Matthew's Gospel localizing Matthew firmly within Judaism has gradually emerged. As is the case with the new perspective on Paul, there are of course, first, still some dissenting voices and, second, there is some variety within this new perspective on Matthew. I would categorize my own understanding of Matthew as part of this new perspective,[1] but I do not belong to its 'radical wing.' Rather,

---
[1] See my monograph *Israel, Kirche und die Völker im Matthäusevangelium*, WUNT 215 (Tübingen: Mohr Siebeck, 2007) and the revised English version *Israel, Church, and the Gentiles in the Gospel of Matthew*, trans. by K. Ess, BMSEC 2 (Waco, TX: Baylor University Press, 2014), further my commentary *Das Evangelium nach Matthäus*, NTD 1 (Göttingen: Vandenhoeck & Ru-

I think – and this might be a third point of convergence with the new perspective on Paul – that it is necessary to move beyond the new perspective.

If we look for an overview of Matthean scholarship as a whole, the common denominator is identified well with a quote from Donald Senior, who noted the *magnus consensus* in the year 1999: "Matthew's interface with Judaism [...] is the fundamental key to determining the social context and theological perspective of this gospel."[2] But this minimal definition also includes approaches according to which Matthew already looks back on his own group's painful process of separation from Judaism and seeks to work through this process, a position that has been prominently supported by Ulrich Luz.[3] In this view, the sharp anti-Pharisaic polemic of the Gospel of Matthew is read against the backdrop of a 'post-decision conflict.' Differently, in the perspective that locates Matthew within Judaism the vehemence of the conflict with the Pharisees is regarded as an indication of a current conflict that ought to be categorized as a debate taking place within Judaism,[4] which can be historically located in the context of the Jewish reformation processes in the aftermath of the Roman-Jewish War. This position, which was largely initiated in the 1990s through the works of Andrew Overman and Anthony Saldarini,[5] has been taken up by David Sim,[6] among others, and notably pursued by Anders Runesson[7] and most recently by John Kampen.[8] These ap-

---

precht, 2015), and the slightly revised English version *The Gospel according to Matthew: A Commentary*, trans. by E. Boring (Waco, TX: Baylor University Press, 2020), and finally my collection of essays *Studien zum Matthäusevangelium*, WUNT 358 (Tübingen: Mohr Siebeck, 2016).

2 D. Senior, "Between Two Worlds. Gentiles and Jewish Christians in Matthew's Gospel," *CBQ* 61 (1999): 1–23, here 5 (cf. also D. Senior, "Matthew at the Crossroads of Early Christianity. An Introductory Assessment," in *The Gospel of Matthew at the Crossroads of Early Christianity*, ed. D. Senior, BETL 243 [Leuven: Peeters, 2011], 3–23, here 6–15). In addition to Senior, see for example U. Luz, *Das Evangelium nach Matthäus, Vol. 1: Mt 1–7*, 5th ed., EKK 1.1 (Düsseldorf and Zürich: Benziger; Neukirchen-Vluyn: Neukirchener Verlag, 2002), 85–89.

3 See Luz, *Evangelium nach Matthäus* I[5] (see n. 2), 96; U. Luz, "Der Antijudaismus im Matthäusevangelium als historisches und theologisches Problem. Eine Skizze," *EvT* 53 (1993): 310–327, here 319.

4 Cf. above all J.A. Overman, *Matthew's Gospel and Formative Judaism: The Social World of the Matthean Community* (Minneapolis, MN: Fortress, 1990), 35–38, 68–70, 79–90, 115–116, and A.J. Saldarini, *Matthew's Christian-Jewish Community*, CSHJ (Chicago, IL, and London: The University of Chicago Press, 1994), 44–67.

5 See the references in note 4.

6 D.C. Sim, *The Gospel of Matthew and Christian Judaism: The History and Social Setting of the Matthean Community*, SNTW (Edinburgh: T&T Clark, 1998).

7 A. Runesson, *Divine Wrath and Salvation in Matthew: The Narrative World in the First Gospel* (Minneapolis, MN: Fortress, 2016). See also idem, "Rethinking Early Jewish–Christian Relations: Matthean Community History as Pharisaic Intergroup Conflict," *JBL* 127 (2008): 95–132; idem,

proaches, which consequently tend to prefer to designate the Matthean communities using the label "Christian" or "Matthean *Judaism*" instead of "Jewish *Christianity*,"[9] share both an emphasis on the Jewish thought found in Matthew and a substantial marginalization of Matthew's universalistic features, which other scholars regard as the true aim of the Gospel.

In my opinion, the marginalization of these universalistic features constitutes one of the points in which the new perspective outlined here can be criticized, for it can hardly be meaningfully disputed that the opening of salvation for gentiles was an essential concern for the first evangelist. When one thinks in the established lines of thought in the debate about the contextualization of the Matthean group(s), this raises the question of whether a substantial inclusion of Matthean universalism in the overall picture fundamentally contradicts locating the Matthean group within Judaism, or is in fact entirely compatible with this view. It seems to me, however, that the usual binary logic of this simple alternative, according to which the Matthean believers in Christ are located either within or outside of Judaism – in metaphorical terms: either *intra* or *extra muros* – leads us astray. This is not just about the fact that the *intra/extra muros* alternative is to some extent a question of perspective and the *muri* thus turn out to be "cognitive wandering dunes."[10] Instead, the central point is that this simple alternative is not well-suited to adequately capturing the complex historical circumstances in which Matthew came to be.

This simultaneously raises an objection to the metaphor of the 'Parting of the Ways'[11] – irrespective of whether one focuses on convergences and divergen-

---

"Judging Gentiles in the Gospel of Matthew. Between 'Othering' and Inclusion," in *Jesus, Matthew's Gospel and Early Christianity: Studies in Memory of G. N. Stanton*, ed. D.M. Gurtner, J. Willitts, and R.A. Burridge, LNTS 435 (London and New York, NY: T&T Clark, 2011), 133–151.
8 J. Kampen, *Matthew within Sectarian Judaism*, AYBRL (New Haven, CT, and London: Yale University Press, 2019).
9 For a critical discussion of these labels see W. Carter, "Matthew's Gospel: Jewish Christianity, Christian Judaism, or Neither?," in *Jewish Christianity Reconsidered: Rethinking Ancient Groups and Texts*, ed. M. Jackson-McCabe (Minneapolis, MN: Fortress, 2007), 155–179.
10 Thus the apt description by K. Backhaus, "Entgrenzte Himmelsherrschaft: Zur Entdeckung der paganen Welt im Matthäusevangelium," in *"Dies ist das Buch ...". Das Matthäusevangelium. Interpretation – Rezeption – Rezeptionsgeschichte. Für H. Frankemölle*, ed. R. Kampling (Paderborn et al.: Schöningh, 2004), 75–103, here 79 (in German: "kognitive Wanderdünen").
11 For an early critique see J.M. Lieu, "'The Partings of the Ways': Theological Construct or Historical Reality?," *JSNT* 56 (1994): 101–119 (repr. in J.M. Lieu, *Neither Jew Nor Greek? Constructing Early Christianity*, SNTW [London and New York, NY: T&T Clark, 2002], 11–29). See further the discussion in A. Reinhartz, "A Fork in the Road or a Multi-Lane Highway? New Perspectives on the 'Parting of the Ways' Between Judaism and Christianity," in *The Changing Face of Judaism, Christianity, and Other Greco-Roman Religions in Antiquity*, ed. I.H. Henderson and G.S. Oe-

ces of theological systems,¹² on themes that are identified as core topics, such as monotheism, election, Torah and Temple, as James Dunn once proposed,¹³ or on social contacts and interaction or whether one tries to integrate both aspects. The basic problem is that the 'Parting of the Ways' approach also essentially operates within a binary logic; a group is either in or out. This binary logic is further burdened by the assumption of monodirectionality: a once-shared path is bifurcated into two ways that diverge from this point on. But as I will try to show in this essay with regard to the Gospel of Matthew, there is a complex evidence, with different aspects pointing to different directions. There are indicators for organizational and institutional autonomy, and there are distinctive elements in the convictions of the Christ-believers, but there are also facets of (deep) integration into and interconnectedness with the Jewish parent body; there is mutual influence and productive competition. Moreover, the 'Parting of the Ways' model tends to treat the relationship between the Matthean communities and the Jewish parent body from only one perspective – in isolation from other aspects of the communities' social relations.

In the following discussion, I will begin with a larger two-part section that will first examine the evidence that illuminates the Jewish context of the Matthean group and pursue the question of the relationship to Judaism that this evidence reveals. In a second step, the universalistic features of the Matthean Jesus story will be considered in terms of the extent to which they indicate anything about the social location of the Matthean group. Third, the aspect of inner-Christian belonging will be considered.

---

gema, JSHRZ.St 2 (Gütersloh: Gütersloher Verlagshaus, 2006), 280–295, esp. 281–288; A.Y. Reed and A.H. Becker, "Introduction: Traditional Models and New Directions," in *The Ways that Never Parted: Jews and Christians in Late Antiquity and the Early Middle Ages*, ed. A.H. Becker and A.Y. Reed, TSAJ 95 (Tübingen: Mohr Siebeck, 2003), 1–33, esp. 16–24.

12 A fundamental problem here is the fact that a decision about whether the ways have parted or not always implies an evaluation of which thematic elements should be given what amount of weight, or how one weighs points of convergence and divergence. Where theological criteria serve to justify the parting of the ways, there is often a tendency to foreground necessary incompatibilities between what can still be regarded as Jewish and the Christian belief system or take them as absolute. Cf. E.K. Broadhead's critical remarks on the 'Parting of the Ways' model: "Almost without exception, this model presumes that there was a sense of inevitability to this separation: something within the teaching of Jesus or Paul or Christianity was ultimately incompatible with any form of Judaism that survived" (*Jewish Ways of Following Jesus: Redrawing the Religious Map of Antiquity*, WUNT 266 [Tübingen: Mohr Siebeck, 2010], 359).

13 Cf. J.D.G. Dunn, *The Partings of the Ways. Between Christianity and Judaism and their Significance for the Character of Christianity* (London: SCM; Philadelphia, PA: Trinity Press International, 1991). Dunn's plural "partings" corresponds to the plurality of core topics.

1 The Matthean Group's Relation to Judaism

If one wants to draw conclusions from a narrative text about the historical location of the group represented by that text, or more precisely, from a factual narrative such as the Gospel of Matthew, a methodological warning first be given: references to the community situation do not emerge from such a narrative in the same way as they do, for example, in some Pauline letters. Inferences are therefore to be drawn with extreme caution. For instance, the fact that the main protagonists of the narrative are Jews hardly provides a clear indication of the evangelist's social location in and of itself, since this fact is simply dictated by the historical foundation of the narrative. One can only attempt to carefully draw conclusions from the *manner in which* the narrative is told, from its tendencies that reveal the narrator's concerns, or from conspicuous details. A substantial result is obtained when a significant number of textual aspects come together in harmony with one another. This is, in my opinion, the case in the Gospel of Matthew. The following considerations are divided into two steps. First, I will discuss the Jewish foundation of the Matthean Jesus story and then, on this basis, turn to the question of the extent to which Judaism appears as the *current* context of the Matthean communities.

1.1 The Jewish Foundation of the Matthean Jesus Story

In terms of reception history, as part of the New Testament the Gospel of Matthew is a foundational document of Christianity. However, this text contains a whole series of indications that the evangelist and his group were rooted in a Jewish milieu. For this reason, one can say that the Gospel of Matthew is not only a foundational document of Christianity, but from a 'history of religions' perspective is also an important witness to Jewish religious history. I limit myself here to three central pieces of evidence:

First: Matthew tells the story of Jesus from 1:1 to 28:20 with constant reference to Israel's Scriptures.[14] The well-known fulfillment quotations[15] are just one especially conspicuous expression of the relevance ascribed to Israel's Scriptures in the Matthean Jesus story as a whole. Alongside these are not only a ser-

---

[14] For an overview cf. M. Konradt, "Israel's Scripture in Matthew," in *The Old Testament in the New: Israel's Scriptures in the New Testament and other Early Christian Writings*, ed. M. Henze and D. Lincicum (Grand Rapids, MI: Eerdmans, forthcoming).
[15] Matt 1:22–23; 2:15, 17–18, 23; 4:14–16; 8:17; 12:17–21; 13:35; 21:4–5; 27:9–10.

ies of further explicit quotations, but above all a multitude of allusions, all of which guide the reader to consider the Jesus story within the horizon of Scripture: the Matthean Jesus story rings out within the resonant space of Scripture, and it acquires a deeper timbre when it is heard within this resonant space. Not only is Jesus's appearance revealed and illuminated by Scripture, but the authorities' resistance to Jesus is also given contours and categorized. The criticism from an Ezekiel or Jeremiah raised against the bad shepherds of the people (Ezek 34; Jer 23:1–4) is realized in the authorities,[16] and they resemble the godless in Psalm 22 who mock the righteous (Matt 27:43),[17] to name only two examples. In addition, appeals to Scripture also play a significant role in justifying the expansion of salvation to include gentiles[18] and thus demonstrate that this expansion is not something completely new taking place, but rather the fulfillment of something that was always inherent in God's history with Israel.

The scriptural references in Matthew are thus so dense that, in my opinion, one must assume that the final form of the Gospel is the result of a longer process of reflection by a Christ-believing Jewish group surrounding or at least with the evangelist – a group that, on the one hand, articulated in its gatherings the Jesus tradition that was handed down to them (with the scriptural quotations and allusions it already contained) and, on the other hand, reflected on Scripture intensely, took both entities in close reference to one another, and interpreted each in light of the other.[19] This extends to the point that the reflection on Scrip-

---

16 Cf. Konradt, *Israel, Church, and the Gentiles* (see n. 1), 38–39. On the central relevance of Ezek 34 as a reference text for Matthew, see J.P. Heil, "Ezekiel 34 and the Narrative Strategy of the Shepherd and the Sheep Metaphor in Matthew," *CBQ* 55 (1993): 698–708, here esp. 700–701; W. Baxter, "Healing and the 'Son of David': Matthew's Warrant," *NovT* 48 (2006): 36–49, here esp. 43–45; and Y.S. Chae, *Jesus as the Eschatological Davidic Shepherd: Studies in the Old Testament, Second Temple Judaism, and in the Gospel of Matthew*, WUNT 2/216 (Tübingen: Mohr Siebeck, 2006), 205–219.
17 In Matt 27:43, Matthew has the authorities speak in the words of the godless who mock the righteous one in Ps 22:9.
18 Cf. C. Ziethe, *Auf seinen Namen werden die Völker hoffen: Die matthäische Rezeption der Schriften Israels zur Begründung des universalen Heils*, BZNW 233 (Berlin and Boston, MA: de Gruyter, 2018).
19 Cf. the apt remark of D. Senior, "The Lure of the Formula Quotations: Re-assessing Matthew's Use of the Old Testament with the Passion Narrative as Test Case," in *The Scriptures in the Gospels*, ed. C.M. Tuckett, BETL 131 (Leuven: Peeters, 1997), 89–115, here 104: "the relationship to the Hebrew Scriptures is dialogic rather than linear. 'Fulfillment' does not mean simply a matter of applying Old Testament quotations to events in the life of Jesus. The events of Jesus' life are illuminated and their authority revealed in the light of the Old Testament and, at the same time, new understandings of the voice of God in the Scriptures and the history of Israel are revealed in the light of Jesus' person and mission."

ture in the elaboration of the Jesus tradition also developed an eminent creative potential, such as in the legends about Jesus's flight to Egypt in Matt 2 or the death of Judas in Matt 27:3–10.

Further, the numerous references to the Jewish authorities' ignorance of Scripture[20] must also be taken into account, as they indicate a dispute over the correct understanding of the Scriptures of Israel. A central concern for the evangelist in his context is to be able to demonstrate that his theological views are in agreement with the testimony of Israel's Scriptures. This also represents the first example of a productive competition between the Matthean group and its Jewish environment, which indicates a shared communicative space. The scriptural references also, at least in part, result from the desire to demonstrate to the competition that the group's positions are in accordance with Scripture.

Secondly, Matthew shows himself to be deeply rooted in Jewish traditions and discourses. The Matthean versions of the Sabbath debates in Matt 12:1–14 provide instructive examples of this (see above all vv. 5–7, 11–12), as does the significant reshaping of the debate over washing hands before a meal in Matt 15, in comparison with Mark 7. The Matthean Jesus does not fundamentally declare certain foods to be pure (see Mark 7:19), but simply rejects the Pharisaic halakah of washing hands.[21] Further, the temple tax pericope in the Matthean special material in 17:24–27 can also be categorized within a halakic debate, since the payment of an *annual* temple tax was by no means uncontroversial in Second Temple Judaism.[22] In this connection, even a small detail is telling, such

---

20 Cf. Matt 9:13; 12:3, 5; 19:4; 21:16, 42; 22:31.
21 On the Sabbath see L. Doering, *Schabbat. Sabbathalacha und -praxis im antiken Judentum und Urchristentum*, TSAJ 78 (Tübingen: Mohr Siebeck, 1999), 432–436, 457–462; A.J. Mayer-Haas, *"Geschenk aus Gottes Schatzkammer" (bSchab 10b): Jesus und der Sabbat im Spiegel der neutestamentlichen Schriften*, NTAbh 43 (Münster: Aschendorff, 2003), 411–493; I.W. Oliver, *Torah Praxis after 70 CE. Reading Matthew and Luke-Acts as Jewish Texts*, WUNT 2/355 (Tübingen: Mohr Siebeck, 2013), esp. 80–99, 114–124, 170–193; on food laws see, for example, S. von Dobbeler, "Auf der Grenze. Ethos und Identität der matthäischen Gemeinde nach Mt 15,1–20," *BZ* 45 (2001): 55–78; Oliver, *Torah Praxis*, 241–293.
22 The biblical basis for the temple tax is Exod 30:11–16. As a tax to be paid *annually* by all adult Jewish males (cf. Neh 10:33), the temple tax was presumably established around the middle of the 1st century BCE on initiative of the Pharisees, while the Sadducees apparently favored the older practice of a voluntary payment for financing the temple cult, and the Essenes understood Exod 30:11–16 as a payment to be made only once in a lifetime (4Q159 2.6–7). Against this background, it becomes clear that the tax collectors' question in v. 24 was not merely an implicit challenge, nor by any means purely rhetorical. On the evidence in the ancient Jewish sources cf. the discussion in J. Liver, "The Half-Shekel Offering in Biblical and Post-Biblical Literature," *HTR* 56 (1963): 173–198 and W. Horbury, "The Temple Tax," in *Jesus and the Politics of His Day*, ed. E.

as the fact that Matthew does not, like Mark, simply write that the woman who suffered from hemorrhages touched Jesus's cloak (Mark 5:27), but rather speaks of the fringe of his cloak (cf. Num 15:38 f.; Deut 22:12).[23] The Matthean world is a world deeply shaped by Judaism. This is also reflected not least in the fundamental significance that Matthew ascribes to the Torah for ethical guidance,[24] which once again in varied form takes up my first point, the scriptural references in Matt.

Third, Matthew emphasizes Jesus's attention to Israel significantly more than Mark.[25] One of Matthew's guiding concerns is to show that the hopes for salvation of God's people Israel have been and continue to be fulfilled in Jesus. The systematic presentation of his ministry in the first main section after the prologue – in 4:17–11:1 – is a presentation of Jesus's ministry *in Israel*. A characteristic expression of Matthew's emphatic location of Jesus's ministry within the history between God and Israel is the significantly greater importance of Jesus's Davidic messiahship in the Gospel of Matthew in comparison with Mark. This christological emphasis is in no way contradicted by an ecclesiological perspective in which Matthew sees Israel as being replaced by the church. Matthew by no means represents a substitution theory; rather, according to Matthew's ecclesiological conception, the church is formed *in* Israel – and then also among the gentiles.[26] The church is thus something like the nucleus of crystallization for the eschatological renewal of the people of God, which had begun with Jesus's ministry and ought to continue through the mission of the disciples.

Alongside this evidence that the evangelist and his group are rooted in Judaism, there are further indications that this rootedness does not simply present

---

Bammel and C.F.D. Moule (Cambridge et al.: Cambridge University Press, 1984), 265–286, here 277–284.

23 It should be pointed out that this divergence from Mark 5:27 also occurs in Luke 8:44, so this is a 'minor agreement.'

24 See, e.g., K. Snodgrass, "Matthew and Law," in *Treasures New and Old. Recent Contributions to Matthean Studies*, ed. D.R. Bauer and M.A. Powell, SBLSymS 1 (Atlanta, GA: Scholars Press, 1996), 99–127; B. Repschinski, *Nicht aufzulösen, sondern zu erfüllen: Das jüdische Gesetz in den synoptischen Jesuserzählungen*, FB 120 (Würzburg: Echter Verlag, 2009), 57–141; M. Konradt, "Rezeption und Interpretation des Dekalogs im Matthäusevangelium," in idem, *Studien zum Matthäusevangelium*, WUNT 358 (Tübingen: Mohr Siebeck, 2016), 316–347; idem, "Das Gebot der Feindesliebe in Mt 5,43–48 und sein frühjüdischer Kontext," in *Ahavah: Die Liebe Gottes im Alten Testament*, ed. M. Oeming, ABIG 55 (Leipzig: Evangelische Verlagsanstalt, 2018), 349–389.

25 For a detailed treatment of this aspect see Konradt, *Israel, Church, and the Gentiles* (see n. 1), 17–88.

26 See Konradt, *Israel, Church, and the Gentiles* (see n. 1), 327–354.

the group's identity-forming past, but rather the group sees itself as belonging to the Jewish community in the present. This brings me to the next point:

1.2 Judaism as the Present Context of the Matthean Communities

This aspect was suggested already when I indicated that the scriptural references in Matthew are also to be read in the context of a productive competition between the Matthean community and its non-Christ-believing Jewish context. I also share the view, mentioned in the introduction, that the vehemence with which the conflict with the Jewish authorities is carried out in the Gospel of Matthew clearly indicates that these debates are of great *current* significance for Matthew and his communities. This hardly just looks back on the past. On the contrary, the severity of the conflict points to an existing social proximity.

A further indication of this is once again the temple tax pericope in Matt 17:24–27. The temple tax is known to have been replaced after 70 CE by the *fiscus Judaicus* that was to be paid to Rome; in connection with the latter, the theological argumentation about the freedom of the children of God is irrelevant. But this by no means necessarily indicates that the pericope should be regarded as simply a historical memory or that it functions solely as a paradigm for the policy of not causing any unnecessary offence. If the instruction to pay the tax now also applies to the *fiscus Judaicus* for the community, or at least for its Jewish members,[27] then the text is instead a clear signal that the Matthean group is connected with the Jewish community as a whole. According to Suetonius (*Dom.* 12.2), Rome adamantly collected the *fiscus Judaicus* primarily under Domitian. In this context, the position of not refusing to pay the tax reads in positive terms as a confession of belonging to Judaism.

If we look for contradictory evidence, we must first address the language of "their" or "your synagogues," which has often been taken as indicating a posi-

---

[27] See, e.g., Saldarini, *Community* (see n. 4), 143–146; W. Carter, "Paying the Tax to Rome as Subversive Praxis: Matthew 17.24–27," *JSNT* 76 (1999): 3–31; and P. Foster, "Vespasian, Nerva, Jesus, and the *Fiscus Judaicus*," in *Israel's God and Rebecca's Children: Christology and Community in Early Judaism and Christianity. Essays in Honor of L. W. Hurtado and A. F. Segal*, ed. D.B. Capes et al. (Waco, TX: Baylor University Press, 2007), 303–320, here 312–315. Contra M. Heemstra, *The* Fiscus Judaicus *and the Parting of the Ways*, WUNT 2/277 (Tübingen: Mohr Siebeck, 2010), 63 n. 125.

tion outside of Judaism.[28] But the evidence is in fact more nuanced. Firstly, the passages taken as evidence must themselves be differentiated. Not all passages exhibit the same sense of distance.[29] When Matthew states that Jesus taught in "their synagogues" in the summaries in Matt 4:23 (par. Mark 1:39) and 9:35, this can be taken in reference to the synagogues in Galilee, without showing a sense of distance. The same applies to Matt 13:54, which deals with the rejection of Jesus in Nazareth: "their synagogues" here are the synagogues of the Nazarenes. However, the situation in other passages is different. According to the context in 12:9, "their synagogue" is that of the Pharisees, and the redactional language of flogging "in their/your synagogues" in 10:17; 23:34 – both occur in Jesus's speech – clearly indicate distance; in addition, in 23:34 the context indicates that, like in 12:9, these are the synagogues of the scribes and Pharisees. We can further point to the fact that Mark's ἀρχισυνάγωγος Jairus (Mark 5:22) becomes simply an ἄρχων in Matt 9:18. Unlike the case of the scribes, some of whom are affiliated with Jesus (13:52; 23:34) in addition to "theirs" (7:29), Matthew never uses 'synagogue' to denote gatherings of Christ-believers or their meeting places, but speaks instead of the ἐκκλησία (16:18; 18:17).

When we seek to interpret this evidence, in my opinion, it cannot be denied that the Matthean community has organized itself as an independent group separate from the synagogue(s), holds independent gatherings and regards the 'synagogue(s)' as a place dominated by their opponents. In other words: it can hardly be disputed that a certain degree of institutional consolidation has taken place apart from synagogue gatherings. The answer to the question of what conclusions can be drawn from the evidence outlined here is dependent upon factors external to the text, namely how one pictures Judaism and its diversity at the time and in the regional environment of Matthew. In this, we also have the problem that the location of the Gospel of Matthew cannot be determined with sufficient certainty.

If the Gospel derives from a regional context in which there was only *one* synagogue and this – with its functions which are known to have been not only religious – was an essential unifying point of reference for local Jews, then the establishment of an independent organization could hardly be regarded as anything other than a significant step in the direction of a process of *separation*. However, a different overall picture could come out if the Gospel of Matthew

---

[28] See, e.g., G.N. Stanton, *A Gospel for a New People: Studies in Matthew* (Edinburgh: T&T Clark, 1992), 128–129.
[29] On the following cf. Saldarini, *Community* (see n. 4), 66–67 and B. Przybylski, "The Setting of Matthean Anti-Judaism," in *Anti-Judaism in Early Christianity*, vol. 1: *Paul and the Gospels*, ed. P. Richardson, SCJud 2 (Waterloo: Wilfrid Laurier University Press, 1986), 181–200, here 193–194.

emerged in an urban context with a large Jewish population in which there were multiple meeting places – as has been demonstrated in the case of metropolises like Alexandria,[30] Rome,[31] or, in the Syrian region where the Gospel probably originated, Damascus, as shown by Acts 9:2, and certainly also Antioch.[32] If there were multiple synagogues in one place, this raises the question of possible factors that determine membership in a synagogue. As I see it, the current state of our sources does not allow us to draw conclusions with sufficient certainty in either direction regarding the decisive question in this context, namely, the extent to which membership in a synagogue was (also) determined by a certain religious character. One might point to the reference to Essene synagogues in Philo, *Prob.* 81. But can this reference be generalized or transferred to the Diaspora? For Alexandria, for example, it would be necessary to ask specifically: where did the so-called consistent allegorists, whom Philo criticizes in *Migr.* 89–93, actually meet? In independent gatherings? Was there an institutional background of differing influences in synagogue communities that accounts for the fact that, after the anti-Jewish pogroms in Alexandria (38/39 CE) under Gaius Caligula, two delegations from the Jews of Alexandria appeared before Claudius (41–54; cf. CPJ I 153, lines 90–92)? If 'differences of direction' played a role, it would become more plausible to differentiate between an attitude toward the (Pharisee dominated) synagogue and belonging to Judaism, even if there would remain the special feature that the Matthean theological consciousness of difference – or that of all Christ-believing groups – goes hand in hand with the preference for ἐκκλησία as a group name. The use of the term ἐκκλησία in and of itself, however, is not an indication of distancing. Its use can likely be traced back to the Christ-believing Jerusalem Hellenists,[33] where it does not mark a position outside of Judaism, but rather 'only' gives expression to the particular self-understanding of the group. In the same way, we can conceive of the differentiation of synagogue and *ecclesia* in the Matthean context within the framework of *inner*-Jewish processes of differentiation.

---

30 For the existence of multiple synagogues in Alexandria, see Philo, *Legat.* 132–138.
31 See, e.g., Philo, *Legat.* 156–157 and, further, the overview based on the analysis of funerary inscriptions in H.J. Leon, *The Jews of Ancient Rome*, updated edition (Peabody, MA: Hendrickson, 1995), 135–166. Cf. further, e.g., C. Claußen, *Versammlung, Gemeinde, Synagoge: Das hellenistisch-jüdische Umfeld der frühchristlichen Gemeinden*, SUNT 27 (Göttingen: Vandenhoeck & Ruprecht, 2002), 103–111.
32 Unfortunately, the source material situation in Syria, where most scholars locate the emergence of the Gospel, is not the best (especially with regard to inscriptions; see L.I. Levine, "Synagoge," *TRE* 32 [2001]: 499–508, here 501).
33 See P.R. Trebilco, *Self-designations and Group Identity in the New Testament* (Cambridge et al.: Cambridge University Press, 2012), 183–198.

It should also be noted that, in any case, distancing from the Pharisaic synagogue need not signify a complete detachment. Matthew twice points out that Jesus's disciples must be prepared for flogging in 'their/your synagogues' (10:17: καὶ ἐν ταῖς συναγωγαῖς αὐτῶν μαστιγώσουσιν ὑμᾶς; 23:34: καὶ ἐξ αὐτῶν μαστιγώσετε ἐν ταῖς συναγωγαῖς ὑμῶν). This suggests that community members still attend meetings in the synagogue – and probably not just as silent listeners, but rather with a promotional, missionary intent, namely, as part of the ongoing effort for the "lost sheep of the house of Israel." (10:6; 15:24)[34] The conflicts presupposed in 10:17 and 23:34, which could end in a flogging, can hardly be explained otherwise.[35] If we take into account the fact that synagogues serve more than just a religious function, this can be given clearer contours with the idea that, in any case, the gatherings of Christ-believers do not occupy the same social position as the synagogues.

To summarize what has been suggested thus far: the Matthean addressees meet in independent gatherings, but appear to be an integral part of Judaism, at least from their own perspective. The Christ-believers emerge here with the self-understanding that they are the true custodians of Israel's theological traditions, and – this is a central point for the location of the Matthean communities, in my opinion – they still want to win over their Jewish contemporaries for the message of Christ. If 17:24–27 in its altered form is currently relevant to the addressees, this underscores the feeling of belonging to Judaism.

However, the other side of the evidence must also be illuminated: the Matthean addressees differ fundamentally in many aspects from other contemporaneous Jewish groups. One of these aspects is the programmatic universality of the offer of salvation, which reconfigures the contrast between the people of God and other people that is fundamental to Israel's self-understanding. With this I come to the second main point, Matthean universalism and the significance of gentile Christians in the Matthean community.

---

[34] This fits with the fact that the first occurrence (10:17) is found in the context of the mission discourse and the second also appears where ἀποστέλλειν is mentioned once again (23:34).
[35] Unless one shifts the occurrence of floggings in the synagogue to the past. Particularly in view of the two-fold reference to it, however, this could hardly be taken as anything other than arbitrary.

2 Matthean Universalism and the Significance of Gentile Christians in the Matthean Community

While it is clear that the Matthean group has *its origins* in Judaism and that Judaism continues to be the group's central life context, there is less clarity about the exact composition of the group at the time that the Gospel was composed. As indicated at the beginning of this paper, representatives of the radical wing of the perspective that sees Matthew within Judaism seek to marginalize the universalistic features of the Matthean Jesus story and usually connect this with the thesis that gentile Christians did not play a role among the Matthean addressees. The alternative, supported by many, is that at the time of the Gospel's composition the character of the Matthean group had already changed due to the addition of believers from among the nations. If one follows this variant, it must further be asked how strong this gentile-Christian element already was. Should we speak of a still primarily Jewish-Christian community[36] or of a mixed community?[37] The transitions here must be defined as fluid rather than clear. Depending on how one decides this question, the relation of the Matthean community to Judaism from a social perspective will be differently nuanced. The following basic principle may apply here: the greater the percentage of gentile Christians one estimates in the community is, the less likely it becomes that the community should be regarded as simply a (deviant) part of Judaism.[38] In other words,

---

36 See, e.g., D.J. Harrington, *The Gospel of Matthew*, SP 1 (Collegeville, MN: Liturgical Press, 1991), 2 ("a largely Jewish-Christian community"); W.D. Davies and D.C. Allison Jr., *A Critical and Exegetical Commentary on the Gospel according to Saint Matthew*, 3 vols., ICC (Edinburgh: T&T Clark, 1988–1997), 3:695, 702 (but see also below n. 37); D. Senior, *Matthew*, ANTC (Nashville, TN: Abingdon, 1998), 21 ("but a growing number of Gentile converts were beginning to swell its membership"); Przybylski, "Setting" (see n. 29), 192.
37 See, e.g., Davies and Allison, *Commentary* (see n. 37), 2:192 ("a mixed community"); K.-C. Wong, *Interkulturelle Theologie und multikulturelle Gemeinde im Matthäusevangelium: Zum Verhältnis von Juden- und Heidenchristen im ersten Evangelium*, NTOA 22 (Freiburg, CH: Universitätsverlag; Göttingen: Vandenhoeck & Ruprecht, 1992), esp. 187–195; H.-J. Eckstein, "Die Weisung Jesu Christi und die Tora des Mose nach dem Matthäusevangelium," in *Jesus Christus als die Mitte der Schrift: Studien zur Hermeneutik des Evangeliums*, ed. C. Landmesser, H.-J. Eckstein, and H. Lichtenberger, BZNW 86 (Berlin and New York, NY: de Gruyter, 1997), 379–403, here 387–390; W. Weren, "The History and Social Setting of the Matthean Community," in *Matthew and the Didache: Two Documents from the Same Jewish-Christian Milieu?*, ed. H. van de Sandt (Assen: Van Gorcum; Minneapolis, MN: Fortress, 2005), 51–62, here 60.
38 Cf. for example the thesis of P. Foster, *Community, Law and Mission in Matthew's Gospel*, WUNT 2/177 (Tübingen: Mohr Siebeck, 2004), 79 "that the attitude towards Gentile Mission more naturally reflects a community that had stepped outside the bounds of Judaism."

this brings with it the question of whether the evangelist seeks to initiate a new course of action with the universal commission in 28:18–20, or whether the community was already pursuing a mission to gentiles (for some time?).

The radical view, that the mission to the gentiles was theoretically accepted by the Matthean community as a(n eschatological) program, but was not in fact put into practice,[39] has not yet gained acceptance. This view already fails because it is unable to account for the weight of 28:16–20 as the goal of the entire narrative. And the reference to the fact that the Gospel of Matthew contains some derogatory statements about the ἐθνικοί (Matt 5:47; 6:7; 18:17[40]) or the ἔθνη (6:32)[41] may well corroborate Matthew's Jewish perspective, but it cannot be taken as evidence for a rejection of the mission to the gentiles. Paul is also able to speak quite pejoratively of the 'gentiles,' as the example of 1 Thess 4:5 clearly demonstrates.[42] Further, the fact that Matthew has no illusions about the hostility facing the disciples in the pagan world (cf. 24:9: καὶ ἔσεσθε μισούμενοι ὑπὸ πάντων τῶν ἐθνῶν διὰ τὸ ὄνομά μου) cannot be invoked as evidence here; persecution is likewise a characteristic of the mission to Israel.[43]

However, an answer to the question of *how long* the community has devoted itself to the mission to the gentiles cannot be deduced from the Gospel of Matthew with adequate certainty. The task of mediating between the specific attention to Israel and the universality of salvation is a central concern of the Matthean retelling of the Jesus story, from 1:1 on. This evidence can hardly be read in any other way than as indicating that this question was of great *current* significance.[44] And this, in turn, could mean that the mission to the gentiles was not

---

[39] See, e.g., Sim, *The Gospel of Matthew and Christian Judaism* (see n. 6), 242–245 (cf. D.C. Sim, "The Gospel of Matthew and the Gentiles," *JSNT* 57 [1995]: 19–48, here 41–44); J.L. Houlden, "The Puzzle of Matthew and the Law," in *Crossing the Boundaries. Essays in Biblical Interpretation in Honour of M. D. Goulder*, ed. S.E. Porter, P. Joyce, and D.E. Orton, BibInt 8 (Leiden et al.: Brill, 1994), 115–131, here 123.

[40] Matthew consistently uses ἐθνικός in a pejorative sense.

[41] Cf. Sim, *The Gospel of Matthew and Christian Judaism* (see n. 6), 226–231.

[42] In Matt 5:46; 18:17, the tax collectors also appear as a negative example or as outsiders without precluding the evangelist from regarding them as valid recipients of Jesus's attention (9:9–13; 11:19; 21:31–32).

[43] This reference does, however, make it clear that, conversely, the resistance brought against Jesus's messengers in Israel is not grounds for abandoning these missionary activities. Otherwise the same would have to apply for the mission to the gentiles. On this see Konradt, *Israel, Church, and the Gentiles* (see n. 1), 9.

[44] Matthew makes a great effort at justification with regard to the emphasis on the fulfillment of the promises of salvation for Israel in Jesus's messianic work as well as in the justification of the mission to the gentiles and in particular its foundation in Israel's Scriptures. On this see Konradt, *Israel, Church, and the Gentiles* (see n. 1), esp. 17–87, 265–325.

uncontroversial among the addressees.⁴⁵ Yet these assumptions do not form a solid basis for assertions about the composition of the community, because this great interest *could* indicate that the evangelist is attempting to *establish* the mission to the gentiles⁴⁶ in the face of disagreement – in this case, a Jewish-Christian community should be assumed, which Matthew tries to move in a new direction. But it can just as well indicate that he is defending the mission against *new resentments* that have come up in his *mixed* community (perhaps because of the influx of Jewish Christians who fled Palestine after the war). As a further possibility, it could be that the Matthean community was exposed to criticism from Pharisees due to the acceptance of non-Jews as full members and that some members of the community were (increasingly) affected by that criticism.⁴⁷ The textual evidence thus permits various historical imaginings. On this example, it becomes clear that conclusions about the historical situation of a group

---

45 On the suggestion that Matthew saw himself as confronted with reservations about the integration of non-Jews among conservative members of the community, cf., e.g., M. Slee, *The Church in Antioch in the First Century CE: Communion and Conflict*, JSNTSup 244 (London and New York, NY: Sheffield Academic, 2003), 134; Foster, *Community* (see n. 38), 20; Konradt, *Israel, Church, and the Gentiles* (see n. 1), 365–366 as well as V. Balabanski, "Mission in Matthew against the Horizon of Matthew 24," *NTS* 54 (2008): 161–175, here 170–171. M. Lohmeyer, *Der Apostelbegriff im Neuen Testament. Eine Untersuchung auf dem Hintergrund der synoptischen Aussendungsreden*, SBB 29 (Stuttgart: Katholisches Bibelwerk, 1995), 385–386, conversely, has postulated that, faced with a neglect of the mission to Israel, the evangelist seeks a renewed emphasis on its significance. In this vein see also Davies and Allison, *Commentary* (see n. 36), 2:192; H. Frankemölle, "Die matthäische Kirche als Gemeinschaft des Glaubens. Prolegomena zu einer bundestheologischen Ekklesiologie," in *Ekklesiologie des Neuen Testaments. Für K. Kertelge*, ed. R. Kampling and T. Söding (Freiburg et al.: Herder, 1996), 85–132, here 124.
46 Consider the position of S. Brown, "The Matthean Community and the Gentile Mission," *NovT* 22 (1980): 193–221, here 217–221 as well as U. Luz in the first edition of vol. 1 of his commentary, where he posits that the community "mit ihrer Israelmission scheiterte, das göttliche Gericht der Zerstörung Jerusalems erlebte und nun vom Evangelisten zu einem neuen Aufbruch gerufen wird" (*Das Evangelium nach Matthäus*, vol. 1: *Mt 1–7*, EKK 1.1 [Zürich et al.: Benziger; Neukirchen-Vluyn: Neukirchener Verlag, 1985], 67, see also Harrington, *Matthew* [see n. 36], 416 and Slee, *Church* [see n. 45], 126, 131, 144). Luz then revised his view in the course of the continued commentary – namely, interpreting 24:9–14 as an indication of a mission to the Gentiles already under way (see U. Luz, *Das Evangelium nach Matthäus*, Vol. 4: *Mt 26–28*, EKK 1.4 [Düsseldorf and Zürich: Benziger; Neukirchen-Vluyn: Neukirchener Verlag, 2002], 451).
47 Consider the similar consideration of Senior, "Between Two Worlds" (see n. 2), 19: "Evidence in Matthew's Gospel may suggest that some in Matthew's community resisted that idea of a Gentile mission, perhaps in part under the pressure of Jewish attacks on the validity of the Jewish character of Matthew's community."

that are drawn from that group's narrative texts can hardly be reached with much certainty.⁴⁸

The significance of the question as to when the Matthean community began evangelizing to gentiles would of course be undermined if the admission of gentiles to the community were conditional upon conversion to Judaism. This position has been prominently and emphatically posited in recent Matthean scholarship. While Matthew's silence on circumcision in the great commission was previously taken to mean that baptism had replaced circumcision as the ritual marking entry into the community⁴⁹ – sometimes with nearly unquestioned certainty – the exact opposite view is taken from the silence on this point in 28:19 by the radical wing of the 'Matthew within Judaism' perspective: Matthew had no need to discuss circumcision here because it was a self-evident prerequisite for the admission of gentile believers into the Matthean *ecclesia* anyway.⁵⁰ The central anchor for this interpretation is the statement in 5:18 that not one iota will pass from the law until the end of the world.⁵¹ Based on this, it is concluded that the commandment of circumcision also remains in effect. If one were to follow this new interpretation, there would be no question about the Jewish nature of the group; gentile Christians in Matthew would be proselytes. Within Christi-

---

48 Donald A. Hagner has formulated this basic problem even more pointedly: "the reconstruction of the life-situation of an evangelist is necessarily a speculative enterprise. It is a kind of educated guesswork" ("The *Sitz im Leben* of the Gospel of Matthew," in *Treasures New and Old. Recent Contributions to Matthean Studies*, ed. D.R. Bauer and M.A. Powell, SBLSymS 1 [Atlanta, GA: Scholars Press, 1996], 27–68, here 27).
49 Cf., among others, J.P. Meier, *Law and History in Matthew's Gospel. A Redactional Study of Mt. 5:17–48*, AnBib 71 (Rome: Biblical Institute Press, 1976), 28.
50 David Sim's position is presented with great decisiveness. See Sim, *The Gospel of Matthew and Christian Judaism* (see n. 6), 251–254 (cf. D.C. Sim, "Christianity and Ethnicity in the Gospel of Matthew," in *Ethnicity and the Bible*, ed. M.G. Brett, BibInt 19 [Leiden et al: Brill, 1996], 171–195, here 184–194), further R. Mohrlang, *Matthew and Paul: A Comparison of Ethical Perspectives*, SNTSMS 48 (Cambridge: Cambridge University Press, 1984), 44–45; A.-J. Levine, *The Social and Ethnic Dimensions of Matthean Salvation History*, SBEC 14 (Lewiston, NY et al.: Mellen, 1988), 181–185; L.M. White, "Crisis Management and Boundary Maintenance: The Social Location of the Matthean Community," in *Social History of the Matthean Community: Cross-Disciplinary Approaches*, ed. D.L. Balch (Minneapolis, MN: Fortress, 1991), 211–247, here 241–242, n. 100; Slee, *Church* (see n. 45), 141–144; Runesson, *Divine Wrath* (see n. 7), 31–36 and also Saldarini, *Community* (see n. 4), 157 and W. Kraus, "Zur Ekklesiologie des Matthäusevangeliums," in *The Gospel of Matthew at the Crossroads of Early Christianity*, ed. D. Senior, BETL 243 (Leuven et al.: Peeters, 2011), 195–239, here 208–211; with some caution W.R.G. Loader, *Jesus' Attitude towards the Law: A Study of the Gospels*, WUNT 2/97 (Tübingen: Mohr Siebeck, 1997), 252–253, 264.
51 See, e.g., D.C. Sim, "Paul and Matthew on the Torah: Theory and Practice," in *Paul, Grace and Freedom: Essays in Honour of J. K. Riches*, ed. P. Middleton, A. Paddison, and K.J. Wenell (London and New York, NY: T&T Clark, 2009), 50–64, here 58–59; Slee, *Church* (see n. 45), 142.

anity, the Matthean community would then be a close relative of the Galatian opponents.

However, this reading has not gained acceptance as the majority position thus far, and I still think this option is highly unlikely. Since I have already commented on this point in detail elsewhere,[52] I will briefly summarize here:

First: Positions on the question of circumcision were by no means uniform in ancient Judaism,[53] which can hardly be surprising given that Hellenistic culture was hostile to circumcision. Ancient Judaism met the pressure of acculturation resulting from this negative attitude in various ways. This includes the fact that even for the period after the failure of the Hellenistic reform in Jerusalem in the first third of the 2nd century BCE there is evidence that circumcision was neglected by some.[54] Even more significant than the attitude toward the importance of circumcision as a Jewish identity marker, however, is that there were various attitudes toward the necessity of circumcision by *non-Jews*, as demonstrated by the conversion of Izates of Adiabene depicted in Josephus, *Ant.* 20.34–48.[55] Even if the question of whether there were uncircumcised pros-

---

[52] See M. Konradt, "Matthäus im Kontext. Eine Bestandsaufnahme zur Frage des Verhältnisses der matthäischen Gemeinde(n) zum Judentum," in idem, *Studien zum Matthäusevangelium*, WUNT 358 (Tübingen: Mohr Siebeck, 2016), 3–42, here 23–36.

[53] For a comprehensive analysis of the texts, see A. Blaschke, *Beschneidung. Zeugnisse der Bibel und verwandter Texte*, TANZ 28 (Tübingen and Basel: Francke, 1998).

[54] Laxity regarding circumcision (of children) to the point of epispasm also occurred among at least some (hellenized) Jews after the failure of the Hellenistic reform (cf. Jub. 15:33–34 as a reflection of the Hellenistic reform), as the adoption of the motif of epispasm in T.Mos. 8:3 suggests. Paul also alludes to epispasm in 1 Cor 7:18. In the so-called consistent allegorists, Philo attests to a group that rejected (physical) circumcision (*Migr.* 89–93). In 2 Bar. 66:5, the killing of uncircumcised compatriots in zeal for the law is presented as part of the reforms of Josiah. Since this has no basis in the Old Testament depictions (2 Kgs 23:4–25; 2 Chr 34:1–7, 33; 35:1–19), it can be presumed that the enforcement of circumcision is due to a present concern. The connection between zeal for the law and circumcision do not need to mean, with regard to the Jews being opposed, that they have fundamentally renounced the Torah; it is enough to assume that they did not share the understanding of the Torah presupposed in 2 Bar. If one follows the reconstruction by P. Schäfer, *Der Bar Kokhba-Aufstand. Studien zum zweiten jüdischen Krieg gegen Rom*, TSAJ 1 (Tübingen: Mohr Siebeck, 1981), 46–50, it should further be considered that assimilated Jews had their foreskin restored in the run-up to the Bar Kochba revolt. In addition, Martial (*Epigrammata* 7.82) depicts with his unique satire how a Jew tried to hide his circumcised penis with a fibula in the public spaces of the baths and the palaestra.

[55] Two positions are contrasted here: while the Galilean Eleazar, probably a Pharisee, considers Izates's status as a God-fearer to be unacceptable, referencing the circumcision commandment in Gen 17 (43–45), Josephus has the merchant Ananias, who originally inspired Izates's enthusiasm for Judaism, present the view that it is possible "to worship God without being circumcised" (41). With this Ananias represents a position that apparently was not an exception, as evi-

elytes at the turn of the centuries, which has been proposed as a possibility on the basis of (an isolated reading) of Philo, *QE* 2.2 (on Exod 22:21),[56] should probably be answered in the negative,[57] it can be established that non-Jewish sympathizers' participation and (partial) integration in synagogal life laid the groundwork for the development and success of the idea of a circumcision-free mission to the gentiles in the movement of Christ-believers.

A *second* piece of evidence arises from the history of early Christian development and the location of the Gospel of Matthew within the spectrum of early Christianity. I will not discuss here the question of the localization of the Gospel – in my opinion, the south of Syria, such as a city like Damascus, constitutes the best option,[58] but I do not wish to develop this in detail here. In terms of contextualization within the history of theology with regard to the question that interests us here, it seems more significant to me that the Matthean emphasis on Peter's central role among the disciples and especially Matt 16:18–19 might indicate the high esteem in which he was held in Matthean Christianity. At the Apostolic Council, Peter was one of the leading figures of the Jerusalem community, who accepted and supported the Antiochene practice of a circumcision-free mission to the gentiles, and there is no indication that his position subsequently changed. In view of the specific position of authority that Peter is given in Matthew and which in Matt 16:17–19 includes the faithful tradition and development of Jesus's interpretation of Torah, it is unlikely that the Matthean community affirmed the mission to the gentiles but rejected the decision of the Apostolic Council that Peter had supported.

Third, 5:18 must be considered within the larger context of the Matthean understanding of the law, in which a differentiation between major and minor com-

---

denced by the existence of God-fearers in diaspora synagogues. In other words, the phenomenon of God-fearers indicates that Ananias's position was not just an emergency solution based on political considerations, but rather had a more widespread social background.

56 Philo here defines the proselyte as "one who circumcises not his uncircumcision but his desires and sensual pleasures and the other passions of the soul." Philo further asks: "What is the mind of the proselyte if not alienation from belief in many gods and familiarity with honouring the one God and Father of all?"

57 Cf. J. Nolland, "Uncircumcised Proselytes?," *JSJ* 12 (1981): 173–194, here 173–179; W. Kraus, *Das Volk Gottes: Zur Grundlegung der Ekklesiologie bei Paulus*, WUNT 85 (Tübingen: Mohr Siebeck, 1996), 102–103. For a different view N.J. McEleney, "Conversion, Circumcision, and the Law," *NTS* 20 (1974): 319–341, here 328–333. On this question cf. also J.J. Collins, "A Symbol of Otherness: Circumcision and Salvation in the First Century," in *"To See Ourselves as Others See Us": Christians, Jews, "Others" in Late Antiquity*, ed. J. Neusner and E.S. Frerichs (Chico, CA: Scholars Press, 1985), 163–186, here 173–174.

58 Cf. Konradt, *The Gospel according to Matthew* (see n. 1), 22–23.

mandments emerges alongside the statement of the validity of *all* commandments.⁵⁹ Matthew works with a hierarchy of commandments, for which the quotation "I desire mercy and not sacrifice" from Hos 6:6 serves as a programmatic maxim. An important aspect in this regard is that, for Matthew, a failure to observe the minor commandments does not exclude people from salvation. Two passages are pertinent here, 5:19–20 and 19:16–22. In 5:19, the Matthean Jesus says that those who annul one of the least of these commandments, and teach others to do so, shall be called least in the kingdom of heaven. He does not say that they are excluded. This possibility only appears in v. 20: "unless your righteousness surpasses *that* of the scribes and Pharisees, you shall not enter the kingdom of heaven." This implies that the scribes and Pharisees neglect not just "iotas and pen-strokes" (5:18), but, in the words of 23:23, they neglect τὰ βαρύτερα τοῦ νόμου, namely the socio-ethical commandments that are of central importance to Matthew. In Matt 19:16–22, Matthew has thoroughly reworked Mark's version of the encounter between Jesus and a rich young man. In Matthew, Jesus answers the young man's question, "what good thing shall I do that I may obtain eternal life?" with a clear statement: "keep the commandments." However, the dialogue continues, because now the young man asks: "Which ones?" The Matthean Jesus now answers with the quotation of the commandments from the second table of the Decalogue and the love command. The implication is clear: these are the commandments whose observance is crucial for obtaining eternal life. This fits perfectly with 5:19–20, and it should be noted that such an understanding of the law paves the way for the inclusion of gentiles apart from the option of full proselytism. To prevent misunderstandings: this is not about the question of the commandment of circumcision *for Jews*, but only whether the formal conversion to Judaism *for Christ-believing people from among the gentiles* and their salvation depends upon their practice of commandments such as circumcision, observation of the Sabbath, and dietary laws – that is, the so-called 'boundary markers.' In my opinion, the correct answer is that the Matthean understanding of the law is oriented such that gentile Christians keep the (soteriologically) truly important commandments without circumcision or commitment to the dietary laws. Matthew's gospel articulates a *moderate* Jewish-Christian position. The fact that a fundamental affirmation of the Torah can go hand in hand with a circumcision-free mission to the gentiles is shown by the tradition Paul cites in 1 Cor 7:19, which might be of Antiochene

---

59 On Matthew's Torah hermeneutics cf. M. Konradt, "Die vollkommene Erfüllung der Tora und der Konflikt mit den Pharisäern im Matthäusevangelium," in idem, *Studien zum Matthäusevangelium*, WUNT 358 (Tübingen: Mohr Siebeck, 2016), 288–315.

origin: "Circumcision is nothing and uncircumcision is nothing, but keeping the commandments of God is what matters." In this connection, a reference to the testimony of the Didache is also instructive. For converts from the gentiles, the social commandments presented in Did 1–5 are obligatory. But with regard to food, Did 6:3a says succinctly: "Bear what you are able (περὶ δὲ τῆς βρώσεως, ὃ δύνασαι βάστασον)!" Only food sacrificed to idols is strictly forbidden (Did 6:3b, cf. the Apostolic Decree in Acts 15:20, 29; 21:25). This, too, does not refer to circumcision, but once again mentions baptism (Did 7). This expresses a moderate Jewish-Christian position, which in my view also applies to the Gospel of Matthew.[60]

Fourth, the justification of the turn toward the gentiles in Matthew's theological concept must be considered. Two elements are of primary significance to this question. First, there is the legitimation of the mission to the gentiles on the basis of Israel's Scriptures, as mentioned above. Here I will limit myself to three brief examples. In the triad of the gifts of the Magi in Matt 2:11, the first two, χρυσὸς καὶ λίβανος, allude to Isa 60:6,[61] such that the arrival of the Magi in Matt 2 invokes the motif of the pilgrimage of nations[62] and is at the same time transformed messianically: their pilgrimage does not end on Mount Zion, but with Jesus. There is also a broad consensus that the inclusion of the phrase Γαλιλαία τῶν ἐθνῶν in the quotation of Isa 8:23 in Matt 4:15 foreshadows the commission of the disciples in Matt 28:16–20, so that this emerges as justified by Scripture. Alongside this, there is the quotation of Isa 42:1–4 in Matt 12:18–21,[63] according to which "the gentiles hope in his name." Thus, according to Matthew, the inclusion of the 'gentiles' in salvation is anchored in Scripture and he locates this inclusion within foundational notion that the promises found in Scripture have been fulfilled in Jesus. The targeted missionary attention to the gentiles takes into account this new salvation-historical situation. Second, the legitimation of the mission to the gentiles is a matter of the Matthean interpretation of the Christ event, specifically his reading of the death and resurrection of Jesus. Here, too, I must limit myself to a brief sketch.[64] Jesus's earthly

---

60 Cf., e.g., Luz, *Das Evangelium nach Matthäus I* (see n. 2), 317.
61 Contra D.C. Sim, "The magi: Gentiles or Jews?," *HTS* 55 (1999): 980–1000, here 997.
62 Cf., e.g., Davies and Allison, *Commentary* (see n. 36), 1:249–250, 253; W. Carter, "Matthew and the Gentiles: Individual Conversion and/or Systemic Transformation?," *JSNT* 26 (2003–2004): 259–282, here 273–274.
63 For a detailed study on this quotation see R. Beaton, *Isaiah's Christ in Matthew's Gospel*, SNTSMS 123 (Cambridge: Cambridge University Press, 2002).
64 For an extensive treatment of this aspect see Konradt, *Israel, Church, and the Gentiles* (see n. 1), esp. 282–311.

ministry is emphatically focused on Israel in Matthew. The turn to the nations is still programmatically ruled out at this stage (15:24), although salvation is already granted to non-Jews *extra ordinem* in the episodes in 8:5–13; 8:28–34; and 15:21–28. In the Matthean conception, the expansion of salvation to the world of the nations is based on the soteriological interpretation of the death of *God's son*[65] as a salvific death, with which the fulfillment of the promises is brought to completion (cf. Matt 26:54, 56). As has often been noted, Matthew apparently understood the reference to the "many" for whom the blood of Jesus is poured out for the forgiveness of sins (Matt 26:28) in a universal sense.[66] The mission to the ἔθνη in Matt 28:18–20 is immediately connected with the proclamation by the resurrected Jesus that he has been installed as lord of the world (28:18b). The universal mission appears as a consequence of the resurrected Christ's universal position of authority. However, this aspect should not be seen as an alternative to the soteriological interpretation of Jesus's death as the reason for the universality of salvation, especially since Matthew has consolidated Jesus's death and resurrection into *a single* nexus of events.[67]

If it is right that the sending of the disciples to all nations in Matt 28:18–20 is connected with the new salvation-historical situation, which is established with the culmination of Matthew's narrative of the fulfillment of the scriptural promises in Jesus's death, resurrection, and installation as universal lord, then in view of this theological context of justification, in my opinion, it would make little sense for the Matthean community to have continued only the other elements of Jewish praxis for conversion to Judaism. For Matthew would not have had to justify this specifically.

To conclude: Matt 28:18–20 does not refer to people from the nations who must become Jews before their integration into the *ecclesia*. After what has been said above, this, however, does not mean that the Matthean gentile Christians should not be differentiated from Pauline gentile Christians.[68] Rather, the

---

65 On the relevance of the 'son of God' motif in the passion narrative see W. Kraus, "Die Passion des Gottessohnes. Zur Bedeutung des Todes Jesu im Matthäusevangelium," *EvT* 57 (1997): 409–427 and Konradt, *Israel, Church, and the Gentiles* (see n. 1), 297–307.
66 Cf., e.g., J.P. Heil, *The Death and Resurrection of Jesus: A Narrative-Critical Reading of Matthew 26–28* (Minneapolis, MN: Fortress, 1991), 38; W. Carter, *Matthew: Storyteller, Interpreter, Evangelist* (Peabody, MA: Hendrickson, 1996), 215, 219; W.G. Olmstead, *Matthew's Trilogy of Parables: The Nation, the Nations and the Reader in Matthew 21.28–22.14*, SNTSMS 127 (Cambridge: Cambridge University Press, 2003), 85; Konradt, *Israel, Church, and the Gentiles* (see n. 1), 307–308.
67 On this see the insertion of ἀπ' ἄρτι in Matt 26:64 and the Easter dimension that Jesus's death acquires through the events in 27:51–53.
68 Cf. Senior, "Between Two Worlds" (see n. 2), 20.

position on the Torah is clearly different. The extent to which the integration of non-Jews had already progressed at the time of the Gospel's composition depends on the question of when the community turned to the mission to the gentiles and with what intensity – a question which, as we have seen, cannot be answered with sufficient certainty. However, it is possible that the mission to the gentiles with which the disciples are tasked in 28:16–20 – regardless of where exactly in this process the Matthean group found itself at the time of the Gospel's composition – indicates a development that must have gradually marginalized the community within Judaism, which was redefining itself after 70 CE. At the same time, this cannot simply be taken to imply a strict separation from Judaism, at least not in Matthew's own perspective. In the Matthean communities, 'pagan' converts are not only obliged to keep Torah's social laws, as Jesus has interpreted them, but they also encounter a version of the Jesus story that strongly emphasizes the focus on Israel in Jesus's ministry, and demonstrates that with their entry into the *ecclesia* gentile Christians are incorporated into a salvation history that began with Abraham, the patriarch of Israel, and in which attention to the 'lost sheep' of Israel is an ongoing task in the context of the eschatological renewal of God's people.[69] Thus, once again, we are left with an ambiguous evidence.

To go one step further, it is significant that the programmatic universalism, as indicated above, is only one point in which the Matthean Christ-believers differed fundamentally from other Jewish groups in their environment. These fundamental differences include the foundational reference to a new salvific act of God in Jesus – a reference that is constitutive for their own identity, which is rejected by other Jews but unites the Matthean community with other Christ-believing groups in other places. This brings me to a short third section:

3 Membership in the Christ-believing Movement

Matthew emphasizes the continuity of the Christ event with God's history with Israel and positions the former within the latter. At the same time, however, the Christ event is not one event alongside others among the vicissitudes of God's history with God's people; rather, the genealogy of Jesus in Matt 1 already

---

[69] Cf. Senior, "Between Two Worlds" (see n. 2), 20: "Matthew anticipated those Gentiles who not only exhibit faith in Jesus but also understand that the Jewish character of Jesus and his teaching is essential to the gospel."

shows that for Matthew, God's history moves toward Jesus.[70] In addition, this orientation toward the Jesus Christ event is not only manifest in the composition of the Jesus story as a new foundational story, but is also connected with the formation of new ritual forms of rendering Christ present in baptism and the eucharist. Moreover, in the Lord's Prayer the communities have a characteristic prayer. The thoroughly Jewish nature of the prayer's content does not change the fact that it constitutes a specific marker of group identity.[71]

Further, the topic of the second section can be taken up again here: Matthew understands the Christ event such that it is significant not only for Israel, but for the entire world. Independent of the question of the precise composition of the Matthean community, this universal significance is connected with the fact that for Matthew, theologically speaking, the church is not just a community of salvation within Israel. Furthermore, the role of Israel in the theological system is changed by the establishment of the church and the expansion of salvation. To be sure, Matthew does not abrogate Israel's special significance as God's chosen people, but he transfers to the church central aspects that mark Israel as God's people in Israel's self-understanding.[72] All these points also fundamentally differentiate Jesus's significance from, for example, the role of the teacher of righteousness for the *yahad* of Qumran.

At the same time, it is important that the Matthean believers in Christ share the orientation toward the Christ event as a central aspect of their own identity with other groups in other places in the ancient Mediterranean, with whom they are in contact. The significant others for Matthew are not only other local Jewish groups, but also other Christ-believing groups in the *oikoumene*. This includes that the Matthean groups distinguish themselves within emergent Christianity from other interpretations of the Christ event, as becomes apparent for example in the warning against pseudoprophets in 7:15–23. But this demarcation does not change the fact that the social location of the Matthean Christ-believers should not be considered only in terms of their belonging to Judaism; instead, a multi-perspective approach must be chosen.

With few exceptions, the aspect of the Matthean communities' relationships within the Christ-believing movement has been given short shrift in recent re-

---

70 See esp. Matt 1:17, where the division of the genealogy into three segments, each with fourteen generations, evokes the idea that the salvation history that began with the election of Abraham runs its course towards Jesus, its intended goal.
71 Cf. K.-H. Ostmeyer, "Das Vaterunser. Gründe für seine Durchsetzung als 'Urgebet' der Christenheit," *NTS* 50 (2004): 320–336.
72 For details see Konradt, *Israel, Church, and the Gentiles* (see n. 1), 345–352.

search,[73] with its strong focus on the relation to Judaism. But these two aspects ought to be connected with one another. The question of the Matthean group's relationship to Judaism can only be adequately addressed if it is pursued alongside consideration of the group's position within emergent Christianity. For example, Matthew not only highlights his understanding of Torah in contrast with his Pharisaic opponents, but also attempts to validate this understanding in contrast with other views within the Christ-believing movement. Moreover, a comprehensive analysis of the communities' social ties must also include relations to their pagan social environment, as well as the wider political contexts, but this can only be suggested briefly here.

4 Conclusion

The metaphor of the 'Parting of the Ways' is, first, unsuited to adequately examine the *complexity* of the relationships between the Christ-believing groups behind the Gospel of Matthew and their Jewish environment. For this metaphor allows only mono-directional thought and involves the problem that it tends to set certain aspects more dominantly over others, which then in the context of a binary, either-or logic are supposed to serve as evidence for a position still within or already outside of Judaism. Second, the metaphor is also unsuited to embedding the analysis of the relationship to Judaism within a comprehensive analysis of the communities' social ties, which also include relationships to other Christ-believing groups and to their pagan social environment. In the next phase of Matthean research, a primary task will be to bring together these various perspectives in a more sophisticated model of multifaceted relationships. For this, it is fundamentally necessary to move beyond the within or outside alternative and the binary and mono-directional approach of the 'Parting of the Ways' metaphor.

It would be attractive to find a new metaphor to describe the complex evidence, a metaphor which is able to connect and integrate the different aspects which I mentioned in the introduction and tried to flesh out a bit in this paper: the coexistence of elements of organizational and institutional autonomy,

---

[73] An important exception is D.C. Sim and B. Repschinski, eds., *Matthew and His Christian Contemporaries*, LNTS 333 (London: T&T Clark, 2008). Some attention has also been paid in recent scholarship to the relationship to Paul. On this see M. Konradt, "Matthäus als Zeuge eines unpaulinischen Christentums. Anmerkungen zur These einer antipaulinischen Ausrichtung des Matthäusevangeliums," in idem, *Studien zum Matthäusevangelium*, WUNT 358 (Tübingen: Mohr Siebeck, 2016), 69–94 (further literature there).

facets of (deep) integration into and interconnectedness with the Jewish parent body, mutual influence and productive competition, theological divergences and convergences. But other metaphors like for example "Rebecca's children"[74] are again not sufficiently complex. Christianity and Judaism did not emerge from one coherent entity, as Early Judaism was highly diverse, as we all know. Nevertheless, one could consider a variation of this kinship metaphor. I thought about the metaphor of a widely ramified family: of relatives who have their own houses, which symbolizes elements of autonomy and independent evolution, but whose members also have contact to other branches of the family. New ramifications can develop, especially through marriage. This would, for example, relate to the inclusion of Gentile members into the Christ-believing groups. In some branches of this family tree, this new element gains the upper hand. The network of relations is thus reconfigured, but there are still links to other members of the wider family, sometimes only indirect links. In this image, Matthew could be regarded as a branch on the family tree with close connections and contacts both to non-Christ-believing parts of the family and to other Christ-believing members of the family.

All metaphors, however, tend to illuminate only some facets of a complex configuration and are inappropriate for others. Maybe, for the time being, we should work without a new metaphor because of its inherent tendency to reduce complexity and just try to describe the complex processes, developments and multi-faceted relations as differentiated and nuanced as possible. This differentiated manner includes that with regard to the question of whether Matthew represents a form of Christ-believing Judaism or a form of Jewish Christianity, one should not give an either-or-answer. It is both. If this is correct, it is fundamentally necessary in Matthean research to move beyond the new perspective on Matthew within Judaism.

Bibliography

Backhaus, K., "Entgrenzte Himmelsherrschaft: Zur Entdeckung der paganen Welt im Matthäusevangelium," in *"Dies ist das Buch ..."*. *Das Matthäusevangelium. Interpretation – Rezeption – Rezeptionsgeschichte. Für H. Frankemölle*, ed. R. Kampling (Paderborn et al.: Schöningh, 2004), 75–103.

Balabanski, V., "Mission in Matthew against the Horizon of Matthew 24," *NTS* 54 (2008): 161–175.

---

[74] Cf. A.F. Segal, *Rebecca's Children. Judaism and Christianity in the Roman World* (Cambridge, MA, and London: Harvard University Press, 1986).

Baxter, W., "Healing and the 'Son of David': Matthew's Warrant," *NovT* 48 (2006): 36–49.
Beaton, R., *Isaiah's Christ in Matthew's Gospel*, SNTSMS 123 (Cambridge: Cambridge University Press, 2002).
Blaschke, A., *Beschneidung. Zeugnisse der Bibel und verwandter Texte*, TANZ 28 (Tübingen and Basel: Francke, 1998).
Broadhead, E. K., *Jewish Ways of Following Jesus: Redrawing the Religious Map of Antiquity*, WUNT 266 (Tübingen: Mohr Siebeck, 2010).
Brown, S., "The Matthean Community and the Gentile Mission," *NovT* 22 (1980): 193–221.
Carter, W., *Matthew: Storyteller, Interpreter, Evangelist* (Peabody, MA: Hendrickson, 1996).
Carter, W., "Paying the Tax to Rome as Subversive Praxis: Matthew 17.24–27," *JSNT* 76 (1999): 3–31.
Carter, W., "Matthew and the Gentiles: Individual Conversion and/or Systemic Transformation?," *JSNT* 26 (2003–2004): 259–282.
Carter, W., "Matthew's Gospel: Jewish Christianity, Christian Judaism, or Neither?," in *Jewish Christianity Reconsidered: Rethinking Ancient Groups and Texts*, ed. M. Jackson-McCabe (Minneapolis, MN: Fortress, 2007), 155–179.
Chae, Y. S., *Jesus as the Eschatological Davidic Shepherd: Studies in the Old Testament, Second Temple Judaism, and in the Gospel of Matthew*, WUNT 2/216 (Tübingen: Mohr Siebeck, 2006).
Claußen, C., *Versammlung, Gemeinde, Synagoge: Das hellenistisch-jüdische Umfeld der frühchristlichen Gemeinden*, SUNT 27 (Göttingen: Vandenhoeck & Ruprecht, 2002).
Collins, J. J., "A Symbol of Otherness: Circumcision and Salvation in the First Century," in *"To See Ourselves as Others See Us": Christians, Jews, "Others" in Late Antiquity*, ed. J. Neusner and E. S. Frerichs (Chico, CA: Scholars Press, 1985), 163–186.
Davies, W. D., and D. C. Allison Jr., *A Critical and Exegetical Commentary on the Gospel according to Saint Matthew*, 3 vols., ICC (Edinburgh: T&T Clark, 1988–1997).
Doering, L., *Schabbat. Sabbathalacha und -praxis im antiken Judentum und Urchristentum*, TSAJ 78 (Tübingen: Mohr Siebeck, 1999).
Dunn, J. D. G., *The Partings of the Ways. Between Christianity and Judaism and their Significance for the Character of Christianity* (London: SCM; Philadelphia, PA: Trinity Press International, 1991).
Eckstein, H.-J., "Die Weisung Jesu Christi und die Tora des Mose nach dem Matthäusevangelium," in *Jesus Christus als die Mitte der Schrift: Studien zur Hermeneutik des Evangeliums*, ed. C. Landmesser, H.-J. Eckstein, and H. Lichtenberger, BZNW 86 (Berlin and New York, NY: de Gruyter, 1997), 379–403.
Foster, P., *Community, Law and Mission in Matthew's Gospel*, WUNT 2/177 (Tübingen: Mohr Siebeck, 2004).
Foster, P., "Vespasian, Nerva, Jesus, and the *Fiscus Judaicus*," in *Israel's God and Rebecca's Children: Christology and Community in Early Judaism and Christianity. Essays in Honor of L. W. Hurtado and A. F. Segal*, ed. D. B. Capes et al. (Waco, TX: Baylor University Press, 2007), 303–320.
Frankemölle, H., "Die matthäische Kirche als Gemeinschaft des Glaubens. Prolegomena zu einer bundestheologischen Ekklesiologie," in *Ekklesiologie des Neuen Testaments. Für K. Kertelge*, ed. R. Kampling and T. Söding (Freiburg et al.: Herder, 1996), 85–132.

Hagner, D. A., "The *Sitz im Leben* of the Gospel of Matthew," in *Treasures New and Old. Recent Contributions to Matthean Studies*, ed. D. R. Bauer and M. A. Powell, SBLSymS 1 (Atlanta, GA: Scholars Press, 1996), 27–68.

Harrington, D. J., *The Gospel of Matthew*, SP 1 (Collegeville, MN: Liturgical Press, 1991).

Heemstra, M., *The Fiscus Judaicus and the Parting of the Ways*, WUNT 2/277 (Tübingen: Mohr Siebeck, 2010).

Heil, J. P., *The Death and Resurrection of Jesus: A Narrative-Critical Reading of Matthew 26–28* (Minneapolis, MN: Fortress, 1991).

Heil, J. P., "Ezekiel 34 and the Narrative Strategy of the Shepherd and the Sheep Metaphor in Matthew," *CBQ* 55 (1993): 698–708.

Horbury, W., "The Temple Tax," in *Jesus and the Politics of His Day*, ed. E. Bammel and C. F. D. Moule (Cambridge et al.: Cambridge University Press, 1984), 265–286.

Houlden, J. L., "The Puzzle of Matthew and the Law," in *Crossing the Boundaries. Essays in Biblical Interpretation in Honour of M. D. Goulder*, ed. S. E. Porter, P. Joyce, and D. E. Orton, BibInt 8 (Leiden et al.: Brill, 1994), 115–131.

Kampen, J., *Matthew within Sectarian Judaism*, AYBRL (New Haven, CT, and London: Yale University Press, 2019).

Konradt, M., *Israel, Kirche und die Völker im Matthäusevangelium*, WUNT 215 (Tübingen: Mohr Siebeck, 2007).

Konradt, M., *Israel, Church, and the Gentiles in the Gospel of Matthew*, trans. by K. Ess, BMSEC 2 (Waco, TX: Baylor University Press, 2014).

Konradt, M., *Das Evangelium nach Matthäus*, NTD 1 (Göttingen: Vandenhoeck & Ruprecht, 2015).

Konradt, M., "Die vollkommene Erfüllung der Tora und der Konflikt mit den Pharisäern im Matthäusevangelium," in idem, *Studien zum Matthäusevangelium*, WUNT 358 (Tübingen: Mohr Siebeck, 2016), 288–315.

Konradt, M., "Matthäus als Zeuge eines unpaulinischen Christentums. Anmerkungen zur These einer antipaulinischen Ausrichtung des Matthäusevangeliums," in idem, *Studien zum Matthäusevangelium*, WUNT 358 (Tübingen: Mohr Siebeck, 2016), 69–94.

Konradt, M., "Matthäus im Kontext. Eine Bestandsaufnahme zur Frage des Verhältnisses der matthäischen Gemeinde(n) zum Judentum," in idem, *Studien zum Matthäusevangelium*, WUNT 358 (Tübingen: Mohr Siebeck, 2016), 3–42.

Konradt, M., "Rezeption und Interpretation des Dekalogs im Matthäusevangelium," in idem, *Studien zum Matthäusevangelium*, WUNT 358 (Tübingen: Mohr Siebeck, 2016), 316–347.

Konradt, M., *Studien zum Matthäusevangelium*, WUNT 358 (Tübingen: Mohr Siebeck, 2016).

Konradt, M., "Das Gebot der Feindesliebe in Mt 5,43–48 und sein frühjüdischer Kontext," in *Ahavah: Die Liebe Gottes im Alten Testament*, ed. M. Oeming, ABIG 55 (Leipzig: Evangelische Verlagsanstalt, 2018), 349–389.

Konradt, M., *The Gospel according to Matthew: A Commentary*, trans. by E. Boring (Waco, TX: Baylor University Press, 2020).

Konradt, M., "Israel's Scripture in Matthew," in *The Old Testament in the New: Israel's Scriptures in the New Testament and other Early Christian Writings*, ed. M. Henze and D. Lincicum (Grand Rapids, MI: Eerdmans, forthcoming).

Kraus, W., *Das Volk Gottes: Zur Grundlegung der Ekklesiologie bei Paulus*, WUNT 85 (Tübingen: Mohr Siebeck, 1996).

Kraus, W., "Die Passion des Gottessohnes. Zur Bedeutung des Todes Jesu im Matthäusevangelium," *EvT* 57 (1997): 409–427.

Kraus, W., "Zur Ekklesiologie des Matthäusevangeliums," in *The Gospel of Matthew at the Crossroads of Early Christianity*, ed. D. Senior, BETL 243 (Leuven et al.: Peeters, 2011), 195–239.

Leon, H. J., *The Jews of Ancient Rome*, updated edition (Peabody, MA: Hendrickson, 1995).

Levine, A.-J., *The Social and Ethnic Dimensions of Matthean Salvation History*, SBEC 14 (Lewiston, NY et al.: Mellen, 1988).

Levine, L. I., "Synagoge," *TRE* 32 (2001): 499–508.

Lieu, J. M., "'The Partings of the Ways': Theological Construct or Historical Reality?," *JSNT* 56 (1994): 101–119 (repr. in J. M. Lieu, *Neither Jew Nor Greek? Constructing Early Christianity*, SNTW [London and New York, NY: T&T Clark, 2002], 11–29).

Liver, J., "The Half-Shekel Offering in Biblical and Post-Biblical Literature," *HTR* 56 (1963): 173–198.

Loader, W. R. G., *Jesus' Attitude towards the Law: A Study of the Gospels*, WUNT 2/97 (Tübingen: Mohr Siebeck, 1997).

Lohmeyer, M., *Der Apostelbegriff im Neuen Testament. Eine Untersuchung auf dem Hintergrund der synoptischen Aussendungsreden*, SBB 29 (Stuttgart: Katholisches Bibelwerk, 1995).

Luz, U., *Das Evangelium nach Matthäus*, vol. 1: *Mt 1–7*, EKK 1.1 (Zürich et al.: Benziger; Neukirchen-Vluyn: Neukirchener Verlag, 1985).

Luz, U., "Der Antijudaismus im Matthäusevangelium als historisches und theologisches Problem. Eine Skizze," *EvT* 53 (1993): 310–327.

Luz, U., *Das Evangelium nach Matthäus*, vol. 1: *Mt 1–7*, 5th ed., EKK 1.1 (Düsseldorf and Zürich: Benziger; Neukirchen-Vluyn: Neukirchener Verlag, 2002).

Luz, U., *Das Evangelium nach Matthäus*, vol. 4: *Mt 26–28*, EKK 1.4 (Düsseldorf and Zürich: Benziger; Neukirchen-Vluyn: Neukirchener Verlag, 2002).

Mayer-Haas, J., *"Geschenk aus Gottes Schatzkammer" (bSchab 10b): Jesus und der Sabbat im Spiegel der neutestamentlichen Schriften*, NTAbh 43 (Münster: Aschendorff, 2003).

McEleney, N. J., "Conversion, Circumcision, and the Law," *NTS* 20 (1974): 319–341.

Meier, J. P., *Law and History in Matthew's Gospel. A Redactional Study of Mt. 5:17–48*, AnBib 71 (Rome: Biblical Institute Press, 1976).

Mohrlang, R., *Matthew and Paul: A Comparison of Ethical Perspectives*, SNTSMS 48 (Cambridge: Cambridge University Press, 1984).

Nolland, J., "Uncircumcised Proselytes?," *JSJ* 12 (1981): 173–194.

Oliver, I. W., *Torah Praxis after 70 CE. Reading Matthew and Luke-Acts as Jewish Texts*, WUNT 2/355 (Tübingen: Mohr Siebeck, 2013).

Olmstead, W. G., *Matthew's Trilogy of Parables: The Nation, the Nations and the Reader in Matthew 21.28–22.14*, SNTSMS 127 (Cambridge: Cambridge University Press, 2003).

Ostmeyer, K.-H., "Das Vaterunser. Gründe für seine Durchsetzung als 'Urgebet' der Christenheit," *NTS* 50 (2004): 320–336.

Overman, J. A., *Matthew's Gospel and Formative Judaism: The Social World of the Matthean Community* (Minneapolis, MN: Fortress, 1990).

Przybylski, B., "The Setting of Matthean Anti-Judaism," in *Anti-Judaism in Early Christianity*, vol. 1: *Paul and the Gospels*, ed. P. Richardson, SCJud 2 (Waterloo: Wilfrid Laurier University Press, 1986), 181–200.

Reed, A. Y., and A.H. Becker, "Introduction: Traditional Models and New Directions," in *The Ways that Never Parted: Jews and Christians in Late Antiquity and the Early Middle Ages*, ed. A. H. Becker and A. Y. Reed, TSAJ 95 (Tübingen: Mohr Siebeck, 2003), 1–33.

Reinhartz, A., "A Fork in the Road or a Multi-Lane Highway? New Perspectives on the 'Parting of the Ways' Between Judaism and Christianity," in *The Changing Face of Judaism, Christianity, and Other Greco-Roman Religions in Antiquity*, ed. I. H. Henderson and G. S. Oegema, JSHRZ.St 2 (Gütersloh: Gütersloher Verlagshaus, 2006), 280–295.

Repschinski, B., *Nicht aufzulösen, sondern zu erfüllen: Das jüdische Gesetz in den synoptischen Jesuserzählungen*, FB 120 (Würzburg: Echter Verlag, 2009).

Runesson, A., "Rethinking Early Jewish–Christian Relations: Matthean Community History as Pharisaic Intergroup Conflict," *JBL* 127 (2008): 95–132.

Runesson, A., "Judging Gentiles in the Gospel of Matthew. Between 'Othering' and Inclusion," in *Jesus, Matthew's Gospel and Early Christianity: Studies in Memory of G. N. Stanton*, ed. D. M. Gurtner, J. Willitts, and R. A. Burridge, LNTS 435 (London and New York, NY: T&T Clark, 2011), 133–151.

Runesson, A., *Divine Wrath and Salvation in Matthew: The Narrative World in the First Gospel* (Minneapolis, MN: Fortress, 2016).

Saldarini, A. J., *Matthew's Christian-Jewish Community*, CSHJ (Chicago, IL, and London: The University of Chicago Press, 1994).

Schäfer, P., *Der Bar Kokhba-Aufstand. Studien zum zweiten jüdischen Krieg gegen Rom*, TSAJ 1 (Tübingen: Mohr Siebeck, 1981).

Segal, A. F., *Rebecca's Children. Judaism and Christianity in the Roman World* (Cambridge, MA, and London: Harvard University Press, 1986).

Senior, D., "The Lure of the Formula Quotations: Re-assessing Matthew's Use of the Old Testament with the Passion Narrative as Test Case," in *The Scriptures in the Gospels*, ed. C. M. Tuckett, BETL 131 (Leuven: Peeters, 1997), 89–115.

Senior, D., *Matthew*, ANTC (Nashville, TN: Abingdon, 1998).

Senior, D., "Between Two Worlds. Gentiles and Jewish Christians in Matthew's Gospel," *CBQ* 61 (1999): 1–23.

Senior, D., "Matthew at the Crossroads of Early Christianity. An Introductory Assessment," in *The Gospel of Matthew at the Crossroads of Early Christianity*, ed. D. Senior, BETL 243 (Leuven: Peeters, 2011), 3–23.

Sim, D. C., "The Gospel of Matthew and the Gentiles," *JSNT* 57 (1995): 19–48.

Sim, D. C., "Christianity and Ethnicity in the Gospel of Matthew," in *Ethnicity and the Bible*, ed. M. G. Brett, BibInt 19 (Leiden et al: Brill, 1996), 171–195.

Sim, D. C., *The Gospel of Matthew and Christian Judaism: The History and Social Setting of the Matthean Community*, SNTW (Edinburgh: T&T Clark, 1998).

Sim, D. C., "The magi: Gentiles or Jews?," *HTS* 55 (1999): 980–1000.

Sim, D. C., "Paul and Matthew on the Torah: Theory and Practice," in *Paul, Grace and Freedom: Essays in Honour of J. K. Riches*, ed. P. Middleton, A. Paddison, and K. J. Wenell (London and New York, NY: T&T Clark, 2009), 50–64.

Sim, D. C., and B. Repschinski, eds., *Matthew and His Christian Contemporaries*, LNTS 333 (London: T&T Clark, 2008).

Slee, M., *The Church in Antioch in the First Century CE: Communion and Conflict*, JSNTSup 244 (London and New York, NY: Sheffield Academic, 2003).

Snodgrass, K., "Matthew and Law," in *Treasures New and Old. Recent Contributions to Matthean Studies*, ed. D. R. Bauer and M. A. Powell, SBLSymS 1 (Atlanta, GA: Scholars Press, 1996), 99–127.

Stanton, G. N., *A Gospel for a New People: Studies in Matthew* (Edinburgh: T&T Clark, 1992).

Trebilco, P. R., *Self-designations and Group Identity in the New Testament* (Cambridge et al.: Cambridge University Press, 2012).

von Dobbeler, S., "Auf der Grenze. Ethos und Identität der matthäischen Gemeinde nach Mt 15,1–20," *BZ* 45 (2001): 55–78.

Weren, W., "The History and Social Setting of the Matthean Community," in *Matthew and the Didache: Two Documents from the Same Jewish-Christian Milieu?*, ed. H. van de Sandt (Assen: Van Gorcum; Minneapolis, MN: Fortress, 2005), 51–62.

White, L. M., "Crisis Management and Boundary Maintenance: The Social Location of the Matthean Community," in *Social History of the Matthean Community: Cross-Disciplinary Approaches*, ed. D. L. Balch (Minneapolis, MN: Fortress, 1991), 211–247.

Wong, K.-C., *Interkulturelle Theologie und multikulturelle Gemeinde im Matthäusevangelium: Zum Verhältnis von Juden- und Heidenchristen im ersten Evangelium*, NTOA 22 (Freiburg, CH: Universitätsverlag; Göttingen: Vandenhoeck & Ruprecht, 1992).

Ziethe, C., *Auf seinen Namen werden die Völker hoffen: Die matthäische Rezeption der Schriften Israels zur Begründung des universalen Heils*, BZNW 233 (Berlin and Boston, MA: de Gruyter, 2018).

Kylie Crabbe
Character and Conflict: Who Parts Company in Acts?

Abstract: Frühe Verfechter des "Parting of the ways"-Modells haben sich in verschiedener Weise auch auf die Apostelgeschichte bezogen, wogegen andere, die mit schärfer abgrenzenden Modellen zur Beschreibung der frühen Beziehungen zwischen Christen und Juden arbeiteten, Belege für eine feindselige Auseinanderentwicklung von Juden und Christen in der lukanischen Darstellung fanden. Der folgende Beitrag geht davon aus, dass sich einige Erzählfiguren in der Apostelgeschichte tatsächlich voneinander trennen. Er zeigt jedoch, dass diese Konflikte keine grundlegende, strukturelle Trennung bedeuten, ebenso wie auch die schroffe Trennung zwischen Paulus und Barnabas keinen generellen Traditionsbruch zwischen verschiedenen Richtungen der Jesusanhänger markiert. Nach der kurzen Diskussion einiger Hypothesen über die Historizität und die strukturelle Entwicklung des "Christentums" in Studien zur Apostelgeschichte wird als erstes die These aufgestellt, dass die auffällige Hybridität der Identität eingeführter Erzählfiguren zeigt, dass die vom Modell der "getrennten Wege" vorausgesetzte Binarität den Identitäten und Beziehungen in der Apostelgeschichte nicht gerecht wird. Im Anschluss daran werden weitere narrative Zielsetzungen untersucht, die sich aus Charakterisierungen und Konflikten in der Apostelgeschichte ergeben, etwa in Bezug auf die Auseinandersetzungen des Paulus mit eifersüchtigen "Juden aus der Asia", sein Verlassen der Synagogen in Korinth und Ephesus sowie die gespaltene Reaktion der Versammlung der Juden in Rom. Nach einer Analyse der Zusammenkunft in Jerusalem, bei der die Tora-Praxis für Heiden diskutiert wird, kommt der Beitrag schließlich zu dem Schluss, dass die Untersuchung der Apostelgeschichte als literarisches Werk zeigt, dass die entscheidende Frage nicht diejenige nach einem Konflikt zwischen "Christen" und "Juden" ist, sondern diejenige nach der Einbeziehung der Heiden in das endzeitliche Gottesvolk.

Keywords: Acts of the Apostles, Luke-Acts, Historicity of Acts, Hybrid identities, Ἰουδαῖοι, Jealousy, "The Jews from Asia," Lukan eschatology, Inclusion of the gentiles

To speak of a "parting of the ways" in Acts is to conjure parallel traditions, parallel "ways" (using a term native to the Acts narrative),[1] which have at a point diverged. The assumptions behind, and limitations of, the image have been ably interrogated, including by the other excellent contributions to this volume, and I will return to some of these questions below. But importantly for this discussion, the Acts of the Apostles featured in the works that first made use of this image.[2] Nonetheless, as Judith Lieu observes, a model of Jewish-Christian relations that imagines two paths diverging, and yet continuing, would have been unrecognisable to the historical participants,[3] and I likewise suggest that, despite the shared ἡ ὁδός language, it is unfamiliar to the world of Acts.

At base the parting of the ways, understood as a decisive break between "Judaism" and "Christianity," is foreign to Acts because the text contains no such separation – or, indeed, such institutional religious formations implied by this type of language. But there is conflict. Characters known as "the Jews" are portrayed as hostile antagonists. Moreover, if these acrimonious interactions were the core of a narrative about separate religious traditions, then the parting of the ways image would be foreign in a different way – Acts might be seen to support the very anti-Jewish sentiments that proponents of the image sought to counter. That there is conflict within Acts has attracted the attention of those looking for historical evidence of a decisive break between "Christianity" and "Judaism."[4] But identities and literary roles in Acts are more complex than this. While concerns about historicity consistently beleaguer critical Acts scholarship, there is a temptation to overlook the literary techniques at play in the ways that individuals and groups are characterised, their conflicts brought to life, and their functions within the wider narrative purposes of the text performed.

Some characters do part ways in Acts. But just as the fraught separation between Paul and Barnabas does not indicate a decisive rift between different brands of Jesus-followers that founds a separate tradition, Paul's departure from the synagogues in Corinth and Ephesus and the divided response of the

---

[1] Cf. Acts 9:2; 18:25–26; 19:9, 23; 22:4; 24:14, 22.
[2] J. Parkes, *The Conflict in the Church and the Synagogue: A Study of the Origins of Antisemitism* (New York: Meridian Books, 1961), 27–70; J.D.G. Dunn, *The Parting of the Ways: Between Christianity and Judaism and their Significance for the Character of Christianity* (London: SCM Press, 1991), 57–74, 117–30, 149–51.
[3] J.M. Lieu, "'The Parting of the Ways': Theological Construct or Historical Reality?," in *Neither Jew nor Greek? Constructing Early Christianity,* ed. eadem, 2nd ed. (London et al.: T&T Clark, 2016), 31–49, here 35.
[4] See further discussion below about assumptions of historicity in Acts scholarship.

Jewish gathering in Rome do not, I suggest, reflect a wider structural division.⁵ After a brief discussion of some assumptions about historicity and the formal development of "Christianity" in studies of Acts, in this paper I suggest in the first instance that the striking hybridity of identities as characters are introduced confirms that the binary presumed by the parted "ways" does not do justice to identities and relationships in Acts. Secondly, I argue that attention to Acts as a literary work reveals other purposes arising from the characterisation and conflicts, such that the relevant question is not about a conflict between "Christians" and "Jews," but about the inclusion of the gentiles in the end-time people of God.⁶

---

5 Although I generally translate Ἰουδαῖοι as Jews, rather than Judeans, I recognise that such translation decisions need to be contextual; see below on this difficult translation issue and the multivalence of the term.
6 Here I am not making historical claims about the social realities of the "parting," except by exercising caution about imposing later realities onto Acts and thus creating a confirmation bias effect by presupposing evidence of later divisions (on the latter, see A.Y. Reed and A.H. Becker, "Introduction: Traditional Models and New Directions," in *The Ways that Never Parted. Jews and Christians in Late Antiquity and the Early Middle Ages*, ed. A.H. Becker and A.Y. Reed, TSAJ 95 [Tübingen: Mohr Siebeck, 2003], 1–33, esp. 22). Approaching Acts as a literary work, I take the genre to be historiography (although recognising it is more distant from the prototypes of the genre such as those by Thucydides, Polybius, or Tacitus) and consider the relationship to Luke to be one of literary unity to the extent that, at minimum, based on the preface and other common themes, the writer of Acts intended it to be read as a sequel to the gospel. I use "Luke" to refer to the writer of both volumes without making a claim about the historical author, and "Luke/Acts" to indicate literary unity while recognising the relationship is not as certain as "Luke-Acts" implies. Noting that questions about the literary (or, rather, authorial) unity of Luke and Acts have also led some interpreters to prefer a second-century date for the composition of Acts (bearing in mind it must have been circulating by the time of Irenaeus), I still prefer a late first-century date for writing. On these important background questions to the study of Acts, see C.S. Keener, *Acts: An Exegetical Commentary*, 4 vols. (Grand Rapids: Baker Academic, 2012–2015), 1: 90–115; M.C. Parsons and R.I. Pervo, *Rethinking the Unity of Luke and Acts* (Minneapolis, MN: Fortress, 1993); P. Walters, *The Assumed Authorial Unity of Luke and Acts: A Reassessment of the Evidence*, SNTSMS 145 (Cambridge: Cambridge University Press, 2009); A. Gregory, "The Reception of Luke and Acts and the Unity of Luke-Acts," *JSNT* 29.4 (2007): 459–472; B.R. Gaventa, *Acts*, ANTC (Nashville: Abingdon Press, 2003), 51; L.T. Johnson, "Literary Criticism of Luke-Acts: Is Reception History Pertinent?," in *Rethinking the Unity and Reception of Luke and Acts*, ed. A. Gregory and C.K. Rowe, (Columbia: University of South Carolina Press, 2010), 66–69; L. Alexander, "Reading Luke-Acts from Back to Front," in *Acts in Its Ancient Literary Context: A Classicist Looks at the Acts of the Apostles*, eadem, JSNTSup 298 (London: T&T Clark, 2007), 207–229.

1 Historicity and assumptions about the parting of the ways in Acts

As noted by Todd Penner, the book of Acts suffers from a peculiar fate as a unique text within the NT canon, to which readers bring an enduring interest in historical questions.[7] While this in itself is not problematic,[8] Penner observes that even historical Jesus research takes a more pragmatic view of the gospel accounts, where diversity between the four canonical narratives has made addressing literary questions unavoidable, but that treatments of Acts are more likely to bring naïve historical questions.[9] A decade earlier, Loveday Alexander similarly considered investment in historicity to be a significant contributing factor in claims about the genre of Luke's two-volume work, with resistance to challenging the "historiography" attribution lying at least in part with an unhelpful conflation of historiography and historical accuracy.[10] More recently, assumptions about historicity manifest explicitly in projects such as that of the Acts seminar, but they also run as a current below much Acts scholarship.[11] It is in part this use of Acts as a bastion of authenticity that has led generations of readers interested in early church beginnings to turn to its pages for evidence of a decisive break

---

[7] T. C. Penner, "Madness in the Method? The Acts of the Apostles in Current Study," *CurBR* 2 (2004): 223–293, here 224.
[8] See, for instance, the careful discussion in L.T. Johnson, *The Acts of the Apostles*, SP 5 (Collegeville: Liturgical Press, 1992), 3–7.
[9] Penner, "Madness" (see n. 7), 224–225.
[10] L. Alexander, *The Preface to Luke's Gospel: Literary Convention and Social Context in Luke 1:1–4 and Acts 1:1*, SNTSMS 78 (Cambridge: Cambridge University Press, 1993), 3. Whether or not Acts is viewed as a form of Hellenistic historiography, the genre designation does not indicate the kind of concerns with historicity seen in contemporary history. See also Penner, "Madness" (see n. 7), 229, 234, 239; G.E. Sterling, *Historiography and Self-Definition: Josephos, Luke-Acts, and Apologetic Historiography*, NovTSup 64 (Leiden: Brill, 1991), 2.
[11] D.E. Smith and J.B. Tyson, eds., *Acts and Christian Beginnings: The Acts Seminar Report* (Salem: Polebridge, 2013). See also, for instance, the discussion of Paul's beatings and shipwrecks in Keener, *Acts* (see n. 6), 1: 462; cf. 26–29; and, particularly in relation to areas of interest to this paper: various contributions to R. Bauckham, ed., *The Book of Acts in Its Palestinian Setting*, BAFCS (Grand Rapids: Eerdmans, 1995); C.J. Hemer, *The Book of Acts in the Setting of Hellenistic History*, BAFCS (Winona Lake: Eisenbrauns, 1990); J. Taylor, "Why were the Disciples First Called 'Christians' at Antioch? (Acts 11,26)," *RB* 100 (1994): 75–94; C. Bennema, "The Ethnic Conflict in Early Christianity: An Appraisal of Bauckham's Proposal on the Antioch Crisis and the Jerusalem Council," *JETS* 56.4 (2013): 753–763.

with Judaism that they know (or claim) from a contemporary standpoint has at some point taken place.¹²

This interest in Acts as a historical source likewise features in the first explorations of the parting of the ways. In what appears to be the first use of the phrase in 1934, James Parkes discusses Acts as a historical source for the precursor events to the decisive breach, which he in turn dates to 80–90 CE.¹³ James Dunn, in his use of the phrase many decades later, likewise views events narrated in Acts as historical evidence and talks about the "*first*" of many "*further partings of the ways.*"¹⁴ For Dunn, Stephen's speech and its aftermath are the "first" parting in relation to the temple and Paul's mission to the gentiles is an "irreparable breach" for Jews, although the point of no return comes between the first and second revolts.¹⁵ However, while these approaches seek to overcome ideas of a separation as a result of "Jewish failure" and related supercessionism, others find just such a dynamic in Acts.¹⁶ It is a guiding principle of Ernst Haenchen's magisterial commentary that Luke writes from a historical context in which a decisive break has taken place, while literary features present a scenario in which the Christian actors are blameless for the breach.¹⁷ And such views are mapped

---

12 I do not deal here with the question of the ways in which the text of Acts was used by later writers to support a separation and/or anti-Jewish sentiments or institutional claims. That important area would be the topic for a separate paper.
13 Parkes, *The Conflict* (see n. 2), 77–79. Some query whether Parkes used the phrase with the full set of assumptions about the multivalent communities of Judaism and Christianity that parted and both continued to thrive and develop in their own ways, and whether this appeared only with James Dunn's 1991 work. See Lieu, "The Parting" (see n. 3), 31, who also points to F.J. Foakes Jackson's discussion of "the parting of the roads" as an anticipation (although still supercessionist), and discussion in Reed and Becker, "Introduction" (see n. 6), 8.
14 Dunn, *The Parting* (see n. 2), 230 (italics original).
15 Dunn, *The Parting* (see n. 2), 238.
16 From the first use of the phrase by Parkes, it was part of a project designed to respond to concerns about Anti-Semitism in the author's own setting. Dunn's later use, responsive to the context that prompted the New Perspective on Paul, likewise reflects a concern to provide a more respectful and sympathetic account of the diversity of Judaism and Christianity's relationship to it—although Dunn's treatment of Christianity is rather more univocal, despite his attention to diversity among Jewish traditions (e.g. Dunn, *The Parting* [see n. 2], 230). See also discussion in Reed and Becker, "Introduction" (see n. 6), 7–16.
17 E. Haenchen, *The Acts of the Apostles: A Commentary* (Oxford: Blackwell, 1971), 540. Though Haenchen is not, of course, the first, or indeed most extreme, proponent of this view, which spans back in modern biblical scholarship to F.C. Baur and earlier.

onto Acts analysis with greater or lesser degrees of subtlety by others, such as Jack T. Sanders[18] and François Bovon.[19]

Nonetheless, there are many who would challenge both such interpretations of the dynamic in Acts and these historical claims about a parting of the ways.[20] Such approaches include divergent views about the literary portrait of "Judaism" or "Jews" in Luke's text as well as alternative accounts of the relationship between Jewish communities and members of the Jesus movement at the time at which Acts was written (whether that is taken to be a late first- or early second-century dating).[21] Among other concerns, critics of the parting of the ways paradigm caution against importing a fourth-century institutional framework for either "Judaism" or "Christianity" onto an earlier time.[22]

In an important contribution, however, Hubert Cancik suggests that Acts does indicate an increasingly institutionalised form of church life and that this, in fact, is the central purpose of the text.[23] Contributing to the long-running

---

[18] J.T. Sanders, *The Jews in Luke-Acts* (Minneapolis, MN: Fortress, 1987). I am heartened by Jack Sanders' own suggestion that his reader might be grateful for the omission of a detailed footnote on the history of scholarship on this question, and follow at least here, if not elsewhere, in his footsteps (J.T. Sanders, "Who is a Jew and Who is a Gentile in the Book of Acts?," *NTS* 37 [1991]: 434–455, here 435). The history of scholarly engagement on this question is vast and frequently repetitive. It spreads into questions about the nature of the Jews, explanations for Jesus' death, the historical existence (or not) of godfearers, and much more.

[19] F. Bovon, "Israel, die Kirche und die Völker im lukanischen Doppelwerk," *TLZ* 108 (1983): 403–414. See discussion also in R.L. Brawley, *Luke-Acts and the Jews: Conflict, Apology, and Conciliation*, SBLMS 33 (Atlanta: Scholars Press, 1989), 139–154. More recently, Bennema also argues for a decisive break by the second century (Bennema, "The Ethnic Conflict" [see n. 11], 753).

[20] Brawley, *Luke-Acts* (see n. 19), 151; Keener, *Acts* (see n. 6), 1: 462–468; for a different approach, see J. Jervell, "The Divided People of God: The Restoration of Israel and the Salvation of the Gentiles," in idem, *Luke and the People of God: A New Look at Luke-Acts* (Eugene, OR: Wipf and Stock, 2002; originally published 1965), 41–74.

[21] On the dating of Acts, see n. 6 above.

[22] Reed and Becker argue that Parkes had already noted many of the problems that later scholars would find with the parting of the ways, including the need to avoid reading fourth-century conceptions into the text, though they say this was neglected by later work (Reed and Becker, "Introduction" [see n. 6], 16–17). Other concerns they identify include assumptions of a clean break after which there were no further interactions or points of convergence. On anachronism and geographical variation, see respectively Keener, *Acts* (see n. 6), 1: 469, 468.

[23] H. Cancik, "The History of Culture, Religion, and Institutions in Ancient Historiography: Philological Observations Regarding Luke's History," *JBL* 116.4 (1997): 673–695. Cancik avoids the passionate political concerns that animated earlier analysis of "early Catholic" tendencies, see for instance, H. Conzelmann, "Luke's Place in the Development of Early Christianity," in *Studies in Luke-Acts: Essays Presented in Honor of Paul Schubert*, ed. L.E. Keck and J.L. Martyn

debate about the genre of Luke/Acts[24] and citing as comparanda Greek and Latin establishment historiographies about religious traditions and philosophical movements, Cancik presents the provocative thesis that Luke/Acts should be understood as an "institutional history." He argues that, rather than a *bios* of Jesus or any individual apostle, it is, in fact, the church (ἐκκλησία) which is the protagonist of Luke's historiography. Cancik highlights the phenomena which are introduced over the course of the narrative in what he claims follow increasingly bureaucratic processes. This includes presbyters (e.g. 14:23; 15:2, 22; 20:17) and bishops (20:28), methods of electing leadership (1:23–26), a council to address doctrinal dispute (15:6–21) which then issues a statement of its decision to be followed by other members (15:22–29), and so on.[25]

Cancik's approach takes a(n overly) maximalist interpretation of the level of internal organisation within the believers' movement in Acts. Although of course he is right to note the use of some ecclesial language, it is important to avoid imbuing terms like ἐκκλησία and πρεσβύτερος with layers of meaning they would only later take on, and on the question of what is commonly called "the Jerusalem Council," it is worth noting that in fact this is a gathering of key characters and groups who are brought together (συνάγω, 15.6), as characters are brought together elsewhere in the narrative (4:31; 11:26; 13:44; 14:27; 20:7; cf. 4:5, 27). The gathering is prompted by Paul and Barnabas' desire to discuss an emerging problem and its decision is certainly significant, but that does not make this narrative episode akin to later conciliar events. Cancik's underlying insight about the central place of the growing movement to the narrative of Acts is nonetheless well made.[26] Rather than focusing on this as institutionalisation that appears increasingly static, though, I suggest this central focus on the developing movement reflects more the increasing momentum of the apostles'

(Nashville: Abingdon Press, 1966), 298–316; W.G. Kümmel, "Current Theological Accusations against Luke," *ANQ* 16 (1975): 131–145.

24 On this designation, see n. 6.

25 In a slightly similar vein, Wilson makes comparisons with Graeco-Roman foundation narratives, arguing that Luke employs features to make his narrative make sense to a Graeco-Roman (non-Jewish) person as supporting the foundation of a new group. He finds eight shared features between these myths and Acts, though also presumes unhelpfully that Jewish groups would not also be making use of Hellenistic literary forms (W.T. Wilson, "Urban Legends: Acts 10:1–11:18 and the Strategies of Greco-Roman Foundation Narratives," *JBL* 120.1 [2001]: 77–99, esp. 98–99).

26 See the positive reception of the creativity of Cancik's approach, if not complete agreement with what she considers imprecise language for the genre designation, in C.K. Rothschild, *Luke-Acts and the Rhetoric of History: An Investigation of Early Christian Historiography*, WUNT 2/175 (Tübingen: Mohr Siebeck, 2004), 53–55.

proclamation as it gathers people into the unfolding eschatological events begun with Jesus' resurrection (more on this below).

More problematic for the current purposes, however, is Cancik's immediate jump to assuming that the level of internal organisation he identifies supports claims about a decisive break between these Christians and Judaism.[27] The very existence of methods for navigating community life among the early Christians does not in itself indicate the nature of their relationship to non-Jesus-believing Jewish characters (of which there is a great variety in the Acts narrative). Indeed, a trap of the parting of the ways image is to assume that certain identities are mutually exclusive and thus presume a neat distinction between the (two) groups. By contrast, the following shows that the Acts narrative frequently highlights the hybrid nature of its characters' identities.

2 Hybrid identities in Acts

In his elaboration of the parting of the ways, James Dunn claims: "Christianity began by rejecting the ethnocentricity of Judaism and of Jewish Christianity."[28] But it is a striking feature of the characterisation in Acts that people are frequently introduced with the multiplicity of their identity on display. Aquila is a Jew who is a native of Pontus,[29] recently of Italy, and now in Corinth – all of which is revealed within a verse (18:2). There is "a Jew named Apollos, a native of Alexandria" (18:24), Timothy is the son of a Jewish woman "but his father was a Greek" (16:1),[30] and, of course, Paul of Tarsus' hybrid identity is revealed over time, as he is presented with excellent credentials as both Jew and Roman (16:37–38; 21:39; 22:1–3, 25–29).[31] This hybridity demonstrates the complexity of identity in the text, which is retained alongside the characters' identities as believers in Jesus. Eric Barreto rightly criticises Lukan scholarship for an assumption that identity is neatly either Jewish, Christian, or Roman, failing to give due attention to its fluid and persistently hybrid nature.[32] Reading a binary

---

[27] Cancik, "The History" (see n. 23), e.g. 674–675, 678.
[28] Here Dunn is criticising later developments that in his view recreated ethnic exclusivity, by imagining Christians as a "third race" and rejecting Judaism (Dunn, *The Parting* [see n. 2], 248).
[29] Aquila is introduced as Jewish before the reader is given his name (18.2).
[30] Timothy's hybridity relates to another broader theme in the passage introducing Timothy, explaining the context of his circumcision.
[31] See further below.
[32] E.D. Barreto, *Ethnic Negotiations: The Function of Race and Ethnicity in Acts 16*, (PhD diss., Emory University, 2010), 239. This introduces the question of the term χριστιανοί, which appears

like the parting of the ways into such descriptions might in part be read as a failure to account for the indications that multiple facets to identity can coexist.³³

The description of the groups gathered in the temple for Pentecost festival celebrations in Acts 2 highlights such layers of identity. All are Jewish. But there is a complex interplay between this identity and the other geographical locations which determine their "native" origins. After the scene setting of the dramatic events of wind, fire, and spoken languages, the narrative asserts: "Now there were dwelling in Jerusalem Jews, devout men (ἄνδρες) from every nation under heaven" (2:5). They come together as a multitude at the sound, and are astounded because they each hear the words in their own "native" languages: καὶ πῶς ἡμεῖς ἀκούομεν ἕκαστος τῇ ἰδίᾳ διαλέκτῳ ἡμῶν ἐν ᾗ ἐγεννήθημεν; (2:8; cf. v. 6). The long list of locations that follows spans the geographical range and perhaps serves to foreshadow the universal scope of the apostles' preaching.³⁴ But it also shows that all of these identities coexist happily with Jewish identity.

---

twice in Acts. In neither place does it appear to be a self-designated title. The first arises in the narration, through which Luke states that the title χριστιανοί was first used in Antioch (11:26). In the second instance, Agrippa makes a riposte in response to Paul's preaching about the resurrection as in continuity with the promises of Moses and the prophets, saying "would you so easily make me a χριστιανός?" (26:28). Paul's response ignores the title, and simply says he would prefer that everyone were like him but for the chains. Haenchen considers various views but then supports an older traditional argument: "The disciples were first called 'Christians,' 'Christ-people,' in Antioch, and that by the Gentile population, because it was here for the first time that they clearly stood out as a separate sect from the Jews" (Haenchen, *The Acts* [see n. 17], 368 n. 3). However, I suggest that, given the hybrid identities we see throughout Acts, it is possible to have such a feature stand out without necessitating a parting of ways (as in the case of Pharisees). Taylor argues that χριστιανοί was a term immediately associated with sedition, though his historical arguments are less convincing (see, e.g. Taylor, "Why Were" [see n. 11], 94). Despite some puzzling over the term, it is at least clear that other self-designating terms appear frequently in the text, including believers, brothers, and so on, and yet the narration does not go on to use χριστιανοί in this way. Hence, I have not adopted this term throughout the paper, and do not think the two uses in Acts 11 and 26 are convincing evidence of a decisive break with Judaism.

33 D. Boyarin, "Semantic Differences; or, 'Judaism'/'Christianity'," in *The Ways That Never Parted. Jews and Christians in Late Antiquity and the Early Middle Ages*, ed. A.H. Becker and A.Y. Reed, TSAJ 95 (Tübingen: Mohr Siebeck, 2003), 65–85.

34 Cf. 2:39. R.C. Tannehill, *The Narrative Unity of Luke-Acts: A Literary Interpretation*, vol. 2 (Minneapolis, MN: Fortress, 1990), 27. Bauckham notes practical ways in which the message might be presented as being spread by pilgrims moving between Jerusalem and diaspora locations (Bauckham, "James and the Jerusalem Church," in *The Book of Acts in Its Palestinian Setting*, ed. idem, BAFCS [Grand Rapids: Eerdmans, 1995], 415–480, esp. 423). Reflections on the world-wide mission do not, however, necessitate the claim that 1:8 serves as a "table of con-

The translation of Ἰουδαῖοι is notoriously difficult and the subject of considerable recent disagreement. While all agree that the identity behind the term can include both geographical and philosophical/creedal elements, views differ on whether the more accurate and/or socially responsible translation is "Jews" or "Judeans." Critics of the former argue that it ties the use in biblical texts to its meaning in later institutional forms from rabbinic Judaism and thus risks connecting the criticisms of Ἰουδαῖοι in the biblical text to modern Jews; therefore Judean is the more appropriate translation to indicate the kinds of geographical designations for identities seen elsewhere in contemporaneous texts.[35] The opposing view, however, observes that such a move effectively eliminates Jews from history (asserting that there is an important, though not simplistic, connection between earlier Jewish material and later Jews), and that it does this by obscuring – but not actually addressing – the problems of anti-Jewish material in the biblical text.[36] Moreover, many recent contributions have noted that the complex issues of ethnicity cannot be resolved through a single translation choice.[37]

---

tents" for the book as a whole (cf. Gaventa, *Acts* [see n. 6], 65); Rome is neither the theological nor political endpoint to the narrative and neither should it be considered "the ends of the earth" (E.E. Ellis, "The End of the Earth (Acts 1:8)," in *History and Interpretation in New Testament Perspective*, idem, BibInt [Leiden: Brill, 2001], 53–63). An appreciation for Luke's portrait of the spread of the gospel in Acts should be distinguished from assumptions about literary structure.

35 S. Mason, "Jews, Judaeans, Judaizing, Judaism: Problems of Categorization in Ancient History," *JSJ* 38 (2007): 457–512; idem and P.F. Esler, "Judaean and Christ-Follower Identities: Grounds for a Distinction," *NTS* 63 (2017): 493–515; S. Mason, "Ancient Jews or Judeans? Different Questions, Different Answers," in *Jew and Judean: A Marginalia Forum on Politics and Historiography in the Translation of Ancient Texts*, ed. T.M. Law and C. Halton (Los Angeles, CA: Marginalia Review of Books, 2014), 11–17; M. Lowe, "Concepts and Words," in *Jew and Judean: A Marginalia Forum on Politics and Historiography in the Translation of Ancient Texts*, ed. T.M. Law and C. Halton (Los Angeles, CA: Marginalia Review of Books, 2014), 33–37.

36 A. Reinhartz, "The Vanishing Jews of Antiquity," in *Jew and Judean: A Marginalia Forum on Politics and Historiography in the Translation of Ancient Texts*, ed. T.M. Law and C. Halton (Los Angeles, CA: Marginalia Review of Books, 2014), 5–10; J.E. Taylor, "'Judean' and 'Jew', Jesus and Paul," in *Jew and Judean: A Marginalia Forum on Politics and Historiography in the Translation of Ancient Texts*, ed. T.M. Law and C. Halton (Los Angeles, CA: Marginalia Review of Books, 2014), 27–32; J. Klawans, "An Invented Revolution," in *Jew and Judean: A Marginalia Forum on Politics and Historiography in the Translation of Ancient Texts*, ed. T.M. Law and C. Halton (Los Angeles, CA: Marginalia Review of Books, 2014), 38–41.

37 Barreto, "Ethnic Negotiations" (see n. 32), 72; A.Y. Reed, "*Ioudaios* Before and After 'Religion'," in *Jew and Judean: A Marginalia Forum on Politics and Historiography in the Translation of Ancient Texts*, ed. T.M. Law and C. Halton (Los Angeles, CA: Marginalia Review of Books, 2014), 21–26.

The geographical descriptions and accounts of "native" languages in Acts 2 provides a good example that calls into question consistently translating in a way that allows the geographical rendering to dominate. It is a case in point of the translation difficulty for diaspora Ἰουδαῖοι, for whom a native language and origin comes from outside of Judea.[38] The presence of proselytes and godfearers[39] here likewise highlights the problem – although in Jerusalem currently, they have not been born into Jewish tradition. However this is understood, as affirmation of a philosophy or politeia (which can retain an original link to the people of the land which developed this politeia), it is at home in a hybrid identity which includes other geographical locations and diaspora settings.[40] Even here in the heartland of Jerusalem, Luke presents Jewish identity as something of a melting pot.

The scene could be confusing in terms of the range of identities on display, and as Peter variously addresses ἄνδρες Ἰουδαῖοι καὶ οἱ κατοικοῦντες Ἱερουσαλὴμ πάντες (V. 14), Ἄνδρες Ἰσραηλῖται (V. 22; cf. v. 23; 3:12; 13:26), and Ἄνδρες ἀδελφοί (v. 29). For instance, are these terms simply synonyms,[41] and who are the residents of Jerusalem? Are they those who always live there, or those who have attended for the festival? Or is it best to side with Robert Tannehill who argues that this needs to be interpreted as Peter addressing characters who have been in Jerusalem since before Passover and thus personally witnessed Jesus' ministry?[42] Regardless, Peter is not addressing only a subset of the crowd (those whose native region is Judea), but all of them as Jews (or, at the very least, as adherents to the beliefs and practices arising from the Judean politeia).[43] Nonetheless the two identities, as Jews and natives of other locations, fit together. It seems that readers may be able to code switch between these different meanings and identities without causing difficulty, as they play some part in characterisation.

---

38 Reinhartz, "The Vanishing" (see n. 36); J.E. Taylor, "'Judean' and 'Jew'" (see n. 36).
39 Frequently mentioned as a specific (contested) category in Acts scholarship. See discussion in J. Jervell, "The Church of Jews and Godfearers," in *Luke-Acts and the Jewish People: Eight Critical Perspectives*, ed. J.B. Tyson (Minneapolis, MN: Augsburg, 1988), 11–20.
40 Cf. Josephus, *Against Apion* 2.165–167.
41 On meanings for "Israelites" here, see Keener, *Acts* (see n. 6), 1: 941–943.
42 Tannehill, *Narrative Unity* (see n. 34), 27–28. Cf. the different use of the same phrase in Acts 13:27–28, where the residents of Jerusalem, although still responsible for Jesus' death, are not the audience but another group.
43 The ESV and NRSV translations, "Men of Judea," arguably here confuse things, when the audience of Peter's speech comes from a range of locations, whereas the same term for antagonist characters is not translated as Judeans but Jews.

This highlights a difficulty in studies that conflate an interest in ascertaining the historicity of the Acts narrative with a more univocal understanding of Jewish identity. For instance, Cornelis Bennema concludes a study on the historicity of the Jerusalem Council with the claim, reminiscent of Dunn's view cited above, that Christianity's innovation was its trans-ethnic extension: "The critical factor in the formation of early Christian identity was that it was no longer attached to a particular ethno-religious identity. Gentiles could be part of the people of God without exchanging their Gentile identity for a Jewish one."[44] But studies like that of Barreto reveal that this idea of exchanging identities is wrong headed.[45] The literary evidence across Acts is of hybrid identities – including of those who are Jewish but not Jesus-believers – without such a sense of a singular "ethnic" identity.

Two further examples of hybrid identities warrant discussion: Moses and Paul. In Stephen's rendition of the history of Israel in Acts 7 he describes Moses not only in his role as part of the rescue from Egypt and as law giver, but his prowess within his Egyptian setting. During his time being raised by Pharaoh's daughter, he was "instructed in all the wisdom of the Egyptians, and he was mighty in his words and deeds" (7:22). The relatively long description of Moses sets him up as one rejected by his own people (vv. 23–29, 35), who becomes "both ruler and redeemer" (v. 35), establishing a type with Jesus (cf. v. 37).[46] And yet his Egyptian expertise is important enough to mention in his paideia, and seems also to play a role in his ability to perform the rescue as a relative outsider.[47]

Paul's hybrid identity plays to multiple sides even more explicitly. When "the Jews from Asia"[48] incite trouble in the Jerusalem temple so that "all the city was stirred up" (21:30), and they seize and seek to kill Paul, the tribune hears word of the chaos and comes with soldiers. Bound with chains, though in fact saved from the violence for now, Paul speaks first to the tribune in Greek, describing him-

---

[44] Bennema, "The Ethnic Conflict" (see n. 11), 762–763.
[45] Barreto, "Ethnic Negotiations" (see n. 32), e.g. 239.
[46] In terms of the nature of Jewish identity, it is also of interest that Luke has Stephen describe Pharaoh dealing "shrewdly with our γένος" (7:19).
[47] Barreto applies the work of postcolonial theorist Homi Bhabha, among others, who highlights the ways in which subalterns deploy hybridity to survive in different political settings (Barreto, "Ethnic Negotiations" [see n. 32], 211–212). This is relevant to the portrayal of Moses here. Likewise, reflections on the ways that colonised groups make use of the genres and rhetorical techniques of a ruling culture in order to define their own traditions and groups and to present this in a way that would be received positively emerge from Gregory Sterling's work on apologetic historiography (Sterling, *Historiography* [see n. 10], 16–19).
[48] This group is discussed in more detail below, at 3.3.

self: "I am a Jew, from Tarsus in Cilicia, a citizen of no obscure city" (v. 39). The tribune acquiesces to Paul's request to address the crowd. Paul then slips competently into Hebrew and gives his credentials, which begin in the same way but then take a different direction: "I am a Jew, born in Tarsus in Cilicia, but brought up in this city, educated at the feet of Gamaliel according to the strict manner of the law of our fathers, being zealous for God as all of you are this day" (22:3). His track record then extends to his claim that the high priest and "the whole council of elders" can provide witness to his previous persecution of the followers of the Way, which acts as sympathetic background to his dramatic call narrative (cf. 22:17–20).[49] But the rancour of the crowd is again raised when Paul describes his call to the gentiles.

Having spoken in Greek on his Roman identity, and Hebrew for his Jewish credentials and call by Jesus, as he is about to be flogged Paul returns to a further revelation about his Roman identity: he is a Roman citizen. Over four verses, Paul's status is clarified and reiterated: he is a Roman citizen by birth (22:25–29; cf. 16:37). Thus, the structure of the passage itself emphasises the hybridity of Paul's identity, and shows that these facets all go together – Roman, Jewish, and "Christian."[50] And, like Moses, all aspects of Paul's identity are going to come in handy for the diplomacy required to fulfil his mission.

While these various layers demonstrate that identities in Acts are not simplistically distinguished into binaries, or "exchanged" for one another, the characterisation also shows that there is a variety of ways of being Ἰουδαῖοι and of being Jesus-followers. Given that these examples show that multiple aspects of identity *can* coexist, the question remains whether the Acts narrative also indicates any separation of identity in the type indicated by the parting of the ways. Here characterisations emerge that have supported the kinds of pictures of Judaism that writers like Parkes and Dunn sought to counter, and yet I suggest these are not indications of a decisive split but features serving a wider narrative purpose.

---

[49] Even within that call narrative, prominence is given to the figure of Ananias, who is "a devout man according to the law, well spoken of by all the Jews who lived there" (22:12), while Paul's faithful status is likewise emphasised by the content of Ananias' vision (22:14).
[50] On the term "Christian," see n. 32.

3 Jewish character groups and the motif of jealousy in Acts

In speculating on the language surrounding the parting of the ways, Daniel Boyarin wonders about conceptualising "Jewish" and "Christian" identities in a scalar way.[51] In so doing, he makes an important move away from the binaries that dominate discussion on this theme and, even though his focus rests on historical realities, such a move is helpful in approaching the literary groupings of Acts also. Although, I suggest, it may not be possible or helpful to conform the differences to points on a single spectrum, differences arising from characterisation and the combinations of hybrid other identities create a diversity that is important to Acts' narrative world.[52] Ἰουδαῖοι can mean different things in different contexts of the narrative.

3.1 Jewish Jesus-followers

While all of the characters in the early chapters are Jews, and protagonists throughout both self-identify as Jews and are named as such by external characters (16:20; 18:14–15; 25:18–19), this status intersects with believer status in their characterisation and narrative role. There are characters such as Timothy's mother, who is explicitly identified as "a Jewish woman who was a believer (γυναικὸς Ἰουδαίας πιστῆς)" (16:1), and others who are "unbelieving Jews" (14:2; 19:9). Paul is described as from "the sect of the Nazarenes" (24:5, 14; cf. 28:22), an apparently Jewish group, while other sects also feature. For instance, Pharisees appear in four key places across Acts: in the conflict with authorities in Acts 5 where Gamaliel (a respected Pharisee) determines the course of the action (5:34–40); in the gathering about circumcision in Jerusalem (15:5); in the audience of Paul's speech in Acts 23:6–9, where Paul exploits sectarian fault lines over the resurrection of the dead to gain leverage with the Pharisees (who then speak in his favour) over the Sadducees; and Paul's own claim to membership of this sect

---

51 Boyarin, "Semantic Differences" (see n. 33), 74–77.
52 Snyder distinguishes between "pure" gentiles and gentiles with previous experience with Judeans, and discusses the importance of these differences for the "story world" of Acts (J.A. Snyder, "Sociolinguistic Dynamics and Characterization in the Acts of the Apostles," in *Characters and Characterization in Luke-Acts*, ed. F.E. Dicken and eadem, LNTS [London: Bloomsbury, 2016], 169–184). Note also that Brawley talks about characters who are treated positively as "almost" Christian, such as the Pharisees (Brawley, *Luke-Acts* [see n. 19], 98–100, 105–6).

(26:5; cf. 22:3). Rather than attempting to identify Pharisees as consistently positive or negative characters in Acts,[53] a more complex account of each characterisation reflects the hybrid identities which appear together with acknowledgement of this sectarian affiliation.[54] Most importantly, those in Acts 15 are Jesus-followers. This makes them fundamentally different from the Pharisee characters in Acts 5 and 23, even as their intervention in the debate reflects halakhic argumentation and interests that make them a plausible grouping within the Jesus movement to put such a view. The opinion they offer may be at odds with that ultimately put forward by James and affirmed by the gathering (as discussed further below), but they are both Pharisees *and* insiders within the Jesus movement. Moreover, they perform an important narrative function to pose a plausible alternative view of the practices that might be required of gentile converts.[55]

Indeed, the *function* of characterisation is important. This is an essential element of approaching Acts as a literary work rather than simply a source of historical data. As the drama of the Acts narrative plays out, different characters and groups of characters take on certain roles. Some Jewish characters serve to confirm that the believers remain rooted in Jewish heritage (e.g. 22:12). Meanwhile, particular antagonist characters act in opposition to the apostles, including Jewish authorities, as well as more general antagonist Jewish groupings from specific locations as the story develops.

3.2 Jewish authorities

The presentation of Jewish authorities in the early chapters of Acts shows them as fumbling and mistaken. When conflict first emerges in Acts, the apostles are arrested by temple authorities for preaching about Jesus' resurrection in two parallel scenes in Acts 4 and 5. The interactions are hostile, and they also involve

---

[53] See, for a positive account in Acts: M. Marshall, *The Portrayals of the Pharisees in the Gospels and Acts*, FRLANT 254 (Göttingen: Vandenhoeck & Ruprecht, 2015), 158–160; D.B. Gowler, *Host, Guest, Enemy and Friend: Portraits of the Pharisees in Luke and Acts*, Emory Studies in Early Christianity 2 (New York: Peter Lang, 1991), 279; on the negatives: J.A. Darr, "Irenic or Ironic? Another Look at Gamaliel before the Sanhedrin (Acts 5:33–42)," in *Literary Studies in Luke-Acts: Essays in Honor of Joseph B. Tyson*, ed. R.P. Thompson and T.E. Phillips (Macon: Mercer University Press, 1998), 121–140, esp. 125.
[54] See R. Hakola, "'Friendly' Pharisees and Social Identity in Acts," in *Contemporary Studies in Acts*, ed. T.E. Phillips (Macon: Mercer University Press, 2009), 181–200.
[55] Brawley argues Luke uses the "high" status of the Pharisees as a way to build credibility for the Jesus movement (Brawley, *Luke-Acts* [see n. 19], 105–106).

elements of irony bordering on comedy – such as when the high priest gathers the whole council to put the apostles on trial, without knowing (as the reader does) that they have already been released by an angel and are back again preaching in the temple: this is divinely-backed activity that cannot be stopped (cf. 5:38–39).[56]

The characterisation of these Jewish authorities is stylised in the service of a broader narrative purpose. They are shown uncertain about how to respond to this bewildering new sect and, by implication of Luke's rhetoric, unable to recognise what God is doing in their midst in keeping with the scriptures.[57] They are opponents of the apostolic movement, and, moreover, the high priest, who initiates the apostles' arrest with the Sadducees in Acts 5, does so out of jealousy at their popularity with the crowd (5:17) – ζῆλος is an important term, to which I return below. Paul, on the other hand, later employs rhetoric to communicate respect to the high priest (23:5) – demonstrating in the same verse that he considers himself part of the same people, and thus bolstering support that the conflict is of an intramural nature.[58] Likewise, the encounter between Peter, the apostles, and the council in Acts 5 shows, rather than disrespect of the Jewish authorities, an overriding commitment to listening to God over people (5:29), with the negative implication akin to the accusations of the prophets, that the Jewish authorities should likewise be attending to God, the true authority.[59]

3.3 "The Jews" from cities in Asia

Later in Acts, a literary pattern emerges about a series of antagonist Jewish groups. "The Jews" whose ire has been raised in earlier encounters with Paul follow him along his missionary journey to the next cities and cause new trouble along the way. In the course of this repetition, these characters become a literary

---

[56] In keeping with Gamaliel's pragmatic advice (K. Crabbe, "Being Found Fighting Against God: Luke's Gamaliel and Josephus on Human Responses to Divine Providence," *ZNW* 106.1 [2015]: 21–39, esp. 27–36).
[57] As conflict builds across Acts, Jewish authorities will be involved again. They are implicated in the plot against Paul, although they are not the group which forms the plan or makes a vow to take his life in Acts 23:12–15. Jewish authorities are portrayed negatively here, although note that "the rulers of the synagogue" in Pisidian Antioch invite Paul and Barnabas to speak (13:15), and this is successful on that day; they are not presented homogenously.
[58] M. Salmon, "Insider or Outsider? Luke's Relationship with Judaism," in *Luke-Acts and the Jewish People: Eight Critical Perspectives*, ed. J.B. Tyson (Minneapolis, MN: Augsburg, 1988), 76–82.
[59] Crabbe, "Being Found" (see n. 56), 31–32.

group, called "the Jews from Asia" (21:27; 24:19). They perform an important function in furthering the plot, moving from an initial positive response, to jealousy at the inclusion of the gentiles, and then stirring up civic unrest.

This antagonist group emerges soon after the Cornelius episode and the mission to the gentiles has begun. In the synagogue in Pisidian Antioch, Paul accepts the invitation of the ἀρχισυνάγωγοι to address the people (13:15), and his long speech connecting scripture and his preaching about Jesus is so well received that "the people begged that these things might be told them the next Sabbath" (13:42), and many are said to follow Paul and Barnabas. The excitement is such that by the next sabbath "almost the whole city" (13:44) joins to hear the preaching. But this then prompts a negative reaction. "The Jews" are "filled with jealousy (ἐπλήσθησαν ζήλου)" at the size of the crowds and begin to contradict Paul, reviling him (λαλουμένοις βλασφημοῦντες). Paul and Barnabas respond by saying:

> It was necessary (ἦν ἀναγκαῖον) that the word of God be spoken first to you (ὑμῖν). Since you thrust it aside and judge yourselves unworthy of eternal life, behold, we are turning to the Gentiles. For so the Lord has commanded us, saying, 'I have made you a light for the Gentiles, that you may bring salvation to the ends of the earth' (13:46b–47).

Their words link back to Simeon's words in the temple (Luke 2:32) and Jesus' words early in Acts (1:8), and here prompt the gathered gentiles to rejoice and believe. But "the Jews" stir up persecution, driving Paul and Barnabas out of the area, who in turn "shook off the dust from their feet" and move on to Iconium (13:51).

Much more could be said about this passage than space here allows. But I particularly want to note two matters: the action of shaking dust off feet and the role of jealousy. By having Paul and Barnabas shake the dust from their feet, Luke links this passage to Jesus' missionary instructions to the disciples in Luke 10:11: missionaries should say to an unresponsive city, "even the dust of your town that clings to our feet we wipe off against you."[60] This suggests a conflict focused on particular characters in a particular place; as an unresponsive city would not spell the end of missionary activity in Luke 10, the action in Acts 13:51 is not a generalisable pronouncement on all the Jewish characters

---

60 The parallel is even closer in Matt 10:14, potentially supporting arguments that Acts might be considered not simply a sequel to Luke but to have intertextual links to the fourfold gospel (M.C. Parsons, "Hearing Acts as a Sequel to a Multiform Gospel: Historical and Hermeneutical Reflections on Acts, Luke, and the ΠΟΛΛΟΙ," in *Rethinking the Unity and Reception of Luke and Acts*, ed. A. Gregory and C.K. Rowe [Columbia: University of South Carolina Press, 2010], 128–152).

within or beyond the Acts narrative. That the pattern continues in other specific places, where the hostile response comes from a varying subset of the characters, confirms the pattern.

The response of jealousy also plays into the wider pattern. In his study of emotions in classical Greek literature, David Konstan places ζῆλος among a set of rivalrous, competitive emotions. He notes Aristotle's definition of ζῆλος as "a kind of pain at the perceived presence of good and honourable things that are possible to acquire for oneself, belonging to those who are similar in nature ... not because the other has it but because one does not oneself" (*Rhet.* 2.11, 1388a30 – 3).[61] For Aristotle this could be positive – the desire could bring about a rivalrous emulation that leads one to obtain this good, which Ed Sanders also argues became the more common meaning for ζῆλος.[62] But Konstan also notes examples from Stoic sources which demonstrate continuing negative uses of ζῆλος.[63] And, indeed, while Sanders' taxonomy of uses of the terms φθόνος and ζῆλος, argues that the former is more common, he does also note continued crossover, through which ζῆλος can also be used to indicate a series of negative emotional "scripts" in Greek texts.[64]

Of particular relevance to the use in Acts are scripts related to "rivalry," the destructive form of which leads to strife between siblings or neighbours.[65] The possible intersection of scripts such as "covetous envy" is also raised by ζῆλος emerging in relation to the size of the crowd.[66] Indeed, this explains why ζῆλος cannot take a positive emulative form here, because it does not manifest in a shared account of what is the desired "good." As in critical portraits of char-

---

[61] D. Konstan, *The Emotions of the Ancient Greeks: Studies in Aristotle and Classical Literature*, Robson Classical Lectures (Toronto: University of Toronto, 2006), 224.

[62] Although Sanders notes the earlier use by Hesiod does include a range of negative, destructive meanings (E.M. Sanders, *Envy and Jealousy in Classical Athens: A Socio-Psychological Approach*, Emotions of the Past [Oxford: Oxford University Press, 2014], 47).

[63] For instance, in a list in which he distinguishes Stoic views of pity, envy (φθόνος), ζῆλος, and ζηλοτυπία, the second-century Diogenes Laertius describes ζῆλος as "a pain at someone else having what one desires oneself." See discussion in Konstan, *The Emotions* (see n. 61), 223. A key distinction between the latter two, is that the more negative ζηλοτυπία describes the pain at someone else having what one wants, even if one also has the desired object too.

[64] Sanders argues that these negative scripts are more commonly connected to φθόνος from the classical period, however, despite his attention to the lexemes, he advocates attention to the relevant scripts at play in a given text, rather than simply the lexeme (Sanders, *Envy* [see n. 62], 37).

[65] This also connects back to Aristotle's association of ζῆλος prompted by the fortune of "those who are similar in nature," as cited above.

[66] Uses of ζῆλος in this setting also tap into wider disdain for envy of the elites among other parts of the population.

acters concerned about popularity elsewhere in Acts,[67] the desire here is for popularity and influence, not the good news that Paul and Barnabas are sharing that has attracted the crowd.[68] Thus, while perhaps these Jewish characters from Antioch might have responded to their feeling of ζῆλος by seeking to emulate Paul and Barnabas, the narrative shows them failing to do so; they respond by reviling them and then stir up persecution in the crowd.[69]

As in Antioch, so also in Iconium,[70] initially "a great number of both Jews and Greeks believed" (1:41) as a result of Paul and Barnabas' preaching in the synagogue. Here conflict then emerges as a group of "unbelieving Jews (ἀπειθήσαντες Ἰουδαῖοι)" stir up the gentiles "and poisoned their minds against the brothers" (v. 2). When the conflict reaches a head, the narrative observes: "But the people of the city were divided; some sided with the Jews and some with the apostles" (14:4). This then leads to an attempt "by both Gentiles and Jews, with their rulers, to mistreat them and to stone them" (v. 5), prompting Paul and Barnabas to flee.

The pattern is repeated again in Lystra, but here the trouble is caused by Jews who come from Antioch and Iconium, and here again they stir up the crowds against Paul (14:19).[71] A few chapters later, the same pattern emerges in Thessalonica, where Paul discusses the scriptures for three sabbaths, and "some of them were persuaded and joined Paul and Silas, as did a great many of the devout Greeks and not a few of the leading women" (17:4). But, again, "the Jews were jealous (ζηλόω)" and they prompt an uproar, employing "wicked men (ἄνδρας τινὰς πονηρούς)" in a mob. Paul and Silas escape to Berea, where the narrator notes "these Jews were more noble than those in Thessalonica" and "many of them therefore believed, with not a few Greek women of high standing

---

67 In Acts 5:26, 34, the temple authorities are frightened of the people, and then listen to Gamaliel, who is popular (Crabbe, "Being Found" [see n. 56], 31–33).
68 Sanders notes the script for envy or jealousy is often used with hatred (μῖσος/μισέω), which does not appear here (or elsewhere in Acts), though the response does include a verbal attack: λαλουμένοις βλασφημοῦντες, which the ESV translates as "reviling" rather than blaspheming (13:45).
69 Showing that other characters (*not* the disciples) stir up civil unrest is another theme of the Acts narrative.
70 As the action is introduced, the repeated pattern is emphasised in the Greek: Ἐγένετο δὲ ἐν Ἰκονίῳ κατὰ τὸ αὐτό (14:1).
71 After a quick (successful) trip to Derbe, they are then able to return to Lystra, Iconium, and Antioch to strengthen disciples there (14:21–23).

as well as men" (17:11–12).⁷² But as when the Jews from Antioch and Iconium cause trouble in Lystra, here the Jews from Thessalonica come to Berea to stir up the crowds and Paul escapes.⁷³ By the time, then, that Paul is in Jerusalem, the group of antagonising characters whose attentions have followed him causing trouble are now referred to more generally as "the Jews from Asia" (21:27). Following their usual pattern, they stir up the crowd (when Paul, meanwhile, was faithfully keeping a vow). And again, following this, as noted above, it is Paul's description of his call to the gentiles that prompts opposition from the crowd listening to his Hebrew speech (22:22).

Despite a tendency for some interpreters to see in these characters a fundamental falling out between Judaism and Christianity, as Robert Brawley notes, it is important to recognise that these do not represent all Jewish characters in the narrative.⁷⁴ The hostile group, by following the same literary pattern, has become something like an antagonist chorus running through the narrative. Their characteristics merge together, which is confirmed by their general description in Jerusalem, but they still remain distinctive in the sense of particular groups from their locations. In each city from which a group of hostile Jews emerges, the proportions vary. "Some" of the Jews in Thessalonica join Paul and Silas, while "many" in Berea do. In Iconium it is clear that when the city divides and some side with "the Jews" and others with the apostles (14:4), this group of Jews (earlier in the scene described as "unbelieving Jews") is not all the Jews of the city.

The piecemeal nature of the opposition group, in fact, plays an important role in Paul's rhetoric when defending himself before Felix, after his arrest in the temple. Tertullus, speaking on behalf of the high priest and some elders, says that Paul is "one who stirs up riots among all the Jews throughout the world (κατὰ τὴν οἰκουμένην) and is a ringleader of the sect of the Nazarenes"

---

72 The repetition of this phrasing also creates the connection between the passages and a sense of a type-scene. Notably, what makes those in Berea more receptive is daily reading of scripture, confirming that scripture witnesses to what Paul and Silas preach.

73 The pattern is partially present in Ephesus, but interrupted because Paul does not stay on after his initial positive preaching when they ask him to (18:20), but instead goes elsewhere and then returns to a different kind of conflict. See below.

74 Brawley, *Luke-Acts* (see n. 19). Brawley also asserts that opposition to Paul in the Acts narrative should not be interpreted as opposition to Christianity (p. 152; contra Haenchen, *The Acts* [see n. 17], 540). When "the Jews" form a plot, and then take a vow to kill Paul (23:12–13), this does not refer to all Jewish characters. Rather, for instance, it is "over 40" who make the vow. Likewise, Apollo is Jewish, but his contribution is celebrated as he argues persuasively with "the Jews" (18:8, cf. v. 28), who are thus delineated as a separate group.

(24:5).⁷⁵ Paul for his part responds to the charge of stirring up all the empire's Jews by narrowing the focus, explaining this στάσις has been caused by "some Jews from Asia (τινὲς δὲ ἀπὸ τῆς Ἀσίας Ἰουδαῖοι)," who he suggests should be present to make the accusation themselves (24:19). The narration also supports Paul's testimony, by showing that despite Tertullus' rhetoric about "all the Jews," Jewish characters who are not part of this group do exist, and emphasising Paul's continuity with his Jewish heritage.

Thus there are a number of narrative functions performed by this group. They create dramatic tension, drawing out opposition, but at the same time are limited to a subset of characters from some locations. The momentum that they give to the narrative comes also through their response to the success of Paul's ministry. As noted above, an earlier reference to jealousy comes in the high priest's response to the apostles' popularity in Acts 5:17, and Stephen also describes Joseph's brothers as jealous, leading them into their error (7:9). But from the time that the mission to the gentiles is introduced, jealousy emerges for this group of Jews as they see the response among the gentiles (13:45; 17:5).⁷⁶ This drives the action forward into the true conflict of the Acts narrative: the inclusion of the gentiles. The mission to the gentiles likewise contributes to three further scenes in which interpreters have found some kind of parting.

4 Narrative movement: How do characters part company in Acts?

As noted above, Dunn looks to events in Acts as historical evidence of a series of early, multiple partings of the ways,⁷⁷ whereas Haenchen finds in the Lukan Paul's conflicts with the synagogues no evidence of Christianity breaking away (yet), but events which plausibly contributed to a decisive separation before the time in which Luke writes.⁷⁸ Indeed, even though Acts presents Jewish characters diversely and the apostles as faithful Jews, occasionally calling their own people to account, there are striking scenes in which characters do part ways.

---

75 This charge is immediately revealed as hyperbole, when Felix returns with his wife, Drusilla, whom the narration explains is Jewish; yet she is clearly not a part of this hyperbolic, empire-wide Jewish rebellion. This scene paints a similar picture of the distinctions between the Pharisees, Sadducees, and Nazarenes (see n. 82).
76 The role of jealousy here means that even those scenes which follow this pattern but do not use the term directly evoke the emotion through the wider narrative script.
77 Dunn, *The Parting* (see n. 2), 230.
78 Haenchen, *The Acts* (see n. 17), 540.

Might the seemingly intramural relationships earlier in the narrative simply be part of a narrative trajectory to a decisive break towards its end? Both the falling out between Paul and the synagogues in Corinth and Ephesus and the enigmatic ending of Acts are important to this question.

4.1 Paul and the synagogues in Corinth and Ephesus

It is a well-recognised theme in Acts that when Paul arrives in a new city he makes his way to the synagogue. Although the designation "The synagogues of the Jews" (13:5; 14:1; 17:1, 10; cf. 9:20; 18:19) may imply some distance from the author or implied reader, the scope of Paul's mission in each location, which can include marketplaces or other locations, indicates instead that this is a distinction between the gathering place of Jews and places of non-Jewish gentiles.[79] Paul's easy access to and engagement in the synagogues shows that his believer status does not preclude him from participation in the synagogue community. But in two episodes in Acts 18 and 19, Paul emphatically parts company with the synagogue.

In Corinth, Paul reasons daily with Jews and Greeks in the synagogue. After some time, while he is "testifying to the Jews that the Christ was Jesus" (18:5), they "oppose" and "revile" him. He makes a dramatic exit: "he shook out his garments and said to them, 'Your blood be on your own heads! I am innocent. From now on I will go to the gentiles" (18:6). As evidence of a decisive breach between "Judaism" and "Christianity" the scene could seem quite cut and dried – reflecting also a passion and criticism that is unlike the division of two equal partners sought by proponents of the parting of the ways. However, there are at least two indications that this is not the kind of breach that might be initially assumed from Paul's response. First, the mission to and relationship with Jewish characters clearly continues. The very next verses relate Paul's move as far as next door, to the house of Titus Justus (a believer), and then the conversion of Crispus, the ruler of the synagogue. Jewish characters are still becoming Jesus-believers. In fact, Paul's vision of the Lord confirms for him that he should continue with his preaching safely, "for I have many in this city who are my people (λαός ἐστίν μοι)" (18:10). He continues teaching the word of God "among them" for one and half years – but who is "them"? Since Paul's announcement that he would go to the gentiles, Luke has named an existing believ-

---

[79] Similarly, the "synagogue of the Freedmen" (6:9) does not indicate a breakaway religious tradition. On this synagogue, see Keener, *Acts* (see n. 6), 2: 1303.

er who lives next door to the synagogue, and then narrated the conversion of a Jewish household and a vision affirming the continuing, friendly presence of the Lord's λαός in the town, a term frequently used for Jewish people, without any reference to a gentile conversion.

Secondly, the narrative uses a civic leader, Gallio the proconsul of Achaia, to confirm that the believers and Jews remain part of the same group. "The Jews" bring their complaint to Gallio, who cuts off the debate by saying this is just an internal matter (18:14–15; cf. 25:18–19). Despite the violence that emerges here in Corinth, this is not a decisive break between all of Judaism and Christianity, but a falling out with particular people in the Corinthian synagogue. And not even here in Corinth is Paul's ministry then limited to gentiles.

A similar pattern emerges in Ephesus.[80] Paul engages in debate in the synagogue for three months, "But when some became stubborn (σκληρύνω) and continued in unbelief, speaking evil of the Way before the congregation, he withdrew from them and took the disciples with him" (19:9). Having reasoned (διαλέγομαι) in the synagogue, he then reasons (διαλέγομαι) daily in the hall of Tyrannus. This direct exchange between Jewish and gentile locations to continue the same work could be a sign of a wider parting. And yet in the scene that follows, when "Jewish exorcists" invoke the name of Jesus, with dramatic effects that affirm Jesus, and indirectly Paul's authority, it is "all the residents of Ephesus, both Jews and Greeks" who respond, praising Jesus.

There is in these two chapters, then, a pattern of conflict with synagogues. Some Jewish characters are described as stubborn and, despite Paul's consistent and faithful persuasion and reasoning, the negative response eventually causes him to leave. But in neither case does this then lead to a ministry exclusively targeted at gentiles. As in the case of "the Jews of Asia," the falling out reflects a piecemeal conflict with people from particular synagogues, and even then not all the people from those synagogues. The very fact that it happens in two consecutive towns over many months demonstrates that this does not relate to the synagogue in all places. However, the final incident in Rome, where these themes again arise, has been taken by many interpreters as Luke's indication of a final and decisive break.

---

80 A common approach in Acts. Patterns emerge, for instance, through the repetition in the Cornelius episode and Paul's call, or through scenes that are similar to one another, such as the conflicts in various Asian cities. Here again Luke pairs stories.

4.2 Who parts company in Rome?

Three days after Paul's much anticipated arrival in Rome, he calls together "the local leaders of the Jews" (28:17). The longer section here includes an initial conversation (vv. 17–22) and a larger gathering (vv. 23–28) comprised of Paul's preaching (v. 23) and the division of the audience, including a long explanatory citation from Isa 6:9–10 (vv. 24–28), before a two-verse epilogue with which the book ends (vv. 30–31).[81]

In the initial conversation, Paul explains the circumstances of his appeal to Caesar, made necessary through "the Jews'" objecting his release. He situates himself firmly within Judaism, claiming both that, in spite of the Jews' interference in his release, "I had no charge to bring against my nation" (v. 19) and that he wanted to see the Roman Jews "since it is because of the hope of Israel that I am wearing this chain" (v. 20). For their part, the group of Roman Jews are happy to listen to him, given they have no negative report about him, although they note "with regard to this sect we know that everywhere it is spoken against" (v. 22). Thus, like Paul, the Roman Jews also place the Jesus-believers within the Jewish community, indicating that the group is a αἵρεσις (28:22; cf. 24:5, 14), reminiscent of the distinctions between Pharisees and Sadducees, where groups remain recognisably Jewish despite their divergent views.[82]

An even larger group then gathers to hear Paul's preaching. His long day of explaining, drawing on scripture, convinces some, "but others disbelieved" (28:24). Here he cites the long section from Isa 6:9–10.[83] Loveday Alexander helpfully highlights the retrospective focus of verses 17–28, alongside the prospective orientation of verses 30–31.[84] This fits with the use of the Isaiah quotation, which rather than announcing a future change, describes the events that have already taken plan across the course of the narrative. The people's "heart has grown dull, and with their ears they can barely hear, and their eyes they have closed" (v. 27). Following the quotation, Paul announces: "Therefore let

---

[81] Verse 29 is a later addition and thus omitted here and from the main text of the Nestlé-Aland 28. See B.M. Metzger, *A Textual Commentary on the Greek New Testament*, 2nd ed. (Stuttgart: Deutsche Bibelgesellschaft, 1994), 444.

[82] The term is usually employed in the context of divisions of the philosophical schools, and thus is in keeping with the use Josephus puts it to in his description of the Jewish sects (*J.W.* 2.119–166). Acts also appreciates these distinctions.

[83] This is cited by Alexander as possible evidence in favour of a prospective narrative unity to Luke and Acts, where Luke appears to have reserved the citation for the climax of his second volume (cf. Mark 4:12; 8:17–18; Alexander, "Reading Luke-Acts" [see n. 6], 216).

[84] Alexander, "Reading Luke-Acts" (see n. 6), 214.

it be known to you that this salvation of God has been sent (ἀπεστάλη) to the gentiles; they will listen" (v. 28).[85] The aorist verb confirms that this is a summary of events recounted already in Acts.

In a study of uses of Isa 6, Craig Evans argues that during the Second Temple period the focus moves from an emphasis in the Hebrew text on divine activity in stopping eyes, ears, and hearts so that the people might not turn, to an accent instead on repentance and the promise of healing.[86] This is a move from prophetic accusation to promise of restoration. In the LXX (and Acts following), the verbs become indicatives: they closed their eyes (ἐκάμμυσαν). The citation can therefore both describe the events that have taken place in the past throughout Acts and stress the option of turning for healing. This is consistent with the setting here. The response of Paul's departing audience of Roman Jews is not univocal but divided, with some still potentially coming to faith as other Jewish characters have done throughout Acts. And, in the final, prospectively-oriented verses, Paul's continuing welcome to "all who came to him" (v. 30) maintains an emphasis on the opportunity to respond positively to Paul's preaching. Whether or not these characters have any future involvement with the sect of the Nazarenes, the narrative does not indicate that this "sect" now constitutes a parallel tradition that has "parted."

Finally, Paul's statement following the citation is reminiscent of his exit from the synagogue in 18:6, where he says he will go to the gentiles (cf. 13:46).[87] Rather than evidence of a final breach between Christians and Jews, each of these passages which describe going to the gentiles emphasises the inclusion of the gentiles, without cutting off the possibility of participation by the Jewish characters. That these passages contribute to a narrative which is ultimately not about a parting of the ways but a debate about the appropriate inclusion of the gentiles in the end-time people of God is highlighted by the debate over circumcision in Acts 15.

---

[85] Alexander highlights an inclusion between the ending of Acts and the beginning of Luke, here noting the parallels with Simeon's speech (Alexander, "Reading Luke-Acts" [see n. 6], 214).
[86] C.A. Evans, *To See and Not Perceive: Isaiah 6.9–10 in Early Jewish and Christian Interpretation*, JSOTSup 64 (Sheffield: JSOT Press, 1989), 163–164.
[87] The statement that the gentiles will listen (ἀκούω) parallels the citation from Isaiah that "this people" will hear (ἀκούω) but never understand (καὶ οὐ μὴ συνῆτε) (vv. 26, 28).

5 Faithfulness and the inclusion of the gentiles

The inclusion of the gentiles is thus a key site of conflict with an antagonist group of Jews in Acts, and a feature also in interactions at significant moments of disagreement between Jewish characters, some of whom do not then become Jesus-believers. There are, however, a number of places where characters (both Jews and gentiles) rejoice at the news of the inclusion of the gentiles (13:48; 15:3). The growing numbers are a cause for celebration, but it is more than this. The theme indicates the fulfilment of prophecy, cast as an eschatological sign. As in another key theme of the apostles' preaching across Acts, the resurrection of Jesus (1:22; 2:24, 29–32; 3:15; 5:29–32; 10:39–41; 13:26–37; 17:30–31; 23:6; 24:15–21; 26:6–8, 23), the text taps into an underlying scriptural claim which signals to the reader that events of eschatological significance are already underway.[88]

Disagreement over the appropriate practice of the law in Acts is another context in which to view the possibility for a parting. The "covenant focused in Torah" is one of the four pillars of Second Temple Judaism that Dunn identifies as sites of contest in the parting of the ways with Christianity.[89] Indeed, characters who oppose the Jesus movement in Acts often make the criticism that the believers are not following the ancestral customs correctly, or that they are advocating that others do not. The accusation against Stephen (6:14; cf. 18:13)[90] and the believers' strategy for Paul to ward off criticism when arriving in Jerusalem (21:24)[91] raise these questions in order for the text to show such concerns to

---

[88] K. Crabbe, *Luke/Acts and the End of History*, BZNW 238 (Berlin: de Gruyter, 2019), 304–307. Agrippa knows that accepting Paul's claim that Jesus has been raised from the dead would mean becoming a Christian; he knows from Jewish tradition that this is what is at stake in the claim (26:28; cf. 17:31). See n. 32 on the term "Christian."

[89] Dunn, *The Parting* (see n. 2), 23–31.

[90] When Stephen is brought before the council, the accusation is: "This man never stops saying things against this holy place and the law; for we have heard him say that this Jesus of Nazareth will destroy this place and will change the customs that Moses handed on to us" (6:14). But the reader knows not to trust the words: they are spoken by "false witnesses," and to clinch Stephen's own trustworthiness, all see that "his face was like the face of an angel" (v. 15). Stephen's speech is clear that the fault lies in consistent failures to implement the law, but some passages might raise further alarm, such as the treatment of the law in Pisidian Antioch (13:39).

[91] The believers in Jerusalem strategise that Paul should take the purification vow so that "all will know that there is nothing in what they have been told about you, but that you yourself also live in observance of the law" (21:24).

be mistaken.⁹² The inclusion of the gentiles comes as a specific example that raises such antinomian concerns. But in a significant moment in the narrative, in Acts 15, Luke supplies a debate that confirms not only that the Torah itself indicates the appropriate practices of the law for gentiles, but the eschatological significance of the gentiles' presence.

After a significant disagreement with some visitors from Judea who argue that "unless you are circumcised according to the custom of Moses (τῷ ἔθει τῷ Μωϋσέως), you cannot be saved (οὐ δύνασθε σωθῆναι)" (15:1), Paul and Barnabas go with others to Jerusalem to discuss the matter. Believers who are Pharisees confirm the view encountered in v. 1: "It is necessary (δεῖ) to circumcise them and to order them to keep the law of Moses (τὸν νόμον Μωϋσέως)" (v. 5). The apostles and elders then gather, and much (unnarrated) discussion ensues. As the debate nears a conclusion, Luke offers a long speech from Peter, outlining his experience with Cornelius (vv. 7–11), unnarrated words from Paul and Barnabas, who describe God's action among the gentiles (v. 12), and a substantial address from James, who brings these sets of experiences back to scripture (vv. 13–21).

By reiterating Cornelius and his household's experience of the Holy Spirit,⁹³ Peter's speech links back to his speech in Acts 2 and the fulfilment of Joel's prophecy about what will take place "in the last days" (2:17).⁹⁴ This is not simply about affirming that the authentic experience of the Spirit by both groups is the same, but that this comes as evidence of eschatological time. James's use of scripture, as argued by Richard Bauckham, likewise affirms this framework for the inclusion of the gentiles.⁹⁵

James's speech is comprised of two engagements with scripture (vv. 16–18, 19–21). He begins with a substantial citation taken largely from Amos 9:11–12,

---

92 This is in keeping with Sterling's suggestion that Luke/Acts employs an apologetic strategy to bolster the confidence of insider audiences, giving tools for the audience to use in responding to such criticisms themselves (Sterling, *Historiography* [see n. 10], 385–386). This does not require support for some earlier attempts to identify particular parties as the opposition for Luke's community (cf. Sanders, "Who is" [see n. 18], 436–337).
93 Pettem argues that Luke omits Mark 6:45–8:26 and then deals with related issues in the Cornelius episode (M. Pettem, "Luke's Great Omission and His View of the Law," *NTS* 42 (1996): 35–54). As argued below, however, the prohibitions for gentile believers in Acts are also based in the Torah.
94 Crabbe, *Luke/Acts* (see n. 88), 307–308.
95 Much of Bauckham's long article (Bauckham, "James" [see n. 34]) focuses on a particular historical framework through which to understand Acts. That is not my concern here. See also Bennema, "The Ethnic Conflict" (see n. 11), drawing on Bauckham to address historical details between Gal 2 and Acts 15.

introduced as prophetic confirmation of Peter's experience. The passage describes the Lord's promise to restore the tent of David so that "the remnant of humanity (οἱ κατάλοιποι τῶν ἀνθρώπων) may seek the Lord, and all the Gentiles who are called by my name" (Acts 15:17; cf. Amos 9:12).[96] The section cited comes from a larger passage in Amos 9 about an idyllic future, in which natural phenomena are overturned for rich opportunities (the grape harvest overtaking the one who sows the seed, mountains dripping with wine, and so on). There are short citations from Jer 12:15 and Isa 45:21 spliced into the citation as it is given in Acts 15:16–17,[97] with a clause at the beginning and end, and the wider passages from which these verses come likewise affirm not only the kinds of promises of an idyllic future that were interpreted eschatologically in early Christian literature but an accent on the inclusion of all nations. Indeed, the following verse in Isa 45:22 makes this affirmation in language entirely at home in Acts: "Turn to me and be saved, all the ends of the earth! For I am God and there is no other."

Thus, as Bauckham rightly notes, James uses scripture to confirm that this inclusion of the gentiles is firmly grounded in existing promises[98] which act, alongside Peter's experience of the Holy Spirit, to confirm the eschatological nature of the events. This sets the scene for his further discussion of the law's provision for gentiles, given their inclusion is not unexpected but already attested in scripture.

James' second engagement with scripture sets out his judgement about the best course of action in relation to the legal practices to be required of gentile believers. This is not a direct citation, but it brings together a list of requirements from Lev 17 and 18 which "the strangers who sojourn among" Israel/you are also required to observe. Bauckham analyses each of the legal requirements in which

---

[96] ESV translation, adjusted for inclusive language. The parallel is present in both the MT and the LXX, but it is more pronounced in the latter, where the wording is almost exact in the second verse (Acts 15:17 and Amos 9:12).

[97] The first clause, μετὰ ταῦτα ἀναστρέψω, appears to be taken instead from Jer 12:15, although the wording differs from NA28 and Rahlfs' LXX, the latter being: καὶ ἔσται μετὰ τὸ ἐκβαλεῖν με αὐτοὺς ἐπιστρέψω—although Acts 15:16 in D also uses ἐπιστρέψω. The wider context of Jer 12:15 shares a promise of divine restoration similar to that in Amos 9 which lends itself to the eschatological application in Acts 15 including the inclusion even of the nations that had previously taught Israel "to swear by Baal." It also includes a threat about divine action if there is no positive response: "But if any nation will not listen, then I will utterly pluck it up and destroy it, declares the Lord" (Jer 12:17 ESV). The final phrase, "known from of old" is not present in Amos 9:11–12, but is shared with Isa 45:21.

[98] Bauckham, "James" (see n. 34), 452–456.

this phrase appears, namely Lev 17:8, 10, 12,⁹⁹ 13; 18:26,¹⁰⁰ and notes that these verses together list the four stipulations summarised in Acts 15:19–21, and as they are set out in the letter to gentile converts that the group gathered in Jerusalem then writes (vv. 23–29).¹⁰¹ Thus the requirements to "abstain from what has been sacrificed to idols, and from blood, and from what has been strangled, and from sexual immorality" (v. 29) is not a watered down legal practice cooked up to make faith palatable for a gentile audience – something that would no doubt be an insufficient response to the concerns of the believers in verses 1 and 5, who were advocating circumcision. Rather, these requirements arise from both the scriptural promise of the inclusion of the gentiles within the people of God, interpreted as an end-time event, and the existing provisions for the legal practices that the Torah already sets out gentiles must observe when dwelling in the midst of the people. James' speech concludes, following the references to the four requirements, with a summary that clearly implies that the preceding rules are all scriptural: "For in every city, for generations past, Moses has had those who proclaim him, for he has been read aloud every sabbath in the synagogues" (v. 21).

In this way, this passage reflects a debate not about whether the fledgling community will continue to follow the law, but about right interpretation of the law. It is also not a passage that sets out the regulations for a long-term, institutionalised early "Christianity" through a formal council of the type that future centuries would see, but an interpretation of the scripturally-mandated requirements during the end-time events also foretold in scripture, and how to live during this time in between Jesus' resurrection and the final events that have already been put in train (Acts 17:31). Therefore, I suggest, the decision about what constitutes faithful legal practice, and the decision making processes of this group of believers in Acts 15, are not evidence of a growing formal break between "Judaism" and "Christianity," but of an eschatologically-focused movement within Judaism engaging in scripture-based debate about the inclusion of the gentiles.

---

99 Lev 17:10 and 12 are both listed because they both reference the resident alien, but they repeat the same requirement to abstain from blood. Thus the five verses here map onto the four prohibitions in Acts 15:20 and 29 (Bauckham, "James" [see n. 34], 459).
100 This is the verse which includes the requirement for the resident alien to avoid "these abominations," though it is the preceding verses which set out the detail of the sexual immoralities covered by this prohibition.
101 The order in Leviticus is the same as that in the apostolic letter (Bauckham, "James" [see n. 34], 459).

6 Conclusion

Some characters do part ways in Acts, with acrimony on both sides. But Acts is neither simply a history book nor an allegory for broader trajectories in early Christianity. The characters who prompt hostility, were they the only Jewish characters and were there a separation of "Christians" and "Jews" (let alone "Christianity" and "Judaism") evident in the narrative, would reflect the kinds of stereotypes that spurred Parkes and others to seek a new model for understanding the history of Jewish-Christian relationships. But these are literary groups and the conflicts they prompt perform literary functions. They show piecemeal responses that nonetheless cannot quash the new preaching, and build momentum towards the inclusion of the gentiles. Indeed, the enthusiastic responses of the gentiles is what prompts the jealous rivalry of "the Jews from Asia" and what also reveals the eschatological significance of the good news the apostles preach.

But even while some character groups are functioning in this way, identity and characterisation remains more complex than the binary implicit in the parting of the ways imagery. The capacity to hold together Jewish and other "native" identities paves the way for the inclusion of a believer identity that does not require the believer to undergo some kind of exchange. And, as Acts describes some emerging internal organisation among the Jesus-believers, these do not of themselves necessitate either later institutions or a separation from other Jewish community structures. The apostles' preaching is part of a growing movement across Acts, grounded in reasoning over the correct interpretation of scriptures, looking to the inclusion of the gentiles as eschatological sign, but also proclaimed "on account of the hope of Israel" (28:20). And despite the divided response, Acts closes with the continued promise, as Paul "welcomes all" who come to him (28:30).

Bibliography

Alexander, L., *The Preface to Luke's Gospel: Literary Convention and Social Context in Luke 1:1–4 and Acts 1:1*, SNTSMS 78 (Cambridge: Cambridge University Press, 1993).

Alexander, L., "Reading Luke-Acts from Back to Front," in *Acts in Its Ancient Literary Context: A Classicist Looks at the Acts of the Apostles*, eadem, JSNTSup 298 (London: T&T Clark, 2007), 207–229.

Barreto, E. D., *Ethnic Negotiations: The Function of Race and Ethnicity in Acts 16*, (PhD diss., Emory University, 2010).

Bauckham, R., ed., *The Book of Acts in Its Palestinian Setting*, BAFCS (Grand Rapids: Eerdmans, 1995).
Bauckham, R., "James and the Jerusalem Church," in *The Book of Acts in Its Palestinian Setting*, ed. idem, BAFCS (Grand Rapids: Eerdmans, 1995), 415–480.
Bennema, C., "The Ethnic Conflict in Early Christianity: An Appraisal of Bauckham's Proposal on the Antioch Crisis and the Jerusalem Council," *JETS* 56.4 (2013): 753–763.
Bovon, F., "Israel, die Kirche und die Völker im lukanischen Doppelwerk," *TLZ* 108 (1983): 403–414.
Boyarin, D., "Semantic Differences; or, 'Judaism'/'Christianity'," in *The Ways That Never Parted. Jews and Christians in Late Antiquity and the Early Middle Ages*, ed. A. H. Becker and A. Y. Reed, TSAJ 95 (Tübingen: Mohr Siebeck, 2003), 65–85.
Brawley, R. L., *Luke-Acts and the Jews: Conflict, Apology, and Conciliation*, SBLMS 33 (Atlanta: Scholars Press, 1989).
Cancik, H., "The History of Culture, Religion, and Institutions in Ancient Historiography: Philological Observations Regarding Luke's History," *JBL* 116.4 (1997): 673–695.
Conzelmann, H., "Luke's Place in the Development of Early Christianity," in *Studies in Luke-Acts: Essays Presented in Honor of Paul Schubert,* ed. L.E. Keck and J. Louis Martyn (Nashville: Abingdon Press, 1966), 298–316.
Crabbe, K., "Being Found Fighting Against God: Luke's Gamaliel and Josephus on Human Responses to Divine Providence," *ZNW* 106.1 (2015): 21–39.
Crabbe, K., *Luke/Acts and the End of History*, BZNW 238 (Berlin: de Gruyter, 2019).
Darr, J. A., "Irenic or Ironic? Another Look at Gamaliel before the Sanhedrin (Acts 5:33–42)," in *Literary Studies in Luke-Acts: Essays in Honor of Joseph B. Tyson,* ed. R. P. Thompson and T. E. Phillips (Macon: Mercer University Press, 1998), 121–140.
Dunn, J. D. G., *The Parting of the Ways: Between Christianity and Judaism and their Significance for the Character of Christianity* (London: SCM Press, 1991).
Ellis, E. E., "The End of the Earth (Acts 1:8)," in *History and Interpretation in New Testament Perspective*, idem, BibInt (Leiden: Brill, 2001), 53–63.
Evans, C. A., *To See and Not Perceive: Isaiah 6.9–10 in Early Jewish and Christian Interpretation*, JSOTSup 64 (Sheffield: JSOT Press, 1989).
Gaventa, B. R., *Acts*, ANTC (Nashville: Abingdon Press, 2003).
Gowler, D. B., *Host, Guest, Enemy and Friend: Portraits of the Pharisees in Luke and Acts*, Emory Studies in Early Christianity 2 (New York: Peter Lang, 1991).
Gregory, A., "The Reception of Luke and Acts and the Unity of Luke-Acts," *JSNT* 29.4 (2007): 459–472.
Haenchen, E., *The Acts of the Apostles: A Commentary* (Oxford: Blackwell, 1971).
Hakola, R., "'Friendly' Pharisees and Social Identity in Acts," in *Contemporary Studies in Acts*, ed. T. E. Phillips (Macon: Mercer University Press, 2009), 181–200.
Hemer, C. J., *The Book of Acts in the Setting of Hellenistic History*, BAFCS (Winona Lake: Eisenbrauns, 1990).
Jervell, J., "The Church of Jews and Godfearers," in *Luke-Acts and the Jewish People: Eight Critical Perspectives*, ed. J. B. Tyson (Minneapolis, MN: Augsburg, 1988), 11–20.
Jervell, J., "The Divided People of God: The Restoration of Israel and the Salvation of the Gentiles," in *Luke and the People of God: A New Look at Luke-Acts,* idem (Eugene, OR: Wipf and Stock, 2002; originally published 1965), 41–74.
Johnson, L.T., *The Acts of the Apostles*, SP 5 (Collegeville: Liturgical Press, 1992), 3–7.

Johnson, L.T., "Literary Criticism of Luke-Acts: Is Reception History Pertinent?," in *Rethinking the Unity and Reception of Luke and Acts*, ed. A. Gregory and C. Kavin Rowe, (Columbia: University of South Carolina Press, 2010), 66–69.

Keener, C. S., *Acts: An Exegetical Commentary*, 4 vols. (Grand Rapids: Baker Academic, 2012–2015).

Klawans, J., "An Invented Revolution," in *Jew and Judean: A Marginalia Forum on Politics and Historiography in the Translation of Ancient Texts*, ed. T. M. Law and C. Halton (Los Angeles, CA: Marginalia Review of Books, 2014), 38–41.

Konstan, D., *The Emotions of the Ancient Greeks: Studies in Aristotle and Classical Literature*, Robson Classical Lectures (Toronto: University of Toronto, 2006).

Kümmel, W. G., "Current Theological Accusations against Luke," *ANQ* 16 (1975): 131–145.

Lieu, J. M., "'The Parting of the Ways': Theological Construct or Historical Reality?," in *Neither Jew nor Greek? Constructing Early Christianity*, ed. eadem, 2nd ed. (London et al.: T&T Clark, 2016), 31–49.

Lowe, M., "Concepts and Words," in *Jew and Judean: A Marginalia Forum on Politics and Historiography in the Translation of Ancient Texts*, ed. T. M. Law and C. Halton (Los Angeles, CA: Marginalia Review of Books, 2014), 33–37.

Marshall, M., *The Portrayals of the Pharisees in the Gospels and Acts*, FRLANT 254 (Göttingen: Vandenhoeck & Ruprecht, 2015).

Mason, S., "Jews, Judaeans, Judaizing, Judaism: Problems of Categorization in Ancient History," *JSJ* 38 (2007): 457–512.

Mason, S., "Ancient Jews or Judeans? Different Questions, Different Answers," in *Jew and Judean: A Marginalia Forum on Politics and Historiography in the Translation of Ancient Texts*, ed. T. M. Law and C. Halton (Los Angeles, CA: Marginalia Review of Books, 2014), 11–17.

Mason, S., and P. F. Esler, "Judaean and Christ-Follower Identities: Grounds for a Distinction," *NTS* 63 (2017): 493–515.

Metzger, B. M., *A Textual Commentary on the Greek New Testament*, 2nd ed. (Stuttgart: Deutsche Bibelgesellschaft, 1994).

Parkes, J., *The Conflict in the Church and the Synagogue: A Study of the Origins of Antisemitism* (New York: Meridian Books, 1961).

Parsons, M. C., "Hearing Acts as a Sequel to a Multiform Gospel: Historical and Hermeneutical Reflections on Acts, Luke, and the ΠΟΛΛΟΙ," in *Rethinking the Unity and Reception of Luke and Acts*, ed. A. Gregory and C. Kavin Rowe (Columbia: University of South Carolina Press, 2010), 128–152.

Parsons, M. C., and R. I. Pervo, *Rethinking the Unity of Luke and Acts* (Minneapolis, MN: Fortress, 1993).

Penner, T. C., "Madness in the Method? The Acts of the Apostles in Current Study," *CurBR* 2 (2004): 223–293.

Pettem, M., "Luke's Great Omission and His View of the Law," *NTS* 42 (1996): 35–54.

Reed, A. Y., "*Ioudaios* Before and After 'Religion'," in *Jew and Judean: A Marginalia Forum on Politics and Historiography in the Translation of Ancient Texts*, ed. T. M. Law and C. Halton (Los Angeles, CA: Marginalia Review of Books, 2014), 21–26.

Reed, A. Y., and A. H. Becker, "Introduction: Traditional Models and New Directions," in *The Ways that Never Parted. Jews and Christians in Late Antiquity and the Early Middle Ages*, ed. A. H. Becker and A. Y. Reed, TSAJ 95 (Tübingen: Mohr Siebeck, 2003), 1–33.

Reinhartz, A., "The Vanishing Jews of Antiquity," in *Jew and Judean: A Marginalia Forum on Politics and Historiography in the Translation of Ancient Texts*, ed. T. M. Law and C. Halton (Los Angeles, CA: Marginalia Review of Books, 2014), 5–10.

Rothschild, C. K., *Luke-Acts and the Rhetoric of History: An Investigation of Early Christian Historiography*, WUNT 2/175 (Tübingen: Mohr Siebeck, 2004).

Salmon, M., "Insider or Outsider? Luke's Relationship with Judaism," in *Luke-Acts and the Jewish People: Eight Critical Perspectives*, ed. J. B. Tyson (Minneapolis, MN: Augsburg, 1988), 76–82.

Sanders, E. M., *Envy and Jealousy in Classical Athens: A Socio-Psychological Approach*, Emotions of the Past (Oxford: Oxford University Press, 2014).

Sanders, J. T., *The Jews in Luke-Acts* (Minneapolis, MN: Fortress, 1987).

Sanders, J. T., "Who is a Jew and Who is a Gentile in the Book of Acts?," *NTS* 37 (1991): 434–455.

Smith, D. E., and J. B. Tyson, eds., *Acts and Christian Beginnings: The Acts Seminar Report* (Salem: Polebridge, 2013).

Snyder, J. A., "Sociolinguistic Dynamics and Characterization in the Acts of the Apostles," in *Characters and Characterization in Luke-Acts*, ed. F. E. Dicken and eadem, LNTS (London: Bloomsbury, 2016), 169–184.

Sterling, G. E., *Historiography and Self-Definition: Josephos, Luke-Acts, and Apologetic Historiography*, NovTSup 64 (Leiden: Brill, 1991).

Tannehill, R. C., *The Narrative Unity of Luke-Acts: A Literary Interpretation*, vol. 2 (Minneapolis, MN: Fortress, 1990).

Taylor, J., "Why were the Disciples First Called 'Christians' at Antioch? (Acts 11,26)," *RB* 100 (1994): 75–94.

Taylor, J., "'Judean' and 'Jew', Jesus and Paul," in *Jew and Judean: A Marginalia Forum on Politics and Historiography in the Translation of Ancient Texts*, ed. T. M. Law and C. Halton (Los Angeles, CA: Marginalia Review of Books, 2014), 27–32.

Walters, P., *The Assumed Authorial Unity of Luke and Acts: A Reassessment of the Evidence*, SNTSMS 145 (Cambridge: Cambridge University Press, 2009).

Wilson, W. T., "Urban Legends: Acts 10:1–11:18 and the Strategies of Greco-Roman Foundation Narratives," *JBL* 120.1 (2001): 77–99.

Jörg Frey

"John within Judaism?"
Textual, Historical, and Hermeneutical Considerations

Abstract: Der Beitrag diskutiert die Frage, mit welchem Recht und in welcher hermeneutischen Intention das Johannesevangelium ‚innerhalb' oder ‚nicht mehr innerhalb' des zeitgenössischen Judentums verortet werden kann, oder ob es gar in seiner Rhetorik und Wirkung als ‚antijüdisch' gelten muss. Den Ausgangspunkt bildet die einflussreiche Hypothese (J. L. Martyn, R. E. Brown), dass das Evangelium aufgrund seiner ἀποσυνάγωγος-Aussagen als Reaktion auf Entscheidungen der frühen Rabbinen in Javne im Rahmen eines Prozesses der "Trennung der Wege" zwischen Juden und Jesus-Nachfolgenden verortet werden könne. Angesichts der inzwischen erfolgten vielfältigen Kritik dieser Hypothese fragt der Beitrag neu anhand wesentlicher Kriterien, inwiefern Johannes jüdisch oder antijüdisch oder gar beides zugleich sein kann. Ein jüdischer Hintergrund lässt sich für den Autor wahrscheinlich machen: Die Rede von Gott und die christologischen Prädikationen gründen ganz in biblischen und frühjüdischen Traditionen. Schwieriger ist die Bestimmung der Situation der Adressatengemeinde. Vor allem in den Johannesbriefen zeigen sich Spuren eines paganen Umfeldes, und auch einige Passagen des Evangeliums weisen auf eine zumindest aus Juden und Ex-Heiden gemischte Gemeinde hin. Eine verstärkte Trennung von Juden und Jesus-Nachfolgenden wird auch durch die soziopolitische Situation nach dem Jahr 70, v. a. die römische Sonderbesteuerung der Juden durch den *fiscus Iudaicus*, nahegelegt. Wesentlich ist die Argumentation der jüdischen Johannesforscherin Adele Reinhartz, dass die Rhetorik des Evangeliums bei seinen Rezipierenden eine Verbindung mit einer neuen Gemeinschaft von Gotteskindern stimuliert, für die Jesus zentral ist, während es eine Distanzierung von den Ἰουδαῖοι nahelegt. Eine Schlussreflexion bezieht die Daten auf die Probleme der Konzeption der "Trennung der Wege" und erörtert die hermeneutischen Interessen, die hinter dem Trend stehen, möglichst viele neutestamentliche Texte noch 'innerhalb des Judentums' einzuordnen. Gegenüber diesen apologetischen oder vor allem 'politische Korrektheit' erstrebenden Ansätzen ist der aufrichtige Blick auf die Rhetorik des Evangeliums (Reinhartz) vorzuziehen.

Keywords: John, Johannine Community, Jewish Background, Rhetoric, Parting of the Ways

1 The "Parting of the Ways" and the Fourth Gospel: The Evidence of the ἀποσυνάγωγος

In the debates about the so-called "Parting of the Ways" between Judaism and Jesus followers and its historical circumstances, the Gospel of John has always played a pivotal role.[1] Regardless whether scholars want to date the division early or late,[2] or whether they conceptualize it as an extended process, the term ἀποσυνάγωγος, attested for the first time ever in Greek literature in John (John 9:22; 12:42; 16:2) calls for an explanation. If this novel term not only refers to a temporal exclusion but to a definitive separation, it seems to point to an important or even to the decisive step in the process of the separation of Jewish Jesus followers from 'the Synagogue.' Of course such a view can only be based upon the critical insight that the narrative of the Fourth Gospel does not merely refer to events during the time of the earthly Jesus, but also or even primarily reflects problems and insights of the post-Easter community as well as those that existed up to the time of its composition. Such a view is well-established in light of the differences between John and the Synoptic tradition,[3] John's particular

---

[1] See my previous discussion of the matter in J. Frey, "'The Jews' in the Gospel of John and the 'Parting of the Ways'," in *The Glory of the Crucified One. Christology and Theology in the Gospel of John*, trans. W. Coppins and C. Heilig, BMSEC (Waco, TX: Baylor University Press; Tübingen: Mohr Siebeck, 2018), 39–72; idem, "Toward Reconfiguring Our Views on the 'Parting of the Ways': Ephesus as a Test Case," in *John and Judaism: A Contested Relationship in Context*, ed. R.A. Culpepper and P.N. Anderson, RBS 87 (Atlanta, GA: SBL Press, 2017), 221–239; idem, "Von Paulus zu Johannes. Die Diversität 'christlicher' Gemeindekreise und die 'Trennungsprozesse' zwischen der Synagoge und den Gemeinden der Jesusnachfolger in Ephesus im ersten Jahrhundert," in *The Rise and Expansion of Christianity in the First Three Centuries of the Common Era*, ed. C.K. Rothschild and J. Schröter, WUNT 301 (Tübingen: Mohr Siebeck, 2013), 235–278; and idem, "Temple and Identity in Early Christianity and in the Johannine Community: Reflections on the 'Parting of the Ways'," in *Was 70 CE a Watershed in Jewish History? On Jews and Judaism before and after the Destruction of the Second Temple*, ed. D.R. Schwartz and Z. Weiss, AJEC 78 (Leiden and Boston, MA: Brill, 2012), 447–507.

[2] On the patterns of dating the parting and the views of respective scholars, see E.K. Broadhead, *Jewish Ways of Following Jesus: Remapping the Religious Map of Antiquity*, WUNT 266 (Tübingen: Mohr Siebeck, 2010), 354–374. For the suggestion that the separation only happened later in the 4th century, see D. Boyarin, *Border Lines: The Partition of Judaeo-Christianity in Divinations: Rereading Late Ancient Religion* (Philadelphia, PA: University of Pennsylvania Press, 2004); cf. also A.H. Becker and A.Y. Reed, eds., *The Ways that Never Parted: Jews and Christians in Late Antiquity and the Early Middle Ages*, TSAJ 95 (Tübingen: Mohr Siebeck, 2003).

[3] On the relationship between John and the Synoptic tradition, see J. Frey, "Das Johannesevangelium auf dem Hintergrund der älteren Evangelientradition: Zum Problem: Johannes und die Synoptiker," in idem, *Die Herrlichkeit des Gekreuzigten: Studien zu den johanneischen Schriften*

theological language,[4] its high Christology,[5] and – even more so – its anti-Jewish polemic which cannot be explained from the time and context of the earthly Jesus. Particularly after the Shoah, New Testament exegesis has become eager to stress that the anti-Jewish sayings presented in the mouth of Jesus with the Ἰουδαῖοι as "children of the devil" (John 8:44) are not sayings of the earthly Jesus himself[6] but express views of the later community responding to later experiences and developments.

The most influential hypothesis was elaborated by J. Louis Martyn in his book on "History and Theology in the Fourth Gospel."[7] His so-called "community hypothesis"[8] suggests that the narrative of the Fourth Gospel mirrors the his-

---

1, ed. J. Schlegel, WUNT 307 (Tübingen: Mohr Siebeck, 2013), 239–294; idem, *Theology and History in the Fourth Gospel* (Waco, TX: Baylor University Press, 2018), 64–77.

[4] On the making of the particular theological language in John, see J. Frey, "From the 'Kingdom of God' to 'Eternal Life': The Transformation of Theological Language in the Fourth Gospel," in *Glimpses of Jesus through the Johannine Lens*, vol. 3 of *John, Jesus, and History*, ed. P.N. Anderson, F. Just, and T. Thatcher (Atlanta, GA: SBL Press, 2016), 439–458.

[5] On the distinctive high Christology in John, see J. Frey, *Theology and History in the Fourth Gospel* (see n. 3), 27–55; idem, "Jesus as the Image of God in the Gospel of John," in *The Glory of the Crucified One* (see n. 1), 285–312.

[6] On the history of research, see R. Bieringer, D. Pollefeyt, and F. Vandecasteele-Vanneuville, "Wrestling with Johannine Anti-Judaism: A Hermeneutical Framework for the Analysis of the Current Debate," in *Anti-Judaism and the Fourth Gospel*, ed. idem, D. Pollefeyt, and F. Vandecasteele-Vanneuville (Louisville, KY: Westminster John Knox, 2001), 3–37; R. Bieringer, "Anti-Judaism and the Fourth Gospel Fifteen Years after the Leuven Colloquium: A Contested Relationship in Context," in *John and Judaism*, ed. R.A. Culpepper and P.N. Anderson, RBS 87 (Atlanta, GA.: SBL Press, 2017), 243–264.

[7] J.L. Martyn, *History and Theology in the Fourth Gospel*, 3rd ed. (New York, NY: Harper & Row, 1968; repr., Louisville, KY: Westminster John Knox, 2003); similarly R.E. Brown, *The Community of the Beloved Disciple: The Life, Loves, and Hates of an Individual Church in New Testament Times* (London: Chapman, 1979). In German scholarship, Klaus Wengst's attempt at locating the Fourth Gospel within an area of strong Jewish influence provided a similarly influential explanation, see K. Wengst, *Bedrängte Gemeinde und verherrlichter Christus. Der historische Ort des Johannesevangeliums als Schlüssel zu seiner Interpretation*, BThS 5 (Neukirchen-Vluyn: Neukirchener, 1981); cf. the 4th ed., entitled: *Bedrängte Gemeinde und verherrlichter Christus. Ein Versuch über das Johannesevangelium*, 4th ed. (Munich: Kaiser, 1992).

[8] On the community hypothesis and its implications see also R.E. Kysar, "The Expulsion from the Synagogue: The Tale of a Theory," in idem, *Voyages with John: Charting the Fourth Gospel* (Waco, TX: Baylor University Press, 2005), 237–245; D.M. Smith, "The Contribution of J. Louis Martyn to the Understanding of the Gospel of John," in *The Conversation Continues: Studies in Paul and John in Honor of J. Louis Martyn*, ed. R.T. Fortna and B.R. Gaventa (Nashville, TN: Abingdon, 1990), 275–294 (repr., in Martyn, *History and Theology in the Fourth Gospel*, 3rd ed.). For a thorough criticism of the hypothesis, see A. Reinhartz, "The Johannine Community and Its Neighbours: A Reappraisal," in *What is John? Vol. 2 Literary and Social Readings of the Fourth*

tory and intellectual development of the Johannine community, which is viewed as a rather isolated 'sectarian' community or group of communities. It is assumed that this community changed its character from an originally Jewish Christian branch of the synagogual community to an increasingly radicalized view of Christ's divinity. At a certain point in that process, the community was expelled from the Synagogue, with deep and traumatic consequences for its members who lost their social relations and also their legal status and became strangers in a hostile world or even subjected to denunciation and persecution. John's anti-Jewish polemic is, then, explained as a "tragedy of closeness"[9] from the continued debate with the Synagogue, which was fueled by the traumatic experiences of the expelled Jesus followers.

The reconstructions by Martyn and his American colleague Raymond E. Brown differ as to what was first, either a high Christology as the reason of expulsion (thus Brown), or else the expulsion as triggering an even more elevated view of Christ (thus Martyn).[10] Both interpreters presuppose the distinction of various literary layers in John for reconstructing the theological development of the related community.[11] In this construction, the location of the ἀποσυνάγωγος event on the timeline of the development or composition of the Gospel was crucial for answering the question whether the Fourth Gospel (or, according to some authors, a first edition of it) was still composed within the context of the Jewish community or, instead, after the expulsion and from an external or even non-Jewish viewpoint. Was the Gospel composed within the heated debates before the definitive separation or was it composed shortly after expulsion from the Synagogue such that the anti-Jewish polemic could also be explained from a historical and psychological perspective as a reaction of the formerly Jewish

---

Gospel, ed. F.F. Segovia (Atlanta, GA: Scholars Press, 1998), 111–138; eadem, "Reading History in the Fourth Gospel: A Response to J. Louis Martyn," in *"What You Have Heard From the Beginning": The Past, Present, and Future of Johannine Studies*, ed. T. Thatcher (Waco, TX: Baylor University Press, 2007), 191–194, and also Frey, "'The Jews' in the Gospel of John and the 'Parting of the Ways'," (see n. 1), 51–61.

9 Thus the well-phrased title by E. Stegemann, "Die Tragödie der Nähe: Zu den judenfeindlichen Aussagen des Johannesevangeliums," *KuI* 4 (1989): 114–122.

10 See Frey, "'The Jews' in the Gospel of John and the 'Parting of the Ways'" (see n. 1), 69–70 with n. 175.

11 See in particular Brown's pattern of five stages in the Johannine history in Brown, *The Community of the Beloved Disciple* (see n. 7), 171–174. Most significant is the fact that Brown has abandoned this pattern in one of his last works, the introduction to the scheduled revision of his commentary which was, then, edited posthumously by his former student Francis Moloney; see R.E. Brown and F.J. Moloney, *An Introduction to the Gospel of John* (New York, NY: Doubleday, 2003), 62–89.

Jesus followers to the traumatic experiences they endured by their fellow Jews? Or was the Gospel composed sometime after the expulsion, at a certain distance from the Synagogue, and thus from a Gentile Christian viewpoint? In this case, John's anti-Judaism could not so easily be explained as part of an inner-Jewish debate, comparable to the debates between other Jewish factions and sects. Instead, it might already represent an external view, possibly already shaped by the formation of a separate non-Jewish identity or even by Pagan influences.[12]

Martyn's hypothesis[13] was based on the optimism of redaction criticism in the 1960s and 1970s. At that time, scholars were confident that they might be able to reconstruct the history and theological development of the Johannine community from its beginnings to its end.[14] During the most recent decades, scholarship has become much more cautious regarding such hypothetical reconstructions. Martyn's hypothesis was also based on the image of the Johannine community as an isolated sectarian circle, unaware of the Synoptic tradition and with little exchange with other groups of Jesus followers.[15] But the reasoning behind this view, particularly the way of concluding from the shape of John's dualistic language to the social or mental structure of the circles or community behind that language is sociolinguistically invalid.[16] Furthermore, the view of Johannine independence from the Synoptic tradition has been abandoned by

---

[12] Folker Siegert, in his idiosyncratic analysis and 'reconstruction' of the 'original' gospel, even wanted to use supposedly anti-Jewish sayings and the high Christology as a critical tool for separating between an early Jewish or Judaeo-Christian writing and a later anti-Jewish layer of the redaction, see his *Das Evangelium des Johannes in seiner ursprünglichen Gestalt: Wiederherstellung und Kommentar*, SIJD 7 (Göttingen: Vandenhoeck & Ruprecht, 2008), 110–160, in particular 155–156.

[13] See a brief discussion of Martyn's views in Frey, *Theology and History in the Fourth Gospel* (see n. 3), 4–10.

[14] Thus, in particular, the redaction critical approaches by Jürgen Becker and Georg Richter; see J. Becker, *Das Evangelium nach Johannes*, 2 vols., ÖTK 4,1–2, 3rd ed. (Würzburg: Echter; Gütersloh: Gütersloher Verlagshaus, 1991); G. Richter, *Studien zum Johannesevangelium*, ed. J. Hainz, BU 13 (Regensburg: Pustet, 1977); for critical evaluation, cf. J. Frey, *Die johanneische Eschatologie*, vol. 1: *Ihre Probleme im Spiegel der Forschung seit Reimarus*, WUNT 96 (Tübingen: Mohr Siebeck, 1997), 273–297.

[15] Cf. also the influential essay by W.A. Meeks, "The Man From Heaven in Johannine Sectarianism," *JBL* 91 (1972): 44–72.

[16] See the criticism by T. Onuki, "Zur literatursoziologischen Analyse des Johannesevangeliums: Auf dem Wege zur Methodenintegration," *AJBI* 8 (1982): 162–216; and K. Berger, *Exegese des Neuen Testaments*, UTB 658, 2nd ed. (Heidelberg: Quelle & Mayer, 1984), 230–231.

many Johannine scholars.[17] Finally, the quite daring idea developed by Martyn from the analysis of John 9 according to which the Gospel actually is a "two-level drama"[18] cannot be confirmed from the Gospel as a whole. According to that view, the narrative of the healing of the man born blind by Jesus actually reflected the healing of a blind man by a Christian charismatic in the community, so that the narrative of Jesus's actions was generally mirroring events of the later community.

Yet, John's text is not a mere retrojection of what had actually happened in a certain period within the Johannine community. Nor can it be simply considered a means of the internal trauma-therapy of an isolated sectarian circle. Its scope and horizon from its beginning (John 1:1) to its end (John 21:25) is bookish, it refers to the beginning of the Scriptures of Israel, and it finally hints at the libraries that could further be written about its protagonist Jesus. This framework strongly suggests that John not only aims at the narrow circles of an in-group discourse, but is aware of other and earlier Jesus traditions (probably from the Synoptics) and aims at a wider audience.[19]

Particularly devastating criticism has been levelled at the widely-received idea that the expulsion from the Synagogue was caused by a central act of rephrasing the Jewish so-called "benediction of the heretics" (ברכת המינים, *birkat hā-mînîm*) in the daily Jewish prayer, the *Shmone Ezre*, by the rabbis at Javne. The rephrased form of the prayer with its extended curse on the "heretics" (מינים, *mînîm*) and the Jewish Christians (נוצרים, *nôṣᵉrîm*) would have had prohibited Jesus followers from participating in the synagogual service. They would have to stay away if they had not wanted to accurse themselves in the communal prayer. But as numerous specialists have demonstrated,[20] the textual and histor-

---

[17] See the forthcoming volume *John's Transformation of Mark*, ed. E.-M. Becker, H. Bond, and C. Williams (London: Bloomsbury, forthcoming 2021) with an impressive 'new consensus' that Mark is (in a manner yet to be defined) presupposed in the Fourth Gospel.
[18] Martyn, *History*, 1st ed. (see n. 7), 46.
[19] This has been convincingly argued by R. Bauckham, "John for Readers of Mark," in *The Gospels for All Christians*, ed. idem (Grand Rapids, MI: Eerdmans, 1998), 147–171.
[20] See G. Stemberger,"Die sogenannte 'Synode von Jabne' und das frühe Christentum," *Kairos* 19 (1977): 14–21; P. Schäfer, "Die sogenannte Synode von Jabne," in idem, *Studien zur Geschichte und Theologie des rabbinischen Judentums* (Leiden: Brill, 1978), 45–64; R. Kimelman, "Birkat Ha-Minim and the Lack of Evidence for an Anti-Christian Jewish Prayer in Late Antiquity," in *Jewish and Christian Self-Definition*, vol. 2, ed. E.P. Sanders (London: SCM Press, 1981), 226–244; S.T. Katz, "Issues in the Separation of Judaism and Christianity after 70 CE: A Reconsideration," *JBL* 103 (1984): 69–74; M. Hengel, *The Johannine Question* (London: SCM Press, 1991), 115–117; W. Horbury, "The Benediction of the Minim and Early Jewish-Christian Controversy," in idem, *Jews and Christians in Contact and Controversy* (Edinburgh: T&T Clark, 1998), 67–110.

ical foundations of this suggestion are weak. First, the rabbinic testimonies about Javne present various decisions made by the Sages between the first and the second Jewish War as one 'event.' Second, the expansion of the curse on the heretics was certainly not aimed at Jewish Jesus followers to keep them away from the synagogue: The term *mînîm* is related to various apocalyptic groups and other deviant Jews, not specifically to Jesus followers, and the term *nôṣᵉrîm* appears only in late textual forms of the *Shmone Ezre*. Finally, it is quite uncertain how quickly the decisions of the rabbis in Roman Palestine became influential in the Western diaspora where the Johannine communities probably lived. Thus, the link between Javne and the Johannine ἀποσυνάγωγος is invalid.

The Johannine evidence does not support a central act of expulsion or a general view of 'the' parting of the ways. If the term ἀποσυνάγωγος refers to separation processes, they are at best local, and we have no clear evidence to place them at a certain point in the composition history of the Gospel or to precisely reconstruct the reasons for the separation. And, most importantly, such explanations do not help with the problematic polemic of the text. They neither exculpate the author or his community nor remove the dangerous potential of generalization that has contributed to later anti-Judaism.

2 Is John Jewish or Anti-Jewish?

Therefore, we must turn to other pieces of evidence for the discussion of the question whether John is still a Jewish work, or whether it is, instead, a non-Jewish or even an anti-Jewish text. This issue was discussed at length in a recent Enoch Colloquium, held before the SBL Annual Meeting on November 22nd in San Diego, and I would like to resume parts of the discussion in the present context: Is John ultimately characterized by a rhetoric of anti-Judaism, as the Jewish Johannine scholar Adele Reinhartz claims in her most recent book featured at that colloquium?[21] Or is the gospel – as Gabriele Boccaccini argued in his rejoinder – a form of "radical Jewish sectarianism"?[22] Is John (radically) Jewish or anti-Jewish? Or is it both, Jewish and anti-Jewish, at the same time?

---

[21] A. Reinhartz, *Cast Out of the Covenant: Jews and Anti-Judaism in the Gospel of John* (Lanham, MD: Lexington/Fortress Academic, 2018).
[22] Thus Gabriele Boccaccini in his still unpublished paper read at the colloquium: "The Gospel of John as a Product of Radical Jewish Sectarianism."

2.1 Jewish *and* Anti-Jewish at the Same Time?

At first glance, the Gospel of John presents itself as a thoroughly Jewish work: Its main protagonist Jesus is explicitly called a Ἰουδαῖος (John 4:9), the story is exclusively located in Jewish areas of Judaea and Galilee, with only one short episode in Samaria, and a particular focus on Jerusalem. With the few exceptions of the Samaritan woman and her kinspeople as well as the Roman governor and his soldiers, all narrative figures in John are Jews. From the very beginning, John draws on Israel's Scriptures, and the debate about Jesus as the Messiah is an exclusively Jewish one – such religious issues are not of interest to a Pagan like Pilate (cf. John 18:35). Finally, when Jesus is crucified under the Roman governor, he is universally presented in three languages as "the king of the Jews" (John 19:19). Even in history-of-religions terms, scholarship since the discovery of the Dead Sea Scrolls has increasingly demonstrated the thoroughly Jewish background of not only Johannine Christology but furthermore of almost any element of the imaginary world of the gospel narrative.[23]

However, John is also one of the most openly anti-Jewish texts in the New Testament, and the anti-Jewish effects in its reception are undeniable. The term Ἰουδαῖοι, usually translated as "Jews," is increasingly used to characterize a group which acts in a negative or even hostile manner against the main protagonist Jesus and likewise against his followers. They do not understand his words (John 2:19–20) and try to kill him (John 5:16, 18). It is said that they do not believe Moses nor the Scriptures (John 5:38–39, 46–47), and that they are not the true progeny of Abraham but, instead, the progeny of the devil (John 8:44). This is confirmed in the passion narrative where not only the high priests but also the Ἰουδαῖοι pursue Jesus's condemnation and crucifixion, and on Easter day Jesus's disciples hide behind closed doors "for fear of the Ἰουδαῖοι" (John 20:19). What does the hostility of the Ἰουδαῖοι and the distanced image of the Ἰουδαῖοι say about the provenance and background of the gospel? And what is its effect with regard to the gospel's message and impact?

Whatever might be the historical referent for the term, in the history of reception the verdict about them as unbelieving "children of the devil" was often used to fuel hatred against Jews, with deadly consequences. This reception history ought to make us cautious about the terminology we use. And it is in light of this caution that I, nevertheless, use the term 'Jew' largely synonymous

---

23 See J. Frey, "Auf der Suche nach dem Kontext des Johannesevangeliums: Eine forschungsgeschichtliche Einführung," in *Kontexte des Johannesevangeliums Das vierte Evangelium in religions- und traditionsgeschichtlicher Perspektive*, ed. idem and U. Schnelle, WUNT 175 (Tübingen: Mohr Siebeck, 2004), 3–45, here 26–28.

with the Johannine term Ἰουδαῖος and 'Jewish' for everything belonging to the Ἰουδαῖοι. This rendering has been questioned in scholarship.²⁴ However, in my view, all attempts of generally limiting or narrowing down the scope of Ἰουδαῖος, for instance, as 'merely (locally) Judaean' or as a mere sub-group of the Jewish people (e.g., its leaders) are unconvincing. Such semantic limitations have often been introduced for ethical reasons to prevent an undue identification of Ἰουδαῖοι in ancient sources with modern Jews.²⁵ But such an ethically honorable aim does not solve the semantic issues. The Ἰουδαῖοι opposing Jesus in Galilee in John 6 are not 'Judaeans,' nor are they the leaders of the people. Thus, Ἰουδαῖοι refers to an often unspecified group of ethnically and religiously (that is, Judea-oriented and Moses-oriented) 'Jewish' people. In John's generalizing usage, where the former distinctions between Pharisees, Sadducees, Herodians, and other groups are left aside, the term turns into a simplified and thus even more dangerous term, a powerful and rhetorically effective symbol that became so dangerously useful to later polemicists and politicians.²⁶

How Jewish and how anti-Jewish is John's Gospel, then? Of course, the answers depend on how we can determine a 'Jewish' and 'anti-Jewish' character of the work. Therefore, we have to reflect the various relevant categories and factors: the author, the tradition adopted, the theology, the community of addressees, the rhetoric, and further socio-political factors. Things become even more complicated if we do not merely look at the Gospel text but also include the Johannine epistles as a further piece of evidence for the community context in which the Gospel originated.

---

24 Cf. the considerations by D.R. Schwartz, "'Judaean' or 'Jew'? How Should We Translate *Ioudaios* in Josephus?" in *Jewish Identity in the Greco-Roman World: Jüdische Identität in der griechisch-römischen Welt*, ed. J. Frey, D.R. Schwartz, and S. Gripentrog, AJEC 71 (Leiden: Brill, 2007), 3–27.
25 See the remark in the entry on Ἰουδαῖος in BAGD. Of course, ancient Ἰουδαῖοι cannot be confused with modern 'Jews.' However, many modern Jews determine their own identity in the line of the tradition of the 'Judean' texts (the Tanak or Hebrew Bible), and the Jerusalem temple, although in modernity, the link between being Jewish and the shape of religious practice can be determined individually and in a wide variety of options. Contrarily, it is questionable whether in antiquity adherents of the Torah, focused on the Jerusalem temple, but living in Galilee, Antioch, Egypt, Rome, or Mesopotamia would have considered themselves 'Judaeans,' let alone whether proselytes such as the king Izates of Adiabene (Josephus, *Ant.* 20.38) would have wanted to become a 'Judaean' (see Schwartz, "'Judaean' or 'Jew'?" [see n. 24], 14).
26 The development towards a dangerous, symbolically burdened term has been aptly elaborated in T. Nicklas, *Ablösung und Verstrickung: 'Juden' und Jüngergestalten als Charaktere der erzählten Welt des Johannesevangeliums und ihre Wirkung auf den impliziten Leser*, RST 60 (Frankfurt a.M.: Lang, 2001), 391–409.

2.2 Categories for Determining John's 'Jewish' or 'Non-Jewish' Character

a) Author

We can pose several questions about the author (if there is one author primarily responsible for the Gospel): Was he born and raised as a Jew,[27] did he have a Jewish religious background and cultural knowledge, and did he still feel and act as a Jew in his ethnic and religious identity? However, since no certainty about John's authorship can be established, the identification of the real author is largely guesswork, and there are almost no clear statements about his background and identity (unlike, for example, in the uncontested Pauline epistles). Even if we concede that John's implicit author has an abundant knowledge of Jewish culture and Scripture, it is uncertain whether the real person who penned the text was actually a Jew and still behaved as such, whether he was part of a synagogual community and observed the Jewish Law to a certain degree. The implicit author, at least, phrases some statements at a certain distance from the Ἰουδαῖοι. He explains Jewish customs to his implied readers and presents the Jewish Jesus speaking to other Ἰουδαῖοι in a distanced manner about "their" (resp.: "your") Law.[28] Thus, a notable distance from the Ἰουδαῖοι is marked, despite the cultural knowledge about Jews, Jewish customs, and Jewish Scriptures.

b) Traditions

Of course, there is abundant usage of the Jewish Scriptures in John, in explicit quotations and many more allusions.[29] The reference to the Scriptures is also fundamental in the dispute with the Ἰουδαῖοι, who search the Scriptures (John 5:39), claim to be Abraham's children (John 8:33) and disciples of Moses (John

---

[27] This is the historical and biographical question which is answered with a strong 'yes' by Hengel, *The Johannine Question* (see n. 20), who considers the evangelist a Palestinian Jew who went to the Diaspora probably in the context of the Jewish War. I still consider many arguments quite plausible, although numerous interpreters today would prefer to refrain from historically answering that tricky 'Johannine Question.'

[28] On words of Jesus, see John 8:17; 10:34; 15:25 etc.; on festivals, see John 2:13; 5:1; 6:4; 7:2; 11:55); on Jewish customs, see John 2:6; 4:9 etc.

[29] See the still important, comprehensive but relatively concise discussion in M. Hengel, "Die Schriftauslegung des 4. Evangeliums auf dem Hintergrund der urchristlichen Exegese," in idem, *Jesus und die Evangelien: Kleine Schriften 5*, WUNT 211 (Tübingen: Mohr Siebeck, 2007), 601–643.

9:28), but, in view of the implicit author, the Scriptures are also valid and cannot be broken (John 10:35). Apart from the Scriptures, John also draws on Jewish exegetical traditions, e.g., Wisdom traditions in the prologue, interpretations of the Jacob story in 1:45–51, ideas about God's activity on the Sabbath in 5:17, etc. He draws on Jewish Messianic discourses about eschatological figures in John 1:20f., and on debates about the origins of the Messiah, whether he will stay forever etc.[30] Jesus's status and legacy are exclusively debated among the Ἰουδαῖοι, mostly with reference to the Scriptures. Thus, the pivotal point of John's message is firmly based on Jewish traditions.

But does the fact that John so intensely refers to Jewish traditions make it 'Jewish'? Is John's rejection of differing interpretations of those traditions still a debate 'within Judaism'? And what would John have to reject, what would he have to ignore, so that it could no longer be considered Jewish?

We can go even a step further. John can also be read within the context of Graeco-Roman ideas and traditions. There was no strict divide between Judaism and the Greco-Roman world, rather Judaism in the 1st century CE lived within the Greco-Roman world. So, there are also numerous Greco-Roman cultural elements which are addressed or alluded to in John, and readers with the respective cultural knowledge most likely recognized that interplay. At the very beginning, there is the term ὁ λόγος, which is not only prefigured in the biblical word of the creation or in Philonic thought, but also resonates widely with numerous aspects of Greek philosophical and religious thought.[31] There may be additional allusions to stories about Dionysus and Asclepios in Johannine Jesus stories.[32] The dialogues at the last meal can also be read in the cultural context of symposia,[33]

---

30 See the comprehensive article by R. Bauckham, "Messianism according to the Gospel of John," in *Challenging Perspectives on the Gospel of John*, ed. J. Lierman, WUNT II/219 (Tübingen: Mohr Siebeck, 2006), 34–68.
31 See the presentation in J. Frey, "Between Torah and Stoa: How Could Readers Have Understood the Johannine Logos," in *The Prologue of the Gospel of John: Its Literary, Theological, and Philosophical Contexts. Papers read at the Colloquium Ioanneum 2013*, ed. J.G. van der Watt, R.A. Culpepper, and U. Schnelle, WUNT 359 (Tübingen: Mohr Siebeck, 2016), 189–234.
32 See, e.g., W. Eisele, "Jesus und Dionysos. Göttliche Konkurrenz bei der Hochzeit zu Kana (Joh 2,1–11)," *ZNW* 100 (2009): 1–28. In contrast with Eisele's cautious approach, which draws on the findings about Dionysus in Galilee (Beit Shean, Sephoris), the approach chosen by D.R. Macdonald, *The Dionysian Gospel: The Fourth Gospel and Euripides* (Minneapolis, MN: Fortress, 2017) is, in my view, too one-sided and ultimately mistaken.
33 See G. Parsenios, *Departure and Consolation: The Johannine Farewell Discourses in Light of Greco-Roman Literature*, NT.Sup 117 (Leiden: Brill, 2005).

or even in the textual context of Plato's famous dialogues.³⁴ Do these resonances with Graeco-Roman thought imply that John is less Jewish in its character? Further, what kind of education and cultural knowledge can be presupposed for diaspora Jewish circles? If Jews in the diaspora were also well-acquainted with central elements of the Graeco-Roman culture, these textual elements do not make John less Jewish.

c) Theology and Christology

What about John's theology and Christology? When talking about *God*³⁵ we can safely state that the term θεός, which is used from the very beginning of the Gospel (John 1:1c), consistently refers to the one God of Israel's Scriptures. His activity in Israel's history is mentioned (cf. John 10:35), his fundamental invisibility is stressed (1:18), and 17:3 explicitly calls him the "only true God," thus articulating the claims of Jewish monotheism in the midst of more pluralistic and polytheistic views of the surrounding world.

Much more complicated is John's Christology. Numerous scholars held the view that with its high Christology, presenting Jesus as a divine being, as θεός (1:1, 18; 20:28), John violates the Jewish principle of monotheism and thus goes beyond the borders of Judaism. Due to the idea that such a view could only be expressed under pagan influence, the British Aramaist and Jesus scholar Maurice Casey provokingly claims that John has changed or even forged the image of Jesus from the true historical image of a Jewish prophet to the idea of a Pagan deity.³⁶ This suspicion seems to be confirmed by John's narrative: There, the Ἰουδαῖοι consider Jesus's claims³⁷ offensive and pursue his death because he made himself God (John 10:33; cf. 19:7). Instead, the Gospel claims that

---

34 See G.H. van Kooten, "The Last Days of Socrates and Christ: *Eutyphro, Apology, Crito,* and *Phaedo* Read in Counterpoint with John's Gospel," in *Religio-Philosophical Discourses in the Mediterranean World: From Plato, through Jesus, to Late Antiquity,* ed. idem and A.K. Petersen, APhR 1 (Leiden: Brill, 2017), 219–243; idem, "John's Counter-Symposium: 'The Continuation of Dialogue' in Christianity – A Contrapuntal Reading of John's Gospel and Plato's Symposium," in *Intolerance, Polemics, and Debate in Antiquity: Politico-Cultural, Philosophical, and Religious Forms of Critical Conversation,* ed. idem and J. van Ruiten, TBN 25 (Leiden: Brill, 2019), 282–357.
35 See J. Frey, "God in the Gospel of John," in idem, *The Glory of the Crucified One* (see n. 1), 313–344.
36 M. Casey, *From Jewish Prophet to Gentile God: The Origins and Development of New Testament Christology* (Cambridge: T&T Clark, 1991).
37 Of course, these are actually rather the claims made by the Johannine preaching with regard to Jesus's divine character, not claims made by the earthly Jesus himself.

Jesus is not a self-made God, but that his status has been given to him from the Father who has sent him. In John 10:34–36, in a daring exegesis of Psalm 82, the Johannine Jesus even defends the claims of high Christology with biblical language. If the Scriptures (and thus God himself) occasionally call human beings 'Gods,' it cannot be illegitimate when Jesus himself claims to be God's Son. The alleged violation of monotheism is countered by a daring, but still very Jewish argument.

From a history-of-religions perspective,[38] recent research has amply demonstrated that the christological titles used in the Fourth Gospel are all thoroughly shaped by Jewish texts and traditions. This is certainly true for the predication of Jesus as the Prophet, the Messiah, the one who is sent or who is to come, the Son of Man, the Son of God, and even the absolute predication the Son.[39] They are all prefigured in various Jewish texts, from prophecy and psalms, apocalyptic and wisdom traditions. Particularly the Dead Sea Scrolls have demonstrated the wide variety of possible expressions of eschatological expectation within contemporary Judaism.[40]

The question is whether this also applies to the highest claim in John, the presentation of Jesus as θεός. In other words, is the divinity of Jesus as claimed in John, also shaped by Jewish patterns, or is it an element of pagan syncretistic influence, and thus a step beyond Judaism? Is the development of Johannine Christology at least in its last and final step a move away from a Jewish prophet to a Gentile God (as Casey has argued), or is it instead a development from a Jewish Messiah to "a *Jewish* god,"[41] as was provokingly suggested by Gabriele Boccaccini? What about the character of Messianic figures in Ancient Jewish texts? Are there not only superhuman but also strictly divine figures within the spectrum of Jewish eschatological expectations?[42] To explain the development of

---

38 See in particular the contributions in the volume *Reading the Gospel of John's Christology as Jewish Messianism: Royal, Prophetic, and Divine Messiahs*, ed. B. Reynolds and G. Boccaccini, AJEC 106 (Leiden and Boston, MA: Brill, 2018).
39 On these titles, see Frey, *Theology and History in the Fourth Gospel* (see n. 3), 27–38; idem, "Jesus as the Image of God in the Gospel of John," (see n. 5), 295–302.
40 See the comprehensive volumes by J.J. Collins, *The Scepter and the Star* (New York, NY: Doubleday, 1995), and J. Zimmermann, *Messianische Texte aus Qumran*, WUNT II/104 (Tübingen: Mohr Siebeck, 1998).
41 Thus G. Boccaccini, "How Jesus Became Uncreated," in *Sibyls, Scriptures, and Scrolls: John Collins at Seventy*, 2 vols., ed. J. Baden, H. Nayman, and E. Tigchelaar, JSJSup 175/1–2 (Leiden and Boston, MA: Brill, 2016), 1:185–208, here 208 (italics original).
42 See now the dissertation of my student R.A. Bühner, *Hohe Messianologie im Antiken Judentum*, WUNT II/523 (Tübingen: Mohr Siebeck, 2020) with a panorama of ancient Jewish texts pre-

early high Christology from Jewish roots, scholars such as Larry Hurtado have referred to various texts about angelic or heavenly figures such as Melchizedek in the Qumran midrash (11QMelch), to texts about enthroned patriarchs such as Moses or Enoch, or the eschatological figure in the Qumran self-glorification hymn (4Q491), and the phenomenon of the early veneration of Jesus as a divine being in prayers and invocations such as the Aramaic μαραναθά (1 Cor 16:22).[43] However, none of those passages really prefigure what is said in John: that the eternal Logos, then identified with the earthly Jesus, is not a created being, but on the side of the creator, acting as medium or even cooperator in the creation of the universe. This is what in Jewish terms makes Jesus really 'divine,' whereas the category of 'divinity' or a 'god' is much more open and unprecise in Pagan thought. Thus, according to Boccaccini, the decisive question is not "How on earth did Jesus become a God?"[44] but more precisely "How did Jesus become uncreated?"[45] Is this a step beyond what was acceptable in Jewish thought, a step beyond Judaism?

Whenever discussing 'limits' or 'borders' of Judaism, we should keep in mind that there was actually no central authority to officially determine such limits, neither in Second Temple times, nor in the early rabbinic period.[46] Thus, any reference to such 'limits' is historically questionable. There were only limits set or felt by special groups or individuals, and this is what the information about conflicts and the outright rejection of certain views in that period can show. But even the outright rejection of a view in one community or region cannot define a 'border' of Judaism in general.

With these caveats in mind, I have tried to argue in a recent conference paper dedicated to Larry Hurtado that even the step taken in John 1:1–3 is prepared within the Jewish tradition, more precisely in the ideas about Lady Wisdom.[47]

---

senting 'Messianic' or eschatological figures with super-human characteristics from certain LXX Psalms to 4 Ezra and 2 Baruch.

43 Cf. L.W. Hurtado, *One God, One Lord. Early Christian Devotion and Ancient Jewish Monotheism* (Philadelphia, PA: Fortress, 1988); idem, *Lord Jesus Christ. Devotion to Jesus in Earliest Christianity* (Grand Rapids, MI: Eerdmans, 2003).

44 Thus the somewhat popular title by L.W. Hurtado, *How on Earth Did Jesus Become a God?* (Grand Rapids, MI: Eerdmans, 2005).

45 Thus the title by Boccaccini, "How Jesus Became Uncreated," (see n. 41).

46 The whole debate about a place '*intra muros*' or '*extra muros*,' so vividly discussed with regard to the Gospel of Matthew, is, therefore, odd since there were no 'walls' but just various degrees of Jewish affiliation.

47 See the more detailed argument in J. Frey, "Between Jewish Monotheism and Proto-Trinitarian Relations: The Making and Character of Johannine Christology," in *Monotheism and Christol-*

The question is whether the traditions about the hypostatic Logos in Philo or the traditions about Wisdom are more closely related to the Johannine Prologue. In Philo, ὁ λόγος is actually used for a hypostatic being. But although this λόγος can be called "second God" (δεύτερος θεός) and "firstborn" (πρωτότοκος) of all beings, it is still an intermediate being within a Middle-Platonic concept that helps to maintain God's full transcendence at a distance from the material world. In the Jewish Wisdom tradition, in particular in Sirach 24 and in Wisdom 7–10 where the traditions about God's word and his wisdom are conflated, Lady Wisdom is presented as a preexistent divine being, on a heavenly throne, sent to humankind from the heavenly realm meant to lead them to life. Although the term ὁ λόγος is not explicitly used there, the Johannine concept of the λόγος is closer to the traditions about Wisdom than to the philosophical reasoning of Philo. It adopts a way of presenting an uncreated divine figure for shaping the image of the divine Logos and Son. But this means, that even when the Logos is called θεός he is not shaped according to a Pagan understanding of divinity, but clearly prefigured in Jewish traditions. As the eternal and preexistent Logos through whom all things are made (John 1:3),[48] yet who is God (John 1:1, 18; 20:28), the Johannine Jesus is still a kind of 'Jewish God' in a close 'binitarian' relationship with the one God of Israel. Thus, even John's presentation of Jesus as θεός (John 1:1c; 20:28) is not beyond what could be formulated within Judaism, since it does not go beyond any clear limits or boundaries of contemporary Jewish thought.

Having discussed issues of pertaining to authorship, adopted traditions, and theology, we can ask about additional aspects pertaining to John's place 'within Judaism.'

d) Community Situation

Things are more difficult regarding the community of addressees or the image of the community mirrored in the Gospel. Here, the difficulty is whether and how far we can draw conclusions from the data of the text to the realities of the world of the author and his addressees. Does the text reflect a particular commu-

---

ogy in *Greco-Roman Antiquity*, ed. M. Novenson (Leiden: Brill, 2020), 189–221, especially 204–210.

[48] On the function of the motif of preexistence in John, see now R.A. Bühner, "Die theologischen Implikationen der Präexistenzchristologie in Joh 1,1–3," in *Perspektiven zur Präexistenz im Frühjudentum und frühen Christentum*, ed. J. Frey, F. Kunath, and J. Schröter, WUNT 457 (Tübingen: Mohr Siebeck, 2021), 185–208.

nity or circle of communities as its background, and to what extent is this relevant for interpretation? In view of the methodological difficulties and the shortcomings of the traditional "Community Hypothesis," Adele Reinhartz in her most recent book[49] has now abandoned this question to merely focus on the text and its pragmatics or rhetoric. In my view, such a cautious restriction goes too far. Methodological difficulties may cause uncertainty of the results but can never lead to the conclusion that there was no such community within which the real author of the gospel lived and theologized. In her book, Reinhartz decides to merely look at the gospel, not at the Johannine epistles. Yet, it is the epistles in particular wherein a circle of communities is implied and addressed, and a particular crisis is mentioned.[50] The similarities in language as well as common sayings traditions confirm that the epistles and the Gospel draw on the same traditions and thus probably originate from the same circle of communities or 'school.'[51] So we cannot avoid reckoning with a circle of communities in the background of both, the Gospel and the epistles, regardless of their sequence and authorship,[52] even if our possibilities of reconstructing a particular community situation or milieu are limited.

It is mostly agreed that in the Gospel, the Farewell discourses (John 13:31–17:26) are the part in which the issues of the later community are most densely reflected. More generally, the words and discourses of Jesus are more clearly shaped by the language and theology of the evangelist while the setting of the Johannine narration as a whole and also the various narrated scenes are more densely linked to the world of Jesus and his contemporaries. Time, places, names, and at least some of the narrated events are rooted in the world of the earthly Jesus and depend on earlier traditions about his ministry. What does this mean for reconstructing the community context of the Gospel? Can we iden-

---

49 Reinhartz, *Cast Out of the Covenant* (see n. 21).
50 See my argument in J. Frey, "'Ethical' Traditions, Family Ethos, and Love in the Johannine Literature," in idem, *Die Herrlichkeit des Gekreuzigten* (see n. 3), 767–802, here 769–773.
51 The term 'school' is often contested, as the comparison with philosophical or later gnostic schools and also with the 'Pauline school' as evident in the deutero-Pauline epistles shows numerous differences, so the term is used only in a restricted sense for those members of the Johannine communities who were involved in the theologizing activities (see U. Schnelle, *Das Evangelium nach Johannes*, ThHK 4, 5th ed. [Leipzig: Evangelische Verlagsanstalt, 2016], 3).
52 In my view, the epistles are not a late product of the 'deutero-Johannine' history but rather written before the completion and distribution of the gospel, so they have to be considered the closest commentary to the gospel; see Frey, *Die johanneische Eschatologie* (see n. 14), 451–455; idem, *Die johanneische Eschatologie*, vol. 3: *Die eschatologische Verkündigung in den johanneischen Texten*, WUNT 110 (Tübingen: Mohr Siebeck, 2000), 46–60.

tify the primary rival or opponent of the Johannine communities with contemporary 'Jews' (i.e., the diaspora Synagogue)?

Things are more complicated. The fact that in John the earthly Jesus is in discussion with Ἰουδαῖοι in a narrative setting located in Jewish Palestine cannot force us to locate the composition of the Gospel also within a completely Jewish environment. Instead, it is remarkable that, unlike in John 2–12, within the Farewell discourses (with the only exception of John 16:2–3 where the ἀποσυνάγωγος is mentioned), the 'Jews' only play a marginal role. This also corresponds to the Johannine Epistles where the Ἰουδαῖοι are also absent. In the Farewell discourses and in the Epistles, a more general term is used, namely 'the world' (ὁ κόσμος) which cannot be simply identified with Jews but represents opposition from a wider angle[53] which may imply Jewish but also non-Jewish rejection of Jesus followers (cf. especially John 15:18 ff). If the Farewell discourses are the most significant part of the Gospel with regard to the situation of the addressees, the community context or background might better be reconstructed from the evidence in these passages, which is additionally confirmed by the epistles, rather than from the disputes of John 2–12.

With these considerations in view, we can again ask whether the Johannine communities are (still) Jewish in their practical life, affiliated to the Jewish 'ethnos' of their province or city. What is their ethnic profile?[54] If we look first to the evidence of the Epistles, where the communities are directly addressed, we can see that the members are called brothers, born from God, and gifted by the anointment (χρῖσμα). According to 2 and 3 John, they meet in houses and the only individual names we know from those communities, Gaius (3 John 1), Demetrios, and Diotrephes (3 John 9) are quite unlikely to be Jewish. Especially the latter two names strongly point to a Pagan background of the individuals mentioned, so that at least these two representatives of the community linked with the authoritative 'Elder' (3 John 1) were probably followers of Jesus from a Pagan background.

Interestingly, however, the messengers of the 'Elder' seem to practice some Jewish forms of behavior. They do not take shelter and food from Pagans (3 John 7: ἐθνικοί), but only from members of the community (i.e., Jesus followers), and at the end of the first epistle (1 John 5:21), the addressees are also warned to

---

[53] See especially John 15:18. On the analogies and between the usage of Ἰουδαῖοι and κόσμος in John, see L. Kierspel, *The Jews and the World in the Fourth Gospel*, WUNT II/200 (Tübingen: Mohr Siebeck, 2006).

[54] For the following argument, see my extensive discussion in "Heiden – Griechen – Gotteskinder: Zu Gestalt und Funktion der Rede von den Heiden im vierten Evangelium," in *Die Herrlichkeit des Gekreuzigten* (see n. 3), 297–338, here 303–308.

keep apart from certain "idols." Whatever these "idols" may be, the term points to a phenomenon within the context of Paganism. Therefore, the communities addressed in the Johannine epistles appear, at least partly, to be of Pagan origin and to live within a marked Pagan context in which they seem to practice some originally (diaspora) Jewish forms of behavior, such as avoiding idols and idolatrous houses or food. Apart from the avoidance of contact with idols and pagan cultic elements (possibly in the houses) or food, there is no further evidence of more specific Jewish forms of observance regarding purity, food, Sabbath, or other aspects of the Law. Are the members of these communities Gentiles or 'Ex-Pagans' who had adopted some kind of originally Jewish habits when joining the community of Jesus followers? Could they be considered to be to some degree Judaizing from an external perspective? Or are they already aware of a new identity, different from that of Jews and Pagans? In my view, the evidence from 1 John in particular points in that direction.

The evidence of the Gospel leads to similar conclusions. Of course, Jesus travels to Jerusalem for the Jewish feasts, and we must imagine that he underwent the purity rites demanded in the temple when he visited as a festival pilgrim (John 2:13). But in the further discourses, the Mosaic Law is primarily characterized as a testimony to Jesus (John 5:39, 46), whereas in diaspora Judaism, it is characterized as instruction that shapes the conduct of those who follow 'Moses.' Furthermore, issues related to circumcision, purity, and food laws are neither discussed nor the focus of the narrative. This is also confirmed by the only exceptions, Jesus's healings on the Sabbath (John 5:1–18; 9:1–7), which are only discussed because they relate to Jesus's legacy and identity, not because of their significance to other halakhic issues. Furthermore, the mention of a meeting of the disciples on Easter day and an additional meeting one week later (John 20:19, 26) might indicate that the community in the background of the Gospel already observed the day of the Lord instead of the Jewish Sabbath. There is no evidence that the Johannine community still practiced the Jewish Law with regard to circumcision, purity, and dietary regulations. Also the focus on the earlier holy places, such as Jerusalem and Mt. Gerizim, is clearly overcome in John 4:21–26.

More telling are some further passages in the Gospel in which Gentiles are explicitly mentioned. First, there is mention of "Greeks" coming to see Jesus before his death (John 12:20–23), where Jesus answers (not directly to the Greeks, but to his disciples) that, after his exaltation, he would "draw all humans to himself" (12:32). The Greeks who could not meet him directly before his exaltation, will enjoy the encounter in the time thereafter. In the Gospel, they are a kind of vanguard for those coming to faith in a later period.⁵⁵ As "Greeks" who could not get to know Jesus before his death, they are probably meant to be Gentiles, rather than merely Diaspora Jewish pilgrims.⁵⁶ This is supported by two interconnected passages in John 10 and 11:⁵⁷ The Good Shepherd is said to lead a flock consisting not only of sheep from the (well-known) stable, but also including other sheep from outside the stable (John 10:16). The advice of the high priest Caiaphas that Jesus would die "for the people" (John 11:50: ὑπὲρ τοῦ λαοῦ) is explained in a notable commentary by the narrator (John 11:51–52) that he would not only die for the people (ὑπὲρ τοῦ ἔθνους), but also in order to lead the scattered children of God to unity. Even if these statements may draw on earlier traditions about the recollection of the Jewish diaspora, they now refer to a new unity of Jewish and originally non-Jewish believers, rather than only to the return of diaspora Jews. Thus, the Fourth Gospel envisages a community that unites Jewish believers in Jesus with Gentiles who have come to belief in a new, mixed community.

Is this community still ethnically Jewish, or considered Jewish or 'Judaizing' from the perspective of its Pagan neighbors? Or is it already a novel entity of Jews and Gentiles with a new, distinctly Jesus-oriented identity, yet without following the lifestyle of diaspora Judaism? It is difficult to negotiate between these various perspectives since there were no unified and clear-cut doctrinal or institutional 'membership requirements' for Jews in Antiquity. But it is also reasonable that from the perspective of Diaspora Jews following the Mosaic Law, as far as that was possible in their area, a communal life together with others who did not follow the purity and dietary laws would have been quite complicated and increasingly impossible. Would an 'average' synagogual community have accepted such Jesus followers as part of their group or not?

According to the evidence of the Gospel and the epistles, the Johannine groups most probably lived as voluntary associations, a circle of friends with flat hierarchies, strongly linked to its founder and hero Jesus and the one

---

55 Thus already J.A. Bengel, *Gnomon Novi Testamenti*, 2ⁿᵈ ed. (Ulm: Gaum, 1763), 407: "*Praeludium regni Dei a Iudaeis ... ad gentes transituri.*"
56 On the reference to "Greeks" in John, see also John 7:35 where, in a misunderstanding, Jesus's Jewish opponents speculate about his enigmatic prediction that they will "seek and not find" him, that he might go εἰς τὴν διασπορὰν τῶν Ἑλλήνων to teach the "Greeks." Here, διασπορὰ τῶν Ἑλλήνων means not the 'dispersion of the Greeks,' but the (Jewish) 'dispersion among the Greeks.' Thus, the 'Greeks' in this context are the Pagan inhabitants of the regions in which Jews live in dispersion. From here, it is rather plausible that the Greeks mentioned in 12:20–23 should also be viewed as Gentiles coming to Jerusalem, not merely Diaspora Jews. See the extensive argument in Frey, "Heiden – Griechen – Gotteskinder," (see n. 54), 322–334.
57 See the argument in Frey, "Heiden – Griechen – Gotteskinder," (see n. 54), 309–322.

God, but without the decisive Jewish identity markers, even though some (formerly, but not exclusively) Jewish practices, such as abstaining from idolatry, were still practiced. Were they already aware of a new identity that differed from the Jewish ethnos or local synagogue as well as from the Pagan world around? Or were they on the way to such an awareness? And how does the rhetoric of the Johannine writings contribute to such an identity formation?

e) The Gospel's Rhetoric

In her inspiring book *Cast Out of the Covenant*,[58] Adele Reinhartz focuses on the rhetoric and the rhetorical effect of the Gospel. Her question is to what affiliation the Gospel's rhetoric inspires or encourages its readers and, on the contrary, what disaffiliation it suggests.

Reinhartz's contribution is most remarkable as she herself draws on a lifelong career of "befriending the beloved disciple"[59] and incorporating that Christian text into the literary heritage of her Jewish tradition, while always struggling with how to cope with John's anti-Jewish rhetoric. In her recent book, she now draws the consequences from her earlier criticism of Martyn's community hypothesis,[60] abandoning the attempts of characterizing the community behind the Gospel but merely focusing on the text and its rhetoric. From here, she concludes that the Gospel is in effect anti-Jewish, rather than a part of an inner-Jewish dialogue/fight. It is not a reaction to expulsion, but instead promotes a "parting of the ways."[61] Her stimulating book has caused me to rethink and sharpen my own approach towards these issues, beyond the mere explanation of the development of John's Christology from Jewish sources.

Reinhartz asks if the identity and affiliation of a model reader could be drawn from reading or hearing the Gospel.[62] An important part of John's rhetoric are the stories of character transformation in which a figure comes to be healed, gains insight, or believes and is therefore attached to a new community, the community of the disciples of Jesus in which a new identity as "children of God" who

---

[58] Reinhartz, *Cast Out of the Covenant* (see n. 21).
[59] A. Reinhartz, *Befriending the Beloved Disciple: A Jewish Reading of the Gospel of John* (New York, NY: Continuum, 2001).
[60] See Reinhartz, "The Johannine Community and Its Neighbours: A Reappraisal," (see n. 8). See now Reinhartz, *Cast Out of the Covenant* (see n. 21), 111–130
[61] Reinhartz, *Cast Out of the Covenant* (see n. 21), 146–157.
[62] The model reader Reinhartz introduces with the avatar "Alexandra" is a younger woman, possibly Jewish, or interested in Jewish culture, but not necessarily, who lives in Ephesus.

have new and eternal life is shaped. This "rhetoric of affiliation"[63] is matched by a "rhetoric of disaffiliation"[64] with regard to the Ἰουδαῖοι or to aspects of Jewish life. Not only is the Gospel silent on Jewish practices such as circumcision, dietary laws, or Sabbath observance, it also dissociates its readers from the main elements of Jewish tradition, Torah and Temple, claiming that they are all fulfilled in Jesus. Finally, it presents the Ἰουδαῖοι as a group hostile to Jesus and his followers, so that readers are also distanced from them and might even start to fear them. Thus, regardless of the historical relation between those Ἰουδαῖοι and 'real Jews' in the world of the readers, the Gospel's narrative rhetoric leads its readers to disassociate themselves from the Ἰουδαῖοι or 'disciples of Moses' in their world and to associate themselves with Jesus and his disciples. Finally, as Reinhartz lucidly observes, "the Gospel's Jewishness was itself mobilized to support the anti-Jewishness that is so deeply embedded in the Gospel's rhetorical project."[65]

We may question whether we should call the Gospel anti-Jewish or whether we should call it "anti-Ioudaioi,"[66] thus avoiding anachronistic images of 'Judaism.' But such an artificial use of language is unlikely to be helpful in the discussion, and leaving a term untranslated may keep an awareness of the problems, but does not solve them. It might also be an overinterpretation when Reinhartz argues that the Jews are "cast out of the covenant" in John, as this is never clearly stated, and the image of the fruitless branches to be cut off from the vine and thrown away (John 15:6)[67] is far from being clear. There is a major difference between John and, say, the Epistle of Barnabas. Furthermore, Reinhartz underestimates, in my view, the positive role model of Nathanael (John 1:45–50) which is openly designed with references to the Jacob tradition and thus addresses particularly Jews who are encouraged to follow their fellow Jew Nathanael and come to believe in Jesus. There is a hope for the eschatological peace of Israel, albeit not without the "King of Israel" (John 1:49), Jesus. John clearly argues against a type of Judaism that rejects its Messiah and king, and thus exclusively promotes a kind of – if one may say – "sectarianism" that finds the fulfilment of all Jewish traditions exclusively in Jesus. But can we still label this "sectarianism," "Jew-

---

63 Cf. Reinhartz, *Cast Out of the Covenant* (see n. 21), 1–48, here 1.
64 Cf. Reinhartz, *Cast Out of the Covenant* (see n. 21), 49–92, here 49.
65 Reinhartz, *Cast Out of the Covenant* (see n. 21), 160.
66 Thus the suggestion uttered by Gabriele Boccaccini in the oral discussion in San Diego, Nov. 22, 2019.
67 See Reinhartz, *Cast Out of the Covenant* (see n. 21), 60–61.

ish," or even "radically Jewish"?[68] Or does the rhetoric of the text outweigh the Jewish roots of the author, the traditions, and the christological thought patterns? Does the rhetoric of disaffiliation with the Ἰουδαῖοι and their customs and new affiliation with a new "family" of "God's children" through faith in Jesus already suggest the development of a new, different category, between or beyond Jews and Pagans? Is the new affiliation inspired by John – not merely the community in which the traditions of the Gospel may be rooted – already discernible as a third group, a group that is predominantly Gentile from the viewpoint of synagogual and law-observant diaspora Judaism, but still Judaizing from the viewpoint of the surrounding Pagan society?

f) Socio-Political Circumstances

Apart from the theological debates focused on Christology, the wider socio-political factors should not be ignored. I have pointed to them in earlier essays,[69] as I am convinced that theological debates actually overestimate theological arguments or reasons given for the split between the majority of Jews and the groups of Jesus-followers. Contrary to what some theological writings suggest, including the Fourth Gospel, there was not only the debate about Jesus, his Messianic identity, or divine dignity. For the period after 70 CE, in the Diaspora, the new factor of the *fiscus iudaicus* must be considered. After the final defeat of the Jewish revolt and the destruction of the Jerusalem temple, Roman authorities imposed a new tax on all Jews in the Roman empire instead of the former temple tax. Whereas the former *didrachmon* was paid voluntarily by male Jews between 20 and 50, now all Jews, men, women, and children from age 3 to 62, were forced to pay the same amount to the Pagan god Jupiter Capitolinus in Rome. Furthermore, a special authority was established for collecting the tax which was clearly aimed at humiliating the Jews. All Jews had to be registered as such and inscribed into tax lists. This is the first time in history that affiliation with a Jewish community or belonging to the Jewish people was not a matter of that community but a matter of public administration. Jews had to be registered as such with

---

68 Thus the suggestions by Gabriele Boccaccini in his unpublished rejoinder to Reinhartz' book (see n. 21).
69 See Frey, "'The Jews' in the Gospel of John and the 'Parting of the Ways,'" (see n. 1), 61–68; and idem, "Temple and Identity in Early Christianity and in the Johannine Community," (see n 1), 500–502. See the thorough investigation by M. Heemstra, *The Fiscus Judaicus and the Parting of the Ways*, WUNT II/277 (Tübingen: Mohr Siebeck, 2010).

their names appearing in the appropriate tax lists. Suetonius[70] reports that especially under Domitian, the tax was collected with all rigor (*acerbissime*) both from those who had adopted a Jewish lifestyle (i.e., Proselytes or even God-fearers) and from those who had denied their Jewish origin (i.e., apostates, and perhaps also Gentile or even some Jewish Jesus followers). We must reckon with the possibility that the new legal and socio-political situation strongly triggered the need for a decision about who was Jewish and had to pay the tax and who was not. The socio-political circumstances that could influence group affiliation and also processes of separation should not be ignored in the discussion about the background, theological intention, and rhetorical effect of our texts.

3 Concluding Remarks and Perspectives

How can we come to a conclusion for these complicated issues? Is John still 'within Judaism' or is its place of origin or at least the direction it points to a place beyond the synagogual assemblies and – even in Roman eyes – beyond the legal place of the Jews as a largely tolerated ethnic group? Does the hatred expressed towards others and fear for one's existence addressed in the Farewell discourses (cf. John 16:2–3), as well as the warning against the idols in 1 John 5:21 ultimately point to a new, insecure legal situation of Jesus followers who were now stripped of the generally granted tolerance of Jewish ethnic traditions and behavior? Does their situation within "the world" come close to what is later reported as an established legal practice within the correspondence of Pliny the Younger[71] from the province of Bithynia in Northern Asia Minor?

3.1 The New Identity Encouraged in John

If ethnically non-Jewish readers read the Gospel, they are clearly encouraged to believe in Jesus (John 20:30–31), which will imply reading the Jewish Scriptures with a christological perspective and abstaining from idolatrous practices. Although such behavior might have been considered 'Judaizing' in the Pagan world, there is certainly no encouragement to continue the practice of circumcision, purity, food regulations, or other aspects of Torah observance, nor is there any encouragement to affiliate with a diaspora synagogue. Furthermore, we can-

---

70 Suetonius, *Dom.* 12.2.
71 Pliny the Younger, *Ep.* 10.96–97.

not assume that such Gentile converts would have wanted to start paying the *fiscus Iudaicus* for mere solidarity with the *ethnos* of the Ἰουδαῖοι if they had never been affiliated with a Jewish community before.

If ethnically Jewish readers read the Gospel, they are encouraged to affiliate with the 'true Israelites' who believe and confess Jesus, with the family of his disciples in the one flock of the one shepherd. There is, however, no explicit call to disaffiliate from the Jewish ethnos, or from a synagogual community, but as the narrative conveys the idea that such Jesus followers might be rejected by the dominant group of the Ἰουδαῖοι or even fear hostile actions from their side, the rhetoric of the Gospel and the socio-political circumstances might actually lead to the consequence of disaffiliation or separation.

The new identity as children of God and disciples or even friends of Jesus is not yet named; they are not called "*Christianoi*" (Acts 11:26), nor a "new"[72] or even "third race,"[73] but considered according to the imagery of the Gospel to be the one flock of the one shepherd, the unity of those from the ἔθνος and others not from that ἔθνος, a group that venerates God neither in Jerusalem nor on Mt. Gerizim, but in spirit and truth. All these images actually point to a new identity that differs from Greco-Roman Paganism but is also independent of the various group-formations of contemporary Judaism, yet they constitute a 'new' identity of strangers within the unbelieving 'world' whose true affiliation is only the friendship with Jesus and the love of God.

3.2 The Johannine Data and the Conceptualization of the Parting of the Ways

Regarding the scholarly pattern(s) of the "Parting of the Ways," the Johannine contribution is less precise than earlier scholarship had assumed. There is no hint at a general, decisive point of separation, and if the ἀποσυνάγωγος still refers to separation processes, they are merely local and occasional. There is also no clarity about how and why the separations actually happened. Was the reason Christology, or other conflicts about purity or issues of daily life? Were there personal conflicts, as it is so often the case in authority-oriented religious groups, or were the socio-political circumstances much more influential than the strictly doctrinal elements? In any case, we have to consider the wide range of factors, the evidence for a thoroughly Jewish background and conceptual framework in

---

72 Diogn. 1:1 καινὸν τοῦτο γένος.
73 Thus Kerygma Petri 2 (in Clement of Alexandria, *Strom.* 6.5.41).

John as well as the rhetoric that ultimately leads to a disaffiliation with the Ἰουδαῖοι. And we have to reckon with the fact that still after an organizational separation and even after a fierce conflict, there might have been additional interactions between groups of Jesus followers and local Jewish communities, as those communities – in Asia Minor quite sizeable and well-established – still formed an important point of reference for the emerging communities of Jesus-followers, apart from the wider civic context.[74]

However, we should not underestimate the effects of the Johannine rhetoric which might have distanced its readers gradually from Judaism. The general effect of this rhetoric is not at least shown by the fact that in the debates of the 3rd and 4th century, the anti-Jewish passages in John were not only used against real Jews but also (and perhaps even more frequently) against deviant Christians, just as we can see during the Reformation period when the polemical stance against the Jews, Jewish institutions, and the Law could be reused against teachings of the traditional Roman church, which were considered to be 'legalistic' by (at least some of) the Reformers.

This leads finally to the question of how the Johannine texts with all their valuable and deep theological ideas can be read without such polemical effects. Any attempts of 'rescuing' them, by censoring or purifying them from dangerous passages, by translating them differently (e. g., with Ἰουδαῖοι rendered by "Judeans"), or by historically explaining their background and composition as a mere reaction to troublesome experiences, does not rid them of their dangerous dynamics of disaffiliation and denigration. The problems are almost unsurmountable, and they leave us, Christian theologians, with the steady task of maintaining an awareness about the Jewish traditions at our own roots. We have to consider that our own identity formation could only happen through harmful processes of conflict and rejection, but that within our own identity, there still exists, and necessarily so, the 'other' that was once rejected.[75]

3.3 Hermeneutical Reflections

There is further need for a critical reflection of the scholarly tendencies in which we participate. The rediscovery of the Jewish roots of the New Testament in New Testament scholarship can only be understood as a late effect of the deadly out-

---

[74] See the contribution by Paul Trebilco in the present volume (p. 273–306).
[75] See the reflections in J. Frey, "New Testament Scholarship and Ancient Judaism: Problems – Perceptions – Perspectives," in idem, *Qumran, Early Judaism, and New Testament Interpretation. Kleine Schriften 3*, ed. J. Cerone, WUNT 424 (Tübingen: Mohr Siebeck, 2019), 19–44, here 44.

bursts of anti-Judaism in the 20th century and the Christian theological interest in the renewal of Jewish-Christian relations thereafter. It was further fortuitously supported by new textual discoveries, especially the Dead Sea Scrolls. Although the initial enthusiasm after their early publication was undue, and no direct links between the Scrolls and the New Testament (including John) can be established, the insights from these sources have strongly changed the scholarly image of Second Temple Judaism, scriptural interpretation, Messianism, and many other subjects. This has also led to the reconfiguration of our views of the development of Christology in contrast with the views of the earlier History-of-Religions school or the German Bultmann school. As is often the case, the pendulum has swung back again in some parts, and indeed, the rediscovery of Jewish elements in the New Testament does not exclude the need to contextualize all these texts within their Greco-Roman context. In history-of-religions terms, any one-sidedness is to be avoided.

The internationalization and widening of New Testament scholarship has also led to due criticism of some earlier theological paradigms and views about Judaism, matters pertaining to the law, and history, not only in Pauline research but also in other fields, including Johannine interpretation. Scholars from various Christian backgrounds or with no religious affiliation at all have entered the discussion, and, not least, Jewish scholars who now freshly embrace texts from the early Jesus movement as part of their own literary heritage.

In parts of Christian theology and exegesis, however, the inclination to an inner-Jewish contextualization is also motivated by the moral strife to avoid anti-Jewish patterns in Christian exegesis and teaching, and, not least, by the attempt to save a dear and valuable canonical text from the devastating charge of being anti-Jewish. To consider all the polemic, including John 8:44, as a still inner-Jewish dialogue, similar to the Qumranites' polemic against other Jews, is a more 'comfortable' view than the idea that even the canonical texts contain anti-Jewish polemic from a stance outside of Judaism, which strengthens the dangerous connections between ancient text and contemporary anti-Judaism within our modern societies. The ethical strife to avoid anti-Jewish effects in the churches and in society can only be applauded. But the desire to safely integrate John 'within Judaism' can neither remove the dangerous elements from the text, nor can it exculpate the text or its author from the possible charge of dangerous generalization and anti-Jewish rhetoric.

In this context, it is significant that a Jewish scholar such as Adele Reinhartz does not embrace the strategy or policy of a completely 'inner-Jewish' reading of John. Her approach is challenging for all those who hold John as a central canonical text, even as the "climax of New Testament theology"[76] in high esteem. Scholarship, however, needs the critical approach that can also name difficult and inacceptable elements in otherwise valuable and insightful texts. Compared with a false 'political correctness,' such honesty is to be preferred.

Bibliography

Bauckham, R., "John for Readers of Mark," in *The Gospels for All Christians*, ed. idem (Grand Rapids, MI: Eerdmans, 1998), 147–171.
Bauckham, R., "Messianism according to the Gospel of John," in *Challenging Perspectives on the Gospel of John*, ed. J. Lierman, WUNT II/219 (Tübingen: Mohr Siebeck, 2006), 34–68.
Becker, A. H., and A. Y. Reed, eds., *The Ways that Never Parted: Jews and Christians in Late Antiquity and the Early Middle Ages*, TSAJ 95 (Tübingen: Mohr Siebeck, 2003).
Becker, E.-M., H. Bond, and C. Williams, eds., *John's Transformation of Mark* (London: Bloomsbury, forthcoming 2021).
Becker, J., *Das Evangelium nach Johannes*, 2 vols., ÖTK 4,1–2, 3rd ed. (Würzburg: Echter; Gütersloh: Gütersloher Verlagshaus, 1991).
Bengel, J. A., *Gnomon Novi Testamenti*, 2nd ed. (Ulm: Gaum, 1763).
Berger, K., *Exegese des Neuen Testaments*, UTB 658, 2nd ed. (Heidelberg: Quelle & Mayer, 1984).
Bieringer, R., "Anti-Judaism and the Fourth Gospel Fifteen Years after the Leuven Colloquium: A Contested Relationship in Context," in *John and Judaism*, ed. R. A. Culpepper and P. N. Anderson, RBS 87 (Atlanta, GA.: SBL Press, 2017), 243–264.
Bieringer, R., D. Pollefeyt, and F. Vandecasteele-Vanneuville, "Wrestling with Johannine Anti-Judaism: A Hermeneutical Framework for the Analysis of the Current Debate," in *Anti-Judaism and the Fourth Gospel*, ed. idem, D. Pollefeyt, and F. Vandecasteele-Vanneuville (Louisville, KY: Westminster John Knox, 2001), 3–37.
Boccaccini, G., "How Jesus Became Uncreated," in *Sibyls, Scriptures, and Scrolls: John Collins at Seventy*, 2 vols., ed. J. Baden, H. Nayman, and E. Tigchelaar, JSJSup 175/1–2 (Leiden and Boston, MA: Brill, 2016), 1:185–208.
Boyarin, D., *Border Lines: The Partition of Judaeo-Christianity in Divinations: Rereading Late Ancient Religion* (Philadelphia, PA: University of Pennsylvania Press, 2004).
Broadhead, E. K., *Jewish Ways of Following Jesus: Remapping the Religious Map of Antiquity*, WUNT 266 (Tübingen: Mohr Siebeck, 2010).
Brown, R. E., *The Community of the Beloved Disciple: The Life, Loves, and Hates of an Individual Church in New Testament Times* (London: Chapman, 1979).
Brown, R. E., and F. J. Moloney, *An Introduction to the Gospel of John* (New York, NY: Doubleday, 2003).

---

[76] Cf. J. Frey, "Johannine Theology as the Climax of New Testament Theology," in idem, *The Glory of the Crucified One* (see n. 1), 347–375.

Bühner, R. A., *Hohe Messianologie im Antiken Judentum*, WUNT II/523 (Tübingen: Mohr Siebeck, 2020).

Bühner, R. A., "Die theologischen Implikationen der Präexistenzchristologie in Joh 1,1–3," in *Perspektiven zur Präexistenz im Frühjudentum und frühen Christentum*, ed. J. Frey, F. Kunath, and J. Schröter, WUNT 457 (Tübingen: Mohr Siebeck, 2021), 185–208.

Casey, M., *From Jewish Prophet to Gentile God: The Origins and Development of New Testament Christology* (Cambridge: T&T Clark, 1991).

Collins, J. J., *The Scepter and the Star* (New York, NY: Doubleday, 1995).

Eisele, W., "Jesus und Dionysos. Göttliche Konkurrenz bei der Hochzeit zu Kana (Joh 2,1–11)," *ZNW* 100 (2009): 1–28.

Frey, J., *Die johanneische Eschatologie*, vol. 1: *Ihre Probleme im Spiegel der Forschung seit Reimarus*, WUNT 96 (Tübingen: Mohr Siebeck, 1997).

Frey, J., *Die johanneische Eschatologie*, vol. 3: *Die eschatologische Verkündigung in den johanneischen Texten*, WUNT 110 (Tübingen: Mohr Siebeck, 2000).

Frey, J., "Auf der Suche nach dem Kontext des Johannesevangeliums: Eine forschungsgeschichtliche Einführung," in *Kontexte des Johannesevangeliums. Das vierte Evangelium in religions- und traditionsgeschichtlicher Perspektive*, ed. idem and U. Schnelle, WUNT 175 (Tübingen: Mohr Siebeck, 2004), 3–45.

Frey, J., "Temple and Identity in Early Christianity and in the Johannine Community: Reflections on the 'Parting of the Ways'," in *Was 70 CE a Watershed in Jewish History? On Jews and Judaism before and after the Destruction of the Second Temple*, ed. D. R. Schwartz and Z. Weiss, AJEC 78 (Leiden and Boston, MA: Brill, 2012), 447–507.

Frey, J., "Das Johannesevangelium auf dem Hintergrund der älteren Evangelientradition: Zum Problem: Johannes und die Synoptiker," in idem, *Die Herrlichkeit des Gekreuzigten: Studien zu den johanneischen Schriften I*, ed. J. Schlegel, WUNT 307 (Tübingen: Mohr Siebeck, 2013), 239–294.

Frey, J., "'Ethical' Traditions, Family Ethos, and Love in the Johannine Literature," in idem, *Die Herrlichkeit des Gekreuzigten: Studien zu den johanneischen Schriften* 1, ed. J. Schlegel, WUNT 307 (Tübingen: Mohr Siebeck, 2013), 767–802.

Frey, J., "Heiden – Griechen – Gotteskinder: Zu Gestalt und Funktion der Rede von den Heiden im vierten Evangelium," in idem, *Die Herrlichkeit des Gekreuzigten: Studien zu den johanneischen Schriften* 1, ed. J. Schlegel, WUNT 307 (Tübingen: Mohr Siebeck, 2013), 297–338.

Frey, J., "Von Paulus zu Johannes. Die Diversität 'christlicher' Gemeindekreise und die 'Trennungsprozesse' zwischen der Synagoge und den Gemeinden der Jesusnachfolger in Ephesus im ersten Jahrhundert," in *The Rise and Expansion of Christianity in the First Three Centuries of the Common Era*, ed. C. K. Rothschild and J. Schröter, WUNT 301 (Tübingen: Mohr Siebeck, 2013), 235–278.

Frey, J., "Between Torah and Stoa: How Could Readers Have Understood the Johannine Logos," in *The Prologue of the Gospel of John: Its Literary, Theological, and Philosophical Contexts. Papers read at the Colloquium Ioanneum 2013*, ed. J. G. van der Watt, R. A. Culpepper, and U. Schnelle, WUNT 359 (Tübingen: Mohr Siebeck, 2016), 189–234.

Frey, J., "From the 'Kingdom of God' to 'Eternal Life': The Transformation of Theological Language in the Fourth Gospel," in *Glimpses of Jesus through the Johannine Lens*, vol. 3

of *John, Jesus, and History*, ed. P. N. Anderson, F. Just, and T. Thatcher (Atlanta, GA: SBL Press, 2016), 439–458.

Frey, J., "Toward Reconfiguring Our Views on the 'Parting of the Ways': Ephesus as a Test Case," in *John and Judaism: A Contested Relationship in Context*, ed. R. A. Culpepper and P. N. Anderson, RBS 87 (Atlanta, GA: SBL Press, 2017), 221–239.

Frey, J., "God in the Gospel of John," in idem, *The Glory of the Crucified One. Christology and Theology in the Gospel of John*, trans. W. Coppins and C. Heilig, BMSEC (Waco, TX: Baylor University Press; Tübingen: Mohr Siebeck, 2018), 313–344.

Frey, J., "Jesus as the Image of God in the Gospel of John," in *The Glory of the Crucified One. Christology and Theology in the Gospel of John*, trans. W. Coppins and C. Heilig, BMSEC (Waco, TX: Baylor University Press; Tübingen: Mohr Siebeck, 2018), 285–312.

Frey, J., "Johannine Theology as the Climax of New Testament Theology," in idem, *The Glory of the Crucified One. Christology and Theology in the Gospel of John*, trans. W. Coppins and C. Heilig, BMSEC (Waco, TX: Baylor University Press; Tübingen: Mohr Siebeck, 2018), 347–375.

Frey, J., "'The Jews' in the Gospel of John and the 'Parting of the Ways'," in *The Glory of the Crucified One. Christology and Theology in the Gospel of John*, trans. W. Coppins and C. Heilig, BMSEC (Waco, TX: Baylor University Press; Tübingen: Mohr Siebeck, 2018), 39–72.

Frey, J., *Theology and History in the Fourth Gospel* (Waco, TX: Baylor University Press, 2018).

Frey, J., "New Testament Scholarship and Ancient Judaism: Problems – Perceptions – Perspectives," in idem, *Qumran, Early Judaism, and New Testament Interpretation. Kleine Schriften 3*, ed. J. Cerone, WUNT 424 (Tübingen: Mohr Siebeck, 2019), 19–44.

Frey, J., "Between Jewish Monotheism and Proto-Trinitarian Relations: The Making and Character of Johannine Christology," in *Monotheism and Christology in Greco-Roman Antiquity*, ed. M. Novenson (Leiden: Brill, 2020), 189–221.

Heemstra, M., *The Fiscus Judaicus and the Parting of the Ways*, WUNT II/277 (Tübingen: Mohr Siebeck, 2010).

Hengel, M., *The Johannine Question* (London: SCM Press, 1991).

Hengel, M., "Die Schriftauslegung des 4. Evangeliums auf dem Hintergrund der urchristlichen Exegese," in idem, *Jesus und die Evangelien: Kleine Schriften 5*, WUNT 211 (Tübingen: Mohr Siebeck, 2007), 601–643.

Horbury, W., "The Benediction of the Minim and Early Jewish-Christian Controversy," in idem, *Jews and Christians in Contact and Controversy* (Edinburgh: T&T Clark, 1998), 67–110.

Hurtado, L. W., *One God, One Lord. Early Christian Devotion and Ancient Jewish Monotheism* (Philadelphia, PA: Fortress, 1988).

Hurtado, L. W., *Lord Jesus Christ. Devotion to Jesus in Earliest Christianity* (Grand Rapids, MI: Eerdmans, 2003).

Hurtado, L. W., *How on Earth Did Jesus Become a God?* (Grand Rapids, MI: Eerdmans, 2005).

Katz, S. T., "Issues in the Separation of Judaism and Christianity after 70 CE: A Reconsideration," *JBL* 103 (1984): 69–74.

Kierspel, L., *The Jews and the World in the Fourth Gospel*, WUNT II/200 (Tübingen: Mohr Siebeck, 2006).

Kimelman, R., "Birkat Ha-Minim and the Lack of Evidence for an Anti-Christian Jewish Prayer in Late Antiquity," in *Jewish and Christian Self-Definition*, vol. 2, ed. E. P. Sanders (London: SCM Press, 1981), 226–244.

Kysar, R. E., "The Expulsion from the Synagogue: The Tale of a Theory," in idem, *Voyages with John: Charting the Fourth Gospel* (Waco, TX: Baylor University Press, 2005), 237–245.

Macdonald, D. R., *The Dionysian Gospel: The Fourth Gospel and Euripides* (Minneapolis, MN: Fortress, 2017).

Martyn, J. L., *History and Theology in the Fourth Gospel*, 3rd ed. (New York, NY: Harper & Row, 1968; repr., Louisville, KY: Westminster John Knox, 2003).

Meeks, W. A., "The Man From Heaven in Johannine Sectarianism," *JBL* 91 (1972): 44–72.

Nicklas, T., *Ablösung und Verstrickung: 'Juden' und Jüngergestalten als Charaktere der erzählten Welt des Johannesevangeliums und ihre Wirkung auf den impliziten Leser*, RST 60 (Frankfurt a. M.: Lang, 2001).

Onuki, T., "Zur literatursoziologischen Analyse des Johannesevangeliums: Auf dem Wege zur Methodenintegration," *AJBI* 8 (1982): 162–216.

Parsenios, G., *Departure and Consolation: The Johannine Farewell Discourses in Light of Greco-Roman Literature*, NT.Sup 117 (Leiden: Brill, 2005).

Reinhartz, A., "The Johannine Community and Its Neighbours: A Reappraisal," in *What is John? Vol. 2 Literary and Social Readings of the Fourth Gospel*, ed. F. F. Segovia (Atlanta, GA: Scholars Press, 1998), 111–138.

Reinhartz, A., *Befriending the Beloved Disciple.: A Jewish Reading of the Gospel of John* (New York, NY: Continuum, 2001).

Reinhartz, A., "Reading History in the Fourth Gospel: A Response to J. Louis Martyn," in *"What You Have Heard From the Beginning": The Past, Present, and Future of Johannine Studies*, ed. T. Thatcher (Waco, TX: Baylor University Press, 2007), 191–194.

Reinhartz, A., *Cast Out of the Covenant: Jews and Anti-Judaism in the Gospel of John* (Lanham, MD: Lexington/Fortress Academic, 2018).

Reynolds, B., and G. Boccaccini, eds., *Reading the Gospel of John's Christology as Jewish Messianism: Royal, Prophetic, and Divine Messiahs*, AJEC 106 (Leiden and Boston, MA: Brill, 2018).

Richter, G., *Studien zum Johannesevangelium*, ed. J. Hainz, BU 13 (Regensburg: Pustet, 1977).

Schäfer, P., "Die sogenannte Synode von Jabne," in idem, *Studien zur Geschichte und Theologie des rabbinischen Judentums* (Leiden: Brill, 1978), 45–64.

Schnelle, U., *Das Evangelium nach Johannes*, ThHK 4, 5th ed. (Leipzig: Evangelische Verlagsanstalt, 2016).

Schwartz, D. R., "'Judaean' or 'Jew'? How Should We Translate *Ioudaios* in Josephus?" in *Jewish Identity in the Greco-Roman World: Jüdische Identität in der griechisch-römischen Welt*, ed. idem, J. Frey, and S. Gripentrog, AJEC 71 (Leiden: Brill, 2007), 3–27.

Siegert, F., *Das Evangelium des Johannes in seiner ursprünglichen Gestalt: Wiederherstellung und Kommentar*, SIJD 7 (Göttingen: Vandenhoeck & Ruprecht, 2008).

Smith, D. M., "The Contribution of J. Louis Martyn to the Understanding of the Gospel of John," in *The Conversation Continues: Studies in Paul and John in Honor of J. Louis Martyn*, ed. R. T. Fortna and B. R. Gaventa (Nashville, TN: Abingdon, 1990), 275–294 (repr., in Martyn, *History and Theology in the Fourth Gospel*, 3rd ed.).

Stegemann, E., "Die Tragödie der Nähe: Zu den judenfeindlichen Aussagen des Johannesevangeliums," *KuI* 4 (1989): 114–122.

Stemberger, G., "Die sogenannte 'Synode von Jabne' und das frühe Christentum," *Kairos* 19 (1977): 14–21.

van Kooten, G. H., "The Last Days of Socrates and Christ *Eutyphro, Apology, Crito,* and *Phaedo* Read in Counterpoint with John's Gospel," in *Religio-Philosophical Discourses in the Mediterranean World: From Plato, through Jesus, to Late Antiquity*, ed. idem and A. K. Petersen, APhR 1 (Leiden: Brill, 2017), 219–243.

van Kooten, G. H., "John's Counter-Symposium: 'The Continuation of Dialogue' in Christianity – A Contrapuntal Reading of John's Gospel and Plato's Symposium," in *Intolerance, Polemics, and Debate in Antiquity: Politico-Cultural, Philosophical, and Religious Forms of Critical Conversation*, ed. idem and J. van Ruiten, TBN 25 (Leiden: Brill, 2019), 282–357.

Wengst, K., *Bedrängte Gemeinde und verherlichter Christus. Der historische Ort des Johannesevangeliums als Schlüssel zu seiner Interpretation*, BThS 5 (Neukirchen-Vluyn: Neukirchener, 1981).

Wengst, K., *Bedrängte Gemeinde und verherrlichter Christus. Ein Versuch über das Johannesevangelium*, 4th ed. (Munich: Kaiser, 1992).

Zimmermann, J., *Messianische Texte aus Qumran*, WUNT II/104 (Tübingen: Mohr Siebeck, 1998).

James Carleton Paget
The Epistle of Barnabas, Jews and Christians

Abstract: Ein Merkmal des Barnabasbriefes, einer Schrift, die zu den sogenannten Apostolischen Vätern gerechnet wird, ist die – zumeist polemische – Beschäftigung mit jüdischen Themen. Allerdings verwendet der Verfasser die griechischen Begriffe für ‚Juden' und ‚Judentum' an keiner Stelle. Vor dem Hintergrund der neueren Kritik an den Grundannahmen des "Parting of the Ways"-Paradigmas untersucht der Aufsatz verschiedene Ansätze zum Verständnis der spezifischen Sicht des Barnabasbriefes auf die Juden. Besondere Aufmerksamkeit wird dabei der Vorstellung gewidmet, der Brief versuche, eine Trennung zwischen Juden und Christen in einer Situation zu konstruieren, in der es gar keine Juden gibt. Angesichts nur sehr spärlicher Informationen zum historischen Kontext des Briefes erscheint es allerdings unmöglich festzustellen, warum der Autor eine solche Position gegenüber denen einnimmt, die er nirgendwo als ‚Juden' bezeichnet.

Keywords: Jew, Christian, separatist, constructivist, Alexandria, reality, contextual, polemic

1 Introduction: the parting of the ways in recent discussion

Up until the turn of the current century and continuing up to the present day, the majority of those scholars who have interested themselves in the study of the early history of Jewish-Christian relations argued for a model known as "the parting of the ways." In broad terms it suggested that the early followers of Jesus remained for some time within the Jewish fold, Judaism understood as a diverse entity. Gradually, however, as a result of the growing Gentile profile of the burgeoning Christian community, which by and large did not observe the Jewish law, the growing hostility of the emerging rabbinic movement, given expression in the so-called 12th benediction of the *Amidah*, which had the effect of excluding Christians from the synagogue, and as a result of the Jewish revolts against Rome, which aggravated hostility between the two communities, the ways of these two movements separated, a separation which was more or less complete by the early part of the 2nd century, with the only outliers being the so-called Jewish Christians, who came to be viewed as heretics by Jew and Christian alike. The paradigm, consciously a response to an earlier supersessionist model, which came close to positing the birth of a separate Christianity with Jesus, who was perceived as a critic of Judaism and saw Christians as the appropriators of the best aspects of a solipsistic, decaying Judaism,[1] was attractive. It was neat, ecumenical and in different ways suited both Jews and Christians, and as a result, an aura of normativity seemed to hang over it.[2]

In spite of refinements, it has come under severe attack. Scholars have questioned the extent to which we can pinpoint institutional instruments, like the 12th Benediction,[3] or particular events like the Jewish revolts, as causative of separation.[4] More importantly, but related to the same point, others have argued that the paradigm is based upon a misplaced view of an early post-70 Rabbinic hegemony within Judaism, and a similarly dominant 'proto-orthodox' Christianity.[5] Once both religions had been de-institutionalised, and their diverse character affirmed (as much for the period following the writing of the New Testament as for

---

[1] See A. von Harnack, *The Expansion of Christianity in the First Three Centuries*, vol. 1 (London: ET Williams & Norgate, 1904–1905), 82–83.

[2] The term is often associated with the work of J. Parkes, *The Conflict of the Church and the Synagogue: A Study in the Origins of Anti-Semitism* (London: Soncino Press, 1934), though earlier uses, including that of F.J. Foakes Jackson, are discussed by Christoph Markschies in this volume. For an account of the main tenets of the parting paradigm, see J.M. Lieu, "'The parting of the ways': theological construct or historical reality?," in *Neither Jew nor Greek. Constructing early Christianity*, ed. eadem, 2nd ed. (London: T&T Clark, 2016), 31–40; and A.H. Becker and A.Y. Reed, eds., *The Ways That Never Parted. Jews and Christians in Late Antiquity and the Early Middle Ages*, TSAJ 95 (Tübingen: Mohr Siebeck, 2003), 1–16.

[3] The difficulties connected with interpreting this prayer, especially as these relate to original wording, extent of influence and related matters are set out in P.W. van der Horst, "The Birkat ha-minim in recent research," in *Hellenism-Judaism-Christianity*, ed. idem (Kampen: Kok, 1994), 99–111. See also J. Marcus, "Birkat ha-minim revisited," *NTS* 55 (2009): 523–551, for an endorsement of the view that the prayer refers to Christians but a qualification of its influence on Jewish-Christian relations.

[4] See J. Carleton Paget, "The Jewish revolts and Jewish-Christian relations," in *Jews and Christians in the First and Second Centuries. The Interbellum 70–132 CE*, ed. J. Schwartz and P.J. Tomson, CRINT 15 (Leiden: Brill, 2017), 276–306.

[5] See C. Hezser, *The Social Structure of the Rabbinic movement in Roman Palestine*, TSAJ 66 (Tübingen: Mohr Siebeck, 1997). This view had been entertained much earlier by Erwin Goodenough; and has now found expression in the idea of synagogal Judaism. For a recent discussion and broad endorsement of this phenomenon see J. Costa, "Qu'est-ce que le 'judaïsme synagogal'?," *JAAJ* 3 (2015): 63–218. See also A.Y. Reed, "Rabbis, 'Jewish Christians', and Other Late Antique Jews: Reflections on the Fate of Judaism(s) After 70 C. E.," in *The Changing Faces of Judaism, Christianity, and other Greco-Roman Religions in Antiquity*, ed. I.H. Henderson, G.S. Oegema, and S. Parks Ricker (Gütersloh: Gütersloher Verlagshaus 2006), 323–346.

the period before), the neat formulations of the partings looked fragile. As Judith Lieu wrote: "The problem with the model of the 'partings of the ways' is that [...] it operates essentially with the abstract or universal conception of each religion, Judaism and Christianity, when what we know about is the local and the specific."[6] In the face of this scholars had to avoid generalisations about how and when Christians and Jews separated, and concentrate on each text and archaeological piece of evidence in its particularity. Indeed, the evidence pointed away from interconnected, evolutionary narratives with specific endpoints to something more fragmentary, localized and complex.[7] Scholars opposed to the paradigm also called for more nuanced engagements with relevant texts. It was no longer acceptable to read Ignatius's reference to "Judaism" and "Christianity" (the first time these entities are mentioned together),[8] or Justin's *Dialogue with Trypho*, with its clearly developed sense of the difference between its Jewish and Christian protagonists, as reflective of a reality in which Jews and Christians were clearly and statically different. Rather scholars should see these texts as performative, that is, as attempts to create and construct a 'desirable' situation in which difference and separation were unambiguously articulated. The truth about Jewish and Christian interaction "on the ground" was much more complex, one in which identities were blurred and there was a complex criss-crossing along mudded tracks[9] – hence the persistence of *adversus Judaeos* texts from the middle of the 2nd century onwards. As Fonrobert stated: "It is perhaps this inability to control the borderland (between Judaism and Christianity) that finally accounts for the anti-Jewish rhetoric in early Christianity."[10] In this view "Judaism" and "Christianity" are evolving constructs and in the controversial and striking work of Daniel Boyarin, they only become realities in any meaningful sense in the post-Constantinian era, where state power allows them to come into being, as religions, which before this point, "Judaism" never was. Up until

---

6 Lieu, "Parting" (see n. 2), 38.
7 A.Y. Reed, "*Epilogue:* After 'Origins,' Beyond 'Identity,' and Before 'Religion(s)'," in eadem, *Jewish Christianity and the History of Judaism*, TSAJ 171 (Tübingen: Mohr Siebeck, 2018), 389–438, here 396 and 398, in particular has emphasized the effect of "narratives of dramatic change." "Whatever date is deemed determinative [...] the very question of *when* serves tidily to collapse any local specificities into the service of a monolithic narrative about two 'religions' [...] The task of cultural history is thereby flattened into a simple narrative of before and after, and the past is construed as a reservoir of precedents for the presumed *telos* of our present."
8 Ign.*Magn.* 8:1; 10:3 and Ign.*Phld* 6:1.
9 The metaphor appears in Lieu, "Parting" (see n. 2), 49.
10 C.E. Fonrobert, "Jewish Christians, Judaisers, and Christian Anti-Judaism," in *A People's History of Christianity. Vol. 2: Late Ancient Christianity,* ed. V. Burrus (Minneapolis, MN: Fortress, 2005), 234–254, here 254.

that point, according to Boyarin, all we have are various types of Jews occupying different positions along a Judaeo-Christian spectrum, ranging from Jews who had no belief in Jesus to Marcion, who attacked the God of the Hebrew Scriptures.[11] In this view there is no attempt to deny that there were from an early stage individuals who called themselves Jews and Christians, but a desire to differentiate between that identification, and the more discursive creation of "Judaism" and "Christianity", whose progenitors sought to create a sense of absolute separation between the evolving groups as if the two were entirely different.[12] Against such a background it becomes meaningless, for instance, to refer to texts as "Jewish Christian"[13] – texts traditionally designated as such become examples of a complex, evolving identity, less strange and exceptional than previously considered.[14]

Critics of the parting paradigm have sought to emphasize the significance of the presence of texts, or of other kinds of evidence, which do not fit the separatist paradigm, avoiding a sense that they are somehow exceptional or regressive in the way that both the heresiologists and, from a different perspective, scholars supportive of the parting paradigm, have thought. In this context one might highlight Annette Yoshiko Reed's work on the *Pseudo-Clementine Homilies* and *Recognitions*.[15] She eschews attempts at stratigraphic studies, which attribute so-called "Jewish Christian" material to an early stage in the textual history of the documents, as has been traditionally the case since the work of F. C. Baur, and instead reads them holistically as products of the 4th century whose so-called Jewish element is a significant feature of their 4th century identity rather than evidence of the concerns of an earlier era. Indeed the stance of these popular texts, in which Christian identity is strongly Jewish and followers of Jesus

---

11 D. Boyarin, "Semantic Differences; or, 'Judaism'/'Christianity'," in *The Ways That Never Parted. Jews and Christians in Late Antiquity and the Early Middle Ages*, ed. A.H. Becker and A.Y. Reed, TSAJ 95 (Tübingen: Mohr Siebeck, 2003), 65–85, here 76.

12 See A.Y. Reed, "Beyond 'Judaism' and 'Christianity' in the Roman Near East," in eadem, *Jewish Christianity and the History of Judaism*, TSAJ 171 (Tübingen: Mohr Siebeck, 2018), 57–84, here 59, who asserts how important it is to avoid mixing up the categories Jew/Christian and Judaism/Christianity "lest the social histories of Jews and Christians, in their localities and specificities, become elided with the account of how certain elites innovated the terminologies and taxonomies which ultimately lie behind our modern notions of 'Judaism,' 'Christianity,' and perhaps even 'religion.'"

13 See M. Jackson-McCabe, *Jewish Christianity: The Making of the Christianity-Judaism Divide* (New Haven, CT, and London: YUP, 2020).

14 See Reed, *Jewish Christianity* (see n. 7), 1–14.

15 A.Y. Reed, "'Jewish Christianity' as Counterhistory?," in eadem, *Jewish Christianity and the History of Judaism*, TSAJ 171 (Tübingen: Mohr Siebeck, 2018), 175–216.

and followers of Moses are presented as similar in their claims, and arraigned against a gentile/Hellenistic world, contrasts strongly to the polemics of the contemporary Eusebius, whose view of Christianity is heavily predicated upon a view of its separateness from Judaism and in which the customary binary is between Jew and Christian. Such creative juxtaposing of works with quite different views on the Jewish-Christian divide, but from the same rough chronological period, is accompanied by attempts to play up the ambiguous identity of a range of other supposedly Christian texts, including works thought to be originally Jewish but which have undergone Christian redaction, like the *Testaments of the Twelve Patriarchs*. Here questions of classification are ranged in such a way as to question attempts to talk in absolute terms about a Jewish or Christian identity.[16] Opponents of the partings paradigm have also emphasized evidence for ongoing contact between Jews and Christians, arguing that such interaction implies that the two never really split with the decisiveness or finality needed to render either tradition irrelevant to the self-definition of the other, or to make participation in both unattractive or inconceivable.[17]

What, then, to make of all of this?

First, this assault on the old "parting" paradigm has not led to an agreed upon alternative paradigm. Just to take one example. Participants in the debate differ as to how they understand the description "never parted". So in the volume of 2003, entitled *The Ways That Never Parted*, for Boyarin, and perhaps also for Reed, the title implied literally what it asserted, at least well beyond the date posited by those in favour of the Partings paradigm. To others it implied ongoing contact between groups who were, at least institutionally, separate. Here, strangely, it is possible to discern a convergence between separatist scholars and supposed non-separatists. For instance, William Horbury, who could reasonably be described as a defender of a version of the "parting" paradigm, is a passionate supporter of the idea that Jews continued to influence Christians (much more so than the other way round, which tends to be an emphasis of some anti-partings advocates);[18] and in a recent article defending the "parting" paradigm,

---

[16] See D. Frankfurter, "Beyond 'Jewish Christianity': Continuing religious sub-cultures of the second and third centuries and their documents," in *The Ways That Never Parted. Jews and Christians in Late Antiquity and the Early Middle Ages*, ed. A.H. Becker and A.Y. Reed, TSAJ 95 (Tübingen: Mohr Siebeck, 2003), 131–143.
[17] Reed, *Jewish Christianity* (see n. 7), 10–11.
[18] See W. Horbury, *Jews and Christians in contact and controversy* (Edinburgh: T&T Clark, 1998).

Shaye Cohen lambasted those who seemed to imply that endorsement of a "parting" paradigm necessarily meant support for a view that opposed ongoing interaction.[19]

Secondly, the assault on the "parting" paradigm emerges not only from trends in Jewish and Christian studies, which favour a view both of ancient Jews and Christians as diverse and fragmented and are skeptical of any idea of centralized powers, at least until the 4th century, but also from aspects of post-modernity. Significant in this context are a dislike of essentializing definitions, scepticism toward master narratives, with their inevitable deferral to teleologies of various kinds, accompanied by a concomitant concern with voices which too often fall outside the narrative, leading to a concentration on the particular and the specific; and a strongly developed sense of the performative and constructivist character of texts.

Thirdly, the assault has, inevitably, encountered criticism. So, for instance, while a performative view of *adversus Judaeos* texts has a *prima facie* appeal, one might wonder to what extent it can be demonstrated that lying beneath the purpose of such texts is a desire to patrol a border (between Jews and Christians) which "on the ground" remained blurred. How might we prove such a claim? Or would we do better to treat such an assertion as little more than a warning not to read off an assumed separatist reality from a separatist text? Related to this is the question of weighting. After all, there are many more broadly separatist texts in the extant collection of Christian sources from antiquity than there are texts, which traditionally have been called Jewish Christian, or texts which give evidence of what one might term intensive forms of Jewish and Christian interaction. While such an observation can be treated skeptically as little more than the tendency of history to be kinder to the literary outputs of winners, in the end we have to explain why the musings of a few separatists led to the establishment of a 'Judaism' and 'Christianity'. Should we not only reckon with the influence of such individuals over significant figures like Constantine, but also with the possibility that the works of the separatists reflected a reality to a greater extent than Boyarin and others imagine? Relevance here may be attached to the fact that in a relatively consistent manner pagans do not appear to associate Christians with Jews, or if they do, like Celsus, do so in the firm belief that Christians are clearly separate from Jews. A possible response to this lies in asserting that a person like Celsus is voicing the opinions of a separatist Jew and

---

[19] S.J.D. Cohen, "The Ways That Parted: Jews, Christians, and Jewish Christians," in *Jews and Christians in the First and Second Centuries: The Interbellum 70–132 CE*, ed. J. Schwartz and P.J. Tomson, CRINT 15 (Leiden: Brill, 2018), 307–339, here 308.

doing so because it suits his purpose; that the failure of Pliny the Younger (*Ep.* 10.96), Tacitus (*Ann.* 15.44), and Suetonius (*Nero* 16.2) to associate Jews and Christians emerges from ignorance or the particular circumstances of the Christians (and Jews) they encountered; and that, moreover, some of the available pagan evidence might point in another direction.[20] Finally, and related to the pagan evidence, we might argue that the critics of the "parting" paradigm insist too much upon a distinction between, on the one hand, evidence from an early stage when there were people who called themselves 'Jews' and 'Christians,' and, on the other, the process by which there evolved two separate systems called 'Judaism' and 'Christianity'. To some the reality of the former is proof of separation at the institutional level, which is supported by other evidence; the latter simply consists of a commonplace truth that the theorizing of the precise nature of the difference is a process, which does not detract from the social reality of difference, and the implicit, if often unarticulated, sense of a boundary between Jew and Christian.[21]

However we assess the critique of the old partings paradigm, at the minimum it demonstrates that we can no longer assume a simple narrative of 'inevitable' separation; and that in spite of the fact that no proven alternative history emerges from this critique, it constitutes a set of admonitory observations, which sensitize us in appropriate ways to the complexities of the available evidence. Such a view is captured in the question asked by Becker and Reed: "What happens," they write, "when we approach our evidence from a different perspective, treating the 'parting of the ways' as a principle that needs to be proved rather than presupposed?"[22]

---

20 For conflicting assessments of the pagan evidence see Lieu, "Parting" (see n. 2), 41–44; and Cohen, "The Ways" (see n. 19), 310–313.
21 So, for instance, Cohen, "The Ways" (see n. 19), 336–337, believes that Christians, who "Judaized," as is evidenced in graphic terms in John Chrysostom's *Eight Discourses against the Judaizing Christians* (*Adv. Jud.*), were always conscious of the boundaries between Judaism and Christianity, though he produces no support for this view. See S. Schwartz, "How many Judaisms were there: a critique of Neusner and Smith on definition and Mason and Boyarin on categorization," *JAJ* 2 (2011): 208–238, for a more nuanced critique of the distinction between 'Jew/Christian' and 'Judaism/Christianity.'
22 Becker and Reed, *The Ways* (see n. 2), 22.

2 The Epistle of Barnabas

What, then, to make of the *Epistle of Barnabas* against the background of such a discussion? Or put another way, how might such a discussion impact upon the study of this epistle?

Preliminary Observations
Most would agree that out of all the non-New Testament writings preceding the writing of Justin's *Trypho*, *Barnabas* is the most preoccupied with subjects thought to be significant in any discussion of Jewish-Christian relations. These relate principally to the interpretation of scripture, both as this relates to the Torah and Jesus's own life, in particular his death, and to some Christian practices. True, Ignatius, to some extent the *Didache*, Polycarp and *Diognetus* engage with subjects of this kind but not to the same extent and not in the same manner.[23] Strikingly, however, and in contradistinction to most of the preceding texts, save the *Didache*, *Barnabas* never mentions the words 'Jew' or 'Judaism,' Christian or Christianity. In strict terms, then, *Barnabas* should not be termed an *adversus Judaeos* text, an observation supported by the fact that in its introductory chapter, in contrast, for instance, to Justin's *Trypho* or Tertullian's *Adversus Judaeos*, there is almost no hint of the presence of an external opponent, let alone one who is identified *explicitly* as a Jew. Signs of polemical interaction may be said to exist within the main body of the epistle but these make an intermittent appearance.[24]

Barnabas's frequent appellation for those one might call Jews is "Israel," though apart from a reference at 5:2 (the scripture concerned relates partly to Israel and partly to us), the word relates to biblical Israel (4:14; 5:8; 6:7; 8:1, 3; 12:2, 5; 16:5). The most common designation is the neutral "they." Sometimes designations are more negative (e.g., the men whose sins are complete [8:1]; and those who had driven the prophets to death [8:1], the wretched men [16:1]). The characterization of 'them,' understood as the Jews, is negative: they have lost the cov-

---

[23] Unlike *Barnabas*, these texts are not strongly exegetical in content. Even where some texts in the collection of Apostolic Fathers are exegetical, like 1 Clement, they are not so in a polemical context. J.M. Lieu, *Image and Reality: The Jews in the World of the Christians in the Second Century* (Edinburgh: T&T Clark, 1996), 4, notes the relative absence of anti-Jewish polemic in the Apostolic Fathers in relation to the New Testament. She rejects an explanation of this disparity by reference to the fact that the former are principally concerned with the internal workings of the church, rightly noting that this could be said for almost all the documents of the New Testament.
[24] Note Barn. 3:6; 4:6b; 9:6.

enant (4:7; 14:4) as a result of their sinful worship of the Golden Calf and their disinherited state was anticipated in earlier moments in their history when God chose Jacob above Esau or Manasseh above Ephraim (13). They did not understand what God commanded, and failed to understand that their scriptures pointed to Christ which led them to kill him (5–7). Such failure to understand scripture is related to the lust of the flesh (10:9) and a failure to listen to God (8:7; 9:1–3) as well as to the activities of a wicked angel (9:4). Their hopes are void (16:2), and Christ's arrival, rather than serving to bring about their redemption, merely brings their sins to completion (5:11; 14:5). They stand utterly rejected, the covenant which should have been theirs now the exclusive possession of the gentiles (13:7).

Lying beneath this harsh polemic, is a distinctive hermeneutical position. For Barnabas there is one law, and if that law is interpreted correctly (that is, non-literally), it is in and of itself perfect. *Barnabas*, it would seem, has no time for a view like Justin's, that the Mosaic law was a temporary entity,[25] given to curb the idolatrous tendencies of the Jews after their worship of the Golden Calf, and one which would fall by the wayside once Christ had come; or more benevolent versions of the same. *Barnabas*, in contrast to this position can affirm the excellence of the law, at one point stating how well Moses has legislated (10:11); and consistent with this position, he nowhere links the law's fate to that of Christ, even if Christ's coming allows us to understand the law as it should have been understood (6:10; 9:9). Following on from this, the author believes only in the one covenant, lost by the Jews as result of their worship of the Golden Calf (a view which contradicts the story as found in Exodus) but now the possession of the Christians. Christians may be the new people (5:7; 7:5), the Jews may even be described as the first people (13:1), but the former inherit what the latter should have possessed and they interpret the law as it always should have been interpreted (2:4; 3:1–6; 9:1f.; 10; 15). This flat, strikingly conservative, view of scripture, which seems to exclude a developed view of the modern construction known as 'salvation history' is reflected in the author's understanding of Christ's relationship to scripture. Here the sense that events referred to the past and taken to point to Christ have some kind of validity in and of themselves is at best muffled. In chapter 12, for instance, *Barnabas* assumes that the sole function of Moses's piling up of shields referred to in Exod 17 was "so that they might learn that they cannot be saved unless they place their hope on

---

25 E.g., Justin, *Dial.* 19–21.

him" (12:3).²⁶ How to understand the origins of such a view of scripture and how to relate it to the negative portrayal of the Jews, just outlined, has been an ongoing concern of study of the epistle.

Attempts to create a trajectory of early Christian hermeneutical thought into which *Barnabas*'s strikingly conservative position fits have by and large been unconvincing. It is also difficult to be clear about his influence, in spite of the fact that the letter stood for some time on the fringes of the Christian canon and was much appreciated by Clement, Origen and Didymus the Blind.²⁷ Philip Vielhauer's observation of many years ago would still be endorsed by some: "Barnabas ist wohl das seltsamste Dokument der urchristlichen Literatur."²⁸

And yet the apparent hostility against non-Christian Jews does not detract from the fact that the document has a Jewish profile. Not only is it a text almost exclusively about scripture (here in contrast to *Diognetus* and Ignatius, both of whom take negative attitudes to Jews) but it betrays knowledge of extra-biblical traditions found in Jewish sources, as well as reflecting at one point in the Epistle, knowledge of extra-biblical Jewish practice.²⁹

There are indications that the author uses sources in the construction of his position. In the opening chapter of his epistle he claims that he is handing over a portion of what he has received (1:5), and this claim is supported by the presence of the Two Ways section of the epistle (found not just in chapters 17–20, but also spread throughout the epistle),³⁰ of collections of biblical passages, which appear as testimonia in other sources apparently independent of *Barnabas*, by the clumsy and loosely connected character of some of his arguments, and indications in the epistle of the presence of points of view which could be understood contradict the overall ideological stance of the author.³¹

---

26 For this argument, see K. Wengst, *Tradition und Theologie des Barnabasbriefes*, AKG 42 (Berlin and New York, NY: de Gruyter, 1971), 76–77.
27 See J. Carleton Paget, *The Epistle of Barnabas. Outlook and Background*, WUNT 2/64 (Tübingen: Mohr Siebeck, 1994), 200–260.
28 P. Vielhauer, *Geschichte der urchristlichen Literatur. Einleitung in das Neue Testament, die Apokryphen und die Apostolischen Väter* (New York, NY, and Berlin: de Gruyter, 1975), 612.
29 See n. 61 below.
30 See below.
31 For well-known advocates of a source approach to the epistle see H. Windisch, *Der Barnabasbrief*, HNT Erg. Die Apostolischen Väter 3 (Tübingen: Mohr Siebeck, 1920); R.A. Kraft, *The Epistle of Barnabas: Its Quotations and Their Sources* (PhD diss., Harvard University, MA, 1961); idem, *The Apostolic Fathers: A New Translation and Commentary, III: Barnabas and the Didache* (New York, NY: Nelson, 1965); P. Prigent, *Les testimonia dans le christianisme primitive: l'Épître de Barnabé et ses sources* (Paris: Gabalda, 1961); K. Wengst, *Tradition und Theologie* (see n. 26).

As with so many early Christian texts, it is difficult to contextualize *Barnabas*.[32] Its author is unknown (the work is clearly pseudonymous; and its attribution may have been late as the letter makes no attempt to fictionalize its association with *Barnabas*),[33] its provenance is unclear, its date disputed, and its purpose difficult to reconstruct. A date after 70 is established by 16:4, which is the earliest unambiguous reference to the destruction of the temple in extant Christian literature, and the possibility arises that at least in one form or another, the author refers to events associated with the Bar Kokhba revolt (more of this later), putting it somewhere in the first half of the 130s. Others would demur and place the date a lot earlier, possibly in the time of Nerva.[34] Many scholars have settled upon Alexandria as a possible provenance for the epistle. The arguments are well known – the presence within the epistle of Philo-like traditions, the fact that a number of Alexandrian authors quote it, including Clement of Alexandria,[35] and that there are arguments in favour of the view that *Barnabas* sheds some light on the origins of a significant stream of tradition in Clement.[36] None of these arguments are in themselves compelling and suffer from the fact that, notoriously, we know almost nothing about early Christianity in Alexandria. Some scholars have, less convincingly, suggested other provenances, e.g., Syria-Palestine and Asia Minor.[37] Some have, understandably, cast aside any attempt to situate the text geographically.[38] This lack of clarity on such significant issues is especially important in the context of the present discussion because, as already noted, scholars who have sought to revise or overturn the model of the parting of the ways have, in their arguments against any generalized master narrative, spoken about the importance of the local and the particular. But if the local and the particular are difficult to determine, how are we to assess the bearing of this text in relation on the question under discussion?

---

32 See R. Hvalvik, *The Struggle for Scripture and Covenant: The Purpose of the Epistle of Barnabas and Jewish-Christian Competition in the Second Century*, WUNT 2/82 (Tübingen: Mohr Siebeck, 1998), 17–53; and F.R. Prostmeier, *Der Barnabasbrief*, KAV 8 (Göttingen: Vandenhoeck & Ruprecht, 1999), 111–134.
33 See Carleton Paget, *Barnabas* (see n. 27), 7, reflecting comments made by Windisch, *Barnabasbrief* (see n. 31), 413.
34 Prostmeier, *Barnabasbrief* (see n. 32), 111–119.
35 Clement of Alexandria, *Strom.* 2.6.31; 2.7.35; 2.15.67; 2.18.84; 2.20.116; 5.8.51–52; 5.10.63.
36 Prostmeier, *Barnabasbrief* (see n. 32), 120–123.
37 Hvalvik, *Struggle* (see n. 32), 39–41, for a summary of these arguments.
38 Hvalvik, *Struggle* (see n. 32), 141–142.

3 Jews and Christians in Barnabas

The observations above act as an introduction to the following discussion which describes the diverse positions which have been taken on the question of Barnabas's relevance to the so-called "parting of the ways." In the process I shall show how such positions reflect broader assumptions about Jewish-Christian relations. It will be contended that discussion of *Barnabas* reveals some of the problems attending the discussion of the parting of the ways more generally.

In the interpretation of *Barnabas* some scholars have argued that the author has little or no interest in the Jewish community, in fact that he and his community are to be seen as distant from it, that Jews as such provide no threat or attraction to the individuals being addressed, that they are not a proximate entity. As Windisch commented, the Jewish people and its cult stand "gerichtet und vernichtet" in the mind of the author and were of no danger to the wider Christian community.[39]

The position is supported by a number of observations. (a) The author assumes an absolute separation between the two communities, exemplified in the use of "them" and "us," and in the strikingly negative assessment of the temple in chapter 16, an assessment which betrays an attitude of almost distant insouciance.[40] (b) The opening and closing chapters barely hint at a crisis or the desire to take on an enemy. True, the author wants to bring his audience to perfect knowledge (Barn. 1:5) but such knowledge is hermeneutical in form and is not presented as if there are those who would oppose it. The closing chapter is similarly vague. (c) The evidence, already referred to, that the author has made use of sources, has led some to argue that whatever anti-Jewish sentiment there may be in the letter is attributable to the sources and not to *Barnabas*. (d) Moreover, in so far as the epistle witnesses to anti-Jewish sentiment, it does so unevenly.[41] (e) According to some, the author is more interested in ethical paranaesis than he is in polemising against Jews – this is a text filled with calls to seek, learn or do what God commands (2:1, 9; 4:1; 10:11; 21:1, 4, 5, 6, 8), and

---

[39] Windisch, *Barnabasbrief* (see n. 31), 323; and Prostmeier, *Barnabasbrief* (see n. 32), 88 and 506.

[40] Such a view is encouraged by the references to "them" and "us" (see below), by the reference to "their" law (3:6), by the possible reference to the covenant belonging to "them" and "us" (4:6b: on the textual difficulties see below), by the claim that the Jews are πρῶτος λαός understood as the former people (13:1f.), and by the striking distancing of Barnabas from the Jewish temple, whose construction he associates with wretched men whose God he describes as "their" God (16:1). On this see Prostmeier, *Barnabasbrief* (see n. 32), 506–507.

[41] Windisch, *Barnabasbrief* (see n. 31), 322–323.

one deeply affected by the Two Ways, not only in its final three chapters but at regular intervals throughout the main part of the epistle.[42] (f) Others have noted that an examination of later interpretation of the text, especially as seen in Clement of Alexandria, is not of an anti-Jewish kind.[43] More recently Clare Rothschild has added two further arguments,[44] first that the polemic against the Jews is banal (it seems entirely to exclude the possibility that Jews could argue allegorically);[45] and secondly, that if a mooted date for *Barnabas* of around 132 CE is accepted, then assuming an Egyptian provenance, the epistle was written in an environment, where as a result of the Trajanic revolt, Jews were at best an exiguous presence.[46] Further on in her article she notes, without a sense that she may be saying something controversial, that "the issues explicitly addressed in the text have been largely solved between Christians and Jews by the beginning of the second century."[47]

Few of those who argue this broad position do so on the basis of what might be termed more generalized observations about the parting of the ways, as, for instance, Rothschild does, though some may be influenced by wider assumptions relating to this matter.[48] Most attempt to provide alternative purposes for

---

[42] For the ethical emphasis of the epistle, allied to what is termed a "nomistic" vocabulary, see esp. J.N. Rhodes, *The Epistle of Barnabas and the Deuteronomic Tradition*, WUNT 2/188 (Tübingen: Mohr Siebeck, 2004), though his work, at least in broad terms, has a pedigree going back to Kraft. On the importance of "Two ways" language in the epistle see Hvalvik, *Struggle* (see n. 32), 64; and J.N. Rhodes, "The Two Ways Tradition in the Epistle of Barnabas: Revisiting an Old Question," *CBQ* 73 (2011): 797–816, here 802f. and 809, commenting that the Two Ways constitutes "the most foundational elements of the author's theology." Note, for instance, the use of the word for "way" (of the 15 occurrences in the letter, seven occur in chap. 1–16), language to do with walking, life and death, light and darkness, salvation and destruction, words for righteousness, sin and evil, and the idea of going astray.
[43] See F.R. Prostmeier, "Antijüdische Polemik im Rahmen christlicher Hermeneutik. Zum Streit über christliche Identität in der Alten Kirche. Notizen zum Barnabasbrief," *ZAC* 6 (2002): 38–58, here 38.
[44] C.K. Rothschild, "Soteriology and the Allegorical Construction of opponents in the Epistle of Barnabas," in *Sōtēria: Salvation in Early Christianity and Antiquity*, ed. D.S. du Toit, C. Gerber, and C. Zimmermann, NovTSup 175 (Leiden: Brill, 2019), 561–576.
[45] Rothschild, "Soteriology" (see n. 44), 561.
[46] For a recent endorsement of this view, see A.-M. Schwemer, "Zum Abbruch des jüdischen Lebens in Alexandria – Der Aufstand in der Dispora unter Trajan (115–117)," in *Alexandria*, ed. T. Georges, F. Albrecht, and R. Feldmeier, COMES 1 (Tübingen: Mohr Siebeck, 2013), 381–399.
[47] Rothschild, "Soteriology" (see n. 44), 566.
[48] Some scholars have operated on the assumption that after about 100 CE or so Jews and Christians failed to interact with each other. This position has an ancient lineage stretching back to Harnack, who adopts a very similar position to Windisch on the nature of *Barnabas*'s anti-Judaism (see A. von Harnack, *Geschichte der altchristlichen Literatur bis Eusebius 1*, vol. 2

the epistle, all of which in different ways, point to inner-Christian concerns: these range from Windisch's generalized view that the work is written "zur Erbauung der Leser" (here aping words found in Jerome's *Vir. ill.* 6, where he speaks of the letter as written *aedificationem ecclesiae*),[49] to Wengst's claim that *Barnabas* is involved in a defence of a particular hermeneutical position, best described as an exaggerated version of *sola scriptura*,[50] to Rothschild's claim that the author is using Jews to argue against a variety of internal Christian enemies, whose mindset was marked by "particularism" "and for which Judaism was an ideal symbol."[51]

This position would seem an unconvincing one, not least to those who argue against the old paradigm of the parting of the ways. It assumes something which seems unlikely to such scholars, namely an engagement with broadly Jewish subjects without reference to Jews. If Christians remained meaningfully entwined with Jews for a relatively long time, well into the 3rd century and considerably beyond that, then, surely a text like *Barnabas*, written at a relatively early stage in Christian history, must be read against such a background? How it is read will vary but it cannot be read without reference to Jews, however one conceives of their presence. Such a position is based upon a number of broad, and for some, disputable, assumptions. The case for the irrelevance of Jews and Judaism for an interpretation of *Barnabas* by and large has its origins, as we noted, in features of the epistle. Before moving on to some alternative readings which take seriously 'the ways that never parted' assumptions, let me respond briefly to these more detailed observations.

First, the content of *Barnabas* is what the author terms "perfect knowledge" (1:5). It is clear that such knowledge is bound up with scriptural interpretation. After stating in 1:6 what perfect knowledge might be, *Barnabas* continues, in the following verse, to speak of the interpretation of the prophets. Moreover, picking up on the binary nature of the language of "them" and "us," the author claims in

---

[Leipzig: Hinrichs, 1992], 415 n. 3 and the words: "Die Kirche hat jedenfalls gar nicht mit dem Judenthum zu tun."). See J. Carleton Paget, "Barnabas and the Outsiders: Jews and their World in the Epistle of Barnabas," in *Early Christian Communities between Ideal and Reality*, ed. M. Grundeken and J. Verheyden, WUNT 342 (Tübingen: Mohr Siebeck, 2015), 179–180.

49 Windisch, *Barnabasbrief* (see n. 26), 323.

50 Wengst, *Tradition* (see n. 26).

51 She writes that Barnabas "employs an anti-Jewish exegetical strategy, like Athanasius, to stigmatize *Christian* opponents." She goes on: "[…] this study construes the Letter of Barnabas not as a challenge to a belligerent Jewish community but to their symbolic Christian equivalents." "Barnabas writes for the purpose of standardizing Christian practices in a city in which Christians were neither the majority nor a single unified community." (Rothschild, "Soteriology" [see n. 44], 562).

1:7 that the Master has made the past and present known to us, here clearly alluding to right understanding of scripture. At 2:4 he goes on to assert that he has made plain to us that he needs neither sacrifices nor burnt offerings, picking up on the language of 1:7. Indeed in the rest of the epistle "gnosis" related words often appear in scriptural contexts.[52] The fact that *Barnabas* often expresses the view that exegesis associated with "them" is false (see 8:7 and 10:12), contrasting what has been revealed to "us" and what has been revealed to "them," clearly indicates that it is a matter of contention, and that the opinion of "them" is in some way relevant to the context being addressed.[53] It is also of consequence that the only other place where there appears to be a repetition of the idea of perfect knowledge is 13:7 where perfection of knowledge is associated with an affirmation of the covenantal status of the Christians.

Secondly, the subjects *Barnabas* discusses, whether these pertain to distinctive Jewish laws such as sacrifice (2), fasts (3), circumcision (9), the dietary laws (10), the sabbath (15) the covenant (4 and 13), the land (6), or the temple (2 and 16), all touch upon issues which are central to Jewish identity. Moreover, his concerns with these and such subjects as Christ's death (5–8), the cross (12) and Christian baptism (11), all reflect concerns found in later *adversus Judaeos* literature and they are all discussed with Jewish opposition in mind.[54] This is especially the case with the death of Christ.[55] That questions to do with the law oc-

---

[52] For explicit association of "gnosis" related words to exegetical contexts see 6:9; 9:8 and 10:10. For associated terms, see *Barnabas*'s use of σοφία at 2:3; 16:9 and 21:5, σύνεσις at 2:3 and 21:5, and ἐπιστήμη at 2:3 and 21:5. Also note *Barnabas*'s use of γνωρίζω (1:7; 5:3) and νοέω (4:14; 6:10; 7:1; 8:2; 10:12). See Hvalvik, *Struggle* (see n. 32), 83–84.

[53] *Barnabas* frequently refers to "us" and "them," though not always by way of a straightforward contrast (e.g., see 1:7) but often the contrast is emphasized. See 2:4, 7, 9, 10; 3:1, 3, 6; 4:7, 8, 14; 5:2, 11, 12; 6:7, 8, 12–13; 7:1, 2, 5; 8:7; 9:4; 10:9, 12; 11:1, 11; 13:1; 14:4, 5; 15:8. For this material see Hvalvik, *Struggle* (see n. 32), 137–139. Interestingly, the Latin translator (L), whose translation may date from the early 3rd century, always translates ἐκεῖνος by the appropriate form of *ille*. Ἰσραήλ, contrarily, is normally translated by *populus Iudaeorum*.

[54] As an example of such concerns see Justin's *Dialogue*, where he discusses circumcision (16; 19; 23), fasts (15), sacrifice (22), sabbath (12; 19; 21) and the covenant (25), along with baptism (14) and crucifixion (40 f.; 86 f.; 90). Similar parallels could be made with a range of *adversus Judaeos* literature.

[55] Hvalvik, *Struggle* (see n. 32), 144–146, who notes how Christ's death is presented as something with negative consequences for "them" (Barn. 5:11; 6:6–7; 14:5) but positive consequences for "us" (5:1; 7:2, 3, 5; 14:5). 12:3 is thought by some to imply the possibility of salvation for them through Christ's death but this is a muted theme at best and one contradicted by 13:7b. On this see below.

cupy structurally significant parts of the letter,[56] is also important, as is the fact that Christian interpretations of these are often contrasted with Jewish ones.[57]

Third, references in the body of the letter to a fear of conversion to their law (3:6) and to those who declare the covenant to be theirs and ours (4:6b)[58] as well as to people who see circumcision as a sign or seal should be taken seriously (9:6). These rare indicators of purpose or of a potential threat are best understood if we assume Jews as somehow in the background.

Fourth, it is difficult to defend the view that polemic is unevenly distributed throughout the epistle. At 2:9 "they" are described as "deceived"; at 3:6 conversion to "their" law is described as "shipwreck"; at chapters 4 and 14 the worship of the golden calf is said to have led to the loss of the covenant; at 5:11 they are described as having persecuted the prophets and completed their sins by killing Christ (for further references to their sin see 8:1 and 14:5); at 8:7 things are obscure to them; at 9:4 their belief in literal circumcision is attributed to an evil angel; at 10 they are upbraided for misunderstanding the food laws, which is attributed to the lust of their flesh (10:9); at 11:1 they are upbraided for rejecting baptism, an act which is portrayed as desertion from God (11:2) and impiety (11:7); at 12:3 their failure to believe in Christ condemns them to damnation; at 15:8 their sabbaths are rejected; and 16:2 their building of a temple is likened to the actions of gentiles. Indeed it is difficult to see why "so much polemic would have been gathered together in circumstances to which it did not speak."[59]

Fifth, there may be indications of contact with Jews. So *Barnabas* betrays knowledge of extra-biblical Jewish traditions, exemplified in his Christological interpretation of events associated with the day of Atonement in chapters 7

---

56 Note how such concerns appear at the beginning (2 and 3), the middle (9 and 10) and the end (15–16) of the main section.

57 See Barn. 8:7 and 10.

58 This reading is based on an acceptance of the Latin reading (*illorum et nostrum est; nostrum est autem*) (with some additions from the Greek: on this see Prostmeier, *Barnabasbrief* [see n. 32], 191). Two different readings are witnessed by the Greek (ἡ διαθήκη ὑμῶν ὑμῖν μένει [H] or ἡ διαθήκη ἡμῶν μέν [S]), the latter of which makes little sense. Although there are no decisive arguments in favour of the Latin reading, this reading seems the least unconvincing. For another view, see J.N. Rhodes, "Barnabas 4.6B: The Exegetical Implications of a Textual Problem," *VC* 58 (2004): 365–392, which is discussed in Carleton Paget, "Outsiders" (see n. 48), 182–183, n. 26, and rejected in favour of the Latin reading.

59 W. Horbury, "Jewish-Christian Relations in Barnabas and Justin Martyr," in idem, *Jews and Christians in contact and controversy* (Edinburgh: T&T Clark, 1998), 127–161, here 135.

and 8.⁶⁰ Better evidence for such contact may come in chapter 3 with its strong emphasis on Jewish fasting, which, while reflecting contemporary Jewish practice, is not so heavily emphasized in the Hebrew Bible.⁶¹

Reference in this context should be made to *Barnabas*'s comments on the temple, in particular at 16:3–4, which consists of a loose citation of Isa 49:17 with its reference to those who tore down the temple building it, and the claim that this is somehow now taking place. While much discussion of this passage focuses on whether the events referred to in v. 4 concern a plan to rebuild the Jerusalem temple by the Romans, for which there is no unambiguous external evidence, or to replace it with a newly built pagan temple, here possibly supported by references in Cassius Dio and Eusebius to events surrounding either the outbreak of the Bar Kokhba revolt or its conclusion,⁶² it seems clear that the events are contemporary, as long as we retain the reading of γίνεται in v. 4, for which there is strong support.⁶³ To some, the reference is sufficiently brief to support the view that *Barnabas* is distant from the event, and by extension the Jews. Equally, however, his interest in contemporary events, exemplified at 1:7 (the reference to things present), can add more importance to the reference,⁶⁴ an importance possibly reflected in the regularity with which temple imagery appears in the letter.⁶⁵

---

60 For the extra-biblical details in the account, especially as these relate to traditions in m. Yoma 6 and m. Parah 3, see Carleton Paget, *Barnabas* (see n. 27), 137–142.
61 This point is well made by Horbury, "Jewish-Christian Relations" (see n. 59), 136–137; and by M. Kok, "The True Covenant People: Ethnic Reasoning in the Epistle of Barnabas," SR 40 (2011): 81–97, here 88. See Carleton Paget, "Outsiders" (see n. 48), 185–186, n. 38, for a summary of the relevant evidence.
62 See Cassius Dio, *Hist*. 69.12; and Eusebius, *Hist. eccl*. 4.6.4. For the most recent discussions of Barn. 16:3–4 along slightly different lines, see W. Horbury, *Jewish war under Trajan and Hadrian* (Cambridge: CUP, 2017), 298–307; and A. Sheppard, "The Letter of Barnabas and the Jerusalem Temple," *JSJ* 48 (2017): 531–550.
63 Γίνεται is omitted by S and H, but witnessed in G and in the Latin translation as *fiet*. Retention of γίνεται is supported by its starkly asyndetic quality, which appears to be supported by the presence of other asyndeta in the epistle (see inter alia Barn. 4:2, 3, 10, 12; 5:6; 6:5; 7:5, 6; 8:2; 9:5, 9; 12:10, 11 and 15:4), by the presence of νῦν, and the indicative of ἀνοικοδομήσουσιν, which unlike the subjunctive form of the same verb in Sinaiticus (ἀνοικοδομήσωσιν), points to the fact that a definite decision has been made. Also 16:5c with its use of ἐγένετο and its reference to a fulfillment of the prophecy would point in this direction. See Prostmeier, *Barnabasbrief* (see n. 32), 503.
64 Rhodes, *Barnabas* (see n. 42), 82, who argues that the reference in 1:7 to "things present" is reflected in 16:3–4, indicating a strong concern with the event, however understood (Rhodes understands it as a reference to Hadrian's decision to build the temple of Zeus in Jerusalem).
65 See Rhodes, *Barnabas* (see n. 42), 35–87.

All of this makes it unlikely that Jews are simply a foil for some kind of internal dispute, as a number of scholars have argued.[66]

The view that *Barnabas* is little more than the hapless reproducer of sources suffers from all the weaknesses of any such argument. Even if true, the thoughtful exegete is still forced to ask why the author chose such sources he did. But

---

[66] The "foil" argument had already been presented by Windisch but has been given detailed expression by Rothschild, "Soteriology" (see n. 44). Her article largely assumes that the ways have parted ("[...] the issues explicitly addressed in the text have been largely solved between Christians and Jews by the beginning of the second century") and that *Barnabas*'s "anti-Jewish" polemic is directed against Christian groups known to *Barnabas*, whose exegetical strategies he disputes. She rejects the view that those who say that the covenant is both theirs and ours could be Jews (4:6), though few, if any scholars have asserted that. As she rightly asserts, it does refer to a Christian rival but not perhaps the one she imagines (someone willing to share the covenant with Barnabas, but with whom he is unwilling to be united). Other opponents are identified as those who fail to acknowledge the necessity of Jesus's suffering, an argument that was originally Jewish but has no Jewish referent now. 9:6, which seems most naturally to be a defense of circumcision, is seen to be evidence that "a literal reading of the Jewish scriptures constitutes the opponents' ground for rejecting them" (the opponent understood as a Marcionite [ibid. 567–568]). Chapters 11 and 12 refer to those who object to certain baptismal practices rather than a condemnation of Jews who have failed to be baptized (where are the practices in chapter 11?). At 13:1 "protos" may well indicate that the opponent is older in age than the author rather than being a reference to the Jewish people as 13:7 seems to make clear. 14:4 is another reference to those who reject divine suffering, its focus no longer, it would seem, on the loss of the covenant through worship of the golden calf. Chapter 16 refers to Christians worshipping Jesus in a temple, though nothing is explicitly said about this (the reference in 16:1a–2 can only be to the Jews). Turning to more specific exegetical errors on the part of the opponents, chapter 2 indicates disagreement with Christians involved in some form of literal sacrifice to God, here possibly Basilideans at the Serapeion. Chapter 3 opposes ascetics, an interpretation which seems only to be possible if one omits any reference to 3:6! Chapter 10 can be taken as referring to Gnostics who upheld dietary regulations together with abstinence from sexual relations and other behaviours including a communal economy and voluntary poverty. Chapter 16 emphasizes the universal and the anti-particular and in so doing calls into question the sanctity of local temples and their relevance for Christians. The opponents, conceived of as Montanists, Basilideans, Marcionites and Valentinians (and perhaps others, too) are united by their affiliation to non-universal separatist dogmatic positions. The argument seems artificial and often appears to ditch the most obvious reading of a text, often omitting discussion of subjects which seem so central for Barnabas (covenant etc.) without showing with any degree of conviction why these ideas might be applicable to the groups Rothschild invokes. While I accept that Jews may not be addressed in the letter – in fact it seems unlikely that they are (cf. "them" and "us"), it seems most convincing to assume that it is their practices and their interpretations, which are being referred to (Rothschild's interpretation hardly gives a convincing account of verses which address opponents directly, e. g., 3:6; 4:6c; and 9:6). Rothschild's alternative view, in part predicated upon a wholesale acceptance of a particular view of the early and absolute separation of Jews and Christians, posits a set of hypothetical opponents, whose existence is questionable.

there are grounds to argue that he is in fact a redactor of material he has received, the combiner of material from a variety of provenances brought together to support a particular viewpoint.[67]

Rothschild's point that the banality of the representation of Jewish interpretation in *Barnabas* is enough to render Jews irrelevant to the epistle's interpretation is unconvincing. Unlike her, I do not see the principal concern of the letter as hermeneutical in the sense that the letter is a call for a deeper/allegorical interpretation of the Bible against a more particularist, literalist one. It is in some sense an attack upon specific interpretations, often associated with "them." Representing Jews as literal interpreters of laws relating to certain important identity markers is not banal, even if it may be presented in an obviously tendentious way (note the characterization of Jewish interpretation at 10:6). Certainly we do know that most Jews would have accorded importance to a literal interpretation of such laws as Sabbath, sacrifice, circumcision and the food laws, however else they may have interpreted these. Moreover, in polemical settings, the manner in which opponents are presented is often tendentious, or indeed banal. This need not imply anything about the extent to which they are present in the setting of the author who is describing them. This is a point which is often lost on those who have approached *adversus Judaeos* literature with a view to showing that Jews cannot be opponents because of the unrealistic/caricatured way in which they are represented. The image in which *Barnabas* is creating "them" does not exclude, though it may occlude, a mooted reality that lies beneath the surface.[68] A reality is no less great for it being caricatured or treated unfairly. It is true that if we look for distinctive, even vivid, elements in *Barnabas*'s portrayal of the Jews, if we wish to say something about their lives, even as lived communally, nothing will be found. But that need not be because there was nothing "behind the text."

It is certainly true that the *Barnabas* has a strongly ethical aspect. As already noted, the call to seek out the commandments of God occurs frequently, and it is true that the moralizing language of the Two Ways is spread throughout the epistle. But the moral interpretation of commandments relating to well-known Jewish prescriptions is simply the positive side of an emphatic negation of their lit-

---

[67] For these arguments see Carleton Paget, *Barnabas* (see n. 27).
[68] See Lieu, *Image* (see n. 23), 12, for a nuanced discussion of the relationship between image and reality in the presentation of Jews in some 2nd century Christian texts. She notes that when a Christian text "speaks of Jews and Judaism there is a contemporary reality, one of which, in differing degrees, its authors are aware. Yet their own needs, the logic of their own argument, and the tradition they draw on, especially the Old Testament, help create and mould the terms in which they speak—to create an 'image.'"

eral implementation. More importantly, it should be noted that Two Ways language and language about "them" converge. At 9:4 the author presents the Jews as deluded by an evil angel and at 18:1 the way of darkness is associated with the angels of Satan; at 18:2 he talks about the ruler of the present time of iniquity, which is reflected in terminology about them at 4:1 and 9b. At 2:9 *Barnabas* can speak about going astray like them "so that the evil one may not smuggle some error in among us." This evil one is the black one at 4:10 and the same title is used in the description of the way of darkness in 20:1.[69] Hvalvik suggests that the Two Ways tradition is no longer, as it is among Jews, used to distinguish between Jew and Gentile, but followers of Christ and Jews, a point which comes home in his description of the Jews as almost like the gentiles (16:1), a description possibly justified by their idolatrous actions.[70]

4 Jews as a proximate reality

Let me turn now to interpretations, which on the basis of some of the arguments made above, posit a proximate relationship to Jews. In the first of these what we are dealing with is a concern with the fact that Christians are or will take up Jewish practices, perhaps in the face of reignited hopes in the possibility of a rebuilt Jewish temple.[71] Broadly speaking it assumes institutionally separate entities but also relative proximity. *Barnabas*, then, has a performative dimension in that it is seeking to police a border, which exists but is porous. Beneath the surface of his text lies a more complex map of intertwining realities. His attitude may be supersessionist, but that is not the attitude of those he is addressing. Here particular significance is attached to 4:6, reading the text, "the covenant is both theirs and

---

69 Hvalvik, *Struggle* (see n. 32), 141–143. For a similar argument about the role of the Two Ways language in *Barnabas*, in which the former is seen as strengthening in-group awareness by sharpening the contrast between those who accept the author's view of the Jewish law and those who do not, see J.C.H. Smith, "The 'Epistle of Barnabas' and the Two Ways of Teaching Authority," *VC* 68 (2014): 465–497.
70 See 4:8 and 14:3. Hvalvik, *Struggle* (see n. 32), 143, suggests that idolatry may have been put at the top of the list of sins associated with the way of darkness (20:1) because of his strong belief that Jews were guilty of such a sin (see 4:8 and 14:3 and also references to their man made institutions, not least the temple).
71 This interpretation of 16:3–4 is supported because: (a) it makes better sense of the citation of Isa 49:17 (on this see Horbury, *Jewish War* [see n. 62], 298–299); and (b) it better explains the unglossed nature of 16:3–4. The case is by no means a clear cut one, not least because scholars have struggled to find any reference to a hope in a rebuilt temple, supported by the Romans, in the period after 70 CE.

ours";[72] to 3:6 with its warning not to become shipwrecked by becoming proselytes to their law; and 9:6 with intimations that circumcision was an area of discussion. The significance of language to do with ethnicity is stressed, whether it be related to the word λαός, applied both to "them" (9:3; 10:2; 12:8; 16:5) and to "us" (3:6; 5:7; 7:5), the latter being designated the new people, whose relationship to Abraham is especially stressed (as Kok points out, there are seven references to the patriarch [6:8; 8:4; 9:7, 8; 13:7 x 3], more than we find in any writer between John and Justin Martyr). Patriarchal stories are referenced to demonstrate that Christians *qua* gentiles are the chosen people, and they are such in an exclusive manner.[73] All pretensions to claims to the covenant on the part of non-Christian Jews are rejected (13:7). Central symbols of Judaean identity are reinterpreted in a manner that questions their customary Jewish application – in fact it is now "us" who become the correct observers of the commandments; it is "us", who are the inheritors of the promised land (6), "us" who embody the true temple. The sense of the polarity of the choices facing those addressed is intensified by the use of Two Ways language, which, as has been noted, occurs not only at the end of the epistle but throughout its main part. In a thoughtful article, Kok makes much of what, reflecting a term used by Denise Buell,[74] he terms the "ethnic reasoning" of *Barnabas* (his attempt, already referenced, to emphasize language of ethnic belonging, seen in his use of λαός, and of kinship through his use of language related to Abraham and other patriarchs). Drawing on J. Z. Smith's claim that "a major part of identity formation is a preoccupation with boundaries," and the opposition in/out, which serves to generate an Other who exists beyond the limits of the group, Kok notes that the remote Other is perceived as less threatening to a distinctive ethnic and cultural identity than the proximate one, who is not so different to us, in this case the Jews. Kok concludes,

> The alarm underlying the fierce rhetoric in *Barnabas* is that the borders remained fluid and many Christians saw no logical contradiction between devotion to Jesus and adopting Judaean praxis or fellowship in synagogues. Ethnic reasoning was utilized to reinforce Christian claims to naturalness and to construct sharp divisions between Christians and Judaeans.[75]

---

72 See n. 58 above.
73 It is possible that Barnabas's reference to Abraham at 13:7 shows knowledge of Rom 4. Interestingly, where Paul affirms the partial inheritance of Israel, Barnabas does not.
74 D.K. Buell, *Why This New Race? Ethnic Reasoning in Early Christianity* (New York, NY: Columbia University Press, 2005). The book seeks to expose the myth, as Buell sees it, that Christianity was a religion which transcended what she terms "ethnic reasoning" in its self-understanding.
75 Kok, "True Covenant" (see n. 61), 93.

Another version of this proximate reading takes the implications of the relationship between "them" and "us" further along this trajectory. Here it is assumed that the absence of the words for 'Jew' and 'Christian' and 'Judaism' and 'Christianity,' and the presence of simple references to "them" and "us" imply that the text operates from within Judaism. Geoffrey Dunn, for instance, argues that the epistle did not so much contrast Jew and Christian or Judaism with Christianity as old people of the covenant with new people of the covenant or one type of Jew with another type.[76] Rather than understanding two distinct religions (Judaism and Christianity), *Barnabas*

> saw a struggle between two peoples claiming to be the one, true, legitimate heirs [sic] of the one true covenant (6.19). In his division of 'them' and 'us', 'them' referred to the rebellious people of the Exodus and their spiritual descendants, while 'us' referred to the authentic Israel, the authentic Israel, who interpreted God's commandments correctly.[77]

Dunn continues: "Support for this interpretation can be found in the mentioning of the prophecy to Rebekah (ch. 13), where the author of the letter indicated that the prophecy was in reference to who was the legitimate heir to the covenant, not to a struggle between two covenants."[78] He argues that the twins in the womb (Jacob and Esau) represent the false heirs and the true heirs rather than the Jews and the Christians, in contrast, for instance, to the way Tertullian understood the biblical passage.[79] "It would seem that *Barnabas* was composed at a time when 'Jew' and 'follower of Jesus' had not yet become mutually exclusive terms. Jewish people were not excluded from being 'us' provided that they

---

[76] G.D. Dunn, "Tertullian and Rebekah: A Re-Reading of an 'Anti-Jewish' Argument in Early Christian Literature," *VC* 52 (1998): 121–145, here 128.
[77] Dunn, "Tertullian" (see n. 76), 129.
[78] Ibid., 130 (see n. 76). The combination of passages (Gen 25:21–23 and Gen 48:8f.) is not witnessed anywhere else in Christian literature, and only once before in Philo, *Leg.* 3.88–94.
[79] See Tertullian, *Adv. Jud.* 1.5–6. He is only interested in the story of Jacob and Esau in Gen 25 (he fails to refer to Gen 48:18–19 and the story of Jacob's blessing of Manasseh and Ephraim). Dunn, ibid. (see n. 76), 142, notes that in Tertullian's version of Gen 25, in contrast to *Barnabas*, there is a direct identifying of Esau with the Jews and Jacob with the Christians ("Beyond doubt, through the edict of the divine utterance, the *prior* and 'greater' people—that is, the Jewish—must necessarily serve the 'less;' and the 'less' people—that is, the Christian—overcome the 'greater.' For, withal, according to the memorial records of the divine Scriptures, the *people* of the Jews—that is, the more ancient—quite forsook God [...]"), and that his whole presentation of the passage has a different feel to *Barnabas* in that Tertullian is explicit about the existence of two covenants (Tertullian, *Adv. Jud.* 2.9–10; 6.1–2).

were followers of Jesus."[80] Dunn tentatively suggests that the epistle might have been written on the cusp of a clear and permanent division emerging between Jew and Christian. In his explanation of why the author avoids this clear cut distinction (at least in terms of vocabulary), Dunn cannot decide as to whether the vocabulary of Jew and Christian was not yet available to him, or whether he was forced in to adopting the position for pragmatic reasons (there were too many so-called Christian Jews in his community).[81]

More recently, Julien Smith has added further to Dunn's argument, arguing that *Barnabas* "constitutes an historical instance of intra-mural debate concerning basic matters of identity."[82] In this respect, he quotes Philo's famous passage in *Migr.* 88–94, in which the latter gives evidence of arguments from within the Jewish community about the correct way to understand the law, with some arguing for an exclusively allegorical viewpoint. Key to Smith's argument is the point that Philo does not consider these individuals to be non-Jews. "The intra-mural Jewish dispute regarding Torah observance on display in Philo raises the possibility that the relationship between Torah observance and identity in *Barnabas* is a genuine, rather than academic, issue. Author and audience are not engaged in a struggle between two separate religions, 'Judaism' and 'Christianity'. Rather [...] the struggle is between the 'twins of Rebekah, between the non-authentic and the authentic people of the covenant' (here quoting Dunn)."[83] The polemic of the letter, then, is best understood as "intra-Jewish," though the author is engaged in an attempt to deconstruct his "Jewish" audience's understanding of their ethnic identity.[84] To the argument that *Barnabas*'s polemic undermines this thesis, Smith replies by asserting that such polemic is the same as that evidenced among Hellenistic philosophical schools, present also in Philo's sharp language aimed at those who forsake the Torah, whom he describes as "incontinent, shameless, and unjust," (*Virt.* 192) but who are clearly still Jews.[85]

---

80 A quotation from an email correspondence with Prof. David Lincicum of Notre Dame University.
81 Ibid. (see n. 76), 132–133.
82 Smith, "Two Ways" (see n. 69), 491.
83 Smith, "Two Ways" (see n. 69), 493.
84 Smith, "Two Ways" (see n. 69), 493. He is calling upon them radically to redefine their "Jewishness."
85 Smith, again reflecting Dunn, argues that the avoidance of language for Jew and Christian, "strongly suggests that Jewish and gentile Christians are still relating to each other in the authorial audience, and that he cannot afford to alienate those who still have high regard for the markers of Jewish identity. When one considers the author's intimate and expansive knowledge of Jewish traditions, the possibility emerges that he himself was a Jewish Christian who has come to find the practices of his ancestral religion, as interpreted by certain of his co-religion-

In Dunn's interpretation a lot hangs on the failure of *Barnabas* to use words like Jew or Christian and on the apparent difference between identifying "us" as inheritors of the single covenant and them as forfeiting it, rather than the idea that we inherit a new and different covenant. I remain to be persuaded. Dunn's claim that the absence of what could be termed a replacement theology, that is the replacement of one covenant by another, makes a material difference to the way one perceives separation or difference, seems unjustified. It is still the followers of Christ who are the inheritors of that one covenant. Moreover, can it be said that the claim that the covenant is now ours (4:6b) is not the equivalent of asserting a distinction of two peoples, especially when one group is called "the new people," and another group has been referred to as the first people?[86] Note should also be taken of 5:2 where Israel appears to refer to a more contemporary entity. But more importantly, what should be made of the claim in 13:7 that the gentiles appear to be the exclusive inheritors of the covenant (here in contrast to Paul): "Behold I have established you, Abraham, as the father of the nations who believe in God without being circumcised." The statement stands in stark contrast to assertions made by Paul both in Rom 9–11 (where, interestingly, the passage about Esau and Jacob occurs but without reference to the issue of a covenant), but more especially in Rom 4 to which Barnabas may possibly allude in 13:7b, where he quotes a version of Gen 15:6, and appears to recall Rom 4:11 and 17.[87] Here Paul, while at pains to argue that Abraham is the father of the uncircumcised, is also clear that he remains the father of the circumcised. I find it difficult to interpret 13:7 in a way that is compatible with Dunn's overall view of *Barnabas* as assuming no kind of separation, and only being on the cusp of such a reality. Certainly 13:7 does not appear to pander to the anxieties of his Christian Jewish audience.

---

ists, incompatible with the worship of Jesus as Lord." His avoidance of the term 'Jew' and 'Christian' suggests that they were not available to him in the sense that they had not come to denote mutually exclusive communities in the mid 2nd century (Smith, "Two Ways" [see n. 69], 493).

86 Smith, ibid., invokes Kok, "Ethnic Reasoning" (see n. 57), in defence of his thesis and there are certainly continuities between the positions of Kok and Smith. Kok, however, is keener than Smith, with his use of the idea of ethnic reasoning, to show that *Barnabas* wants to separate any view that Christians and Jews are the same. In fact far from showing some level of scrupulosity towards the sensitivities of the mooted audience of *Barnabas* whose understanding of their identity was more inclusive than the author's, he seeks to separate Jew from Christian in a radical and binary way. Smith prefers to call this *Barnabas*'s radical redefinition of Jewishness.

87 Arguments in J. Carleton Paget, "Paul and the *Epistle of Barnabas*," in *The Apostolic Fathers and Paul*, ed. T.D. Still and D.E. Wilhite (London and Oxford: T&T Clark 2016), 79–100, here 88–90.

Moreover, Smith's attempts to contextualize *Barnabas*'s debate about the Torah, particularly the laws that are significant identity markers, within a debate about its allegorisation and application within Judaism, seems to take insufficient account of the other matters *Barnabas* is arguing about – ownership of the covenant, identity of the people of God, commitment to the figure of Jesus. Against such a backcloth one has to wonder to what extent the debates about the law in *Barnabas* are intra-mural, debates about different understandings of the relationship between the allegorical interpretation of texts and their literal application. Such arguments may have had a very different resonance, I suspect, in the situation envisaged by Philo in *Migr*.

Dunn and Smith are right, however, to problematize the absence of any language specifically relating to Jews and Judaism/Christians and Christianity. What was to prevent *Barnabas* from using terms, which, for instance, Ignatius was quite at ease using, as well as Diognetus?[88] If the author is involved in an act of separatism, then why not determine that through explicit vocabulary ("Christians" and "Jews" rather than "them" and "us")? Perhaps their absence is accounted for by assuming that in the circumstances in which *Barnabas* found himself reference to "them" and "us" was sufficient to indicate identities, such was the proximity of each group to the other. It is also possible that *Barnabas* could not rely on an understanding of "Christian" as entailing "non-Jewish" and therefore did not want to risk this, or simply that he was squabbling over the same piece of turf as multiple other groups that could not be reduced to a simple binary. These suggestions are all compatible with the view that *Barnabas* may have been addressing his letter to a situation where identities were less clear than he wished. The cry at 4:6b that the covenant is both theirs and ours, alluded to at 13:1, points to a reality unacceptable to *Barnabas*. It is telling that the "perfect knowledge" (1:7) he offers, is arrived at with an affirmation that the covenant belongs exclusively to the gentiles (13:7).[89]

It is also the case, and this is a more general point applicable to all the positions examined above, that *Barnabas* cannot be categorized as anything other than a Jewish text – its concerns are Jewish – the interpretation of scripture, in particular the law; its interest in the commandments; its apocalyptic tone; the

---

[88] Ignatius's use of "christianismos" and "ioudaismos" as binaries at Ign.*Magn.* 8:1; 10:3 and Ign.*Phld* 6:1 is not witnessed again until Tertullian in the 3rd century. *Diognetus*'s relatively frequent use of the terms "Jew" and "Christian" is unique among those writings termed 'Apostolic Fathers'. This might imply that the vocabulary, deployed contrastively, was not in frequent use until the end of the 2nd century.

[89] The decision to restrict the binaries to "them" and "us" may have been determined by the usage of the vocabulary found in 4:6.

categories in which it understands ethnicity; its knowledge of extra-biblical traditions; its concern with imagery relating to the temple and the land. The exclamation, "See how well Moses legislated," which acts as a partial conclusion to a discussion of the food laws, could easily have been raised from a Hellenistic Jewish sermon.[90] That the author promotes a Christocentric vision of the Old Testament, that he thinks the covenant has come to those who follow Christ, that he thinks Christ is a key to understanding the truths of scripture, is only significant insofar as we hold these assertions to be non-Jewish. This letter may betray institutional separation, or the hope of it, but it cannot be said to display ideological separation.

Before moving to some concluding remarks, the issue of context needs to be considered. As already stated, this is very difficult to determine. The letter rarely deals in specifics (the only reference to an external event may be found in 16:3–4; and insofar as the author engages with the reality of the Jewish and Christian community, he does so without reference to any Jewish realia like the synagogue, or related manifestations of that community); and no consensus has been arrived at with regard to the provenance of the epistle. Hvalvik's agnosticism on these matters leads him to situate *Barnabas* in the 2nd century more generally, and specifically within the context of 2nd century Jewish-Christian interaction. This involves him in a generalized account of such interaction, all in the service of showing that *Barnabas*'s polemic finds its natural place in a widely evidenced atmosphere of polemical exchange and proselytizing competition, a position which does owe a lot to a conventional understanding of the parting of the ways, seeking, as it does, to subsume a particular text into an assumed and generalized setting.[91] Others, as we have seen, who suggest a date in the 130s and an Egyptian/Alexandrian provenance ask how in a post-Trajanic revolt setting, one in which it is assumed that the Jewish population in Alexandria was considerably diminished, any Christian could appear to be as preoccupied as *Barnabas* with Jews. As already noted, Rothschild has argued that acceptance of such a setting should lead to a reading of the supposedly anti-Jewish polemic in a way that places only secondary significance on Jews. Others, such as Tobias Nicklas, have argued that the polemic is understandable in such a setting, stressing that *Barnabas*, writing in a situation where association with Jews is thought dangerous, and perhaps more so in the wake of the outbreak of the Bar Kokhba revolt, wants to disassociate the Christians absolutely from the Jews.

---

[90] Prostmeier, *Barnabasbrief* (see n. 32), 407, notes the broad similarity of these words to *Let.Aris.* 128–131; 169–171 and also 144. Carleton Paget, *Barnabas* (see n. 27), 151, for further arguments supporting the Jewish provenance of Barn. 10.
[91] Hvalvik, *Struggle* (see n. 32), 213–321.

> The author of Barn's purpose was two-fold: on the one hand, the anti-Jewish propaganda text serves to convince as many members of his community as possible not to follow Christ believers who behaved like Jews. On the other hand, the author did not want to abandon scripture – that is why it is claimed [...] for his group of Christians alone.[92]

In this interpretation the Jews remain a reality but one determined by a context in which they are not really present as such, an interpretation not entirely different from Nicklas's explanation of the anti-Jewish polemic in the *Epistle of Diognetus*.[93] Another possibility lies in assuming that any understanding of the text's engagement with Jews should not be determined by some preconceived view of what the situation of Jews was like in Egypt post-revolt, but rather that *Barnabas* should be seen as a document which illuminates such a context in unexpected ways, perhaps allowing us, for instance, to make better sense of the important role of Jewish opinion in Celsus's *True Word* which some have wanted to date before 175 and to situate in Egypt.[94]

However we decide to proceed, the student of *Barnabas* should acknowledge how fragile his or her conclusions are in the face of such uncertainty about the epistle's context. Insistence on the local and the particular, a mark, as already noted, of the ways that never parted approach, is at a theoretical level compelling. Whether it is, in many cases, little more than a cautionary admonition thrown into a cauldron of ignorance is worthy of reflection.

5 Conclusion

I began this paper by noting how the old paradigm of the parting of the ways had come under assault, and how this had been forged not only by 'historical' concerns, but also by an intellectual atmosphere, reflecting aspects of post-modernity. This was marked by a suspicion of master narratives with their assumed

---

[92] T. Nicklas, *Jews and Christians? Second Century Christian Perspectives on the "Parting of the Ways"* (Tübingen: Mohr Siebeck, 2014), 73.
[93] See T. Nicklas, "Identitätsbildung durch Konstruktion der 'Anderen' in *Ad Diognetum*," in *Early Christian Communities between Ideal and Reality*, ed. M. Grundeken and J. Verheyden, WUNT 342 (Tübingen: Mohr Siebeck, 2015), 203–217, here 217, where he argues that *Diognetus* exemplifies a form of polemic, which reflects pagan/Alexandrian criticisms of Judaism, but avoids traditional Christian criticisms (e.g., those relating to Christology and scripture), and so "schneidet [...] so konsequent wie möglich alle Verbindungen zwischen Christentum und Judentum ab," making it plain that separatist instincts could function in different ways.
[94] See M.R. Niehoff, "A Jewish Critique of Christianity from Second-Century Alexandria: Revisiting the Jew mentioned in the *Contra Celsum*," *JECS* 21 (2013): 151–175.

teleologies, a concern with complex issues relating to identity, and an alertness to the constructivist nature of texts. While I noted that these criticisms of a previously regnant paradigm had not themselves led to a clear and agreed upon alternative, and were themselves subject to some sharp criticisms, the methodological assumptions underlying the critique forced the scholar interested in the subject of ancient Jewish-Christian relations to return to texts in a fresh way.

What did the *Epistle of Barnabas* look like against this background? In a necessarily broad-based account, I showed how discussion of *Barnabas*'s relevance to the study of Jewish-Christian relations had thrown up a wide gamut of opinions, ranging from the view that Jews barely impinged upon the author's consciousness, functioning rather as foils in internal 'Christian' arguments, to views that the epistle gave evidence of a complex attempt on the part of the author to forge an identity, based around a separatist outlook, in a setting in which distinctions between Jew and Christian were much less obvious to some than to the author. In this view the epistle is a performative text, seeking to create a reality of separation, which did not reflect the environment in which *Barnabas* found himself. I also discussed the view that the epistle could be seen as a document seeking to forge a Christ-based identity from within the Jewish community, or within the framework of that community. This view was encouraged by the absence of the use in the text of words for Jew or Christian, and of a conventional replacement theology in which a second or new covenant was argued for (a view in part encouraged by *Barnabas*'s own scriptural hermeneutic); and by the possibility that some of *Barnabas*'s most striking positions about the law were evidenced within known Jewish sources.

These latter two positions, the second of which seems less likely than the first, reflect elements of the ways that never parted outlook, though arguably, aspects of the first emerge in a much earlier era, insofar as these concern themselves with the threat of Judaizers, though here the emphasis is different – people from outside infiltrate the community and seek to turn it from what it was before, and *Barnabas* reacts; rather than *Barnabas* seeking to change a blurred vision – the covenant is both theirs and ours – which is perhaps the norm.

Whatever we think of where the text lies on some scale of Jewish-Christian separation, it remains a Jewish document ideologically, a point which stands in spite of the text's separatist tendencies.

In all of this one must note the underdetermined presence of Jews. The word 'Jew' does not occur in the text. Arguments are not placed in the mouth of Jews, at least at any length. Moreover, beyond the fact of false interpretation, often associated with the past, almost no activity in a discernible present is attributed to Jews. Even reference to their conversionary activity appears in pallid form. *Barnabas*'s image of the Jew is strikingly general – their day-to-day world invisible, their actions in the face of the Christian community invisible, their views monochrome. That does not mean they are absent from the context *Barnabas* is addressing, simply that the reality of that presence is occluded by the constructed image.

Related to this observation is the question of context, not least as this relates to provenance and date. A scholar who holds *Barnabas* to be written in Alexandria after the Trajanic revolt may view his aims and self-understanding differently from someone who places him elsewhere or in the same city at an earlier date. Insistence on the local and the specific, a *cri de cœur* of those who oppose the partings paradigm, is often little more than the expression of a desideratum which cannot be attained, whatever the truth of the principle.

The *epistle of Barnabas*, then, throws up a medley of issues which highlight and reflect aspects of the present debate about Jews and Christians. The limits of what we can define as Jewish; the relationship between ideological and institutional separation; texts as creators or reflectors of reality; the significance of context in the determination of a set of questions relating to separation; the need for caution about placing a text within a wider narrative. These are issues which will go on being discussed without any final resolution. Given the nature of the evidence available to us, and the complexity of these issues, this is entirely appropriate.

Bibliography

Becker, A. H., and A. Y. Reed, eds., *The Ways That Never Parted. Jews and Christians in Late Antiquity and the Early Middle Ages*, TSAJ 95 (Tübingen: Mohr Siebeck, 2003).

Boyarin, D., "Semantic Differences; or, 'Judaism'/'Christianity'," in *The Ways That Never Parted. Jews and Christians in Late Antiquity and the Early Middle Ages*, ed. A. H. Becker and A. Y. Reed, TSAJ 95 (Tübingen: Mohr Siebeck, 2003), 65–85.

Buell, D. K., *Why This New Race? Ethnic Reasoning in Early Christianity* (New York, NY: Columbia University Press, 2005).

Carleton Paget, J., *The Epistle of Barnabas. Outlook and Background*, WUNT 2/64 (Tübingen: Mohr Siebeck, 1994).

Carleton Paget, J., "Barnabas and the Outsiders: Jews and their World in the Epistle of Barnabas," in *Early Christian Communities between Ideal and Reality*, ed. M. Grundeken and J. Verheyden, WUNT 342 (Tübingen: Mohr Siebeck, 2015), 179–180.

Carleton Paget, J., "Paul and the *Epistle of Barnabas*," in *The Apostolic Fathers and Paul*, ed. T. D. Still and D. E. Wilhite (London and Oxford: T&T Clark 2016), 79–100.

Carleton Paget, J., "The Jewish revolts and Jewish-Christian relations," in *Jews and Christians in the First and Second Centuries. The Interbellum 70–132 CE*, ed. J. Schwartz and P. J. Tomson, CRINT 15 (Leiden: Brill, 2017), 276–306.

Cohen, S. J. D., "The Ways That Parted: Jews, Christians, and Jewish Christians," in *Jews and Christians in the First and Second Centuries: The Interbellum 70–132 CE*, ed. J. Schwartz and P. J. Tomson, CRINT 15 (Leiden: Brill, 2018), 307–339.

Costa, J. "Qu'est-ce que le 'judaïsme synagogal'?," *JAAJ* 3 (2015): 63–218.

Dunn, G. D., "Tertullian and Rebekah: A Re-Reading of an 'Anti-Jewish' Argument in Early Christian Literature," *VC* 52 (1998): 121–145.

Fonrobert, C. E., "Jewish Christians, Judaisers, and Christian Anti-Judaism," in *A People's History of Christianity. Vol. 2: Late ancient Christianity*, ed. V. Burrus (Minneapolis, MN: Fortress, 2005), 234–254.

Frankfurter, D., "Beyond 'Jewish Christianity': Continuing religious sub-cultures of the second and third centuries and their documents," in *The Ways That Never Parted. Jews and Christians in Late Antiquity and the Early Middle Ages*, ed. A. H. Becker and A. Y. Reed, TSAJ 95 (Tübingen: Mohr Siebeck, 2003), 131–143.

Hezser, C., *The Social Structure of the Rabbinic movement in Roman Palestine*, TSAJ 66 (Tübingen: Mohr Siebeck, 1997).

Horbury, W., "Jewish-Christian Relations in Barnabas and Justin Martyr," in idem, *Jews and Christians in Contact and Controversy* (Edinburgh: T&T Clark, 1998), 127–161.

Horbury, W., *Jews and Christians in contact and controversy* (Edinburgh: T&T Clark, 1998).

Horbury, W., *Jewish war under Trajan and Hadrian* (Cambridge: CUP, 2017).

Hvalvik, R., *The Struggle for Scripture and Covenant: The Purpose of the Epistle of Barnabas and Jewish-Christian Competition in the Second Century*, WUNT 2/82 (Tübingen: Mohr Siebeck, 1998).

Jackson-McCabe, M., *Jewish Christianity: The Making of the Christianity-Judaism Divide* (New Haven, CT, and London: YUP, 2020).

Kok, M., "The True Covenant People: Ethnic Reasoning in the Epistle of Barnabas," *SR* 40 (2011): 81–97.

Kraft, R. A., *The Epistle of Barnabas: Its Quotations and Their Sources* (PhD diss., Harvard University, MA, 1961).

Kraft, R. A., *The Apostolic Fathers: A New Translation and Commentary, III: Barnabas and the Didache* (New York, NY: Nelson, 1965).

Lieu, J. M., *Image and Reality: The Jews in the World of the Christians in the Second Century* (Edinburgh: T&T Clark, 1996).

Lieu, J. M., "'The parting of the ways': theological construct or historical reality?," in *Neither Jew nor Greek. Constructing early Christianity*, ed. eadem, 2nd ed. (London: T&T Clark, 2016), 31–40.

Marcus, J., "Birkat ha-minim revisited," *NTS* 55 (2009): 523–551.

Nicklas, T., *Jews and Christians? Second Century Christian Perspectives on the "Parting of the Ways"* (Tübingen: Mohr Siebeck, 2014).

Nicklas, T., "Identitätsbildung durch Konstruktion der 'Anderen' in *Ad Diognetum*," in *Early Christian Communities between Ideal and Reality*, ed. M. Grundeken and J. Verheyden, WUNT 342 (Tübingen: Mohr Siebeck, 2015), 203–207.

Niehoff, M. R., "A Jewish Critique of Christianity from Second-Century Alexandria: Revisiting the Jew mentioned in the *Contra Celsum*," *JECS* 21 (2013): 151–175.

Parkes, J., *The Conflict of the Church and the Synagogue: A Study in the Origins of Anti-Semitism* (London: Soncino Press, 1934).

Prigent, P., *Les testimonia dans le christianisme primitive: l'Épître de Barnabé et ses sources* (Paris: Gabalda, 1961).
Prostmeier, F. R., *Der Barnabasbrief*, KAV 8 (Göttingen: Vandenhoeck & Ruprecht, 1999).
Prostmeier, F. R., "Antijüdische Polemik im Rahmen christlicher Hermeneutik. Zum Streit über christliche Identität in der Alten Kirche. Notizen zum Barnabasbrief," *ZAC* 6 (2002): 38–58.
Reed, A. Y., "Rabbis, 'Jewish Christians', and Other Late Antique Jews: Reflections on the Fate of Judaism(s) After 70 C. E.," in *The Changing Faces of Judaism, Christianity, and other Greco-Roman Religions in Antiquity*, ed. I. H. Henderson, G. S. Oegema, and S. Parks Ricker (Gütersloh: Gütersloher Verlagshaus 2006), 323–346.
Reed, A. Y., "Beyond 'Judaism' and 'Christianity' in the Roman Near East," in eadem, *Jewish Christianity and the History of Judaism* TSAJ 171 (Tübingen: Mohr Siebeck, 2018), 57–84.
Reed, A. Y., "*Epilogue:* After 'Origins,' Beyond 'Identity,' and Before 'Religion(s)'," in eadem, *Jewish Christianity and the History of Judaism*, TSAJ 171 (Tübingen: Mohr Siebeck, 2018), 389–438.
Reed, A. Y., "'Jewish Christianity' as Counterhistory?," in eadem, *Jewish Christianity and the History of Judaism*, TSAJ 171 (Tübingen: Mohr Siebeck, 2018), 175–216.
Rhodes, J. N., "Barnabas 4.6B: The Exegetical Implications of a Textual Problem," *VC* 58 (2004): 365–392.
Rhodes, J. N., *The Epistle of Barnabas and the Deuteronomic Tradition*, WUNT 2/188 (Tübingen: Mohr Siebeck, 2004).
Rhodes, J. N., "The Two Ways Tradition in the Epistle of Barnabas: Revisiting an Old Question," *CBQ* 73 (2011): 797–816.
Rothschild, C. K., "Soteriology and the Allegorical Construction of opponents in the Epistle of Barnabas," in *Sōtēria: Salvation in Early Christianity and Antiquity*, ed. D. S. du Toit, C. Gerber, and C. Zimmermann, NovTSup 175 (Leiden: Brill, 2019), 561–576.
Schwartz, S., "How many Judaisms were there: a critique of Neusner and Smith on definition and Mason and Boyarin on categorization," *JAJ* 2 (2011): 208–238.
Schwemer, A.-M., "Zum Abbruch des jüdischen Lebens in Alexandria – Der Aufstand in der Dispora unter Trajan (115–117)," in *Alexandria*, ed. T. Georges, F. Albrecht, and R. Feldmeier, COMES 1 (Tübingen: Mohr Siebeck, 2013), 381–399.
Sheppard, A., "The Letter of Barnabas and the Jerusalem Temple," *JSJ* 48 (2017): 531–550.
Smith, J. C. H., "The 'Epistle of Barnabas' and the Two Ways of Teaching Authority," *VC* 68 (2014): 465–497.
van der Horst, P. W., "The Birkat ha-minim in recent research," in *Hellenism – Judaism – Christianity*, ed. idem (Kampen: Kok, 1994), 99–111.
Vielhauer, P., *Geschichte der urchristlichen Literatur. Einleitung in das Neue Testament, die Apokryphen und die Apostolischen Väter* (New York, NY, and Berlin: de Gruyter, 1975).
von Harnack, A., *The Expansion of Christianity in the First Three Centuries*, vol. 1 (London: ET Williams & Norgate, 1904–1905).
von Harnack, A., *Geschichte der altchristlichen Literatur bis Eusebius 1*, vol. 2 (Leipzig: Hinrichs, 1992).
Wengst, K., *Tradition und Theologie des Barnabasbriefes*, AKG 42 (Berlin and New York, NY: de Gruyter, 1971).
Windisch, H., *Der Barnabasbrief*, HNT Erg. Die Apostolischen Väter 3 (Tübingen: Mohr Siebeck, 1920).

Benjamin A. Edsall
Justin Martyr without the "Parting" or the "Ways"

Abstract: Obwohl sich das Modell der "Trennung der Wege" seit 1961 etabliert hat, ist es in jüngerer Zeit deutlich in die Kritik geraten. Der vorliegende Beitrag wendet sich diesem Modell mit besonderer Konzentration auf Justin den Märtyrer zu. Dabei zeigt sich, dass Justins Schriften die Vorstellung von einer "Trennung" von Judentum und Christentum nicht unterstützen. Statt der Rede von "Trennung" finden sich dort vielmehr die Auffassung einer Kontinuität des christlichen Glaubens mit *verus Israel* sowie Hinweise auf einen andauernden Dialog und die Gemeinschaft von Juden und Christen.

Keywords: Justin Martyr, Parting of the Ways, Jewish-Christian Relations, Early Judaism, Early Christianity

> Christian texts (like Justin's *Dialogue with Trypho the Jew*) emphasize that Christianity is right and that Judaism is wrong, because Christians, not Jews, properly understand the Hebrew Scriptures. There certainly is a parting of the ways here, at least in the reality as constructed by these texts.

This is the conclusion drawn by Shaye Cohen in his recently updated essay, entitled "The Ways that Parted."[1] I begin here because Cohen's view represents a form of what is still the majority position, despite some notable challenges in recent years, perhaps most famously in the volume edited by Adam Becker and Annette Yoshiko Reed.[2] If scholars are no longer happy with Harnack's description of Judaism and Christianity as distinct religions whose "hot war" is largely

---

[1] S.J.D. Cohen, "The Ways That Parted: Jews, Christians, and Jewish-Christians, ca. 100–150 CE," in *Jews and Christians in the First and Second Centuries: The Interbellum 70–132 CE*, ed. J. Schwartz and P.J. Tomson, CRINT 15 (Leiden: Brill, 2018), 338–339.
[2] A.H. Becker and A.Y. Reed, eds., *The Ways that Never Parted: Jews and Christians in Late Antiquity and the Early Middle Ages*, TSAJ 95 (Tübingen: Mohr Siebeck, 2003), built on in a recent *Festschrift*, L. Baron, J. Hicks-Keeton, and M. Thiessen, eds., *The Ways That Often Parted: Essays in Honor of Joel Marcus*, ECL (Atlanta, GA: Society of Biblical Literature Press, 2018); cf. also J.M. Lieu, *Neither Jew nor Greek?: Constructing Early Christianity* (Edinburgh: T&T Clark, 2002), 31–49 and D. Boyarin, *Border Lines: The Partition of Judaeo-Christianity* (Philadelphia, PA: University of Pennsylvania Press, 2004), among others. Notably, however, Boyarin argues that while we should not read Justin's work as reflecting an *already* parted way, he is nevertheless "participating in producing it." (67)

https://doi.org/10.1515/9783110742213-010

over by the time of Justin,³ the apologist is still often taken as evidence that Christians and Jews maintained tight boundaries by the mid 2ⁿᵈ century;⁴ or that Justin represents the "point of cleavage" between Jewish and Christian interpretive traditions;⁵ or that he offers evidence of a clear distinction between church and synagogue;⁶ or that Justin sees Judaism and Christianity as "two separate religions [...] in direct conflict."⁷ In view of this widespread opinion, it is not surprising that the Reed and Becker volume does not include a chapter on Justin Martyr.⁸

The way in which Cohen phrases his position, moreover, is important: "there *certainly* is a parting of the ways here, *at least in the reality as constructed by these texts*."⁹ In what follows I want to question precisely this certainty and the view that such a parting is a reality that Justin's writings construct in themselves. The evidence provided by his first *Apology* and the *Dialogue with Trypho* is

---

3 A. von Harnack, *Ist die Rede des Paulus in Athen ein ursprünglicher Bestandteil der Apostelgeschichte? Judentum und Judenchristentum in Justins Dialog mit Trypho, nebst einer Collation der Pariser Handschrift Nr. 450*, TU39/1 (Leipzig: Hinrichs, 1913), 92.
4 G.N. Stanton, *Studies in Matthew and Early Christianity*, WUNT 309 (Tübingen: Mohr Siebeck, 2013), 363–375.
5 L. Misiarczyk, *Il midrash nel* Dialogo con Trifone *di Giustino Martire* (Płock: Płocki Instytut Wydawniczy, 1999), 26; cf. also B.G. Bucur, "Justin Martyr's Exegesis of Biblical Theophanies and the Parting of the Ways between Christianity and Judaism," *TS* 75.1 (2014): 34–51, here 51, "christological exegesis of theophanies [...] sowed the seeds of a *communal separation* between those who advocated and those who rejected this exegetical avenue."
6 M.W. Bates, "Justin Martyr's Logocentric Hermeneutical Transformation of Isaiah's Vision of the Nations," *JTS* 60.2 (2009): 538–555, here 554.
7 A. Gregerman, *Building on the Ruins of the Temple: Apologetics and Polemics in Early Christianity and Rabbinic Judaism*, TSAJ 165 (Tübingen: Mohr Siebeck, 2016), 57, cf. p. 21 – "Justin is in no doubt about the separation of Judaism and Christianity." Part of the difficulty in this formulation is that the abstract concepts 'Judaism' and 'Christianity' suggest fixed systems of thought and/or ways of life and obscure the variety of ways in which Justin depicts the relationship of 'Jews' and 'Christians' in his writings. On p. 21 n. 9 Gregerman notes that Justin, *Dial.* 46–47 "suggest that the division is not yet firm to everyone." I suggest that Justin is one of those for whom the division is not yet firm; see further below.
8 This holds true also for the volume edited by Baron et al., *The Ways That Often* (see n. 2).
9 My emphasis. "The reality as constructed by" Justin Martyr's *Dialogue* is addressed earlier in the same piece on pp. 315–317. Following from his conclusion that Christians and non-Christian Jews were viewed by the Roman government as different socio-religious groups by the time of Nerva (96 CE; cf. n. 15 below), he argues that these social distinctions appear in Justin's construal of Christianity and Judaism: his "anti-Jewish stance" shows that he understood "Christianity to be not-Judaism" such that he "thinks there is an unbridgeable divide between Jews who do not believe in Christ and gentiles (like Justin) who do" (315, 317). The difficulties with this account will be addressed below.

more ambivalent than such a conclusion indicates – rather than constructing a Jewish and Christian parting of the ways, I suggest that Justin's works undermine those very categories.[10] After brief general reflections on the "parting of the ways" metaphor, I turn to a more detailed engagement with Justin's writings, focusing first on his rhetorical construction of 'Jewish' and 'Christian' identities and, second, on socio-historical evidence that Justin presents, somewhat despite himself, for an ongoing fuzziness of Jewish/Christian boundaries.

1 Parting of the Ways: Implications, Strengths and Weaknesses

At least since the republication of James Parkes's work in 1961, the metaphor of the "parting of the ways" has served as a useful image for the process of self-definition by which 'Jews' and 'Christians' became distinct and distinctly separate groups.[11] This image has two principal strengths. In the first place, it borrows

---

10 The bulk of relevant information is found in the *Dialogue*. There is no space here to address the differences in genre and rhetorical argumentation between the *Apology* and *Dialogue*. In the course of the thematic approach to Justin's works here, the focus will rest on material from the latter with other corroborating cross-currents from the former; distinctive emphases of each work are mentioned where relevant in the notes below.

11 J. Parkes, *The Conflict of the Church and Synagogue: A Study in the Origins of Antisemitism* (Cleveland, OH, and New York, NY: Soncino Press, 1934; repr., Cleveland, OH, and New York, NY: Meridian, 1961), 71–122; note the comments in Cohen, "The Ways that Parted" (see n. 1), 307–308 on his preference for "Jews" and "Christians" over their counterparts, Judaism and Christianity. Despite his efforts at terminological clarity, Cohen's formulation still requires a certain homogenization of both Jews and Christians such that they can, in fact, part. (Notably, he continues to use the abstract nouns Judaism and Christianity.) Furthermore, his recognition that Judaism and Christianity are variegated phenomena undermines his certainty of their parting, nor is it true that *"all* the extant evidence points in the same direction" (p. 335, emphasis added). If the question of the parting is, at root, a question about social realities "on the ground" – about "life as lived by real people in historical time, not some theological abstraction or some hypostasized reality that exists only in the mind" (S.J.D. Cohen, "Common Judaism in Greek and Latin Authors," in *Redefining First-century Jewish and Christian Identities: Essays in Honor of Ed Parish Sanders*, ed. F.E. Udoh [Notre Dame, IN: Notre Dame University Press, 2008], 69–87, here 70.) – then as long as there is some congruence, as long as some Christians claim to be Jews and vice versa, where does that leave such a model? On defining "Jews" in antiquity, see S.J.D. Cohen, "'Those Who Say They are Jews, and are Not': How Do You Know a Jew in Antiquity When you See One?," in *The Diasporas in Antiquity*, ed. idem and E.S. Frerichs (Atlanta, GA: Scholars Press, 1993), 1–45 whose conclusion emphasizes the difficulties in drawing boundaries around the concept of "Jew" in antiquity.

its language from the ancient sources, at least insofar as early Christians and Jews wrote about the "ways": the ways of life and death, light and darkness, God's way, the ways of the *kosmos* or gentiles, etc. The metaphor itself, then, does not operate at a purely etic level. Second, and probably more importantly, the metaphor is effective by means of its simplicity. It goes almost without saying that today there are two religious traditions called, respectively, Judaism and Christianity. However much these two traditions have in common, late 20th century efforts at rapprochement presuppose a clear distinction between the two groups at least on a social, if not also religious, level.[12] Given that Jesus and Paul and the earliest disciples operated within the bounds of first century Judaism, the argument runs, identifying a point of separation is an obvious task.

At a conceptual level, to ask a question about *the* "parting" between Jews and Christians is, in terms borrowed from Reinhart Koselleck and Paul Ricœur, to inquire about the relation of a particular event to more enduring historical structures.[13] Following Ricœur a little farther, if we construct a simplified historiographical narrative of the parting metaphor, the structures of 'Judaism' and 'Christianity' constitute historical agents, 'quasi-characters,' who take part in a specific event, namely the parting of ways. This narrative implies – even if subtly – that both characters have a relatively stable identity such that one can coherently attribute agency to them. Both must predate the event in which they participate, even as they continue on afterwards. In fact, this is an important factor to remember in the "parting" metaphor: that it is not, strictly speaking, the fork in the road that is the parting of ways, but that it is the fact that different groups go in different directions at the fork in the road. That is, the metaphor implies that Jews and Christians were happily (or unhappily?) walking along together on the same path and then, as the path splits, so also do they.

---

12 The very concept of rapprochement requires (at least) two separate parties. It remains the case, however, that such a view does not allow space for the contemporary Messianic Jewish communities (cf. the comments in the introduction to D.J. Rudolph and J. Willitts, eds., *Introduction to Messianic Judaism* [Grand Rapids, MI: Zondervan, 2013]) among other marginal Jewish or Christian groups.

13 See R. Koselleck, *Futures Past: On the Semantics of Historical Time*, trans. K. Tribe (Cambridge, MA: MIT Press, 1985), 105–115 and particularly the appropriation of this terminology by P. Ricœur, *Time and Narrative*, trans. K. McLaughlin and D. Pellauer, 3 vols. (Chicago, IL: University of Chicago Press, 1984), 1: 175–225 where he discusses the role of "singular causal imputation" in historical "quasi-events" in which second-order entities, i.e., generalized historical "structures," act as "quasi-characters." Note that Ricœur later nuanced his account of narrative, disentangling descriptive "explanatory intelligibility" and "narrative intelligibility" in their respective accounts of structures and events; cf. P. Ricœur, *Memory, History, Forgetting* (Chicago, IL: University of Chicago Press, 2004), 236–248.

The problems with this are well known but are worth rehearsing briefly here. Speaking about Judaism and Christianity, just as much as speaking collectively of Jews or Christians, is to work with abstractions.[14] Indeed, every statement about 'Christianity' or 'Judaism,' every claim about what 'Christians' or 'Jews' do or believe, in history or today is necessarily to engage in abstraction, to move away from particular communities or individuals – with their idiosyncrasies and inconsistencies – toward generalized formulations. Such generalizations are essentializing and involve tacit normative claims about what qualifies as Christian or Jewish or otherwise. This is necessarily true, it seems to me, because the very process of isolating key aspects of 'Jews' or 'Christians' requires that one make determinations about which groups need to be covered by the explanatory force of the generalization.[15]

One solution to this problem is to break down the abstract 'structures' into their component parts of individual Jews or Christians and their various communities, who may be in conflict with others who claim the same moniker. This provides a more nuanced historical account – identifying multiple partings of multiple ways[16] – but doing so enervates the principal strength of the metaphor. As Judith Lieu noted, the resulting image resembles less a parting of ways than it does "a criss-crossing of muddy tracks which only the expert tracker, or poacher, can decipher."[17] This approach, moreover, struggles to explain the very experience of difference between Judaism and Christianity that scholars set out to address in the first place. Somewhat like the sorites paradox, if the separation of one particular Christian community from a particular Jewish communi-

---

14 Cf. n. 11 above.
15 On the character and pervasiveness of normative claims within Religious Studies, see esp. T.A. Lewis, *Why Philosophy Matters for the Study of Religion – and Vice Versa* (Oxford: Oxford University Press, 2015), 43–61. It is not the presence of normative claims as such that pose the problem here but rather the fact that their normative dimension is often unacknowledged. Every definition of "Christian" or "Jew" excludes and, for the question of the "parting," what is excluded is historically – and methodologically – as significant as what is included. (This, of course, is a normative stance of my own, related to a broader commitment that historiography is obligated to attend to excluded terms, privileging the variegated detail to the neat explanation; see the argument in M. de Certeau, *The Practice of Everyday Life*, trans. S. Rendall [Berkeley, CA: University of California Press, 1984], 45–61.)
16 As in the title of the recent Joel Marcus *Festschrift* in Baron, Hicks-Keeton, and Thiessen, *The Ways that Often Parted* (see n. 2). This is also the approach followed by Cohen in the chapter which leads off the present argument.
17 Lieu, *Neither* (see n. 2), 49; cf. the difficulty of modeling the "parting" visually highlighted in M. Goodman, "Modeling the 'Parting of the Ways'," in *The Ways that Never Parted: Jews and Christians in Late Antiquity and the Early Middle Ages*, ed. A.H. Becker and A.Y. Reed, TSAJ 95 (Tübingen: Mohr Siebeck, 2003), 119–129.

ty does not constitute the "parting," the rather obvious question arises: how many groups have to "part ways" across the whole set of early Jewish and Christian phenomena before *the* parting has been accomplished?[18] Whose point of view is being adopted in attempting to answer this question?[19] When examined in light of fine-grained distinctions between different Jewish and Christian groups in antiquity, the vague quality of the image of "the parting" quickly becomes an impediment to clear discussion.[20] Questions inevitably remain. Who is a Jew or a Christian or both?[21] Is it enough for someone simply to claim the title? Where, when and how did these people interact and in what way did they understand what they were doing?

The burden of what follows is to show that explicit testimony and tacit witness of Justin's *Apology* and *Dialogue* do not support the image of the "parting of the ways." That is to say, in light of the fact that Judaism and Christianity, as abstractions, do not lend themselves easily to the project of identifying a particular rupture between the two, even on the scale of a single writer, Justin's account bears witness to a complex reality not readily captured with the image of "parting" ways.

---

18 The sorites paradox, attributed to Euboulides of Miletus, is famously formulated in relation to grains of sand: when is an unquantifiable "heap" of sand no longer a heap (that is, when is it quantifiable) when removing grains one by one? See the extensive introduction to this paradox in D. Hyde and D. Raffman, "Sorites Paradox," in *The Stanford Encyclopedia of Philosophy*, ed. E.N. Zalta (Stanford, CA: Stanford University Press, 2018), https://plato.stanford.edu/archives/sum2018/entries/sorites-paradox/ last accessed on 15 July 2020.
19 For instance, if one opts for a Roman legal point of view, which Cohen appears to privilege, then the imposition and alleviation of the *fiscus Iudaicu*s has been proposed as that point at which Jews and Christians were distinguishable by outsiders; see Cohen, "The Ways that Parted" (see n. 1), 310–313 following the work of M. Heemstra, *The Fiscus Judaicus and the Parting of the Ways*, WUNT 2/277 (Tübingen: Mohr Siebeck, 2010).
20 To a degree, this critique of the "parting" reflects a difference in historical scale: the "parting of the ways" attempts to account for shifts among social groups in the *longue durée* while attending to Justin's particular voice operates at a micro-historical scale (on the importance of "scale" in historiography, see esp. the discussion in Ricœur, *Memory* [see n. 13], 204–216). Even so, the greater the number of individual voices that undermine a macro-historical *longue durée* explanation, the less explanatory power they hold and they may eventually be discarded entirely.
21 On the difficulties of defining "Jewish Christianity" in scholarship on antiquity, see esp. the chapter entitled "The definition of the term 'Jewish Christian' / 'Jewish Christianity' in the history of research" in J. Carleton Paget, *Jews, Christians and Jewish Christians in Antiquity*, WUNT 251 (Tübingen: Mohr Siebeck, 2010), 289–324.

2 The Ways: Justin and the Continuity of True Israel

As I hope to show, Justin's construction of Christian and Jewish identities is highly theological; he does not directly describe sociological realities, nor is he interested in offering an impartial account.²² Moreover, the implicit premise of the "parting" imagery – that Jew and Christian are roughly equivalent and mutually exclusive conceptual categories (ignoring the excluded middle) – is not shared by Justin, for whom Christianity both participates in and comprehends ethno-racial discourse.²³ In other words, for Justin, there are not "two ways" capable of parting.

Now, to a certain degree, Justin appears to be clear that "Jews" and "Christians" are distinct.²⁴ The Jews have their synagogues and the Christians their churches. The former denounce the latter in their weekly meetings while the latter possess the proper interpretation of scripture, worship the true Christ and constitute *verus Israel*, the latter point being prominent particularly in the *Dialogue*.²⁵

---

22 Cf. Bobichon's: "Sa [viz. Justin's] vision du monde est essentiellement théologique, et une analyse critique de ses affirmations doit prendre en compte cette priorité"; P. Bobichon, *Justin Martyr, Dialogue avec Tryphon: Édition critique, traduction, commentaire*, 2 vols., Paradosis (Freiburg, CH: Éditions universitaires de Fribourg, 2003), 74.
23 While the language of "race" is hotly debated, the present analysis follows D. Kimber Buell in assuming that "race" is always a socially constructed category (i.e., not genetically determined) and, to that extent, it maps onto the consistent efforts to define γένος in antiquity. The present analysis of Justin's reasoning is indebted to Buell's compelling work; D. Kimber Buell, *Why This New Race: Ethnic Reasoning in Early Christianity* (New York, NY: Columbia University Press, 2005).
24 Note that, while the terms Χριστιανός and Ἰουδαῖος are present in Justin's writings, he never uses the abstract nouns Χριστιανισμός or Ἰουδαισμός, in contrast with writers such as Ignatius of Antioch.
25 "Your" Synagogues: Justin, *Dial*. 16.4; 47.4; 53.4; 72.3 ("the Jews in Synagogues"); 96.2. Synagogue of the wicked in Ps 22:17: Justin, *Dial*. 98.4; 104.1. Church as possessor of scriptures: Justin, *Dial*. 29.2 etc. Jewish persecution (and cursing) of Christians: Justin, *1 Apol*. 31.6; *Dial*. 16.4; 96.2. Justin's testimony about cursing Christians in the synagogue is largely distinguished from the (later) use of the *birkat ha-minim*; see J.M. Lieu, "Accusations of Jewish Persecution in Early Christian Sources, with Particular Reference to Justin Martyr and the *Martyrdom of Polycarp*," in *Tolerance and Intolerance in Early Judaism and Christianity*, ed. G.N. Stanton and G.G. Stroumsa (Cambridge: Cambridge University Press, 1998), 279–295; Boyarin, *Border Lines* (see n. 2), 67–71; Cohen, "The Ways that Parted" (see n. 1), 333 and more generally R. González Salinero, "*Sinagogae Iudaeorum, fontes persecutionum? Il supposto intervento degli ebrei nelle persecuzioni antichristiane durante l'Impero Romano*," *VetChr* 43 (2006): 93–104, on Jewish persecution of

For we are the true, spiritual, Israelite γένος – that of Judah and Jacob and Issac and Abraham, who was witnessed by God in his uncircumcision because of his faith and was blessed and called a father of many nations – who have been led to God by this crucified Christ, as we will show in the following arguments.[26]

A short passage toward the end of the *Dialogue* similarly asserts a strong distinction: "The marriages of Jacob were types of the deeds that were about to be completed by Christ [...] Leah is *your* people and synagogue and Rachel is *our* church."[27] To appreciate the significance of this, it is important to remember that Justin's theme of the church as "true Israel" is linked closely with his view that prophecies about Jacob and Israel in the scriptures refer properly to Jesus. "So then, as [scripture] calls Christ 'Israel' and 'Jacob,' so also are we who are hewn from Christ's womb the true Israelite γένος."[28] In appealing to Jacob's marriages as τύποι in this way, then, Justin distinguishes between *you* – Trypho and the Jewish "people" with their synagogues – and *us* – the Church, who always had the real favor of Christ.[29]

This simple account of Justin's view is quickly complicated, however. As Denise Buell put it, "While seeking to differentiate them [*viz.* Jews and Christians] [...] Justin also repeatedly blurs their boundaries."[30] Indeed, the very claim that Christians are the true γένος of Israel in the *Dialogue* invites this blurring. Justin's inclusion of Judah among the other patriarchs in *Dial.* 11.5 (quoted above) is calibrated specifically to address his literary interlocutor *as a Jew* – Judah is aligned

---

Christians. Note that for the *Dialogue* I have used the critical edition of Bobichon, *Dialogue avec Tryphon* (see n. 22) and occasionally consulted the translation in T.B. Falls and T.P. Halton, trans., *St. Justin Martyr: Dialogue with Trypho*, Selections from the Fathers of the Church 3 (Washington, DC: Catholic University of America Press, 2003); for the *1 Apology* I have relied on the text in D. Minns and P. Parvis, *Justin, Philosopher and Martyr: Apologies* (Oxford University Press, 2009). Page numbers for primary source editions are only noted where the Greek text is quoted.
26 Justin, *Dial.* 11.5 (Bobichon, 212) – Ἰσραηλιτικὸν γὰρ τὸ ἀληθινόν, πνευματικόν, καὶ Ἰούδα γένος, καὶ Ἰακὼβ καὶ Ἰσαὰκ καὶ Ἀβραάμ, τοῦ ἐν ἀκροβυστίᾳ ἐπὶ τῇ πίστει μαρτυρηθέντος ὑπὸ τοῦ Θεοῦ καὶ εὐλογηθέντος καὶ πατρὸς πολλῶν ἐθνῶν κληθέντος, ἡμεῖς ἐσμεν, οἱ διὰ τούτου τοῦ σταυρωθέντος Χριστοῦ τῷ Θεῷ προσαχθέντες, ὡς καὶ προκοπτόντων ἡμῖν τῶν λόγων ἀποδειχθήσεται. Note that all translations are mine unless otherwise indicated.
27 Justin, *Dial.* 134.3 (Bobichon, 544) – Ἀλλὰ Λεία μὲν ὁ λαὸς ὑμῶν καὶ ἡ συναγωγή, Ῥαχὴλ δὲ ἡ ἐκκλησία ἡμῶν.
28 Justin, *Dial.* 135.3 (Bobichon, 546–548) – Ὡς οὖν Ἰσραὴλ τὸν Χριστὸν καὶ Ἰακὼβ οὕτως λέγει, καὶ ἡμεῖς ἐκ τῆς κοιλίας τοῦ Χριστοῦ λατομηθέντες, ἰσραηλιτικὸν τὸ ἀληθινόν ἐσμεν γένος. Cf. also Justin, *Dial.* 123.8–9 et passim.
29 Note also the strong "you" vs. "us" rhetoric in Justin, *Dial.* 93.4–5, as elsewhere.
30 Buell, *Why This New Race* (see n. 23), 97. The present analysis of Justin's ethnic reasoning is indebted to Buell's compelling work.

with Trypho's γένος in *Dial.* 52.3. At the same time, Jesus's own family is noted as being "of the tribe of Judah" while in *1 Apol.* 32.3 Justin notes explicitly that "Judah is the forefather of the Jews."[31] His use of γένος terminology highlights the ethnic-racial discourse by which Justin will *both* relativize Trypho's claims about Jewish identity, placing them on par with those of other nations, *and* establish the spiritual-genetic continuity of true Israel throughout history.[32]

Despite the fact, then, that Christians are "us" and Jews are "you" in Justin's rhetoric, it is also true that some Jews are numbered among the Christians. As it is with members of the other nations (οἱ ἀπὸ παντὸς ἔθνους ἀνθρώπων) who have been persuaded to become Christians, so also is it with "those from the Jews and Samaritans" (οἱ ἀπὸ Ἰουδαίων καὶ Σαμαρέων), according to Justin in the first *Apology*.[33] Similarly, speaking to Trypho in the *Dialogue*, Justin notes that some of those "from your people" have believed in Christ.[34] If Justin prefers the term γένος to ἔθνος in relation to the Jews – perhaps because of his knowledge that the scriptures typically distinguish between τὰ ἔθνη and Israel[35] – he nevertheless also identifies the Jews as an ἔθνος in a variety of ways.[36] In *Dial.* 17.1, for instance, he states "no other nation has engaged in this injustice against us and against Christ, to the extent that you have."[37] Like the Greeks, Romans or

---

31 Justin, *Dial.* 78.4 (Bobichon, 398) – ἀπὸ γὰρ τῆς κατοικούσης τὴν γῆν ἐκείνην φυλῆς Ἰούδα τὸ γένος ἦν; *1 Apol.* 32.3 (Minns and Parvis, 168, my translation) – Ἰούδας γὰρ προπάτωρ Ἰουδαίων, ἀφ' οὗ καὶ τὸ Ἰουδαῖοι καλεῖσθαι ἐσχήκασι.
32 Cf. the observation in Bobichon, *Dialogue avec Tryphon* (see n. 22), 974 – "En diluant la distinction entre 'race', 'peuple', ou 'nation', c'est l'identité nationale et religieuse des Juifs que l'Apologiste s'efforce de mettre en question, afin d'inscrire l'ensemble des nations dans la perspective universaliste qui est la sienne."
33 Justin, *1 Apol.* 53.3 (Minns and Parvis, 214). There are some textual difficulties in this passage, particularly in relating 53.3 to what precedes it; cf. the discussion in Minns and Parvis, *Justin, Philosopher and Martyr* (see n. 25), 215 n. 2.
34 Justin, *Dial.* 47.3 (Bobichon, 300) – [...] οἱ ἀπὸ τοῦ γένους τοῦ ὑμετέρου πιστεύειν [...].
35 Cf. Justin, *1 Apol.* 49; 53.2–3; *Dial.* 11; 16.2 *et passim*; note also the comments in Bobichon, *Dialogue avec Tryphon* (see n. 22), 973 – "En Dial. 117, 4.5, le mot γένος, qui désigne les Juifs, est opposé à ἔθνη (= les nations). De même, en *Dial.* 131, 1, le peuple juif (λαός) est distingué de l'ensemble que constituent les nations (ἔθνη). En *I Apol.* 53, 3s., Samaritains et Juifs, appelés φῦλον Ἰσραήλ et οἶκος Ἰακώβ, sont dissociés des autres races d'hommes (τὰ ἄλλα πάντα γένη), appelées 'nations' (ἔθνη)."
36 See Justin, *Dial.* 19.5 where the circumcized (cf. Trypho's claim in 1.3) are called both a λαός and ἔθνος, with an appeal to Hosea; cf. the comments in B.L. White, "Justin between Paul and the Heretics: The Salvation of Christian Judaizers in the *Dialogue with Trypho*," *JECS* 26.2 (2018): 163–189, here 166, 170 about the equivalence of non-Christian Jews and other ἔθνη in the *Dialogue*.
37 Justin, *Dial.* 17.1 (Bobichon, 224) – Οὐχ οὕτως γὰρ τὰ ἄλλα ἔθνη εἰς ταύτην τὴν ἀδικίαν τὴν εἰς ἡμᾶς καὶ τὸν Χριστὸν ἐνέχονται, ὅσον ὑμεῖς [...].

other ἔθνη/γένη, Jews have a land,[38] local government,[39] a language,[40] and a common genealogy.[41] Similarly, they have a common set of religious/ritual observances which are intimately linked with what we might term their cultural or religious identity.[42] Trypho expresses bewilderment at Christians on exactly this point. Christians, he says, "claim to be pious and different from others" but in no way distinguish themselves from the nations (τὰ ἔθνη). The examples that he adduces for distinctive practices are notably Jewish: observing a specific (implicitly Jewish) festal calendar and the sabbath, practicing circumcision.[43] In other words, Trypho's Jewish people are treated as an ἔθνος among all the other ἔθνη in the world.[44]

As noted above, Justin appropriates a similar ethnic reasoning to describe Christians.[45] As "true Israel," and therefore the true descendants of Abraham,

---

38 Justin, *1 Apol.* 32.4; 47.1; 53.3; *Dial.* 78.4 (linking land and genealogy).
39 Justin, *1 Apol.* 31.2; 40.6; *Dial.* 49.4.
40 Justin, *1 Apol.* 31.1; 33.7 (Hebrew); *Dial.* 103.5 (Judean and Syrian language). Bobichon notes a textual difficulty here with the presence of the doubled explanation of σατᾶ, the second of which is glossed with τῇ Ἑβραίων ἑρμηνευθείσῃ φωνῇ. While Otto deletes this the phrase from ταυτόν to φωνῇ, Marcovich and Semisch keep it with some minor emendation. See the apparatus in Bobichon, *Dialogue avec Tryphon* (see n. 22), 464 n. 11.
41 Justin, *1 Apol.* 32.1–4; cf. *Dial.* 78.4 where the "land of Judah" is linked with the "γένος of the tribe of Judah."
42 Cf. the summary of "an important cluster of ancient conventions" around "ethnic reasoning" (drawn from Herodotus *Hist.* 8.144.2) in Buell, *Why This New Race* (see n. 23), 37–38; cf. the similar account of conventions in J.M. Lieu, *Christian Identity in the Jewish and Graeco-Roman World* (Oxford: Oxford University Press, 2004), 104–108.
43 Justin, *Dial.* 10.3 (Bobichon, 208) – Εκεῖνο δὲ ἀποροῦμεν μάλιστα, εἰ ὑμεῖς, εὐσεβεῖν λέγοντες καὶ τῶν ἄλλων οἰόμενοι διαφέρειν, κατ' οὐδὲν αὐτῶν ἀπολείπεσθε, οὐδὲ διαλλάσσετε ἀπὸ τῶν ἐθνῶν τὸν ὑμέτερον βίον, ἐν τῷ μήτε τὰς ἑορτάς, μήτε τὰ σάββατα τηρεῖν, μήτε τὴν περιτομὴν ἔχειν. It is perhaps worth noting that the Samaritans were also known to practice circumcision, no doubt linked by the second century with their devotion to their version of the Pentateuch.
44 So also Bobichon, *Dialogue avec Tryphon* (see n. 22), 974 on Justin, *Dial.* 130.3 – "En *Dial.* 130, 3, Israël est présenté comme une race élue parmi d'autres races." Note the citation of Isa 1:3–4 in Justin, *1 Apol.* 37.2 (Minns and Parvis, 178), where Israel is called an ἔθνος ἁμαρτωλόν. It is perhaps worth noting the argument of O. Skarsaune, *The Proof from Prophecy: A Study in Justin Martyr's Proof-Text Tradition: Text-Type, Provenance, Theological Profile*, NovTSup 56 (Leiden: Brill, 1987), 158 that, while two citations from Isaiah in Justin, *1 Apol.* 37 probably originate in an anti-cultic testimonium, the appeal to Isa 1:3–4 is Justin's own appropriation of the prophecy for "anti-Jewish" purposes, even if one wants to qualify the latter description.
45 This is demonstrated convincingly in Buell, *Why This New Race* (see n. 23), 98–109, who notes the consistent efforts at constructing "race" (γένος) in antiquity; cf. the comments in Bobichon, *Dialogue avec Tryphon* (see n. 22), 971 – "En plusieurs passages, Justin se montre préoccupé par leur définition, à laquelle il n'accorde pas seulement une dimension terminologique."

Isaac and Jacob, Christians too are characterized by a common lineage.⁴⁶ Accordingly, they are described explicitly as a people, race and nation (λαός, γένος, ἔθνος). Of course, Justin is not the first writer to use ethno-racial language with respect to Christians. In a way very similar to the apologist, the *Epistle to Diognetus* refers to Christians as a "new race" (καινὸν γένος) which is both entirely distinctive in worship (θεοσεβεία) from other people but also indistinguishable by other typical ethnic indicators such as language, geography or customs.⁴⁷ When applied to Christians, ethnic distinctives undergo necessary modifications in Justin's work: Christians lack a common geography or language and their forefathers are inherited by faith, rather than by physical descent.⁴⁸ Nevertheless, in Justin's account, Christians are not "merely a people [λαός], but [...] also a *holy people*" who were prophesied by Isaiah.⁴⁹ As the people whom God chose, Christians are not like just any other people (δῆμος), tribe (φῦλον), or nation (ἔθνη) such as the Carians, Phrygians, Arabs, Egyptians or Idumaeans, but they are the ἔθνος promised to Abraham.⁵⁰ How does this non-biological genealogy work? Just as Abraham was called by Christ's voice to leave his land (ἐξελθεῖν ἀπὸ τῆς γῆς), so also have Christians been called by the same voice to leave their former way of life (ἐξήλθομεν [...] ἀπὸ τῆς πολιτείας) that they shared with inhabitants of the land (τὰ κοινὰ τῶν ἄλλων τῆς γῆς οἰκητόρων).⁵¹ In short, Christians gain Abraham as their forefather through a shared calling by and obedience to Christ.⁵²

That this obedience entails a new way of life that is distinct from "other inhabitants of the land" – implying broad applicability to any Christian in any "land" whatsoever – points toward Justin's concern to highlight the religious

---

46 Justin, *Dial.* 11.5; 119, et passim.
47 Diogn. 1; 5 (B.D. Ehrman, ed., *The Apostolic Fathers*, LCL [Cambridge, MA: Harvard University Press, 2003]). Not accidentally, this is the work from which Buell draws the title of her work; cf. her discussion in Buell, *Why This New Race* (see n. 23), 29–32.
48 Cf. comments in Buell, *Why This New Race* (see n. 23), 99–100.
49 Justin, *Dial.* 119.3 (Bobichon, 502); citing Isa 62:12 – καὶ καλέσει αὐτὸν λαὸν ἅγιον λελυτρωμένον ὑπὸ κυρίου [...].
50 Justin, *Dial.* 119.4 (Bobichon, 502) – Οὐκοῦν οὐκ εὐκαταφρόνητος δῆμός ἐσμεν, οὐδὲ βάρβαρον φῦλον, οὐδὲ ὁποῖα Καρῶν ἢ Φρυγῶν ἔθνη· ἀλλὰ καὶ ἡμᾶς ἐξελέξατο ὁ Θεός [...].
51 Justin, *Dial.* 119.5 (Bobichon, 503), citing and commenting on the Gen 12:1; cf. the brief comments in Skarsaune, *Proof from Prophecy* (see n. 44), 346.
52 Justin's argument here appears to draw on Paul's comments on Abraham in Galatians and Romans, on which see recently, K.B. Neutel, "'Neither Jew nor Greek': Abraham as a Universal Ancestor," in *Abraham, the Nations and the Hagarites: Jewish, Christian, and Islamic Perspectives on Kinship with Abraham*, ed. M. Goodman, G.H. van Kooten, and J.T.A.G.M. van Ruiten, TBN 13 (Leiden: Brill, 2010), 291–306.

boundaries of the Christian γένος (including doctrinal and ritual boundaries). As is well known, Justin wrote an entire treatise against "all the heresies that have arisen" and these divergent forms of Christianity remain a clear concern in the *Dialogue*.[53] For example, following Justin's assurance that no Christian from among the Gentiles would ever worship idols or eat idol meat (εἰδωλόθυτον), Trypho interjects that some Christians do in fact eat such food.[54] Justin admits that, of course, there are some who profess to be Christians but whose teaching proceeds from "the spirits of error," in contradistinction to those who are "disciples of the true and pure teaching about Jesus Christ."[55] The former "call themselves Christians" (Χριστιανοὺς ἑαυτοὺς λέγουσιν) but Justin considers them ill-suited to the name and calls them instead according to their supposed founders: the "Marcionites, Valentinians, Basilideans, Saturnalians, and others with other names."[56] That is, the "chosen nation" in Christ, descending from Abraham, is delimited by specific practices and teachings.

So too the Jews, on Justin's telling. Jews are those who keep the law of Moses and can distinguish between those groups who *are* Jews and who only claim to be so. In the former case, we have already seen Trypho's evident perplexity at the fact that Christians do not follow the Mosaic Law.[57] Further, Justin regularly identifies Trypho as a follower of particular "teachers," who are presented as leading the Jewish people astray in their scriptural interpretations.[58] Indeed, Justin's literary avatar links Trypho's teachers directly with the Pharisees, opposing contemporary Christians as the latter opposed Christ: "do not revile the Son of God nor, trusting your Pharisaic teachers, scorn the king of Israel (as your syn-

---

[53] Justin, *1 Apol.* 26.8 (Minns and Parvis, 152) – Ἔστι δὲ ἡμῖν καὶ σύνταγμα κατὰ πασῶν τῶν γεγενημένων αἱρέσεων συντεταγμένον. On the anti-heretical concern of the *Dialogue*, see below and esp. the recent argument in M. den Dulk, *Between Jews and Heretics: Refiguring Justin Martyr's Dialogue with Trypho* (London and New York, NY: Routledge, 2018).

[54] Justin, *Dial.* 34.8–35.1. Justin here displays dependence on Paul's comments in 1 Cor 8–10, where the term εἰδωλόθυτος appears for the first time; cf. B.A. Edsall, *Paul's Witness to Formative Early Christian Instruction*, WUNT 2/365 (Tübingen: Mohr Siebeck, 2014), 102.

[55] Justin, *Dial.* 35.2 (Bobichon, 270) – Κἀγὼ ἀπεκρινάμην· Καὶ ἐκ τοῦ τοιούτους εἶναι ἄνδρας, ὁμολογοῦντας ἑαυτοὺς εἶναι Χριστιανοὺς καὶ τὸν σταυρωθέντα Ἰησοῦν ὁμολογεῖν καὶ κύριον καὶ Χριστόν, καὶ μὴ τὰ ἐκείνου διδάγματα διδάσκοντας, ἀλλὰ τὰ ἀπὸ τῶν τῆς πλάνης πνευμάτων, ἡμεῖς, οἱ τῆς ἀληθινῆς Ἰησοῦ Χριστοῦ καὶ καθαρᾶς διδασκαλίας μαθηταί, πιστότεροι καὶ βεβαιότεροι γινόμεθα ἐν τῇ ἐλπίδι τῇ κατηγγελμένῃ ὑπ' αὐτοῦ.

[56] Justin, *Dial.* 35.6 (Bobichon, 270) – Καί εἰσιν αὐτῶν οἱ μέν τινες καλούμενοι Μαρκιανοί, οἱ δὲ Οὐαλεντινιανοί, οἱ δὲ Βασιλειδιανοί, οἱ δὲ Σατορνιλιανοί, καὶ ἄλλοι ἄλλῳ ὀνόματι, ἀπὸ τοῦ ἀρχηγέτου τῆς γνώμης ἕκαστος ὀνομαζόμενος.

[57] Justin, *Dial.* 10–11; cf. 45.2 et passim.

[58] On the Jewish religious authorities in the *Dialogue* generally, see P. Bobichon, "Autorités religieuses juives et 'sectes' juives dans l'œuvre de Justin Martyr," *REAug* 48 (2002): 3–22.

agogue leaders teach you to do after prayer)."⁵⁹ Justin's construal of Jewish religious boundaries is granted further clarity, somewhat ironically, by the famously opaque list of Jewish heresies in *Dial.* 80.4.⁶⁰ Justin begins by telling Trypho that if he hears someone claim to be a Christian while not professing belief in the physical resurrection of the dead, he should not think of them as a Christian. The apologist drives his point home with an appeal to Trypho's recognition of diverse claims to being Jewish:

> [...] do not think them Christian just as you would not confess Sadducees to be Jews, if one were to consider it carefully, or the similar heresies of the Genistai, Meristai, Galileans, Hellenians and Pharisee-baptists [...] who claim to be Jews and the children of Abraham and 'confess God with their lips,' as God himself cries, 'but their hearts are far from him.'⁶¹

Matthijs den Dulk has rightly noted that Justin's list here is prescriptive, rather than strictly descriptive, insofar as he appears to admit that Trypho would have to consider the matter carefully rather than have such heresiological dis-

---

59 Justin, *Dial.* 137.2 (Bobichon, 550) – μὴ λοιδορῆτε ἐπὶ τὸν υἱὸν τοῦ θεοῦ, μηδὲ Φαρισαίοις πειθόμενοι διδασκάλοις τὸν βασιλέα τοῦ Ἰσραὴλ ἐπισκώψητέ ποτε [...]; cf. e.g., *Dial.* 102.5 (Bobichon, 460) – Ἡ γὰρ τοῦ ἰσχυροῦ αὐτοῦ λόγου δύναμις, δι' ἧς ἀεὶ ἤλεγχε τοὺς συζητοῦντας αὐτῷ Φαρισαίους καὶ γραμματεῖς καὶ ἁπλῶς τοὺς ἐν τῷ γένει ὑμῶν διδασκάλους [...], and *Dial.* 117.3–4 (Bobichon, 498) with its reference to οἱ ἀρχιερεῖς τοῦ λαοῦ ὑμῶν καὶ διδάσκαλοι leading Trypho's people astray. On this, see B.A. Edsall, "Scribes, Pharisees, Sadducees and Trypho: Jewish Leadership and Jesus Traditions in Justin's Construal of Christian and Jewish Identity," in *The Reception of Jewish Tradition in the Social Construction of Early Christianity*, ed. J.M.G. Barclay and K. Crabbe (London: T&T Clark/Bloomsbury, forthcoming).
60 See the recent discussion in den Dulk, *Between Jews and Heretics* (see n. 53), responding to G.S. Smith, *Guilt by Association: Heresy Catalogues in Early Christianity* (Oxford: Oxford University Press, 2014) and Boyarin, *Border Lines* (see n. 2); cf. the brief but illuminating treatment in Bobichon, "Autorités religieuses" (see n. 58) and the still relevant discussion in A. Le Boulluec, *La notion d'hérésie dans la littérature grecque, IIe-IIIe siècles*, 2 vols. (Paris: Etudes augustiniennes, 1985), 1:70–77.
61 Justin, *Dial.* 80.4 (Bobichon, 406) – [...] μὴ ὑπολάβητε αὐτοὺς Χριστιανούς, ὥσπερ οὐδὲ Ἰουδαίους, ἄν τις ὀρθῶς ἐξετάσῃ, ὁμολογήσειεν εἶναι τοὺς Σαδδουκαίους ἢ τὰς ὁμοίας αἱρέσεις Γενιστῶν καὶ Μεριστῶν καὶ Γαλιλαίων καὶ Ἑλληνιανῶν καὶ Φαρισαίων Βαπτιστῶν (καὶ μὴ ἀηδῶς ἀκούσητέ μου πάντα ἃ φρονῶ λέγοντος), ἀλλὰ λεγομένους μὲν Ἰουδαίους καὶ τέκνα Ἀβραάμ, καὶ χείλεσιν ὁμολογοῦντας τὸν θεόν, ὡς αὐτὸς κέκραγεν ὁ θεός, τὴν δὲ καρδίαν πόρρω ἔχειν ἀπ' αὐτοῦ. On reading the final "heresy" with the manuscript witness, see esp. Bobichon, "Autorités religieuses" (see n. 58). While arguments for scribal intervention have been made in a variety of directions, perhaps the most plausible remains that of Harnack, that Φαρισαίων was added by a later copyist who wanted to bring it closer to the well-known list of seven Jewish sects, also seen in Hegisippus's list (in Eusebius, *Hist. eccl.* 4.22.7); cf. Harnack, *Rede des Paulus in Athen?* (see n. 3), 57–58.

course immediately ready to hand.⁶² Even so, the list itself entails that Justin's portrayal of Judaism is such that certain doctrines – among them resurrection, given the context and the prominence of the Sadducees – are requisite to qualify for the name "Jew."

The parallels established by means of Justin's ethno-racial reasoning enable him to highlight the contrasts between his Christianity and Trypho's Judaism. It is based, however, on a presumption that both parties share a common discursive space, not only with respect to the familiar cluster of ethno-racial entailments but also with respect to a shared (though disputed) scriptural basis, a common religious vocabulary and even certain common practices, such as a rejection of "idolatry."⁶³ As Judith Lieu noted, "Justin could not have had the same sort of dialogue with a Greek philosopher as he has with Trypho, for Judaism and Greek philosophy do not stand on a par as 'preparations for the Gospel.'"⁶⁴ Justin's sketch of a shared discursive space and his argumentative logic might seem to lead to a view that "Christian" and "Jewish" *are* mutually exclusive categories. The problem with this conclusion, though, is that Jewish religious practices inhabit a rather tricky space for Justin. Explored in more detail below, Justin admits it is possible for both Jewish and Gentile Christians to continue practicing the Mosaic Law while being Christians.⁶⁵ Unlike those of other nations, then, Jews *can* continue living in line with their ancestral πολιτεία while also living in Christ.⁶⁶

---

62 den Dulk, *Between Jews and Heretics* (see n. 53), 112, 143.
63 Cf. Justin, *Dial.* 34.8 (Bobichon, 268) in which King Solomon is criticized for his idolatry even as Christians are vindicated by their rejection of it – Ἀλλὰ καὶ τολμῶ λέγειν ἃ γέγραπται ἐν ταῖς Βασιλείαις ὑπ' αὐτοῦ πραχθέντα, ὅτι διὰ γυναῖκα ἐν Σιδῶνι εἰδωλολάτρει· ὅπερ οὐχ ὑπομένουσι πρᾶξαι οἱ ἀπὸ τῶν ἐθνῶν διὰ Ἰησοῦ τοῦ σταυρωθέντος ἐπιγνόντες τὸν ποιητὴν τῶν ὅλων Θεόν, ἀλλὰ πᾶσαν αἰκίαν καὶ τιμωρίαν μέχρις ἐσχάτου θανάτου ὑπομένουσι περὶ τοῦ μήτε εἰδωλολατρῆσαι, μήτε εἰδωλόθυτα φαγεῖν; cf. the comments in *Dial.* 19, 22 et passim. In *1 Apology*, Justin links idols with the work of demons; e.g., *1 Apol.* 41.1; 64.1 (*pace* the interpretive note in Minns and Parvis, 251); see *1 Apol.* 49.5 for his praise of gentile Christians for rejecting idols.
64 J.M. Lieu, *Image and Reality: The Jews in the World of the Christians in the Second Century* (London and New York, NY: T&T Clark, 1996), 113. The issue of the σπερματικὸς λόγος (*2 Apol.* 8) might be seen to complicate this point, though the philosophical auto-biography Justin provides in *Dial.* 1–8 clearly subordinates any truth present in Stoic or Platonic philosophy to the truth present in the scriptures, which are a shared point of contact between Trypho and Justin.
65 Esp. in Justin, *Dial.* 47, see below.
66 See his claim about nations leaving their ancestral πολιτεία in Justin, *Dial.* 119.5, discussed above, and cf. the comments in Buell, *Why This New Race* (see n. 23), 112 – "Justin [...] never entertains the possibility that a Phrygian, Egyptian, or Greek could maintain their ancestral customs after having become a follower of Christ." On the link between Jewish religious practices

Moreover, the apparent equivalence (and, therefore, exclusivity) in Justin's use of ethno-racial logic for Jewishness and Christianness breaks down to the degree that his construal of the latter tends toward a view of Christians as the universal γένος.⁶⁷ Justin not only claims that Christians are made up of people from every nation, as noted above, but also that they follow laws and practices that are universally valid and have been anticipated and prophesied in scripture.⁶⁸ Indeed, the idea that God – who is always the same (ὁ αὐτὸς ὢν ἀεί) – would not want everyone to practice the same righteous deeds throughout history is declared "laughable and stupid" (γελοῖα καὶ ἀνόητα).⁶⁹ Christians, then, are the ideal people, able to persuade those from any other nation who are willing to live according to the perfect law of Christ, enacting both perfect philanthropy and perfect piety.⁷⁰

There is, undoubtedly, more than a hint of what Judith Lieu referred to as "the language of competition and take over" in Justin's writings.⁷¹ Incorporating people from every nation into a new nation appears to entail a certain amount of erasure: leaving their previous ways of life for the new way of Christ. But this is not Justin's focus when it comes to his debate with Trypho. Rather, it is here that

---

and their identity as the Jewish πολιτεία, see the discussion in B.A. Edsall, "Persuasion and Force in 4 Maccabees: Appropriating a Political Dialectic," *JSJ* 48.1 (2017): 92–112.

67 Cf. the comments in Buell, *Why This New Race* (see n. 23), 110, though her argument that Justin's view that the "universal" and "eternal" aspects of Christianity connote fluidity in comparison with the fixity of Judaism seems to miss the fixity in God's laws, plan, will and people implied by Justin in the *Dialogue*. That which is seen to be grounded in the unchanging will of God is not a likely contender for marking fluidity.

68 Justin, *Dial.* 67.6–10 (Bobichon, 366–368), where those righteous before Moses and the promised "new covenant" from Jer 31:31 show τί μὲν ὡς αἰώνιον καὶ παντὶ γένει ἁρμόζον, καὶ ἔνταλμα καὶ ἔργον ὁ Θεὸς ἐπίσταται [...].

69 Justin, *Dial.* 23.1–2 (Bobichon, 240) – Ἐὰν δὲ ταῦτα οὕτως μὴ ὁμολογήσωμεν, συμβήσεται ἡμῖν εἰς ἄτοπα ἐμπίπτειν νοήματα, ὡς τοῦ αὐτοῦ θεοῦ μὴ ὄντος τοῦ κατὰ τὸν Ἐνὼχ καὶ τοὺς ἄλλους πάντας, οἳ μήτε περιτομὴν τὴν κατὰ σάρκα ἔχοντες μήτε σάββατα ἐφύλαξαν μήτε δὲ τὰ ἄλλα, Μωϋσέως ἐντειλαμένου ταῦτα ποιεῖν, ἢ τὰ αὐτὰ αὐτῶν δίκαια μὴ ἀεὶ πᾶν γένος ἀνθρώπων βεβουλῆσθαι πράσσειν· ἅπερ γελοῖα καὶ ἀνόητα ὁμολογεῖν φαίνεται. Δι' αἰτίαν δὲ τὴν τῶν ἁμαρτωλῶν ἀνθρώπων, τὸν αὐτὸν ὄντα ἀεὶ ταῦτα καὶ τὰ τοιαῦτα ἐντετάλθαι ὁμολογεῖν, καὶ φιλάνθρωπον καὶ προγνώστην καὶ ἀνενδεῆ καὶ δίκαιον καὶ ἀγαθὸν ἀποφαίνειν ἐστίν.

70 On the nexus of persuasion (and force), piety and philanthropy in Greek, Roman and Jewish political discourse, see Edsall, "Persuasion and Force in 4 Maccabees" (see n. 66); a presentation of Christians as the ideal πολιτεία is found as early as the book of Acts; see esp. T.C. Penner, "Civilizing Discourse: Acts, Declamation, and the Rhetoric of the *Polis*," in *Contextualizing Acts: Lukan Narrative and Greco-Roman Discourse*, ed. idem and C. Vander Stichele, Symposium (Atlanta, GA: Society of Biblical Literature, 2003), 65–104.

71 Lieu, *Image and Reality* (see n. 64), 136.

his argument that Christians are "true" Israel comes back in force.[72] Jews and Christians are not simply an opposed binary because Christians are not a *new* universal people, but are universal through time precisely as *verus Israel*. Even more pointedly, relative to his portrayal of Trypho, Christians are the true descendants of Judah – in Christ, they are also true Jews.[73] Christians, then, predate the Mosaic Law and include all those who lived "with the Logos."[74] Moses and Melchizedek were Christians *avant la lettre* and, by Justin's logic, so were all faithful Israelites and Jews. Any who were unfaithful had already departed from the way of life, and so were also already the targets of prophetic critique in scripture. Put differently, if one wants to speak of a "parting" in Justin's terms, it is one that happened long ago and continues to happen whenever an Israelite or Jew rejects God's will or his Messiah. It is not principally distinction between actual social groups but rather a claim about theological legitimacy. Justin does not, therefore, construct a reality of a parting of ways between Christians and Jews, but rather works to establish a line of direct continuity between true Israel past and true Israel present – running from Abraham to Christ and

---

[72] This is not to enter into the debate about the audience of the *Dialogue*; this view holds whether Justin's concerns are internal polemic or external apologetic. While a number of recent writers have opted for an entirely internal Christian audience – esp. M.S. Taylor, *Anti-Judaism and Early Christian Identity: A Critique of the Scholarly Consensus*, Studia post-Biblica 46 (Leiden: Brill, 1995); den Dulk, *Between Jews and Heretics* (see n. 53); T. Rajak, *The Jewish Dialogue with Greece and Rome: Studies in Cultural and Social Interaction* (Leiden: Brill, 2001), 511–533; D. Rokéah, *Justin Martyr and the Jews*, JCPS 5 (Leiden: Brill, 2002); Boyarin, *Border Lines* (see n. 2) et al. – the careful and somewhat agnostic treatment in Lieu, *Image and Reality* (see n. 64), 108–109 remains compelling.

[73] In addition to the place of Judah in Justin, *Dial.* 11.5, discussed earlier, see esp. *Dial.* 120.2 (Bobichon, 504–506) – Εἴγε δὲ καὶ τὴν εὐλογίαν Ἰούδα καταμάθοις, ἴδοις ἂν ὃ λέγω. Μερίζεται γὰρ τὸ σπέρμα ἐξ Ἰακώβ, καὶ διὰ Ἰούδα καὶ Φαρές, καὶ Ἰεσσαὶ καὶ Δαβὶδ κατέρχεται. Ταῦτα δ᾽ ἦν σύμβολα ὅτι τινὲς τοῦ γένους ὑμῶν εὑρεθήσονται τέκνα Ἀβραάμ, καὶ ἐν μερίδι τοῦ Χριστοῦ εὑρισκόμενοι, ἄλλοι δὲ τέκνα μὲν τοῦ Ἀβραάμ, ὡς ἡ ἄμμος δὲ ἡ ἐπὶ τὸ χεῖλος τῆς θαλάσσης ὄντες, ἥτις ἄγονός τε καὶ ἄκαρπος, πολλὴ μὲν καὶ ἀναρίθμητος ὑπάρχουσα, οὐδὲν δὲ ὅλως καρπογονοῦσα, ἀλλὰ μόνον τὸ ὕδωρ τῆς θαλάσσης πίνουσα. He continues, arguing that the prophecy about a ruler from Judah (Gen 49:10) "was not spoken to Judah but to Christ" (Καὶ τοῦτο ὅτι οὐκ εἰς Ἰούδαν ἐρρέθη, ἀλλ᾽ εἰς τὸν Χριστόν, φαίνεται).

[74] Justin, *1 Apol.* 46.3 (Minns and Parvis, 200) – καὶ οἱ μετὰ λόγου βιώσαντες Χριστιανοί εἰσι, κἂν ἄθεοι ἐνομίσθησαν, οἷον ἐν Ἕλλησι μὲν Σωκράτης καὶ Ἡράκλειτος καὶ οἱ ὅμοιοι αὐτοῖς, ἐν βαρβάροις δὲ Ἀβραὰμ καὶ Ἀνανίας καὶ Ἀζαρίας καὶ Μισαὴλ καὶ Ἠλίας καὶ ἄλλοι πολλοί, ὧν τὰς πράξεις ἢ τὰ ὀνόματα καταλέγειν μακρὸν εἶναι ἐπιστάμενοι, τὰ νῦν παραιτούμεθα; cf. *Dial.* 19.4–6; 45.3–4; etc.

then on to Christians.⁷⁵ As far as Justin is concerned, Jews have not "parted" from Christians *en masse*; rather, true Israel and true Jews have been a constant line, while *some* Jews (now and then, in Justin's view) reject Christ as the true *logos* of scripture.⁷⁶

Justin's formulation of Judaism and Christianity, then, is highly theological and, to that extent, leaves relatively untouched the scholarly question which drives the use of the "parting of the ways" imagery, namely, the social realities of early Jewish Christian relations. The apologist appears unconcerned with such social-historical questions. Even so, Justin does occasionally provide clues, even despite himself, about the social realities of his day. I turn to one particularly important passage now.

3 The Parting: "I suppose they will probably be saved [...]"

In an oft discussed section of the *Dialogue*, Trypho directly poses the question: does observing the Law necessarily disqualify a person from being saved? The exchange that follows constitutes the clearest witness to the potential for ongoing religious and social relations between Jews and Christians in Justin's time, that is, to the question of whether Justin offers evidence about a parting of the ways. Trypho asks:

> If some even now desire to live observing those matters commanded by Moses while they believe in this crucified Jesus – acknowledging that he is God's Christ and that it has been given to him to judge simply everyone and that his is the eternal kingdom – are they still able to be saved?⁷⁷

---

75 Pace Cohen, "The Ways that Parted" (see n. 1), 314, Justin does not refer to Christians as the *new* Israel vs. *old* Israel but rather as *true* Israel, which points not toward a construction of rupture but of continuity.
76 See e.g., Trypho's recognition that Justin's interpretation of prophecies against the faithless in Israel are directed against himself in Justin, *Dial.* 25.6 (Bobichon, 246) – Καὶ ὁ Τρύφων Τί οὖν ἐστιν ὃ λέγεις; ὅτι οὐδεὶς ἡμῶν κληρονομήσει ἐν τῷ ὄρει τῷ ἁγίῳ τοῦ Θεοῦ οὐδέν;
77 Justin, *Dial.* 46.1 (Bobichon, 296) – Ἐὰν δέ τινες καὶ νῦν ζῆν βούλωνται φυλάσσοντες τὰ διὰ Μωϋσέως διαταχθέντα, καὶ πιστεύσωσιν ἐπὶ τοῦτον τὸν σταυρωθέντα Ἰησοῦν, ἐπιγνόντες ὅτι αὐτός ἐστιν ὁ Χριστὸς τοῦ Θεοῦ, καὶ αὐτῷ δέδοται τὸ κρῖναι πάντας ἁπλῶς, καὶ αὐτοῦ ἐστιν ἡ αἰώνιος βασιλεία, δύνανται καὶ αὐτοὶ σωθῆναι;

Justin's initial response appears negative but does not directly answer the question.[78] Trypho presses him for a clear answer: even granting all of Justin's points, can a person who confesses Jesus to be the Christ *and* follows the Law be saved? Justin's response reveals a significant variety in Christian views and practices in relation to the Law. His view is summed up by his first answer:

> In my view, Trypho, I say that such a person will be saved, unless he tries to convince other people to observe these things in every situation, while saying that they will not be saved unless they observe these things (I'm speaking about those Gentiles circumcised from error by Christ).[79]

Famously, Trypho asks whether Justin's caveat – "in my view" – indicates that other Christians would disagree with his position. This gives the apologist the opportunity to differentiate his view from those of a more stringent anti-Jewish group of Christians. "There are some," he admits, "who dare not to share conversation or fellowship" with law-observant Christians, though he does not agree with them.[80] The language of hospitality (κοινωνεῖν) is not insignificant for Justin: Christians share with those in need; God commands to avoid any fellowship with thieves; (true) Christians have no κοινωνία with those who blaspheme Christ while claiming to be Christian.[81] This is more than mere fellowship-as-

---

78 Justin, *Dial*. 46.2–7 (Bobichon, 296–298) – Justin reiterates his denial that observing the whole Law is possible (Συσκεψώμεθα κἀκεῖνο, εἰ ἔνεστιν, ἔλεγον, φυλάσσειν τὰ διὰ Μωϋσέως διαταχθέντα ἅπαντα νῦν); notes the righteous who preceded the Mosaic Law and were not beholden to it (Ἀβραάμ, καὶ Ἰσαάκ, καὶ Ἰακώβ, καὶ Νῶε, καὶ Ἰώβ, καὶ εἴ τινες ἄλλοι γεγόνασι πρὸ τούτων ἢ μετὰ τούτους ὁμοίως δίκαιοι […] Ὅτι δὲ μέχρι Μωϋσέως οὐδεὶς ἁπλῶς δίκαιος οὐδὲν ὅλως τούτων περὶ ὧν ἐζητοῦμεν ἐφύλαξεν, οὐδὲ ἐντολὴν ἔλαβε φυλάσσειν, πλὴν τὴν ἀρχὴν λαβούσης ἀπὸ Ἀβραὰμ τῆς περιτομῆς, ἐπίστασθε.); claims that the Mosaic commandments given on account of hard-heartedness do not conduce to just actions or piety (Διὰ τὸ σκληροκάρδιον τοῦ λαοῦ ὑμῶν πάντα τὰ τοιαῦτα ἐντάλματα νοεῖτε τὸν Θεὸν διὰ Μωϋσέως ἐντειλάμενον ὑμῖν).
79 Justin, *Dial*. 47.1 (Bobichon, 300) – Κἀγώ. Ὡς μὲν ἐμοὶ δοκεῖ, ὦ Τρύφων, λέγω ὅτι σωθήσεται ὁ τοιοῦτος, ἐὰν μὴ τοὺς ἄλλους ἀνθρώπους, λέγω δὴ τοὺς ἀπὸ τῶν ἐθνῶν διὰ τοῦ Χριστοῦ ἀπὸ τῆς πλάνης περιτμηθέντας, ἐκ παντὸς πείθειν ἀγωνίζηται, ταὐτὰ αὑτῷ φυλάσσειν, λέγων οὐ σωθήσεσθαι αὐτούς, ἐὰν μὴ ταῦτα φυλάξωσιν; cf. 47.3.
80 Justin, *Dial*. 47.2 (Bobichon, 300) – Εἰσίν, ἀπεκρινάμην, ὦ Τρύφων, καὶ μηδὲ κοινωνεῖν ὁμιλίας ἢ ἑστίας τοῖς τοιούτοις τολμῶντες. οἷς ἐγὼ οὐ σύναινός εἰμι.
81 Christians share their goods in common in Justin, *1 Apol*. 14.2 (Minns and Parvis, 112 – καὶ παντὶ δεομένῳ κοινωνοῦντες; cf. 15.10); avoiding fellowship with thieves in Justin, *Dial*. 27.2 (Bobichon, 248 – μήτε κοινωνοὶ κλεπτῶν; alluding to Isa 1:15); rejecting the fellowship of blasphemers in *Dial*. 35.5 (Bobichon, 270 – ὧν οὐδενὶ κοινωνοῦμεν). Similarly, Justin's Trypho suggests that Jewish teachers urge Jews to cease fellowship with Christians as blasphemers; *Dial*. 38.1 (Bo-

conversation. From the perspective of "the parting," Justin appears to know of a group of Christians who would argue for complete separation from those who follow any Jewish religious or cultural practices. In this light, the fact that Justin *rejects* Christians who refuse fellowship with Jews immediately places the "parting" model in question. His view is decidedly more moderate, even if it is hard to know how representative he is.[82]

To these groups, Justin adds another. His concern to keep Jewish believers in Christ from imposing the Law on their fellow Gentile (or even Jewish) believers leads him to consider the fate of Gentiles who are persuaded by their law-proselytizing friends. "Those who are convinced in favor of a law-observant way of life while maintaining the confession in God's Christ, I suppose they will probably be saved."[83] Whatever else happens, though, Justin denies salvation to those who deny that Jesus is the Christ and especially to those who curse Christians "in their synagogues."[84]

In total, Justin's answer points toward six groups of people with distinct views of the Law and Christ. The first two groups are found among those law-observant Jewish believers that Trypho posits. Justin divides this group between proselytizing and non-proselytizing varieties of law-observant believers. While it is possible that these groups include law-observant Gentiles, the larger context of Justin's argument indicates that Jewish believers are principally in view here.[85] Alongside these two groups of Jewish believers, Justin identifies three groups of Gentile Christians. The first, whose views are rejected by Justin, are strictly anti-Jewish. The second are more moderate in their rejection of the Law while accepting non-proselytizing Jewish believers as "brothers," and are represented by Justin himself. The third group are the Gentiles who are convinced by their Jewish "brethren" that they ought to observe the Mosaic Law. Finally, there is a group of

---

bichon, 276) – Καὶ ὁ Τρύφων εἶπεν Ὦ ἄνθρωπε, καλὸν ἦν πεισθέντας ἡμᾶς τοῖς διδασκάλοις νομοθετήσασι μηδενὶ ἐξ ὑμῶν ὁμιλεῖν, μηδέ σοι τούτων κοινωνῆσαι τῶν λόγων.

82 On the relative moderation of Justin's views, see A. Laato, "Justin Martyr Encounters Judaism," in *Encounters of the Children of Abraham from Ancient to Modern Times: Encounters of the Children of Abraham from Ancient to Modern Times*, ed. eadem and P. Lindqvist, Studies on the children of Abraham 1 (Leiden: Brill, 2010), 97–123.

83 Justin, *Dial.* 47.4 (Bobichon, 302) – Τοὺς δὲ πειθομένους αὐτοῖς ἐπὶ τὴν ἔννομον πολιτείαν μετὰ τοῦ φυλάσσειν τὴν εἰς τὸν Χριστὸν τοῦ θεοῦ ὁμολογίαν καὶ σωθήσεσθαι ἴσως ὑπολαμβάνω.

84 Justin, *Dial.* 47.4; cf. the comments and bibliography regarding Justin's claims of persecution in n. 25 above.

85 In Justin, *Dial* 47.3, Justin refers explicitly to "those of your race" and he notes in 47.1 that his concern about proselytism is mainly related to "those from the Gentiles."

anti-Christian Jews.[86] If, on the basis of Justin's comments, one were to produce a spectrum of engagement between Jews and Christians in the middle of the second century, it would perhaps look something like this.

| Anti-Jewish Christians | Justin's Moderate Christians | Law-observant Gentile Christians | Non-proselytising Jewish Christians | Proselytising Jewish Christians | Anti-Christian Jews |

←——→

In fact, such a spectrum would undoubtedly be more complicated than it is possible to represent here since, for instance, law-observant Gentile believers might have differing views on whether they ought to persuade other Gentiles and Jews to follow the Law. Moreover, within each group, there would no doubt be a variety of views on other theological, ritual, and practical matters, implicating all manner of sectarian and so-called gnostic groups.

Even so, of these groups, only the extreme ends of the spectrum would constitute a parting of the ways in any strict sense. The other four collectively point toward an ongoing common life and there is no compelling reason to deny the label of either Jew or Christian to these middling groups, that is, to deny them a label they would claim for themselves. According to Justin's testimony, there remains an intra-Christian discussion about the place of the Law in Christian life. These different Christian groups receive (or ought to receive, in Justin's view) each other as "brothers," and engage in hospitality and socio-religious communion. If some Christians and Jews wanted to effect a "parting," Justin himself explicitly did not do so. While the size, social significance and even existence of each of these groups may be disputed, there is no reason to think that Justin's spectrum of Jewish and Christian views is entirely fictitious, given what we know about the variety of Christian and Jewish groups in the second century. Indeed, the very fact of law-observant Jews undermines Justin's argument that Christians from *all* backgrounds have left their ancestral practices, not to mention the fact that law-observant Gentiles belies his tendency to claim all real

---

86 The discussion of this passage in M. Simon, *Verus Israel: A Study of the Relations Between Christians and Jews in the Roman Empire, AD 135–425*, trans. H. McKeating (Oxford and Portland, OR: Littman Library of Jewish Civilization, 1996), 243–244 remains insightful. He notes the implication that "Jewish Christianity" still remains within the Church, for Justin, and he highlights the importance of ritual practice for defining community boundaries.

Christians agree with his view of the Law.[87] In allowing these two categories, Justin admits facts which run against the grain of his argument in important ways.

4 Conclusion

By way of conclusion, I want to return to the title of this chapter and the opening quotation from Cohen. His argument makes two closely related claims: first, that Christians and Jews had parted ways by the mid-second century and, second, that the "reality […] constructed" by Justin's writings bear witness to this. As I noted earlier, the claim that Jews and Christians (or, to a greater extent, that Judaism and Christianity) had parted ways involves a necessary level of abstraction from the particularities of individual Christian or Jewish communities, a certain essentializing of both groups that enables one to attribute agency to them. On all counts, the argument here has been that these claims do not hold up to scrutiny vis-à-vis the works of Justin Martyr. Rather than a "parting of the ways," Justin describes neither a "parting" nor two "ways." Instead, the ambiguity and messiness of his account bears witness to the ambiguous and messy reality of Jewish and Christian relations in his period.

To take the latter first, Christians and Jews, for Justin, are not described or implied to be two equivalent and mutually exclusive social-religious or even ethnic groups. Christians may well be the γένος and ἔθνος that constitutes *verus Israel*, but this is a group that also includes Jews – among those from other nations – and also allows for a continued observance of the Jewish Law by both Jewish and Gentile believers. Similarly, rather than a "parting," Justin emphasizes *continuity* between true Israel and the church as well as continuity in those who were not true Israel both then and now. The prophetic critiques are, in that sense, timeless and apply to those who reject God's *logos* in scripture and in Christ in all periods. Christians and Jews, according to Justin, however, are still in contact – not only in a generalized sense of living side by side in the Roman empire, but also in the sense of having very fuzzy boundaries and continuing to participate in a common life to varying degrees. That is to say, if some Jews and some Christians had parted ways, Justin shows that there had been no

---

[87] Cf. Justin, *Dial.* 119.5, discussed above. I am indebted to Tobias Georges for this observation; "Justin's 'Dialogue' and the Search for Contemporary Discourse between Christians and Jews: A closer look at 'Dialogue,' chapter 47" XVIII. International Conference on Patristic Studies, Oxford, 19 August – 24 August 2019.

decisive break and, perhaps more interestingly, that he anticipated no such break to be necessary or inevitable in the future.[88]

Bibliography

Baron, L., J. Hicks-Keeton, and M. Thiessen, eds., *The Ways That Often Parted: Essays in Honor of Joel Marcus*, ECL (Atlanta, GA: Society of Biblical Literature Press, 2018).

Bates, M.W., "Justin Martyr's Logocentric Hermeneutical Transformation of Isaiah's Vision of the Nations," *JTS* 60.2 (2009): 538–555.

Becker, A. H., and A. Y. Reed, eds., *The Ways that Never Parted: Jews and Christians in Late Antiquity and the Early Middle Ages*, TSAJ 95 (Tübingen: Mohr Siebeck, 2003).

Bobichon, P., "Autorités religieuses juives et 'sectes' juives dans l'œuvre de Justin Martyr," *REAug* 48 (2002): 3–22.

Bobichon, P., *Justin Martyr, Dialogue avec Tryphon: Édition critique, traduction, commentaire*, 2 vols., Paradosis (Freiburg, CH: Éditions universitaires de Fribourg, 2003).

Boyarin, D., *Border Lines: The Partition of Judaeo-Christianity* (Philadelphia, PA: University of Pennsylvania Press, 2004).

Bucur, B. G., "Justin Martyr's Exegesis of Biblical Theophanies and the Parting of the Ways between Christianity and Judaism," *TS* 75.1 (2014): 34–51.

Carleton Paget, J., *Jews, Christians and Jewish Christians in Antiquity*, WUNT 251 (Tübingen: Mohr Siebeck, 2010).

Cohen, S. J. D., "'Those Who Say They are Jews, and are Not': How Do You Know a Jew in Antiquity When you See One?," in *The Diasporas in Antiquity*, ed. idem and E. S. Frerichs (Atlanta, GA: Scholars Press, 1993), 1–45.

Cohen, S. J. D., "Common Judaism in Greek and Latin Authors," in *Redefining First-century Jewish and Christian Identities: Essays in Honor of Ed Parish Sanders*, ed. F. E. Udoh (Notre Dame, IN: Notre Dame University Press, 2008), 69–87.

Cohen, S. J. D., "The Ways That Parted: Jews, Christians, and Jewish-Christians, ca. 100–150 CE," in *Jews and Christians in the First and Second Centuries: The Interbellum 70–132 CE*, ed. J. Schwartz and P. J. Tomson, CRINT 15 (Leiden: Brill, 2018), 338–339.

de Certeau, M., *The Practice of Everyday Life,* trans. S. Rendall (Berkeley, CA: University of California Press, 1984).

den Dulk, M., *Between Jews and Heretics: Refiguring Justin Martyr's Dialogue with Trypho* (London and New York, NY: Routledge, 2018).

Edsall, B. A., *Paul's Witness to Formative Early Christian Instruction*, WUNT 2/365 (Tübingen: Mohr Siebeck, 2014).

---

[88] So I disagree with Boyarin, *Border Lines* (see n. 2), 73 when he writes, "After the time of Justin and his promulgation of Verus Israel, becoming a Christian (or follower of Christ) meant something different-it no longer entailed becoming a Jew-, and once becoming a Christian became identified with 'entering [the true] Israel,' the whole semantic/social field shifted." This is giving too much power to Justin, I think, and does not appreciate his recognition of differing Christian views and practices.

Edsall, B. A., "Persuasion and Force in 4 Maccabees: Appropriating a Political Dialectic," *JSJ* 48.1 (2017): 92–112.
Edsall, B. A., "Scribes, Pharisees, Sadducees and Trypho: Jewish Leadership and Jesus Traditions in Justin's Construal of Christian and Jewish Identity," in *The Reception of Jewish Tradition in the Social Construction of Early Christianity*, ed. J. M. G. Barclay and K. Crabbe (London: T&T Clark/Bloomsbury, forthcoming).
Ehrman, B. D., ed., *The Apostolic Fathers*, LCL (Cambridge, MA: Harvard University Press, 2003).
Falls, T. B., and T. P. Halton, trans., *St. Justin Martyr: Dialogue with Trypho,* Selections from the Fathers of the Church 3 (Washington, DC: Catholic University of America Press, 2003).
González Salinero, R., "*Sinagogae Iudaeorum, fontes persecutionum?* Il supposto intervento degli ebrei nelle persecuzioni antichristiane durante l'Impero Romano," *VetChr* 43 (2006): 93–104.
Goodman, M., "Modeling the 'Parting of the Ways'," in *The Ways that Never Parted: Jews and Christians in Late Antiquity and the Early Middle Ages*, ed. A. H. Becker and A. Y. Reed, TSAJ 95 (Tübingen: Mohr Siebeck, 2003), 119–129.
Gregerman, A., *Building on the Ruins of the Temple: Apologetics and Polemics in Early Christianity and Rabbinic Judaism*, TSAJ 165 (Tübingen: Mohr Siebeck, 2016).
Heemstra, M., *The Fiscus Judaicus and the Parting of the Ways*, WUNT 2/277 (Tübingen: Mohr Siebeck, 2010).
Hyde, D., and D. Raffman, "Sorites Paradox," in *The Stanford Encyclopedia of Philosophy*, ed. E. N. Zalta (Stanford, CA: Stanford University Press, 2018), https://plato.stanford.edu/archives/sum2018/entries/sorites-paradox/ last accessed on 15 July 2020.
Kimber Buell, D., *Why This New Race: Ethnic Reasoning in Early Christianity* (New York, NY: Columbia University Press, 2005).
Koselleck, R., *Futures Past: On the Semantics of Historical Time,* trans. K. Tribe (Cambridge, MA: MIT Press, 1985).
Laato, A., "Justin Martyr Encounters Judaism," in *Encounters of the Children of Abraham from Ancient to Modern Times: Encounters of the Children of Abraham from Ancient to Modern Times*, ed. eadem and P. Lindqvist, Studies on the children of Abraham 1 (Leiden: Brill, 2010), 97–123.
Le Boulluec, A., *La notion d'hérésie dans la littérature grecque, IIe-IIIe siècles,* 2 vols. (Paris: Etudes augustiniennes, 1985).
Lewis, T. A., *Why Philosophy Matters for the Study of Religion – and Vice Versa* (Oxford: Oxford University Press, 2015).
Lieu, J. M., *Image and Reality: The Jews in the World of the Christians in the Second Century* (London and New York, NY: T&T Clark, 1996).
Lieu, J. M., "Accusations of Jewish Persecution in Early Christian Sources, with Particular Reference to Justin Martyr and the *Martyrdom of Polycarp*," in *Tolerance and Intolerance in Early Judaism and Christianity*, ed. G. N. Stanton and G. G. Stroumsa (Cambridge: Cambridge University Press, 1998), 279–295.
Lieu, J. M., *Neither Jew nor Greek?: Constructing Early Christianity* (Edinburgh: T&T Clark, 2002).

Lieu, J. M., *Christian Identity in the Jewish and Graeco-Roman World* (Oxford: Oxford University Press, 2004).
Minns, D., and P. Parvis, *Justin, Philosopher and Martyr: Apologies* (Oxford University Press, 2009).
Misiarczyk, L., *Il midrash nel* Dialogo con Trifone *di Giustino Martire* (Płock: Płocki Instytut Wydawniczy, 1999).
Neutel, K. B., "'Neither Jew nor Greek': Abraham as a Universal Ancestor," in *Abraham, the Nations and the Hagarites: Jewish, Christian, and Islamic Perspectives on Kinship with Abraham*, ed. M. Goodman, G. H. van Kooten, and J. T. A. G. M. van Ruiten, TBN 13 (Leiden: Brill, 2010), 291–306.
Parkes, J., *The Conflict of the Church and Synagogue: A Study in the Origins of Antisemitism* (Cleveland, OH, and New York, NY: Soncino Press, 1934; repr., Cleveland, OH, and New York, NY: Meridian, 1961).
Penner, T. C., "Civilizing Discourse: Acts, Declamation, and the Rhetoric of the *Polis*," in *Contextualizing Acts: Lukan Narrative and Greco-Roman Discourse*, ed. idem and C. Vander Stichele, Symposium (Atlanta, GA: Society of Biblical Literature, 2003), 65–104.
Rajak, T., *The Jewish Dialogue with Greece and Rome: Studies in Cultural and Social Interaction* (Leiden: Brill, 2001).
Ricœur, P., *Time and Narrative*, trans. K. McLaughlin and D. Pellauer, 3 vols. (Chicago, IL: University of Chicago Press, 1984).
Ricœur, P., *Memory, History, Forgetting* (Chicago, IL: University of Chicago Press, 2004).
Rokeah, D., *Justin Martyr and the Jews*, JCPS 5 (Leiden: Brill, 2002).
Rudolph, D. J., and J. Willitts, eds., *Introduction to Messianic Judaism* (Grand Rapids, MI: Zondervan, 2013).
Simon, M., *Verus Israel: A Study of the Relations Between Christians and Jews in the Roman Empire, AD 135–425*, trans. H. McKeating (Oxford and Portland, OR: Littman Library of Jewish Civilization, 1996), 243–244.
Skarsaune, O., *The Proof from Prophecy: A Study in Justin Martyr's Proof-Text Tradition: Text-Type, Provenance, Theological Profile*, NovTSup 56 (Leiden: Brill, 1987).
Smith, G. S., *Guilt by Association: Heresy Catalogues in Early Christianity* (Oxford: Oxford University Press, 2014).
Stanton, G. N., *Studies in Matthew and Early Christianity*, WUNT 309 (Tübingen: Mohr Siebeck, 2013).
Taylor, M. S., *Anti-Judaism and Early Christian Identity: A Critique of the Scholarly Consensus*, Studia post-Biblica 46 (Leiden: Brill, 1995).
von Harnack, A., *Ist die Rede des Paulus in Athen ein ursprünglicher Bestandteil der Apostelgeschichte? Judentum und Judenchristentum in Justins Dialog mit Trypho, nebst einer Collation der Pariser Handschrift Nr. 450*, TU 39/1 (Leipzig: Hinrichs, 1913).
White, B. L., "Justin between Paul and the Heretics: The Salvation of Christian Judaizers in the *Dialogue with Trypho*," *JECS* 26.2 (2018): 163–189.

Paul R. Trebilco

Beyond "The Parting of the Ways" between Jews and Christians in Asia Minor to a Model of Variegated Interaction

Abstract: Im ersten und zweiten Jahrhundert n. Chr. florierten die jüdischen und christlichen Gemeinschaften in Kleinasien. Welche Formen der Begegnung und welche Wechselwirkungen zwischen diesen Gemeinschaften lassen sich feststellen? Es gibt Belege für negative Interaktionen, die entweder zu einem, wahrscheinlich lokalen, "Parting of the ways" führten oder möglicherweise reflektieren, dass sich eine Trennung ereignet hatte und nun eine Feindschaft zwischen diesen Gemeinschaften bestand. Jedoch gibt es auch andere Hinweise, die auf positivere Interaktionen verweisen, die entweder auf eine gewisse Vermischung zwischen den Gemeinschaften oder auf den Einfluss einer Gruppe auf die andere hindeuten, oder aber darauf, dass sich die Gemeinschaften gegenseitig nicht als antagonistisch betrachtet haben. Das lässt darauf schließen, dass das "Parting of the ways"-Modell zur Beschreibung der Verhältnisse in den ersten beiden Jahrhunderten unzureichend ist. Ein differenzierterer Ansatz, die bemerkenswerte Vielfalt von Interaktionsformen zwischen jüdischen und christlichen Gemeinschaften in Kleinasien zu betrachten, stellt das Modell der "vielfältigen Interaktionen" dar. Mit diesem sind auch die Belege für die Diversität sowohl innerhalb der jüdischen als auch der christlichen Gemeinschaften in Kleinasien vereinbar.

Keywords: Asia Minor, "Parting of the Ways," Intermixing, Variegated Interaction, Diversity

1 Introduction

Asia Minor was a very significant region for both Jewish and early Christ-believing communities. We have substantial evidence for Diaspora Jewish communities. Philo, in *Legatio ad Gaium* 214, writes that the Jewish people are "spread abroad over all the continents and islands so that it seems to be not much less than the indigenous inhabitants."[1] Certainly, there is no doubt that the Jew-

---

[1] See also Philo, *Legat.* 281–282; Josephus, *J.W.* 2.398; 7.43; *Ant.* 14.115 (quoting Strabo); Sib.Or. 3.271.

ish Diaspora in Asia Minor was "very large"[2] and very significant. Van der Horst notes that we have epigraphic evidence, mostly from the first few centuries CE, for Jews from at least seventy-five cities and villages in Asia Minor.[3] The cities where there were significant Jewish communities included Acmonia, Andriake, Apamea, Aphrodisias, Çatiören, Ephesus, Hierapolis, Korykos, Priene, Sardis and Smyrna.[4] Settlement in some places goes back at least to the 3rd century BCE,[5] so by the 1st century CE many communities were well established.

Asia Minor was also a very significant area for the early Christian movement. Early Christian communities grew quickly in Asia Minor, and these communities have left us a significant portion of the New Testament. David Aune notes that "In the aftermath of the fall of Jerusalem following the first Jewish revolt in 66–73 CE, Anatolia had become perhaps the most important geographical center of Christianity in the ancient world."[6]

How then do we understand the relationship between these very significant Jewish communities and Christian communities in Asia Minor? What sort of interactions occurred between them?

---

[2] P.W. van der Horst, "Jews and Christians in Aphrodisias in the Light of their Relations in Other Cities of Asia Minor," *NedTT* 43 (1989): 106–121, here 107.

[3] P.W. van der Horst, "Judaism in Asia Minor," in *The Cambridge History of Religions in the Ancient World. Vol. 2: From the Hellenistic Age to Late Antiquity*, ed. M.R. Salzman and W. Adler (Cambridge: Cambridge University Press, 2013), 321–340, here 325–326. Some of the evidence is given in E. Schürer, rev. and ed. G. Vermes, F. Millar, and M. Goodman, vol. III.1 of *The History of the Jewish People in the Age of Jesus Christ (175 B.C. – A.D. 135)* (Edinburgh: T&T Clark, 1986), 17–36. Complete evidence is now given in W. Ameling, ed., *Inscriptiones Judaicae Orientis: Vol. II: Kleinasien*, TSAJ 99 (Tübingen: Mohr Siebeck, 2004). See also Map B VI 18 of the *Tübinger Atlas des Vorderen Orients*, which has the title *Die jüdische Diaspora bis zum 7. Jahrhundert n.Chr.*, and shows how many settlements there were.

[4] See Schürer et al., *History* (see n. 3), 17–36; for Çatiören and Korykos, see M.R. Fairchild, "Turkey's Unexcavated Synagogues: Could the world's earliest known synagogue be buried amid rubble?," *BAR* 38.4 (2012): 34–41, esp. 65.

[5] See Josephus, *Ant.* 12.147–153; see further P.R. Trebilco, *Jewish Communities in Asia Minor*, SNTSMS 69 (Cambridge: Cambridge University Press, 1991), 5–7.

[6] D.E. Aune, *Revelation 1–5*, WBC (Dallas, TX: Word, 1997), 131. Christianity continued to flourish in Asia Minor, as a number of recent studies have shown; see U. Huttner, *Early Christianity in the Lycus Valley*, AJEC 85; ECAM 1 (Leiden: Brill, 2013); C. Breytenbach and J.M. Ogereau, eds., *Authority and Identity in Emerging Christianities in Asia Minor and Greece*, AJEC 103 (Leiden: Brill, 2018); C. Breytenbach and C. Zimmermann, *Early Christianity in Lycaonia and Adjacent Areas: From Paul to Amphilochius of Iconium*, AJEC 101, ECAM 2 (Leiden: Brill, 2018); S. Mitchell and P. Pilhofer, eds., *Early Christianity in Asia Minor and Cyprus: From the Margins to the Mainstream*, AJEC 109, ECAM 3 (Leiden: Brill, 2019); P. McKechnie, *Christianizing Asia Minor: Conversion, Communities, and Social Change in the Pre-Constantinian Era* (Cambridge: Cambridge University Press, 2019).

The paradigm of the "parting of the ways" posits a period when early Christ-believers were within the synagogue, although perhaps also meeting as groups separately as well, followed by a period of conflict, leading to a time when the two groups were separate. Of course, I doubt if any scholars have ever thought the process was quite so straight-forward and linear. But here I wish to show how much more complicated the relationships were between Jewish communities and Christ-believing communities in Asia Minor.

I will begin by giving some indications from Asia Minor which suggest that the situation in the 3rd and 4th centuries CE was complex, and that at this time there was at least some intermixing of Jews and Christians. The paradigm which suggests that there was a definitive and permanent "parting of the ways" between these two communities by this time is clearly inadequate.

When we look from this vantage point back at the earlier period of the first two centuries CE, I suggest we see a variety of relationships. Some of our evidence suggests some "parting," while other evidence suggests significant intermixing between the two communities. The picture in Asia Minor is one of great variability and variety, with local and regional differences. Accordingly, I suggest we should think of a model of variegated interaction.

I also want to argue that the paradigm of "parting" misleads us in another way. It tends to suggest that the *key* relationship for Jewish and Christian groups was the relationship with the other group. That is, that the key relationship for a Jewish group in a city was the Christian group, and the key relationship for a Christian group was the Jewish group. I want to argue that this is not the case. Certainly for Christian groups, the relationship with the local Jewish community was important at first. But after some time, the wider city was the key context within which Christian groups in Asia Minor needed to negotiate their communal life. In addition, I will suggest that the key relationship for Jewish groups was with their wider Greco-Roman city.

One issue faced in this discussion is the lack of texts written by Jews in Asia Minor from this period. We presume that Jews in Asia Minor did write some literature, but it is very unfortunate that no texts have survived or been found. Hence, our evidence for Jewish communities here is from inscriptions and from archaeology,[7] or from what Christian texts say about Jewish communities. This limitation of the nature of our evidence does provide some constraints on

---

[7] It should be noted that inscriptions, archaeological sites and texts all need to be placed in some sort of context in order to interpret them. So our dependence on "stones" for evidence of Jewish communities and the need to interpret these aright, is not qualitatively different from the challenges we face in interpreting texts.

what can be said and must be borne in mind here. However, we do have a significant amount of evidence that can be discussed.

2 Complex intermixing of communities in the 3rd and 4th centuries CE

I start by taking the "long view." What do we know about the relationship of Christian and Jewish communities in Asia Minor in the 3rd and 4th centuries? We might think that by this point, they had become "separate religions." However, some evidence tells a different story, and strongly questions the idea of "parting," at least in some places and at some times.

2.1 The Eumeneian Formula: A Formula shared by Jews and Christians

A series of funerary inscriptions from Phrygia end with the phrase ἔσται αὐτῷ πρὸς τὸν θεόν, normally translated as "he or she will have to reckon with God."[8] The formula sought to protect tombs against violation or unauthorized burials by invoking divine wrath on any potential vandal.[9] A number of variants of the formula have also been found. This formula is extremely common in and around Eumeneia,[10] and so has been called "the Eumeneian formula," although it is found elsewhere too.[11] The dated inscriptions are from 246 to 273/4 CE,[12] and

---

[8] On this formula, and for more detail on the argument given here see P.R. Trebilco, "The Christian *and* Jewish Eumeneian Formula," in *Negotiating Diaspora: Jewish Strategies in the Roman Empire*, ed. J.M.G. Barclay, LSTS 45 (Sheffield: Sheffield Academic Press, 2004), 66–88; see also McKechnie, *Christianizing* (see n. 6), 210–231, 288–296.

[9] On the protection of tombs from violation in Asia Minor see J.H.M. Strubbe, "'Cursed be he that moves my bones'," in *Magika Hiera. Ancient Greek Magic and Religion*, ed. C.A. Faraone and D. Obbink (New York, NY: Oxford University Press, 1991), 33–59; idem, *ARAI EPITUMBIOI. Imprecations against Desecrators of the Grave in the Greek Epitaphs of Asia Minor. A Catalogue*, IGSK 52 (Bonn: Habelt, 1997).

[10] In 1939 Calder knew of 47 examples from Eumeneia and Apamea alone and the number has increased since then; see W.M. Calder, "The Eumeneian Formula," in *Anatolian Studies Presented to William Hepburn Buckler*, ed. W.M. Calder and J. Keil (Manchester: Manchester University Press, 1939), 15–26, here 21–22.

[11] It is found in the upper Maeander basin (in Eumeneia, Apamea, Hieropolis, Sebaste) as well as in Eastern Phrygia (e.g., Synnada) (see W. Tabbernee, *Montanist Inscriptions and Testimonia: Epigraphic Sources Illustrating the History of Montanism*, North American Patristic Society Patris-

the undated examples are thought to be from the first quarter of the 3rd century to the early 4th century CE.¹³

A number of clearly Christian inscriptions used the Eumeneian formula and it seems likely that at least two inscriptions with the formula are Jewish.¹⁴ There are many other cases where we cannot tell whether the inscription is Christian or Jewish and in my view these should be described as "either Christian or Jew-

---

tic Monograph Series 16 [Macon, GA: Mercer University Press, 1997], 144 n. 45) and in the Upper Tembris Valley and sporadically further afield in places like Caesarea in Cappadocia, Kyzikos and Rome; on its distribution see *MAMA* VII, xxxvii–xxxviii. Those examples found outside Phrygia are probably on the tombs of Phrygian immigrants; see Tabbernee, *Montanist Inscriptions and Testimonia*, 144 n. 45.

12 The inscription dated to 246 CE is given in W.M. Calder, "Early Christian Epitaphs from Phrygia," *AnSt* 5 (1955): 25–38, here 38. See also *MAMA* VII, xxxvii. The inscription dated to 273/274 is in *MAMA* IV.357. For a list of the dated inscriptions see S. Mitchell, *Anatolia. Land, Men and Gods in Asia Minor. Vol. II: The Rise of the Church* (Oxford: Clarendon Press, 1993), 40 n. 243 and for all the dated inscriptions see McKechnie, *Christianizing* (see n. 6), 288–296. He notes that one other inscription (296 n. 19) should be dated after 282.

13 See Tabbernee, *Montanist Inscriptions* (see n. 11), 145. For the earliest undated inscription see *MAMA* IV.31, dated by M. Waelkens, "Ateliers lapidaires en Phrygie," in *Actes du VIIe Congress international d'épigraphie grecque et latine, Constantza, 9–15 septembre 1977*, ed. D.M. Pippidi (Bucharest: Editura Academie; Paris: Société d'Édition "Les Belles Lettres", 1979), 105–128, here 127. It is an example of the simple Eumeneian formula.

14 With regard to the Christian inscriptions, for example, one inscription with the simple formula begins with Χριστιανοί (see *MAMA* VI.235; see also Tabbernee, *Montanist Inscriptions* [see n. 11], 167–170 n. 20), and another includes the Christogram (see Tabbemee, *Montanist Inscriptions* [see n. 11], 223–229 n. 33; see also *MAMA* VI.234). For other Christian examples, see Trebilco, "Christian *and* Jewish" (see n. 8), 68–70. With regard to the inscriptions which are probably Jewish, see Trebilco, "Christian *and* Jewish" (see n. 8), 70–72. One inscription (Text from W.M. Ramsay, *The cities and bishoprics of Phrygia: being an essay of the local history of Phrygia from the earliest time to the Turkish conquest [Band 1,2]: West and West-Central Phrygia*, [Oxford: Clarendon Press, 1897], 562–564, nos. 455–457 – with date) was identified as a Jewish inscription by Louis Robert on the basis of the name Μαθιος – Mathios, a Semitic rather than an indigenous name in the text, and a name which has been found in Jewish inscriptions; see L. Robert, *Hellenica: Recueil d'epigraphie de numismatique et d'antiquites grecques*, vol. 11–12 (Limoges: Bontemps, 1960), 411 n. 1–3; see also D. Noy, *Jewish Inscriptions of Western Europe. Vol. 2: The City of Rome* (Cambridge: Cambridge University Press 1995), n. 338. The other inscription includes the phrase "sickle of the curse" (ἀράς δρέπανον) which is generally thought to be derived from the Septuagint of Zechariah 5,1–5 (Text in W.M. Ramsay, *The cities and bishoprics*, 652 n. 563; *CIJ* 769; *IJO* II, n. 176). On the inscription, see P.W. van der Horst, *Ancient Jewish Epitaphs. An introductory survey of a millennium of Jewish funerary epigraphy (300 BCE – 700 CE)*, CBET 2 (Kampen: Kok Pharos, 1991), 58. With regard to this inscription, we need to leave open the possibility that it could be Christian, although it seems far more likely to be Jewish. McKechnie, *Christianizing* (see n. 6), 212 n. 12 is dubious that either are Jewish. Some pagan use of the formula well beyond Phrygia is also known; see Trebilco, "Christian *and* Jewish" (see n. 8), 72.

ish."¹⁵ I suggest then that Christians and Jews shared the Eumeneian formula in 3rd century Phrygia.

What does this mean with respect to relations between the two groups? It seems likely that Christians and Jews were aware that the other group also used the formula and also expanded it in various ways.¹⁶ Its continued use by both groups suggests that they were willing to have the formula in common and that there were close relations between Christians and Jews.¹⁷ The two communities may have shared a good deal of common vocabulary, perhaps even with borrowing of ideas between them. This would explain why it is very difficult, and in many cases impossible, for us to distinguish which inscriptions come from which community.¹⁸ The boundaries between some Christians and some Jews may have been hazy; the communities may have been far less demarcated than has often been thought.¹⁹

---

15 See Trebilco, "Christian *and* Jewish" (see n. 8), 72–79.
16 It is possible that the two groups were unaware that they shared the Eumeneian formula. However, if some of the considerable number of inscriptions which contain the simple formula were Christian and others were Jewish, then Christians and Jews from the same place probably used the same formula; doing so without realising the other group also used the formula seems very unlikely, though possible. Recall that we have no evidence that Jews had their own cemeteries in Asia Minor in this period. See M.H. Williams, "The Meaning and Function of *Ioudaios* in Graeco-Roman Inscriptions," *ZPE* 116 (1997): 249–262, here 256.
17 L.H. Kant, "Jewish Inscriptions in Greek and Latin," *ANRW* 20.2 (1987): 671–713, here 685–686.
18 From this and other evidence, Kant ("Jewish Inscriptions" [see n. 17], 686) suggests that "the Jewish and Christian communities, in some places until late antiquity, had such close affinities that it is often difficult and artificial to make distinctions between them. Thus, the boundary between Christians [and] Jews [...] is often hazy. [...] [I]t suggests that a great diversity of expression and self-understanding was open to Jews in the Greco-Roman world."
19 See also A.J. Bij de Vaate and J.W. van Henten, "Jewish or Non-Jewish? Some Remarks on the Identification of Jewish Inscriptions from Asia Minor," *BO* 53 (1996): 16–28, here 28. It is possible that the writers of the inscriptions did not identify themselves clearly as Christians or Jews, but this seems less likely, particularly given the strong Christian identity obvious in the use of the term "Christian" and other Christian identifiers, and the clear indications of Jewish identity in some other Jewish inscriptions from the area. Note for example the clear indications that someone is a Jew in the inscriptions from Hierapolis (see e.g., *IJO* II nos 187, 188, 190, 192, 193) and *IJO* II, n. 179 from Apamea.

2.2 The Synods of Laodicea and Pazon: Christians involved in Jewish practices

The Synod of Laodicea strongly questions the idea of "parting." The Synod, which was a regional council with representatives from various parts of Asia, was probably held around 380 CE and relates to Christians in Asia.[20] The Synod prohibited Christians from practising their religion with Jews, in particular, "celebrating festivals with them," "keeping the Sabbath," and "eating unleavened bread" during the Passover. The Synod decreed that Christians should work on the Sabbath and read the Gospels as well as the Jewish scriptures on Saturday (Canons 16, 29, 37, 38).[21] This is highly revealing and suggests that close contact between Christian and Jewish communities seem to have been quite normal. It indicates the attraction of Judaism and of Jewish practices to many Christians, and points to significant Jewish influence on the life of Christian communities in the mid 4th century, influence that the Synod was seeking to combat.[22] It suggests that, even in the 4th century, there was at times a blurring of the boundary lines between Jewish and Christian communities. Christians were clearly involved in synagogue life and we can speak of some real convergences of practice between the two communities.

Van der Horst points to the wider significance of this evidence from the Synod of Laodicea:

> These canons can only be explained on the assumption that keeping the sabbath, celebrating Pesach and other Jewish religious festivals, etc., were not marginal but frequently occurring and tenacious phenomena among Christians in Asia Minor in the second half of the fourth century. John Chrysostom's and Aphraat's testimonies make it highly probable that this assumption is correct. Only the fact that Judaism continued to make itself strongly felt and to make effective propaganda throughout the first five centuries of our era makes it explicable that during these centuries there was a persistent tradition of judaizing in the church of Asia Minor which defied all the anathemas of the church authorities.[23]

This is significant evidence for the impact of Jewish communities on Christian groups in the mid 4th century in Asia Minor. While this impact may have been

---

[20] For the date, see Huttner, *Early Christianity* (see n. 6), 294–296, who notes the possible range is between 341 and 381, and who on page 389 opts for around 380.
[21] See Huttner, *Early Christianity* (see n. 6), 291–314.
[22] See further van der Horst, "Jews and Christians" (see n. 2), 118; F.J.E. Boddens Hosang, *Establishing Boundaries: Christian-Jewish Relations in Early Council Texts and the Writings of Church Fathers*, JCPS 19 (Leiden: Brill, 2010), 91–107.
[23] Van der Horst, "Jews and Christians" (see n. 6), 118.

simply sporadic, we can suspect that it was more likely to have been continuous and enduring, since this is not isolated evidence.

The Synod of Laodicea is not alone as evidence for ongoing contact between Jews and Christians at this time. In the time of Valens (364–378), a Synod of Novatian bishops met at a village called Pazon in Phrygia. Mitchell notes that "Socrates's account of the synod at Pazon indicates explicitly that the rural Novatians not only celebrated Easter on the same date as the Passover, but actually attended the Jewish Passover festival."[24] Similarly, in Theophanes's *Chronographia*, we are told that in 367, Christians in Phrygia celebrated Passover together with the Jews.[25]

We can see then that in the mid 4th century, the evidence suggest that for these particular communities, "the ways have not parted." Of course, they may have "parted" at a particular place at some point in time and then come back together again. Or the situation may have been highly variable from place to place. But it seems more likely that "the ways" have not actually parted in the first place – at least in some places.

2.3 Christians becoming Jewish God-fearers in Aphrodisias and Philadelphia

In 1976 a now famous stele was discovered in Aphrodisias. It is now recognised that it contains two inscriptions, one probably to be dated to the 4th century, and the other to the early 5th century or later.[26] The first inscription has a list of

---

[24] S. Mitchell, "An Apostle to Ankara from the New Jerusalem: Montanists and Jews in Late Roman Asia Minor," *SCI* 24 (2005): 207–223, here 220; see Socrates, *Hist. eccl.* IV.28; V.22. Significant contact continued later too. An early 6th century Montanist inscription records that one Trophimus who is from Pepuza but was buried in Ankara and who is called an "apostle," had died on the Sabbath day. Mitchell discusses the inscription in detail (see "An Apostle," 207–223) and concludes that "the Montanist church, in Ankara at least, was closely modelled on Jewish organisations in Asia Minor and maintained significant contacts with them"; see Mitchell, "An Apostle," 220; date in ibidem, 214.

[25] See Theophanes's *Chronographia* 62.17–19; see also van der Horst, "Judaism" (see n. 3), 335.

[26] See A. Chaniotis, "The Jews of Aphrodisias: New Evidence and Old Problems," *SCI* 21 (2002): 209–242, here 213–218; idem, "The Conversion of the Temple of Aphrodite at Aphrodisias in Context," in *From Temple to Church: Destruction and Renewal of Local Cultic Topography in Late Antiquity*, ed. J. Hahn, S. Emmel, and U. Gotter, RGRW 163 (Leiden: Brill, 2008), 243–273, here 247; also Ameling, *Inscriptiones* (see n. 3), 77–82. Van der Horst, "Judaism" (see n. 3), 328 dates it to "probably – but not certainly [...] the late fourth or fifth century CE"; cf., G. Gilbert, "Jews in Imperial Administration and its Significance for Dating the Jewish Donor Inscription from Aphrodisias," *JSJ* 35 (2004): 169–184, who dates both inscriptions to the fourth century.

around 55 Jews followed by a list of 52 God-fearers. The second inscription has an introduction that indicates that the names that follow are members of an association "of the lovers of learning also [known as] those who wholly praise," which probably indicates their devotion to the study of Torah and to the praise of God.[27] Then follows a list of names, of which three are proselytes, two are designated *theosebēs*, and the other 14 are clearly Jews by birth, judging by their names.[28] The inscriptions give evidence for a large and flourishing Jewish community in Aphrodisias.

What is significant here is the indication that the Jewish community in Aphrodisias may have attracted members of Christian families as God-fearers. Chaniotis points out that one of the theosebeis in the 4th century inscription "has the characteristic Christian name Gregorios,[29] which alludes to the duty of the Christian to be alert and watchful (gregorein), particularly with regard to sins."[30] The name is a characteristically Christian name,[31] and there is only one known Jewish use of this name, in its female form Glegoria, for a Jewish woman.[32]

It is also noteworthy that at Deliler, near Philadelphia in a 3rd–4th century inscription, one person who is θεοσεβής, which in the inscription probably indi-

---

However, M.H. Williams, "Semitic Name-Use by Jews in Roman Asia Minor and the Dating of the Aphrodisias Stele Inscriptions," in *Old and New Worlds in Greek Onomastics*, ed. E. Matthews, PBA 148 (Oxford: Oxford University Press, 2007), 173–197, has argued for a fifth or sixth century date for both inscriptions on the basis of the use of Hebrew forms for personal names.

27 See D.-A. Koch, "The God-fearers between facts and fiction. Two theosebeis-inscriptions from Aphrodisias and their bearing for the New Testament," *Studia Theologica – Nordic Journal of Theology* 60 (2006): 62–90, here 71.

28 The inscription probably relates to the foundation by this association of a collective burial place; see Ameling, *Inscriptiones* (see n. 3), 91–92; A. Chester, "Jewish Inscriptions and Jewish Life," in *Neues Testament und hellenistisch-jüdische Alltagskultur. Wechselseitige Wahrnehmungen*, ed. R. Deines, J. Herzer, and K.-W. Niebuhr, WUNT 274 (Tübingen: Mohr Siebeck 2011), 383–441, here 413–415.

29 It is Face I, line 44; the actual name is Γληγόριος. J. Reynolds and R. Tannenbaum, *Jews and Godfearers at Aphrodisias*, Cambridge Philological Society Supplementary Volume 12 (Cambridge: Cambridge Philological Society, 1987), 107 note "Greek Γληγόριος, with a common change from *rho* to *lambda*, from γρηγορέω, 'be wakeful, watchful'; widely disseminated, both in the east and in the west, as a name and as a *signum*, from the later 2nd century onwards; of 54 cases at Rome a few are men of status, most uncertain. For a Jewish example of Γληγορία, CIJ II.927."

30 Chaniotis, "Jews of Aphrodisias" (see n. 26), 231. He notes being watchful with regard to sins is "a meaning attested, e.g., in the Gospel of Matthew 24.43." Williams, "Semitic Name-Use" (see n. 26), 186–191, does not discuss the name Gregorios.

31 Chaniotis, "Jews of Aphrodisias" (see n. 26), 231.

32 Chaniotis, "Jews of Aphrodisias" (see n. 26), 231 n. 78; see Frey, CIJ 927.

cates a "God-fearer,"[33] had the name Eustathios and another person, who is not explicitly said to be a God-fearer, is named Athanasia.[34] Chaniotis argues that both these names are almost exclusively attested for Christians,[35] and "allude to Christian beliefs and virtues: faith and immortality of the soul."[36]

Accordingly, Chaniotis suggests that Gregorios at Aphrodisias and Eustathios and Athanasia at Philadelphia may have originated from Christian families.[37] That they became God-fearers of Jewish synagogues (or in the case of Athanasia, perhaps a proselyte, since she is not said to be a "God-fearer") enables us to personalise and individualise the decrees of the Synods of Laodicea and Pazon. Here are the types of individuals who may have been in the minds of those who formulated the canons of the Synods. They help us to see the intermixing of Jewish and Christian communities in actual practice.

2.4 The Seven Sleepers Cemetery in Ephesus – Jewish artifacts in a Christian cemetery

In Ephesus there is a very significant church and burial site that has become known as the Cemetery of the Seven Sleepers. This is related to a legend which tells of seven men who were walled up in a cave during the Decian persecution of 250 and fell asleep. They woke up during the time of the Christian Emperor Theodosius II (402–450), and were subsequently buried, and a church was then built over the graves.[38] The Cemetery of the Seven Sleepers in Ephesus

---

33 There is debate as to whether this is a "God-fearer" or a pious Jew; see Trebilco, *Jewish Communities* (see n. 5), 162; Ameling, *Inscriptiones* (see n. 3), 205–206.
34 See *IJO* II, n. 49; CIJ, 754. Chaniotis, "Jews of Aphrodisias" (see n. 26), 231 is convinced that both Eustathios and Athanasia are God-fearers.
35 Chaniotis, "Jews of Aphrodisias" (see n. 26), 231 n. 80: "There is only one attestation of the name Athanasios in Jewish context: Frey 1952: no 796 (Noy, *Jewish Inscriptions of Western Europe*, Vol. 2 (see n. 14), no 400 is not certain) and two for Eustathia: Frey 1952: nos 804 and 813." Ameling, *Inscriptiones* (see n. 3), 206 n. 32 cites a number of people named Anastasia (Ἀναστασία) but this is a different name.
36 Chaniotis, "Jews of Aphrodisias" (see n. 26), 231.
37 This phenomenon is found elsewhere; Chaniotis, "Jews of Aphrodisias" (see n. 26), 231 notes that the proselyte Anastasios at Venosa was probably the offspring of Christian parents; see D. Noy, *Jewish Inscriptions of Western Europe: Vol. 1: Italy (excluding the City of Rome), Spain and Gaul* (Cambridge: Cambridge University Press, 1993), n. 52, from the 5th century.
38 See P. Scherrer, *Ephesus: The New Guide* (Istanbul: Ege Yaginlari, 2000), 30. On this and other similar legends see P.W. van der Horst, "Pious Long-Sleepers in Greek, Jewish, and Christian Antiquity" in idem, *Studies in Ancient Judaism and Early Christianity* (Leiden: Brill, 2014), 248–266.

is associated with this legend. The earliest building period in the Seven Sleepers complex has recently been dated to the mid 3rd century, although parts of the complex dates to the 5th and 6th centuries, and it was clearly in use over a long period of time.[39]

The point of interest here is that there are two Jewish finds in this Christian cemetery. Two Jewish lamps with menorahs have been discovered; they probably date from the 4th to the 6th century.[40] One is particularly interesting, since a cross is depicted as part of the central branch of the menorah.[41]

What are these Jewish finds doing there? Were a few Jews buried in this predominantly Christian cemetery? Or did Jews visit Christian graves? Or were Jews and Christians in the same family? Or was the lamp with the menorah and the cross from a Jewish Christian? We do not know, but this is very intriguing and seems to be evidence for intermixing between Jews and Christians in Ephesus.

These four 'case studies' then provide us with evidence which suggests there was some intermixing of Jewish and Christian communities in Asia Minor in the 3rd century and beyond.[42] I suggest that if our knowledge was more extensive, we would find more evidence of this kind. It suggests that "parting" is not a good metaphor for the relationship of Jewish and Christian communities in Asia Minor. A good deal of 'intermixing' seems to have occurred.

---

39 See N. Zimmermann, "Das Sieben-Schläfer-Zömeterium in Ephesos: Neue Forschungen zu Baugeschichte und Ausstattung eines ungewöhnlichen Bestattungskomplexes," *JÖAI* 80 (2011): 365–407; for dating see 372–392.
40 See R. Pillinger, "Jüdische Alltagskultur in Ephesos und Umgebung im Spiegel der Denkmäler," in *Neues Testament und hellenistisch-jüdische Alltagskultur. Wechselseitige Wahrnehmungen*, ed. R. Deines, J. Herzer, and K.-W. Niebuhr, WUNT 274 (Tübingen: Mohr Siebeck, 2011), 85–98, here 89; the lamps are given in F. Miltner, *Das Cömeterium der Sieben Schläfer*, FiE IV/2 (Wien: Rohrer, 1937) 188, Plate 12, n. 167; 188, Plate 12, n. 164. For other Jewish finds from Ephesus see Pillinger, "Jüdische Alltagskultur" (see n. 40), 86–94; see also C. Foss, *Ephesus After Antiquity: A Late Antique, Byzantine and Turkish City* (Cambridge: Cambridge University Press, 1979), 45 n. 48, 85 and n. 80; G.H.R. Horsley, "The Inscriptions of Ephesos and the New Testament," *NovT* 34 (1992): 105–168, here 125.
41 See Pillinger, "Jüdische Alltagskultur," (see n. 40), 89 and 96, Abb. 17.
42 The *Martyrdom of Pionius* could be an additional case study. It suggests significant interaction (both positive and negative) between Jews and Christians in Smyrna in 250 CE, although its interpretation is disputed. See further Trebilco, *Jewish Communities* (see n. 5), 30–31; W. Ameling, "The Christian *lapsi* in Smyrna, 250 A.D. (Martyrium Pionii 12–14)," *VC* 62 (2008): 133–160.

3 The variety of relationships between Jewish communities and Christian communities in the first two centuries

What do we know then about interactions between Jews and Christians in Asia Minor in the first two centuries? Here I will seek to highlight various facets of the evidence rather than being comprehensive.[43] This evidence can be seen to fall into two groups. Some evidence points to negative interactions, which either lead to a, probably local, "parting," or perhaps reflect that a parting had occurred and now there was antagonism between the two communities. Other evidence points to more positive interactions, which either suggests some intermixing between communities, or that the communities did not view each other antagonistically. Overall, this evidence suggests that in the first two centuries the "parting" model is inadequate, and a more nuanced way of viewing the significant variety of forms of interaction between Jewish and Christian communities is needed. I will deal with the evidence for negative interactions first.

3.1 Evidence for negative interactions between Jews and Christians

3.1.1 The opposition to Jewish and non-Jewish Christ-believers by Jews according to Acts

According to Acts, Paul preached in a number of synagogues in Asia Minor. He regularly received a mixed reaction, with some Jews becoming Christ-believers (for example, in Ephesus [Acts 19:9–10]), and others opposing him. According to Acts, Jewish opposition to Paul occurred in Pisidian Antioch (Acts 13:45, 50), Iconium (14:2, 5), Lystra (though involving Jews from Antioch and Iconium; see 14:19),[44] and Ephesus (19:9), with a general reference to opposition from Jews in Asia in Acts 20:19. Often it is said that Jewish opposition relates to the fact that

---

[43] See further S.C. Mimouni, "Les Judéens chrétiens et les Judéens synagogaux en Anatolie au IIe siècle: Confrontation ou coexistence (Ignace, Polycarpe et Méliton)," in *Jews and Christians in Antiquity: A Regional Perspective*, ed. P. Lanfranchi and J. Verheyden (Leuven: Peeters, 2018), 143–162.

[44] This incident is almost certainly referred to in 2 Cor 11:25.

Christian preaching had some success among *both* Jews and Gentiles (e. g., in Pisidian Antioch, Acts 13:16, 42–48; in Iconium, Acts 14:1–2).

In Acts 21 Luke says that Jews from Asia, probably primarily from Ephesus,[45] took the lead in charging Paul with attacking the people, the law and the Temple, that is, fundamental dimensions of Jewish identity. The paramount charge was that Paul had brought a Gentile into the Temple, thus defiling it (see Acts 21:27–29). This seems to have occurred at Pentecost (see Acts 20:16), so these Jews from Asia probably had come to Jerusalem as pilgrims. The references to Jewish opposition to Paul and others in Paul's letters increase our confidence that this evidence from Acts is historical, even though Paul never mentions preaching in synagogues in his letters.[46]

Here then is evidence of opposition towards Christ-believers from Jewish communities in Asia Minor in the 1st century.

3.1.2 John's Gospel?

In my view strong arguments can be mounted that John's Gospel was written in Asia Minor, probably in Ephesus, although of course this issue is much debated.[47]

---

45 Since they recognise Trophimus who had recently been in Ephesus; see Acts 20:4.

46 See 2 Cor 11:24, 26 and references to general persecution in Rom 8:35; 1 Cor 4:12; 2 Cor 4:9; 6:4–5; 12:10; Gal 5:11; it is likely that one element of these general references is persecution by Jews. These passages predate Paul's return to Jerusalem (see Acts 21; Rom 15:25–31) and so these instances of Jewish opposition belong to the period of Paul's mission in Asia Minor, Macedonia and Achaia. Gal 5:11, with its ἔτι ("still"), suggests Paul's controversies with Jews were not confined to any one period of his ministry. Paul also speaks of the Gospel as addressed "to the Jew first and also to the Greeks"; see Rom 1:16; also Rom 2:9–10; 3:9; 9:1–5; 10:1, 12; 1 Cor 1:24; 7:18; Gal 3:28. This suggests he would preach in synagogues if at all possible. The punishment in 2 Cor 11:24 is based on Deut 25:1–3. We have no record of where any of these floggings occurred, but Acts portrays several occasions prior to the writing of 2 Corinthians when Paul could have received the thirty-nine lashes; see Acts 13:45, 50; 14:5; 18:12. In 2 Cor 11:26 Paul also speaks of being in danger from his own people. The consistent pattern in Acts of Paul being in conflict with the synagogue (see e.g., 13:44–52; 17:1–5, 13–14, 18:5–7) is quite plausible then. See further Trebilco, *Jewish Communities* (see n. 5), 20–27; J.M.G. Barclay, "Paul among Diaspora Jews: Anomaly or Apostate," *JSNT* 60 (1995): 89–120, here 115–119; E.J. Schnabel, "Jewish Opposition to Christians in Asia Minor in the First Century," in idem, *Jesus, Paul, and the Early Church: Missionary Realities in Historical Contexts. Collected Essays*, WUNT 406 (Tübingen: Mohr Siebeck, 2018), 289–332.

47 See P.R. Trebilco, *The Early Christians in Ephesus from Paul to Ignatius*, WUNT 166 (Tübingen: Mohr Siebeck, 2004), 241–263.

Stephen Wilson, like many others, thinks John's Gospel can be read as evidence for both the history and the present situation of the Johannine community. On this view, to quote Wilson, "the depiction of Jews and Judaism in John expresses the troubled history of the relationship between his community and the synagogue."[48] On such a view, all that is said about "the Jews" in John's Gospel does indeed "fit" with what we know of the actual Jewish community in Ephesus, in the sense that "the Jews" in the Gospel are presented as a strong community, opposed to the Christ-believing group, and able to act forcibly against them.[49] This is compatible with our evidence for the *actual* Jewish community in the city of Ephesus, which was a sizable and significant group.[50] Clearly, there is antagonism between "the Jews" and the followers of Jesus in the Gospel.

However, I do not think that we can include John's Gospel here as evidence for interaction between Jewish communities and Christ-believing communities *in Ephesus*, since, following Bauckham and a number of other scholars, I take the view that the Gospels were written for all Christians and so I do not think John's Gospel can be used to reconstruct the history of a particular community.[51] But I note that many would want to follow the view that Stephen Wilson propounds and so I include this evidence here as a further indication for many scholars of negative interactions between Jews and Christ-believers in Asia Minor.[52]

3.1.3 Revelation

In Rev 2:9 and 3:9 John writes of "the synagogue of Satan" in Smyrna and Philadelphia. Rev 2:9 reads: "I know your affliction and your poverty, even though you are rich. I know the slander on the part of those who say that they are Jews and are not, but are a synagogue of Satan."

---

48 S.G. Wilson, *Related Strangers: Jews and Christians, 70–170 C.E.* (Minneapolis, MN: Fortress, 1995), 73; he regards this as "a universally recognized fact."
49 They can cast them out of the synagogue (John 9:22; 12:42; 16:2) and may even be able to put some Christians to death (John 16:2; cf. 10:28; 15:18).
50 See Trebilco, *Early Christians* (see n. 47), 37–51.
51 See Trebilco, *Early Christians* (see n. 47), 237–241; see R. Bauckham, ed., *The Gospels for All Christians. Rethinking the Gospel Audiences* (Grand Rapids, MI: Eerdmans, 1998).
52 Another example of this approach is by Jörg Frey, in his recent essay, "Toward Reconfiguring Our Views on the 'Parting of the Ways': Ephesus as a Test Case," in *John and Judaism: A Contested Relationship in Context*, ed. R.A. Culpepper and P.N. Anderson (Atlanta, GA: Society Biblical Literature, 2017), 221–239.

In my view, the most likely interpretation of these verses – though it is hotly disputed – is that they concern people who are non-Christian Jews, but whom John considers have now forfeited the right to call themselves Jews because they reject Christ and attack his followers.⁵³ Hence in John's view, they "say that they are Jews and are not." Because they actively oppose and slander Christians (βλασφημία; 2:9),⁵⁴ John regards them as aligning themselves with Satan, the Great Accuser (Rev 12:10). Hence for John, they are a synagogue not of God (as the Jews themselves would have claimed) but of Satan.⁵⁵ In John's eyes, they are not true Jews.⁵⁶ This suggests that the Jewish and Christ-believing

---

53 The other view is that they are Gentile Christians; see Wilson, *Related Strangers* (see n. 48), 163; D. Frankfurter, "Jews or Not? Reconstructing 'the Other' in Rev 2:9 and 3:9," *HTR* 94 (2001): 403–425; M. Murray, *Playing a Jewish Game: Gentile Christian Judaizing in the First and Second Centuries CE*, SCJud 13 (Waterloo: Wilfrid Laurier University Press, 2004), 73–81. On 99 she writes that Rev 2:9 and 3:9 refers to Christians who "are accused of falsely identifying themselves as Jews." These Gentile Christians would have kept some Jewish customs and affiliated with a synagogue to avoid persecution; see Wilson, *Related Strangers* (see n. 48), 163. However, C.R. Koester, *Revelation: A New Translation with Introduction and Commentary*, AYB (New Haven, CT: Yale University Press, 2014), 275 notes (italics original): "Problems with this approach include the fact that individuals might affiliate with a synagogue, but they would not *constitute* a synagogue. Moreover, it is unlikely that one group of Christians would denounce another to the Roman authorities," which is what this view suggests had occurred. Hence, it is more likely that they are ethnically Jewish.
54 βλασφημία is strong language, used elsewhere in Revelation of the activity of the beast and the Whore; see Rev 13:1, 5, 6; 17:3. J. Lambrecht, "Jewish Slander: A Note on Rev 2,9–10," in idem, *Collected Studies on Pauline Literature and on The Book of Revelation* (Rome: Pontificio Istituto Biblico, 2001), 329–339, argues that here it refers to slander against Christians rather than blasphemy against God and Christ.
55 See E. Schüssler Fiorenza, *The Book of Revelation: Justice and Judgment* (Philadelphia, PA: Fortress, 1985), 116.
56 Bauckham notes on the phrase, "those who say they are Jews but are not" in Rev 2:9 and 3:9: "No doubt this description throws back at non-Christian Jews what non-Christian Jews said about Christian Jews. Such polemic suggests at least incipient schism of the Jewish/Samaritan kind, rather than mere diversity, and it suggests two groups, like Jews and Samaritans, both understanding their self-identity as Jewish, while denying Jewish identity to the other." See R. Bauckham, "The Parting of the Ways: What Happened and Why?" in idem, *The Jewish World Around the New Testament. Collected Essays I*, WUNT 223 (Tübingen: Mohr Siebeck, 2008), 175–192, here 181–182. See also L.L. Thompson, *The Book of Revelation: Apocalypse and Empire* (Oxford: Oxford University Press 1990), 90; J. Lambrecht, "Synagogues of Satan (cf. Rev 2,9 and 3,9): Anti-Judaism in the Apocalypse," in idem, *Collected Studies on Pauline Literature and on The Book of Revelation* (Rome: Pontificio Istituto Biblico, 2001), 341–356. On the polemic of the passage, see E.-M. Becker, "Jews and Christians in Conflict? Polemical and Satirical Elements in Revelation 2–3," in *Critique and Apologetics: Jews, Christians and Pagans in Antiquity*, ed. A.-C. Jacobsen, J. Ulrich, and D. Brakke (Frankfurt a.M.: Lang, 2009), 111–136.

communities in Smyrna and Philadelphia were quite separate communities and that there was significant negative interactions and conflict between them.

3.1.4 The Acts of John

The *Acts of John* are probably to be dated to around 150–160 CE,[57] and many of the activities of John recounted in the *Acts of John* occur in Ephesus. Although the provenance of this work is debated, Lalleman and others have argued that it was written in Asia Minor, and this is the most likely possibility.[58] Accordingly, the text may well have some knowledge of the contemporary situation in Ephesus and wider Asia Minor at the time it was written.

The only place in the text where Jews are mentioned is *Acts of John* 94 where we read: "Now, before he [Jesus] was arrested by the lawless Jews, who received their law from a lawless serpent, he [Jesus] gathered us all together and said, 'Before I am delivered up to them, let us sing a hymn to the Father, and go forth to what lies before us'."[59] This reflects the Gospels, where Jesus is arrested by other Jews.[60] However, *Acts of John* 94 clearly demonstrates a strong anti-Jewish sentiment,[61] since it describes them as "lawless Jews," and adds that the Jewish law was delivered by "a lawless serpent," which is clearly a reference to Satan.[62] Perhaps in this, *Acts of John* is influenced by, but goes beyond, the Gospel of John,[63] which the author of *Acts of John* clearly knows.[64]

---

[57] See P.J. Lalleman, *The Acts of John: A Two-Stage Initiation into Johannine Gnosticism*, Studies on the Apocryphal Acts of the Apostles 4 (Leuven: Peeters, 1998), 268–270; H.W. Attridge, "The Acts of John and the Fourth Gospel," in *From Judaism to Christianity: Tradition and Transition. A Festschrift for Thomas H. Tobin, S.J., on the Occasion of His Sixty-fifth Birthday*, ed. P. Walters, NovTSup 136 (Leiden: Brill, 2010), 255–265, here 256.

[58] See Lalleman, *Acts of John* (see n. 57), 256–268; H. Engelmann, "Ephesos und die Johannesakten," *ZPE* 103 (1994): 297–302; J.N. Bremmer, "Jews, Pagans and Christians in the Apocryphal Acts," in *Juden, Christen, Heiden? Religiöse Inklusion und Exklusion in Kleinasien bis Decius*, ed. S. Alkier and H. Leppin, WUNT 400 (Tübingen: Mohr Siebeck, 2018), 333–362, here 335, argues for composition in the area of Northern Lycia or Caria.

[59] Note R.I. Pervo, "Johannine Trajectories in the Acts of John," *Apocrypha* 3 (1992): 47–68, here 48, who writes that the *Acts of John* "display scarcely a trace of affinity with or derivation from Judaism."

[60] See Mark 14:43–47; Matt 26:47–56; Luke 22:47–53; John 18:2–12.

[61] H.-J. Klauck, *The Apocryphal Acts of the Apostles: An Introduction* (Waco, TX: Baylor University Press, 2008), 33 writes that this is "a vehement anti-Jewish polemic."

[62] See Pervo, "Johannine Trajectories" (see n. 59), 48 n. 6.

[63] See John 8:44.

Thus, there may simply be a textual explanation for what is said in *Acts of John* 94 and it is hard to know if this antipathy is in any way influenced by interactions between the Christ-believing author of *Acts of John* and contemporary Jews. There is no further evidence in *Acts of John* for any such interaction and it is noteworthy that the author of *Acts of John* makes no other comments about Jews. But it is significant that there is such strong antagonism towards Jews in this text, although we do need to emphasise that the *Acts of John* give no clear evidence about contemporary interactions between himself and the Jewish community.[65]

3.1.5 Jewish involvement in the Martyrdom of Polycarp?

The *Martyrdom of Polycarp* portrays the Jews of Smyrna as playing a part in Polycarp's death, probably sometime between 155–161 CE.[66] The Jews in the city are portrayed as having contacts in high places in the city and as being prepared to work with Gentiles against the Christ-believers.

But is this historically accurate?[67] The Jews are portrayed as involved, along with others in the city, in denouncing Polycarp as "the destroyer of our gods,"

---

64 See Lalleman, *Acts of John* (see n. 57), 110–123; Attridge, "Acts of John" (see n. 57), 258–265. E. Junod and J.-D. Kaestli, *Acta Iohannis, Tomis 2: Textus alii Commentarius*, CCSA 2 (Turnhout: Brepols, 1983), 643–644 relate this reference to the serpent to John 8:44. See also J.M. Lieu, *Christian Identity in the Jewish and Graeco-Roman World* (Oxford: Oxford University Press, 2004), 291 who notes other texts that associate Jews with demons or Satan.
65 Lalleman, *Acts of John* (see n. 57), 121 thinks that the community behind *Acts of John* "has gained a considerable distance from the Jewish context in which its Gospel [of John] originated." The *Acts of Peter*, probably written in Asia Minor in the last two decades of the 2nd century, perhaps in Bithynia (see Bremmer, "Jews, Pagans and Christians" [see n. 58], 342) mention "the Jews" a number of times. Bremmer, "Jews, Pagans and Christians" (see n. 58), 343 notes: "It is evident that we find here a clear distancing of the Jews, which perhaps presupposes a readership that was still interested in them. In any case, Jews are well attested in Pontus and Bithynia and thus could possibly be seen as opponents."
66 See Mart.Pol. 12:2; 13:1; 17:2–18:1. For the date range see P. Hartog, *Polycarp's Epistle to the Philippians and the Martyrdom of Polycarp: Introduction, Text, and Commentary* (Oxford: Oxford University Press, 2013), 191–200.
67 It has been argued that the story does not portray social reality; see E.L. Gibson, "The Jews and Christians in the *Martyrdom of Polycarp*: Entangled or Parted Ways?," in *The Ways that Never Parted: Jews and Christians in Late Antiquity and the Early Middle Ages*, ed. A.H. Becker and A.Y. Reed, TSAJ 95 (Tübingen: Mohr Siebeck, 2013), 145–158; L. Gaston, "Jewish Communities in Sardis and Smyrna," in *Religious Rivalries and the Struggle for Success in Sardis and Smyr-*

complaining that he is "teaching many neither to sacrifice nor to worship" (12:2). As Hartog notes, "Faithful Jews would not have claimed the 'gods' as their own, nor would they have been upset at a waning of pagan sacrifices."[68] Further, members of the Jewish community are said to assist with collecting kindling, even though it was a "great Sabbath" (13:1), an activity that seems unlikely on the Sabbath.[69] These details have rightly been questioned.[70] However, this does not mean that the text has no historical value whatsoever, and it is entirely credible that the Jewish community was opposed to Christians in Smyrna.[71]

In addition, the Christian author of the account, writing perhaps in the 160s or 170s,[72] clearly thought the Jewish community was strongly opposed to Polycarp, as is shown by the narrative portrayal of the Jewish community in the book. This almost certainly reflects significant conflict between Jewish and Christ-believing communities at this later time.[73]

---

na, ed. R.S. Ascough, SCJud 14 (Waterloo: Wilfrid Laurier University Press, 2005), 17–24, here 21–23.
68 Hartog, *Polycarp's* Epistle (see n. 66), 228; see also 303–304.
69 See Hartog, *Polycarp's* Epistle (see n. 66), 303–304, 306.
70 Hartog, *Polycarp's* Epistle (see n. 66), 228 notes these points "stretch historical credibility."
71 See Hartog, *Polycarp's* Epistle (see n. 66), 230. He notes the historical issues with the text but adds, "This is not to claim that Jews had no part in the suppression of Christianity in Smyrna." Similarly, J.M. Lieu, "Accusations of Jewish Persecution in Early Christian Sources, with particular Reference to Justin Martyr and the *Martyrdom of Polycarp*," in *Tolerance and Intolerance in Early Judaism and Christianity*, ed. G.N. Stanton and G.G. Strousma (Cambridge: Cambridge University Press 1998), 279–295, here 288, notes that in the Mart.Pol., Polycarp's death is in imitation of Jesus's death, and hence "the Jews" are involved in Polycarp's death, as they are in Jesus's death, but she notes "It is unlikely that the imitation theme has created the presence of the Jews entirely [in *Mart. Poly.*] – if it had, more explicit verbal echoes [of the Gospels] could be expected." See also Mimouni, "Les Judéens chrétiens" (see n. 43), 152–153.
72 See Hartog, *Polycarp's* Epistle (see n. 66), 186.
73 Hartog, *Polycarp's* Epistle (see n. 66), 231. As Hartog notes, "if *Mart. Pol.* was written (or even edited) in the ensuing years after the event, the resultant materials may reflect later tensions" between the two groups. I am not dealing with Melito of Sardis here. Although his anti-Judaism is clear from his *Peri Pascha*, it is difficult to know what his attitude was to contemporary Jews; see L. Cohick, "Melito of Sardis's *Peri Pascha* and its 'Israel'," *HTR* 91 (1998): 351–372. She argues (371–372): "that this homily does not reflect any second- or third-century rivalry between Jews and Christians but rather highlights the developing theological arguments concerning identity among Christians. [...] I have suggested that this homily reveals little regarding Jews or Judaism in the author's time. Indeed, it centers on defining Christianity over against a hypothetical 'Israel' that the unknown author has created largely for rhetorical purposes. This approach in no way discredits the evidence that Judaism in the early centuries was active and vibrant in some cities. It simply suggests that this homily's anti-Jewish rhetoric is not the place to find evidence for Jews or Judaism of its time."

3.1.6 Christians writing "Against the Jews"

Eusebius tells us that two Christian authors from Asia Minor, Apollinaris, bishop of Hierapolis, Phrygia, and Miltiades both wrote two-volume works entitled "Πρὸς Ἰουδαίους – Against the Jews."[74] Unfortunately, both these works are lost, and we know only their titles. Both wrote in the time of Marcus Aurelius (161–180 CE).[75]

We see then that there is significant evidence for negative interactions between Jewish communities and Christian communities in Asia Minor, and at least some of this evidence suggests a strong antipathy between distinct and separated communities.

3.2 Evidence for positive interactions or Jewish influence on Christian communities

I now turn to the evidence for more positive interaction or for Jewish influence on Christian communities, which suggests either some intermixing between communities, or that the Jewish and Christian communities did not view the other community antagonistically.

3.2.1 Ignatius

Ignatius wrote to a number of Christian groups in Asia Minor, probably between 105–110 CE.[76] In his *Letter to the Magnesians*, Ignatius warns Magnesian Christ-believers against living "according to Judaism" and keeping the Sabbath (Ig-

---

74 For Apollinaris see Eusebius, *Hist. eccl.* 4.27.1; for Miltiades see Eusebius, *Hist. eccl.* 5.17.5. It is not absolutely certain that Miltiades is from Asia Minor, but this seems likely; see Mimouni, "Les Judéens chrétiens" (see n. 43), 155–156. Huttner, *Early Christianity* (see n. 6), 238 notes that πρός may be translated here as "to" the Jews, which would give the books a less polemical ring.
75 On Apollinaris, see R.M. Grant, *Greek Apologists of the Second Century* (Philadelphia, PA: Westminster Press, 1988), 85–97; on Miltiades, see Grant, *Greek Apologists* (see n. 75), 90–91. See also Mimouni, "Les Judéens chrétiens" (see n. 43), 155–156.
76 See Trebilco, *Early Christians* (see n. 47), 629–631. In support of this date see M.J. Edwards, "Ignatius and the Second Century: An Answer to R. Hübner," *ZAC* 2 (1998): 214–226; J. Lookadoo, *The High Priest and the Temple: Metaphorical Depictions of Jesus in the Letters of Ignatius of Antioch*, WUNT 2/473 (Tübingen: Mohr Siebeck, 2018), 15–22; McKechnie, *Christianizing* (see n. 6), 69–71.

n.*Magn.* 8–10).⁷⁷ In Ign.*Magn.* 10:3 he writes: "it is outlandish to proclaim Jesus Christ and practice Judaism," which suggests that some Christians were involved in Jewish practices, of which the Sabbath is clearly one.⁷⁸

In the *Letter to the Philadelphians* (Ign.*Phld.*) 6:1 we read: "But if anyone should interpret Judaism to you, do not hear him. For it is better to hear Christianity from a man who is circumcised than Judaism from one who is uncircumcised." In the second sentence of this quotation, Ignatius refers first of all to a Jewish Christian who is promoting Christian faith and then to a Gentile who is promoting Judaism. What Ignatius goes on to say in the letter suggests this latter group are Gentile *Christians*;⁷⁹ that is, there are Gentile Christians who, according to Ignatius, were preaching or promoting Jewish practices. We do not know *why* these Gentile Christians were doing this. As Murray comments:

> Gentile Christians in Asia Minor may have continued with prior practices of Jewish rites adopted when they were God fearers on the periphery of the synagogue: they simply did not change their lifestyle when they became Christians [...]. Or, perhaps in the setting of a vibrant diaspora Judaism, gentile Christians became exposed to Judaism through social interaction with Jews.⁸⁰

Here is a quite different situation for Christ-believers from Philadelphia in comparison with the conflict that is apparent in Revelation, for here in Ignatius some ethnic Jews are promoting belief in Christ and some Gentile Christians are promoting Judaism. It is noteworthy with regard to Philadelphia then that from Revelation we learn of Christians being in intense conflict with Jews, whereas from Ignatius, just a few years later, we learn that some Gentile Christians are promoting Judaism. The situation is clearly fluctuating, or does the different evidence relate to quite different Christian groups? We simply do not know and can only ask the question.

Accordingly, we see that in Magnesia, Christ-believers were involved in Jewish practices and in Philadelphia, Gentile Christ-believers were promoting Judaism, undoubtedly including Jewish practices.

---

77 See Murray, *Playing a Jewish Game* (see n. 53), 84–86
78 Murray, *Playing a Jewish Game* (see n. 53), 86–87, thinks it is not clear that the Christ-believers who were involved in Jewish practices did so under the direct influence of Jews.
79 See Wilson, *Related Strangers* (see n. 48), 164; Murray, *Playing a Jewish Game* (see n. 53), 88–91.
80 Murray, *Playing a Jewish Game* (see n. 53), 91.

3.2.2 Justin Martyr

Justin's *Dialogue with Trypho,* written around 155–160 CE[81] in Rome, was set in Ephesus according to Eusebius (*Hist. eccl.* 4.18.6), perhaps on the basis of a well-established tradition. It purports to be a historical dialogue. Lieu argues that it is entirely reasonable to think that Justin did have discussions with a "Trypho" in Ephesus in the way suggested in the *Dialogue*. His readers would also regard this as reasonable.[82]

Although we cannot regard Justin's work as a reliable record of an actual debate, both Justin and his readers could well have seen Ephesus as a suitable and realistic venue for a debate between a learned Christ-believer and a learned Jew concerning matters such as Jesus and the law.[83] This suggests that it is reasonable to think that there were these sorts of discussions in Ephesus around 160 CE.

What does this suggest about the interaction between Jews and Christ-believers in Ephesus at this time? At the least, it suggests that each community was reasonably knowledgeable about the other and that there may have been in-depth debates and disputes "conducted in a civilized tone,"[84] about a range of matters.

3.2.3 Polycrates and the Quartodeciman controversy

We learn of the Quartodeciman controversy from Bishop Polycrates of Ephesus, who wrote to Bishop Victor of Rome c. 190–195,[85] in a letter which has been pre-

---

81 See J.M. Lieu, *Image and Reality: The Jews in the World of the Christians in the Second Century* (Edinburgh: T&T Clark, 1996), 103.
82 See Lieu, *Image and Reality* (see n. 81), 103–104; see also T.J. Horner, *Listening to Trypho: Justin Martyr's* Dialogue *Reconsidered*, CBET 28 (Leuven: Peeters, 2001), 179–189.
83 See Thompson, *Book of Revelation* (see n. 56), 143.
84 Wilson, *Related Strangers* (see n. 48), 283; see also Horner, *Listening to Trypho* (see n. 82), 187–188.
85 The dates for Polycrates can only be determined from the fact that he wrote to Victor, who was bishop of Rome from c. 189–199 CE (see P. Lampe, *From Paul to Valentinus: Christians at Rome in the First Two Centuries* [Minneapolis, MN: Fortress, 2003], 336). O. Skarsaune, "Evidence for Jewish Believers in Greek and Latin Patristic Literature," in *Jewish Believers in Jesus: The Early Centuries*, ed. idem and R. Hvalvik (Peabody, MA: Hendrickson, 2007), 505–567, here 516, dates Polycrates to ca. 195. R. Bauckham, *Jesus and the Eyewitnesses: The Gospels as Eyewitness Testimony*, 2nd ed. (Grand Rapids, MI: Eerdmans, 2017), 438 dates him to "c. 190–195."

served by Eusebius.[86] In the letter, Polycrates defended the Asian practice of celebrating Easter at the same time as the Jewish Passover, and so beginning on the eve of Nisan 14. Victor objected that this was out of step with the rest of the Church and sought to excommunicate the Asian Churches en masse because of their practice in this regard. Only the fact that Irenaeus stepped in prevented this. The Quartodeciman controversy continued for over 200 years and was mainly focussed in Asia Minor.

In his letter to Victor of Rome, Polycrates described 14 Nisan as the day "when the people remove the leaven (ὅταν ὁ λαὸς ἤρνυεν τὴν ζύμην)."[87] Bauckham notes that this expression cannot simply be derived from Exod 12:15, but rather reflects contemporary Jewish practice of removing the leaven and the language that was used for that practice.[88] We note also the Jewish use of ὁ λαός for the Jewish people; this term is found in Jewish inscriptions in Asia Minor from Nysa, Smyrna, Appia and Hierapolis,[89] and so probably reflects contemporary Jewish language. Accordingly, Bauckham notes that Polycrates "can speak of things Jewish in an authentically Jewish way."[90] This may in part be due to Polycrates living in close proximity to the large Jewish community of Ephesus and perhaps being part of a church with a strongly Jewish-Christian background. He knows about Jewish language and Jewish customs. It probably also relates to his claim to partly Jewish descent, reflected in his claim to be descended from one of Philip's daughters.[91] In this small way then, we see the interaction of Jews in Ephesus with some Christians towards the end of the 2nd century.

As I have noted, Quartodeciman practice followed the local Jewish dating of Passover, which began on 14 Nisan. This is clear when Polycrates says "my kinsmen ever kept the day when the people put away the leaven."[92] Polycrates is clearly speaking of "the day" when he also keeps the Pascha. Thus he relates

---

[86] Polycrates, quoted in Eusebius, *Hist. eccl.* 5.24.2–7.
[87] Eusebius, *Hist. eccl.* 5.24.6.
[88] Bauckham, *Jesus and the Eyewitnesses* (see n. 85), 447. Note that Melito, *Peri Pascha* 39–41, 43 uses ὁ λαός of "the Jewish people" four times. For example, *Peri Pascha* 39: "For the very salvation and reality of the Lord were prefigured in the people." Melito is probably also reflecting contemporary Jewish language.
[89] See *IJO* II.26.4 (Nysa), 44.3 (Smyrna), 181.2 (Appia), 206.5 (Hierapolis); see also Schürer et al., *History* (see n. 3), 89–90.
[90] Bauckham, *Jesus and the Eyewitnesses* (see n. 85), 447. The *Didascalia Apostolorum*, written in Syriac, also uses "the People" to speak of the Jews; see *Didascalia Apostolorum* 5.17.1; 5.19.9–10; P.F. Bradshaw, "The Origins of Easter," in *Passover and Easter*, ed. idem and L.A. Hoffman (Notre Dame: University of Notre Dame Press, 1999), 5:81–97, here 87. It has a strongly anti-Jewish tone.
[91] Bauckham, *Jesus and the Eyewitnesses* (see n. 85), 447.
[92] Eusebius, *Hist. eccl.* 5.24.6.

the timing of the Christian festival to the timing of the Jewish Passover.[93] Those following Quartodeciman practice accordingly needed to know when Passover occurred each year and it seems certain that they would find this out from the local Jewish community. As Polycrates says, he observes the Pascha "when the people [that is, the Jewish people] put away the leaven." We can also be confident that Polycrates would learn of the dating of Passover from the local Jewish community in Ephesus because of the significant complexities facing Diaspora Jewish communities themselves when it came to determining the dating of Passover. Bradshaw writes:

> The determination of the correct date for the celebration of the Passover each year was a difficult enough matter for Jewish Diaspora communities. Strictly speaking, they depended upon the sighting of the new moon in Jerusalem, which occurred on average every 29 1/2 days, making each new month either the 30th or 31st day after the old one. By the time that Passover arrived, two weeks later, communities far from Jerusalem would still not know which of the two days had been declared the new moon. Sometimes, too, the decision to insert an extra month into the Jewish year might be made so late that very distant Diaspora communities would not know about it in time, and so would celebrate their Passover a month early. Having the date of Easter dependent upon the determination of the Passover presented an even greater problem for early Christians. While some seemingly felt no embarrassment in having to ask their Jewish neighbors when they should celebrate their festival, others found this demeaning and so sought alternative solutions.[94]

Given this complex system for finding out the timing of Passover each year for a Diaspora Jewish community, there seems to be no way for a Christian community in Asia Minor to find out the dating of Easter, other than to ask the local Jewish community. According, Quartodecimans in Asia Minor followed the Jewish dating of Passover, which was itself determined by the local Jewish community.[95]

---

93 See A. Stewart-Sykes, *The Lamb's High Feast: Melito, Peri Pascha and the Quartodeciman Paschal Liturgy at Sardis*, SVigChr 42 (Leiden: Brill, 1998), 165.
94 Bradshaw, "The Origins of Easter" (see n. 90), 91–92. T.C.G. Thornton, "Problematical Passovers. Difficulties for Diaspora Jews and Early Christians in determining Passover Dates during the First Three Centuries A.D," in *Studia Patristica Vol. XX: Papers Presented to the Tenth International Conference on Patristic Studies held in Oxford 1987: Critica, Classica, Orientalia, Ascetica, Liturgica*, ed. E.A. Livingstone (Leuven: Peeters, 1989), 402–408 has also shown the considerable problems facing Diaspora Jewish communities with regard to knowing the calendar, particularly with regard to intercalating an extra month, since until the second half of the 4th century such decisions were made year-by-year in Palestine.
95 Sozomen, *Hist. eccl.* 7.18 tells us that some Montanists fixed the date of the Pascha by tying it to the fourteenth day of the first month of spring, Artemisios, according to their local Julian calendar; see also T.J. Talley, *The Origins of the Liturgical Year* (Collegeville, PA: Liturgical Press 1991), 8–9. However, Sozomen, *Hist. eccl.* 7.18 contrasts this Montanist practice with that of

There must then have been some lines of communication between Jewish and Christian communities in Asia Minor.

It is important to note that Quartodeciman practice was quite widespread in Asia Minor at this time. Polycrates claims that a whole range of past Christian leaders were all Quartodecimans, and lists Polycarp of Smyrna, Thraseas of Eumeneia, Sagaris of Laodicea, Papirius and Melito of Sardis, as well as seven previous bishops of Ephesus.[96] In addition, he claims many other contemporary bishops in Asia were also Quartodecimans. The practice was widespread then.

Of course, all the Christian communities in Asia Minor need not have found out the date of Pascha from their local Jewish community, since word could travel around Christian communities. But clearly, some Christian communities found out the dating from their local Jewish community.

We can say then that Polycrates and other Christians in Ephesus and some other Christian communities in Asia Minor were influenced by the local Jewish community, at least to the extent of the dating of their Pascha. But it is also completely clear that Jewish and Christian practices were quite distinct – on 14 Nisan Christians celebrated, not Passover, but Christ's death and resurrection.

We can also ask the more general question of *why* the Asian Churches followed the practice of celebrating Pascha on 14 Nisan? This *could* be seen to be very 'Jewish,' for they commemorated the death and resurrection of Jesus at the same time that Jewish communities were celebrating Passover. But did they celebrate Easter *on 14 Nisan* under local Jewish influence?[97] Or did they celebrate at the same time to make the point that they were celebrating something different – not the Passover and the liberation from Egypt, but the death and resurrection of Jesus? Or was Quartodeciman practice derived exclusively from John's Gospel and the traditions written there that Jesus died at the same time as the Passover sacrifice was being offered in the Temple,[98] and so was their Easter practice without any "local" influence from local Jewish communities – either positively or negatively? This would then simply be to follow ancient Christian

---

the Quartodecimans, so we do not have evidence that Quartodecimans fixed the date in this way. Further, the Quartodeciman practise is regularly tied to Nisan 14 (Polycrates letter in Eusebius, *Hist. eccl.* 5.24.1–7 says: "All these kept the fourteenth day of the passover according to the gospel"), which is clearly the Jewish calendar, not the Julian one.

96 See Eusebius, *Hist. eccl.* 5.24.3–8.

97 Destephen thinks Quartodeciman practice was because of Jewish influence; see S. Destephen, "Les courants religieux en Asie Mineure du IVe au VIIe siècle," in *Hierapolis di Frigia XII. Le abitazioni dell'insula 104 a Hierapolis di Frigia*, ed. A.Z. Ruggiu (Istanbul, Yayinlari, 2019), 655–665, here 655, where he writes: "L'influence du judaïsme reste toutefois si forte que les chrétiens d'Asie Mineure célèbrent Pâques selon le calendrier juif, le 14e jour de Nisan."

98 See John 19:14, 31, 42.

tradition.[99] Thus, it is very difficult to know *why* the Christian communities did what they did! For we do not have any texts that explain *why* Christian communities in Asia celebrated the Pascha on 14 Nisan. Polycrates simply says that this was their traditional practise.

Being a Quartodeciman *in itself* does not mean that there were positive relationships with the local Jewish community. As I have noted, Melito of Sardis is a Quartodeciman and he was clearly anti-Jewish. He follows the Jewish dating of Pascha, but writes in a strongly negative way about Judaism.[100] However, even in this case, we do not know what Melito's attitude was to *contemporary* Jews, although we can suspect it was very negative. That a Christian community followed a custom that was related to Jewish practice, does not necessarily mean they had positive relations with living Jewish communities then.

But as we have noted, Polycrates in Ephesus knows about Jewish language and practice, and knows about the dating of Easter and hence Pascha from the local Jewish community. To this extent, there is some interaction between the two communities and Polycrates is influenced by the local Jewish community. But we cannot be more specific than this about on-going contact between Jewish and Christian communities or about Polycrates's attitude towards or relationship with the contemporary Jewish community in Ephesus – we simply do not know!

I have spent some time on this particular evidence because it also demonstrates how complicated the situation can be, and how very complex and difficult it can be to determine when interaction between real Jews and real Christians "on the ground" has *actually* happened, or when "Jewish influence" on Christians has *really* occured!

We see then that there is evidence for positive interaction or for Jewish influence on Christian communities, which suggests either some relationship or intermixing between communities, or that the Jewish and Christian communities did not view the other community antagonistically. This goes with the similar evidence from the 3rd century onwards with which I began this paper, which similarly suggested some on-going interaction and intermixing between Jewish and Christian communities in Asia Minor.

---

99 This is what Polycrates claims; he lists the "luminaries" in Asia, going back to "Philip of the twelve apostles," and then says: "All these kept the fourteenth day of the passover according to the gospel (κατὰ τὸ εὐαγγέλιον), never swerving but following according to the rule of the faith (κατὰ τὸν κανόνα τῆς πίστεως ἀκολουθοῦντες)." See Polycrates in Eusebius, *Hist. eccl.* 5.24.1–7.
100 See Melito, *Peri Pascha* 37–45; 74–105. For example, 43: "the people was made void when the church arose."

4 What are the key relationships for each community?

Let me raise one more issue in relation to "the parting of the ways" paradigm for Asia Minor. As we think about the ongoing development of both Jewish and Christian communities from the vantage point of "the parting of the ways" paradigm, we might think that each community was the context for the development of the other. Thus, on this view, the context for the development of Christian communities would be Jewish communities and the context for the development of Jewish communities would be the Christian communities.

Certainly, Christian groups at the very beginning of the movement were regularly formed from within the Jewish community. In the earliest period, Gentiles would understand themselves to be joining a Jewish group. Outsiders would also see Christians as a Jewish group. Accordingly, a key context for early Christian life, at least at first, was the Jewish community.

However, the wider city was also an important and often a challenging context for the early Christians. As the Christian groups became increasingly Gentile, the Christian groups grew away from Jewish communities and their context increasingly became the city. Accordingly, key issues in books from Asia Minor like 1 Peter, 1 and 2 Timothy and Revelation are not relationships with the Jewish community but rather relationships with the wider society. How, as a community of Christ-believers, did one negotiate life in the Greco-Roman city? This was a key issue.

Further, to look at the reverse side of this issue, there is very little evidence that the Christian groups formed the context for the Jewish communities in Asia Minor, at least not in the 1st and 2nd centuries CE.[101] The primary context for the Jewish communities, their most proximate "other," was the wider city and it was within the context of the wider Greco-Roman city that the Jewish communities had to negotiate their life. As far as we can tell, generally the impact of the growing Christian movement on the Jewish communities in Asia Minor was small. Certainly we have early evidence from Acts that Jewish communities acted to discipline Jewish Christians in their midst,[102] but there is little evidence that interaction with Christian thought, for example, was a significant feature of synagogue life. Perhaps for a considerable period, most Jewish communities could

---

[101] See J. Magness, "The Date of the Sardis Synagogue in Light of the Numismatic Evidence," *AJA* 109 (2005): 443–475, here 467.
[102] See 3.1.1 above.

ignore Christian groups.[103] Accordingly, the "parting of the ways" paradigm is partly a Christian theological way of considering the matter. From a Jewish perspective in Asia Minor, relationships with the Christian group, at least in the 1st–2nd centuries, may have been a matter of minor significance.

5 Conclusions

We see then that "the parting of the ways" paradigm is inadequate when it comes to discussing the relationships between Jewish and Christian communities in Asia Minor in the first few centuries. It is better to talk about a variety of relationships in different places and over time – some negative relationships, some positive relationships, some influence from one community to the other, and some intermixing between communities. There is no one pattern, but rather significant variety and diversity. Accordingly, we can speak of a picture of variegated interaction.

For we have seen a significant amount of evidence from Ignatius, Justin Martyr, Polycrates and the Quartodeciman controversy, the Synods of Laodicea and Pazon, as well as evidence relating to a shared funerary formula in Eumeneia, to people from a Christian family being God-fearers in Aphrodisias and Philadelphia, and probably to Jewish visitors to a Christian Cemetery in Ephesus, which all indicates that real and on-going interaction did occur between Jews and Christians in Asia Minor. Of course, I have also discussed significant evidence for negative interaction between Jewish and Christian communities, from Acts, Revelation, the Acts of John, the Martyrdom of Polycarp, and two later writers, but this was not the situation everywhere and at all times. What we have is a picture or model of variegated interaction.

Here I think of the recent Festschrift in honour of Joel Marcus: *The Ways that Often Parted*. Baron, Hicks-Keeton and Thiessen, the editors of the volume, write:

> The unifying thesis of this volume is that Christianity's eventual distinction from Judaism was messy and multiform, occurring at difference paces in diverse geographies with varied literary resources, theological commitments, historical happenstance, and political maneuvering. [...] So, while the title of this current volume might be read as a polemical response to Reed's and Becker's *The Ways That Never Parted*, the cumulative findings of the following essays in fact provide additional evidence for the argument their volume makes. After all, ways that eventually did part can only be understood to have parted often, if indeed

---

[103] Here though we must bear in mind that our evidence for Jewish communities is limited and we have no texts written by Jews from Asia Minor themselves.

there was no one single, definitive, early parting of the ways between Judaism and Christianity.[104]

What I have said about a picture of variegated interaction is in keeping with the generally recognised diversity of both Jewish and Christian communities in Asia Minor. This diversity in both cases is well known across Asia Minor.[105] It seems likely that Jewish communities in Asia Minor were often quite different from each other. This diversity is demonstrated by comparing the excavated synagogues in Sardis, Priene and Andriake, which are different from each other in size, architecture and decoration.[106] Clearly the three communities were different, perhaps because of a whole range of local factors including when the communities were originally founded and under what circumstances, the community's size at its foundation and over time, its leadership, the relationships with city officials, and its relationship to and influence within the wider community. With regard to early Christianity, I suggest that Ephesus, the leading city of Asia, is a cameo of diversity. Virtually all those who have considered the evidence recently would suggest that there were a number of different Christian communities in the city.[107] In addition, early Christian diversity across Asia Minor in the first few centuries is very clear from the range of evidence that we have.

---

[104] L. Baron, J. Hicks-Keeton, and M. Thiessen, "Introduction," in *The Ways that Often Parted: Essays in Honor of Joel Marcus*, ed. L. Baron, J. Hicks-Keeton and M. Thiessen, SBLECL 24 (Atlanta, GA: Society of Biblical Literature Press, 2018), 1–13, here 2, 4. Becker and Reed write that in choosing the title, *The Ways that Never Parted: Jews and Christians in Late Antiquity and the Early Middle Ages*, "we wish to call attention to the ample evidence that speaks against the notion of a single and simple 'Parting of the Ways' in the first or second century CE and, most importantly, against the assumption that no meaningful convergence ever occurred thereafter. [...] we suggest that Jews and Christians (or at least the elites among them) may have been engaged in the task of 'parting' throughout Late Antiquity and the early Middle Ages, precisely because the two never really 'parted' during that period with the degree of decisiveness or finality needed to render either tradition irrelevant to the self-definition of the other, or even to make participation in both an unattractive or inconceivable option." See A.Y. Reed and A.H. Becker, "Introduction: Traditional Models and New Directions," in *The Ways that Never Parted: Jews and Christians in Late Antiquity and the Early Middle Ages*, ed. A.H. Becker and A.Y. Reed, TSAJ 95 (Tübingen: Mohr Siebeck, 2003), 1–33, here 22–23.
[105] For Jewish communities, see Trebilco, *Jewish Communities* (see n. 5); for early Christianity see R.E. Oster, "Christianity in Asia Minor," in *The Anchor Bible Dictionary*, ed. D.N. Freedman (New York, NY: Doubleday, 1994), 1:938–954 and the studies noted in n. 6 above.
[106] See P.R. Trebilco "Jews in Asia Minor," in *Routledge Handbook of Jews and Judaism in Late Antiquity*, ed. C. Hezser (London: Routledge, forthcoming 2021).
[107] See for example, M. Tellbe, *Christ-Believers in Ephesus. A Textual Analysis of Early Christian Identity Formation in a Local Perspective*, WUNT 242 (Tübingen: Mohr Siebeck, 2009), 39–47. He

This means that different Jewish communities and different groups within the early Christian communities in Asia Minor might well sustain different levels of interaction and different relationships with the other grouping. Some Christians might have had virtually no interaction with Jews,[108] while other Christian groups may have had significant and on-going interaction with Jewish groups (as shown by Justin and Polycrates). Such diversity and difference may have been evident amongst the different Jewish communities in Asia Minor too. This would explain the variegated nature of our evidence. This also means that there might well have been other groups of both Jews and Christians who would have told a quite different story again.[109]

Finally, in *The Ways that Never Parted*, Becker and Reed write of

> the inadequacy of any monolithic model that seeks to theorize the relationships between 'Judaism' and 'Christianity' without considering the socio-cultural and discursive specificities that shaped interactions between Jews and Christians in different cultural contexts, geographical locales, and social strata.[110]

I hope this study has shown the importance of specific context and of geographical locale and again underlines the point that it is problematic to generalise from one area to another.

Bibliography

Ameling, W., ed., *Inscriptiones Judaicae Orientis: Vol. II: Kleinasien*, TSAJ 99 (Tübingen: Mohr Siebeck, 2004).
Ameling, W., "The Christian *lapsi* in Smyrna, 250 A.D. (Martyrium Pionii 12–14)," *VC* 62 (2008): 133–160.

---

thinks (47) "there were various types or groups of Christ-believers in Ephesus towards the end of the first and the beginning of the second century."
108 The group represented in the Johannine Letters would probably fall into this category. It has not been discussed here because it provides no evidence for Christians interacting with Jews.
109 See J.M. Lieu, "'The Parting of the Ways': Theological Construct or Historical Reality?," in *Neither Jew Nor Greek? Constructing Early Christianity*, SNTW (London: T&T Clark, 2002), 11–29, here 18.
110 Preface to A.H. Becker and A.Y. Reed, eds., *The Ways that Never Parted: Jews and Christians in Late Antiquity and the Early Middle Ages* (Minneapolis, MN: Fortress, 2007), X; emphasis added.

Attridge, H. W., "The Acts of John and the Fourth Gospel," in *From Judaism to Christianity: Tradition and Transition. A Festschrift for Thomas H. Tobin, S.J., on the Occasion of His Sixty-fifth Birthday*, ed. P. Walters, NovTSup 136 (Leiden: Brill, 2010), 255–265.

Aune, D. E., *Revelation 1–5,* WBC (Dallas, TX: Word, 1997).

Barclay, J. M. G., "Paul among Diaspora Jews: Anomaly or Apostate," *JSNT* 60 (1995): 89–120.

Baron, L., J. Hicks-Keeton, and M. Thiessen, "Introduction," in *The Ways that Often Parted: Essays in Honor of Joel Marcus*, ed. L. Baron, J. Hicks-Keeton, and M. Thiessen, SBLECL 24 (Atlanta, GA: Society of Biblical Literature Press, 2018), 1–13.

Bauckham, R., ed., *The Gospels for All Christians. Rethinking the Gospel Audiences* (Grand Rapids, MI: Eerdmans, 1998).

Bauckham, R., "The Parting of the Ways: What Happened and Why?" in idem, *The Jewish World Around the New Testament. Collected Essays I*, WUNT 223 (Tübingen: Mohr Siebeck, 2008), 175–192.

Bauckham, R., *Jesus and the Eyewitnesses: The Gospels as Eyewitness Testimony*, 2nd ed. (Grand Rapids, MI: Eerdmans, 2017).

Becker, A. H., and A. Y. Reed, eds., *The Ways that Never Parted: Jews and Christians in Late Antiquity and the Early Middle Ages* (Minneapolis, MN: Fortress, 2007).

Becker, E.-M., "Jews and Christians in Conflict? Polemical and Satirical Elements in Revelation 2–3," in *Critique and Apologetics: Jews, Christians and Pagans in Antiquity*, ed. A.-C. Jacobsen, J. Ulrich, and D. Brakke (Frankfurt a.M.: Lang, 2009), 111–136.

Bij de Vaate, A. J., and J. W. van Henten, "Jewish or Non-Jewish? Some Remarks on the Identification of Jewish Inscriptions from Asia Minor," *BO* 53 (1996): 16–28.

Boddens Hosang, F. J. E., *Establishing Boundaries: Christian-Jewish Relations in Early Council Texts and the Writings of Church Fathers*, JCPS 19 (Leiden: Brill, 2010).

Bradshaw, P. F., "The Origins of Easter," in *Passover and Easter*, ed. idem and L. A. Hoffman (Notre Dame: University of Notre Dame Press, 1999), 5:81–97.

Bremmer, J. N., "Jews, Pagans and Christians in the Apocryphal Acts," in *Juden, Christen, Heiden? Religiöse Inklusion und Exklusion in Kleinasien bis Decius*, ed. S. Alkier and H. Leppin, WUNT 400 (Tübingen: Mohr Siebeck, 2018), 333–362.

Breytenbach, C., and J. M. Ogereau, eds., *Authority and Identity in Emerging Christianities in Asia Minor and Greece*, AJEC 103 (Leiden: Brill, 2018).

Breytenbach, C., and C. Zimmermann, *Early Christianity in Lycaonia and Adjacent Areas: From Paul to Amphilochius of Iconium*, AJEC 101, ECAM 2 (Leiden: Brill, 2018).

Calder, W. M., "The Eumeneian Formula," in *Anatolian Studies Presented to William Hepburn Buckler*, ed. W. M. Calder and J. Keil (Manchester: Manchester University Press, 1939), 15–26.

Calder, W. M., "Early Christian Epitaphs from Phrygia," *AnSt* 5 (1955): 25–38.

Chaniotis, A., "The Jews of Aphrodisias: New Evidence and Old Problems," *SCI* 21 (2002): 209–242.

Chaniotis, A., "The Conversion of the Temple of Aphrodite at Aphrodisias in Context," in *From Temple to Church: Destruction and Renewal of Local Cultic Topography in Late Antiquity*, ed. J. Hahn, S. Emmel, and U. Gotter, RGRW 163 (Leiden: Brill, 2008), 243–273.

Chester, A., "Jewish Inscriptions and Jewish Life," in *Neues Testament und hellenistisch-jüdische Alltagskultur. Wechselseitige Wahrnehmungen*, ed. R. Deines, J. Herzer, and K.-W. Niebuhr, WUNT 274 (Tübingen: Mohr Siebeck 2011), 383–441.

Cohick, L., "Melito of Sardis's *Peri Pascha* and its 'Israel'," *HTR* 91 (1998): 351–372.
Destephen, S., "Les courants religieux en Asie Mineure du IVe au VIIe siècle," in *Hierapolis di Frigia XII. Le abitazioni dell'insula 104 a Hierapolis di Frigia*, ed. A. Z. Ruggiu (Istanbul, Yayinlari, 2019), 655–665.
Edwards, M. J., "Ignatius and the Second Century: An Answer to R. Hübner," *ZAC* 2 (1998): 214–226.
Engelmann, H., "Ephesos und die Johannesakten," *ZPE* 103 (1994): 297–302.
Fairchild, M. R., "Turkey's Unexcavated Synagogues: Could the world's earliest known synagogue be buried amid rubble?," *BAR* 38.4 (2012): 34–41.
Foss, C., *Ephesus After Antiquity: A Late Antique, Byzantine and Turkish City* (Cambridge: Cambridge University Press, 1979).
Frankfurter, D., "Jews or Not? Reconstructing 'the Other' in Rev 2:9 and 3:9," *HTR* 94 (2001): 403–425.
Frey, J., "Toward Reconfiguring Our Views on the 'Parting of the Ways': Ephesus as a Test Case," in *John and Judaism: A Contested Relationship in Context*, ed. R. A. Culpepper and P. N. Anderson (Atlanta, GA: Society Biblical Literature, 2017), 221–239.
Gaston, L., "Jewish Communities in Sardis and Smyrna," in *Religious Rivalries and the Struggle for Success in Sardis and Smyrna*, ed. R. S. Ascough, SCJud 14 (Waterloo: Wilfrid Laurier University Press, 2005), 17–24.
Gibson, E. L., "The Jews and Christians in the *Martyrdom of Polycarp:* Entangled or Parted Ways?," in *The Ways that Never Parted: Jews and Christians in Late Antiquity and the Early Middle Ages*, ed. A. H. Becker and A. Y. Reed, TSAJ 95 (Tübingen: Mohr Siebeck, 2013), 145–158.
Gilbert, G., "Jews in Imperial Administration and its Significance for Dating the Jewish Donor Inscription from Aphrodisias," *JSJ* 35 (2004): 169–184.
Grant, R. M., *Greek Apologists of the Second Century* (Philadelphia, PA: Westminster Press, 1988).
Hartog, P., *Polycarp's* Epistle to the Philippians *and the* Martyrdom of Polycarp: *Introduction, Text, and Commentary* (Oxford: Oxford University Press, 2013).
Horner, T. J., *Listening to Trypho: Justin Martyr's* Dialogue *Reconsidered*, CBET 28 (Leuven: Peeters, 2001).
Horsley, G. H. R., "The Inscriptions of Ephesos and the New Testament," *NovT* 34 (1992): 105–168.
Huttner, U., *Early Christianity in the Lycus Valley*, AJEC 85, ECAM 1 (Leiden: Brill, 2013).
Junod, E., and J.-D. Kaestli, *Acta Iohannis, Tomis 2: Textus alii Commentarius*, CCSA 2 (Turnhout: Brepols, 1983).
Kant, L. H., "Jewish Inscriptions in Greek and Latin," *ANRW* 20.2 (1987): 671–713.
Klauck, H.-J., *The Apocryphal Acts of the Apostles: An Introduction* (Waco, TX: Baylor University Press, 2008).
Koch, D.-A., "The God-fearers between facts and fiction. Two theosebeis-inscriptions from Aphrodisias and their bearing for the New Testament," *Studia Theologica – Nordic Journal of Theology* 60 (2006): 62–90.
Koester, C. R., *Revelation: A New Translation with Introduction and Commentary*, AYB (New Haven, CT: Yale University Press, 2014).
Lalleman, P. J., *The Acts of John: A Two-Stage Initiation into Johannine Gnosticism*, Studies on the Apocryphal Acts of the Apostles 4 (Leuven: Peeters, 1998).

Lambrecht, J., "Jewish Slander: A Note on Rev 2,9–10," in idem, *Collected Studies on Pauline Literature and on The Book of Revelation* (Rome: Pontificio Istituto Biblico, 2001), 329–339.

Lambrecht, J., "Synagogues of Satan (cf. Rev 2,9 and 3,9): Anti-Judaism in the Apocalypse," in idem, *Collected Studies on Pauline Literature and on The Book of Revelation* (Rome: Pontificio Istituto Biblico, 2001), 341–356.

Lampe, P., *From Paul to Valentinus: Christians at Rome in the First Two Centuries* (Minneapolis, MN: Fortress, 2003).

Lieu, J. M., *Image and Reality: The Jews in the World of the Christians in the Second Century* (Edinburgh: T&T Clark, 1996).

Lieu, J. M., "Accusations of Jewish Persecution in Early Christian Sources, with particular Reference to Justin Martyr and the *Martyrdom of Polycarp*," in *Tolerance and Intolerance in Early Judaism and Christianity*, ed. G. N. Stanton and G. G. Strousma (Cambridge: Cambridge University Press 1998), 279–295.

Lieu, J. M., "'The Parting of the Ways': Theological Construct or Historical Reality?," in *Neither Jew Nor Greek? Constructing Early Christianity*, SNTW (London: T&T Clark, 2002), 11–29.

Lieu, J. M., *Christian Identity in the Jewish and Graeco-Roman World* (Oxford: Oxford University Press, 2004).

Lookadoo, J., *The High Priest and the Temple: Metaphorical Depictions of Jesus in the Letters of Ignatius of Antioch*, WUNT 2/473 (Tübingen: Mohr Siebeck, 2018).

Magness, J., "The Date of the Sardis Synagogue in Light of the Numismatic Evidence," *AJA* 109 (2005): 443–475.

McKechnie, P., *Christianizing Asia Minor: Conversion, Communities, and Social Change in the Pre-Constantinian Era* (Cambridge: Cambridge University Press, 2019).

Miltner, F., *Das Cömeterium der Sieben Schläfer*, FiE IV/2 (Wien: Rohrer, 1937).

Mimouni, S. C., "Les Judéens chrétiens et les Judéens synagogaux en Anatolie au IIe siècle: Confrontation ou coexistence (Ignace, Polycarpe et Méliton)," in *Jews and Christians in Antiquity: A Regional Perspective*, ed. P. Lanfranchi and J. Verheyden (Leuven: Peeters, 2018), 143–162.

Mitchell, S., *Anatolia. Land, Men and Gods in Asia Minor. Vol. II: The Rise of the Church* (Oxford: Clarendon Press, 1993).

Mitchell, S., "An Apostle to Ankara from the New Jerusalem: Montanists and Jews in Late Roman Asia Minor," *SCI* 24 (2005): 207–223.

Mitchell, S., and P. Pilhofer, eds., *Early Christianity in Asia Minor and Cyprus: From the Margins to the Mainstream*, AJEC 109, ECAM 3 (Leiden: Brill, 2019).

Murray, M., *Playing a Jewish Game: Gentile Christian Judaizing in the First and Second Centuries CE*, SCJud 13 (Waterloo: Wilfrid Laurier University Press, 2004).

Noy, D., *Jewish Inscriptions of Western Europe. Vol. 1: Italy (excluding the City of Rome), Spain and Gaul* (Cambridge: Cambridge University Press, 1993).

Noy, D., *Jewish Inscriptions of Western Europe. Vol. 2: The City of Rome* (Cambridge: Cambridge University Press 1995).

Oster, R. E., "Christianity in Asia Minor," in *The Anchor Bible Dictionary*, ed. D. N. Freedman (New York, NY: Doubleday, 1994), 1:938–954.

Pervo, R. I., "Johannine Trajectories in the Acts of John," *Apocrypha* 3 (1992): 47–68.

Pillinger, R., "Jüdische Alltagskultur in Ephesos und Umgebung im Spiegel der Denkmäler," in *Neues Testament und hellenistisch-jüdische Alltagskultur. Wechselseitige*

Wahrnehmungen, ed. R. Deines, J. Herzer, and K.-W. Niebuhr, WUNT 274 (Tübingen: Mohr Siebeck, 2011), 85–98.

Ramsay, W. M., *The Cities and Bishoprics of Phrygia*, Vol. I, Part 2 (Oxford: Clarendon Press, 1897).

Reed, A. Y., and A. H. Becker, "Introduction: Traditional Models and New Directions," in *The Ways that Never Parted: Jews and Christians in Late Antiquity and the Early Middle Ages*, ed. A. H. Becker and A. Y. Reed, TSAJ 95 (Tübingen: Mohr Siebeck, 2003), 1–33.

Reynolds, J., and R. Tannenbaum, *Jews and Godfearers at Aphrodisias*, Cambridge Philological Society Supplementary Volume 12 (Cambridge: Cambridge Philological Society, 1987).

Robert, L., *Hellenica: Recueil d'epigraphie de numismatique et d'antiquites grecques*, vol. 11–12 (Limoges: Bontemps, 1960).

Scherrer, P., *Ephesus: The New Guide* (Istanbul: Ege Yaginlari, 2000).

Schnabel, E. J., "Jewish Opposition to Christians in Asia Minor in the First Century," in idem, *Jesus, Paul, and the Early Church: Missionary Realities in Historical Contexts. Collected Essays*, WUNT 406 (Tübingen: Mohr Siebeck, 2018), 289–332.

Schürer, E., rev. and ed. G. Vermes, F. Millar, and M. Goodman, *The History of the Jewish People in the Age of Jesus Christ (175 B.C. – A.D. 135)*, vol. III.1 (Edinburgh: T&T Clark, 1986).

Schüssler Fiorenza, E., *The Book of Revelation: Justice and Judgment* (Philadelphia, PA: Fortress, 1985).

Skarsaune, O., "Evidence for Jewish Believers in Greek and Latin Patristic Literature," in *Jewish Believers in Jesus: The Early Centuries*, ed. O. Skarsaune and R. Hvalvik (Peabody, MA: Hendrickson, 2007), 505–567.

Stewart-Sykes, A., *The Lamb's High Feast: Melito, Peri Pascha and the Quartodeciman Paschal Liturgy at Sardis*, SVigChr 42 (Leiden: Brill, 1998).

Strubbe, J. H. M., "'Cursed be he that moves my bones'," in *Magika Hiera. Ancient Greek Magic and Religion*, ed. C. A. Faraone and D. Obbink (New York, NY: Oxford University Press, 1991), 33–59.

Strubbe, J. H. M., *ARAI EPITUMBIOI. Imprecations against Desecrators of the Grave in the Greek Epitaphs of Asia Minor. A Catalogue*, IGSK 52 (Bonn: Habelt, 1997).

Tabbernee, W., *Montanist Inscriptions and Testimonia: Epigraphic Sources Illustrating the History of Montanism*, North American Patristic Society Patristic Monograph Series 16 (Macon, GA: Mercer University Press, 1997).

Talley, T. J., *The Origins of the Liturgical Year* (Collegeville, PA: Liturgical Press 1991).

Tellbe, M., *Christ-Believers in Ephesus. A Textual Analysis of Early Christian Identity Formation in a Local Perspective*, WUNT 242 (Tübingen: Mohr Siebeck, 2009).

Thompson, L. L., *The Book of Revelation: Apocalypse and Empire* (Oxford: Oxford University Press 1990).

Thornton, T. C. G., "Problematical Passovers. Difficulties for Diaspora Jews and Early Christians in determining Passover Dates during the First Three Centuries A.D," in *Studia Patristica Vol. XX: Papers Presented to the Tenth International Conference on Patristic Studies held in Oxford 1987: Critica, Classica, Orientalia, Ascetica, Liturgica*, ed. E. A. Livingstone (Leuven: Peeters, 1989), 402–408.

Trebilco, P. R., *Jewish Communities in Asia Minor*, SNTSMS 69 (Cambridge: Cambridge University Press, 1991).

Trebilco, P. R., "The Christian *and* Jewish Eumeneian Formula," in *Negotiating Diaspora: Jewish Strategies in the Roman Empire*, ed. J. M. G. Barclay, LSTS 45 (Sheffield: Sheffield Academic Press, 2004), 66–88.

Trebilco, P. R., *The Early Christians in Ephesus from Paul to Ignatius*, WUNT 166 (Tübingen: Mohr Siebeck, 2004).

Trebilco, P. R., "Jews in Asia Minor," in *Routledge Handbook of Jews and Judaism in Late Antiquity*, ed. C. Hezser (London: Routledge, forthcoming 2021).

van der Horst, P. W., "Jews and Christians in Aphrodisias in the Light of their Relations in Other Cities of Asia Minor," *NedTT* 43 (1989): 106–121.

van der Horst, P. W., *Ancient Jewish Epitaphs. An introductory survey of a millennium of Jewish funerary epigraphy (300 BCE – 700 CE)*, CBET 2 (Kampen: Kok Pharos, 1991).

van der Horst, P. W., "Judaism in Asia Minor," in *The Cambridge History of Religions in the Ancient World. Vol. 2: From the Hellenistic Age to Late Antiquity*, ed. M. R. Salzman and W. Adler (Cambridge: Cambridge University Press, 2013), 321–340.

van der Horst, P. W., "Pious Long-Sleepers in Greek, Jewish, and Christian Antiquity" in idem, *Studies in Ancient Judaism and Early Christianity* (Leiden: Brill, 2014), 248–266.

Waelkens, M., "Ateliers lapidaires en Phrygie," in *Actes du VIIe Congress international d'épigraphie grecque et latine, Constantza, 9–15 septembre 1977*, ed. D. M. Pippidi (Bucharest: Editura Academie; Paris: Société d'Édition "Les Belles Lettres", 1979), 105–128.

Williams, M. H., "The Meaning and Function of *Ioudaios* in Graeco-Roman Inscriptions," *ZPE* 116 (1997): 249–262.

Williams, M. H., "Semitic Name-Use by Jews in Roman Asia Minor and the Dating of the Aphrodisias Stele Inscriptions," in *Old and New Worlds in Greek Onomastics*, ed. E. Matthews, PBA 148 (Oxford: Oxford University Press, 2007), 173–197.

Wilson, S. G., *Related Strangers: Jews and Christians, 70–170 C.E.* (Minneapolis, MN: Fortress, 1995).

Zimmermann, N., "Das Sieben-Schläfer-Zömeterium in Ephesos: Neue Forschungen zu Baugeschichte und Ausstattung eines ungewöhnlichen Bestattungskomplexes," *JÖAI* 80 (2011): 365–407.

Joseph Verheyden
Living Apart Together: Jews and Christians in Second-Century Rome – Re-visiting Some of the Actors Involved

Abstract: Der vorliegende Aufsatz untersucht Material aus römischen Quellen oder aus Quellen, die mit Rom in Verbindung stehen. Die Einführung bietet einige allgemeinere Überlegungen zur Verwendung von Paradigmen, insbesondere des "Parting of the Ways"-Paradigmas, um die Beziehungen zwischen Juden und Christen im zweiten Jahrhundert zu untersuchen. Der erste Abschnitt gibt einen Überblick über einige Autoren, denen die Frage entweder gleichgültig zu sein scheint (*1 Clemens*, der *Hirt des Hermas*) oder die eine sehr dezidierte Sichtweise vertreten, aber nicht im unmittelbaren Dialog mit jüdischen Gegnern stehen (Ignatius). Der zweite Abschnitt behandelt Justins *Dialog mit dem Juden Tryphon*. Er konzentriert sich dabei auf die rhetorischen Strategien, die Justin benutzt, um den Gegner in die Enge zu treiben, und zeigt, dass Justin nicht so sehr darauf bedacht war, die andere Seite für sich zu gewinnen, sondern vielmehr Argumente für die Verteidigung des Standpunkts der Christen zu liefern, um seinen Lesern eine Hilfestellung bei der Bewahrung ihrer Identität zu geben. In einem kurzen dritten Abschnitt wird Justins Standpunkt demjenigen von Marcion gegenübergestellt, mit besonderem Blick darauf, wie der Erstgenannte seinen Gegner darstellt. In der Zusammenfassung wird dargelegt, dass Justins *Dialog*, das Hauptthema dieses Aufsatzes, nicht darauf abzielt, eine "Parting of the Ways"-Theorie zu propagieren, sondern pragmatisch nach Wegen sucht, wie beide Seiten zusammenleben können, wobei sie gleichzeitig ihre Differenzen in der Interpretation eines gemeinsamen Erbes anerkennen.

Keywords: 1 Clement, Shepherd of Hermas, Ignatius of Antioch, Justin Martyr, Marcion, Roman Christianity

Allow me to begin this paper with a famous citation that I hope will illustrate the wider context in which I would like to situate my topic. The passage was originally written in French, but it has been translated into English and German, and since the phrase sounds even more impressive in the latter version I cite it according to that translation:

> Nehmen wir einmal an, das moderne Europa wäre Zeuge davon gewesen, wie die Gläubigen die christlichen Kirchen verließen, um Allah oder Brahma zu verehren, die Gebote des Kon-

> fuzius oder des Buddha zu befolgen, die Grundsätze des *shinto* anzunehmen; denken wir uns ein großes Durcheinander von allen Rassen der Welt, in dem arabische Mullahs, chinesische Literaten, japanische Bonzen, tibetanische Lamas, hinduistische Pandits zu gleicher Zeit den Fatalismus und die Prädestination, den Ahnenkult und die Anbetung des vergötterten Herrschers, den Pessimismus und die Erlösung durch Selbstvernichtung verkündigten, und dass alle diese Priester in unseren Städten fremdartig stilisierte Tempel erbauten und in diesen ihre verschiedenen Riten zelebrierten – dann würde dieser Traum, den die Zukunft vielleicht einmal verwirklichen wird, uns ein ziemlich genaues Bild von der religiösen Zerrissenheit gewähren, in der die alte Welt vor Konstantin verharrte.

The text was written by the great Franz Cumont. It is found in his book *Die orientalischen Religionen im römischen Heidentum,* in which he developed his impressive thesis on the influx of oriental religions in late-republican and early imperial Rome and how it changed the ancient world.[1] One may dispute the overall thesis, which I will not do here. Instead I wish to offer four brief comments on the basis of this one passage that may help to get a better picture of how the topic we are dealing with in this volume should best be assessed. First, Cumont speaks of a vision in which he saw a world that had not yet come into existence in his days, but that he apparently does not think to be a mere chimera. Today, we can see this world realised in many of our major Western cities. The dream became true and we are coping with the consequences of it, and this probably still for a very long time. Second, Cumont's vision speaks of two phenomena that are only syntactically distinguished, but not really as to their content, unless one reads the text more carefully. On the one hand, he sees a massive move from established religion, however this is to be defined, towards new groups and religious practices of foreign origin; on the other, he sees an apparently equally massive influx of people adhering to external or "strange" cults and practices. Together these two cause a revolution in the world the local population was familiar with. Third, one can question certain aspects of Cumont's presentation and the imagery he used for sketching "the world before Constantine," such as the degree of visibility all these groups had in society, but one should probably to a large part agree with the overall picture and with the consequences, in

---

1 The German translation: F. Cumont, *Die orientalischen Religionen im römischen Heidentum* (Repr. Darmstadt: Olms, 1975 [²1914]), 227. Originally published as *Les religions orientales dans le paganisme romain,* 4th ed. (Paris: Annales du Musée Guimet, 1929). English: *The Oriental Religions in Roman Paganism* (Repr. New York: Dover, 1956 [1911]). The French version was re-published, with an introduction by C. Bonnet and F. Van Haeperen, in 2006 as part of the *Bibliotheca Cumontiana* project (F. Cumont, *Les religions orientales dans le paganisme romain,* ed. C. Bonnet and F. Van Haeperen with B. Toune, *Bibliotheca Cumontiana. Scripta Maiora* 1 [Turin: Nino Aragno Editore, 2006]).

terms of revolutionising society and creating new sorts of tensions between religious groups, he implicitly connects with it. Fourth and final, in his book Cumont paid relatively little attention to Judaism and Christianity as representatives of this "oriental invasion," probably because they were not really "visible" in these early days through their places of worship, but he would certainly reckon the two amongst them. It is to these two that I will turn in the following, because they are the topic of this volume and because they have a special bound to each other, a bound unlike any of the other players on the field of religion had in early imperial Rome. I will first draw attention to the overall situation, and then deal with a work that I think is illustrative and symptomatic for a particular way in which Christians tried to handle the question of their relationship towards Judaism in second-century Rome.

Much has been written in the past three or so decades about "the parting of the ways" between Judaism and Christianity in the first two centuries of our era.[2] The image itself is a most vivid and also a most intriguing one.[3] It expresses the

---

[2] The "mother of all books" on the matter is, of course, the collection of essays, the proceedings of a Durham conference of 1989, edited by James Dunn under the title *Jews and Christians. The Parting of the Ways A.D. 70 to 135*, WUNT 66 (Tübingen: Mohr Siebeck, 1992). As is well known, the majority of the contributors took a nuanced stance on the delicate question of whether the earliest Christian writings and the communities they addressed and stemmed from were truly anti-Semitic. The essay by Dunn himself is a good example of this, cautioning against all too simplistic positions ("The Question of Anti-semitism in the New Testament Writings of the Period," in *Jews and Christians* [cf. above], 177–211) and putting a question mark in the title of each section dealing with a particular New Testament writing (e.g., "Is Acts 'Anti-Semitic'?"). In his conclusion he points out again his general thesis that these texts were written at a time that "'Judaism' (or Judaisms) was under dispute and its boundaries in process of being redrawn" (210). Dunn also pays attention to the pastoral aspect, warning against attempts at ignoring or even removing such passages that are deemed "difficult." "But this is no answer and quickly becomes as manipulative as the abuses it seeks to avoid" (211). As always, "the answer is not to run away from our historical roots and the hurt of the earliest 'parting of the ways', but to enter more fully into it, to understand it afresh 'from inside' as far as that is possible, and to re-evaluate the whole period and its outworkings [sic] in company with those who also regret that parting." It sounds like a (political) programme, and that is how it was meant by the author.
[3] Actually, the paradigm or model is used for denoting change or separation in related fields, and far beyond. Here are a few titles to illustrate this: G. Boccaccini, *Beyond the Essene Hypothesis: The Parting of the Ways between Qumran and Enochic Judaism* (Grand Rapids, MI: Eerdmans, 1998); on a more theoretical level, arguing that scholars of Rabbinic and Early Christian literature often tend to obscure the similarities in the topics they are studying: M.A. Tong, "Protective Difference: Protectionist Strategies and the Parting of the Ways," *Method and Theory in the Study of Religion* (2020): 1–9. In other disciplines or areas: A.D. Wright, *The Divisions of French Catholicism, 1629–1645: "The Parting of the Ways"* (Burlington VT: OUP, 2013); J. Bos, "Before the Parting of the Ways: Nederlandse filosofen over geschiedenis en geschiedweten-

dynamics of a process, all while evoking connotations of radicality and irreversibility. It is no surprise, then, that the model, or paradigm, has continued to appeal to quite some scholars.⁴ Yet it has also increasingly met with mild and more severe criticism from various corners. Most of these more critical voices do not wish to ignore the phenomenon of gradual separation it describes, but for different reasons are more or less sceptical about the usefulness of the model to do so.⁵ A few have gone one step further and have not just questioned the appropri-

---

schap, 1920–1970," *Tijdschrift voor Geschiedenis* 129 (2016): 35–56. In the paramedical sphere: I. Norman, "'... and Midwifery': Time for a Parting of the Ways or a Closer Union with Nursery?," *International Journal of Nursing Studies* 44 (2007): 521–522. In philosophy: M. Friedman, *A Parting of the Ways: Carnap, Cassirer, and Heidegger* (Chicago: Open Court Press, 2000); at the intersection of epistemology and the philosophy of science: M.D. Beni, *Cognitive Structural Realism: A Radical Solution to the Problem of Scientific Representation* (Cham: Springer International Publishing, 2019), 11–36 ("The Parting of the Ways"). And from a much further past, pedagogy: H. Lucas, *At the Parting of the Ways: Considerations and Meditations for Boys* (London: Sands and Co., 1906).

4 See V. Martin, *A House Divided: The Parting of the Ways between Synagogue and Church. Studies in Judaism and Christianity* (New York and Mahwah, NJ: Paulist Press. A Stimulus Book, 1995); S. Spence, *The Parting of the Ways: The Roman Church as a Case Study*, Interdisciplinary Studies in Ancient Culture and Religion 5 (Leuven: Peeters, 2003), focusing on the first century, mainly based on evidence from Paul; D. Stökl Ben Ezra, "Weighing the Parts. A Papyrological Perspective on the Parting of the Ways," *NT* 51 (2009): 168–186; M. Heemstra, *The Fiscus Judaicus and the Parting of the Ways*, WUNT 2/277 (Tübingen: Mohr Siebeck, 2010); I. Ramelli, "The Jesus Movement's Flight to Pella and the 'Parting of the Ways'," *Augustinianum* 54 (2014): 35–51 (all while recognising that the model is "a construal" (47), Ramelli assesses it positively); B.G. Bucur, "Justin Martyr's Exegesis of Biblical Theophanies and the Parting of the Ways between Christianity and Judaism," *Theological Studies* 75 (2014): 34–51, arguing that the "consistently Christological interpretation of theophanic texts" (50) is not Justin's invention but has its roots in New Testament writings; from an archaeological perspective, E.C. Smith, *Jewish Glass and Christian Stone: A Materialist Mapping of the "Parting of the Ways,"* Routledge Studies in the Early Christian World (Abingdon: Routledge, 2017); S.J.D. Cohen, "The Ways That Parted: Jews, Christians, and Jewish-Christians, ca. 100–150 CE," in *Jews and Christians in the First and Second Centuries: The Interbellum 70–132 CE*, ed. J. Schwartz and P.J. Tomson, CRINT 15 (Leiden and Boston, MA: Brill, 2018), 307–339; M. Rosik, *Church and Synagogue (30–313 A.D.): Parting of the Ways*, European Studies in Theology, Philosophy and History of Religions 20 (Berlin: P. Lang, 2019); K. Schenck, *A New Perspective on Hebrews: Rethinking the Parting of the Ways* (Lanham, MD: Lexington Books and Fortress Academic, 2019).

5 See, e.g., J.M. Lieu, *Image and Reality. The Jews in the World of the Christians in the Second Century* (Edinburgh: T&T Clark, 1996); eadem, *Neither Jew nor Greek? Constructing Early Christianity* (Edinburgh: T&T Clark, 2002), 31–49; M. Zetterholm, *The Formation of Christianity in Antioch: A Social-Scientific Approach to the Separation between Judaism and Christianity* (London: Routledge, 2003); J. Carleton Paget, "Introduction," in *Jews, Christians and Jewish Christians in Antiquity*, ed. idem, WUNT 251 (Tübingen: Mohr Siebeck, 2010), 1–39, here 3–24 (a good critical survey of recent literature); E.K. Broadhead, *Jewish Ways of Following Jesus: Redrawing the Reli-*

ateness of the model but also the reality it points to. This criticism can take two very different formats. One option is simply to deny that there ever was a common basis from which to depart.[6] The other is to argue that there was no parting going on in that early period; it was not until much later than is usually assumed by the adherents of the model that the two sides started to drift apart, and even then one should be cautious in using such a radical definition.[7] There seems to

---

gious Map of Antiquity, WUNT 266 (Tübingen: Mohr Siebeck, 2010), 354–391; B. Green, *Christianity in Ancient Rome: The First Three Centuries* (London and New York: T&T Clark, 2010); S.C. Mimouni and B. Pouderon, eds., *La croisée de chemins revisitée: Quand l'église et la synagogue se sont-elles distinguées? Actes du colloque de Tours, 18–19 juin 2010* (Paris: Cerf, 2012); T. Nicklas, *Jews and Christians? Second Century 'Christian' Perspectives on the 'Parting of the Ways,'* Annual Deichmann Lectures 2013 (Tübingen: Mohr Siebeck, 2014); idem, "Parting of the Ways? Probleme eines Konzepts," in *Juden – Heiden – Christen?*, ed. S. Alkier and H. Leppin, WUNT 400 (Tübingen: Mohr Siebeck, 2018), 21–41. Cf. the bibliography in Ramelli, "Jesus Movement" (see n. 4), 47 nn. 29–30.

[6] This is the option taken by U. Schnelle, *Die getrennten Wege von Römern, Juden und Christen* (Tübingen: Mohr Siebeck, 2019). The final clause of his book says it all: "Entscheidend war die Position der Römer: Ihre christentumsfeindliche Haltung forderte geradezu die Distanzierung des Judentums vom entstehenden Christentum. Deshalb konnte es auch keine 'Trennung der Wege' geben, denn alle drei sind nie gemeinsame, sondern von Anfang an getrennte Wege gegangen" (190).

[7] See A.H. Becker and A.Y. Reed, eds., *The Ways that Never Parted. Jews and Christians in Late Antiquity and the Early Middle Ages,* TSAJ 95 (Tübingen: Mohr Siebeck, 2003). The book contains a combination of case studies and more theoretical reflections. Those familiar with the work will no doubt have noted the various ways in which the model is questioned in the way it is referred to in the titles of the essays: using question marks (P. Frederiksen, A. Cameron), pointing out difficulties and "pitfalls" in studying the matter (D. Boyarin, R.A. Kraft), using terms such as "reconsidering" (A.S. Jacobs), "entangled or parted ways?" (E.L. Gibson), "continuing [...] sub-cultures" (D. Frankfurter; in a slightly different format also Reed), or even "convergence" (A. Salvesen). Perhaps the most telling essay of all is the short contribution by Martin Goodman (119–129: "Modeling the 'Parting of the Ways'") that consists almost entirely of diagrams illustrating in various ways the intertwining, or at least the ongoing significance of the common originals, of Jewish and Christian groups and perspectives, even when their representatives thought they had truly separated. Specifically with regard to Tertullian, S.E. Binder, *Tertullian, on Idolatry and Mishnah Avodah Zarah: Questioning the Parting of the Ways between Christians and Jews*, Jewish and Christian Perspectives 22 (Leiden and Boston, MA: Brill, 2012). Note how both Schnelle (see n. 6) and Becker and Reed squarely announce their position in the title of their book. Cf. also D. Boyarin, *Border Lines: The Partition of Judaeo-Christianity*, Divinations: Rereading Late Ancient Religion (Philadelphia, PA: University of Pennsylvania Press, 2004), with the critical remarks of Carleton Paget, "Introduction" (see n. 5), 15 ("to play up continuities" at the cost of accusing Justin of intentionally misrepresenting Jewish Logos theology). The difficulty with the model is that it actually does not say "never," but rather "some time," as is made most clear by a comment of Boyarin on how to read Justin: "we miss important possibilities for a historical reading of Justin's text because of a persistent misreading (a century old) that takes it as

be no place for a middle way. Either the two communities were working hard to break, or stay, away from each other, or they were doing their best to avoid this. As usual, reality was most probably more nuanced, and therefore also more complicated.[8] The asset, which at the same time is also the drama, of Jewish-Christian relationships, then as now, is that the two share a common heritage that none of them wishes to forsake and that one party says has been abused by the other for its own agenda, while the other thinks the full potentials of this heritage have never been truly explored and recognised by the original claimants. The links between the two are so intricate and the issues at stake so vital for both parties that the problem cannot be ignored and that a solution that satisfies both is probably never to be produced. The two are stuck in a dilemma that constitutes itself a crucial part of their raison d'être. We need others to be "us" or "ourselves." Yet in the case of Judaism and Christianity at the same time one of the two has long urged the other to become like them, and thus to give up or ignore the differences that gave both their identity, while the other wished its counterpart to recognise it was mistaken about its claims and assumptions, and thus in a sense also to ignore its own identity.[9]

Two things emerge from the above that perhaps need further scrutiny, which is what I will try to provide in this paper. One is briefly to show that the Jewish-Christian divide was perhaps not that all-embracing as one might be led to think in reading the "parting of the ways" literature. The other, partly linked to the former, is that some of the more important evidence for treatments of the question

---

reflecting an existing situation (an alleged "parting of the ways") rather than participating in producing it (a partitioning of religious territory)" ("Justin's Dialogue with the Jews: The Beginnings of Orthodoxy," in *Border Lines* [see n. 7], 37–73, here 67). Division is in the process of being created, even by those who are said to be intent on keeping the sides together.

8 The complexity of Jewish-Christian relations in antiquity (and beyond), which to a large part was caused by contingencies, such as local traditions, the role of individuals, and specific events that created a crisis situation, was duly emphasised in several of the essays collected in P. Lanfranchi and J. Verheyden, eds., *Jews and Christians in Antiquity. A Regional Perspective*, Interdisciplinary Studies in Ancient Culture and Religion 18 (Leuven et al.: Peeters, 2018). The purpose was to show how such "regional factors" play their role in shaping these relations.

9 The complexity of the situation for all parties involved is well described by S.C. Mimouni, "Introduction. Sur la question de la séparation entre 'jumeaux' et 'ennemis' aux Ier et IIe siècles," in *La croisée de chemins revisitée: Quand l'église et la synagogue se sont-elles distinguées? Actes du colloque de Tours, 18–19 juin 2010*, ed. idem and B. Pouderon (Paris: Cerf, 2012), 7–20, here 19: "De toute façon, parler de rupture et de séparation est une question idéologique qui suppose une tout autre question: celle de la distinction entre un christianisme et un rabbinisme qui se veulent différents, afin d'empêcher toute confusion dans les esprits – car si l'un ou l'autre se confondaient, comment alors pourrait-on les distinguer de manière aussi radicale que l'un et l'autre le voudraient?"

does not so much seem to be intent on forcing a solution in one way or the other ("staying or parting"), but rather on looking for settling the issue in such a way that both sides can go on with their lives, while realising that they will continue to be neighbours and live side-by-side, whether they like it or not. The prime and major concern for community leaders in such a model is to find ways to ascertain that one's own side is sheltered against possible attacks or criticisms, adequately equipped to withstand these when they happen, and sufficiently enthused to respect the barriers and to stay within its own territory. All of this may sound a bit abstract at this stage, but I hope to clarify my position in studying specific aspects of one writing in particular.

1 The relation to Judaism, a "non-issue" in second-century Christian writings in Rome

Peter Lampe's fine survey of Roman Christianity in the second century has become a classic in the field. Lampe is not specifically interested in the question of how Roman Christian communities and their leaders positioned themselves over against Judaism, but as he deals with all possible aspects that help draw a full picture of these communities, he can of course not avoid speaking of it when necessary. The topographical analysis with which he begins his work shows that traces of Christian presence can be found, to different degrees, in several areas of the city. Not unexpectedly, the so-called "Jewish quarter" of Trastevere also harboured a significant number of Christian communities: "Mit grosser Sicherheit können wir Trastevere, die XIV. augusteische Region, als frühes christliches Wohnviertel ausmachen."[10] The same goes for the area around the Via Appia/Porta Capena within the walls of the city.[11] For other areas the evidence is less univocal, but not completely absent. The sociographical analysis that completes this part of Lampe's study gives the same results. A few areas are predominantly occupied by people of lower classes, obviously not just of Jewish descent, for these quarters are also hotbeds of other oriental religions. That is where one may expect also to find Christian communities. Other areas, such as the quarters on the Aventine and the Mars Field, show a mixed population, which does not mean that Christians were totally absent from them. As a matter of fact, this was where openings could be made to recruit converts from some-

---

10 P. Lampe, *Die stadtrömischen Christen in den ersten beiden Jahrhunderten. Untersuchungen zur Sozialgeschichte*, 2nd ed., WUNT 2/18 (Tübingen: Mohr Siebeck, 1989), 30.
11 Ibid.

what higher social classes. In sum, like other religious groups, Christians were not bound to one or two quarters, though they must have been more prominent in certain areas than in others. The image of Jews and Christians emancipating from Judaism finding themselves together in some sort of ghetto, if one would wish to maintain such a model at all, is most probably a fiction. The situation was rather more diverse and "mixed," which means, inter alia, that the two groups were not exclusively bound up with each other.

Literary evidence that Christians were not constantly obsessed by how to situate themselves towards Judaism can be found in at least two writings that are commonly said to have originated in Rome. Writing most probably at the turn of the century, or perhaps even as late as the 120s,[12] the author of 1 Clement had other problems to face when writing to the Corinthian community. In bolstering his argument, he frequently refers to Jewish traditions, both in a positive and a rather more negative way, to instruct his addressees and draw comparisons between what is said in these traditions and what the Corinthian Christians are doing, but he does not use that material in any way to suggest that Christians should distance themselves from Judaism. It is rather the contrary: they can find there good examples to explain and master situations or events occurring in their own communities. Two examples may illustrate this. In the opening chapters, envy and jealousy are identified as the major cause for the troubles that shake the Corinthian community. They can lead to terrible things, including fratricide, as Clement shows in a long list of references to biblical cases of envy, starting with Cain and Abel and going all the way to Saul and David (1 Clem. 4).[13] Useful lessons can be taught from them, and the overall picture is that the Christians misbehaving in Corinth are no better than their Jewish ancestors and are playing with fire. The remarkable thing is that the comparison is not used polemically against Judaism, as if Christians were better, but at best only pedagogically, as what one should not wish to follow, and actually above all merely practically and realistically: what happened then, is still happening today, as if nothing had changed. No moral judgement is spoken against Judaism as a whole; the examples are merely that, examples from a common tradition

---

[12] So the somewhat "unorthodox" opinion of O. Zwierlein, *Petrus in Rom. Die literarischen Zeugnisse. Mit einer kritischen Edition der Martyrien des Petrus und Paulus auf neuer handschriftlicher Grundlage*, Untersuchungen zur antiken Literatur und Geschichte 96 (Berlin and New York: de Gruyter, 2009) 13 and 330. I mention this position as an illustration of both the uncertainty that continues to exist about the dating and other introductory issues of this earliest Christian literature and of the tenacity of "common opinion."

[13] Cf. H.E. Lona, *Der erste Clemensbrief*, KAV 2 (Göttingen: Vandenhoeck & Ruprecht, 1998), 147–155.

known also to the addressees and meant to educate and frighten them back into discipline.[14] In 1 Clem. 43 is told the famous story of the confrontation between Moses and the heads of the twelve tribes concerning the priesthood that is settled with the example of the blossoming rod (Num 17) and will lead to establishing Aaron as head of the priests.[15] The story serves as an introduction and a parallel to the issue that interests Clement above anything else – the way the apostles have arranged for the leadership of the communities to be settled orderly. This is dealt with in chapter 44. The passage is part of the overall argument as developed in 1 Clem. 40 – 44 that strife leads to nothing and unity in recognition of officially established leadership is the only viable way forward. I have no wish to discuss the quality of the argument in this context, but just want to point out that once again an example from Israel's past is used to illustrate an eternal truth: able leaders should always stay aware of the fact that strife and conflict lurk behind any incident that may occur. The Jewish leaders challenging Moses are not worse than those opposing the received leadership structures, and there is not even the idea that things could have developed since then towards a more realistic position on these matters; on the contrary, just as Moses knew what was coming and prepared to deal with it and solve the problem, so the apostles knew their flock and took similar measures to keep things in hand.[16] In short, Judaism (or "Israel") is not a topic for itself, "it rather is an instrument to achieve something else."[17]

Like Clement, the author of the Shepherd of Hermas has his own problems to deal with and sees no reason even to touch upon the question of Jewish-Christian relations in his otherwise endlessly long exhortation of his flock and the many descriptions of its flaws and deficiencies. The latter are numerous and of all sorts, but nowhere the danger of hanging out with Jewish neighbours is brought on the table or even hinted at. Its author is not unfamiliar with Jewish tradition, even with elements that are rather on the fringes of that tradition as is

---

14 "Die Haltungen von markanten Gestalten der Geschichte stellen Vorbilder dar, die – positiv oder negativ – vom Leser als solche erkannt und auf die eigene Wirklichkeit übertragen werden sollen. [...] Das Interesse ist nicht historisch, sondern rhetorisch-pragmatisch" (ibid., 154).
15 Ibid., 448 – 455.
16 Lona speaks in this respect, and with reference to 43:1, of "die Parallelisierung der Rolle des Mose und der der Apostel" and notes that Clement in 44:1 emphasises that the apostles had been instructed by the Lord about such troubles (ibid., 454).
17 J. Verheyden, "Israel's Fate in the Apostolic Fathers. The Case of 1 Clement and the Epistle of Barnabas," in *The Separation between the Just and the Unjust in Early Judaism and in the Sayings Source – Die Scheidung zwischen Gerechten und Ungerechten in Frühjudentum und Logienquelle*, ed. M. Tiwald, BBB 172 (Göttingen: V&R Press; Bonn: Bonn University Press, 2015), 237–262, here 239.

shown in two subsequent chapters of the first part of the work. Vis. 2.3.4 cites or refers to "the Book of Eldad and Modat," "the only attributed quote in *Hermas*."[18] The precise extent of the citation is unclear, but this lost apocryphal book said to have been written in the name of two prophets mentioned in Num 11:26 is cited to exhort one Maximus not to despair and to realise that the Lord always welcomes the one who finally repents. It is a nice thought, but one can easily find evidence from other biblical books to the same effect and maybe even Hermas could have relied on a word of Jesus to state the same; but he does not and prefers to rely on an almost completely unknown book of Jewish origin.[19] The second case is perhaps even slightly more disturbing. In an ensuing vision Hermas sees a young man questioning him about the identity of the elderly woman who gave him the little book. The best answer he can come up with is that she is "the Sibyl," which she is not, for she represents the Church (Vis. 2.4.1). It is not clear whether Hermas thinks of a pagan or a Jewish sibyl, but the second option can certainly not be excluded.[20] So here again, Jewish tradition, not per force biblical tradition, is probably referred to in an attempt to make sense of a vision. Jewish tradition, if that is what the sibyl represents, is a viable option for the Christian Hermas who is otherwise not interested in things Jewish and makes no particular efforts to cite from that tradition. Jewish tradition is "an open book" for this author and apparently also for his intended readership; nothing is wrong with citing from it and no polemical intentions are connected with it whatsoever, but at the same time one has the impression that the author could as well have cited from Christian or pagan tradition to make his point, as he shows no special interest in Judaism as such.

This was certainly different in other quarters. One traveller to Rome, forced to make the journey and taken up with addressing all sorts of questions in his own communities, finds it necessary to set aside his personal problems and situation and to lecture his readership in two of his letters on the dangers of com-

---

18 C. Osiek, *The Shepherd of Hermas*, Hermeneia (Minneapolis, MN: Fortress, 1999), 57.
19 The prophetic character of the quotation adds to the threatening effect, but similar wording could also be found in Jesus tradition. The choice of the author is all the more remarkable, and unusual, because of the combination with the motif of the "book from heaven"; cf. N. Brox, *Der Hirt des Hermas*, KAV 7 (Göttingen: Vandenhoeck & Ruprecht, 1991), 103.
20 As a matter of fact, this possibility is strengthened if one opts against reading "Cumae" in 1.1.3, for then the "natural" association with the Cumaean Sibyl is off the table, or at least far less prominent. Jewish tradition contains many examples of identifying Israel or Jerusalem with a woman, and that may well be the more plausible context. So Osiek, *Hermas* (see n. 18), 58: "a wisdom motif already adapted to Jewish purposes."

ing too close to Judaism.²¹ Ignatius of Antioch warns the community in Magnesia not to give in to attempts to lure it back into its old way of life "according to Judaism," as this will cost them God's grace (*Magn.* 8:1).²² "Judaizing" is a constant threat for newly converted members of the community. By that, Ignatius is probably referring, first and foremost, to perceived threats from inside, by Jewish converts who wished to stick to some of their traditional practices and tried to impose these on other converts.²³ Ignatius is more outspoken still in *Magn.* 10:3 when calling "proclaiming Jesus Christ and practising Judaism outlandish" (ἄτοπον). He continues by noting that Judaism is the forerunner, but Christianity the real thing: "For Christianity did not believe in Judaism, but Judaism in Christianity – in which every tongue that believes in God has been gathered together."²⁴ The same sound is heard in the letter to the Philadelphians (*Phld.* 6:1). The threat of being exposed to Jewish propaganda – from the inside, but maybe also from the outside, in an attempt to lure away aspiring Christians – is considered real, all while recognising that there is a close bound between the two religions and even valuing the potential of being taught on Christ by a Jew rather than by a Gentile on Judaism. The comparison seems a bit strange, but its clue is clear when it is added that none of these options is valid if these teachers do not speak of Christ, for then "they both appear to me as monuments and tombs of

---

21 He thereby clearly took his perception of the situation in Antioch as the standard to address other communities. On the former, see T.A. Robinson, *Ignatius of Antioch and the Parting of the Ways. Early Jewish-Christian Relations* (Peabody, MA: Hendrickson, 2009) and the general observation on how Ignatius judged the ethnic situation in the city: "Ignatius reflects a more developed but intentionally less nuanced sense of the divisions. For him, there are but two camps – Judaism and Christianity. Whatever the nuances within these camps, they are irrelevant to his main distinction" (103–104). On Ignatius' take on the Jews/Christians divide, see Nicklas, *Jews and Christians?* (see n. 5), 124–129.
22 W.R. Schoedel, *A Commentary on the Letters of Ignatius of Antioch*, Hermeneia (Philadelphia: Fortress, 1985), rightly considers *Magn.* 8–10 to represent "the heart of the letter" (118). Judaism "is not even granted a historically limited role in the unfolding of God's plan" (119). This distances Ignatius from Paul. Actually, "the negative view of Judaism is more emphatic in Ignatius than in the Pastorals and approaches the extreme position of *Barnabas*" (ibid.). On the latter writing, see Verheyden, "Israel's Fate" (see n. 17), 247–161; Nicklas, *Jews and Christians?* (see n. 5), 67–74, 177–182.
23 So emphatically, Zetterholm, *Formation* (see n. 5), 203–211: "*a realistic conflict within a close group that eventually acquired non-realistic elements*" (210; italics original).
24 This strange formula should not be read as if Ignatius gives in to his previous position and allows Judaism a place in salvation history, but rather as a reference to how former Jews in the city once converted to Christianity and should be held as models for future generations. So rightly Schoedel, *Ignatius* (see n. 22), 126.

the dead, on which are written merely human names."[25] Christianity is intrinsically linked to Judaism, but should by definition prevail, because both are supposed to look towards Christ Jesus. No such thoughts are met in Ignatius' letter to the Roman community. They are above all, and repeatedly, warned not to intervene on behalf of the martyr *in spe*, evoking a situation in which it is taken for granted that Roman Christians were able to do so if they had wished. Maybe Ignatius knew of people with connections in high places and is not speaking in blue air, but no names are given. Not a word is said about the threat to Christians he signalled in the letters to Magnesia and Philadelphia. This may be because he is now all-focused on his own fate, but it is at least remarkable how he emphasises that the Roman community is solely oriented to Christ and the Father (note the *bi-nomen* χριστόνομος πατρώνυμος in the prescript of the letter, with χριστώνυμος as a variant), ruled by the former (*Rom.* 9:1), who is repeatedly called God (prescript; 3:3 "being in the Father"), and empowered by the hatred it suffers from the world (3:3).[26] The way Ignatius presents it and for all the parallelism between his fate and that of Christ he indulges in, the true enemy are the Roman, and not, as in Jesus' passion, the Jewish authorities.[27]

These few examples, the last of which featuring an author who is looking at the question from a rather unexpected angle, show that crucial things could be dealt with in the Roman orbit in and among Christian communities without bringing up the question of the latter's relationship with Judaism. That is not to say, of course, that it was completely a non-issue, as I will show in the second part of the paper.

---

25 Possibly a faint allusion at Matt 23:37, though others prefer to look for parallels in Greek literature (so Schoedel, *Ignatius* [see n. 22], 203). The mention of Gentiles in this context in a sense complicates the argument, but it also makes it possible for Ignatius to speak out even more radically: Christ is the key.

26 Translated in terms of obedience to the Law, this means that the latter (and Scripture as a whole) matter only in so far as they are "prophesying the 'Christ-event'" (Nicklas, *Jews and Christians?* [see n. 5], 129).

27 Cf. Schoedel, *Ignatius* (see n. 22), 172: "it is significant that whereas elsewhere Ignatius is mildly disposed to pagan society despite its hostility (*Eph.* 10; cf. *Tr.* 8:2), in this letter he treats the importance of being hated by the world as the essence of Christianity (besides 3:3, see also John 7:7; 15:18–19; 17:14; 1 John 3:13)." In Ign.*Rom.* 5 he plays heavily on this theme when considering the Roman authorities he has to deal with as almost non-human and their city as the place for Christians to attain salvation through martyrdom.

2 The *Dialogue with Trypho*, or how Christians are to behave towards Jews

Justin's *Dialogue with Trypho* is not the only such work from the second century we know of, but it is the only one that has been preserved,[28] and it is the only one that, through its author, can be linked with Rome.[29] The latter aspect is of course not without some importance for the topic of this paper, but it should be added that Justin does not seem to have made any special effort to bring out the specific situation in Rome and rather gives the impression that what he is presenting is of a more general nature and would work also in other contexts. In the following I will focus on two things. I will give a general characterisation of Justin's approach, as I understand it, and of his idea of what a discourse with benevolent Jewish opponents should look like; I will then illustrate this from one case study.[30]

Scholars have invested a lot of energy in debating in how far the dialogue reflects a real-life situation and whether the dialogue partner was an historical

---

[28] Of a few others we have merely the title: cf. the *Altercatio Jasonis et Papisci*, which may have been preserved in the Latin *Altercatio Simonis Judaei et Theophili Christiani*, though this is difficult to ascertain. On its possible influence on Justin, see W. Rutherford, "*Altercatio Jasonis et Papisci* as a Testimony Source for Justin's 'Second God' Argument," in *Justin Martyr and His Worlds*, ed. S. Parvis and P. Foster (Minneapolis, MN: Fortress, 2007), 137–144.

[29] On Justin Martyr and his œuvre, see most recently J. Ulrich, *Justin Apologien*, KfA 4/5 (Freiburg et al.: Herder, 2018), 18–30. For a history of research on the *Dialogue*, see S.J.G. Sanchez, *Justin apologiste chrétien. Travaux sur le* Dialogue avec Tryphon *de Justin Martyr*, CahiersRB 50 (Paris: Gabalda, 2000), 25–67. A good survey of all introductory questions concerning the Dialogue in A. Rudolph, "*Denn wir sind jenes Volk ...". Die neue Gottesverehrung in Justins Dialog mit dem Juden Tryphon in historisch-theologischer Sicht*, Hereditas 15 (Bonn: Borengässer, 1999), 21–66.

[30] The first nine chapters have been commented by J.C.M. van Winden, *An Early Christian Philosopher. Justin Martyr's Dialogue with Trypho Chapters One to Nine. Introduction, Text, Commentary*, Philosophia Patrum 1 (Leiden: Brill, 1971). As yet, there is no systematic commentary on the work. The one that comes closest to such a commentary is the very valuable companion volume to the critical edition published by P. Bobichon, *Justin Martyr. Dialogue avec Tryphon. Édition critique, traduction, commentaire*, 2 vols., Paradosis 47/1–2 (Fribourg: Academic Press, 2003). I have used Bobichon's edition and have extensively referred to his notes. As much as I like Lukyn Williams's translation, I have opted for Falls's all through, even if it is sometimes perhaps a bit too free, because it is probably more easily accessible, but I have added an occasional reference to the other in the notes. See A.L. Williams, *Justin Martyr The Dialogue with Trypho. Translation, Introduction and Notes* (London: SPCK, 1930); T.B. Falls, *Saint Justin Martyr*, Fathers of the Church 6 (Washington, D.C.: CUA Press, 1948).

figure (rabbi Tarphon?).³¹ These are obviously legitimate questions, but as there are no firm indications for answering any of these positively, it is perhaps safer not to give too much weight to this aspect, realising that the thoughts and opinions that are put forward in the text are doubtless more important for Justin than the question whether this actually "happened" in the way he presents it.³² Information on the setting is sparse and never said to be in any way relevant for the subject to be discussed. In that respect, one should not forget that the dialogue is not set in Rome. It takes place under a colonnade (*Dial.* 1.1; 9.3) in a city that is not further identified, but Eusebius says was Ephesus (*Hist. eccl.* 4.18.6), before Justin set sail for Rome (*Dial.* 142.1–3). The debate is not centred on analysing the situation in a specific place, but tackles the questions that are on the table on a more general level, as philosophers are supposed to do, for both parties behave and consider themselves as such. Justin is addressed in this way by Trypho and does not object to it, and the latter prides himself on his training by one Corinthus "the Socratic" (1.2). This is of quite some importance, as the Jewish partner in the dialogue is identified as anything but a professionally trained rabbi. Actually, he has a far more open mind towards Christianity, so it seems, than the rabbis who are met later on in the Mishnah or the Talmud. He wants to hear the truth (87.1), something any true philosopher should aim at. Little can be drawn from this to decide on where the text was composed, but Rome, Justin's

---

31 A balanced presentation of these questions in Lieu, *Image and Reality* (see n. 5), 109–113; cf. also T.J. Horner, *Listening to Trypho. Justin Martyr's Dialogue Reconsidered*, Contributions to Biblical Exegesis & Theology 28 (Leuven et al.: 2001), 16–32; the attempt to give Trypho a place within "Asian Jewry" is interesting, but remains a bit experimental (169–190).

32 In this respect, the in se innovating approach Horner offers when trying to unearth Trypho's perspective from the *Dialogue* is methodologically difficult to substantiate. See his reconstruction of the "Trypho text" (*Listening to Trypho* [see n. 31], 39–56). Decidedly going beyond the "yes or no" question about the historicity of the character is M.R. Niehoff, "A Jew for Roman Tastes: The Parting of the Ways in Justin Martyr's *Dialogue with Trypho* from a Post-Colonial Perspective," *JECS* 27 (2019): 549–578. Niehoff considers Justin's Trypho to be a construct fabricated to upset a Roman audience by bringing on the table such "horrible" topics as circumcision, Jewish exclusivism that Romans naturally associate with xenophobia, and futile questions on principles of textual exegesis (549: "a spiritually sterile activity"). The approach is innovative, though perhaps a bit too one-sided, for one can easily imagine that part at least of Justin's teaching in countering Trypho, say, on the double Parousia or on the figure of a divine saviour from the East, would probably also be rather difficult to digest for a Roman taste. With the issue of exegesis vs. philosophy, Justin may well have been catering to a Roman audience, as there is some evidence that Roman-based or -schooled philosophers were rather caustic in their comments on the great tradition of commenting upon "the classics." Referring to a comment made by Seneca, Niehoff notes, "Philosophy has in his view nothing to do with commentary. It is instead a therapy of the individual self" (571).

hometown for some years, is evidently a good candidate. The dialogue is presented as the result of a chance encounter between Justin "the philosopher" and a wandering Jew who readily introduces himself as such, giving his name and briefly referring to his own situation. He says he is a refugee from the war, which should most probably be taken as referring to the Bar Kochba war, who divides his time between Greece (more particularly, Corinth) and Asia Minor (1.3).[33] Rome is not in sight and the man apparently has no intention to visit it soon. It is also important to note that the outcome of the dialogue remains open. The two are said to part ways good-humoured, without having been able to convince the other. Trypho's friendly invitation to continue the debate on another occasion sounds rather hollow as he knows Justin is leaving for Rome, and in the same way the latter's expectation that Trypho and his companions might one day find happiness in worshipping "the Christ of God," with which he takes leave, is little more than a pious hope.

In between the opening and closing setting is a long tractate on basic aspects of the Jewish and the Christian faith presented as a dialogue, but actually it rather takes the form of a Socratic dialogue in which the two partners are not speaking on equal terms and are not given the same opportunity to voice their opinion, but one merely functions as a sparring partner for the other who does most of the talking and throughout very much stays in command of the scene and the contents of the talk.[34] Obviously, Trypho is not completely passive.[35] He does fight back and uses four types of criticism to counter Justin, calling him out of his mind (39.3), biased in the choice of his arguments (27.1),[36] blasphemous (38.1; 79.1), and sophistic (79.1)[37] – all of them classical strategies in polemics, but none of these is able to shake Justin's confidence, who in turn does not scare away of challenging Trypho (64.2; 67.4, 7), nor are they expected to confuse the reader into doubting Justin's presentation. So several elements – the presentation and overall behaviour of the Jewish partner in the encounter, not your typical Jewish opponent, and of the Christian partner, Justin himself,

---

[33] On the impact the revolt may have had on raising tensions between Christians and Jews, see J. Carleton Paget, "Jewish Revolts and Jewish-Christian Relations," in *Jews and Christians in the First and Second Centuries: The Interbellum 70–132 CE*, ed. J. Schwartz and P.J. Tomson, CRINT 15 (Leiden and Boston, MA: Brill, 2018), 276–306, here 298–302.

[34] Martin, *A House Divided* (see n. 4), 170: "a monologue rather than a dialogue."

[35] A survey of the interaction is sketched in Bobichon, *Justin* (see n. 30), 921–941; the list gives a first general idea of how the dialogue develops.

[36] Cf. P.J. Donahue, *Jewish-Christian Controversy in the Second Century. A Study in the* Dialogue *of Justin Martyr* (PhD diss., Yale University, 1973), 160–163.

[37] On the latter, see Horner, *Listening to Trypho* (see n. 31), 73–78.

probably more a teacher than a polemicist, the tone of the dispute, its setting and its format – all seem to suggest that the work bears more the character of a tractate than of a real dialogue. It is not particularly interested in addressing daily-life situations of Jewish-Christian co-existence but aims higher and tackles principled questions of both religious traditions.[38] In so far as this is indeed the case and purpose of the *Dialogue*, one might ask if it should not rather be defined as a manual for how to behave towards Judaism, hence a text of a far more normative nature than the title and format at first sight would seem to suggest. That this, as a matter of fact, is what Justin intended it to be will be shown from a couple of examples.

The *Dialogue* does not really display a clear and systematic structure.[39] Several topics show up on more than one occasion, but overall one could say that the Law and Christ form the two major topics that have Justin's attention; they are dealt with throughout the *Dialogue* with apparently not much concern for order. The first is covered by chapters 9–47, the second by chapters 48–108, including some smaller sections on specific beliefs (mostly centred around chapters 79–82, but not limited to these). A third and final part argues, based on the outcome of the previous ones, that it is the Christians who have correctly understood the promises that were made to the Jewish people, and invites the latter to join them in recognising this and hopefully drawing the appropriate conclusions from it (chapters 109–141). The *Dialogue* contains some pretty harsh statements on the part of Justin (and also of Trypho) and a few passages smell of supersessionism, but this in itself is not a sufficient basis to conclude that Justin is writing "the dialogue to end all dialogue."[40] The way the dialogue ends may be revealing in this respect. The cheerful goodbye at the end of chapter 142 may well be more than a mere literary *topos* and reflect Justin's opinion that the discourse with Judaism can go on even after the harsh words that have been said about it. It is not the end of the story. A brief look at the text itself may help to support this view.

---

38 On the delicate and difficult question of the quality and the roots of Justin's expertise and its origin in matters Jewish, see D. Rokéah, *Justin Martyr and the Jews*, Jewish and Christian Perspectives Series 5 (Leiden and Boston, MA: 2002), 20–42.
39 "La littérature consacrée à Justin foisonne de jugements réservés sur son aptitude de composer" (Bobichon, *Justin* [see n. 30], 17). On the difficulties and various proposals, see ibidem, 17–48.
40 On verbal rivalry and the notion of "take-over," see Lieu, *Image and Reality* (see n. 5), 136–140. It is one of the more delicate and emotional topics in the *Dialogue* (see Trypho's reply in 124.1).

Unlike Trypho and Justin, I am not interested in finding "the truth about Judaism or Christianity" or in assessing the strength of the arguments Justin puts forward, but in the tactics and strategies that are being used, in what they provoke, and in whether they point towards a push for parting ways or rather should be read as an invitation somehow to stay together. It is not easy to come across such traces as this involves a bit of reading between the lines and looking for the impression certain statements may make and for the consequences these might have for one party or the other. Justin rarely spells out any of these. So I am aware there might be a dose of subjectivity involved in this kind of approach, but I hope to make it clear that it is not only about subjective impressions.

2.1 On tactics and strategies

Justin uses a number of strategies and tactics in confronting his Jewish discussion partner. Probably the most important one is the decision basically to argue almost exclusively from Jewish Scripture. It may look as if this is just inevitable, but we will see below that this is not necessarily the case. Jews and Christians share a common heritage, and hence in an all-embracing way, a common fate. Scripture is "theirs" as a source of truth and as the major tool, for both sides, in making sense of their own existence and indeed of the world as a whole. It is a blessing and a curse at the same time. Scripture is not only a source for identity creation, it is also the battlefield par excellence on which any dispute between Judaism and Christianity is to be fought. On a few occasions Justin relies on references to Greek mythology (67.2 and 70.5) or philosophy (6.3; 8.3), as a rule in an unfavourable comparison with Judeo-Christian tradition.[41] But overall,

---

[41] The former is about the story of the birth of Perseus from Zeus and the virgin Danae. Trypho brings it up to counter Christian opinion on the birth of Jesus. Justin retorques with the same argument he also uses in *1 Apol.* 54.8: such a story is the work of the devil. That is the line of thought in *Dial.* 69.1–3 and his conclusion in 70.5. In *1 Apol.* 21.2 and 22.5 he argues differently and in a sense more convincingly when urging the emperor to accept the virgin birth of Jesus as he also does with Perseus. In 69.2–3 are mentioned Alcmene, Asclepius, Dionysus, Hercules, Semele, and Zeus again. Cf. Bobichon, *Justin* (see n. 30), 756 n. 3 and 4, 765 n. 14. On the parallel with *1 Apol.* 21 and the hypothesis of a common source, see P. Prigent, *Justin et l'Ancien Testament. L'argumentation scripturaire du traité de Justin contre toutes les hérésies comme source principale du Dialogue avec Tryphon et de la Première Apologie*, 2nd ed., Études Bibliques (Paris: Gabalda, 1966), 158–171. On the criticism of ancient philosophy, Rudolph, *Gottesverehrung* (see n. 29), 84–87; Green, *Christianity in Ancient Rome* (see n. 5), 81–92: "where philosophy can only glimpse aspects of the truth, Christianity can be certain" (87).

Scripture is immensely more important. Hence the innumerable and often endlessly long citations. For many of the latter, the reader may wonder what is the point of getting so much context, if only a few lines, and sometimes even less, are then also explained in some more detail. In not a few cases it looks as if for Justin citing Scripture is in itself proof and argument for his position.[42] The proof is in the citing.

In line with this general attitude and his hesitance to introduce arguments that are not based on Scripture, Justin can agree with Trypho that one should not try to explain what happens on earth by merely referring to God's will, because it is too easy and it usually does not answer the problem. In order to avoid any impression that this is what he is after, he insists that he solely relies on evidence from Scripture and on facts (28.1–2).[43] It is an interesting way of putting things, as it assumes that these two always go together.[44]

Citing Scripture comes with a few basic hermeneutical principles. The three most important of these are the conviction that Scripture reveals its own truth if interpreted correctly, that it cannot contradict itself or be mistaken, and that its true meaning as a rule is not to be found in the literal or historical interpretations championed by Jewish tradition as represented by Trypho. The first of

---

Greek philosophy is made a topic above all in the opening chapters of the work, in which both parties refer to Plato and Pythagoras. Trypho seems to take a double stand on its usefulness when he first says he does not care much about whether he agrees with them (6.1) and a bit later urges Justin to keep away from his profound aspirations for knowing the divine and stick with philosophical virtues (8.3). It is not an open contradiction, but Justin at least manages to build in some tension in Trypho's replies. On Justin's somewhat dubious knowledge and handling of Greek philosophy in these passages, see N. Hyldahl, *Philosophie und Christentum. Eine Interpretation der Einleitung zum Dialog Justins*, Acta Theologica Danica 9 (Copenhagen: Munksgaard, 1966), esp. pp. 91–99; van Winden, *An Early Christian Philosopher* (see n. 30), 100–101, 121–122; Sanchez, *Justin* (see n. 29), 163–177.

42 Scripture is the cornerstone of any dispute between Jews and Christians, and not infrequently the latter probably felt they were lagging behind in their command of exegetical techniques when confronting Jewish intellectuals (so Lieu, *Image and Reality* [see n. 5], 128–129), though Justin does not seem to be particularly concerned about this.

43 *Dial.* 28.2: Ἐπειδὴ ἀπό τε τῶν γραφῶν καὶ τῶν πραγμάτων τάς τε ἀποδείξεις καὶ τὰς ὁμιλίας ποιοῦμαι, ἔλεγον, μὴ ὑπερτίθεσθε μηδὲ διστάζετε πιστεύσθαι ("Then I replied, 'Since I base my arguments and suggestions on the Scriptures and facts, you should not hesitate to believe me"). Falls fails to translate the emphatic double verb; Lukyn Williams translates more correctly as "do not put the matter off, or hesitate." Justin had used the motif before in 23.4 and will use it again in 39.6 and 53.5.

44 Cf. Bobichon, *Justin* (see n. 30), 649 n. 22: "c'est surtout la *coïncidence* de ces deux types de preuves qui constitue pour lui un argument décisif en faveur de la conception chrétienne de l'histoire du Salut."

these principles is never spelled out as such, but it is continually tested and "demonstrated" all through the *Dialogue* in the many instances in which Justin compares Jewish with Christian interpretation.⁴⁵ The second is brought on the table in only a few instances.⁴⁶ The third is the backbone of Justin's Christological exegesis. Passages which Judaism traditionally explained as referring to one of its kings – Hezekiah, David, or Solomon – are in truth to be read in light of what happened to Jesus as the Christ.⁴⁷ Justin indulges in this sort of exegesis,

---

45 In *Dial*. 79, to name one such instance, Justin counters Trypho's objection that his interpretation of the motif of the fallen angels is artificial and even blasphemous (79.1 τετεχνασμέναι ... καὶ βλάσφημοι) by citing two passages from the Prophets that would support his position (Isa 30:1 and Zech 3:1–2) without much of a comment, as if the texts speak for themselves. On the motif, though not on Justin's method, see Prigent, *Justin* (see n. 41), 20–24; Bobichon, *Justin* (see n. 30), 783 n. 2. On the role of the Prophets as Justin's "allies," see C.D. Allert, *Revelation, Truth, Canon and Interpretation: Studies in Justin Martyr's* Dialogue with Trypho, SupVigChr 64 (Leiden and Boston, MA: Brill, 2002), 92–98.
46 A clear case is found in *Dial*. 65.2 where Justin accuses Trypho of provoking him to say that Scripture is inconsistent. His reaction is fierce and emotional: "you are sadly mistaken if you did so in the hope of embarrassing me into admitting that some passages of Scripture contradict others, for I would not be so bold as to assert, or even imagine, such a thing. […] I am positive that no passage contradicts another, I would rather openly confess that I do not know the meaning of the passage" (εἰ δὲ χάριν τοῦ νομίζειν δύνασθαι εἰς ἀπορίαν ἐμβάλλειν τὸν λόγον, ἵν᾽ εἴπω ἐναντίας εἶναι τὰς γραφὰς ἀλλήλαις, πεπλάνησαι· οὐ γὰρ τολμήσω τοῦτό ποτε ἢ ἐνθυμηθῆναι ἢ εἰπεῖν ... ἐκ παντὸς πεπεισμένος ὅτι οὐδεμία γραφὴ τῇ ἑτέρᾳ ἐναντία ἐστίν, αὐτὸς μὴ νοεῖν μᾶλλον ὁμολογήσω τὰ εἰρημένα). "Le principe de non contradiction est fondamental dans la conception que Justin a des Écritures" (Bobichon, *Justin* [see n. 30], 755 n. 3).
More implicit is 51.1, where Trypho thinks little of Justin's long citation of Isa 39:8–40:17 to support his position that the Baptist is the forerunner of the Messiah: "the words of the prophecy which you just quoted are ambiguous, and they certainly do not prove what you want them to prove" (ἀμφίβολοι μὲν πάντες οἱ λόγοι τῆς προφητείας, ἣν φῇς σύ, ... καὶ οὐδὲν τμητικὸν εἰς ἀπόδειξιν οὗπερ βούλει ἀποδεῖξαι ἔχοντες). Justin replies that what John announced was fulfilled in Jesus and combines with it the objection that since no other prophets have come forward anymore in Judaism, Isaiah's prophecy must apply to John, thereby implying that otherwise Scripture would contain promises that were never fulfilled, hence wrong. The line of argument is tricky, to say the least, in part also because the text is slightly uncertain (on the latter, see Bobichon, *Justin* [see n. 30], 722 n. 2). Cf. also G.N. Stanton, "Other Early Christian Writings: *Didache*, Ignatius, *Barnabas*, Justin Martyr," in *Early Christian Thought in Its Jewish Context*, ed. J.M.G. Barclay and J.P.M. Sweet (Cambridge: CUP, 1996), 174–190, here 185–188.
47 Two examples out of several to illustrate this. In *Dial*. 33.1 Justin declares void any interpretation that explains Ps 109:1–5 as referring to king Hezekiah: "you are wrong" (πεπλάνησθε). The correct interpretation obviously is to read it as a prophecy on Christ who for Justin is the only one rightly to be identified as a priest in the order of Melchisedech. He repeats the argument in *Dial*. 77.1, now with reference to Isa 8:4. In *Dial*. 34.1 he uses the same reasoning to oppose identifying the king addressed in Ps 71 with Solomon. One wonders whether such arguments could ever convince the opponent. On Justin's handling of these identifications, which

much at the incomprehension and distress of Trypho, at least initially. The overarching criticism that covers these three approaches is the observation that the Jews do not understand their own tradition, because their spirit is hardened, as it is said more than once with reference to Isa 29:13–14.[48] Occasionally, Justin ventilates his frustration that Jewish exegesis loses itself in minutiae, a critique that is perhaps true in part, but certainly does not apply all through.[49] It turns out then that, even though Justin and Trypho are working from the same source material, they are usually not "on the same page."

One strategy Justin particularly seems to like is that of repeating or coming back on an interpretation he had given before. Sometimes he is urged by Trypho to do so, but elsewhere he does so of his own initiative (63.1; 85.6–7). Apart from the obvious pedagogical purpose behind such a move, the strategy also serves two further purposes in this kind of literature. It forces a particular opinion upon the audience, and it provides the author with an excellent opportunity to show what he considers to be the truly important topics and to picture his protagonist as being in command of the situation and capable of defending his position time and again without being caught in contradictions or tensions of any sort. Two such topics are the double advent of the Messiah/Christ[50] and the Virgin birth.[51]

---

had deep roots in Jewish tradition, see P. Bobichon, "Salomon et Ézéchias dans l'exégèse juive des prophéties royales et messianiques, selon Justin Martyr et les sources rabbiniques," *Tsafon. Revue d'études juives du Nord* 44 (2002–03): 149–165.

48 In *Dial.* 78.11 Justin concludes his reading of the visit of the magi at the birth of Jesus with this passage and the firm statement that the grace to understand Scripture has been transferred to the Christians: δίο καὶ εἰς ἡμᾶς μετετέθη ἡ χάρις αὕτη. The same motif had been developed before in 30.2 and 32.5 (with a shorter citation from Isaiah), and occurs also in *1 Apol.* 60.1, but here with reference to a transfer of wisdom from the Greeks to the Christians, another favourite of Justin (Bobichon, *Justin* [see n. 30], 671 n. 23). On the concept of grace in Justin, see Donahue, *Controversy* (see n. 36), 211–222; Sanchez, *Justin* (see n. 29), 86–95.

49 The criticism may sound ironic, as when Justin recalls Jewish exegetes disputing the correct spelling of the names of Abraham and Sarah (113.2), but is not totally justified, as a change in meaning can be involved. Cf. Bobichon, *Justin* (see n. 30), 853 n. 6.

50 In *Dial.* 32.2, Justin summarises his position on the double Parousia by emphasising that his argument is completely based on Jewish Scripture: νῦν δὲ διὰ πάντων τῶν λόγων ἀπὸ τῶν παρ' ὑμῖν ἁγίων καὶ προφητικῶν γραφῶν τὰς πάσας ἀποδείξεις ποιοῦμαι, ἐλπίζων τινὰ ἐξ ὑμῶν δύνασθαι εὑρεθῆναι ἐκ τοῦ κατὰ χάριν τὴν ἀπὸ τοῦ κυρίου Σαβαὼθ περιλειφθέντος εἰς τὴν αἰώνιον σωτηρίαν ("Now, I shall derive all my proofs from all the words I adduce from your sacred and prophetic Scriptures, in the hope that some one may be found among you to be of that seed which, by the grace of the Lord of Sabaoth, is reserved for everlasting salvation"). Note the emphatic double πᾶς and the double qualification of Scripture in combination with the first person singular and the firm expression of hope and confidence that this should suffice to convince

Every now and then, the dispute is peppered with quite provocative statements on the part of Justin, usually relying on standard criticisms, some of these quite harsh ones, that were commonly made against Judaism. Early in the dispute Justin brings up the standard critique that the Jews are not only liable of the death of Jesus, but have gone at great lengths to discredit Christianity all over the world (17.1).[52] Justin also repeatedly declares common Jewish ritual praxis void while useless for obtaining salvation.[53] It is a variant on the objection

---

even the most sceptic opponent. On the motif of hope, see Bobichon, *Justin* (see n. 30), 670 n. 11: "C'est ainsi que Justin définit, à plusieurs reprises, ce qui motive son activité missionnaire." In 52.1–2, Justin comes back to the topic and now, citing Gen 49:8, calls upon none less than the Patriarch Jacob to confirm once again what had been argued and "demonstrated" before with the help of the prophets. On the significance of the concept of the double advent in Justin, see Allert, *Revelation* (see n. 45), 231–239. On his use of the biblical passage, see O. Skarsaune, "Justin and His Bible," in *Justin Martyr and His Worlds*, ed. S. Parvis and P. Foster (Minneapolis, MN: Fortress, 2007), 53–76, here 55–56.

51 This time the tone and presentation are different, as Justin says in 66.1 that he will pick up where he had left the topic and continues by citing once more Isa 7:10 as he had done already in *Dial.* 43.5–6, before he was interrupted by Trypho who wanted to hear instead about the conditions for salvation. Justin gave in to the request, but now brings Trypho back to the "real issue." On Justin's use of the concept, see Rudolph, *Gottesverehrung* (see n. 29), 184–187.

52 Οὐξ οὕτως γὰρ τὰ ἄλλα ἔθνη εἰς ταύτην τὴν ἀδικίαν τὴν εἰς ἡμᾶς καὶ τὸν Χριστὸν ἐνέχονται, ὅσον ὑμεῖς, οἳ κἀκείνοις τῆς κατὰ τοῦ δικαίου καὶ ἡμῶν τῶν ἀπ' ἐκείνου κακῆς προλήψεως αἴτιοι ὑπάρχετε ("The other nations have not treated Christ and us, His followers, as unjustly as have you Jews, who, indeed, are the very instigators of that evil opinion they have of the Just One and of us, His disciples"). Note the chiasm in associating Christ ("the Just One") and "us" (Bobichon, *Justin* [see n. 30], 633 n. 1). Cohen, "The Ways That Parted" (see n. 4), 314–317, is critical of such claims on the part of Justin for the simple reason that "Jerusalem" did not have the means to organise such a project (316).

Another such general accusation is that of the Jews "cursing" the Christians. The topic is addressed in 96.1–2 citing Torah (Deut 21:23) while explicitly noting that the curse is not pronounced by God (ὑπὸ θεοῦ) and, contrary to Paul in Gal 3:13, that it did not refer to Christ. Justin manages to turn the verse into an accusation against the Jews. Cf. Bobichon, *Justin* (see n. 30), 824 n. 1. For the use of Deut 21:23, see J. Smit Sibinga, *The Old Testament Text of Justin Martyr* (Leiden: Brill, 1963), 96–98; O. Skarsaune, *The Proof from Prophecy. A Study of Justin Martyr's Proof-Text Tradition: Text-Type, Provenance, Logical Profile*, SupNT 65 (Leiden: Brill, 1987), 118 and 216–220; Rudolph, *Gottesverehrung* (see n. 29), 187–191. On tensions with the synagogue in this respect, see Donahue, *Controversy* (see n. 36), 191–192 (*Dial.* 17.1) and 222–227; Lieu, *Image and Reality* (see n. 5), 129–132; Boyarin, *Border Lines* (see n. 7), 54–58 and 67–73.

53 A good example is 19.2. Justin argues that circumcision offers no help and as a matter of fact is a sign marking out the Jewish people for suffering. The argumentation is rather twisted, to say the least. Cf. Donahue, *Controversy* (see n. 36), 153–157; Niehoff, "Roman Tastes" (see n. 32), 554–566. The same is true of Jewish ablutions, "your useless baptism" (τὸ βάπτισμα ἐκεῖνο τὸ ἀνωφελές). The latter topic picks up on what Justin had said in 14.1.

that the Jews do not understand their own religious tradition and have to be instructed about it by Christians to see its real value and meaning.[54] In the same line, and also applying to religious praxis, it is said that the Jews had continually to be taught and directed by God, "for you have always been disposed to forget Him, as Moses himself testifies [Exod 32:6]" (εὐκατάφοροι ὄντες καὶ εὐχερεῖς πρὸς τὸ ἀφίστασθαι τῆς γνώσεως αὐτοῦ, ὡς καὶ Μωϋσῆς φησιν).[55] And then there is of course the accusation of corrupting Scripture (72.1).[56]

Equally vivid and rhetorically useful are occasional objections *ad hominem*.[57] The standard critique on the Jews' liability for Jesus' death in 17.1 is fol-

---

[54] A particularly harsh statement of that sort is found in 38.2, when countering Trypho's objections to read Ps 44 in the light of Christ. Justin begins by pitying the Jews for not understanding their own Scriptures, then tells Trypho he will do his utmost to offer him the correct reading "out of fear for being judged" (Justin likes this motif; cf. Bobichon, *Justin* [see n. 30], 684–685), and concludes with an urgent exhortation to turn away from Jewish tradition because his teachers cannot see beyond their own narrow perspective. The last part of the section runs as follows: καταφρονοῦντες τῆς παραδόσεως τῶν ὑμετέρων διδασκάλων, ἐπεὶ οὐ τὰ διὰ τοῦ θεοῦ ὑπὸ τοῦ προφητικοῦ πνεύματος ἐλέγχονται νοεῖν δυνάμενοι, ἀλλὰ τὰ ἴδια μᾶλλον διδάσκειν προαιρούμενοι ("forsake the tradition of your teachers, for they are convicted by the Prophetic Spirit of being incapable of understanding the truths spoken by God, and of preferring their own opinions"). In 39.5, he states, without further ado, that only the Christians possess the truth: ἡμεῖς ... οἱ ἐκ πάσης τῆς ἀληθείας μεμαθητευμένοι ("We [...] who have been well instructed in His whole truth"). Justin uses the motif also elsewhere to make clear its unique character and its superiority over all other claims of wisdom. Cf. Bobichon, *Justin* (see n. 30), 687 n. 14. Such a position naturally calls for Trypho to ask on what basis Justin can say that he possesses this kind of knowledge. The topic is addressed in 58.1–2, and Justin's answer is as surprising as it is obvious: it is not a matter of rhetorical skills; he just enjoys a particular grace: χάρις παρὰ θεοῦ μόνη εἰς τὸ συνιέναι τὰς γραφὰς αὐτοῦ ἐδόθη μοι ("this grace alone was given me from God to understand His Scriptures"). Fortunately for Trypho, he is willing to share it with anyone who is open to his message. There is little one can bring against such a claim.

[55] When dealing with kashrut (20.1); the same line of arguing is developed in 21.1 on the Sabbath commandment. "Ces prescriptions [...] auraient donc essentiellement une fonction prophylactique" (Bobichon, *Justin* [see n. 30], 642 n. 1). On the status of Moses' Law in Justin's argument, see Rokéah, *Justin Martyr* (see n. 38), 43–60, esp. 54–55 (on Exodus).

[56] It is perhaps the nastiest objection, because it is mixed up with insinuations about diabolical interventions: "ce rapprochement entre les contrefaçons diaboliques d'une part, les mutilations des Écritures de l'autre, est lourd de sens" (Bobichon, *Justin* [see n. 30], 765 n. 1). Justin gives it all its weight, comparing it negatively to the idolatry of the golden calf (73.6).

[57] In arguing that Jewish exegesis cannot solve the apparent contradictions in Torah, Justin replies in 112.1, ὑμεῖς δε, ταῦτα ταπεινῶς ἐξηγούμενοι, πολλὴν ἀσθένειαν καταψηφίζεσθε τοῦ θεοῦ, εἰ ταῦτα οὕτως ψιλῶς ἀκούοιτε καὶ μὴ τὴν δύναμιν ἐξετάζοιτε τῶν εἰρημένων ("But you explain these passages in a repulsive manner, imputing to God every sort of weakness, when you interpret them baldly, without analysing the spirit of the words"). The vivid opposition

lowed by the apparently innocent observation that Trypho has read about Christ – it is not said what and how he did so –, which gives Justin the right to cite also directly from Jesus' teaching (18.1).⁵⁸ The move has the double advantage of enabling Justin to cite Christian material almost in line with Scriptural material, as he does in 17.2–4, a strategy, it must be said, he will not abuse, and of accusing Trypho in not-so-hidden language of not seeing the truth when it is presented to him. A similar case is found in 29.2, now applied to the Jewish Scripture, when Justin prides himself on arguing from writings that are part of Trypho's own religious tradition: "Aren't you acquainted with them, Trypho?" (ἐπιγνώσκεις αὐτούς, Τρύφων;).⁵⁹

A useful tool in disputes is to seemingly give in to the objections of the opponent, in order to counter them. A fine example is found in the way Justin replies to Trypho's comment that God will not forsake his people (25.6), to which Justin assents all while specifying that the rule does not apply as such, but only for those who do not harm the Christians (26.1).⁶⁰ That is a quite singular interpretation of a basic belief in Judaism and a fundamental modification of the old covenant theology which Justin is fond to bring up and turn in his advantage.

In some instances the strategy consists in bluntly negating what the other side holds against you. Trypho accuses Justin of citing Scripture selectively and of cherry-picking (27.1). The other just denies it – "'My friends', I replied, 'I have not purposely omitted such passages from the Prophets [he is speaking of Isaiah] because they do not coincide with my teaching'" – and then goes in the offense by claiming he kept silent about certain passages because they are so embarrassing for the other party: "although God through His Prophets gives

---

between ἀσθένεια and δύναμις adds force to the argument. It is just one of many such instances of direct reply.

58 Note the direct address: ἐπειδὴ γὰρ ἀνέγνως, ὦ Τρύφων, ὡς αὐτὸς ὁμολογήσας ἔφης, τὰ ὑπ' ἐκείνου τοῦ σωτῆρος ἡμῶν διδαχθέντα ... ("Since you, Trypho, admit that you have read the teachings of Him who is our Saviour ..."). Implied in the address is the critique that Trypho may well have read, but not understood what he was reading. So Bobichon, *Justin* [see n. 30], 635 n. 1); the motif is known to Justin (see *Dial.* 29.2 below; 55.3).

59 Cf. Donahue, *Controversy* (see n. 36), 163–165. There is some unintended irony in Justin's ironic question, as he had just misidentified a passage from Malachi, cited in 28.5, as stemming from Zechariah. On this kind of mistakes, see Bobichon, *Justin* (see n. 30), 663 n. 11.

60 The judgement goes for οἱ τὸν Χριστὸν διώξαντες καὶ διώκοντες καὶ μὴ μετανοοῦντες οὐ κληρονομήσουσιν ἐν τῷ ὄρει τῷ ἁγίῳ οὐδέν ("those who have persecuted Christ in the past and still do, and do not repent, shall not inherit anything on the holy mountain"). Justin links to it the more universalistic perspective that he naturally connects with Christianity. For Justin, the Jews can pose a deadly threat to the Christian community. Lieu calls it the "most specific among the charges of Jewish hostility" (Lieu, *Image and Reality* [see n. 5], 135).

you identical commands as He did through Moses, this was done only on account of your hardness of heart and ingratitude toward Him" (27.2).[61]

Justin occasionally likes to use hyperboles and a hyperbolic style, such as when he insists and takes for granted that Christianity has conquered the world and the Jews have become invisible, which is obviously not the case and rather reflects some wishful thinking on Justin's part (117.1–2).[62] But within the rhetoric of the discussion such comments can serve a purpose, as they show which side is in decline and which one is rising. Hyperbole of a rather different kind is used when contrasting the universal character of the Christian message over against the exclusiveness Judaism is aiming at. Now salvation is offered to all who wish to repent, including the Jews, but not privileging them in any way (141.2–4).[63] This can be connected with evoking a sense of urgency, as when Justin calls upon the Jews not to delay repentance (28.2).[64]

Occasionally also, but far less than one might perhaps expect in this sort of literature, Justin uses logical arguments to corner Trypho. A nice example, partly mixed up with irony, another strong strategy in disputes, is found in 27.5, when Justin first challenges Trypho to explain why God, who installed the Law, allowed circumcision to take place on Sabbath, and then calls upon him to explain why the Law appeared only with Moses.[65]

Many more, and more diversified, lines of argumentation should be mentioned, but these samples may hopefully suffice to show how the dispute is con-

---

[61] Οὐκ ὡς ἐναντιουμένων μοι τῶν τοιούτων προφητειῶν, ὦ φίλοι, παρέλιπον αὐτάς, ... κἂν διὰ πάντων τῶν προφητῶν κελεύῃ ὑμῖν τὰ αὐτὰ ποιεῖν ἃ καὶ διὰ Μωυσέως ἐκέλευσε, διὰ τὸ σκληροκάρδιον ὑμῶν καὶ ἀχάριστον εἰς αὐτόν. The latter motif is dear to Justin, as was shown already above.

[62] The whole passage breathes the tension between Christian sacrificial praxis (the Eucharist), which is celebrated ἐν παντὶ τόπῳ τῆς γῆς and which God accepts with no further ado (προλαβών) and Jewish praxis which was always limited to Jerusalem, and moreover not agreeable to God (ἀπαναίνεται), as Justin illustrates from Mal 1:10–12.

[63] The principle is formulated in 141.2: ἐὰν μετανοήσωσι, πάντες βουλόμενοι τυχεῖν τοῦ παρὰ θεοῦ ἐλέους δύνανται, καὶ μακαρίους αὐτοὺς ὁ Λόγος προλέγει ("everyone who repents can, if he desires, obtain the mercy of God, and he is called blessed by the Scripture"). The whole chapter focuses on repentance. In what follows none less than the great king David is referred to as a model of a penitent sinner after his crime against Uriah. Israel is not excluded, but its sacrifice will have to be great.

[64] See the citation above (n. 43).

[65] These are of course two different things, but they have in common that they inspire objections of a logical character. The question of inconsistencies in Torah is a consequence of the wrong approach Jewish exegesis sticks to: "une lecture 'littérale' de la Loi rend, selon Justin, les prescriptions divines incohérentes ou incompatibles entre elles" (Bobichon, *Justin* [see n. 30], 659 n. 18).

ceived. In the end, Justin's indefatigable efforts to interpret Scripture for Trypho's company pay off, as the latter are gradually silenced or forced into consenting to Justin's position. One can see the development when merely looking at the way the interaction between the two parties is shifting both in content and in frequency. Trypho starts off with a quite vivid exchange in *Dial.* 8–11, and several other such instances can be found (see 19–21, 45–47, 56–58, 67–68), but this changes in the latter part of the encounter. In *Dial.* 123.7, in reply to Justin citing Exod 36:12 ("my people Israel"), Trypho asks, "Do you mean to say that you are Israel, and that God says all this about you?," only to be rebuked quite ironically by Justin: "I might think that your question was prompted by your ignorance, but since, to prove this point, I offered arguments to which you agreed, I cannot believe that your question was the result of ignorance of what was said, or another example of your desire to quibble, but a challenge to repeat my arguments for the sake of the newcomers here present."[66] Trypho cannot but consent and allow Justin to cite Isa 42:1–4 as further proof of his position. Shortly after, he is challenged to give his own opinion on how he sees "the significance of the name of *Israel*" (125.1), but all he and his party can do is stay silent and leave the talking to Justin. The same situation is found in 126.1 and 128.1 – Trypho's company does not reply anymore; they only assent to what Justin has been saying (130.1) and give way to their opponent who goes on lecturing them, as in 130.3: "Now, gentlemen, I wish to call to your attention other passages from Moses ...."

---

[66] Τί οὖν; φησὶν ὁ Τρύφων. Ὑμεῖς Ἰσραήλ ἐστε, καὶ περὶ ὑμῶν λέγει ταῦτα; – Εἰ μέν, ἔφην αὐτῷ, μὴ περὶ τούτων καὶ πολὺν λόγον πεποιήμεθα, κἂν ἀμφέβαλον μή τι οὐ συνίων τοῦτο ἐρωτᾷς· ἐπειδὴ δὲ καὶ μετὰ ἀποδείξεως καὶ συγκαταθέσεως καὶ τοῦτο συνηγάγομεν τὸ ζήτημα, οὐ νομίζω σε ἀγνοεῖν μὲν τὰ προειρημένα οὐδὲ πάλιν φιλεριστεῖν, ἀλλὰ προκαλεῖσθαί με καὶ τούτοις τὴν αὐτὴν ἀπόδειξιν ποιήσασθαι. The politeness of the exchange should not be mistaken. Justin's reply is harsh for he accuses Trypho of simply not being able or, worse, willing to understand what he had been saying. Trypho's nod shows he got the point. From the perspective of Justin (and the reader) it is like a surrender, though in the end it will turn out that Trypho has not come over to Justin's side. The passage recalls the statement Justin had made in 11.5 at the end of the introduction about how the Christians have become the "true and spiritual" (ἀληθινόν, πνευματικόν) Israel of Abrahamic descent through Christ crucified (see below). Note the Pauline flavour of the qualification. Cf. Bobichon, *Justin* (see n. 30), 615 n. 27 and 28; on Justin as interpreter of Paul and the debate it has produced, see, e.g., M.J. Thomas, *Paul's "Works of the Law" in the Perspective of Second Century Reception*, WUNT 2/468 (Tübingen: Mohr Siebeck, 2018), 151–163. Thomas is probably right when noting that the difficulty in assessing Justin's handling of Paul is in part due to the latter's ambiguity (161). A comparative approach to Paul's and Justin's reading of Scripture is offered by Rokéah, *Justin Martyr* (see n. 38), 61–95.

2.2 A case study: *Dial.* 8–14

Justin's insistence at the very beginning of the encounter on being a Christian philosopher, a philosopher who believes in the Messiah (8.1–2), is countered by Trypho with a double argument.[67] A philosopher Justin may be, but he should above all make sure to keep the Law, which is first summarised as getting circumcised and keeping Sabbath and other Jewish feasts, and then generalised as "in brief, fulfill the whole written law" (8.4 ἁπλῶς τὰ ἐν τῷ νόμῳ γεγραμμένα πάντα ποίει).[68] Moreover, he should turn away from his obsession with a Messiah, for no such figure will appear without having been anointed and made known through this by the prophet Elijah (8.4). The brutal and ridiculing intervention of Trypho's companions makes Justin almost leave the scene, only to be called back by Trypho to continue the dispute at another place, without the troublemakers (9.2–3). Justin repeats Trypho's criticism, mentioning only circumcision and the Sabbath and leaving out the "other feasts," and asks whether he also believes in the more savvy accusations of Christian immorality that are said to be told among Jews about Christians and involve cannibalism and promiscuity (10.1).[69] Trypho distances himself from the latter[70] and asserts he knows what is in "your Gospel" (in the singular) which he thinks is "marvelous and great" (θαυμαστὰ καὶ μεγάλα), but repeats the charges about ignoring circumcision and the Sabbath and invites Justin to plead his cause on these, adding that one cannot have one's cake and eat it by saying one firmly believes in God while disrespecting His commandments (10.3–4).[71]

---

[67] On Justin's "conversion," see van Winden, *An Early Christian Philosopher* (see n. 30), 118–121; Horner, *Listening to Trypho* (see n. 31), 103–107.

[68] "To Trypho Greek philosophy apparently has a preparatory function" (van Winden, *An Early Christian Philosopher* [see n. 30], 121). What really matters, however, is whether Justin still keeps Torah, which he obviously does not for Trypho and his company.

[69] See Rudolph, *Gottesverehrung* (see n. 29), 96–99, and the comment, "Missachtung des Gesetzes (stellt) Tryphons Hauptvorwurf gegenüber den Christen dar" (98).

[70] *Dial.* 10.2: "those other charges which the rabble lodge against you are not worthy of belief, for they are too repulsive to human nature" (περὶ δὲ ὧν οἱ πολλοὶ λέγουσιν, οὐ πιστεῦσαι ἄξιον· πόρρω γὰρ κεχώρηκε τῆς ἀνθρωπίνης φύσεως). The motif is well known from other Christian authors as well (cf. Bobichon, *Justin* [see n. 30], 606 n. 4). Trypho knows the limited power of pure slander and does not wish to identify with such people who have nothing else to bring against Christianity.

[71] On the motif of circumcision in the *Dialogue*, see Donahue, *Controversy* (see n. 36), 152–153; Lieu, *Image and Reality* (see n. 5), 113–124, who points out that the topic had received quite some attention as a consequence of Hadrian's ban on the practice (121); Thomas, *Reception* (see n. 66), 163–166.

The criticism is straightforward, but not unfair, for based on facts as far as Trypho is concerned. It leaves open the possibility to find common ground, if Justin manages to explain the situation. This is not said in so many words, but it is reflected by the tone and the wording Trypho uses to voice his argument. If this is not just Justin daydreaming, wishing for the impossible, or being naive, it might indeed reflect the position of at least some in the Roman Jewish community.

Justin feels the heat and immediately moves to reply. His opening words read like a confession of his belief in the one true God who unites Jews and Christians: "Trypho, there never will be … any other God … Furthermore, we do not claim that our God is different from yours … Nor have we placed our trust in any other (for, indeed, there is no other)" (11.1).[72] Can there be a stronger expression of the sense for unity? But there is of course also difference, and the latter should not be belittled. Justin starts from the observation that the old Law and covenant[73] have been superseded by another and final Law, Christ himself, which has widened the horizon from a strict application to the Jewish people towards a universal perspective: "(the covenant) which now must be respected by all those who aspire to the heritage of God" (11.2 ἣν νῦν δέον φυλάσσειν πάντας ἀνθρώπους, ὅσοι τῆς τοῦ θεοῦ κληρονομίας ἀντιποιοῦνται).[74] Proof of this is to be found in the prophecies of old, Isa 51:4–5 and Jer 31(38):31–32, both of them cited in full, which announce, respectively, "a light to the nations" and "a new covenant" (*Dial.* 11.3).[75] At first sight it looks like a strong argument for concluding that something beyond the old Law is indeed being expected, but the argument is weaker than it looks. The sting is, of course, to find out when and how this is to happen. Christians believe that this has taken place in Christ; Jews see it as still outstanding. The juxtaposition of the two citations marks out the neat difference in perspective on who will benefit from the turnabout. Isaiah speaks of

---

[72] Οὔτε ἔσται ποτὲ ἄλλος θεός, ὦ Τρύφων, … Οὐδὲ ἄλλον μὲν ἡμῶν, ἄλλον δὲ ὑμῶν ἡγούμεθα θεόν, … οὐδ᾿ εἰς ἄλλον τινὰ ἠλπίκαμεν, οὐ γὰρ ἔστιν. It is a confession that not all Roman Christians would have subscribed to. "La réponse que Justin offre ici constitue une réfutation simultanée des thèses de Marcion (cf. *I Apol.* 26,5; 58,1) et des accusations juives (cf. *Rom.* 3,29–30 et 10,12)" (Bobichon, *Justin* [see n. 30], 610 n. 1). On the details of Justin's reply, see Rudolph, *Gottesverehrung* (see n. 29), 99–105.
[73] Lukyn Williams (*Dialogue* [see n. 30], 22 n. 3) opposes the translation "covenant" for διαθήκη here and elsewhere, "for that implies more co-operation than mere receiving"; he suggests instead "disposition," but "law and covenant" is a well-known combination. For the list of references that connect the word with Christ, see Bobichon, *Justin* (see n. 30), 984.
[74] "Thème directeur dans le *Dialogue*" (Bobichon, *Justin* [see n. 30], 612 n. 7).
[75] On these prophetic passages and the topic in general, see Skarsaune, *Proof* (see n. 52), 353–359 and 228–229.

"the nations"; Jeremiah's "covenant" is meant for the Jewish people – "with the house of Israel, and with the house of Juda."[76] The gap seems unsurmountable, but Justin would not have launched himself onto this path if he did not know where it would be leading him. The solution is not found in Christ – that would just not work to convince an opponent – but in Abraham, the father of all nations (11.4–5).[77] It started with Abraham, the father of the "true and spiritual Israel," but this reality was transformed by Christ being crucified (see the quote above).[78] Christ is "merely" the instrument – these are my words, not Justin's, but I think they reflect his position – who made it possible for non-Jews to come home again.[79] The idea clearly is that the prophecies do not materialise of themselves, they have to be realised, first by Christ, then by humankind acting upon God's call through Christ.

So common ground there is and there has always been. It is just a matter of reading Scripture correctly and seeing the implications of any prophecies found in it. That does not sound like trying to get away from the others, but rather like pointing to a difference and a difficulty, all while offering the way out of the latter.

The tone becomes somewhat nastier, or in any case more polemic, in the next chapter. A second citation from Isaiah, now Isa 55:3–5 (*Dial.* 12.1),[80] once again emphasising the universal perspective of God's "everlasting covenant" that will draw all nations towards Him by the new "Lawgiver" (Justin's, not Isaiah's words) He sent to the world, is turned into a critique of the harshness and stubbornness of the Jews who disregard this call. They remain blind in the sight of wondrous miracles being performed and refuse to understand that

---

[76] Cf. M.W. Bates, ""Justin Martyr's Logocentric Hermeneutical Transformation of Isaiah's Vision of the Nations," *JTS* 60 (2009): 538–555, esp. 554. On Justin's handling of Isaiah's prophecies, see S. Wendel, *Scriptural Interpretation and Community Self-Definition in Luke-Acts and the Writings of Justin Martyr*, SupNT 139 (Leiden and Boston, MA: Brill, 2011), 247–254; "Justin attempts to depict non-Jewish Christ-believers as the rightful heirs of the scriptural promises and legacy originally designated for Jews" (247).

[77] On the importance of Abraham and the promise made to him in the dispute, see Horner, *Listening to Trypho* (see n. 31), 122–126; Rokéah, *Justin Martyr* (see n. 38), 117–127 (including the other patriarchs); Wendel, *Scriptural Interpretation* (see n. 76), 226–235. In comparison to Luke, "Justin more typically presents non-Jewish Christ-believers as the descendants of Abraham and rightful heirs of the promises originally made to Jews" (235).

[78] On the crucial meaning of this concept of "the new and true Israel," see Rudolph, *Gottesverehrung* (see n. 29), 254–261.

[79] Note the phrase τῷ θεῷ προαχθέντες to describe Christ's role in the process. He is the new Moses implicitly referred to in 11.1.

[80] On this passage, see Skarsaune, *Proof* (see n. 52), 63–64.

change has come (12.2). Circumcision, the Sabbath law, and any other feast have been transformed into something new – a call for living an ethical life not bound to place and time: "the New Law demands that you observe a perpetual Sabbath" (12.3 Σαββατίζειν ὑμᾶς ὁ καινὸς νόμος διὰ παντὸς ἐθέλει).[81] The concepts remain the same, but their meaning has been changed, or rather, their true meaning, which they always had, has finally been revealed. Purity laws are not about material washing, which is what one should keep doing if one is dirty (12.3), but about having faith in Christ and about the salvific effect of his suffering and death (13.1).[82] For a Christian, real water has been replaced by real blood, but we are not asked to sprinkle us with the latter as one was expected to do with the former according to the Law, but to accept in faith that this is how we were saved. The change is radical and complete. It requires a new mind set, a totally new way of looking at God's commandments.[83] The rest of the chapter consists of an interminably long citation from Isa 52:10 – 54,6 which Christians from early on had taken to refer to Christ's passion.[84] As such, it does not so much contribute to criticise Jewish ritual practices as provide a basis for the Christian interpretation of Jesus' death. The lack of balance between citation and comment could be said to weaken the argument in so far as the emphasis is shifted from re-interpreting Jewish praxis to offering a Scriptural basis for the God-willed passion, but obviously that is not how Justin wishes to see things.

The situation has become somewhat more uneasy, but all hope is not given up. As a matter of fact, the argument is similar to the previous one, only that it now has been combined with explaining the true meaning of Jewish ritual praxis and the role of Christ in the process. It consists of offering a correct understanding of a passage from Scripture which leads one to correctly understand the divine commandments. Being lectured about one's own sacred tradition may seem hard to suffer, but the argument basically remains Scriptural and so at least leaves an opportunity for Trypho to challenge it on his own premises, if he wishes to do so.

Justin then brings the discussion to the issue of concrete practices, as Trypho had done initially. The first one he mentions did not figure in Trypho's list, but is

---

[81] The phrase obviously sounds familiar to a Christian reader and the topic was addressed by several other authors. See Bobichon, *Justin* (see n. 30), 616 n. 12.
[82] Note that the contrast is not between ritual bathing and Christian baptism, but between ritual and faith, though the cleansing aspect is not lost on Justin, neither is the connotation of offering sacrifices.
[83] Cf. Rudolph, *Gottesverehrung* (see n. 29), 146–162.
[84] "Justin est le premier à citer intégralement – et à des moments stratégiques – ce poème" (Bobichon, *Justin* [see n. 30], 621 n. 33); he does so here and also in *1 Apol.* 50.1–51.6.

picked up from what he just had said about true purity (14.1). Like Jews, Christians too use real water when cleansing a person in baptism, but the ritual receives a new meaning, as this is not about becoming clean again, but about receiving life as an expression of one's altered state upon repenting and coming to know God. As far as Justin is concerned, baptism is not allegorised – Christians do perform a ritual –, but it concerns the soul, not the body. This distinction, not based on any further argument and not allowing for the possibility that also in Judaism the purity ritual may express a cleansing of the inner person, recalls Jesus' criticism of the "hypocrites" in Matt 23:25 par. Luke 11:39–40; this is then combined with the motif of its usefulness for changing a person, which reminds one of Paul's argument in 1 Cor 15:32 (see also James 2:14, 16).[85] In the same way, returning to eating leavened bread after the azyma, for which Justin obviously cannot cite any Christian counterpart, should be understood as expressing the will to practice "other deeds," new ones, true ones (*Dial.* 14.3).[86] As an illustration of this, Justin treats Trypho to another long citation in 14.4–7, picking up Isa 55:3–5 again. However, he now extends it to include all of vv. 3–13 announcing the coming of Christ and what it will bring about in terms of renewing everything. The reader may wonder how this can be turned into an argument for the case he is pleading here. Justin does not care to comment on the text, apart from adding, quite generally, that other, mostly unidentified, passages from Scripture also speak about a second coming in glory when all, including the Jews (ὁ λαὸς ὑμῶν), will recognise Him. In Justin's opinion, Scripture apparently speaks for itself.

---

[85] Τί γὰρ ὄφελος ἐκείνου τοῦ βαπτίσματος, ὃ τὴν σάρκα καὶ μόνον τὸ σῶμα φαιδρύνει; ("For, of what value is that baptism which cleanses only the flesh and body?"). Justin returns to it in 29.1, explaining that it is the Spirit who makes Christian baptism superior to Jewish purification ritual. Cf. J.E. Morgan-Wynne, "The Holy Spirit and Christian Experience in Justin Martyr," *VigChr* 38 (1984): 172–177, esp. 172–173. Jesus' discourse against the Pharisees in Matt 23 plays a not unimportant role in Justin's argumentation. See the "contextualisation" of the discourse proposed by A.Y. Reed, "When Did Rabbis Become Pharisees?," in *Envisioning Judaism: Essays in Honor of Peter Schäfer on the Occasion of his Seventieth Birthday*, ed. R.S. Boustan et al., vol. 2, TSAJ 119 (Tübingen: Mohr Siebeck, 2013) 859–896 (repr. in eadem, *Jewish-Christianity and the History of Judaism. Collected Essays*, TSAJ 171 [Tübingen: Mohr Siebeck 2018], 295–329).
[86] Διὸ καὶ μετὰ τὰς ἑπτὰ ἡμέρας τῶν ἀζυμοφαγιῶν νέαν ζύμην φυρᾶσαι ἑαυτοῖς ὁ θεὸς παρήγγειλε, τουτέστιν ἄλλων ἔργων πρᾶξιν καὶ μὴ τῶν παλαιῶν καὶ φαύλων τὴν μίμησιν ("Therefore, after eating unleavened bread for seven days, you were ordered by God to prepare new leaven for yourselves, that is, to practise other deeds, not to repeat your old sinful ones"). Torah does not prescribe the preparation of new leaven, as Justin seems to think. Bobichon (*Justin* [see n. 30], 625 n. 14) considers it a mere slip of the pen. Justin was probably influenced by what Paul wrote in 1 Cor 5:7–8 (ibid., 943–945), which he interpreted in his favour.

The discussion has not really been moved forward, so it seems, except that Trypho is once more reminded of the fact that it is all about correctly interpreting Scripture. The two parties stay in the same orbit. Scripture is the battle field and at the same time the source for all interpretation of religious praxis. As much as it may seem to be a divisive factor, both parties of necessity have to recognise that it is also what keeps them together. This same conclusion, with perhaps some nuancing, could be made after analysing other subsections of the *Dialogue*.

As said before, we do not know in how far Justin's arguments reflect real-life disputes in reply to provocative questions from Jewish opponents, or should rather be seen as a pre-emptive strike from the Christian side, preparing fellow Christians for how to respond to criticism from the other side.[87] Whatever can possibly be said about the former, the latter definitely is the more important aspect of this whole dispute. It is not so much about winning over the others as building up a defence for one's own. In that respect, the *Dialogue* is rather more like a catechism or a manual for handling criticism from the Jewish side and for instructing Christians on how to resist the latter and construct an identity that is, at least in part, built on positioning themselves vis-à-vis the Judaism of their time.[88]

This first confrontation with Trypho, which was analysed in some detail above, shows that Justin is not intent on creating a break or making futile any further encounter, even though he does not give in an inch on what Trypho has objected to. The tension continues to exist, maybe, one might add, to the benefit of both parties.[89] The debate continues, Justin seems victorious, certainly towards the end of the work, but the ultimate goal of converting the other side to come over to one's own, if that was the goal at all, is definitely not reached.

In reading the *Dialogue* we hear one particular Christian voice, Justin's, speaking out on the relation between Judaism and Christianity. We do not

---

87 The quite implausible suggestion that Justin was writing for (interested) gentiles is discussed in some detail and dismissed by Allert, *Revelation* (see n. 45), 445–453.

88 On the identity marking and identity constructing aspect of Justin's work in view of confronting the Greco-Roman world, see Wendel, *Scriptural Interpretation* (see n. 76), 137–142. Wendel's concluding comment of how "Justin uses the Jewish scriptures to demonstrate the antiquity of the origins of his community as well as the superiority of its knowledge and practices over competing non-Jewish traditions" (142) can *mutatis mutandis* also be used for describing his goal in discussing with Jewish opponents. On the use of such "protectionist strategies" in preserving one's world, be it in a contemporary academic context, see Tong, "Protective Difference" (see n. 3), 1–9.

89 And this is well understandable: "Radical differences in the context of great similarity tend to awaken deep feelings of self-justification and strong rejection of the other" (Martin, *A House Divided* [see n. 4], 173).

know for sure in how far it represents merely a personal meaning or the opinion of a group, nor in how far it was effective, but as it is not just an isolated attempt by a nobody there is reason to think it also made an impact. We also hear one particular Jewish voice, Trypho's, but as shaped and circulated by a Christian. Here as well, we do not know how it was received by "the other side," but it certainly was not devastatingly negative and so may have met with some support at least. One might be tempted to ask whether Justin was deluding himself when engaging in a dispute he could not fully bring to an end, or just being naïve, or perhaps rather more a pragmatist who knows how to distinguish between what is possible and what cannot be changed and should perhaps better left unchanged. Of the three, I hope to have made it clear that I am inclining towards the latter, which is certainly not the worst option. The *Dialogue* reflects a situation Justin could not change and perhaps even somehow wanted to be perpetuated.[90]

3 But what about "that other guy"?

The third, final and far too short part of this quick survey of opinions on Judaism that have left a trace in Christian Rome deals with "the elephant in the room," the person I have so far tried to avoid mentioning. Justin's is but one voice. A totally different voice is heard when turning from Justin to Marcion.[91] Things are much more complicated here, not in the least because access to the latter's work and opinions is difficult as they have come down to us only in a fragmentary form and through his adversaries. It has not prevented some scholars from advancing big theories, or rather it may have encouraged them to do so, theories in which the speculation at times matches the spectacular.[92]

---

[90] One might be tempted to summarise this as if the *Dialogue* shows us flashes from "two different thought worlds" (so Nicklas, *Jews and Christians?* [see n. 5], 142), though the image only works on condition that one keeps aware of the fact that in many places these worlds were constantly meeting each other in daily life. Whether one calls them "siblings," or "jumeaux," or "enemies," fact is that the two sides were condemned to live together. "Jews and Christians were neighbors in the cities of the Empire; they could not ignore each other" (Martin, *A House Divided* [see n. 4], 173).

[91] Green's suggestion that "it was perhaps no accident that Marcion developed his view of the status of the Old Testament in Rome," because that is where the divide between Jews and Christians is first evidenced, while appealing, is difficult to substantiate (Green, *Christianity in Ancient Rome* [see n. 5], 73).

[92] I am thinking of recent hypotheses on the relation between Marcion and the synoptic gospels. See M. Vinzent, *Marcion and the Dating of the Synoptic Gospels*, Studia Patristica. Supple-

Justin was familiar with at least part, and probably more, of Marcion's teaching, and he did not like it at all.[93] He mentions him twice in the *First Apology* (26.5 and 58.1) and his followers once in the *Dialogue* (35.6). His verdict on both is short and equally harsh. Marcion teaching "to believe in another and greater god than the Creator" is said to be possessed by demons.[94] He is mentioned in the company of Simon Magus and his disciple Menander, never a good sign in mainstream authors, as representing people who are wrongly called Christians, just as others are misidentified as philosophers. Justin seemingly takes his distances from certain vile accusations that were brought against the Marcionites, including promiscuity and cannibalism, which recalls Trypho's attitude in *Dial*. 10.1, but calls for taking action against them, including the death penalty, and refers to his (now lost) treatise against all heresies. He repeats the accusation of being possessed in *1 Apol*. 58.1 where he adds some more comments on the dangers of Marcion's teachings.[95] In *Dial*. 35.6, he lists Marcion's followers together with the Valentinians, Basilidians and Saturnilians, not the kind of people one wishes to be associated with in orthodox circles, and compares, no doubt ironically, their decision to call themselves after their founder to how philosophical schools received their name.[96]

---

ment 2 (Leuven et al.: Peeters, 2014) and M. Klinghardt, *Das älteste Evangelium und die Entstehung der kanonischen Evangelien*, 2 vols., TANZ 60/1–2 (Tübingen: Francke, 2015).
  For a brief, balanced view on Marcion's position towards Judaism, see Nicklas, *Jews and Christians?* (see n. 5), 142–156.
93 Cf. Donahue, *Controversy* (see n. 36), 240–244, esp. 240: "the issue between Justin and the Jews was much the same as that between orthodox Christians and Marcionites: the relation of the Old Testament to the New"; the comparison, as so often with comparisons, is probably only partially correct. S. Moll, "Justin and the Pontic Wolf," in *Justin Martyr and His Worlds*, ed. S. Parvis and P. Foster (Minneapolis, MN: Fortress, 2007), 145–151, esp. 151.
94 Cf. Ulrich, *Apologien* (see n. 29), 285–289. Ulrich rightly notes, "Justin beschränkt sich auf Markion's Kernthesen, der theologische Hintergrund dieser Lehre wird nicht mitgeteilt" (286). Cf. also M. den Dulk, *Between Jews and Heretics. Refiguring Justin Martyr's Dialogue with Trypho*. Routledge Studies in the Early Christian World (London and New York: Routledge, 2018), 19–25. On Justin's demonology, see now D.E. Nyström, *The Apology of Justin Martyr: Literary Strategies and the Defence of Christianity*, WUNT 2/462 (Tübingen: Mohr Siebeck, 2018), 137–151.
95 Ulrich, *Apologien* (see n. 29), 445–447. Perhaps more important still than the teaching is the fact that Marcion is the last example, after Simon Magus (56) and those persecuting the Christians (57), of the ongoing activities of the demons which Justin is dealing with in chapters 56–58. In him is revealed "der Kulminationspunkt der dämonischen Tätigkeit" (445).
96 Maybe it is also implied that Christians, by contrast, derive their name not from a mere man. So A. Le Boulluec, *La notion d'hérésie dans la littérature grecque (IIe-IIIe siècles), vol. I: De Justin à Irénée* (Paris: Études augustiniennes, 1985), 61; Bobichon, *Justin* (see n. 30), 678 n. 14. On Justin's wider interest in "heresy hunting," including in the *Dialogue*, see now den Dulk, *Between Jews and Heretics* (see n. 94).

That much of Marcion's opinions is clear, it seems, to allow for the conclusion that he was at least laying the foundations for radically breaking away from Judaism. The dialogue, any sort of dialogue, has to stop. In a way it seems to be the easiest solution, taking the path of the shorter pain. On further thought, however, such a solution comes at a price. For one, it may easily be taken by the other side as an act of cowardice; but there is more. By giving up the debate one leaves the others untouched and strengthened in their conviction they had it all right. But perhaps the most devastating part of such a move is that it throws out an integral element on which Christian identity is built, and hence also an already relatively longstanding tradition of interpreting Christianity from Judaism, as this was developed by Paul, the evangelists and early Christian authors of the first few generations. As far as this can be deduced from the evidence preserved among his opponents, Marcion saw the consequences, and acted accordingly. One cannot do away with Jewish Scripture without also giving up part of the own tradition and its writings. In the end, the move is largely self-destructive.

In the two passages referred to above, Justin does not elaborate on the consequences of Marcion's teachings for the relation with Judaism, but he cannot have ignored them. In any case, Marcion's efforts were lost on Justin. His purpose in the *Dialogue* is not to expel Judaism from the Christian orbit, but rather to keep the two somehow connected, even if they will not merge into one. We do not know how successful Justin was, but there is every reason to assume that his more realistic and workable solution may well have had some influence in local communities and that he may have had some effect in silencing other, more radical voices,

4 A brief conclusion

We have met two contrasting opinions on how to go about with Judaism and have also referenced a few apparently rather more uncommitted positions, though the latter is very much a conclusion from silence. It is not easy to decide which of the two positions, Justin's or Marcion's, got the upper hand in mainstream Christianity. One might think that Marcion's was a lost cause and that Justin came out victorious, but that may be too simplistic a conclusion. Marcion's cause was taken up and continued and even developed into a church of its own that persisted for several centuries, even though it was gradually more and more marginalised and we do not have as much clear and strong evidence as we would like of how much of his initial views were still held till the very end. Hence, at least a part of Christianity was lost for the mainstream church, which is quite a heavy price to pay for trying to solve a question that cannot be solved in an absolute way. So one is perhaps entitled to say that Justin's side won, but that it did not win unconditionally. Debates with representatives of Judaism went on for a much longer time than Marcion's church survived, but the very fact that such disputes were held or put in scene is in itself proof that any intention of winning a final battle should be given up. Hence, that there will always be another side and that it is as much, or perhaps even more, a matter of fencing off the own position than of winning over that other side. It is certainly a better option than merely ignoring the other. Reality does not disappear by pretending it does not exist. Jews are a given, and so are Christians, and both are here to stay. Justin realised that; Marcion tried to do away with it. Or put differently, Jew is Jew and Christian is Christian, and always the two will continue to meet – as others. Perhaps that is, in this context, a fair definition of living apart together.[97]

Bibliography

Allert, C. D., *Revelation, Truth, Canon and Interpretation: Studies in Justin Martyr's* Dialogue with Trypho, SupVigChr 64 (Leiden and Boston, MA: Brill, 2002).
Bates, M. W., "Justin Martyr's Logocentric Hermeneutical Transformation of Isaiah's Vision of the Nations," *JTS* 60 (2009): 538–555.
Becker, A. H., and A. Y. Reed, eds., *The Ways that Never Parted. Jews and Christians in Late Antiquity and the Early Middle Ages*, TSAJ 95 (Tübingen: Mohr Siebeck, 2003).
Beni, M. D., *Cognitive Structural Realism: A Radical Solution to the Problem of Scientific Representation* (Cham: Springer International Publishing, 2019).

---

[97] In this respect, I do agree with one aspect of the double conclusion my fellow contributor and co-editor of this volume, Ben Edsall, has reached in his essay on Justin Martyr (see pp. 248–272). The *Dialogue* does not give the impression that Justin had the intention to halt the discussion with representatives of Judaism, but one has the strong feeling that he is convinced the discussion should be held on his terms and in as far as he stays in command. I am less convinced by Edsall's suggestion that the concept of *verus Israel* is the basis for Justin to hope the conversation can continue. His claim of being a member of a "new Israel" in *Dial.* 123.7, immediately raises the ire of Trypho, as we have noted above, who cannot see the continuity and naturally thinks it constitutes a break. That is also how M. Simon long ago interpreted the passage: *Verus Israël. Étude sur les relations entre chrétiens et juifs dans l'empire romain (135–425)*, 2nd ed. (Paris: de Boccard, 1964), 206. On the difficulties with the concept, see also Green, *Christianity in Ancient Rome* (see n. 5), 73, with regard of how to handle Marcion: "His Christian opponents found themselves in the difficult position of endorsing the split with Judaism while wanting to claim that Christianity was its true successor, the true Israel." If Justin was hoping this was a valid basis for continuing a shared tradition, he was badly mistaken in the eyes of Trypho, as he himself indicates with the latter's reaction.

Binder, S. E., *Tertullian, on Idolatry and Mishnah Avodah Zarah: Questioning the Parting of the Ways between Christians and Jews*, Jewish and Christian Perspectives 22 (Leiden and Boston, MA: Brill, 2012).

Bobichon, P., "Salomon et Ézéchias dans l'exégèse juive des prophéties royales et messianiques, selon Justin Martyr et les sources rabbiniques," *Tsafon. Revue d'études juives du Nord* 44 (2002–03): 149–165.

Bobichon, P., *Justin Martyr. Dialogue avec Tryphon. Édition critique, traduction, commentaire*, 2 vols., Paradosis 47/1–2 (Fribourg: Academic Press, 2003).

Boccaccini, G., *Beyond the Essene Hypothesis. The Parting of the Ways between Qumran and Enochic Judaism* (Grand Rapids, MI: Eerdmans, 1998).

Bos, J., "Before the Parting of the Ways: Nederlandse filosofen over geschiedenis en geschiedwetenschap, 1920–1970," *Tijdschrift voor Geschiedenis* 129 (2016): 35–56.

Boyarin, D., *Border Lines: The Partition of Judaeo-Christianity*, Divinations: Rereading Late Ancient Religion (Philadelphia, PA: University of Pennsylvania Press, 2004).

Boyarin, D., "Justin's Dialogue with the Jews: The Beginnings of Orthodoxy," in idem, *Border Lines, The Partition of Judaeo-Christianity*, Divinations: Rereading Late Ancient Religion (Philadelphia, PA: University of Pennsylvania Press, 2004), 37–73.

Broadhead, E. K., *Jewish Ways of Following Jesus: Redrawing the Religious Map of Antiquity*, WUNT 266 (Tübingen: Mohr Siebeck, 2010).

Brox, N., *Der Hirt des Hermas*, KAV 7 (Göttingen: Vandenhoeck & Ruprecht, 1991).

Bucur, B. G., "Justin Martyr's Exegesis of Biblical Theophanies and the Parting of the Ways between Christianity and Judaism," *Theological Studies* 75 (2014): 34–51.

Carleton Paget, J., *Jews, Christians and Jewish Christians in Antiquity*, WUNT 251 (Tübingen: Mohr Siebeck, 2010).

Carleton Paget, J., "Introduction," in *Jews, Christians and Jewish Christians in Antiquity*, ed. idem, WUNT 251 (Tübingen: Mohr Siebeck, 2010), 1–39.

Carleton Paget, J., "Jewish Revolts and Jewish-Christian Relations," in *Jews and Christians in the First and Second Centuries: The Interbellum 70–132 CE*, ed. J. Schwartz and P. J. Tomson, CRINT 15 (Leiden and Boston, MA: Brill, 2018), 276–306.

Cohen, S. J. D., "The Ways That Parted: Jews, Christians, and Jewish-Christians, ca. 100–150 CE," in *Jews and Christians in the First and Second Centuries: The Interbellum 70–132 CE*, ed. J. Schwartz and P. J. Tomson, CRINT 15 (Leiden and Boston, MA: Brill, 2018), 307–339.

Cumont, F., *Les religions orientales dans le paganisme romain*, 4th ed. (Paris: Annales du Musée Guimet, 1929).

Cumont, F., *Les religions orientales dans le paganisme romain*, ed. C. Bonnet and F. Van Haeperen with B. Toune, *Bibliotheca Cumontiana. Scripta Maiora* 1 (Turin: Nino Aragno Editore, 2006).

Cumont, F., *The Oriental Religions in Roman Paganism* (Repr. New York: Dover, 1956 [1911]).

Cumont, F., *Die orientalischen Religionen im römischen Heidentum* (Repr. Darmstadt: Olms, 1975 [²1914]).

Donahue, P. J., *Jewish-Christian Controversy in the Second Century. A Study in the Dialogue of Justin Martyr* (PhD diss., Yale University, 1973).

den Dulk, M., *Between Jews and Heretics. Refiguring Justin Martyr's Dialogue with Trypho*. Routledge Studies in the Early Christian World (London and New York: Routledge, 2018).

Dunn, J. D. G., ed., *Jews and Christians. The Parting of the Ways A.D. 70 to 135*, WUNT 66 (Tübingen: Mohr Siebeck, 1992).
Dunn, J. D. G., "The Question of Anti-semitism in the New Testament. Writings of the Period," in *Jews and Christians. The Parting of the Ways A.D. 70 to 135*, ed. idem, WUNT 66 (Tübingen: Mohr Siebeck, 1992), 177–211.
Falls, T. B., *Saint Justin Martyr*, Fathers of the Church 6 (Washington, D.C.: CUA Press, 1948).
Friedman, M., *A Parting of the Ways: Carnap, Cassirer, and Heidegger* (Chicago: Open Court Press, 2000).
Green, B., *Christianity in Ancient Rome: The First Three Centuries* (London and New York: T&T Clark, 2010).
Heemstra, M., *The Fiscus Judaicus and the Parting of the Ways*, WUNT 2/277 (Tübingen: Mohr Siebeck, 2010).
Horner, T. J., *Listening to Trypho. Justin Martyr's Dialogue Reconsidered*, Contributions to Biblical Exegesis & Theology 28 (Leuven et al.: 2001).
Hyldahl, N., *Philosophie und Christentum. Eine Interpretation der Einleitung zum Dialog Justins*, Acta Theologica Danica 9 (Copenhagen: Munksgaard, 1966).
Klinghardt, M., *Das älteste Evangelium und die Entstehung der kanonischen Evangelien*, 2 vols., TANZ 60/1–2 (Tübingen: Francke, 2015).
Lampe, P., *Die stadtrömischen Christen in den ersten beiden Jahrhunderten. Untersuchungen zur Sozialgeschichte*, 2nd ed., WUNT 2/18 (Tübingen: Mohr Siebeck, 1989).
Lanfranchi P., and J. Verheyden, eds., *Jews and Christians in Antiquity. A Regional Perspective*, Interdisciplinary Studies in Ancient Culture and Religion 18 (Leuven et al.: Peeters, 2018).
Le Boulluec, A., *La notion d'hérésie dans la littérature grecque (IIe-IIIe siècles)*, vol. I: *De Justin à Irénée* (Paris: Études augustiniennes, 1985).
Lieu, J. M., *Image and Reality. The Jews in the World of the Christians in the Second Century* (Edinburgh: T&T Clark, 1996).
Lieu, J. M., *Neither Jew nor Greek? Constructing Early Christianity* (Edinburgh: T&T Clark, 2002).
Lona, H. E., *Der erste Clemensbrief*, KAV 2 (Göttingen: Vandenhoeck & Ruprecht, 1998).
Lucas, H., *At the Parting of the Ways: Considerations and Meditations for Boys* (London: Sands and Co., 1906).
Martin, V., *A House Divided: The Parting of the Ways between Synagogue and Church. Studies in Judaism and Christianity* (New York and Mahwah, NJ: Paulist Press. A Stimulus Book, 1995).
Mimouni, S. C., "Introduction. Sur la question de la séparation entre 'jumeaux' et 'ennemis' aux Ier et IIe siècles," in *La croisée de chemins revisitée: Quand l'église et la synagogue se sont-elles distinguées? Actes du colloque de Tours, 18–19 juin 2010*, ed. idem and B. Pouderon (Paris: Cerf, 2012), 7–20.
Mimouni, S. C., and B. Pouderon, eds., *La croisée de chemins revisitée: Quand l'église et la synagogue se sont-elles distinguées? Actes du colloque de Tours, 18–19 juin 2010* (Paris: Cerf, 2012).
Moll, S., "Justin and the Pontic Wolf," in *Justin Martyr and His Worlds*, ed. S. Parvis and P. Foster (Minneapolis, MN: Fortress, 2007), 145–151.
Morgan-Wynne, J. E., "The Holy Spirit and Christian Experience in Justin Martyr," *VigChr* 38 (1984): 172–177.

Nicklas, T., *Jews and Christians? Second Century 'Christian' Perspectives on the 'Parting of the Ways,'* Annual Deichmann Lectures 2013 (Tübingen: Mohr Siebeck, 2014).

Nicklas, T., "Parting of the Ways? Probleme eines Konzepts," in *Juden – Heiden – Christen?*, ed. S. Alkier and H. Leppin, WUNT 400 (Tübingen: Mohr Siebeck, 2018), 21–41.

Niehoff, M. R., "A Jew for Roman Tastes: The Parting of the Ways in Justin Martyr's *Dialogue with Trypho* from a Post-Colonial Perspective," *JECS* 27 (2019): 549–578.

Norman, I., "'... and Midwifery': Time for a Parting of the Ways or a Closer Union with Nursery?," *International Journal of Nursing Studies* 44 (2007): 521–522.

Nyström, D. E., *The Apology of Justin Martyr: Literary Strategies and the Defence of Christianity*, WUNT 2/462 (Tübingen: Mohr Siebeck, 2018).

Osiek, C., *The Shepherd of Hermas*, Hermenia (Minneapolis, MN: Fortress, 1999).

Prigent, P., *Justin et l'Ancien Testament. L'argumentation scripturaire du traité de Justin contre toutes les hérésies comme source principale du Dialogue avec Tryphon et de la Première Apologie*, 2nd ed., Études Bibliques (Paris: Gabalda, 1966).

Ramelli, I., "The Jesus Movement's Flight to Pella and the 'Parting of the Ways'," *Augustinianum* 54 (2014): 35–51.

Reed, A. Y., "When Did Rabbis Become Pharisees?," in *Envisioning Judaism: Essays in Honor of Peter Schäfer on the Occasion of his Seventieth Birthday*, ed. R. S. Boustan et al., vol. 2, TSAJ 119 (Tübingen: Mohr Siebeck, 2013) 859–896 (repr. in eadem, *Jewish-Christianity and the History of Judaism. Collected Essays*, TSAJ 171 [Tübingen: Mohr Siebeck 2018], 295–329).

Robinson, T. A., *Ignatius of Antioch and the Parting of the Ways. Early Jewish-Christian Relations* (Peabody, MA: Hendrickson, 2009).

Rokéah, D., *Justin Martyr and the Jews*, Jewish and Christian Perspectives Series 5 (Leiden and Boston, MA: 2002).

Rosik, M., *Church and Synagogue (30–313 A.D.): Parting of the Ways*, European Studies in Theology, Philosophy and History of Religions 20 (Berlin: P. Lang, 2019).

Rudolph, A., *"Denn wir sind jenes Volk ...". Die neue Gottesverehrung in Justins Dialog mit dem Juden Tryphon in historisch-theologischer Sicht*, Hereditas 15 (Bonn: Borengässer, 1999).

Rutherford, W., "*Altercatio Jasonis et Papisci* as a Testimony Source for Justin's 'Second God' Argument," in *Justin Martyr and His Worlds*, ed. S. Parvis and P. Foster (Minneapolis, MN: Fortress, 2007), 137–144.

Sanchez, S. J. G., *Justin apologiste chrétien. Travaux sur le* Dialogue avec Tryphon *de Justin Martyr*, CahiersRB 50 (Paris: Gabalda, 2000).

Schenck, K., *A New Perspective on Hebrews: Rethinking the Parting of the Ways* (Lanham, MD: Lexington Books and Fortress Academic, 2019).

Schnelle, U., *Die getrennten Wege von Römern, Juden und Christen* (Tübingen: Mohr Siebeck, 2019).

Schoedel, W. R., *A Commentary on the Letters of Ignatius of Antioch*, Hermeneia (Philadelphia: Fortress, 1985).

Simon, M., *Verus Israël. Étude sur les relations entre chrétiens et juifs dans l'empire romain (135–425)*, 2nd ed. (Paris: de Boccard, 1964).

Skarsaune, O., *The Proof from Prophecy. A Study of Justin Martyr's Proof-Text Tradition: Text-Type, Provenance, Logical Profile*, SupNT 65 (Leiden: Brill, 1987).

Skarsaune, O., "Justin and His Bible," in *Justin Martyr and His Worlds*, ed. S. Parvis and P. Foster (Minneapolis, MN: Fortress, 2007), 53–76.

Smit Sibinga, J., *The Old Testament Text of Justin Martyr* (Leiden: Brill, 1963).

Smith, E. C., *Jewish Glass and Christian Stone: A Materialist Mapping of the "Parting of the Ways,"* Routledge Studies in the Early Christian World (Abingdon: Routledge, 2017).

Spence, S., *The Parting of the Ways: The Roman Church as a Case Study*, Interdisciplinary Studies in Ancient Culture and Religion 5 (Leuven: Peeters, 2003).

Stanton, G. N., "Other Early Christian Writings: *Didache*, Ignatius, *Barnabas*, Justin Martyr," in *Early Christian Thought in Its Jewish Context*, ed. J. M. G. Barclay and J. P. M. Sweet (Cambridge: CUP, 1996), 174–190.

Stökl Ben Ezra, D., "Weighing the Parts. A Papyrological Perspective on the Parting of the Ways," *NT* 51 (2009): 168–186.

Thomas, M. J., *Paul's "Works of the Law" in the Perspective of Second Century Reception*, WUNT 2/468 (Tübingen: Mohr Siebeck, 2018).

Tong, M. A., "Protective Difference: Protectionist Strategies and the Parting of the Ways," *Method and Theory in the Study of Religion* (2020): 1–9.

Ulrich, J., *Justin Apologien*, KfA 4/5 (Freiburg et al.: Herder, 2018).

Verheyden, J., "Israel's Fate in the Apostolic Fathers. The Case of 1 Clement and the Epistle of Barnabas," in *The Separation between the Just and the Unjust in Early Judaism and in the Sayings Source – Die Scheidung zwischen Gerechten und Ungerechten in Frühjudentum und Logienquelle*, ed. M. Tiwald, BBB 172 (Göttingen: V&R Press; Bonn: Bonn University Press, 2015), 237–262.

Vinzent, M., *Marcion and the Dating of the Synoptic Gospels*, Studia Patristica. Supplement 2 (Leuven et al.: Peeters, 2014).

Wendel, S., *Scriptural Interpretation and Community Self-Definition in Luke-Acts and the Writings of Justin Martyr*, SupNT 139 (Leiden and Boston, MA: Brill, 2011).

Williams, A. L., *Justin Martyr The Dialogue with Trypho. Translation, Introduction and Notes* (London: SPCK, 1930).

Winden, J. C. M. van, *An Early Christian Philosopher. Justin Martyr's Dialogue with Trypho Chapters One to Nine. Introduction, Text, Commentary*, Philosophia Patrum 1 (Leiden: Brill, 1971).

Wright, A.D., *The Divisions of French Catholicism, 1629–1645: "The Parting of the Ways"* (Burlington VT: OUP, 2013).

Zetterholm, M., *The Formation of Christianity in Antioch: A Social-Scientific Approach to the Separation between Judaism and Christianity* (London: Routledge, 2003).

Zwierlein, O., *Petrus in Rom. Die literarischen Zeugnisse. Mit einer kritischen Edition der Martyrien des Petrus und Paulus auf neuer handschriftlicher Grundlage*, Untersuchungen zur antiken Literatur und Geschichte 96 (Berlin and New York: de Gruyter, 2009).

Tobias Nicklas
Jews and Christians? Sketches from Second Century Alexandria

Abstract: Der Beitrag fordert, an die Stelle des Paradigmas "Parting(s) of the Ways" ein differenziertes Modell von Fragestellungen zu setzen, die in der Lage sind, Trennungs- und Abgrenzungsprozesse im Verhältnis von Juden und Christen in gleicher Weise zu berücksichtigen wie Aspekte gegenseitiger (auch positiver) Einflussnahme und Einwirkungen von außen, also z. B. durch staatliche Repressionen. Wichtige Aspekte dieses Modells werden am Beispiel "Alexandria im 2. Jahrhundert" diskutiert. Dieses bereitet jedoch aus verschiedenen Gründen besondere Schwierigkeiten: Einerseits liegen die Ursprünge des Christentums in Alexandria weitgehend im Dunkeln, andererseits sind nach dem Diasporakrieg unter Trajan (115–117 n. Chr.) kaum noch Zeugnisse jüdischen Lebens in Alexandria zu erkennen. Als ein Schlüsseltext für die Wurzeln des Christentums in Alexandria wird die apokryphe Apokalypse des Petrus identifiziert, die sich als Teil oder wenigstens in der Nähe eines weltoffenen Diasporajudentums einordnen lässt. Trotz aller Schwierigkeiten der Datierung und Zuordnung zeigt sich darüber hinaus ein Spektrum von Texten, das nicht nur Tendenzen scharfer Abgrenzung bezeugt, sondern auch Aspekte gegenseitigen Interesses und gegenseitiger Beeinflussung. Am Ende des zweiten Jahrhunderts finden sich schließlich zunehmend christliche Schriften, die sich – vielleicht aus Mangel an Berührungspunkten mit Juden – dem Judentum gegenüber als eher ‚neutral' erweisen.

Keywords: Alexandria, Parting of the Ways, Apocalypse of Peter, the 'Jew' of Celsus, Epistle of Barnabas, Gospel of the Hebrews, Protevangelium of James

From which point in time can we speak about a "parting of the ways" between Jews, Jewish Christians, and Christians in Alexandria? This is a clear question. I hope that you are not too disappointed if I do not answer it because I think that it is riddled with problems. The problematic nature of the question extends beyond the fact that our data about the origins of what we call 'Christianity' in Alexandria are scarce and that it is still a matter of debate how, when, and by whom a kind of 'Christianity' entered Alexandria (and Egypt).[1] Additionally, although I

---

[1] The number of studies on the origins of Alexandrian Christianity is almost unmanageable. For an overview, see B. Schliesser, "Why Did Paul Skip Alexandria? A Study of Earliest Christianity

am often forced to use the terms 'Jews' and 'Christians' in my research on ancient sources, I usually try to look first for emic categories found in different texts and ask, what these categories might mean, and where they draw their "borderlines"[2] between different groups.[3] As I do not have to repeat how many problems (and what kind of pejorative connotations) are connected with the term "Jewish Christians,"[4] I would like to concentrate on the question of why I am not entirely happy with the use of "parting of the ways"-terminology. As I have done in several previous publications,[5] I concentrate here on a few issues that sometimes lead to misunderstandings. First and foremost, I am not interested in identifying the historical date that marked the decisive break between 'Jews' and 'Christians.'[6] Instead, my main point is that both the categories we use to describe an-

---

in Alexandria," in *Alexandria – Hub of the Hellenistic World*, ed. J. Frey, T.J. Kraus, and B. Schliesser, WUNT (Tübingen: Mohr Siebeck, forthcoming 2021), n. 1. I will not repeat Schliesser's overview here, but use much of this secondary literature in my own discussions.

2 Of course, I allude here (and elsewhere) to D. Boyarin, *Border Lines. The Partition of Judaeo-Christianity*, Divinations (Philadelphia, PA: University of Pennsylvania, 2006).

3 For this kind of research, see, for example, M. Henning and T. Nicklas, "Questions of Self-Designation in the Ascension of Isaiah," in *The Ascension of Isaiah*, ed. J.N. Bremmer, T.R. Karmann, and T. Nicklas, Studies on Early Christian Apocrypha 11 (Leuven: Peeters, 2016), 175–198, and S. Alkier, "Terminologien kollektiver Identitäten in der Apostelgeschichte des Lukas," in *Juden – Heiden – Christen? Religiöse Inklusion und Exklusion in Kleinasien bis Decius*, ed. idem and H. Leppin, WUNT 400 (Tübingen: Mohr Siebeck, 2018), 301–332.

4 Regarding the problems and ambiguities related to the term see M. Jackson-McCabe, "What's in a Name? The Problem of 'Jewish Christianity,'" in *Jewish Christianity Reconsidered. Rethinking Ancient Texts and Groups*, ed. idem (Minneapolis, MN: Fortress, 2007), 7–38; regarding the history of its use see H. Lemke, *Judenchristentum. Zwischen Ausgrenzung und Integration: Zur Geschichte eines exegetischen Begriffes*, HThSt 25 (Münster: LIT, 2001) and J. Carleton Paget, "The definition of the term 'Jewish Christian' / 'Jewish Christianity' in the history of research," in *Jews, Christians and Jewish Christians in Antiquity*, ed. idem, WUNT 251 (Tübingen: Mohr Siebeck, 2010), 289–324 (including an extensive bibliography).

5 See T. Nicklas, *Jews and Christians? Second Century 'Christian' Perspectives on the 'Parting of the Ways,'* Annual Deichmann Lectures 2013 (Tübingen: Mohr Siebeck, 2014); idem, "Getrennte Wege oder verflochtene Linien? 'Juden' und 'Christen' vor der konstantinischen Wende," *KuI* 30 (2015): 35–47; idem, "Parting of the Ways? Probleme eines Konzepts," in *Juden – Heiden – Christen? Religiöse Inklusion und Exklusion in Kleinasien bis Decius*, ed. S. Alkier and H. Leppin, WUNT 400 (Tübingen: Mohr Siebeck, 2018), 21–42 and idem, "Ein Baum mit zwei Ästen, getrennte Wege oder bleibende Vernetzung?," in *Christentum und Europa. XVI. Europäischer Kongress für Theologie (10.–13. September 2017 in Wien)*, ed. M. Meyer-Blanck, VWGTh 57 (Leipzig: EVA, 2019), 321–339.

6 For many, even recent, publications this remains the most important question. See, for example, the overview by U. Schnelle, *Die getrennten Wege von Römern, Juden und Christen: Religionspolitik im 1. Jahrhundert* (Tübingen: Mohr Siebeck, 2018), 3–6 who, however, adds a whole series of questions that must be distinguished.

cient realities (like 'Jews,' 'Christians,' and 'Jewish Christians') and also the related models we use to decide what is important and what is less important drastically influence the results of our research. To give just one example: in his recent article "The Ways That Parted: Jews, Christians and Jewish Christians, ca. 100–150 CE," Shaye J. D. Cohen writes:

> The notion of 'the parting of the ways' does not in the least suggest that Jews and Christians stopped speaking with each other, arguing with each other, and influencing each other. Christian literature of the first centuries CE bears many signs of reaction to Jewish truth claims, and if we believe modern scholarship, Jewish (rabbinic) literature of the first centuries CE bears many signs of reaction to Christian truth claims, but such reactions in of themselves neither prove nor disprove a parting of the ways. They prove only that Jews and Christians continued to speak with each other.[7]

Cohen is certainly right. My only question is, how important is the fact that people whom we would label 'Jews' and others whom we would label 'Christians' continued to speak with each other (and probably not just spoke or had conflicts, but also shared aspects of their lives with each other and may have even learned from each other)? This question becomes even more urgent if we confront it with another of Cohen's claims in the same essay: "The parting of the ways is about people, societies, and institutions, not about disembodied truth claims or the abstractions 'Judaism' and 'Christianity.'"[8]

But what if some of our key sources – like, for example, Ignatius of Antioch – use these abstractions, and what if, at the same time, this usage only makes sense if some people did not behave according to what institutions and their representatives expected them to do?[9] Should we see this as a marginal phenomenon or not? To say it in different words: from which point does the fact that 'Jews' and 'Christians' interacted (in whatever ways and in whatever parts of their lives) matter so much that the image of a "parting" of their ways is misleading?

Let me illustrate this with a few examples. In the 2018 issue of the journal *Apocrypha*, Christa Müller-Kessler edited three fragments of an early version of the *Dormition of Mary* in Christian Palestinian Aramaic, a Christian apocryphon

---

[7] S.J.D. Cohen, "The Ways That Parted: Jews, Christians, and Jewish-Christians, ca. 100–150 CE," in *Jews and Christians in the First and Second Centuries: The Interbellum 70–132 CE*, ed. J. Schwartz and P.J. Tomson, CRINT 15 (Leiden/Boston, MA: Brill, 2018), 307–339, esp. 308. Of course, Cohen's title reacts to the well-known volume by A.H. Becker and A.Y. Reed, eds., *The Ways that Never Parted. Jews and Christians in Late Antiquity and the Early Middle Ages* (Minneapolis, MN: Fortress, 2007).
[8] Cohen, "Ways That Parted" (see n. 7), 307.
[9] See, for example, the short discussion in Nicklas, *Jews and Christians* (see n. 5), 1–12.

containing a (probably early) Peter and Paul story which until now had been understood as a medieval Ethiopic addition to the *Book of Mary's Repose*.[10] The interesting point is that these clearly Christian fragments were not found in a Christian library, but in the Cairo Genizah. Even if we may count this as a pure accident, and even if we do not know whether any member of Cairo's Ben Ezra Synagogue ever used or read these fragments, there must have been at least someone who owned these clearly Christian texts and someone who decided not to destroy them, but to leave them in the Genizah.[11] This may be a marginal phenomenon in a situation where Jews and Christians were certainly differentiated groups, but if we are interested in people and their relations (and not just in truth claims and abstractions), I think this piece of evidence should interest us. Another example: starting with Ignatius of Antioch[12] (and perhaps already in the book of Revelation), we have plenty of evidence for so-called "Judaizers," that is, Christians (or "Christ followers") from a non-Jewish background who in different ways followed Jewish customs that were not accepted by what we usually call the "main church." Their relation to the synagogue (or to local synagogues) may have existed on very different levels – some of them seem to have attended synagogue services and observed the Sabbath or food laws. Even if we certainly should not call them 'Jews' (from whatever perspective), we should decide whether these groups are a phenomenon marginal enough to be completely dismissed. And even if we are not interested in "Judaizers," what do we do about people who liked to participate in Jewish feasts and celebrations? Again, if we are interested in people who mutually influenced each other (and not just in some people whose opinions we regard as decisive), why

---

10 C. Müller-Kessler, "Three Early Witnesses of the 'Dormition of Mary' in Christian Palestinian Aramaic from the Cairo Genizah (Taylor-Schechter Collection) and the New Finds in St Catherine's Monastery," *Apocrypha* 29 (2018): 69–95. I am grateful to Stephen Shoemaker who pointed to this evidence during a research seminar at the Universität Regensburg Centre for Advanced Studies "Beyond Canon."

11 For a thorough approach regarding the question of how material culture can help us understand ancient Jewish-Christian relations, see the fascinating book by E.C. Smith, *Jewish Glass and Christian Stone. A Materialist Mapping of the 'Parting of the Ways'* (London and New York, NY: Routledge, 2018).

12 In many earlier publications I tended toward the traditional date of Ignatius's *Epistles*. In the meantime, however, I am convinced that the evidence against an early date in the Trajanic period is too formidable. For a thorough discussion (placing Ignatius in the middle of the 2nd century) see, for example, J.N. Bremmer, "The Place, Date, and Author of the Ignatian Letters. An Onomastic Approach," in *Das Baujahr hinter der Fassade*, ed. W. Grünstäudl et al., WUNT (Tübingen: Mohr Siebeck, forthcoming 2021).

should we describe their situation with the help of a "parting of the ways" model?

We could go on with different examples but perhaps it is better to come to a preliminary conclusion regarding the concepts I am using. If I am reluctant to use the model of one or more "parting(s) of the ways," this does not mean that I am not aware of the fact that it was possible for outsiders (like members of the Roman administration) to distinguish 'Christians' – or at least some groups of Jesus followers – from Jews or members of other religious groups quite early in the first and/or second centuries.[13] I am also aware of the fact that we can speak of Christians who cannot be called 'Jews' (and who did not want to be identified with Jews) quite early. My own approach simply wants to show that the 'borderlines' drawn in the dynamic religious landscapes of antiquity were certainly not always identical to the ones drawn even in cases where we use the same (or comparable) terminologies. I would like to stress that where people drew borderlines their opinions did not always mirror what others thought (or, even more, they can be positions made *against* others' thoughts). And I would like to remind us of the fact that ancient people's constructions of "identities" – both social and individual – and their related "lived religion" were certainly less stable and consistent than we would like to presume.[14] In other words: the image of one or more "parting(s) of the ways" can only describe parts of ancient realities and is in danger of excluding others. The concept is not complex enough because it presupposes categories that do not do justice to the complexity both of ancient groups and the situational formation of individual lives. At the same time, the model is in danger of overemphasizing aspects of separation and – where it sees contact – conflict. Again, this is not to say that we do not see dimensions of separation or conflict – the model we use, however, influences our perspective. That is why I would like to re-model the question of how and when we can see one or more "partings of the ways" between Jews and Christians. Instead, I want to distinguish between three historical questions and reformulate the introductory question in the following manner:

(1) *Where can we see processes of distinction between groups we would label 'Jewish' and 'Christian' today? How can we describe these groups more concretely (and*

---

13 See also Cohen, "Ways That Parted" (see n. 7), 310–313, and – with a strong focus on this issue – Schnelle, *Die getrennten Wege* (see n. 6), 17–44.

14 Regarding the problems of speaking about "a," that is, one "Christian identity" in antiquity, see É. Rebillard, *Christians and Their Many Identities in Late Antiquity, North Africa, 200–450 CE* (New York, NY: Cornell University, 2012); regarding the use of the term "lived religion" in relation to antiquity, see J. Rüpke, *On Roman Religion: Lived Religion and the Individual in Ancient Rome* (New York, NY: Cornell University, 2016).

how do they possibly relate to other groups)? How do these processes relate to concrete historical circumstances?

While this first group of questions – following a proposal by Simon Claude Mimouni[15] – concentrates on matters of separation, a second cluster of questions moves in the opposite direction:

(2) *How do our sources reflect aspects of positive contact and mutual influence between at least certain 'Christian' and certain 'Jewish' groups and individuals? Which dimensions of life are affected by these contacts and in which situations are they possible?*

One may add a third dimension that has only recently been emphasized by Udo Schnelle:[16]

(3) *To what extent do "outside" influences – we may call them "historical contexts" – like, for example, Roman politics, create new situations which influence the developments described in questions (1) and (2)?*

A history of Jewish-Christian relations in antiquity should thus be at least three-dimensional. It should include aspects of distinction and differentiation between groups, but at the same time be interested in contact and interaction (both between groups and individuals). And it should, finally, be emphasized that Jewish-Christian interactions did not develop in a vacuum. At the same time, this approach remains an ideal. At least in some cases the available evidence makes it almost impossible to describe all three dimensions in an adequate manner.

My concrete task is to attempt this three-dimensional approach, focusing on developments in Alexandria. Several reasons make this task extremely difficult: first, we do not know very much about Alexandrian Judaism *after* the Diaspora War of 115–117 CE, and, second, we cannot be sure which 'Christian' texts emerged in 2nd or even 1st century Alexandria. In other words, an extreme outward influence (see question 3!), that is, the almost complete destruction of Jewish life in Alexandria, makes it extremely difficult to say anything reliable about questions (1) and (2). It will thus certainly not be possible to give concrete answers to *all* the above guiding questions. I will only be able to discuss examples of writings that can probably (or possibly) be traced to Alexandria and try to show how my approach

---

15 S.C. Mimouni, "Sur la question de la séparation entre 'jumeaux' et 'ennemis' aux Ier et IIe siècles," followed by A.Y. Reed, "Parting Ways over Blood and Water? Beyond 'Judaism' and 'Christianity' in the Roman Near East," both in *La Croisée des Chemins revisitée. Quand l'Église et la Synagogue se sont-elles distinguées? Actes du colloque de Tours 18–19 juin 2010*, ed. S.C. Mimouni and B. Pouderon, Patrimoines. Judaïsme antique (Paris: Cerf, 2012), 7–20 and 227–260, esp. 230.

16 Schnelle, *Die getrennten Wege* (see n. 6).

creates a difference. I will start with a few examples of evidence for the survival of a Jewish community in Alexandria.

1 Evidence for Jewish Survival after 117 CE

It is very difficult to determine whether and when, after the catastrophic Diaspora war, Jewish life in Alexandria started to flourish again.[17] Eldon Jay Epp's overview of papyrological witnesses has shown that evidence for Jewish life in Oxyrhynchus stopped almost entirely for several centuries;[18] the results of Tal Ilan's more recent overview of evidence in the whole of Egypt is not much different.[19] As we do not have comparable opportunities for Alexandria, we cannot make direct conclusions. We also may assume a considerable or even radical break for Alexandria, but perhaps at least a limited recovery of Alexandria's Jewish life should not be completely excluded because the city may have become a destination for Jewish refugees.[20] Even if this was the case, as far as I see, the evidence for Jewish life in 2nd century post-war Alexandria is scarce. The question whether the *Acta Pauli et Antonini* (P.Lond. inv. 1; P.Louvre 2376 bis) describe a conflict between a Greek and a Jewish delegation to be decided by Hadrian in Rome (or by Trajan in Antioch) is matter of a debate we do not have to resolve as the *Acta* do not give any evidence regarding "Jewish-Christian" relations.[21]

---

[17] Regarding the number of Jews in pre-war Alexandria, see, for example, the discussion of A. Martin, "Origines de l'Alexandrie chrétienne: Topographie, Liturgie, Institutions," in *Origeniana Octava. Origen and the Alexandrian Tradition 1*, ed. L. Perrone, BETL 164 (Leuven: Peeters, 2003), 105–119, esp. 106–107.
[18] See E.J. Epp, "The Jews and the Jewish Community in Oxyrhynchus: Socio-Religious Context for the New Testament Papyri," in *New Testament Manuscripts. Their Texts and their World*, ed. T.J. Kraus and T. Nicklas, TENT 2 (Leiden and Boston, MA: Brill, 2006), 13–52.
[19] See T. Ilan, "The Jewish Community in Egypt before and after 117 CE in Light of Old and New Papyri," in *Jewish and Christian Communal Identities in the Roman World*, ed. Y. Furstenberg (Leiden and Boston, MA: Brill, 2016), 203–224, esp. 215: "[T]he evidence for Jews in the two first centuries after the revolt is scant, and they are recognizable only by their names."
[20] This is suggested by A.M. Schwemer, "Zum Abbruch des jüdischen Lebens in Alexandria. Der Aufstand in der Diaspora unter Trajan (115–117)," in *Alexandria*, ed. T. Georges, F. Albrecht, and R. Feldmeier, COMES 1 (Tübingen: Mohr Siebeck, 2013), 381–399, esp. 393–395.
[21] Schwemer, "Abbruch" (see n. 20), 394–395; but see also B. Pouderon, "'Jewish', 'Christian' and 'Gnostic' Groups in Alexandria during the 2nd Cent. Between Approval and Expulsion," in *Beyond Conflicts: Cultural and Religious Cohabitations in Alexandria and Egypt between the 1st and 6th Century CE*, ed. L. Arcari, STAC 103 (Tübingen: Mohr Siebeck, 2017), 155–176, esp. 157. Schwemer also mentions the *Acta Hermaisci*, but, as far as I can see, this text is better dated into a period shortly before the war (see also the detailed discussion by H.A. Musurillo, *The*

While the *Acta* do not offer any witness for our overall question, two others are more intriguing. In several of his writings, Origen speaks about a Jew with whom he is in contact regarding exegetical problems.[22] The most detailed but also problematic of these passages can be found in Origenes, *Hom. Jer.* 20(19).2:[23]

> Καὶ πρῶτον χρήσομαι παραδόσει Ἑβραϊκῇ, ἐληλυθυίᾳ εἰς ἡμᾶς διά τινος φυγόντος διὰ τὴν τοῦ Χριστοῦ πίστιν καὶ διὰ τὸ ἐπαναβεβηκέναι ἀπὸ τοῦ νόμου καὶ ἐληλυθότος ἔνθα διατρίβομεν.
>
> And first, I want to make use of a Hebrew tradition, which was given to us by one who fled because (his) belief in Christ and (his) rise from the law, and came to the place where we live.

This passage, of course, sounds highly interesting. Origen seems to speak about a Jew who obviously had to leave the synagogue (or, even more, had to flee from his home town?) because of his conversion into a Christ believer and a somehow-related transgression of the (Jewish) law. It does not become clear to what extent the two reasons for this flight are related and, of course, we have only Origen's (not very friendly) perspective on the situation. The main point regarding our question, however, is this text's final passage. Because he thinks that this Jew must be identified with the one mentioned, for example, in Origen's *Epistula ad Africanum* 7, P. Nautin, the editor of the text in the Sources Chrétiennes, changed the extant verbal form διατρίβομεν ("we live") to διετρίβομεν ("we lived").[24] As the *Homilies on Jeremiah*, however, were delivered in Caesarea, the text only then refers to an Alexandrian Jew if we follow Nautin's (unnecessary) conjecture. In other words: Origen met this Jew probably in Caesarea.[25] Other passages, however, attest contacts between Origen and a "learned Hebrew, the son of a Rabbi" (*Ep. Afr.* 7), a "Hebrew teacher" (*Princ.* 1.3.4), or "a certain Hebrew" (*Sel. Ezech.* 9.2). Origen, who shared the view of many ancient Christian

---

Acts of the Pagan Martyrs. Acta Alexandrinorum [Oxford: Oxford University Press, 1954], 164–168).

22 For more details, see G. Dorival and R. Naiweld, "Les interlocuteurs hébreux et juifs d'Origène à Alexandrie et à Césarée," in *Caesarea Maritima e la scuola origeniana. Multiculturalità, forme di competizione culturale e identità cristiana*, ed. O. Andrei (Brescia: Paideia, 2013), 121–138.

23 For a short note, see Pouderon, "'Jewish'" (see n. 21), 157–158. Regarding the text, see A. Fürst and H.E. Lona, eds., *Die Homilien zum Buch Jeremia*, Origenes. Werke mit deutscher Übersetzung 11 (Berlin and Boston, MA: de Gruyter, 2018), 490.

24 For an even more detailed discussion of the problem, see Fürst and Lona, *Homilien* (see n. 23), 491–492 n. 772. Nautin's edition appeared in SC 238 (see p. 256 n. 1).

25 That's why Pouderon's ("'Jewish'" [see n. 21], 158) conclusion that this Jew must have been a migrant from Palestine to Alexandria is probably wrong. Regarding Jewish-Christian relations in Origen's Caesarea, see Fürst and Lona, *Homilien* (see n. 23), 41–48.

authors that Israel had lost its status as God's elected people and thus could sound very anti-Jewish,[26] seems to have fostered contacts with at least one learned Jew already in his Alexandrian period. This does not say very much about group relations, but it offers a nice example for the fact that an individual could behave quite differently in different situations of his life.

Much more interesting, however, is a second figure – an anonymous Jew whose arguments against Christianity were used by Celsus in his *Alethes Logos* and preserved in Origen's *Contra Celsum*. In a 2013 article, Niehoff argues convincingly that this Jew is not just a fictional figure (as Origen supposes in *Cels*. 1.28; 2.1.28 and 54) but an authentic Jewish voice from mid-2nd century Alexandria,[27]

> a well educated Jew, who continued the intellectual as well as the scholarly tradition of Philo and his colleagues from the 1st century CE. He apparently responded to the increasing popularity of the Christian faith among his fellow Jews, being concerned especially about the *Letter of Barnabas*, which advocated a novel theology of supersession and used the Jewish Scriptures to support exclusive Christian claims.[28]

Niehoff not only follows earlier authors who pointed to differences between Celsus's and the Jew's views;[29] she shows that Celsus must have worked with a the-

---

[26] The classical work on Origen's relation to Jews is N.R.M. de Lange, *Origen and the Jews. Studies in Jewish-Christian Relations in Third-Century Palestine* (Cambridge: Cambridge University Press, 1972); but see also G. Sgherri, *Chiesa e Sinagoga nelle opere di Origene*, Studia Patristica Mediolanensia 3 (Milan: Vita e Pensiero, 1982) and (for a short overview) Fürst and Lona, *Homilien* (see n. 23), 35–41.

[27] M.R. Niehoff, "A Jewish Critique of Christianity from 2nd Century Alexandria. Celsus' Jew Revisited," *JECS* 21 (2013): 151–175 and (later) eadem, "Jüdische Bibelinterpretation zwischen Homerforschung und Christentum," in *Alexandria*, ed. T. Georges, F. Albrecht, and R. Feldmeier, COMES 1 (Tübingen: Mohr Siebeck, 2013), 341–360, esp. 357–359. For the different opinion (following Origen himself who considered Celsus's Jew a rhetorical device), see H.E. Lona, *Die 'Wahre Lehre' des Kelsos*, Kommentar zu den frühchristlichen Apologeten. Erg. 1 (Freiburg et al.: Herder, 2005), 172–177 who starts his excursus on Celsus's Jew with the words: "Herabsetzend vergleicht Origenes die Einführung des Juden durch Kelsos mit der rhetorischen Übung eines Kindes (1,28), d. h. mit der schulischen Aufgabe, einer fiktiven Person eine Rede in den Mund zu legen. Der Jude des Kelsos ist seine literarische Schöpfung, und als solche soll sie zunächst betrachtet werden."

[28] Niehoff, "Jewish Critique" (see n. 27), 153.

[29] See E. Bammel, "Der Jude des Celsus," in idem, *Judaica. Gesammelte Schriften*, WUNT 37 (Tübingen: Mohr Siebeck, 1986), 265–283; L. Troiano, "Il Giudeo di Celso," in *Discorsi di Verita*, ed. L. Perrone (Roma: Institutum Patristicum Augustinianum, 1998), 115–128, and L. Blumell, "A Jew in Celsus's *True Doctrine*? An Examination of Jewish Anti-Christian Polemic in the Second Century C.E.," *SR* 36 (2007): 299–310.

matically well-structured written source[30] that can be divided in two parts: a criticism directed against Jesus (or claims about Jesus) in book 1 and a discussion with "fellow Jews who had embraced the new doctrine and left their fathers' customs"[31] in book 2. Even more important is the fact that this anonymous Jew's discussion of the emerging early Christian Gospels followed the hermeneutics of the Alexandrian school, which was highly influential on Alexandrian Jewish exegesis of biblical texts. This reconstruction demonstrates a certain training in the critical interpretation of Homer that focuses on problems of implausible passages and discusses textual contradictions.[32] This unknown author must have had access to several Gospel writings which he understood as consisting of two layers: "a primitive layer created by Jesus himself and a subsequent layer added by his disciples" who "subsequently embellished the Jesus traditions with fanciful stories."[33] The Jew's second part is interested in why "citizens" (πολῖται) of his community left "the law of our fathers" (τὸν πάτριον νόμον) "in favor of another name" (εἰς ἄλλο ὄνομα).[34] Niehoff understands this as a reference to the gematric discussion of Jesus's name (plus a representation of the T) in Barn. 9:8.[35] The Jew's main point of critique becomes clear somewhat later; according to him, "Christ-believers blame Jews for not having believed in Jesus as God" (Cels. 2.8b). Even if I am not absolutely sure how far we should understand the *Epistle of Barnabas* (to which we will return later) as a background of the Jew's argument, it seems clear that the Jew – I quote Maren Niehoff – "writes these lines with a clear sense that an ineffaceable borderline has been drawn between Christians and Jews. He moreover relies on a Christian self-definition that relies

---

30 Niehoff, "Jewish Critique" (see n. 27), 157: "The sheer amount of material quoted from the mouth of the Jew and especially its consistency make the assumption of a written source mandatory. It is unwise to imagine that Celsus either received such an extended and coherent tradition in oral form or that he himself made it up or that he created an amalgam of different Jewish voices."
31 Niehoff, "Jewish Critique" (see n. 27), 157.
32 Cf. Niehoff, "Jewish Critique" (see n. 27), 161–163. For an overview of the mutual relations, see M.R. Niehoff, *Jewish Exegesis and Homeric Scholarship in Alexandria* (Cambridge: Cambridge University Press, 2012).
33 Niehoff, "Jewish Critique" (see n. 27), 160.
34 See Origen, *Cels.* 2.1 also quoted by Niehoff, "Jewish Critique" (see n. 27), 171 who understands this formulation as another sign that the "anonymous author once more shares his basic outlook with Philo."
35 Cf. Niehoff, "Jewish Critique" (see n. 27), 172. This is an intriguing observation. A certain interest in Jesus's name, however, is already visible in Matt 1:21 (where the name Jesus is understood as a sign that he will save his people) or even Phil 2:9, according to which Jesus is given a "name which is greater than all other names," that is, "Kyrios," the "Lord."

on the notion of progress by dismissing its Jewish roots."[36] In other words, Celsus's Jew may be an important voice in a history of distinction, a voice that positions itself in an emerging spectrum of groups. Of course, we have only his perspective, but his perspective presupposes not just 'Jews' and 'Christians,' but several groups of them: (1) 'Jews' who were open to following his argument and who wanted to remain distinct from 'Christians'; (2) 'Jews' who (for whatever reason) regarded it as attractive to follow the 'Christian' movement; and (3) 'Christians' who developed a Christology that could be understood as venerating Jesus as a God.

Perhaps we can also get some indirect evidence from another perspective. Some of the most well-known early Jewish writings that did not make it into the Old Testament canon come from Alexandria. How is it possible that they survived – and even more – how is it possible that they survived in mainly 'Christian' hands? It is clear that there is no simple answer to this broad question. It would be necessary to discuss this problem for every text in a different way. And every answer to this question would have to construct something like a bridge, a moment of contact and interest and perhaps a moment where boundaries were less clear than in later times. One could discuss, for example, the works of Philo of Alexandria which did not only survive, but were used by a whole series of Christian authors, many of whom spent at least parts of their life in Alexandria.[37] While Maren Niehoff thinks that parts of Philo's work could have been rescued by his Roman audience, David T. Runia thinks "the survival of Philo's writings was entirely dependent on the intervention of Christian authors."[38] Following a suggestion by D. Barthélemy, he sees the Alexandrian *Didaskaleion* (founded by Pantaenus, Clement of Alexandria's enigmatic teacher)[39] as key for the survival of Philo's works.[40] But even if this is the case, we have to fill a gap of several decades in which there must have been a time where Philo's writings made it into the hands of people we call 'Christians' today.

Another example may be even more intriguing. At least some of the Sibylline Oracles go back to Alexandrian Judaism before they made it into today's 'Christian' collection. One of the most fascinating examples is book 5. Large sections of

---

36 Niehoff, "Jewish Critique" (see n. 27), 173.
37 For an overview, see D.T. Runia, *Philo in Early Christian Literature. A Survey* (Minneapolis, MN: Fortress, 1993); reg. Origen and Philo see esp. A. van den Hoek, "Philo and Origen. A Descriptive Catalogue of Their Relationship," *SPhiloA* 12 (2000): 44–121.
38 Runia, *Philo* (see n. 37), 16–17.
39 Regarding Pantaenus, see A. Jakab, *Ecclesia alexandrina. Evolution sociale et institutionelle du christianisme alexandrine (II*^{e}* et III*^{e}* siècles)* (Bern et al.: Lang, 2001), 107–115.
40 See Runia, *Philo* (see n. 37), 22.

this writing focus on Egypt (see vv. 60–114.179–99.458–463.484–511). V. 53 even understands the Sibyl as a confidant of Isis (v. 53: Ἴσιδος ἡ γνωστή) and the oldest extant quote of Sib. Or. 5 can be found in Clement of Alexandria, *Protr.* 4.50 and *Paed.* 2.10.99.[41] All this points to a very probable origin of this writing in Egypt (or even in Alexandria). Two aspects are highly intriguing: the *Oracle*'s first 51 verses allude to a series of Roman Emperors from Hadrian (vv. 47f.), who is described in extremely favorable terms, to (perhaps) Antoninus Pius (v. 49f.), and, finally, Marcus Aurelius and Lucius Aurelius Verus (v. 51). Does this mean that we have a piece of evidence that is relevant not just for ongoing Alexandrian Jewish literary activities in Hadrianic and even post-Hadrianic times?[42] If we follow John J. Collins and Olivia Stewart Lester, who date the text to the times of Hadrian (*before* the Bar Kochba war of 132–135) and view v. 51 or 49–51 as a later interpolation, this seems to be the case.[43] But this is not the only interesting point: vv. 256–259 speaks about the appearance of an "admirable man from heaven" (256) who had "stretched his hands on fruitful wood" (257) – clearly an allusion to Jesus's passion. Vv. 258–259, in turn, which call him the one who had made the sun stand still, of course, refers first and foremost to Joshua (see Josh 10:13–14), a figure who is called "Jesus" in the LXX. Of course, one can describe this (or at least v. 257) as a 'Christian' interpolation into an otherwise purely 'Jewish' text. All this suggests that an Egyptian (perhaps Alexandrian) 'Jewish' text was (at least partly) composed after 117 CE. This text was not only updated up to the middle of the 2nd century, but was also used and, again, slightly revised by Christians. We cannot know exactly when and where this was the

---

41 For these arguments, see J.-D. Gauger, *Sibyllinische Weissagungen. Griechisch-deutsch*, 2nd ed., Tusculum (Zürich and Düsseldorf: Artemis & Winkler, 2002), 455.

42 See, for example, the suggestion by Schwemer, "Abbruch" (see n. 20), 395 who, however, reckons with an end of the community after Hadrian's times (which contradicts the *Sibylline Oracles*'s evidence!). D. Frankfurter, "The Legacy of Jewish Apocalypses in Early Christianity: Regional Trajectories," in *The Jewish Apocalyptic Heritage in Early Christianity*, ed. J.C. VanderKam and W. Adler, CRINT III/4 (Assen: Van Gorcum; Minneapolis, MN: Fortress, 1996), 129–200, esp. 145, even sees a close connection between the text's attack against Memphis (Sib.Or. 5.60–92 and 179–186) and "an apparent massing of Jewish forces there in 116, presumably to destroy Egyptian shrines."

43 See J.J. Collins, *The Sibylline Oracles of Egyptian Judaism*, SBL.DS 13 (Missoula, MT: Society of Biblical Literature, 1974), 94–95 and (more recently) O. Stewart Lester, *Prophetic Rivalry, Gender, and Economics. A Study in Revelation and Sibylline Oracles 4–5*, WUNT 2/466 (Tübingen: Mohr Siebeck, 2018), 144 n.10. But see the older discussion in Gauger, *Sibyllinische Weissagungen* (see n. 41), 454–455 who even seems to contradict himself when he writes later (508) about v. 49: "Also ist das Orakel unter den Antoninen vor 180 n.Chr. verfaßt worden."

case. All of this, however, is not understandable without at least some moment of contact, mutual interest, and interactions.

2 Stories about the Origins of the Christian movement in Alexandria[44]

Unfortunately, the short and enigmatic note about a certain Alexandrian named Apollos (Acts 18:24–25), a figure we also know from 1 Corinthians, is only partly helpful. The passage is highly interesting as it reveals the categories that Acts uses to describe its figures.[45] As Acts, however, does not claim that Apollos received his "catechesis in the way of the Lord" (ἦν κατηχημένος τὴν ὁδὸν τοῦ κυρίου) *in Alexandria*, it does not offer evidence for the roots of Alexandrian 'Christianity.'[46] Codex Bezae Cantabrigiensis (D), the most important witness of the so-called 'Western text' of Acts (represented also by some Latin manuscripts), however, offers a slightly different text. The most important variants are the following: instead of the words Ἀπολλῶς ὀνόματι, D offers ὀνόματι Ἀπολλώνιος (*nomine Apollonius*); instead of Ἀλεξανδρεὺς τῷ γένει, we read γένει Ἀλεξανδρεύς (*natione Alexandrinus*; v. 24). Moreover, D offers an additional ἐν τῇ

---

44 I do not regard the *Letter of Claudius to the Alexandrians* edited by H.I. Bell, *Jews and Christians in Egypt. The Jewish Troubles in Alexandria and the Athanasian Controversy* (Repr. Westport, CT: Greenwood, 1972 [1924]), 1–37, as a source regarding the origins of Christianity in Alexandria. For a critical discussion of this evidence, see also Jakab, *Ecclesia alexandrina* (see n. 39), 43–45.
45 Apollos *is* a Ἰουδαῖος, that is, a "Jew," but at the same time an Ἀλεξανδρεύς and instructed in the "way of the Lord." As such he speaks and teaches thoroughly the things about Jesus (τὰ περὶ Ἰησοῦ; Acts 18:25). He is not just an ἀνὴρ λόγιος, which we could translate "an eloquent man" or "a man who knows how to speak (properly)," but also δυνατὸς ἐν ταῖς γραφαῖς, that is, "an expert in the Scriptures" (what certainly refers to the Scriptures of Israel) (both 18:24). In other words, he comes from Alexandria, is a Jew, *and* a follower of Christ (even if he only knows the baptism of John; 18:25). As someone who seems to have Greek rhetorical training, an expertise in the scriptures of Israel, and is instructed about Jesus, he starts to teach in the (Jewish) synagogue of Ephesus. After having received additional instruction about the "way [of God]" by Priscilla and Aquila, he plans to go to Achaia where he becomes helpful to the "believers" because he is able to refute the "Jews" through the scriptures. I think it becomes clear that a simple distinction between the categories 'Jews' and 'Christians' does not do justice to this passage. This is just another example of what S. Alkier ("Terminologien kollektiver Identitäten" [see n. 3]) has shown in more detail for other passages of the book of Acts.
46 For a broader treatment (including earlier secondary literature), see J. Wehnert, "Apollos," in *Alexandria*, ed. T. Georges, F. Albrecht, and R. Feldmeier, COMES 1 (Tübingen: Mohr Siebeck, 2013), 403–412.

πατρίδι (d [gig]: *in patria*) after κατηχημένος.⁴⁷ The Bezan text of Acts 18:24–25 thus does not only transform Apollos into an Apollonios, it also stresses his Alexandrian background slightly more than Acts and places his first instruction about "the word of the Lord" (B τὸν λόγον τοῦ κυρίου instead of "way of the Lord") in Alexandria. It is not necessary to follow Josep Rius-Camps and Jenny Read-Heimerdinger and understand the Bezan version as the (more or less) original text of Acts to regard this as interesting complex of variants.⁴⁸ The passage may not be understood as a reliable witness for the origins of Alexandrian 'Christianity,' but it reflects a (probably) 2nd century redactor's interest. According to this version of Acts, the roots of the Alexandrian 'Christian' movement do not only go back to a very early period, they are described as an inner Jewish movement. Apollonios is a Ἰουδαῖος, a learned man and powerful in the Scriptures (of Israel). At the same time, he teaches "the things about Jesus," but only knows about the baptism of John. That's why he needs more detailed instruction by Aquila and Priscilla.⁴⁹ For this text, it is thus not a contradiction to be a Jew and teach about Jesus. To say it again: I do not say that the Bezan text's claim is historically reliable. This text, however, shows that claims like this were possible even in the (certainly not too early) 2nd century.

Unfortunately, Eusebius of Caesarea's *Ecclesiastical History* does not offer very much reliable (and even less pertinent) information relevant for our questions, Eusebius mentions a certain Annianus as the first bishop of Alexandria (after Mark) (*Hist. eccl.* 2.24) and offers names of his successors. Even if some later apocryphal writings do not transmit historically reliable evidence regarding the roots of the Christian movement in Alexandria, their way of describing it may well be interesting. The (perhaps late 4th century) *Martyrdom of Mark*, for example, relates the origins of the Alexandrian church to a more or less random meeting between Mark and a cobbler whose reactions to Mark's message do not sound as if he were a Jew. Even more, the text is mainly interested in whether the Alexandrian community can be understood as an apostolic foundation (by Mark who is understood as an apostle and evangelist) and also in the early Christians' fight against the demons of the past among which Serapis figures as the

---

47 For even more details, see J. Rius-Camps and J. Read-Heimerdinger, *The Message of Acts in Codex Bezae. A Comparison with the Alexandrian Tradition IV: Acts 18.24 – 28.31: Rome*, LNTS 415 (London and New York, NY: Continuum, 2009), 17–18.

48 See their four volume commentary *The Message of Acts in Codex Bezae*, but also their respective articles in T. Nicklas and M. Tilly, eds., *The Book of Acts as Church History. Texts, Textual Traditions and Ancient Interpretations*, BZNW 120 (Berlin and New York, NY: de Gruyter, 2003), 263–280 and 281–296.

49 Contrary to what we find in the critical editions, the Bezan text offers this order of names.

key antagonist.[50] Even if § 1 of the *Martyrdom* calls Egypt "uncircumcised at its heart" (see Rom 2:29 and Acts 7:51), Jews are never mentioned. The only possible piece of counter-evidence can be seen in § 10, where different calendrical systems are used to fix the date of Mark's memory, the last of which is κατὰ δὲ Ἑβραίους Νισαθρίων ἑπταδεκάτῃ, that is, "according to the Hebrews, at the 17th of Nisan." Of course, this does not say anything more than that the (probably late 4th century) author of the *Martyrdom* is aware of the existence of "Hebrews" in Alexandria and that these "Hebrews" are clearly distinguished from "us, the Christians" who are mentioned only a few lines later.

Besides the *Martyrdom*, a second apocryphal tradition connects the origins of the Alexandrian Church with the mission of Barnabas. The oldest witness for this idea can be found in the *Pseudoclementine Homilies* according to which Clement, who is on his way to Caesarea Stratonis, has to stop in Alexandria (*Ps.-Clem.Hom.* I.8.3–4).[51] There, he meets a group of philosophers who have heard of the rumors regarding a man from Judea who performs miracles and is called a "Son of God," that is, of course, Jesus. As Clement asks them for firsthand information, they refer to Barnabas who is present in Alexandria. Interestingly, the text emphasizes that Barnabas is an eyewitness of Jesus, but also that he comes from his home-country, that is, he is a "Hebrew" (*Ps.-Clem.Hom.* I.9.1). Clement finds him, listens to his words, and understands that he tells the truth. Barnabas stays for a few days with Clement and instructs him (*Ps.-Clem.Hom.* I.13.3); after this, he tells him that he has to leave Alexandria, will go to Judea "because of a festival required by true divine service," and stay there with the members of his people (*Ps.-Clem.Hom.* I.13.4). Clement leaves only a few days after Barnabas. When he reaches Caesarea, he meets Barnabas who introduces him to Peter (*Ps.-Clem.Hom.* I.15.5–6), the story's main protagonist. According to the *Homilies*, all this happens during Jesus's lifetime (see, for example, *Ps.-Clem.Hom.* I.6).[52] Barnabas, in turn, who is probably understood as one of the

---

50 For a more detailed treatment of this text, see T. Nicklas, "The *Martyrdom of Mark* in Late Antique Alexandria," in *Alexandria – Hub of the Hellenistic World*, ed. J. Frey, T.J. Kraus, and B. Schliesser (Tübingen: Mohr Siebeck, forthcoming 2021), and idem, "Martyrdom of Mark," in *More New Testament Apocrypha*, ed. T. Burke (Grand Rapids, MI: Eerdmans, forthcoming 2021).
51 For a detailed discussion of the figure of Barnabas in the *Pseudoclementine Homilies*, see J. Verheyden, "Presenting Minor Characters in the Pseudo-Clementine Novel. The Case of Barnabas," in *Nouvelles intrigues pseudo-clémentines. Plots in the Pseudo-Clementine Romance*, ed. F. Amsler et al., PIRSB 6 (Prahins, CH: Éditions du Zèbre, 2008), 249–257.
52 According to the *Recognitions*, Barnabas and Clement meet in Rome. As many scholars tend to understand the *Homilies* as more reliable than the *Recognitions*, it seems probable that this passage was a part of the alleged *Grundschrift*.

70/72 disciples who were sent out as missionaries by Jesus himself, is presented a Hebrew who follows Jewish customs. Of course, one should not treat this as reliable evidence regarding the roots of Alexandrian Christianity. The *Homilies*, however, can be understood as a writing that still *claimed* very early "Palestinian Hebrew" origins of an Alexandrian mission.

Interestingly, the *Pseudoclementine Homilies* are not completely alone in this idea. Although the *Acts of Barnabas*, for example, focus on a second missionary journey in Cyprus (after the one told in Acts 13:4–13), they close with Mark's arrival in Alexandria (§ 26) and thus connect the mission of Alexandria at least indirectly with Barnabas.[53] The somewhat later *Barnabas Encomium* by the Monk Alexander, finally, seems to connect this with traditions as we find them in the *Homilies*[54] and makes Barnabas both a direct disciple of Jesus (l. 238ff.) and a successful missionary who not only operates in Cyprus, but also in Rome (l. 367–369) and in Alexandria (l. 381–384).[55] Again, all this does not tell us very much about the historical origins of the Alexandrian Church. If we, however, take together the so-called 'Western' text of Acts, the *Pseudoclementine Homilies*, and related Barnabas writings, we can see that the claims for the Jewish origins of Alexandrian Christianity remained influential even in times where other claims – that is, traditions about a Markan mission in 'pagan' Alexandria – became dominant. In other words, these traditions cannot help us to answer the question of what the first Christian movement in Alexandria *really* looked like, but they show us *what kind of stories* about this earliest movement could be told for quite a long time.

3 The Witness of (Probably) Alexandrian 'Christian' Writings

If we, finally, want to go a step further and understand how early groups of Christ-followers may have appeared, how they distinguished themselves from what kind of Judaism, and how they interrelated, we have to look into texts that arguably originated in Alexandria. I can only offer a small selection that offers a spectrum of views.

---

53 For a broader treatment, see T. Nicklas, "Barnabas Remembered: Apokryphe Barnabastexte und die Kirche Zyperns," in *Religion als Imagination*, ed. L. Seehausen et al. (Leipzig: EVA, 2020), 167–188.
54 I do not claim that the text *knew* both *Homilies* and *Recognitions* and reworked them literally.
55 For more details, see Nicklas, "Barnabas Remembered" (see n. 53).

3.1 An Earliest Group of Writings?

3.1.1 The Apocalypse of Peter

In a series of articles, Jan Bremmer and I offered arguments for an Alexandrian provenance of the Greek/Ethiopic *Apocalypse of Peter*.⁵⁶ It is extremely difficult to give an exact date of this text; perhaps we may think about the first decades of the 2nd century, but we may have to go somewhat later.⁵⁷ In any case, it seems that we have a very ancient writing, the problematic transmission of which, however, makes it difficult to deal appropriately with its details. Two aspects of the *Apocalypse of Peter* are especially interesting for our question. First, while it is clear that this text was written by Christ-followers, our usual categories of 'Christians' vs. 'Jews' vs. 'Greeks' do not fit for this writing.⁵⁸ We are, for example, informed about a resurrection of the dead which seems in no way connected to Jesus's resurrection and could stem from an early Jewish writing based on an exegesis of Ezek 37 and other Old Testament passages (Apoc.Pet. 4).⁵⁹ This resurrection scene, however, is followed by a description of the world's destruction in fire, an *ekpyrosis* that is first and foremost related to the myth of Phaeton, but that also made its way both into texts like Sib.Or. 5 and 2 Peter. Salvation of sinners is related to the Acherusian Lake and the Elysian field (Apoc.Pet. 14:4); Hebrew theophoric angel names like Uriel (Apoc.Pet. 4:9–10) and Ezrael (Apoc.-Pet. 9) meet with Tartarouchos (Apoc.Pet. 13) and Temlakos (Apoc.Pet. 8) and

---

56 See J.N. Bremmer, "The *Apocalypse of Peter*. Greek or Jewish?" and idem, "The *Apocalypse of Peter*. Place, Date and Punishments," both in *Maidens, Magic and Martyrs in Early Christianity*, idem, WUNT 379 (Tübingen: Mohr Siebeck, 2017), 269–280 and 281–294, and T. Nicklas, "'Insider' und 'Outsider'. Überlegungen zum historischen Kontext der Darstellung 'jenseitiger Orte' in der Offenbarung des Petrus," in *Topographie des Jenseits. Studien zur Geschichte des Todes in Kaiserzeit und Spätantike*, ed. W. Ameling (Stuttgart: Steiner, 2011), 35–48 and idem, "Jewish, Christian, Greek? The Apocalypse of Peter as a Witness of Early 2nd-Cent. Christianity in Alexandria," in *Beyond Conflicts. Cultural and Religious Cohabitations in Alexandria and Egypt between the 1st and the 6th Century CE*, ed. L. Arcari, STAC 103 (Tübingen: Mohr Siebeck, 2017), 27–46.
57 While I have defended an early 2nd century date in most of my writings on this text (see, for example, Nicklas, "Jewish" [see n. 56]), J.N. Bremmer, "The *Apocalypse of Peter* as the First Christian Martyr Text: Its Date, Provenance and Relationship with 2 Peter," in *2 Peter and the Apocalypse of Peter. Towards a New Perspective*, ed. J. Frey, M. den Dulk, and J.G. van der Watt, BibInt 174 (Leiden/Boston, MA: Brill, 2019), 75–98, esp. 91, proposes the time "around 150."
58 For more details, see Nicklas, "Jewish" (see n. 56), 27–35.
59 For a detailed analysis, see T. Nicklas, "Resurrection – Judgment – Punishment. Apocalypse of Peter 4," in *Resurrection of the Dead. Biblical Traditions in Dialogue*, ed. G. van Oyen and T. Shepherd, BETL 249 (Leuven et al.: Peeters, 2012), 461–474.

a description of hell appears that is influenced by Orphic traditions.[60] All this points to a context in which our usual distinctions do not work very well. The *Apocalypse of Peter* thus probably originated among Christ-followers who were both interested in Jewish eschatology and heavily influenced by Greek ideas of the end of time and the otherworld.

How did the group behind the text understand its relationship to Israel? If we can trust the transmission of chapter 2, its relation to Israel seems to have been ambivalent. In chapter 2, the text offers an interesting version of the parable of the fig tree (see also Mark 13:28–29 par Matt 24:32–34; Luke 13:6–9). I quote only the decisive passages, which start with a saying of Jesus:

> But as for you, learn from the fig tree its lesson. As soon as its sprout emerges and its branches bud at that time will be the end of the world (Apoc.Pet. 2:1).

After Peter has asked him about the meaning of this parable, Jesus responds with another parable:

> Do you not understand that the fig tree is the house of Israel? It is like a man (who) planted a fig tree in his garden and it did not produce fruit. And he sought its fruit many years, but he did not find it. And he said to his gardener, 'Uproot this fig tree so that it won't make your soil worthless for us.' And the gardener said to the master of the land, 'Send (us). We will weed it and dig ashes beneath it and irrigate it with water. And if it does not bear fruit this time we will remove its roots from the garden and plant another in its place.' Did you not perceive that the fig tree is the house of Israel? And indeed, I have told you, when its branches bud in the end, false messiahs will come. And when they see his evil deeds, they will turn away. And they will reject him who is called the 'glory of our ancestors,' who crucified the first Christ and erred exceedingly. But this liar is not the Christ. And when they resist him, he will wage war with the sword. And there will be many martyrs. Then at that time when the branches of the fig tree, this alone is the house of Israel, have budded, there will be many martyrs by his hand [...] Indeed, Enoch and Elijah will be sent in order to instruct them that this is the deceiver who will come into the world and perform signs and wonders to deceive it (Apoc.Pet. 2:4–12).[61]

Even if this passage provides many difficulties, it becomes clear that this writing has a rather optimistic view of Israel's future. While the passage starts with a fierce warning that the fig tree could be uprooted and removed (see Luke 13:6–9), this is not seen as being already accomplished (see Matt 21:43). Instead,

---

60 See, for example, Bremmer, "*Apocalypse of Peter*. Greek or Jewish?" (see n. 56), 273.
61 Translations by E.J. Beck, *Justice and Mercy in the Apocalypse of Peter. A New Translation and Analysis of the Purpose of the Text*, WUNT 427 (Tübingen: Mohr Siebeck, 2019), 66–67.

the text seems to prophecy that the "branches of the fig tree" will indeed bud again and thus – I quote Joel Marcus –

> 'the house of Israel' will be restored by God's good graces. [...] The Apocalypse of Peter, then, removes the ambiguity found in the Lukan parable: 'the keeper of the garden' will not labour in vain. Rather, the Israel-tree's shoot will burst forth and its branches will sprout, and that will be the sign of the end of the world. [...] The Israel-tree will *not* be replaced by another tree, because the fig tree is the house of Israel alone.[62]

Besides this passage, the *Apocalypse of Peter* is highly interested in the theme of mercy, even going so far as to develop the idea that the elect will not only escape eternal fire (Apoc.Pet. 6:4) but have the chance to ask for whomever they want to be rescued from eternal punishment (Apoc.Pet. 14:1–3):

> I (i.e. Christ; TN) will give to my called and my elect whomever they ask of me out of punishment, and I will give them a good baptism in the salvation of the so-called Acherusian lake in the Elysian field, a part of righteousness with my holy ones. And I will depart, I and my elect, rejoicing with the patriarchs to my eternal kingdom. And I will accomplish with them my promises, which I promised to them, I and my father who is in heaven.[63]

The *Apocalypse of Peter* thus speaks about two levels of salvation. One level is for the elect, who can be called "the righteous, the ones perfect in all righteousness" (Apoc.Pet. 13:1) or "my called and my elect" (Apoc.Pet. 14:3).[64] This group will follow Christ to his "eternal kingdom." A second level of salvation is reserved for all who would deserve to be punished but who are rescued via the intercession of the elect.[65] If I understand the text correctly, this second group will not enter the kingdom, but will dwell in the Elysian field (Apoc.Pet. 14:1). Interestingly, the text never emphasizes belief in Christ as a decisive criterion for being counted among the elect. And even if this is implied, it seems clear that not *all* Christ-believers will follow Christ in his kingdom. Even more, *everybody* can at least reach the second level of salvation. It is only necessary that an elect person in-

---

62 J. Marcus, "The Gospel of Peter as a Jewish Christian Document," *NTS* 64 (2018): 473–494, esp. 493 (also referring to R. Bauckham, "The Two Fig Tree Parables in the Apocalypse of Peter," *JBL* 104 [1985]: 269–287). I think this conclusion remains possible even if one does *not* identify the "liar" mentioned in the text with Bar Kochba.
63 Translation: Beck, *Justice and Mercy* (see n. 61), 72.
64 Translations: Beck, *Justice and Mercy* (see n. 61), 71–72.
65 For a broader discussion, see T. Nicklas, "Petrusoffenbarung, Christusoffenbarung und ihre Funktion: Autoritätskonstruktion in der Petrusapokalypse," in *Autorschaft und Autorisierungsstrategien in apokalyptischen Texten*, ed. J. Frey, M.R. Jost, and F. Tóth, WUNT 426 (Tübingen: Mohr Siebeck, 2019), 347–364, esp. 359–363.

tercedes for him or her. If we take both observations into account, one gets the impression that the text is not only deeply rooted in Judaism and shows hope for the whole of Israel, but also that it is written for a community that is so much connected to people "outside" – perhaps including non-Christ-believing Jews – that it feels the need to include them in their idea of salvation.

3.1.2 The Gospel of the Hebrews

Time and again, it has been argued that the so-called *Gospel of the Hebrews* goes back to a community of Jewish Christ followers in Egypt or – even more precisely – in Alexandria.[66] If this was true, this text would be a wonderful witness for Jewish origins of the Christian movement in Alexandria. It is, however, almost impossible to come to a clear conclusion regarding this text's provenance. According to Eusebius of Caesarea, *Hist. eccl.* 4.22.8, the *Gospel of the Hebrews* was used by Hegesippus (second half of the 2nd century CE). Hegesippus, however, could have accessed this writing anywhere on his travels from Palestine/Asia Minor via Corinth to Rome (Eusebius, *Hist. eccl.* 4.8.1–3; 4.22.1–3);[67] therefore, his use does not provide an argument for the text's Alexandrian origins. A little bit more interesting may be the fact that the oldest extant quote of this writing is located in Clement of Alexandria, *Strom.* 2.9.45.5. This, of course, does not suggest much more than that at least one copy of this writing was accessible in the Alexandrian *Didaskaleion*.

But even if we presuppose that the *Gospel of the Hebrews* played some role among a group of 2nd century Alexandrian 'Christians,' several questions must remain open for now. How, for example, did the group behind the text – very probably Jewish followers of Jesus who was understood as "the Savior" (see Jerome, *Comm. Mich.* 7.5–7; CChrSL 76; 513,306–309) – define its relations to other groups of what we call 'Jews' and 'Christians'? Even the title *Gospel according to*

---

[66] See, for example, J. Frey, "Die Fragmente des Hebräerevangeliums," in *Antike christliche Apokryphen in deutscher Übersetzung, vol. I: Evangelien und Verwandtes*, ed. C. Markschies and J. Schröter (Tübingen: Mohr Siebeck, 2012), 593–606, esp. 598: "kann man [...] mit Vorsicht eine Herkunft aus dem alexandrinischen Judenchristentum vermuten, wenngleich die Anknüpfung an palästinische Traditionen [...] anzunehmen ist."
[67] See A. Gregory, *The Gospel according to the Hebrews and the Gospel of the Ebionites*, OECGT (Oxford: Oxford University Press, 2017), 55 (who also points to Papias of Hierapolis and discusses Eusebius's witness concretely on p. 82–85).

the Hebrews (τῷ καθ᾽ Ἑβραίους εὐαγγελίῳ) used by Clement causes problems:[68] does it imply that this text goes back to a group that could be called "Hebrews" even if its members were followers of Jesus?[69] Is the term 'Hebrews' synonymous with 'Israelites'/'Jews'? Does it, more explicitly, mean Jews with a diaspora background? And does this mean that at least the text's title preserves the memory of a group for whom the boundaries between who we designate 'Jews' and 'Christians' did not count? Or does it resemble the perspective of outsiders who used it to distinguish themselves from the text's alleged audience, that is, the 'Hebrews'? And to what extent does this title relate to the parallel construction *Gospel according to the Egyptians?* There is no fully reliable answer to any of these fascinating questions; the number of 'ifs' to be made does not allow any firm conclusion in whatever direction.

3.2 One or more generations later ...

3.2.1 The Epistle of Barnabas

Interestingly, we do not only have apocryphal traditions connecting Barnabas with Alexandria, but there is also a majority of modern scholars who understand the (pseudepigraphical) *Epistle of Barnabas* as a writing that originated (or was at least heavily influential) in Alexandria. Perhaps one can even go a step further and connect it to events which led to the Bar Kochba War of 132–135.[70] Because James Carleton Paget deals with this writing in another essay in this volume (in addition to a series of outstanding publications),[71] I will not deal extensively with this text. Instead, I simply want to stress two minor points. (1) With its

---

68 For a discussion of the passage (τῷ καθ᾽ Ἑβραίους εὐαγγελίῳ), see Gregory, *Gospel* (see n. 67), 62.
69 Interestingly, the same title is used by Origen (*Comm. Jo.* 2.12: τὸ καθ᾽ Ἑβραίους εὐαγγέλιον), Eusebius of Caesarea (*Hist. eccl.* 3.25.5; 3.39.17 τὸ καθ᾽ Ἑβραίους εὐαγγέλιον; see also 3.27.4 and 4.22.8) and Didymos of Alexandria (*Comm. Ps.*), while Jerome's descriptions of the text show some variation. See, for example, *Comm. Eph.* (in hebraico evangelio), *Comm. Mich.* 7.5–7 (*evangelio, quod secundung Hebraeos editum*), *Comm. Isa.* 40.9–11 (*in evangelio quod iuxta Hebraeos scriptum*) etc. For the textual witnesses, see Gregory, *Gospel* (see n. 67).
70 For a discussion of the text's origins, see, for example, F.R. Prostmeier, *Der Barnabasbrief*, KAV 8 (Göttingen: Vandenhoeck & Ruprecht, 1999), 119–130. But see J. Carleton Paget's contribution in the present volume, pages 217–247.
71 See, for example, J. Carleton Paget, "Barnabas and the Outsiders: Jews and their World in the *Epistle of Barnabas*," in *Early Christian Communities between Ideal and Reality*, ed. M. Grundeken and J. Verheyden, WUNT 342 (Tübingen: Mohr Siebeck, 2015), 177–202.

idea that God's covenant with Israel was broken before it reached the people of Israel and with its allegorical interpretation of Scriptures, the *Epistle of Barnabas* is a very good witness for the history of distinctions that Mimouni calls for.[72] (2) At the same time, this writing offers indirect evidence for the (probable) existence of alternative voices. If we trust the text-critically problematic Barn. 4:6b,[73] there may have been a group (obviously of Christ-followers) who considered God's covenant to be valid for both a non-Christ-believing part of Israel (that is, 'them') and 'us' (that is, a fuzzily defined group of Christ-followers addressed by Barn.). And this is not the only piece of evidence. Does Barn. 3:6 reflect a concern of parts of Barn.'s alleged audience to convert to Judaism (and follow "their Law")? And does Barn. 9:6 reflect a real interlocutor's voice who considered the circumcision a real sealing of Israel?[74] There is at least a good chance that Barn. does not only witness to a process of distinction, but also – at least indirectly – reflects counter-voices who focus on a continuing connection between the groups distinguished by Barn. Connected with the evidence given by Celsus's Jew (see above), it looks like we have evidence for four different positions: the author of Barn. and his followers who claim that they have the only true access to the traditions of Israel, the "anonymous Jew" who prepares a detailed scholarly criticism of Jesus traditions, Jews who seem to be interested in the Christian movement, and Christ followers who do not accept Barn.'s far-reaching ideas about Israel.

3.2.2 Second Peter

Only recently, Wolfgang Grünstäudl and (following him) Jörg Frey have offered good arguments to understand the canonical 2 Peter as a text that both *used* the *Apocalypse of Peter* as its source and that originated in the middle or the second half of the 2nd century in Alexandria.[75] Of course, this idea is controversial,[76]

---

72 See above in the introduction.
73 The usually preferred text is "the covenant is both theirs and ours" (based on the Latin *illorum et nostrum est*). But see the critical discussion by J.N. Rhodes, "*Barnabas* 4.6B: The Exegetical Implications of a Textual Problem," *VigChr* 58 (2004): 365–392 (also discussed by Carleton Paget, "Barnabas and the Outsiders" [see n. 71], 182 n. 26).
74 Regarding circumcision in the *Epistle of Barnabas*, see J. Carleton Paget, "*Barnabas* 9.4 a peculiar verse on circumcision," in *Jews, Christians and Jewish Christians in Antiquity*, idem, WUNT 251 (Tübingen: Mohr Siebeck, 2010), 77–89.
75 See W. Grünstäudl, *Petrus Alexandrinus. Studien zum historischen und theologischen Ort des zweiten Petrusbriefes*, WUNT 2/353 (Tübingen: Mohr Siebeck, 2013), 234–295; he is followed by J. Frey, *Der Brief des Judas und der zweite Brief des* Petrus, THKNT 15/II (Leipzig: EVA, 2015), 170–

but – if it is correct – it may offer a fascinating insight into the development of Alexandrian Christianity between the early and mid-2nd century. 2 Peter still speaks about its audience's call and election (2 Pet 1:10) and hopes for their access into "our Lord and Savior's eternal kingdom" (2 Pet 1:11). Like the *Apocalypse of Peter* (Apoc.Pet. 14:4–5) it reports that Peter's death was foretold by Jesus Christ, the Lord (2 Pet 1:14), and mentions a heavenly voice on the holy mountain (2 Pet 1:18; Apoc.Pet. 17:1). While the *Apocalypse of Peter*, however, seems to be concerned with an imminent expectation of the parousia and eternal judgment, 2 Peter mainly deals with the problem of the delay of parousia (2 Pet 3:1–13). Both texts are concerned with the coming "Day of the Lord" (2 Pet 3:10; see Apoc.Pet. 4:1: "Day of God") and expect a *Weltenbrand* (2 Pet 3:10; see Apoc.-Pet. 5).[77] In this context, it is even more striking that we no longer hear anything about Israel's future. 2 Pet 2:20 is interested in the proper interpretation of scripture, but differing from, for example, *Barn.*, this passage seems not to deal with Jewish scriptural interpretation. Compared to the *Apocalypse of Peter*, 2 Peter could be seen as a witness for an "Israelvergessenheit"[78] that we can observe in several other 2nd century writings as well. Of course, we remain on "thin ice," but if we trust Grünstäudl and Frey, 2 Peter may indicate a development from a form of 'Christianity' that is very much concerned with the fate of Israel to one where Israel's fate no longer plays a major role.

Can we place the *Kerygma Petri* in the same line of development? It seems to represent a form of Christianity using Peter as its key authority, but, at the same time, it is directed towards an audience that is completely different from the one addressed by the *Apocalypse of Peter*. Jörg Frey writes:

> In the Kerygma of Peter, Peter serves as a spokesman of a completely Gentile type of Christianity, rejecting pagan cults as well as Jewish practices and angel veneration. Jesus is

---

174 and 186–189; idem, "Second Peter in New Perspective," in *2 Peter and the Apocalypse of Peter. Towards a New Perspective*, ed. idem, M. den Dulk, and J.G. van der Watt, BibInt 174 (Leiden and Boston, MA: Brill, 2019), 7–74 (plus the following discussion of this proposal).

76 See, for example, the criticism by P. Foster, "Does the *Apocalypse of Peter* Help to Determine the Date of 2 Peter?," in *2 Peter and the Apocalypse of Peter. Towards a New Perspective*, ed. J. Frey, M. den Dulk, and J.G. van der Watt, BibInt 174 (Leiden and Boston, MA: Brill, 2019), 217–260.

77 Regarding the impact of this motif, see W. Grünstäudl, "Petrus, das Feuer und die Interpretation der Schrift: Beobachtungen zum Motiv des Weltenbrandes im zweiten Petrusbrief," in *Der eine Gott und die Völker in eschatologischer Perspektive*, ed. L. Neubert and M. Tilly, BThSt 137 (Neukirchen-Vluyn: Neukirchener, 2013), 183–208.

78 With the use of this term I allude to M. Theobald, *Israel-Vergessenheit in den Pastoralbriefen. Ein neuer Vorschlag zu ihrer historisch-theologischen Verortung im 2. Jahrhundert n.Chr. unter besonderer Berücksichtigung der Ignatius-Briefe*, SBS 229 (Stuttgart: Katholisches Bibelwerk, 2016).

called 'Nomos' and 'Logos'. God is depicted in Platonizing terms as the creator of all things, and he is also said to have the power to set an end. [...] Although the text is only preserved fragmentarily, we may assume that the theological milieu of 2 Peter may be relatively close to the Kerygma of Peter. The Kerygma is also rooted in a predominantly Gentile Christian background and shaped by Hellenistic terms [...] 'Knowledge' [...] of Christ is a central motif, as in 2 Peter. Second Peter only differs from the Kerygma in its eschatological views."[79]

3.2.3 The Protevangelium of James

It was J. N. Bremmer who only recently argued on (mainly) linguistic grounds that the *Protevangelium of James* (which could be one of the earliest Christian writings that used 2 Peter) emerged in late 2nd century (probably 180–190 CE) Alexandria.[80] If we trust Bremmer's conclusion, the *Protevangelium* adds a very nice (and from my viewpoint fitting) additional piece to the overall picture. The *Protevangelium* seems not to be very anti-Jewish and even repeats Matthew's idea that Jesus will be the Savior of his people (Matt 1:21; Prot.Jas. 11:3 and 14:2), whatever the phrase "his people" may mean! At the same time, the text does not have very concrete knowledge of the *real* Jewish worlds of 1st century Palestine. Instead, its story is placed in an almost 'fairy tale' Israel with (not well-specified) Jewish feasts and a Jerusalem Temple full of virgin girls. The text's interest in questions of purity[81] and its extensive use of LXX language indicates that the *Protevangelium* is aware of Christianity's roots in the traditions of Israel.[82] At the same time, its final scene, the story of Zacharias's assassination in the Temple (Prot.Jas. 23–24), seems to put an end to an old (and bygone) cult: Zacharias's blood turns into stone and cannot be removed from the Temple until the avenger will come (Prot.Jas. 24:2–3). In other words: like the Gospel of Matthew, the *Protevangelium* integrates its Jesus story into a story of Israel. Unlike Matthew, who struggles with the question of Israel's fate and future, the *Protevangelium* seems to understand this Israel as belonging to a distant past.

---

79 Frey, "Second Peter" (see n. 75), 23.
80 See J.N. Bremmer, "Author, Date and Provenance of the *Protevangelium of James*," in *The Protevangelium of James*, ed. idem, T. Karmann, and T. Nicklas, Studies on Early Christian Apocrypha 16 (Leuven: Peeters, 2020), 61–85.
81 For a detailed discussion of the evidence, see L. Vuong, *Gender and Purity in the Protevangelium of James*, WUNT 2/358 (Tübingen: Mohr Siebeck, 2013).
82 For a more detailed discussion, see T. Nicklas, "Israel, der Tempel und der theologische Ort des *Protevangeliums Jacobi*," in *The Protevangelium of James*, ed. idem, J.N. Bremmer, and T. Karmann (Leuven: Peeters, 2020), 133–158.

3.2.4 Other Witnesses

It may be striking that I have yet to discuss a few more secure early witnesses to Alexandrian Christianity. Starting in the early 130s, we have increasing evidence for the appearance of 'Christian' teachers in Alexandria, some of whom are usually seen as related to different so-called 'Gnostic' movements.[83] One could mention Basilides and his son Isidor, (perhaps) Valentinus, and Heracleon. These teachers and the groups associated with them, however, represent forms of the 'Christian' movement practiced by intellectuals who had removed themselves quite far from Christianity's Jewish horizon. Perhaps we may integrate the few remaining fragments of the *Gospel according to the Egyptians* into a comparable background.[84] The same could be said about the (perhaps) Alexandrian, (probably) late-2nd century *Ad Diognetum*. This text, which has sometimes been labelled *Epistle to Diognetus* (better described as a *Logos Protrepticos*[85]), runs the risk of advertising Christianity as the "new genos and way of life" (Diogn. 1:1). It disconnects Christianity almost completely from the Jewish past.[86]

4 Conclusion

One thing is clear: It is difficult, perhaps almost impossible, to speak about Jewish-Christian relations in 1st and 2nd century Alexandria as almost every historical conclusion stands on very shaky ground. I tried at least to make clear the presuppositions upon which I rely, adding many 'ifs' and 'maybes' along the way. But perhaps at least a few conclusions begin to emerge. I would like to present them as existing in two dimensions. First, I will offer a (cautious) attempt to describe a diachronic development of the situation in Alexandria and, second, I want to make a (similarly) cautious attempt to connect at least a few of the remaining voices and describe a form of a discourse wherein different voices react with

---

83 For a closer discussion, see A. Fürst, *Christentum als Intellektuellen-Religion. Die Anfänge des Christentums in Alexandria*, SBS 213 (Stuttgart: Katholisches Bibelwerk, 2007), 19–42.
84 For a more detailed discussion, see C. Markschies, "Das Evangelium nach den Ägyptern," in *Antike christliche Apokryphen in deutscher Übersetzung, vol. I: Evangelien und Verwandtes*, ed. idem and J. Schröter (Tübingen: Mohr Siebeck, 2012), 661–682, esp. 679–682.
85 H.E. Lona, *An Diognet*, KFA 8 (Freiburg: Herder, 2001), 23–24.
86 For a broader discussion, see T. Nicklas, "Identitätsbildung durch Konstruktion der 'Anderen': Die Schrift *Ad Diognetum*," in *Early Christian Communities between Ideal and Reality*, ed. M. Grundeken and J. Verheyden, WUNT 342 (Tübingen: Mohr Siebeck, 2015), 203–218.

each other (or at least take position regarding certain sets of questions and problems).

If we see the *Apocalypse of Peter* as a witness to an early Alexandrian group of Christ followers and date the text not too late, we can count it as evidence for an early movement of Christ followers concerned with Israel's future.[87] At the same time, this group must have been in some way connected with an open minded "Hellenistic Judaism" that participated in many ideas of the Greek-speaking culture of its time.[88] The notion that the beginnings of Alexandrian 'Christianity' must be described as an inner-Jewish movement would fit well with the fact that several 2nd century (and later) writings like the Bezan text of Acts, the *Pseudoclementine Homilies*, and even the late antique *Barnabas Encomium* preserved memories of the Jewish roots of the Christian movement in Alexandria.[89] Perhaps even the "strange silence concerning Alexandrian Christianity" before the Diaspora War suggests such a conclusion.[90]

The 115–117 Diaspora War must have been a serious upheaval – or probably better, a catastrophe – for Jewish life in Alexandria,[91] probably *including* the group of Christ followers behind the *Apocalypse of Peter*. At the same time, we have seen that it probably did not completely end Jewish life in Alexandria. In Hadrianic and perhaps slightly later times, both, the 5th *Sibylline Oracle* and the Jew quoted by Celsus (around the middle of the 2nd century?), among others, may point to the fact that we have at least some remains of Jewish life in post-war Alexandria. Perhaps we can even go a step further and say (following Celsus's Jew) that some non-Christ-believing Jews may have been interested in becoming 'Christians' at this time. If we move our attention to writings usually labelled as Christian, the *Epistle of Barnabas* (perhaps written shortly before the Bar Kochba War) tries to define a Christianity that claims all traditions of Israel

---

[87] Of course, I am aware of Bremmer's later date of the *Apocalypse of Peter* (see above). If we date the text long after the Bar Kochba War, it may be difficult to understand its concern with Israel's future.

[88] Regarding evidence for exactly such a kind of Judaism in Alexandria, see, among others, J. Carleton Paget, "Jews and Christians in Alexandria – from the Ptolemies to Caracalla," in *Jews, Christians and Jewish Christians in Antiquity*, idem, WUNT 251 (Tübingen: Mohr Siebeck, 2010), 123–147, esp. 130–134.

[89] If the *Gospel of the Hebrews* played some role in the earliest 'Christian' movement in Alexandria, this can be counted as additional evidence.

[90] Quote from Carleton Paget, "Jews and Christians" (see n. 88), 137.

[91] For a broader view (including the Bar Kochba revolt), see J. Carleton Paget, "Jewish Revolts and Jewish-Christian Relations," in *Jews and Christians in the First and Second Centuries: The Interbellum 70–132 CE*, ed. J. Schwartz and P.J. Tomson, CRINT 15 (Leiden and Boston, MA: Brill, 2018), 276–306.

for itself (and at the same time reacts against Christ followers who do not want to go this way), a claim to which Celsus's Jew may have reacted in his own way.

In the 130s, we stand on somewhat safer ground. These years may have seen the start of a new form of Christianity that Alfons Fürst calls "Intellektuellenreligion."[92] This development can be connected to figures like Basilides and Isidor, perhaps Valentinus and Herakleon, and the start of the *Didaskaleion* related to Pantaenos. Each of these figures represent forms of Christianity that (in different ways) were always distanced from Judaism. The *Gospel of the Egyptians* may also be an example of such a Gentile Christianity. The memories of a Christianity related to Peter's authority – and first represented in the *Apocalypse of Peter* – seem to have endured. Both 2 Peter and the *Kerygma of Peter*, however, represent a Christianity no longer very interested in Jewish matters.[93] While *Ad Diognetum* (if it is an Alexandrian text) understands Christianity as a new *genos* besides Greco-Roman and Jewish cults, the *Protevangelium of James* (like Clement of Alexandria[94]) does not even need to be very anti-Jewish. It places the roots of Jesus's story in the history of Israel using LXX language and imagery. At the same time, it seems to be distanced from any 'real' Judaism.

2nd century Alexandria is an extremely difficult case, and I hope that at least 50% of the above story correspond to historical realities. Crucial parts of the original mosaic are lost, and in many cases we cannot be sure that what we have are pieces that belonged to *this part* of the mosaic.[95] We cannot know how many voices were completely silenced and how much evidence is lost forever. Perhaps this example demonstrates a special difficulty connected to the concept of the "Parting of the Ways," especially if we relate it to Alexandria: it looks like we

---

92 Fürst, *Christentum* (see n. 83).
93 For evidence of an even broader Petrine discourse in Alexandria, see T. Nicklas, "Petrus-Diskurse in Alexandria. Eine Fortführung der Gedanken von Jörg Frey," in *2 Peter and the Apocalypse of Peter: Towards a New Perspective*, ed. J. Frey, M. den Dulk, and J.G. van der Watt, BibInt 174 (Leiden and Boston: Brill, 2019), 99–127.
94 But see J. Carleton Paget, "Clement of Alexandria and the Jews," in *Jews, Christians and Jewish Christians in Antiquity*, idem, WUNT 251 (Tübingen: Mohr Siebeck, 2010), 91–102 (see esp. his conclusions on p. 100–101).
95 Of course, I am well aware of the fact that the texts I discussed are not the only ones that have been attributed as witnesses of 1st or 2nd century Alexandrian or Egyptian Christianity. See, for example, J.J. Gunther, "The Alexandrian Gospel and Letters of John," *CBQ* 41 (1979): 591–603; idem, "The Alexandrian Epistle of Jude," *NTS* 30 (1984): 549–562; M. Frenschkowski, "Τὰ βαΐα τῶν φοινίκων (Joh 12,13) und andere Indizien für einen ägyptischen Ursprung des Johannesevangeliums," *ZNW* 91 (2000): 212–229 or W. Pratscher, "Der zweite Clemensbrief als Dokument des ägyptischen Christentums," in *Das ägyptische Christentum im zweiten Jahrhundert*, ed. idem, M. Öhler, and M. Lang, SNTU NF 6 (Wien and Berlin: LIT, 2008), 81–100.

have (at least some vague) evidence for a form of a Christian movement closely related to the synagogue in pre-war Alexandria. The Diaspora War's results – that is, its outward influences – both made a real "parting" and a real mutual influence quite difficult. There were not many Jews left (and they probably remained almost invisible) while new forms of Christianity entered the town. The only probable two post-war texts which are really relevant for our question, the *Epistle of Barnabas* and the text written by Celsus's Jew, however, could be better understood as part of a history of distinctions which seems to have been necessary because there were people who did not accept these distinctions and remained connected across the 'borderlines.'[96]

Bibliography

Alkier, S. "Terminologien kollektiver Identitäten in der Apostelgeschichte des Lukas," in *Juden – Heiden – Christen? Religiöse Inklusion und Exklusion in Kleinasien bis Decius*, ed. idem and H. Leppin, WUNT 400 (Tübingen: Mohr Siebeck, 2018), 301–332.

Bammel, E., "Der Jude des Celsus," in idem, *Judaica. Gesammelte Schriften*, WUNT 37 (Tübingen: Mohr Siebeck, 1986), 265–283.

Bauckham, R., "The Two Fig Tree Parables in the Apocalypse of Peter," *JBL* 104 (1985): 269–287.

Beck, E. J., trans., *Justice and Mercy in the Apocalypse of Peter. A New Translation and Analysis of the Purpose of the Text*, WUNT 427 (Tübingen: Mohr Siebeck, 2019).

Becker, A. H., and A. Y. Reed, eds., *The Ways that Never Parted. Jews and Christians in Late Antiquity and the Early Middle Ages* (Minneapolis, MN: Fortress, 2007).

Bell, H. I., ed., "Letter of Claudius to the Alexandrians," in *Jews and Christians in Egypt. The Jewish Troubles in Alexandria and the Athanasian Controversy* (Repr. Westport, CT: Greenwood, 1972 [1924]), 1–37.

Blumell, L., "A Jew in Celsus's *True Doctrine*? An Examination of Jewish Anti-Christian Polemic in the Second Century C.E.," *SR* 36 (2007): 299–310.

Boyarin, D., *Border Lines. The Partition of Judaeo-Christianity*, Divinations (Philadelphia, PA: University of Pennsylvania, 2006).

Bremmer, J. N., "The *Apocalypse of Peter*. Greek or Jewish?," in *Maidens, Magic and Martyrs in Early Christianity*, idem, WUNT 379 (Tübingen: Mohr Siebeck, 2017), 269–280.

Bremmer, J. N., "The *Apocalypse of Peter*. Place, Date and Punishments," in *Maidens, Magic and Martyrs in Early Christianity*, idem, WUNT 379 (Tübingen: Mohr Siebeck, 2017), 281–294.

Bremmer, J. N., "The *Apocalypse of Peter* as the First Christian Martyr Text: Its Date, Provenance and Relationship with 2 Peter," in *2 Peter and the Apocalypse of Peter. Towards a New Perspective*, ed. J. Frey, M. den Dulk, and J. G. van der Watt, BibInt 174 (Leiden and Boston, MA: Brill, 2019), 75–98.

---

96 I am grateful to Andrea Allen for the correction of my English.

Bremmer, J. N., "Author, Date and Provenance of the *Protevangelium of James*," in *The Protevangelium of James*, ed. idem, T. Karmann, and T. Nicklas, Studies on Early Christian Apocrypha 16 (Leuven: Peeters, 2020), 61–85.
Bremmer, J. N., "The Place, Date, and Author of the Ignatian Letters. An Onomastic Approach," in *Das Baujahr hinter der Fassade*, ed. W. Grünstäudl et al., WUNT (Tübingen: Mohr Siebeck, forthcoming 2021).
Carleton Paget, J., "*Barnabas* 9.4 a peculiar verse on circumcision," in *Jews, Christians and Jewish Christians in Antiquity*, idem, WUNT 251 (Tübingen: Mohr Siebeck, 2010), 77–89.
Carleton Paget, J., "Clement of Alexandria and the Jews," in *Jews, Christians and Jewish Christians in Antiquity*, idem, WUNT 251 (Tübingen: Mohr Siebeck, 2010), 91–102.
Carleton Paget, J., "Jews and Christians in Alexandria – from the Ptolemies to Caracalla," in *Jews, Christians and Jewish Christians in Antiquity*, idem, WUNT 251 (Tübingen: Mohr Siebeck, 2010), 123–147.
Carleton Paget, J., "The definition of the term 'Jewish Christian' / 'Jewish Christianity' in the history of research," in *Jews, Christians and Jewish Christians in Antiquity*, ed. idem, WUNT 251 (Tübingen: Mohr Siebeck, 2010), 289–324.
Carleton Paget, J., "Barnabas and the Outsiders: Jews and their World in the *Epistle of Barnabas*," in *Early Christian Communities between Ideal and Reality*, ed. M. Grundeken and J. Verheyden, WUNT 342 (Tübingen: Mohr Siebeck, 2015), 177–202.
Carleton Paget, J., "Jewish Revolts and Jewish-Christian Relations," in *Jews and Christians in the First and Second Centuries: The Interbellum 70–132 CE*, ed. J. Schwartz and P. J. Tomson, CRINT 15 (Leiden and Boston, MA: Brill, 2018), 276–306.
Cohen, S. J. D., "The Ways That Parted: Jews, Christians, and Jewish-Christians, ca. 100–150 CE," in *Jews and Christians in the First and Second Centuries: The Interbellum 70–132 CE*, ed. J. Schwartz and P. J. Tomson, CRINT 15 (Leiden and Boston, MA: Brill, 2018), 307–339.
Collins, J. J., *The Sibylline Oracles of Egyptian Judaism*, SBL.DS 13 (Missoula, MT: SBL, 1974).
de Lange, N. R. M., *Origen and the Jews. Studies in Jewish-Christian Relations in Third-Century Palestine* (Cambridge: Cambridge University Press, 1972).
Dorival, G., and R. Naiweld, "Les interlocuteurs hébreux et juifs d'Origène à Alexandrie et à Césarée," in *Caesarea Maritima e la scuola origeniana. Multiculturalità, forme di competizione culturale e identità cristiana*, ed. O. Andrei (Brescia: Paideia, 2013), 121–138.
Epp, E. J., "The Jews and the Jewish Community in Oxyrhynchus: Socio-Religious Context for the New Testament Papyri," in *New Testament Manuscripts. Their Texts and their World*, ed. T. J. Kraus and T. Nicklas, TENT 2 (Leiden and Boston, MA: Brill, 2006), 13–52.
Foster, P., "Does the *Apocalypse of Peter* Help to Determine the Date of 2 Peter?," in *2 Peter and the Apocalypse of Peter. Towards a New Perspective*, ed. J. Frey, M. den Dulk, and J. G. van der Watt, BibInt 174 (Leiden and Boston, MA: Brill, 2019), 217–260.
Frankfurter, D., "The Legacy of Jewish Apocalypses in Early Christianity: Regional Trajectories," in *The Jewish Apocalyptic Heritage in Early Christianity*, ed. J. C. VanderKam and W. Adler, CRINT III/4 (Assen: Van Gorcum; Minneapolis, MN: Fortress, 1996), 129–200.
Frenschkowski, M., "Τὰ βαΐα τῶν φοινίκων (Joh 12,13) und andere Indizien für einen ägyptischen Ursprung des Johannesevangeliums," *ZNW* 91 (2000): 212–229.

Frey, J., "Die Fragmente des Hebräerevangeliums," in *Antike christliche Apokryphen in deutscher Übersetzung, vol. I: Evangelien und Verwandtes*, ed. C. Markschies and J. Schröter (Tübingen: Mohr Siebeck, 2012), 593–606.

Frey, J., *Der Brief des Judas und der zweite Brief des Petrus*, THKNT 15/II (Leipzig: EVA, 2015).

Frey, J., "Second Peter in New Perspective," in *2 Peter and the Apocalypse of Peter. Towards a New Perspective*, ed. idem, M. den Dulk, and J. G. van der Watt, BibInt 174 (Leiden and Boston, MA: Brill, 2019), 7–74

Fürst, A., *Christentum als Intellektuellen-Religion. Die Anfänge des Christentums in Alexandria*, SBS 213 (Stuttgart: Katholisches Bibelwerk, 2007).

Fürst, A., and H. E. Lona, eds., *Die Homilien zum Buch Jeremia*, Origenes. Werke mit deutscher Übersetzung 11 (Berlin and Boston, MA: de Gruyter, 2018).

Gauger, J.-D., *Sibyllinische Weissagungen. Griechisch-deutsch*, 2nd ed., Tusculum (Zürich and Düsseldorf: Artemis & Winkler, 2002).

Gregory, A., *The Gospel according to the Hebrews and the Gospel of the Ebionites*, OECGT (Oxford: Oxford University Press, 2017).

Grünstäudl, W., *Petrus Alexandrinus. Studien zum historischen und theologischen Ort des zweiten Petrusbriefes*, WUNT 2/353 (Tübingen: Mohr Siebeck, 2013).

Grünstäudl, W., "Petrus, das Feuer und die Interpretation der Schrift: Beobachtungen zum Motiv des Weltenbrandes im zweiten Petrusbrief," in *Der eine Gott und die Völker in eschatologischer Perspektive*, ed. L. Neubert and M. Tilly, BThSt 137 (Neukirchen-Vluyn: Neukirchener, 2013), 183–208.

Gunther, J. J., "The Alexandrian Gospel and Letters of John," *CBQ* 41 (1979): 591–603.

Gunther, J. J., "The Alexandrian Epistle of Jude," *NTS* 30 (1984): 549–562.

Henning, M., and T. Nicklas, "Questions of Self-Designation in the Ascension of Isaiah," in *The Ascension of Isaiah*, ed. J. N. Bremmer, T. R. Karmann, and T. Nicklas, Studies on Early Christian Apocrypha 11 (Leuven: Peeters, 2016), 175–198.

Ilan, T., "The Jewish Community in Egypt before and after 117 CE in Light of Old and New Papyri," in *Jewish and Christian Communal Identities in the Roman World*, ed. Y. Furstenberg (Leiden and Boston, MA: Brill, 2016), 203–224.

Jackson-McCabe, M., "What's in a Name? The Problem of 'Jewish Christianity,'" in *Jewish Christianity Reconsidered. Rethinking Ancient Texts and Groups*, ed. idem (Minneapolis, MN: Fortress, 2007), 7–38.

Jakab, A., *Ecclesia alexandrina. Evolution sociale et institutionelle du christianisme alexandrine (IIe et IIIe siècles)* (Bern et al.: Lang, 2001).

Lemke, H., *Judenchristentum. Zwischen Ausgrenzung und Integration: Zur Geschichte eines exegetischen Begriffes*, HThSt 25 (Münster: LIT, 2001).

Lona, H. E., *An Diognet*, KFA 8 (Freiburg: Herder, 2001).

Lona, H. E., *Die 'Wahre Lehre' des Kelsos*, Kommentar zu den frühchristlichen Apologeten. Erg. 1 (Freiburg et al.: Herder, 2005).

Marcus, J., "The Gospel of Peter as a Jewish Christian Document," *NTS* 64 (2018): 473–494.

Markschies, C., "Das Evangelium nach den Ägyptern," in *Antike christliche Apokryphen in deutscher Übersetzung, vol. I: Evangelien und Verwandtes*, ed. idem and J. Schröter (Tübingen: Mohr Siebeck, 2012), 661–682.

Martin, A., "Origines de l'Alexandrie chrétienne: Topographie, Liturgie, Institutions," in *Origeniana Octava. Origen and the Alexandrian Tradition 1*, ed. L. Perrone, BETL 164 (Leuven: Peeters, 2003), 105–119.

Mimouni, S. C., "Sur la question de la séparation entre 'jumeaux' et 'ennemis' aux Ier et IIe siècles," in *La Croisée des Chemins revisitée. Quand l'Église et la Synagogue se sont-elles distinguées? Actes du colloque de Tours 18–19 juin 2010*, ed. idem and B. Pouderon, Patrimoines. Judaïsme antique (Paris: Cerf, 2012), 7–20.

Müller-Kessler, C., "Three Early Witnesses of the 'Dormition of Mary' in Christian Palestinian Aramaic from the Cairo Genizah (Taylor-Schechter Collection) and the New Finds in St Catherine's Monastery," *Apocrypha* 29 (2018): 69–95.

Musurillo, H. A., *The Acts of the Pagan Martyrs. Acta Alexandrinorum* (Oxford: Oxford University Press, 1954).

Nicklas, T., and M. Tilly, eds., *The Book of Acts as Church History. Texts, Textual Traditions and Ancient Interpretations*, BZNW 120 (Berlin and New York, NY: de Gruyter, 2003).

Nicklas, T., "'Insider' und 'Outsider'. Überlegungen zum historischen Kontext der Darstellung 'jenseitiger Orte' in der Offenbarung des Petrus," in *Topographie des Jenseits. Studien zur Geschichte des Todes in Kaiserzeit und Spätantike*, ed. W. Ameling (Stuttgart: Steiner, 2011), 35–48.

Nicklas, T., "Resurrection – Judgment – Punishment. Apocalypse of Peter 4," in *Resurrection of the Dead. Biblical Traditions in Dialogue*, ed. G. van Oyen and T. Shepherd, BETL 249 (Leuven et al.: Peeters, 2012), 461–474.

Nicklas, T., *Jews and Christians? Second Century 'Christian' Perspectives on the 'Parting of the Ways,'* Annual Deichmann Lectures 2013 (Tübingen: Mohr Siebeck, 2014).

Nicklas, T., "Getrennte Wege oder verflochtene Linien? 'Juden' und 'Christen' vor der konstantinischen Wende," *KuI* 30 (2015): 35–47.

Nicklas, T., "Identitätsbildung durch Konstruktion der 'Anderen': Die Schrift *Ad Diognetum*," in *Early Christian Communities between Ideal and Reality*, ed. M. Grundeken and J. Verheyden, WUNT 342 (Tübingen: Mohr Siebeck, 2015), 203–218.

Nicklas, T., "Jewish, Christian, Greek? The Apocalypse of Peter as a Witness of Early 2nd-Cent. Christianity in Alexandria," in *Beyond Conflicts. Cultural and Religious Cohabitations in Alexandria and Egypt between the 1st and the 6th Century CE*, ed. L. Arcari, STAC 103 (Tübingen: Mohr Siebeck, 2017), 27–46.

Nicklas, T., "Parting of the Ways? Probleme eines Konzepts," in *Juden – Heiden – Christen? Religiöse Inklusion und Exklusion in Kleinasien bis Decius*, ed. S. Alkier and H. Leppin, WUNT 400 (Tübingen: Mohr Siebeck, 2018), 21–42.

Nicklas, T., "Ein Baum mit zwei Ästen, getrennte Wege oder bleibende Vernetzung?," in *Christentum und Europa. XVI. Europäischer Kongress für Theologie (10.–13. September 2017 in Wien)*, ed. M. Meyer-Blanck, VWGTh 57 (Leipzig: EVA, 2019), 321–339.

Nicklas, T., "Petrus-Diskurse in Alexandria. Eine Fortführung der Gedanken von Jörg Frey," in *2 Peter and the Apocalypse of Peter: Towards a New Perspective*, ed. J. Frey, M. den Dulk, and J. G. van der Watt, BibInt 174 (Leiden and Boston: Brill, 2019), 99–127.

Nicklas, T., "Petrusoffenbarung, Christusoffenbarung und ihre Funktion: Autoritätskonstruktion in der Petrusapokalypse," in *Autorschaft und Autorisierungsstrategien in apokalyptischen Texten*, ed. J. Frey, M. R. Jost, and F. Tóth, WUNT 426 (Tübingen: Mohr Siebeck, 2019), 347–364.

Nicklas, T., "Barnabas Remembered: Apokryphe Barnabastexte und die Kirche Zyperns," in *Religion als Imagination*, ed. L. Seehausen et al. (Leipzig: EVA, 2020), 167–188.

Nicklas, T., "Israel, der Tempel und der theologische Ort des *Protevangeliums Jacobi*," in *The Protevangelium of James*, ed. idem, J. N. Bremmer, and T. Karmann (Leuven: Peeters, 2020), 133–158.

Nicklas, T., "The *Martyrdom of Mark* in Late Antique Alexandria," in *Alexandria – Hub of the Hellenistic World*, ed. J. Frey, T. J. Kraus, and B. Schliesser (Tübingen: Mohr Siebeck, forthcoming 2021).

Nicklas, T., "Martyrdom of Mark," in *More New Testament Apocrypha*, ed. T. Burke (Grand Rapids, MI: Eerdmans, forthcoming 2021).

Niehoff, M. R., *Jewish Exegesis and Homeric Scholarship in Alexandria* (Cambridge: Cambridge University Press, 2012).

Niehoff, M. R., "A Jewish Critique of Christianity from 2nd Century Alexandria. Celsus' Jew Revisited," *JECS* 21 (2013): 151–175.

Niehoff, M. R., "Jüdische Bibelinterpretation zwischen Homerforschung und Christentum," in *Alexandria*, ed. T. Georges, F. Albrecht, and R. Feldmeier, COMES 1 (Tübingen: Mohr Siebeck, 2013), 341–360.

Pouderon, B., "'Jewish', 'Christian' and 'Gnostic' Groups in Alexandria during the 2nd Cent. Between Approval and Expulsion," in *Beyond Conflicts: Cultural and Religious Cohabitations in Alexandria and Egypt between the 1st and 6th Century CE*, ed. L. Arcari, STAC 103 (Tübingen: Mohr Siebeck, 2017), 155–176.

Pratscher, W., "Der zweite Clemensbrief als Dokument des ägyptischen Christentums," in *Das ägyptische Christentum im zweiten Jahrhundert*, ed. idem, M. Öhler, and M. Lang, SNTU NF 6 (Wien and Berlin: LIT, 2008), 81–100.

Prostmeier, F. R., *Der Barnabasbrief*, KAV 8 (Göttingen: Vandenhoeck & Ruprecht, 1999).

Rebillard, É., *Christians and Their Many Identities in Late Antiquity, North Africa, 200–450 CE* (New York, NY: Cornell University, 2012).

Reed, A. Y., "Parting Ways over Blood and Water? Beyond 'Judaism' and 'Christianity' in the Roman Near East," in *La Croisée des Chemins revisitée. Quand l'Église et la Synagogue se sont-elles distinguées? Actes du colloque de Tours 18–19 juin 2010*, ed. S. C. Mimouni and B. Pouderon, Patrimoines. Judaïsme antique (Paris: Cerf, 2012), 227–260.

Rhodes, J. N., "*Barnabas* 4.6B: The Exegetical Implications of a Textual Problem," *VigChr* 58 (2004): 365–392.

Rius-Camps, J., and J. Read-Heimerdinger, *The Message of Acts in Codex Bezae*, 4 vols. (London and New York, NY: T&T Clark, 2007).

Rius-Camps, J., and J. Read-Heimerdinger, *The Message of Acts in Codex Bezae. A Comparison with the Alexandrian Tradition IV: Acts 18.24–28.31: Rome*, LNTS 415 (London and New York, NY: Continuum, 2009).

Runia, D. T., *Philo in Early Christian Literature. A Survey* (Minneapolis, MN: Fortress, 1993).

Rüpke, J., *On Roman Religion: Lived Religion and the Individual in Ancient Rome* (New York, NY: Cornell University, 2016).

Schliesser, B., "Why Did Paul Skip Alexandria? A Study of Earliest Christianity in Alexandria," in *Alexandria – Hub of the Hellenistic World*, ed. J. Frey, T. J. Kraus, and B. Schliesser, WUNT (Tübingen: Mohr Siebeck, forthcoming 2021).

Schnelle, U., *Die getrennten Wege von Römern, Juden und Christen: Religionspolitik im 1. Jahrhundert* (Tübingen: Mohr Siebeck, 2018).

Schwemer, A. M., "Zum Abbruch des jüdischen Lebens in Alexandria. Der Aufstand in der Diaspora unter Trajan (115–117)," in *Alexandria*, ed. T. Georges, F. Albrecht, and R. Feldmeier, COMES 1 (Tübingen: Mohr Siebeck, 2013), 381–399.
Sgherri, G., *Chiesa e Sinagoga nelle opere di Origene*, Studia Patristica Mediolanensia 3 (Milan: Vita e Pensiero, 1982).
Smith, E. C., *Jewish Glass and Christian Stone. A Materialist Mapping of the 'Parting of the Ways'* (London and New York, NY: Routledge, 2018).
Stewart Lester, O., *Prophetic Rivalry, Gender, and Economics. A Study in Revelation and Sibylline Oracles 4–5*, WUNT 2/466 (Tübingen: Mohr Siebeck, 2018).
Theobald, M., *Israel-Vergessenheit in den Pastoralbriefen. Ein neuer Vorschlag zu ihrer historisch-theologischen Verortung im 2. Jahrhundert n. Chr. unter besonderer Berücksichtigung der Ignatius-Briefe*, SBS 229 (Stuttgart: Katholisches Bibelwerk, 2016).
Troiano, L., "Il Giudeo di Celso," in *Discorsi di Verita*, ed. L. Perrone (Roma: Institutum Patristicum Augustinianum, 1998), 115–128.
van den Hoek, A., "Philo and Origen. A Descriptive Catalogue of Their Relationship," *SPhiloA* 12 (2000): 44–121.
Verheyden, J., "Presenting Minor Characters in the Pseudo-Clementine Novel. The Case of Barnabas," in *Nouvelles intrigues pseudo-clémentines. Plots in the Pseudo-Clementine Romance*, ed. F. Amsler et al., PIRSB 6 (Prahins, CH: Éditions du Zèbre, 2008), 249–257.
Vuong, L., *Gender and Purity in the Protevangelium of James*, WUNT 2/358 (Tübingen: Mohr Siebeck, 2013).
Wehnert, J., "Apollos," in *Alexandria*, ed. T. Georges, F. Albrecht, and R. Feldmeier, COMES 1 (Tübingen: Mohr Siebeck, 2013), 403–412.

List of Contributors

Jan N. Bremmer, Prof. Dr. em., held the Chair of Religious Studies at the Faculty of Religious Studies and Theology of the University of Groningen, Netherlands; currently he is a Fellow at the Centre for Advanced Studies "Beyond Canon_" (FOR 2770) of the University of Regensburg, Germany

James Carleton Paget is a Reader in New Testament Studies at the Faculty of Divinity of the University of Cambridge and a Fellow and Tutor of Peterhouse College, Cambridge, U.K.

Kylie Crabbe is a Senior Research Fellow in Biblical and Early Christian Studies and the Director of Graduate Research Programs at the Institute for Religion and Critical Inquiry of the Australian Catholic University in Melbourne, Australia

Benjamin A. Edsall is a Senior Research Fellow and Institute Research Coordinator at the Institute for Religion and Critical Inquiry of the Australian Catholic University in Melbourne, Australia

Jörg Frey is Professor of New Testament with special focus on Ancient Judaism and Hermeneutics at the Faculty of Theology of the University of Zurich, Switzerland, and Research Associate at the University of the Free State, Bloemfontein, South Africa

Matthias Konradt is Professor of New Testament Theology at the Faculty of Theology of the Ruprecht Karls University Heidelberg, Germany

Christoph Markschies is Professor of Ancient Christianity (Patristics) at the Faculty of Theology of the Humboldt University Berlin, Germany, and President of the Berlin-Brandenburg Academy of Sciences and Humanities

Tobias Nicklas is Professor of New Testament Exegesis and Hermeneutics at the Faculty of Theology of the University of Regensburg, Germany, Research Associate at the University of the Free State, Bloemfontein, South Africa, Adjunct Ordinary Professor at Catholic University of America, Washington, D.C., USA., and Director General of the Centre for Advanced Studies "Beyond Canon_" (FOR 2770) of the University of Regensburg, Germany

Anders Runesson is Professor of New Testament, Vice Dean and Dean of Research at the Faculty of Theology of the University of Oslo, Norway

Jens Schröter is Professor of New Testament and Ancient Christian Apocrypha at the Faculty of Theology of the Humboldt University Berlin, Germany; currently he is a Fellow at the Centre for Advanced Studies "Beyond Canon_" (FOR 2770) of the University of Regensburg, Germany

Paul R. Trebilco is Professor of New Testament Studies at the Theology Programme | Mātai Whakapono Karaitiana of the University of Otago | Te Whare Wānanga o Otāgo in New Zealand

Joseph Verheyden is Professor of New Testament Studies at the Faculty of Theology and Religious Studies of the KU Leuven, Belgium

Index of Ancient Sources
Hebrew Bible / Old Testament / Septuagint

Gen

12:1	259
15:6	240
17	137
25:21–23	238
48:8–9	238
48:18–19	238
49:10	264

Exod

12:15	294
17	225
22:21	138
30:11–16	127
32:6	328
34:15–16	109
36:12	331

Lev

17	178
17:7	109
17:8	179
17:10	179
17:12–13	179
18	178
18:26	179

Num

15:38–39	128
17	315
25:1	109

Deut

21:23	327
22:12	128
25:1–3	285
27–28	108
31:16	109

Josh

10:13–14	358

2 Kgs

23:4–25	137

2 Chr

15:1–19	137
34:1–7	137
34:33	137

Neh

10:33	127

Esth

4:17 (C28)^{LXX}	111
8:17	62

Jdt

10:5	111
12:1–4	108, 111

Tob

1:10–11	108

1 Macc

1:41–64	111

2 Macc

	6, 62–63
2:21	98
5:27	110
6–7	111
8:1	98
14:38	98

Ps

	18
22:9	126
44	328
71	325
82	197
109:1–5	325
142:2	106

Wis

7–10	199
14:12	109

Sir

24	199

Hos

1–3	109
6:6	139

Amos

9	178
9:11–12	177–178

Zech

3:1–2	325
5:1–5	277

Mal

1:10–12	330

Isa

1:3–4	258
6	175
6:9–10	174
6:17–28	174
6:28	175
6:30	175
6:30–31	174
7:10	327
8:4	325
29:13–14	326
30:1	325
39:8–40:17	325
42:1–4	331
42:7	101
45:21–22	178
49:17	233, 236
51:4–5	333
52:10–54:6	335
55:3–5	334, 336
60:6	140

Jer

12:15	178
12:17	178
23:1–4	126
31:31–32	333

Ezek

16:26	109
16:28	109
34	126
37	363

Dan

1:3–17	111
1:12^{LXX}	111

Early Jewish Writings

2 Bar.

66:5	137

1 En.

7:1	109
8:1–3	109
10:7–8	109

4 Macc.

	65–66
4:15–6:35	111

4:26	63, 98	5.458–463	358
5:2	109	5.484–511	358

Jos.Asen.

T.Benj.

7:10	108	8:2	109
8:10	101	9:1	109

Jub.

T.Dan

16:5	109	5:5–6	109
16:8	109		

T.Jud.

20:3–4	109	14:2–6	109
22:16–17	109	15:1–2	109
22:19–23	108	18:2	109
25:1	109		
25:7–8	109		
39:6	109		

T.Levi

		9:9	109
		19:1	101

Let.Aris.

128–131	242		
144	242		
169–171	242		

T.Mos.

8:3	137

Ps.-Phoc.

T.Reu.

31	109	1:6	109
		3:3	109

Sib.Or.

	372	4:6–11	109
3.271	273	5:1–7	109
5.47–51	358	6:1–4	109
5.53	358		

T.Sim.

5.60–114	358	5:3–4	109
5.179–199	358		
5.256–259	358		

Ancient Jewish Authors

Josephus

A.J.

Ag.Ap.

		14.115	273
2.165–167	161	14.252	41
12.147–153	274	16.62	41
		18.63–64	69
		20.34–48	137
		20.267	70

J.W.

2.119–166	174
2.398	273
7.43	273

Vita

14	111
276–281	41, 43, 47
294–295	43, 47

Philo

Decal.

8	109

Ios.

201–202	112

Leg.

3.88–94	238
3.156	112

Legat.

132–138	131

156–157	131
214	273
281–282	273
361–363	111

Migr.

	241
88–94	239
89–93	137

Prob.

81	41, 131

QE

2.2	138

Spec.

2.20	111

Virt.

192	239

Dead Sea Scrolls

1QS

5.21	108
6.18	108

4Q159

2.6–7	127

4Q491

	198

4QMMT

	93
C7	107
C27–32	108

11QMelch

	198

Rabbinic Works

Lev. Rab.

35:12	42

t. Meg.

2:17	42

New Testament

Matt

1:1	125, 134
1:17	143
1:21	356, 370
1:22–23	125
2	127, 140
2:11	140
2:15	125
2:17–18	125
2:23	125
4:14–16	125
4:15	140
4:23	42, 130–131
5:18	136, 138
5:19–20	139
5:46–47	134
6:7	134
6:32	134
7:15–23	143
7:29	130
8:5–13	141
8:17	125
8:28–34	141
9:9–13	134
9:13	127
9:18	130
9:35	42, 130
10:6	132
10:14	167
10:17	42, 130–132
11:13	64
11:19	134
12:1–14	127
12:9	130
12:11–12	127
12:17–21	125
12:18–21	140
13:35	125
13:52	130
13:54	41, 130
15:21–28	141
15:24	132, 141
16:17–19	138
16:18	41, 47, 130
16:18–19	138
17:24–27	127, 129, 132
18:17	41, 130, 134
18:18	47
19:4	127
19:16–22	139
21:4–5	125
21:16	127
21:31–32	134
21:42	127
21:43	364
22:31	127
23:23	139
23:25	336
23:34	130, 132
23:37	318
24:9	134
24:32–34	364
26:26	141
26:28	141
26:47–56	288
26:54	141
26:64	141
27:3–10	127
27:9–10	125
27:43	126
27:51–53	141
28:16–20	134, 140, 142
28:18–20	134, 141
28:19	136
28:20	125

Mark

1:21	41
1:39	42, 130
4:7–11:1	128
4:12	174
5:22	130
5:27	128
6:45–8:26	177
8:17–18	174
13:28–29	364
14:43–47	288

Luke

2:32	167
8:44	128
10	167
11:39–40	336
12:11	41
13:6–9	364
13:31	48
16:16–17	64
19:27	20
22:47–53	288

John

1:1	190, 196, 199
1:1–3	198
1:3	199
1:18	196, 199
1:20–21	195
1:45–50	205
1:45–51	195
2–12	201
2:6	194
2:13	194, 202
2:19–20	192
3:1–2	47
4:9	192
4:21–26	202
5:1	194
5:1–18	202
5:16	192
5:17	195
5:18	192
5:38–39	192
5:39	194, 202
5:46	202
5:46–47	192
6:4	194
7:2	194
7:35	203
8:17	194
8:33	194
8:44	187, 192, 210, 288
9	190
9:1–7	202
9:16	47
9:22	6, 35–36, 186, 286
9:28	195
10:16	203
10:28	286
10:33	196
10:34	194
10:34–36	197
10:35	195–196
11:50–52	203
11:55	194
12:13	373
12:20–23	202–203
12:32	202
12:42	6, 35, 186, 286
13:31–17:26	200
15:6	205
15:18	201, 286
15:25	194
16:2	6, 35, 186, 286
16:2–3	201, 207
17:3	196
18:2–12	288
18:20	37, 41–42
18:35	192
19:7	196
19:14	296
19:19	192
19:31	296
19:39	47
19:42	296
20:19	192, 202
20:26	202
20:28	196, 199
20:30–31	207
21:25	190

Acts

1:2	169
1:8	159, 167
1:22	176
1:41	169
2	159, 161, 177
2:5–6	159
2:8	159
2:14	161
2:16–21	177
2:22–23	161

2:24	176	13:51	167
2:29–32	176	14:1	169, 172
3:12	161	14:1–2	285
3:15	176	14:1–7	49
4	165	14:2	164, 284
4:5	157	14:4	169–170
4:27	157	14:5	169, 284–285
4:31	157	14:19	169, 284
5	165–166	14:21–23	169
5:17	166, 171	14:23	157
5:26	169	14:27	157
5:29	166	15	165, 175, 177, 179
5:29–32	176	15:1	177
5:34	169	15:2	157
5:34–40	164	15:3	176
5:38–39	166	15:5	47, 164, 177
6:9	42, 172	15:6–21	157
6:14–15	176	15:7–21	177
7	162	15:16–17	178
7:9	171	15:19–21	49, 179
7:19	162	15:20	109, 140, 179
7:22–29	162	15:21	179
7:35	162	15:22–29	157
7:37	162	15:23–29	179
7:39	163	15:29	109, 140, 179
7:51	361	16	113
9:2	131, 152	16:1	158, 164
9:20	172	16:13	42
10:39–41	176	16:20	164
11	159	16:37	163
11:26	37, 68, 98, 157, 208	16:37–38	158
13:4–13	362	17:1	172
13:5	172	17:1–4	49
13:15	167	17:1–5	285
13:16	285	17:4	169
13:26	161	17:5	171
13:26–37	176	17:10	172
13:27–28	161	17:10–12	49
13:39	176	17:11–12	170
13:42–48	49, 285	17:13–14	285
13:44	157, 167	17:30–31	176
13:44–52	285	17:31	179
13:45	171, 284–285	18:2	158
13:46	175	18:4–8	49
13:46b–47	167	18:5	172
13:48	176	18:5–7	285
13:50	284–285	18:6	172, 175

18:8	170	24:14	152, 164, 174
18:10	172	24:15–21	176
18:12	285	24:19	167, 171
18:14–15	164, 173	24:22	152
18:19	172	25:18–19	164, 173
18:20	170	26	159
18:24	158, 359	26:5	165
18:24–25	359–360	26:6–8	176
18:25	359	26:23	176
18:25–26	152	26:28	37, 73, 98, 159
18:26	175	28:17–28	174
18:28	170, 175	28:20	174, 180
19	113	28:22	164, 174
19:8–9	49	28:30	180
19:9	152, 164, 173, 284	28:30–31	174
19:9–10	284		
19:23	152	**Rom**	
19:32	99		
19:39–40	99	1–11	104
20:4	285	1:7	103
20:7	157	1:16	103–104
20:16	285	2:9–10	103–104
20:17	152	2:29	102
20:19	284	3:9	104
20:28	157	3:24	113
21	285	3:30	104
21:24	176	4	102, 240
21:25	109, 140	4:11	240
21:27	167, 170	4:17	240
21:27–29	285	5:12–21	104
21:30	162	8:1	103
21:39	158	8:1–13	110
22:1–3	158	9–11	240
22:3	163, 165	9:5	99
22:4	152	10:12–13	103
22:12	163, 165	10:14–22	110
22:14	163	10:25–30	110
22:17–20	163	11	104
22:22	170	11:1	103
22:25–29	158, 163	11:1–32	114
23	165	11:5	103
23:5	166	11:13	106
23:6	47, 176	11:16	106
23:6–9	164	11:17–24	49
23:12–13	170	11:25–26	106
23:12–15	166	11:28	106
24:5	164, 171, 174	14	110–112

14:1–2	111
14:1–15:13	95
14:2–23	102
14:14	112

1 Cor

	100
1:2	103
1:21	102
1:22–24	103–104
1:24	285
3:22	102
4:12	285
5:1	102, 109
5:17	101
6:9	109
6:13	102
6:13–20	109
6:18	102
7:2	102, 109
7:17–24	50, 109
7:18	137, 285
7:19	139
7:23	109
8	111–112
8–10	110–111, 260
8:7–12	111
9:20–21	89, 105
10:14	102
10:14–21	109
10:25	110
10:32	104
14:22	102
15:3	99
15:8–9	101
15:32	336
16:22	198

2 Cor

	100
4:6	101
4:9	285
6:4–5	285
11:22–23	103
11:24	285
11:25	284
11:26	285
12:10	285

Gal

	100
1:13	101
1:13–14	62, 65
1:14	98
1:15	101
1:16	106
1:23	101
2	177
2:11–16	106
2:14	98
2:15	104, 106
2:16	106
3:13	327
3:28	44, 104, 285
4:8	109
5:11	285
5:19	109
5:20	102, 109
6:15	101
6:20	108

Phil

1:1	99
2:9	356
3:2–11	95
3:5	47, 103
3:6–7	101
3:9	33

1 Thess

1:9	109
4:3	109
4:5	134

1 Tim

	298

2 Tim

	298
2:22	103

1 Pet

	298
4:16	37, 73, 98

2 Pet

	373
1:10–11	369
1:14	369
1:18	369
2:20	369
3:1–13	369

1 John

5:21	201, 207

2 John

	201

3 John

1	201
9	201

Rev

2:9	286–287
3:9	286–287
12:10	287
13:1	287
13:5–6	287
17:3	287

Apostolic Fathers

Barn.

	7, 19, 224, 372, 374
1:5	226, 230
1:6	230
1:7	231, 233, 241
2	231–232
2:1	228
2:3	231
2:4	225, 231
2:7	231
2:9	228, 232, 236
2:10	231
3	231–232
3:1	231
3:1–6	225
3:3	231
3:6	224, 228, 231–232, 234, 237
4	231
4:1	228, 236
4:2–3	233
4:6	224, 228, 232, 234, 236, 240–241, 368
4:7	225, 231
4:8	231, 236
4:9	236
4:10	233, 236
4:12	233
4:14	224, 231
5–7	225
5–8	231
5:1–3	231
5:2	224, 240
5:6	233
5:7	225, 237
5:8	224
5:11	225, 231–232
6:5	233
6:6–9	231
6:7	224
6:8	231, 237
6:10	225, 231
6:12–13	231
7	232
7:1–3	231
7:5	225, 231, 233, 237
7:6	233
8	233
8:1	224
8:2	231, 233
8:3	224
8:4	237
8:7	225, 231–232
9	231–232
9:1–3	225
9:3	237

9:4	225, 231–232, 236	21:8	228
9:5	233		
9:6	224, 232, 234, 237, 368	**1 Clem.**	
9:7	237		224, 307
9:8	231, 237, 356	4	314
9:9	225, 233	40–44	315
10	225, 231–232, 234	43:1	315
10:2	237	44:1	315
10:6	235		
10:9	225, 231–232	**Did.**	
10:10	231		224
10:11	225, 228	1–5	140
10:12	231	1:1–3	19
11	231, 234	6:3	140
11:1	231–232	7	140
11:2	232	12:4	37
11:7	232		
11:11	231	**Herm.Vis.**	
12	225, 231, 234	2.3.4	316
12:2	224	2.4.1	316
12:3	226, 231–232		
12:5	224	**Ign.**	
12:8	237	**Magn.**	
12:10–11	233		
13	225, 231		291
13:1	225, 231, 234, 241	2:10	75
13:1–2	228	8–10	317
13:7	225, 231, 234, 237, 240–241	8:1	3, 98, 219, 241, 317
14:3	236	9:1	66
14:4–5	225, 231, 234	10	35
15	225, 232	10:1	3, 66, 75, 98
15:4	233	10:2	75
15:8	231–232	10:3	3, 75, 98, 219, 241, 292, 317
16	231–232, 234		
16:1	224, 228, 236	**Phld.**	
16:1–2	234	5:6	75
16:2	232	6:1	3, 66, 98, 219, 241, 292, 317
16:3–4	233, 236, 242		
16:4	227, 233	**Rom.**	
16:5	224, 233, 237	1:16	285
17–20	226	2:9–10	285
17:3	231	2:29	361
18:1–2	236	3:3	75, 318
20:1	236	3:9	285
21:1	228		
21:4–6	228		
21:5	231		

5	318
5:6	75
6:1	75
8:35	285
9:1	318
9:1–5	285
10:1	285
12:1	285
15:25–31	285

Smyrn.

1:2	66

Mart.Pol.

10:1	74
12:2	289–290
13:1	289–290
17:2–18:1	289

Early Christian Writings

Apoc.Pet.

	368, 372
2:1	364
2:4–12	364
4:1	369
4:9–10	363
5	369
6:4	365
8–9	363
13	363
13:1	365
14:1–3	365
14:4	363

Acts John

	289

94	288

Prot.Jas.

	373
11:3	370
14:2	370
23–24	370

Ps.-Clem.Hom.

I.6	361
I.8.3–4	361
I.9.1	361
I.13.3–4	361
I.15.5–6	361

Ancient Christian Authors

Clement of Alexandria

Paed.

2.10.99	358

Protr.

4.50	358

Strom.

2.7.35	227
2.6.31	227

2.9.45.5	366
2.15.67	227
2.18.84	227
2.20.116	227
5.8.51–52	227
5.10.63	227
6.5.41	208

Eusebius

Dem. Ev.

1.2	67

Praep. Ev.

1.5.12	67

Hist. Eccl.

2.24	360
3.25.5	367
3.27.4	367
3.39.17	367
4.8.1–3	366
4.18.6	293, 320
4.22.1–3	366
4.22.8	366–367
4.27.1	291
5.17.5	291
5.24.1–7	296–297
6.4.6	233
7.18	295

Irenaeus

Haer.

3.3–4	75

Jerome

Comm. Mich.

7.5–7	366

Vir. Ill.

6	230

John Chrysostom

Adv. Jud.

1.2	20
1.2–3	20
1.3	25
1.7	21, 22
5.9	25
8.5	21
8.5–6	25

Justin

1 Apol.

	250
14.2	266
15.10	266
21.2	323
22.5	323
26.5	333
26.8	260
31.1–2	258
31.6	255
32.1–4	258
32.3	257
33.7	258
37.2	258
40.6	258
41.1	262
46.3	264
47.1	258
49	257
49.5	262
50.1–51.6	335
53.2–3	257
53.3	257–258
54.8	323
58.1	333, 339
60.1	326
64.1	262

Dial.

	219, 224, 250, 319
1–8	262
1.1–2	320
1.3	321
6.1	324
6.3	323
8–11	331
8–14	332
8.1–2	332
8.3	323–324
8.4	332
9–47	322
9.2–3	332
9.3	320
10–11	260

10.1	332, 339	35.2	260
10.2	332	35.5	266
10.3	258	35.6	260, 339
10.3–4	332	38.1	266, 321
11	257	38.2	328
11.1–3	333	39.3	321
11.4–5	334	39.6	324
11.5	256, 259	40–41	231
12	231	43.5–6	327
12.1	334	45–47	331
12.2–3	335	45.2	260
13.1	335	45.3–4	264
14	231	46.1	265
14.1	327, 336	46.2–7	266
14.3–13	336	47	51, 262
15–16	231	47.1–2	266–267
16.2	257	47.3	257, 267
16.4	255	47.4	255, 267
17.1	257, 327–328	48–108	322
17.2–4	329	49.4	258
18.1	329	51.1	325
19	231, 262	52.1–3	327
19–21	225, 331	53.4	255
19.4–6	264	53.5	324
19.5	257	55.3	329
21	231	56–58	331
22	262	58.1	339
23	231	58.1–2	328
23.1–2	263	63.1	326
23.4	324	64.2	321
25	231	66.1	327
25.6	265, 329	67–68	331
26.1	329	67.2	323
26.5	339	67.4	321
27.1	321, 329	67.6–10	263
27.2	266, 330	67.7	321
27.5	330	69.1–3	323
28.1–2	324, 330	70.5	323
28.5	329	72.1	328
29.2	255, 329	72.3	255
30.2	326	73.6	328
32.2	326	77.1	325
32.5	326	78.4	257–258
33.1	325	78.11	326
34.1	325	79	325
34.8	262	79–82	322
34.8–35.1	260	79.1	321, 325

80.4	261
85.6–7	326
86–87	231
87.1	320
90	231
93.4–5	256
96.1–2	327
96.2	255
98.4	255
103.5	258
104.1	255
109–141	322
112.1	328
113.2	326
117.1–2	330
117.3–4	261
119.3–5	259
119.5	262, 269
120.2	264
123.7	341
123.8–9	256
126.1	331
128.1	331
130.1	331
130.3	258, 331
134.3	256
135.3	256
137.2	261
141.2–4	330
142.1–3	320

Melito

Peri Pascha

37–45	297
39–41	294
74–105	297

Origen

Cels.

1.1	77
1.1.25	76
1.3	77
1.9	77
1.28	355
2.1	356
2.1.28	355
2.1.54	355
2.8	77, 356
3.13.9	76
3.14.18	76
3.75	62

Comm. Jo.

2.12	367

Ep. Afr.

7	354

Hom. Jer.

20(19).2	354

Princ.

1.3.4	354

Sel. Ezech.

9.2	354

Tertullian

Adv. Jud.

	224
1.5–6	238
2.9–10	238
6.1–2	238

Marc.

4.4.4	65
4.6.3	64
4.33.8	64
5.2.1	65
5.3.8	63

Greco-Roman Literature

Acta Alexandrinorum

Acta Hermaisci

353

Acta Pauli et Antonini

353–354

Aristotle

Rhet.

1388a30–33   168

Cassius Dio

Hist.

69.12   233

Herodotus

Hist.

8.144.2   258

Pliny the Younger

Ep.

10.96	98, 223
10.96–97	37, 207
10.96.1	73
10.96.9–10	49

Suetonius

Claud.

25.4   72

Dom.

12.2   129, 207

Nero

16.2   223

Tacitus

Ann.

15.44	73, 223
15.44.2–3	71

Index of Modern Authors

Abegg, M. G.   107–108
Alexander, L.   153–154, 174–175
Alkier, S.   13, 348, 359
Allert, C. D.   325, 327, 337
Allison, D. C.   133, 135, 140
Ameling, W.   59, 274, 280–283
Ando, C.   80
Arnold, J.   77
Ascough, R. S.   39–41
Attridge, H. W.   288–289
Aune, D. E.   274

Bachmann, M.   93, 107
Backhaus, K.   123
Bady, G.   22
Baker, C.   60
Balabanski, V.   135
Bammel, E.   355
Bar-Asher Siegal, M.   96
Barclay, J. M. G.   78, 108, 111, 285
Bardet, S.   70
Baron, L.   5, 34, 52, 249–250, 253, 299–300
Barreto, E. D.   158, 160, 162
Barrett, C. K.   66
Barthélemy, D.   357
Barton, C.   59
Bates, M. W.   250, 334
Bauckham, R.   154, 159, 177–179, 190, 195, 286–287, 293–294, 365
Baumgarten, A.   78
Baur, F. C.   16, 34, 155, 220
Baxter, W.   126
Beaton, R.   140
Beck, E. J.   364–365
Becker, A. H.   4, 12, 16, 24–25, 34, 96, 124, 153, 155–156, 186, 218, 223, 249–250, 299–301, 311, 349
Becker, E.-M.   190, 287
Becker, J.   189
Bell, H. I.   359
Benbassa, E.   96
Bengel, J. A.   203

Beni, M. D.   310
Bennema, C.   154, 156, 162, 177
Berger, K.   189
Bergjan, S.-P.   21
Bernier, J.   36–37
Berthelot, K.   80
Bhabha, H.   162
Bieringer, R.   187
Bij de Vaate, A. J.   278
Bile, M.   73
Binder, D. D.   41
Binder, S. E.   311
Bird, M. F.   94
Blaschke, A.   137
Bloch, R.   79
Blumell, L.   355
Bobichon, P.   255–261, 263–267, 319, 321–333, 336, 339
Boccaccini, G.   94, 191, 197–198, 205–206, 309
Boddens Hosang, F. J. E.   279
Boer, M. C. de   36–38

Bond, H.   190
Bonnet, C.   308
Bos, J.   309
Botermann, H.   72
Boyarin, D.   15, 24, 27, 59, 66–67, 94, 96–97, 159, 164, 186, 219, 221–222, 249, 255, 261, 264, 270, 311, 327, 348
Bovon, F.   156
Bradshaw, P. F.   294
Brakke, D.   1
Brändle, R.   21
Braun, R.   74
Brawley, R. L.   156, 164–165, 170, 295
Bredekamp, H.   12
Bremmer, J. N.   6, 58, 60, 63, 65, 68, 71, 78, 288–289, 350, 363–364, 370, 372
Breytenbach, C.   274
Broadhead, E. K.   124, 186, 310
Brown, R. E.   185, 187–188
Brown, S.   135

Brox, N. 316
Bucur, B. G. 250, 310
Buell, D. K. 237, 255–256, 258–259, 262–263
Bühner, R. A. 197, 199
Bultmann, R. 93, 210
Burns, J. E. 34, 48, 52

Calder, W. M. 276–277
Cameron, A. 311
Campbell, W. S. 38
Cancik, H. 156–158
Carleton Paget, J. 7, 70, 77, 95, 218, 226–227, 230, 232–233, 235, 240, 242, 254, 310–311, 321, 367–368, 372–373
Carrier, R. 73
Carter, W. 123, 129, 140–141
Casevitz, M. 63
Casey, M. 196
Certeau, M. de 253
Chae, Y. S. 126
Chaniotis, A. 280–282
Chester, A. 281
Chilton, B. D. 47
Cirafesi, W. V. 36–38
Claußen, C. 131
Cohen, S. J. D. 2, 11, 24, 26, 48, 51, 66, 78, 91, 222–223, 249–251, 253–255, 265, 269, 310, 327, 349, 351
Cohick, L. 290
Coinci, G. de 67
Collins, J. J. 138, 197, 358
Conzelmann, H. 156
Cook, J. G. 60, 71–72
Corke-Webster, J. 73
Costa, J. 218
Couzin, R. 59
Crabbe, K. 6, 166, 169, 176–177
Cumont, F. 308
Czajkowski, K. 80

Darr, J. A. 165
Daumier, C. 63
Davies, W. D. 133, 135, 140
Deines, R. 109
Den Dulk, M. 260–262, 264, 339
Destephen, S. 296

Di Segni, L. 48
Dobbeler, S. von 127
Doering, L. 107, 127
Donahue, P. J. 321, 326–327, 329, 332, 339
Dorival, G. 354
Downey, G. 23
Draper, J. 19
Dunn, J. D. G. 3, 15–16, 18, 24, 90, 92–93, 100, 107–108, 124, 152, 155, 158, 162–163, 171, 176, 309
Dunn, G. D. 238–241

Eckhardt, B. 78–80
Eckstein, H.-J. 133
Edsall, B. A. 7, 105, 260–261, 263, 341
Edwards, M. J. 291
Ehrman, B. D. 2, 259
Eisele, W. 195
Eisenbaum, P. 50
Elkins, N. T. 59
Ellis, E. E. 160
Engelmann, H. 288
Epp, E. J. 353
Esler, P. F. 160
Evans, C. A. 175

Fairchild, M. R. 274
Falls, T. B. 256, 319
Finkelstein, A. 22
Foakes Jackson, F. J. 17–18, 91, 155, 218
Fonrobert, C. E. 219
Foss, C. 283
Foster, P. 129, 133, 135, 369
Frankemölle, H. 135
Frankfurter, D. 221, 287, 311, 358
Fredriksen, P. 2, 24–25, 38, 40, 44, 96, 99, 110, 311
Freedman, H. 42–43
Frenschkowski, M. 373
Frey, J. 4, 6, 16, 58, 93, 101, 103, 107–108, 186–189, 192, 195–198, 200–201, 203, 206, 209, 211, 281–282, 286, 366, 368–370
Freyne, S. 2
Friedman, M. 310
Fürst, A. 354–355, 371, 373

Gager, J. G. 44, 52
Gain, B. 73
Gaston, L. 289
Gathercole, S. J. 93
Gauger, J.-D. 358
Gaventa, B. R. 153, 160
Geelhaar, T. 76
Georges, T. 269
Gercke, A. 68
Gerhards, A. 28
Gibson, E. L. 289, 311
Gilbert, G. 280
Gillihan, Y. M. 43
Ginzburg, C. 59
González Salinero, R. 255
Goodenough, E. 218
Goodman, M. 3, 45, 58, 253, 274, 311
Gowler, D. B. 165
Gunther, J. J. 373
Günther, S. 59
Gurtner, D. M. 38
Grabbe, L. L. 69
Grant, R. M. 291
Green, B. 311, 323, 338, 341
Gregerman, A. 250
Gregory, A. 153, 366–367
Gruen, E. 40
Grünstäudl, W. 368–369

Haenchen, E. 155, 159, 170–171
Hagner, D. A. 136
Hakola, R. 165
Halton, C. 60
Halton, T. P. 256
Harland, P. A. 40
Harl, M. 62
Harnack, A. von 218, 229, 250, 261
Harrington, D. J. 133, 135
Hartog, P. 289–290
Hedner Zetterholm, K. 45, 48, 112
Heemstra, M. 58–59, 92, 129, 206, 254, 310
Heil, J. P. 126, 141
Hemer, C. J. 154
Hengel, M. 15, 98, 100–101, 190, 194
Henning, M. 348
Hezser, C. 218

Hicks-Keeton, J. 34, 52, 249, 253, 299–300
Hommel, H. 72
Horbury, W. 16, 127, 190, 221, 232–233, 236
Horner, T. J. 293, 320–321, 332, 334
Horrell, D. G. 73
Horsley, G. H. R. 283
Houlden, J. L. 134
Howell, J. R. 69
Hübner, R. 65
Hurtado, L. W. 198
Huttner, U. 274, 279, 291
Hvalvik, R. 227, 229, 231, 236, 242
Hyde, D. 254
Hyldahl, N. 324

Ilan, T. 353
Imrie, A. 80
Inge, W. R. 17–18

Jackson-McCabe, M. 34, 37, 220, 348
Jacobs, A. S. 311
Jakab, A. 357, 359
Jastrow, M. 42
Jervell, J. 156, 161
Johnson, L. T 154
Jones, C. P. 71
Judge, E. A. 58
Junod, E. 289

Kaestli, J.-D. 289
Kampen, J. 122–123
Kant, L. H. 278
Kato, T. 107
Katz, S. T. 190
Keener, C. S. 153–154, 156, 161, 172
Kierspel, L. 201
Kimelman, R. 190
Kingsley Barrett, C. 15
Kinzig, W. 21
Klauck, H.-J. 288
Klawans, J. 160
Klinghardt, M. 339
Kloppenborg, J. S. 37, 39–41, 43
Koch, D.-A. 102, 281
Koester, C. R. 287
Kok, M. 233, 237, 240

Konradt, M. 6, 38, 106, 121–123, 125–126, 128, 134–135, 137–141, 143–144
Konstan, D. 168
Korner, R. J. 40–41, 99
Koselleck, R. 252
Kraemer, R. S. 60, 110
Kraft, R. A. 226, 229, 311
Krause, A. R. 41
Kraus, W. 92, 136, 138, 141
Kümmel, W. G. 157
Kysar, R. E. 187

Laato, A. 267
Lake, K. 17
Lalleman, P. J. 288–289
Lambrecht, J. 287
Lampe, P. 293, 313
Lanfranchi, P. 312
Lange, N. R. M. de 355
Langer, R. 36
Lassandro, D. 22
Last, R. 40–41
Law, T. M. 60
Le Boulluec, A. 261, 339
Leibniz, G. W. 13
Lemke, H. 348
Leon, H. J. 131
Leonhardt, C. 27–28
Leppin, H. 13, 58, 77
Levine, A.-J. 136
Levine, E. 18
Levine, L. I. 35–37, 42, 131
Lewis, T. A. 253
Lietzmann, H. 98
Lieu, J. M. 4, 16–18, 24, 63–65, 74–75, 91, 110, 123, 152, 155, 218–219, 223–224, 235, 249, 253, 255, 258, 262–264, 289–290, 293, 301, 310, 320, 322, 324, 329, 332
Lightfoot, J. B. 15–17
Lincicum, D. 239
Lindemann, A. 100
Lipsius, R. A. 60
Liver, J. 127
Loader, W. R. G. 136
Lohnmeyer, M. 135
Löhr, H. 110–111

Lona, H. E. 314–315, 354–355, 371
Longenecker, R. N. 101
Lookadoo, J. 291
Lowe, M. 61, 160
Lucas, H. 310
Luz, U. 122, 135, 140

Macdonald, D. R. 195
Magid, S. 67
Magness, J. 298
Marcus, J. 218, 253, 299, 365
Marguerat, D. 113
Markschies, C. 5, 25, 28, 75, 218, 371
Marshall, M. 165
Martin, V. 310, 321, 337–338, 353
Martyn, J. L. 35–36, 185, 187–190, 204
Mason, S. 2, 60–62, 67, 70, 160
Mayer, W. 22, 28
Mayer-Haas, A. J. 127
McEleney, N. J. 138
McKechnie, P. 274, 276–277, 291
McLynn, N. B. 24
Meeks, W. A. 189
Meier, J. P 136
Metzger, B. M. 174
Millar, F. 79, 274
Miltner, F. 283
Mimouni, S. C. 284, 290–291, 311–312, 352, 368
Minns, D. 256–258, 260, 262, 264, 266
Mitchell, S. 274, 277, 280
Mittelstraß, J. 13
Misiarczyk, L. 250
Mohrlang, R. 136
Moll, S. 74, 339
Moloney, F. J. 188
Morgan, H. A. 17
Morgan-Wynne, J. E. 336
Müller-Kessler, C. 349–350
Muñoz-Santos, M.E. 68
Murray, M. 287, 292
Musurillo, H. A. 353

Naiweld, R. 354
Nanos, M. D. 37–38, 94
Neusner, J. 2, 47
Neutel, K. B. 259

Nicklas, T.   4, 7, 11, 24, 57, 61, 65–66, 97–99, 193, 242–243, 311, 317–318, 338–339, 348–349, 360–363, 365, 370–371, 373
Niebuhr, K.-W.   3–4, 95, 98, 111
Niederwimmer, K.   19
Niehoff, M. R.   77–78, 243, 320, 327, 355–357
Nolland, J.   138
Nongbri, B.   59
Norman, I.   310
Novenson, M. V.   62–63
Noy, D.   43, 66–67, 277, 282
Nyström, D. E.   339

Oegema, G. S.   62
Ogereau, J. M.   274
Öhler, M.   60
Oliver, I. W.   38, 50, 127
Olmstead, W. G.   141
Olsson, B.   41
Onuki, T.   189
Osiek, C.   316
Oster, R. E.   300
Ostmeyer, K.-H.   143
Overman, J. A.   95, 122

Pachoumi, E.   73
Parkes, J.   16–17, 152, 155, 163, 180, 218, 251
Parsenios, G.   195
Parsons, M. C.   153, 167
Parvis, P.   256–258, 260, 262, 264, 266
Penner, T. C.   154, 263
Perler, O.   65
Pervo, R. I.   153, 288
Petersen, A. K.   59, 95–96
Pettem, M.   177
Pilhofer, P.   274
Pillinger, R.   283
Pinkau, K.   12
Pischedda, J. B.   73
Pollefeyt, D.   187
Pouderon, B.   311, 353–354
Powell, M. J.   67
Pratscher, W.   373
Price, J.   80

Prigent, P.   226, 323, 325
Prostmeier, F. R.   78, 227–229, 232–233, 242, 367
Przybylski, B.   130, 133

Rabkin, H.   96
Rabkin, Y. M.   96
Raffman, D.   254
Rajak, T.   264
Ramelli, I.   310–311
Ramsay, W. M.   277
Read-Heimerdinger, J.   360
Rebillard, É.   75, 351
Reed, A. Y.   4, 12, 16, 24–25, 34, 63, 67, 96, 124, 153, 155–156, 160, 186, 218–221, 223, 249–250, 299–301, 311, 336, 349, 352
Repschinski, B.   128, 144
Reinhartz, A.   4, 36, 92, 97, 107, 123, 160–161, 185, 187–188, 191, 200, 204–206, 210
Reynolds, B.   197
Reynolds, J.   281
Rhodes, J. N.   229, 232–233, 368
Richardson, P.   43
Richter, G.   189
Ricœur, P.   252, 254
Rickert, H.   14
Ritter, A. M.   21, 72
Rius-Camps, J.   360
Robert, L.   68, 277
Robinson, T. A.   317
Rokéah, D.   264, 322, 328, 331, 334
Romeny, B. ter Haar   4
Rosik, M.   310
Rothschild, C. K.   157, 229–230, 234–235, 242
Rowe, C. K.   153
Rudolph, A.   319, 323, 327, 332–335
Rudolph, D. J.   112, 252
Runesson, A.   2, 4–5, 37–38, 40–41, 44, 47, 50, 95, 97, 99, 122–123, 136
Runia, D. T.   357
Rüpke, J.   351
Rutherford, W.   319
Ryan, J. J.   40

Sacco, G.   67
Sahlins, M.   59
Saldarini, A. J.   4, 122, 129–130, 136
Salmon, M.   166
Salvesen, A.   311
Sanchez, S. J. G.   319, 324, 326
Sanders, E. M.   168–169, 177
Sanders, E. P.   45, 99–100
Sanders, J. T.   156
Sänger, D.   62
Satlow, M.   60
Schäfer, P.   15, 24, 95–96, 137, 190
Schenck, K.   310
Scherrer, P.   282
Schliesser, B.   347–348
Schmithals, W.   78
Schnabel, E. J.   285
Schnelle, U.   3, 11–14, 23, 57–59, 78, 91–92, 102, 200, 311, 348, 351–352
Schoedel, W. R.   317–318
Schröter, J.   6, 101, 113
Schürer, E.   274, 294
Schüssler Fiorenza, E.   287
Schwartz, D. R.   193
Schwartz, S.   35, 60–61, 223
Schwemer, A.-M.   63, 100–101, 229, 353, 358
Seeliger, H. R.   75
Segal, A. F.   2, 94, 97, 145
Senior, D.   122, 126, 133, 135, 141–142
Sgherri, G.   355
Shandruk, W.   73
Shaw, B. D.   71
Sheinfeld, S.   103
Sheppard, A.   233
Shoemaker, S.   350
Siegert, F.   189
Sim, D. C.   122, 134, 136, 140, 144
Simon, M.   42–43, 268, 341
Skarsaune, O.   258–259, 293, 327, 333–334
Slee, M.   135–136
Sleepers, S.   283
Smith, E. C.   310, 350
Smith, D. E.   154
Smith, D. M.   187
Smith, G. S.   261

Smith, J. C. H.   236
Smith, J. Z.   237, 239–241
Smit Sibinga, J.   327
Snodgrass, K.   128
Snyder, J. A.   164
Solin, H.   72
Spence, S.   310
Spicq, C.   68
Stanton, G. N.   130, 250, 325
Staples, J. A.   105
Stegemann, E.   188
Stemberger, G.   35, 190
Sterling, G. E.   154, 162, 177
Stewart-Sykes, A.   295
Stewart Lester, O.   358
Stockhausen, A. von   25
Stökl Ben Ezra, D.   310
Stone, M. E.   43
Stroumsa, G. G.   11
Strubbe, J. H. M.   276
Stuhlmacher, P.   16
Syme, R.   71–72

Tabbernee, W.   276–277
Talley, T. J.   295
Tannehill, R. C.   159, 161
Tannenbaum, R.   281
Taylor, J.   68, 154, 159–161, 264
Teitler, H. C.   72
Tellbe, M.   300
Tepper, Y.   48
Theissen, G.   92
Theobald, M.   369
Thiessen, M.   34, 38, 52, 249, 253, 299–300
Thomas, M. J.   331–332
Thompson, L. L.   287, 293
Thornton, T. C. G.   295
Tilly, M.   102, 360
Tomson, P. J.   60, 102
Tong, M. A.   309, 337
Trebilco, P. R.   7, 70, 131, 209, 274, 276–278, 282–283, 285–286, 291, 300
Troiano, L.   355
Tyson, J. B.   154

Ulrich, J.   319, 339

Van de Sandt, H. 95
Van den Hoek, A. 357
Van der Horst, P. W. 218, 274, 277, 279–280, 282
Van der Lans, B. 60, 68, 71, 77
Vandecasteele-Vanneuville, F. 187
Van Haeperen, F. 308
Van Henten, J. W. 278
Van Kooten, G. H. 196
VanMaaren, J. 38
Van Minnen, P. 58
Verheyden, J. 4, 7, 312, 315, 317, 361
Vermes, G. 274
Vielhauer, P. 226
Vinzent, M. 63–64, 75, 338
Vogel, M. 13
Vuong, L. 370

Waelkens, M. 277
Wagner, J. R. 102
Walters, P. 153
Wander, B. 3, 91
Ward, J. S. 71
Watson, F. 93
Weber, M. 13–14
Wehnert, J. 359
Wendel, S. 334, 337
Wengst, K. 187, 226, 230
Weren, W. 133
Westerholm, S. 93

Whealey, A. 70
White, B. L. 257
White, L. M. 136
Whitmarsh, T. 59
Wilken, R. L. 22
Wilk, F. 102
Williams, A. L. 319, 324, 333
Williams, C. 190
Williams, M. H. 60, 278, 281
Willitts, J. 252
Wilson, S. G. 286–287, 292–293
Wilson, W. T. 157
Winden, J. C. M. van 319, 324, 332
Windisch, H. 226–228, 230, 234
Wischmeyer, W. 75
Wolter, M. 103
Wong, K.-C. 133
Wrede, W. 93
Wright, A. D. 309

Yuval, I. J. 27

Zahn, T. 68
Zara, E. 71
Zetterholm, M. 37–38, 51, 106, 310, 317
Ziethe, C. 126
Zimmermann, C. 274
Zimmermann, J. 197
Zimmermann, N. 283
Zwierlein, O. 73, 314

Index of Subjects

Acts of the Apostles 17, 68, 73, 101, 151–180
 – Historicity of Acts 151–154, 162
Alexandria 5, 7, 42–43, 77–78, 131, 158, 227, 242–243, 245, 347, 352–363, 368–374
Antijudaism 6, 11, 18, 20–23, 50, 93, 131, 152, 155, 160, 187, 188–193, 204–205, 209–210, 228–230, 242–243, 266–268, 288, 290, 297, 355
Antioch on the Orontes 11–12, 20–28, 68–70, 92, 98, 104, 131, 138–139, 159, 317, 353
 – Antioch incident 106, 109
Antioch in Pisidia 166–167, 176, 284–285
Apocalypse of Peter 363–365, 368–369, 372–373
Apostolic Council see Jerusalem Council
Asia Minor 5, 7, 78, 207, 209, 227, 273–276, 278–280, 283–286, 288–289, 291–292, 294–301, 321, 366
Associations 6, 37, 39–44, 47, 49–50, 109, 203

Barnabas 107, 151–152, 157, 167, 169, 177, 361–362
Barnabas Encomium 372

Celsus 77–78, 222, 243, 355–357, 368, 372–374
Christians/Christianity 1–5, 7, 11–12, 14–20, 24, 26–28, 33–35, 37–38, 44, 46, 48–52, 57–58, 60, 64, 67, 75–76, 78, 80, 89, 91–98, 100–102, 123–125, 138, 143–145, 152–153, 155–156, 158, 162, 170–173, 176, 179–180, 218–224, 227, 237–239, 241, 249–255, 260, 262–263, 265, 268–269, 274, 290, 292, 299–301, 309, 312–313, 317–318, 320, 323, 327, 329–330, 332, 337, 340–341, 347, 349, 355, 359–360, 362, 369–374
 – *Christiani* 68, 71–73, 98

 – *Christianismos*/Χριστιανισμός 6, 35, 60–61, 64–67, 73–77, 241, 255
 – *Christianitas* 57, 76
 – *Christianoi*/Χριστιανοί 37, 60, 68, 73–74, 77, 92, 98, 158–159, 208, 255, 260–261, 264, 277
Circumcision 25, 79, 89, 94, 100, 102–103, 108–109, 136–140, 158, 164, 175, 179, 202, 205, 207, 231–232, 234–235, 237, 256, 258, 320, 327, 330, 332, 335, 368
Civic institutions 37–38, 40–41, 47, 49
Constructivism 222, 244
Corinth 103–104, 110, 152, 158, 172–173, 314, 321, 366
Cyprus 362

Didache 4, 18–19, 95, 140, 224
Diversity 1, 43, 45, 51, 91, 130, 154–155, 164, 278, 287, 299–301

Ephesus 65, 99, 151–152, 170–173, 274, 282–288, 293–300, 320
Epistle of Barnabas 7, 19, 205, 224, 244–245, 356, 367–368, 372, 374

Fiscus Iudaicus 58–59, 79, 92, 129, 185, 206, 208, 254
Food laws 4, 89, 94–95, 100, 102, 106, 108–110, 112, 202, 232, 235, 242, 350

Galatia 62, 108–109, 137
Gentile mission 106, 123, 126, 128, 133–142, 145, 153, 155, 167, 171, 175–180
Gospel of the Hebrews 366, 372

Hellenists 3, 92, 131
Hermeneutics 52–53, 139, 185, 209–211, 225–226, 228, 230, 235, 244, 324, 356
History/historiography 12, 14–18, 20, 28, 34, 36, 45–46, 49–50, 52–53, 67, 96, 125–126, 128, 138, 142–143, 153–154, 156–157, 160, 162, 180, 189, 191–192, 196–197, 200, 210, 217, 219–220, 222–

223, 225, 230, 253–254, 257, 263, 286, 317, 352, 357, 368, 373–374

Iconium   167, 169–170, 284–285
Identity   6, 28, 34, 37, 43, 52, 67, 91, 95, 100, 102, 129, 137, 142–143, 158–163, 180, 189, 193–194, 202–204, 206–209, 220–221, 231, 235, 237, 239–241, 244, 252, 257–258, 263, 278, 285, 287, 290, 312, 316, 323, 337, 340, 351
 – Christian identity   7, 28, 91, 162, 164, 220–221, 251, 340
 – Hybrid identity   6, 153, 158–159, 162–165
 – Jewish identity   7, 28, 95, 102, 137, 159, 161–162, 164, 204, 221, 231, 251, 255, 257, 285
Ignatius of Antioch   35, 255, 349–350
Inclusion of the gentiles   see Gentile mission
Intermixing of communities   276–283
Israel as God's chosen people   104

James   106, 165, 177–179
Jealousy   164, 166–169, 171, 314
Jerusalem   42, 92, 131, 137–138, 151, 159, 161–162, 164, 170, 176–177, 179, 192, 202, 208, 233, 274, 285, 295
 – Jerusalem Council (Apostolic Council)   106, 109, 138, 140, 157, 162
 – Jerusalem temple   92, 95, 98, 124, 127, 129, 155, 159, 162, 166–167, 170, 193, 202, 205–206, 227–228, 231–233, 236, 242, 285, 296, 370
 – Second Temple   60, 91–93, 97, 127, 175–176, 198, 210
Jesus movement   1, 4, 39, 44, 48, 58, 67, 156, 165, 176, 210
Jews/Judaism   1–7, 11–12, 14–18, 21, 23–28, 33–35, 37–38, 41, 44–52, 58–62, 64–67, 74–75, 77, 79–80, 89–102, 104–109, 111–114, 121–125, 127–133, 136–137, 139, 141–145, 152, 155–156, 158–160, 163–164, 166–167, 169–170, 172–174, 176, 179–180, 186, 189, 191–199, 202–203, 205–210, 217–226, 228–230, 232–245, 249–257, 260–265, 268–269, 278–279, 281, 285–292, 296–297, 299–301, 309, 312–318, 322–323, 325, 327, 329–330, 336–341, 349, 352, 357, 362, 368, 372–373
 – Early Judaism   5, 16, 18, 39, 145, 357, 363
 – Ἰουδαῖος/Ἰουδαῖοι   20, 25, 69, 104–105, 153, 160–161, 163–164, 169, 171, 185, 187, 192–196, 201, 205–206, 208–209, 255, 257, 261, 291, 360
 – Ἰουδαϊσμός/Judaismus   6, 35, 59, 60–67, 74–76, 80, 98, 100, 241
 – "Jews from Asia" (Acts)   162, 167, 170–171, 180, 285, 299
 – Rabbinic Judaism   5–6, 35–38, 42, 45, 47–48, 50, 95, 97, 160, 191, 198, 217–218, 349
 – Second Temple Judaism   60, 91–93, 97, 127, 176, 210
Jewish-Christian Relations   5–8, 17, 152, 180, 210, 217–218, 224, 228, 244, 312, 315, 350, 352–354, 371
Jewish Christianity   3, 15–17, 34–35, 37–38, 48, 66, 95, 123, 145, 158, 254, 268
Johannine Community   36, 188–190, 202, 286
John Chrysostom   5, 12, 20–23, 25–28, 223, 279
John the Baptist   64
Justin Martyr   6–7, 51, 77, 237, 250, 269, 293, 299, 341

Laodicea   279–280, 282, 299
Lystra   169–170, 284

Maccabees   6, 62–63, 65–66, 76, 98
Marcion   61–66, 74–78, 80, 220, 234, 260, 333, 338–341
Matthew   38, 47, 99, 121–123, 125–130, 132–136, 138–145, 370
 – Matthew within Judaism   122, 133, 136, 145
Metaphor   1, 3, 5, 7, 11–18, 20, 24, 35, 50–51, 90–91, 95–97, 101, 104, 113, 123, 144–145, 219, 251–253, 283

Non-Jewish Christianity 35, 38, 48, cf. Gentile mission

Parting of the Ways 3, 11–12, 14–18, 20, 23–24, 28, 34–35, 39, 50–51, 58–59, 61, 67, 76, 78, 90, 95, 99, 102, 113–114, 123–124, 144, 152, 154–156, 158–159, 163–164, 172, 175–176, 180, 186, 191, 204, 208, 217, 223, 227–230, 242–243, 249–251, 254, 265, 268–269, 275, 298–300, 309–310, 312, 348–349, 351, 373
Paul/Pauline tradition 3–4, 6, 17, 33–34, 38–39, 41, 44, 49–51, 58, 61–63, 65, 76, 89–94, 97–100, 106–114, 121–122, 124–125, 134, 137, 139, 141, 152, 155, 157–159, 162–164, 166–167, 169–177, 180, 194, 200, 210, 237, 240, 252, 259–260, 284–285, 310, 317, 327, 331, 336, 340, 350
 – Paul within Judaism 89, 93–94
Pazon 279–280, 282, 299
Peter 98, 106, 108, 138, 161, 166, 177–178, 361, 364, 369, 373
Polemic 16, 21, 23–24, 26–27, 50, 60, 76–77, 98, 103, 122, 187–188, 191, 193, 209–210, 221, 224–225, 229, 232, 234–235, 239, 242–243, 264, 287–288, 291, 299, 314, 316, 321–322, 334
Purity 92, 108, 110–114, 202–203, 207–208, 335–336, 370

Qumran texts 6, 19, 51, 143, 210

Rabbinic Judaism see Jews/Judaism
Rhetoric 5, 7, 22–23, 49, 51, 127, 162, 166, 170–171, 191, 193, 200, 204–210, 219, 237, 251, 256–257, 290, 328, 330, 355, 359

Rome 5, 7, 43, 59, 65–66, 69–75, 78, 111, 131, 153, 173–174, 293, 307–308, 313–321, 338, 353, 362, 366

Sabbath 4, 25–27, 66, 89, 94–95, 100, 109–110, 113, 127, 139, 167, 179, 195, 202, 205, 231, 232, 235, 258, 279, 290–292, 330, 332, 335, 350
Second Temple see Jerusalem temple
Synagogue 2, 4–6, 20, 24–27, 33, 36–39, 41–43, 47–48, 69, 79, 129–132, 138, 152, 171–173, 179, 237, 255–256, 267, 282, 284–285, 300, 350
Syria 79, 131, 138, 227, cf. Antioch

Table fellowship of Jews and non-Jews 106–109, 111–113, cf. food laws
Temple see Jerusalem temple
Temple tax 127, 129, 206, cf. *fiscus Iudaicus*
Theology 28, 35, 52–53, 78, 89, 91–93, 99, 102, 113–114, 138, 187, 193, 196, 199–200, 210–211, 229, 240, 244, 311, 329, 355
Thessalonica 169–170
Torah 5–6, 65, 92–93, 95–96, 98, 100, 102, 107–108, 110–112, 114, 124, 128, 137–139, 142, 144, 176–177, 179, 193, 205, 207, 224, 239, 241, 281, 328, 330, 332, 336

Variegated Interaction 275, 299–300

Works of the Law 93, 100, 106–108, cf. Torah

www.ingramcontent.com/pod-product-compliance
Lightning Source LLC
Chambersburg PA
CBHW061926220426
43662CB00012B/1821